Sacred Origins of Profound Things

The Stories behind the Rites and Rituals of the World's Religions

CHARLES PANATI

ARKANA
PENGUIN BOOKS

ARKANA
Published by the Penguin Group
Penguin Books Ltd, 27 Wrights Lane, London W8 5TZ, England
Penguin Books USA Inc., 375 Hudson Street, New York, New York 10014, U.S.A.
Penguin Books Australia Ltd, Ringwood, Victoria, Australia
Penguin Books Canada Ltd, 10 Alcorn Avenue, Toronto, Ontario, Canada M4V 3B2
Penguin Books (N.Z.) Ltd, 182–190 Wairau Road, Auckland 10, New Zealand

Penguin Books Ltd, Registered Offices: Harmondsworth, Middlesex, England

First published in the United States of America in Arkana 1996
First published in Great Britain in Arkana 1997

1   3   5   7   9   10   8   6   4   2

Printed in the United States of America
Set in Bembo
Designed by Deborah Kerner

PENGUIN

ARKANA

SACRED ORIGINS OF PROFOUND THINGS

In his varied career Charles Panati has been science editor for *Newsweek,* Professor of Physics at Columbia University, and twice a co-host for television. His recent books include *Panati's Extraordinary Origins of Everyday Things, Panati's Extraordinary Endings of Practically Everything and Everybody,* and *Panati's Fads, Follies and Manias,* as well as two works of fiction, *Links* and *The Pleasuring of Rory Malone.* He has also written for television and has contributed articles to, among others, *Esquire, Cosmopolitan,* and *Reader's Digest.*

ALSO BY CHARLES PANATI

Supersenses: Our Potential for Parasensory Experience

The Geller Papers: Scientists Examine Psychic Uri Geller (editor)

Death Encounters: Evidence of an Afterlife?

Breakthroughs: Advances in Medicine and Technology

The Silent Intruder: Surviving the Radiation Age (with Michael Hudson)

The Browser's Book of Beginnings

Panati's Extraordinary Origins of Everyday Things

Panati's Extraordinary Endings of Practically Everything and Everybody

Panati's Fads, Follies and Manias

FICTION

Links

The Pleasuring of Rory Malone

For my mother,
an American Catholic

Why We Believe
What We Believe

INTRODUCTION

EACH OF US LONGS to believe that our own life—and all life—is not accidental and meaningless but has value and purpose. Assurance that this is so has come from religion for billions of people since the dawn of history.

Anthropologists have never discovered a group of people who did not harbor some sort of religious beliefs—in gods or goddesses, or in supernatural powers. Religion seems to be as old as our species and no doubt has its origins in human reflection. Who am I? Where did I come from? Why am I here? Where will I end up?

Our word "religion" is from the Latin *religio*, which meant "respect for what is sacred, awe," and was rooted in the verb *religare*, "to bind." In medieval Europe, the word evolved to mean "a system of sacred beliefs and practices that binds a people together."

Even the most religious among us tend, over time, to take religion for granted. People have lost sight of the origins of sacred practices and customs, the reasons for religious holidays, rituals, and symbols, the meanings of vestments, sacraments, devotions, and prayers.

Why, for instance, do we pray with hands joined together?

Why are there *nine* classifications of angels?

Who recited the first rosary?

Who made the first hajj?

When did the first boy become bar mitzvah?

How do certain Christian saints come to be patrons of cyberspace? Of hemorrhoids?

Have all religions recognized a Satan?

Are there differences between the Jewish "Yahweh," the Christian "God the Father," and the Islamic "Allah"?

How did millions of people move from the concept of polytheism—the worship of many gods and goddesses—to the adoration of a single male deity?

Why don't Jews eat pork, why don't some Muslims eat certain vegetables, and why did Christians once observe meatless Fridays?

Why does Judaism, but not Roman Catholicism, allow divorce?

How did the pope become infallible on issues of faith and morals? Why did papal infallibility become dogma only in the summer of 1870?

What does sacred scripture—the Jewish and Christian Bibles and the Koran—really say about contraception, abortion, certain sexual practices, and homosexuality?

I have written about origins before, in such books as *Extraordinary Origins of Everyday Things*, which dealt with secular origins. This book deals with sacred origins. I wrote it to clarify the origins of hundreds of religious customs and practices existing in many faiths. I admit to having an obsession with learning about how things started.

It is my hope that by focusing on the fundamental hows and whys underlying religious practices and beliefs, I can rekindle in readers the excitement and awe that we felt when we were first introduced to religion as children.

That awe often dims with the rigors of adult life. Busy with careers and childrearing, we may end up worshiping by rote—and lose out on the magic inherent in the act of worship. Every now and then it is wise and helpful to go back to basics. In these pages you will find the origins of some of the most profound and cherished religious beliefs. Some will be familiar. Others may be shocking.

If, at times, entries seem slightly slanted toward Catholicism that may be due to the fact that I attended Catholic grammar school, high school, and college; for sixteen years I was taught by nuns and priests. I was an altar boy, and I even considered becoming a priest. Writers, it's said, tend to write about what they know best.

Since the book covers many faiths, Eastern and Western, I've used a non-denominational dating system:

B.C.E. = BEFORE THE COMMON ERA (PREVIOUSLY: BEFORE CHRIST).
C.E. = COMMON ERA (PREVIOUSLY: A.D., LATIN, *ANNO DOMINI*, "IN THE YEAR OF THE LORD").

CHARLES PANATI
New York City

Contents

Sacred Origins of Profound Things

PART

I

Popular
Piety

CHAPTER

1

𝔓rayer 𝔓ostures

Hands Joined to Heads Covered

WHAT PRAYER IS ◆

"An intimate friendship, a frequent conversation held alone with the Beloved" is how sixteenth-century Spanish mystic Saint Teresa of Ávila defined prayer.

"Elevation of the mind to God" is what prayer was for Saint John of Damascus.

"Ask, and it will be given you" is how Luke in 11:9 summed up petition as a form of prayer.

"Religion's primary mode of expression," said philosopher William James, who claimed that religion itself could not exist without the concept of prayer.

An Islamic proverb states that to pray and to be a Muslim are synonymous. In Indian mysticism, prayer is considered as vital as breathing.

Christians pray following the example of Jesus Christ, who throughout his lifetime remained in communication with his Father in Heaven through prayer. Christ prayed at the time of his baptism, on performance of his miracles, and before and after his passion. For Saint Augustine, his autobiographical *Confessions* is one single long prayer between the saint and his Creator—in prayer's confessional mode. There are five modes, as we'll see.

When prayer becomes manipulative in its intent, it harks back to its origin: magic incantation. For ancient peoples, superstitious of thunder and lightning, swarms of locusts and torrential monsoons, magical chant, recited in prescribed rhythm before the sacrificing of a lamb or the deflowering of a virgin, was their way to appease a god. "All good fates are in the hands of god," says one of the earliest of Egyptian prayers.

In all likelihood, the very first human prayer fervently uttered was a cry for help—a petitional prayer. We have no way of knowing if it was answered.

BIBLICAL ORIGIN OF PRAYER: GENESIS 4:26 ◆

The first mention of prayer in the Bible comes early in the Book of Genesis, and indeed donates prayer's origin. Adam and Eve already have disobeyed God. Cain has killed Abel. Eve has borne another son, Seth, and Seth has named his own son Enosh when we're told:

At that time men began to call upon the name of the Lord. (Gen. 4:26)

And man would call and call on God. And God makes a promise to hear man's prayers, and woman's, too, if not to answer all of them, in Deuteronomy 4:7:

For what great nation is there that has gods so close to it as the Lord, our God, is to us whenever we call upon him?

Thus early in the Bible, through these quotations, the formula is set: Humans ask, God listens. Maybe God answers.

More than a thousand years after Moses wrote the Book of Genesis, Jesus Christ, God the Son, arrives and assures us with filial frankness: "Whatever you ask in prayer, believe that you receive it, and you will . . . all things are possible to him who believes" (Mark 11:24, 9:23). Thus we feel that if a particular prayer petition is not answered, perhaps our belief was not ardent enough.

The Bible's Book of Psalms is actually a meditation of biblical history presented in the form of prayer, in which the Word of God becomes his people's prayer.

Prayer, as we'll see, is one of the most ancient expressions of religion, cherished in all cultures throughout recorded time. It is a human act of communication with the sacred or holy—with God, or with gods or goddesses, or with any transcendent realm.

FIVE KINDS OF PRAYER: PREHISTORY ◆

Recited either sitting or standing, kneeling or swaying, skull bare or cloaked, eyes closed or cast heavenward, palms joined or arms extended skyward, prayer is divided by theologians into five categories that have existed since primitive times.

ADORATION. This highest form of prayer consists of contemplation of God himself. It is the kind of intense meditation we most accurately associate with the prayers of mystics, and it's the purest form of prayer. We ask no favors; we just adore our Creator.

The word "adore" is from the Latin *adorare*, meaning "to worship."

In Christianity, neither saints nor the Blessed Virgin Mary may be addressed with prayers of adoration. In Islam, adoration is the primary form of prayer.

One of the earliest recorded prayers of adoration in the Bible is the Sanctus or song of Heaven recorded in the prophet Isaiah's vision: "Holy, holy, holy, the Lord God of hosts, all the earth is full of his glory" (Isa. 6:3).

Intellectually, prayer is communication or talk. Emotionally, though, prayer is inseparable from a sense of a sacred presence in our midst. This is especially true of adoration. "Going out of one's self" or a "pilgrimage of the spirit" is a unique ingredient of adorational prayer.

All peoples pray alike. And have for all time. In order to appreciate this cross-cultural uniformity in adorational prayer over the ages, here are several examples, each dated, striking in their similarities, diverse in their deities.

Creator of the germ in woman,
Maker of the seed in man,
Giver of breath to animate everyone he maketh!
O sole God, whose powers no other possesseth.
Thou didst create earth according to thy heart.
TO THE SUN GOD, ATON, EGYPT, FOURTEENTH CENTURY B.C.E.

There is a Spirit which was before heaven and earth were.
The One dwelling in silence beyond earthly forms,
    never changing, omnipresent. I do not know its name.
I call it Tao. I call it the Supreme.
TAOISM, FIFTH CENTURY B.C.E.

There is a light that shines beyond all things.
All the universe is in truth Brahman. He is the beginning and
    the end and life of all.
As such, in silence, give unto him adoration.
EIGHTH CENTURY B.C.E. HINDU UPANISHAD,

I address myself to Thee, to Whom all worship is due.
My heart yearns for thee with a yearning that is
    never stilled. Let me live before Thee, with Thee,

Live in Thy sight, I humbly pray.
AHURA MAZDA, ZOROASTRIAN GOD, SIXTH CENTURY B.C.E.

Ho! Great Spirit, Grandfather, you made everything
  and are in everything, guide everything,
Provide everything and protest everything because
Everything belongs to you.
ANCIENT SIOUX PRAYER

Great and holy is the Lord, the holiest of holy ones.
Majesty precedes him,
Grace and truth surround his presence,
Blessed be he who makes the earth by his power.
DEAD SEA SCROLLS, C. 150 B.C.E.–68 C.E.

To God belongs the praise, Lord of Heaven and Earth,
Lord of all being. His is the dominion in the heavens and in the earth.
He is the Almighty, the everwise.
SEVENTH-CENTURY ISLAMIC PRAYER TO ALLAH

CONFESSION. This is the personal acknowledgment that the believer has sinned and seeks forgiveness. It is a prayer of self-examination, usually recited in private. Many a Christian saint previously a sinner has titled his autobiography *Confession.*

The general form of a confession includes an expression of sorrow for past transgression, a petition for God's forgiveness, and, in some cases, the expression of resolve to amend one's ways.

The word "confess" is from the Latin *confiteri,* meaning "to acknowledge."

Psalm 51, the Miserere, or Prayer of Repentance, is a perfect example of the confessional mode: "Have mercy on me O God. . . . Thoroughly wash me of my guilt [petition] . . . I acknowledge my offense [sorrow] . . . teach me wisdom [resolve]."

Roman Catholicism has elevated confession to the status of a sacrament; a mortal sin can be forgiven only through a formal act of contrition before a priest. Sacramental confession is optional in Anglican churches and many Protestant denominations. (*See* Penance.)

Here is a beautiful ancient Persian prayer of confession, recited today by Muslims; notice how, like many Old Testament psalms, it employs repetition to cast its spell.

All that we ought to have thought and have not thought,
All that we ought to have said and have not said,

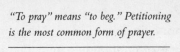

"To pray" means "to beg." Petitioning is the most common form of prayer.

All that we ought to have done and have not done,
All that we ought not to have thought but thought,
All that we ought not to have spoken but have spoken,
All that we ought not to have done but have done,
For thoughts, words, and deeds we pray, God, for forgiveness.

PETITION. Not surprisingly, this is the most common form of prayer, also known as supplication. It is asking God for something we desire, for ourselves, or for others. Mystics have always regarded petition as the lowest form of prayer. But Jesus Christ himself petitioned God in the Garden of Gethsemane that the cup of suffering might pass from him.

In fact, our word "prayer" comes from the Latin *precarius*, meaning "to obtain by begging."

For most peoples, to pray is to beg. Assyrian kings, Babylonian peasants, Hebrew scholars, all petitioned God or gods for good health, long life, prosperity, and victorious battle. "Man is a beggar before God," taught Saint Augustine.

Matthew tells us that petitionary prayer, especially in terms of healing, has the best chance of being answered if it is combined with fasting: "This kind [of illness] can be cast out only by prayer and fasting" (Matt. 17:20).

An early biblical petition comes from the lips of Abraham when he begs God to spare the city of Sodom from total destruction, then humbly concludes: "I have ventured to speak to the Lord though I am but dust and ashes" (Gen. 18:27). This is also an example of a petition that goes ungranted. Jesus' petition in Gethsemane demonstrates the way all petitionary prayer has to be modified by humility: "Thy will be done."

Islamic prayer is unique in that it is an act of pure adoration of God or Allah and it is therefore unsuitable to petition *while* praising. Muslims do not mix worship with solicitation.

An ancient Hindu prayer of pure petition:

From the unreal lead me to the real!
From darkness lead me to light!
From death lead me to immortality!

PRAISE. Here the focus of praise is not only upon God himself, as in adoration, but also, above all, on his many acts of creation in nature. From earliest times, praise involved a recital of God's greatest deeds, beginning with such words as "Praise be to thee, O Lord, who made . . ." The ancient hymn of praise *Te Deum Laudamus* begins with an adoration of God but includes his many wonderworks.

Hymns of praise are a common feature of all church liturgies. And many prayers, as we'll see in the next chapter, contain some expression of praise, as in the Lord's Prayer: "Hallowed by thy name."

From the *Te Deum Laudamus* in the Book of Common Prayer:

We praise thee, O God; we acknowledge thee to be the Lord . . .
The glorious company of the Apostles, praise thee.
The goodly fellowship of the Prophets, praise thee.
The noble army of Martyrs, praise thee.
The holy Church worldwide doth acknowledge thee.

THANKSGIVING. One of the oldest known hymns, dating from the twelfth century B.C.E., is an act of thanksgiving to the Babylonian sun god Marduk, creator of Heaven and earth, for victorious defeat of an enemy. In ancient Egypt, extant prayers of thanksgiving are preserved as engravings on the backs of scarabs, those large, horned, stout-bodied beetles, brightly colored; especially the black-winged dung beetle, sacred to Egyptians.

Thanksgiving Day, first celebrated in 1621 in Plymouth, Massachusetts, was in effect a prayer of thanks to God for an abundance of food. The custom was ancient and universal. The Greeks honored Demeter, goddess of agriculture, with a day of thanksgiving; the Romans paid tribute to Ceres, the goddess of corn; the Hebrews offered thanks to Yahweh for abundant harvests with the eight-day Feast of Tabernacles. Thanks has a way of expressing itself in festivals. (*See* Feast Days.)

The Roman Catholic *grace before meals* is typical in form to the most ancient prayers of thanks ever discovered:

Bless us, O Lord, and these Thy gifts,
which we are about to receive from Thy bounty,
Through Christ Our Lord, Amen.

PHYSICAL MOVEMENT IN RELIGIOUS EXPRESSION ✦

Hand gestures, body postures, and dance steps of all kinds have long been part of the religious expression accompanying prayer. The intentions of some of these acts are obvious; others spring from superstitions. Let's examine their origins.

ARMS EXTENDED: NEAR EAST, PREHISTORY ✦

For our ancestors, one of the most ancient and reverential gestures that accompanied prayer was the spreading heavenward of arms and hands, as if to collect a shower of gifts. This was followed by *folding the arms across the breast*, wrists intersecting above the heart, as if to shield the heart. Both gestures possess an intrinsic logic and obvious intent: God, or gods, resided in the sky, and the heart is the seat of emotion.

A variation on this devotional posture was known to Greeks and Romans as the *orant position*, often captured in art of the period, in which the arms are bent at the elbows but still held upward, forming a *W*. The orant motif is found most commonly in the Christian frescoes that decorated the catacombs from the second century to the sixth century C.E. The *W* posture was used not merely to depict a supplicant in prayer, but also to represent a deceased person's soul ascending into Heaven.

As early as the third century C.E., Christians had modified the orant posture to one of arms fully extended from the shoulders, torso and arms now forming a *cross*. When the rigid stance was held for hours or days without end by fasting monks, the painful, self-inflicted penance was called the "vigil of the cross" and was capable of inducing visions. Pain and sensory deprivation were ancient means for achieving religious highs.

HANDS JOINED: CHRISTIANITY, NINTH CENTURY ✦

Less clear is the origin of the gesture of palms and fingers joined in a kind of steeple.

The familiar practice is mentioned nowhere in the Bible. It appeared in the Christian Church only in the ninth century and did not become widely accepted until the thirteenth century. Later sculptors and painters incorporated the joined-hands gesture into religious scenes whose subject matter predates the origin of the gesture.

Religious historians trace the gesture back to the act of shackling a pris-

Joining hands to pray is a gesture of submission that had its origin in the practice of shackling the hands of prisoners.

oner's hands with vine or rope; joined hands came to symbolize a man's submission to his master. Or Creator. In Roman times, a captured soldier could avert immediate slaughter simply by affecting the joined-hands pose. "I surrender," it graphically shouted. "I'm your humbled servant." The gesture was handy in lieu of a white flag.

Centuries later, European feudal lords adopted the joining of hands as an action by which their vassals did homage and pledged fealty. In taking an oath of loyalty, a serf sandwiched his hands between those of his lord as an expression of subjection and ownership.

From such diverse practices, all with a common intent, Christianity assumed the gesture as a sign of a follower's total obedience to divine authority. Later, many writers within the Christian Church offered, and encouraged, a more pious and picturesque origin: joined hands represent a church's pointed steeple. In Colonial America, pastors often affixed a disciplinary origin: palms locked in prayer prevented children from fidgeting during long services—a form of self-shackling, of self-control.

BODY SWAYING: EARLY JUDAISM ♦

Swaying the body back and forth is an ancient Hebrew custom, with one explanation for its origin found in the Zohar, a mystical commentary on the Five Books of Moses, or the Pentateuch, begun in the second century C.E. by scholar Rabbi Simon bar Yochai. A humble person, as depicted in Proverbs 20:27, is a "candle of the Lord," the light of whose wick flickers harmoniously with the glow from the Torah. In fact, the Hebrew word *zohar* literally means "brightness."

One explanation for *full torso bobbing* from the waist up is given by twelfth-century Spanish philosopher Yehuda Halevi in *The Kuzari*. This custom originated before the printing press, at a time when many people read in sequence from a single handwritten text. Each person, says Halevi, "was compelled to bend down in order to read a passage and to then straighten himself out again. This resulted in continual bending forward and moving backward, the book being on the ground." By the time printed prayer books were plentiful, the practice of bobbing was ingrained.

Yet another explanation for devotional swaying, and/or bobbing, stems from the time when Moses revealed to his followers the Ten Commandments, and the awestruck crowd trembled and shook in prayerful reverence.

Modern psychologists offer a simpler explanation for rhythmic body movement during prayer—a sort of dance still found among primitive tribes: the poetic meter of prayer, or chant, invites the body to beat time through repetitive motion. Swaying and bobbing are thus viewed as ritual dance pared down to minimal movement.

BOWED HEAD AND WAVING HANDS ◆

The *bowed head* in prayer has for centuries been a symbol of humility, a pagan posture originating in the earliest days of religion, when earthly kings claimed divine lineage and demanded shows of subservience.

Waving hands in the air is a devotional practice mentioned in the Jewish Talmud, and it is among the oldest gestures employed to scare off evil spirits. It harks back to such other ancient pagan good luck gestures as crossed fingers and "thumbs up."

KNEELING: LATE JUDAISM, EARLY CHRISTIANITY ◆

This stance during prayer is a sign of servitude. Christians of many denominations believe that the body and blood of Jesus Christ is present in the Eucharist and kneel in reverence to the Lord's Real Presence.

In the Temples of Jerusalem, kneeling was an integral part of ceremonies. But when Christians adopted kneeling as a prayer posture, rabbis prohibited it in Jewish worship. The only exception was on Yom Kippur, when cantor and congregants, during the reading of an account of ancient Temple services, mimic the kneeling (and prostration) once practiced by high priests.

Traditionally, in services, some prayers are recited while standing, others while sitting. Whereas the practice varies from religion to religion, for Jews there is a general rule of thumb: Prayers selected from the Bible and meant to be studied are recited while sitting, that being the position for study.

In early Christianity, kneeling was not a common prayer stance; standing was. The shift came about in Western Church services when it became customary after the *Gloria in Excelsis* for people to engage in a moment of pri-

"To genuflect" means "to bend the knee." Kneeling is an act of adoration.

vate contemplation; the priest's order to kneel was *Flectamus genua,* "Bend your knees"—Latin *flectere* + *genu* = "to bend" + "knee"; the origin of our word "genuflect."

As Christianity splintered into different denominations, favoring different doctrines, kneeling practices varied. The 1552 version of the Book of Common Prayer contains a Declaration on Kneeling which makes clear that kneeling does not imply Christ's Real Presence in the Eucharist and no adoration is called for; rather, kneeling during the Communion part of Mass merely signifies humility. (*See* Real Presence.)

In June of 1995, a group of American Catholic bishops proposed making kneeling optional during Communion, but the innovation was voted down by other bishops and rejected by Rome.

EYES CLOSED: PREHISTORY ◆

The act of praying with eyes closed may have one of the simplest and least superstitious of all explanations: to shut out distractions. The custom is ancient and found in all faiths.

Prayer, purposeful and intense, demands complete concentration, and visual distractions cause the mind to wander, thus disrupting communications with the divine. In the Middle Ages, Christian monks, in prayer and fasting, were known to shut their eyes for days or weeks at a time so that no earthly diversion would sideline their contact with God. This practice of sensory deprivation often evoked apparitions of Jesus Christ, the Blessed Virgin Mary, and one's favorite patron saints.

We do not always obtain what we pray for, and the reasons given throughout time, in various faiths, are many. We have not prayed devoutly enough. We have, unwittingly, asked for something God foresees is not in our best interest. We have not prayed long enough, perseverance being the key to success.

BEATING THE BREAST: EARLY CHRISTIANITY ◆

Striking the breast with the right hand just above the heart is a prayer gesture of penance, one no longer intended to inflict pain, though its ancient antecedent, flagellation, was. Confessional phrases such as "I have sinned" and "through my fault" (*mea culpa*) are the appropriate moments for breast-beating atonement.

The practice has very curious and sexually contradictory roots. In many parts of Europe and Asia, flogging the body with a rough vine, stick, or whip, often drawing blood, is an extremely old gesture of atonement, once inflicted by a priest, later by the penitent himself. The stern noun "discipline" and humble proper noun "disciple" are both rooted in the Latin verb *discere*, "to learn well."

Many clerics, Saint Augustine for one, cautioned congregants not to flagellate themselves too enthusiastically, or too frequently. In the Middle Ages, chaste nuns and monks favored birch rods or knotted leather whips for self-flogging, and Cardinal Peter Damian in the eleventh century acquired fame, and a following, because of his manual in praise of flagellation: sinners were advised to strip to the waist and let themselves be beaten by more pious individuals. Flagellation, in fact, remained a common and often secretive aspect of many religious orders well into the 1960s. In some parts of the world, notably in South America and Central Asia, days of atonement are still marked by lay penitents beating themselves bloody.

It's ironic that the primitive gesture of whipping, which stings and engorges the flesh with blood, was—and remains—a form of sexual stimulation. In the brain, the centers for pain and pleasure cozy side by side to make curious neighbors. Tribes in the past employed flagellation in male sexual initiation rites; saints are known to have beaten themselves into religious frenzies indistinguishable from sexual release; and today a significant segment of the pornography industry focuses on flagellation.

Perhaps we should not be surprised to find sexual practices ritualized into religious gestures. People's oldest religions included sacred prostitutes and phallic worship, mixing ecstasy and procreation in ways we find unacceptable today. Whipping is the dark side of worship.

AMEN: EGYPT, 2500 B.C.E. ◆

One of the most common religious utterances, "amen" makes 13 appearances in the Hebrew Bible, 119 in the New Testament, and is plentiful in Islamic writings.

To the Hebrews, the word meant "so it is," expressing assent or agreement, and also signifying truth. Thus, a Hebrew scholar terminating a speech or sermon with "amen" assured his audience that his statements were trustworthy and reliable. Also, in early times, many congregants were unable to read and thus join their spiritual leader in prayer; "amen" became the illiterate's contribution to, and participation in, textual recitation. Sort of like signing one's name with an *X*.

The Talmud claims that "amen" is an acrostic, that is, an arrangement of words in which certain letters in each line, such as the first or last, are used to spell out a motto. "Amen," it turns out, is an acrostic formed from the first letters of the Hebrew phrase *El Melech Ne'eman*, "the Lord is a trustworthy King."

In the Bible, "amen" first appears in the Book of Numbers, in the "Ordeal for a suspected adulteress":

May the Lord make you an example of malediction. . . . May this water, then, that brings a curse, enter your body and make your belly swell and your thighs waste away! And the woman shall say, "Amen, amen!" (Num. 5:21–22)

Thus, the adulteress gives her assent to the curse.

The word then makes twelve appearances in Deuteronomy (chapter 27), as assent to "the twelve curses." For example: "Cursed be he who dishonors his father or his mother! And all the people shall answer, 'Amen!' " (Deut. 27:16).

Amun, the Egyptian god of
reproduction. His name means
"hidden one," and is the root of
the word "amen."

Actually, the word has pagan roots and originated in Egypt around 2500 B.C.E. To the Egyptians, *Amun* meant "hidden one" and was the name of their highest deity, at one time worshiped throughout the Middle East. As later cultures invoked the god Jupiter with the exclamation "By Jove!," the Egyptians called on their deity, "By Amun!" The Hebrews adopted the affirmation, imbued it with fresh meaning, and passed it on to Christians.

At the conclusion to the Our Father, it is customary to add "Amen." But as the Lord's Prayer is given in early versions of Matthew (6:9–13), the "so be it" response does not appear. (*See* Lord's Prayer.)

HALLELUJAH:
ANCIENT ISRAELITES, OLD TESTAMENT TIMES ◆

One of the richest words in religious liturgy, "hallelujah," meaning "praise ye the Lord," is an ancient Hebrew term that appears in the Old Testament only in the Psalms, where it usually lies outside the main body of text.

The Hebrew spelling of the word reveals its meaning and origin: *halelu! Yah*, literally "praise!" + "Lord," where *Yah* is an abbreviated form of "Yahweh," God's personal name to the Israelites. The verb "praise" is in the plural imperative, clearly implying that the phrase is a command to the entire congregation: *All of you* praise the Lord! The use of the plural imperative was typical of Israelite worship.

"Hallelujah" (this spelling of the word is an Old English translation of the Hebrew) most likely was a liturgical cry independent of any particular prayer, and this is probably why it exists outside the text of the Psalms. It may stand at the beginning of a Psalm, as in 111–12; or at the end, as in 104, 105, 115–17; or in both positions, as in 106, 113, 135, and 146–50.

The joyous cry also appears in the Apocrypha: in the Greek Book of Tobit 13:17, where it is a cry of praise for the New Jerusalem; and in 2 Maccabees 7:13, where rescued Jews erupt into rejoicing. John uses the word several times in the Book of Revelation.

Christians prefer the spelling "Alleluia," which is a second-century B.C.E. Greek, and later Latin, transliteration of the Hebrew *halelu Yah*. Pope Gregory the Great (590–604) suggested that the word was particularly suited for Easter services, and he laid out its use in Roman rite worship.

FACING EAST: NEAR EAST, PREHISTORY ◆

In the earliest days of Christianity, congregants prayed while facing east, in the direction of the rising sun. The custom is pagan and ancient, harking back to an era when a sun worshiper was not someone bent on getting a tan. Early stone altars were set up so the officiating high priest faced east.

For Christians, Jesus Christ was the "sun of righteousness." The east-facing position for the priest remained the norm throughout the Middle Ages. In Roman Catholicism, just a few decades ago, the altar was turned so that the priest faces the congregation; his back might or might not face the rising sun. The use of solar orientation in setting up altars has passed from ritual form to practical function.

Jews face east, toward Jerusalem, the Holy City, as a token of respect. The Ark of synagogues in the Western world is deliberately placed on the eastern wall so the congregation faces east as it prays. (See Mecca.)

PRAYING THROUGH SAINTS: NEW TESTAMENT ◆

"If you ask anything of the Father in my name," Jesus instructs his apostles in John 16:23, "he will give it to you." This quotation is often given as the origin of Christians' recitation of prayers "in the name of Jesus Christ." It marks the beginning of the use of intermediaries between people and God.

In time, many Christians dispensed with the use of Jesus as intermediary, preferring to make their appeal through the Blessed Virgin Mary, or their favorite patron saints. The reason is more superstitious than religious, having to do with purity of soul and proximity of personage. Many people, feeling themselves sinners, assume God will more readily fulfill their requests if presented by someone already pure and conveniently close to him in Heaven. In effect, we're saying: These people have God's ear. This type of prayer through intermediary is particularly common among Roman Catholics and Eastern Orthodox Christians, who chose to communicate through Mary or any of the hundreds of canonized patron saints.

Support for the notion of saints holding God's ear can be found in the New Testament. In the Gospel of Matthew, we're assured that Jesus' disciples will sit with him in judgment; and the Book of Revelation pictures saints standing in front of God's heavenly throne.

Praying through saints also brings up the issue of specialization, which, of course, marks the age in which we live. Antony of Padua is the patron saint of childless women. Martha, the patron of cooks. Saint Eligius, the patron of coin collectors. Thomas, the patron of construction workers. Luke, the patron of butchers. Vitus, the saint for dancers. Hairdressers turn to a duo of male saints, Cosmas and Damian. Even as people seek out medical specialists for specific ailments, so, too, many people will turn to patron saints. (*See* Patron Saints.)

Although statistics are hard to come by, it is commonly claimed in religious journals and from the pulpit that people who petition God through patrons have a better chance of having their prayers answered.

Many Protestant denominations oppose "indirect prayer." The practice, they say, runs counter to biblical teaching; indeed, sixteenth-century Protestant reformers emphasized the concept of the "individual priesthood of all believers." In stressing that any person can petition the Christian Triune Godhead without an intermediary, reformers pointed to the New Testament words of Paul: "There is one mediator between God and man, the man Christ Jesus" (1 Tim. 2:5).

SIGN OF THE CROSS: THIRD CENTURY C.E. ◆

Christian prayer often begins and ends with the making of the "sign of the cross," a touching of the forehead, heart, left, then right, shoulders with the first three fingers of the right hand.

It is commonly held that the three fingers—thumb, index, and middle finger—symbolize the three persons of the Trinity: Father, Son, and Holy Spirit. Whereas the remaining two fingers, joined together and tucked inward toward the palm, signify Christ's dual nature: divine and human. No symbol is wasted.

Tertullian (160–250), Latin Church father from Carthage, makes early mention of the "sign of the Lord," tracing a cross on the forehead: "When we put on our clothes and shoes, when we bathe, when we sit at table, when we light our lamps, in all ordinary actions of life, we trace upon the forehead the sign of the Lord."

Oil or ash was sometimes used, and Saint John Chrysostom speaks eloquently of the practice: "Each day people carry around the sign formed on their foreheads as if it were a trophy on a column. Anyone could see a whole chorus of these signs of the cross in houses, in the marketplaces . . . in bridal chambers."

When the Romans began a wide-scale persecution of Christians, believers used the sign of the cross as a secret code for quick identification of each other. A rapid stroking of forehead, and perhaps the breast and shoulders, silently assured that "I'm one of you."

Saint Augustine is emphatic on the importance of the symbol in receiving the sacraments: "Unless that sign be applied, whether it be to the foreheads of believers, or to the very water out of which they are regenerated, or to the oil with which they receive the anointing charism, none of them is properly administered."

Over the centuries, Roman Catholics resorted to making the sign of the cross not once but three times in succession (with three fingers) as an additional symbol of the Trinity. For a time following the Reformation, Protestants shunned the gesture completely, regarding it as an unwanted reminder of their days under the yoke of Roman Catholicism and the pope. Furthermore, Protestants argued that the cross was a torturous reminder of Christ's cruel death. Only in recent times, and not entirely without reluctance, have more and more Protestants, especially Lutherans and Episcopalians, returned to making the sign of the cross.

COVERING THE HEAD: EXODUS 28:4, 1 CORINTHIANS 11 ◆

Since biblical times, women were required to cover their heads with scarves or veils in churches and temples, as a sign of chastity and modesty, and as an expression of guilt for the sin of Eve. Men, who made the rules, occasionally adopted head coverings for themselves.

IN CHRISTIANITY. The practice of requiring a Christian woman to cover her head in church and during prayer originates with a sexist slight made by Saint Paul in his First Letter to the Corinthians, written about 56 C.E.:

> A man indeed ought not to cover his head, because he is the image and glory of God. But woman is the glory of man. . . . This is why the woman ought to have a sign of authority over her head. (1 Cor. 11:7–10)

Paul goes on to say that a woman without a head covering is an insult to the angels.

IN JUDAISM. The earliest Jewish reference to a head covering exists in Exodus 28:4, which lists the vestments that set the priest apart from the congregation: "a breastpiece, an ephod [a richly embroidered outer garment], a robe, a brocaded tunic, a miter [turban or headband], and a sash."

The miter was called a *mitznefet* and was the tonsorial crown of the priest's wardrobe. Whereas several biblical references view a head covering as a sign of mourning the dead, the Talmud associates headgear with the concept of reverence toward God and a gesture of respect by the faithful.

A full-headed *wig* or *shaytl* (Yiddish for "wig") in time became a popular head covering for Jewish women, its intent being to make a woman's natural hair less of a sexual stimulus for men. On the other hand, a *tichl* is a large *scarf* used today by ultra-Orthodox women to cover their shaved heads. Men have always found women's hair erotic.

YARMULKE: TALMUDIC PERIOD Today, Orthodox Jews and many Conservative Jews believe that covering the head with a yarmulke or skullcap is an expression of "reverence for God," *yirat Shama'yim*. Orthodoxy demands that the head be kept covered at all times, while most Conservative Jews believe the head should be covered during prayer, study, and at mealtime.

The word "yarmulke" is Yiddish, but of uncertain meaning. One view is that the word derives from a medieval head covering called a *armucella*, worn by clergy. An alternative view is that "yarmulke" is related to the French *arme* (Latin *arma*), a round medieval helmet with a movable visor.

A less-used Yiddish word for "yarmulke" is *koppel*, from the Latin *capitalis*, "of the head."

Perhaps the most traditional view is that "yarmulke" is a mispronunciation of the Hebrew phrase *yaray may'Elokim*, "in awe of God." This idea is based in part on the words of fifth-century Talmudic scholar Huna ben Joshua: "I never walked four cubits with uncovered head because God dwells over my head."

PHYLACTERIES To fulfill God's command to bind his laws on the hands and head of man—"And thou shalt bind them for a sign upon thine hand, and they shall be as frontlets between thine eyes" (Deut. 6:8)—some Jewish men began wearing phylacteries, *tefillin* in Hebrew.

Phylacteries are two small leather cases holding slips inscribed with scrip-

Mezuzah (left), *means "doorpost."*
Phylactery (on forehead) *and*
prayer shawl.

tural passages: one box is fastened with leather thongs to the forehead, one to the left arm; a practice followed today by many Orthodox Jews during morning prayer. The word *tefillin* is related to *tefillah*, Hebrew for "prayer."

The English word "phylactery" comes from the Greek *phylax*, meaning "a watchman."

MEZUZAH ♦ *Parchment inscribed with rolled-up Scripture is also contained in the familiar cylindrical mezuzah.*

In Hebrew, the word means "doorpost," and the Bible mandates that doorposts of Jewish homes bear a mezuzah: "And thou shalt write them [the commandments] upon the doorposts of thy house and upon thy gates" (Deut. 6:9). The mezuzah was to remind the homeowner of God's laws, and to serve as a visible symbol of one's Jewish identity as well as membership in the Jewish community.

Today, many Jews continue to observe this tradition by hanging mezuzot (plural) on the doorframes of their homes or apartments. In Israel, they hang from entrances of public buildings. In the United States, a custom has arisen among some Jews of wearing small charmlike mezuzot on neck chains.

PRAYER SHAWL: NUMBERS 15:37–41 ♦

Of all the ritual garments associated with Jewish religious life, the fringed prayer shawl—*tallit*, Hebrew for "cloak" or "cover"—is perhaps the most important to Jews, and the most familiar to non-Jews.

Like the *tefillin*, it—or at least its fringe—also has a biblical source. In Numbers (15:37–41), God instructs Moses to "speak to the Children of Israel and bid them to affix fringes [*zizith*] to the corners of their garments." Whenever fringes are seen, people will be reminded of God's Ten Commandments to Moses. Thus, the prayer shawl exists to support and display the fringes.

Since the biblical mandate requires that the fringes be visible—"a fringe that you may look upon, and remember all the commandments of the Lord"—prayer shawls are not worn at night, only during daylight hours when the fringes are easily seen. The only exception to this law is on the eve of the holy Yom Kippur, though even then a man must don his prayer shawl before nightfall.

The color blue, which the Talmud relates as the favorite color of Jews— since the blue Mediterranean was the largest body of water near Israel—is the preferred color for embroidery on the *tallit*. This color preference also originates from a reference in Numbers: "Put with the fringe of each corner of the garment a thread of blue." At one time, blue thread was woven through the fringes; today, blue is often the color of the prayer shawl's stripes.

CROSS-DRESSING PROHIBITION. Today, we think of sartorial fringe as delicate feminine adornment, but in ancient times, only men wore fringed garments. Thus, the fringed *tallit* is never worn by women, whom the Bible prohibits from wearing men's clothing. Indeed, the Old Testament specifically prohibits cross-dressing by either gender: "A woman shall not wear an article proper to a man, nor shall a man put on a woman's dress; for anyone who does such things is an abomination to the Lord" (Deut. 22:5).

HYMN AND LITANY: EAST AND WEST ◆

Benediction ("a blessing"), litany (alternating phrases), hymns (praises), doxologies (declarations of glorification)—these have been from ancient times the major types of devotion, in the West and in the East.

From the third millennium B.C.E. to the time of Jesus Christ, forms of prayer changed very little from the oldest hymns and litanies unearthed among Assyrians and Babylonian peoples. A hymn (Greek *hymnos*, meaning "festive song") is a song of praise, whereas a litany (Greek *litanos*, "a pledge") is an alternation between clergy and congregation of titles of deities, or of petitions. Numerous ancient battle hymns are preserved in libraries throughout the Middle East.

The ancient Greeks, who prized poetry, couched many prayers in the form of hymns, such as the prayer of Diomedes to the goddess Athena in Homer's *Iliad*. One of the oldest-known Greek hymns is that of women devotees of Dionysus, god of wine and fertility; such songs of praise were not always pure and sublime. "If the people did not hold a procession and sing a hymn to the genitals," wrote a Greek philosopher six centuries before Christ, "it would be an outrageous performance."

By Roman times, the pantheon of gods and goddesses was so overpopulated that a worshiper had to take pains not to invoke the wrong deity and incur a god's wrath. To avoid this error, Romans consulted litanies of gods and goddesses, a Who's Who of the heavens, in order to offer thanksgiving or make a petition. At that time, a popular form of personal prayer was the *votum* or "vow," in which the suppliant strikes a mutual bargain with a deity for exchange of divine favor: "I'll build you a temple, if you grant me victory in battle." This swapping of favors, a sacred quid pro quo, mushroomed

21 ⤵

in Roman times, bequeathing to history a wealth of devotional architecture and artifacts.

For a Roman military commander, the most solemn and extreme form of the *votum* was the *devotio*, or personal "act of devotion," in which he offered his own life to a deity in order to secure a battle victory for his people.

The form of prayer called litany reaches its fullest extent in the East, in Hinduism, where repetition, and progressive absorption in devotion, lead through monotony to ecstasy. In the prayer known as the Thousand Names of Shiva, or the *Sivasahasranaman*, 1,008 titles of the "destroyer god" are invoked, each strophe ending with the same refrain. Recited with concentration and a pure heart, the litany is said to wipe out sin, as well as all sense of self.

In the West, early Christians preserved the hymns, doxologies, and benedictions composed by Jewish scribes. They also adhered to the Hebrew custom of praying three times a day. Christians particularly cherished one of the world's best-known collections of prayer: the Old Testament's 150 Psalms, the Bible's hymnal. These are songs of praise, wisdom, and puzzlement over life's many pitfalls, and remain as relevant today as when they were composed, many as early as the tenth century B.C.E. (*See* Psalms.)

In the seventh century, Islamic liturgy added a ritual daily prayer called the salat, which displays both Jewish and Christian influences. This minutely detailed prayer ritual is recited while the suppliant turns toward Mecca, in Saudi Arabia, five times a day. Since, as mentioned, Islamic prayer is an act of adoration of Allah, it does not accommodate the kind of petitioning for personal wants and desires typical of Christian and Jewish prayer. (*See* Pillars of Islam.)

Prayer, in its long history, has not evolved in any progressive social or personal sense, unlike the people who pray. Then and now, East and West, prayer, in the presence of life's mysteries, seeks a dialogue with the divine.

In the next chapter, we'll examine the origins of some of the best-loved prayers of several faiths.

𝕭est-𝕷oved 𝕻rayers

Apostles' Creed to Agnus Dei

LORD'S PRAYER: MATTHEW 6:9–13, 65–75 c.e. ◆

Although the Lord's Prayer is a unifying bond in Christianity, it is thoroughly Jewish in structure, containing common Hebrew elements of praise and petition, and a yearning for the coming of the Kingdom of God. Technically, the prayer consists of an introductory address, followed by six elements: three praises concerning God's glory, and three petitions acknowledging the human need for sustenance, forgiveness, and deliverance from evil. They are:

ADDRESS: Our Father who art in heaven.

PRAISES: 1. Hallowed be thy name.

               2. Thy kingdom come.

               3. Thy will be done, on earth as it is in heaven.

PETITIONS: 4. Give us this day our daily bread.

               5. And forgive us our debts [or trespasses], as we also have forgiven our debtors.

               6. And lead us not into temptation, but deliver us from evil.

This is the version traditionally used in the Roman Catholic Church. Other churches added a doxology (Greek *doxa*, "exalted praise") that has gained acceptance among Catholics as well in recent decades: "For thine is the kingdom and the power and the glory, forever." These words of sheer exaltation exist in many old manuscripts, and in several Jewish prayers composed in Christ's time, but they are clearly later additions and not part of the original.

Authorship of the original, of course, is traditionally taken to be Jesus Christ himself, in the Sermon on the Mount, delivered somewhere between

*The Sermon on the Mount.
The Lord's Prayer (the
Catholic's "Our Father")
is Christ's example of a
perfect prayer.*

the years 27 to 30 C.E. The words were first recorded some thirty-five years later by Matthew, who gives the full prayer; Luke (11:2–4) gives an abbreviated version.

That the Lord's Prayer is distinctly Jewish is made abundantly clear by Jesus Christ when he suggests to his listeners how they should pray:

"In praying, do not multiply words as the Gentiles do; for they think that by saying a great deal, they will be heard. . . . Your Father knows what you need before you ask him" (Matt. 6:7–9).

Then Christ provides instructions on the ideal parsimonious prayer: "In this manner you shall pray: 'Our Father who art in heaven. . . .' "

Early Christians took Our Lord's command—"In this manner you shall pray"—quite seriously, some clergy reciting three hundred Our Fathers a day, keeping tabs by tossing pebbles into a pile. The earliest commentary on the prayer was that by Tertullian, around 198 C.E., who called it the "epitome of the whole gospel."

Saint Jerome in the fourth century tampered with the wording a bit, changing "give us this day our *daily* [*quotidianum*] bread" to "supernatural [*supersubstantialem*] bread," but no one liked that at all. Around the same time, Saint Augustine, who felt that the Lord's Prayer was the source of all other prayers, instructed that it be the *oratio quotidiana*, the prayer recited three times a day—a Jewish formula.

For centuries, the Lord's Prayer was taught to simple illiterate folk only in Latin as the *Pater Noster*, which they recited by rote, probably not comprehending individual words and phrases. Amazingly, although English versions of the prayer exist before the Reformation, there was before that century no single, hallowed text; the first authoritative prayer appeared in the 1539 *Manuall of Prayers of the Prymer in Englysh.*

EIGHT BEATITUDES:
SERMON ON THE MOUNT, MATTHEW 5:3–12 ◆

The word "beatitude" is from the Latin *beatitudo*, suggesting a state of "perfect happiness" or "perfect blessedness."

Traditionally, Jesus Christ is credited with composing the Lord's Prayer and the Beatitudes, as well as the Golden Rule, all delivered in a single lengthy sermon. But the text that we take today to be the Sermon on the Mount was most likely not a single homily delivered on a single day. Rather, the long passage in Matthew is undoubtedly a compilation by the Gospel writer of Christ's essential teachings.

A shorter passage in the Gospel of Luke presents many of the same ideas, often in similar language, and has Jesus delivering the sermon on level ground. While Matthew lists eight Beatitudes, Luke gives four, in slightly different form (Luke 6:20–22). Biblical scholars suspect that Luke's Gospel passage, shorter and less detailed, may well be closer to an actual sermon delivered by Christ in Aramaic.

The Beatitudes are promises by Christ of specific rewards to those who cultivate certain spiritual qualities or who perform particular good works. As Matthew lists Christ's guarantees:

1. Blessed are the poor in spirit; for theirs is the Kingdom of Heaven.
2. Blessed are the meek; for they shall possess the earth.
3. Blessed are they that mourn; for they shall be comforted.
4. Blessed are they that hunger and thirst after justice; for they shall have their fill.
5. Blessed are the merciful; for they shall obtain mercy.
6. Blessed are the clean of heart; for they shall see God.
7. Blessed are the peacemakers; for they shall be called the children of God.
8. Blessed are they that suffer persecution for justice's sake; for theirs is the Kingdom of Heaven.

The origins of other phrases composed by Jesus Christ that have great spiritual meaning for all Christians:

IN GETHSEMANE: "Abba, Father, all things are possible to thee. Remove this cup from me; yet not what I will, but what thou willest" (Mark 14:36). "Abba" is Aramaic for "father."

ON THE CROSS:	"Father, forgive them; for they know not what they do" (Luke 23:34).
IN AGONY:	"My God, my God, why hast thou forsaken me?" (Mark 15:34).
AT THE MOMENT OF DEATH:	"Father, into thy hands I commit my spirit!" (Luke 23:46).

HAIL MARY: SIXTEENTH CENTURY C.E. ◆

Whereas the Our Father is called a *liturgical* prayer, straight from the Bible, the Hail Mary is known as a *devotional* prayer that evolved over time from the pious practices of monks, nuns, and lay Christians. The Lord's Prayer was voiced by followers in Christ's own time, but Mary's devotion did not become the popular form of prayer we know today until the sixteenth century.

This homage to the Virgin, assembled piecemeal, is divided into two major parts: the salutation and the petition.

SALUTATION. The first salutation, "Hail, full of Grace; the Lord is with thee," is the angel Gabriel's greeting to Mary at the time of the Annunciation of Christ's conception. The words are out of Luke (1:28), to which the Church, for clarity, inserted the proper name "Mary."

"Blessed art thou amongst women, and blessed is the fruit of thy womb" is also from Scripture (Luke 1:42), and the phrase is Elizabeth's salutation to Mary at the Visitation. Again, for clarity, the Church added the proper "Jesus" after "womb" so there could be no mistaking whom Mary was carrying.

During the early Middle Ages, the sentence from the mouth of Gabriel was recommended by priests as a form of physical penance: one genuflected and recited the line scores of times, or hundreds of times, depending on the severity of one's sin.

The Annunciation to Mary by the angel Gabriel opens the Hail Mary.

Most Christians today might be surprised to learn that these two salutations *were* the Hail Mary in its entirety in the twelfth century. In fact, that's the first time both passages were combined to form a devotional prayer to Mary.

PETITIONS. The first petitionary part of the prayer, "Holy Mary, Mother of God," is a phrase that dates specifically from the Council of Ephesus in 431 C.E.

Ephesus was the ancient Ionian Greek city in what is now Turkey. It was important in Greek and Roman times as the site of the Temple of Artemis (Diana, to the Romans), goddess of the moon, wild beasts, and patron of hunters. Ephesus is suspected by some scholars to be where Mary lived out her earthly days.

The Greek city, which the Goths sacked and virtually destroyed in 262, became the location in 431 for Pope Celestine I's ecumenical council. The gathering of bishops debated whether Christ, from the moment of conception, had two distinct natures, human and divine. That is, was Mary the mother of only a human fetus, who after his birth became divine? Or was Mary the mother of God himself? Supporters of the latter proposition rioted for days, literally running through the streets of Ephesus shouting, "Holy Mary! Mother of God!"

When council bishops broke the news that Christ was, from the moment of his conception, divine, and that Mary was indeed the Mother of God, Christians began to pray to her with a new phrase: "Holy Mary, Mother of God, pray for us sinners."

In the sixteenth century, the Church created the full devotional prayer we know today by augmenting the above petition to read: "Holy Mary, Mother of God, pray for us sinners, now and at the hour of our death, Amen."

By this point in history, Mary had become a major figure of Christian devotion, personally appearing around the world in apparitions, and her perpetual virginity had become the heated focus of Reformation debate. The Church felt Mary needed a prayer that spelled out her theology. (*See* Virginity; Visions.)

Had Mary, Christ's mother, really resided in Ephesus? It's known that Saint John, whom Christ charged with his mother's care, lived in Ephesus. The Temple of Artemis was rediscovered in 1869, and the city has been extensively excavated in our own century. There exists the remains of a "house of the Virgin," though whether Mary lived out her earthly days there, or whether the house is merely a shrine erected in her memory, may never be known for certain.

ORIGIN OF THE BLACK MADONNA ◆ *The phrase refers to more than 150 images of the Virgin Mary found throughout Europe, at several major shrines, which portray her as black.*

Why a black-faced Virgin?

In most of the images studied, the facial color seems to be an accident of art. For instance, age and a patina of soot account for some darkenings. In other cases, silver plate or paint has oxidized; or the ripened wooden surface beneath the painting has discolored and bled through.

But there may be more to the mystery. Mary may have lived in Ephesus, and it is known that Greek artists often depicted the moon goddess Artemis of Ephesus as black, as Roman painters occasionally colored their own huntress Diana of Ephesus black—perhaps for the superstitious reason that black females were thought from ancient times to be more potent miracle workers. The cult of Mary is thought to spring from the cult of Diana, and it's possible that early worshipers of the Blessed Virgin Mary felt that a black-faced Madonna would bring them better luck.

APOSTLES' CREED: LATE SIXTH CENTURY c.e. ◆

A creed is a precise statement of beliefs, and all religions cherish their own creeds. The word "creed" is from the Latin *credo*, meaning "I believe."

The major creed used by Roman Catholics, Anglicans, and many Protestants begins with quick affirmations of central truths—the Trinity, the Annunciation, the Virgin Birth, the Crucifixion, the Harrowing of Hell, the Resurrection, the Ascension:

I believe in God, the Father Almighty, Creator of heaven and earth; and in Jesus Christ, His only Son, Our Lord; who was conceived by the Holy Spirit,

A creed, from credo, Latin for "I believe," is composed by clerics as an affirmation of central religious truths.

born of the Virgin Mary, suffered under Pontius Pilate, was crucified, died, and was buried. He descended into hell; the third day He arose again from the dead; He ascended into heaven. . . .

According to tradition, this manifesto of twelve beliefs was penned by the twelve Apostles, each man contributing one article of faith; hence its name. But, actually, the creed came together piecemeal, springing from a list of questions converts had to answer in order to be baptized into the faith.

Typically, a bishop would ask a catechumen (person to be baptized): "Dost thou believe in God the Father almighty?" . . . "Dost thou believe Our Lord was conceived by the Holy Spirit, born of the Virgin Mary?" The convert would respond: "I believe." In fact, an example of such interrogation used to baptize Romans about 200 C.E. is preserved in the *Apostolic Tradition* of Hippolytus.

Such lists of beliefs were then known as baptismal creeds. For Roman Catholics, perhaps the earliest formula is given by Luke in Acts 8:37, in the Confraternity Bible, when Philip converts the Ethiopian. Philip says: "If thou dost believe with all thy heart . . ." And the convert answers: "I believe in Jesus Christ, the Son of God." (This verse 37 is not found in Greek and Vulgate manuscripts, nor is it recognized by other authorities.)

What is recited today as the Apostles' Creed reached its final form late in the sixth century in southwestern France. Gradually, its string of affirmations—I believe in the Holy Catholic Church, the communion of saints, the remission of sins, the resurrection of the flesh . . . —replaced earlier baptismal creeds. During the thirteenth-century reign of Pope Innocent III, it became the official creed of the entire Catholic Church in the West. To this day, the prayer is not recognized by Eastern Orthodox churches.

Into its few sentences, the creed packs a wealth of beliefs, points an accusing finger at Pontius Pilate, and seats the risen Christ *on the right hand of God the Father*. The Apostles' Creed is a concise summary of faith from Creation to Final Judgment.

NICENE CREED: LATE FOURTH CENTURY C.E. ◆

This Christian creed (examined in detail elsewhere in this book) sets forth the official Church teaching on the Trinitarian Godhead. The word *Filioque*, Latin for "and from the Son," was later added to the passage: "I believe in the Holy Spirit, who proceeds from the Father *and from the Son*." The all-important word gave the Holy Spirit equal Godhead status.

CREED OF PIUS IV: SIXTEENTH CENTURY ◆

Called the Profession of Faith of the Council of Trent, this important Christian creed was promulgated in the papal bull *Injunctum Nobis*, issued on November 13, 1564, as Reformation rhetoric heated up. Countering Martin Luther's many charges against Rome, it is a concise summary of Christian doctrines concerning Scripture, original sin, faith, the Mass and sacraments, veneration of saints, indulgences, and the primacy of the papacy at Rome. It was Pius's "Take that, Luther!" fired back at the Reformer.

EASTERN CREEDS ◆

Asian religions have parallels to Christian creeds. Some chanted mantras in Buddhism and Hinduism are actually professions of beliefs not unlike the Apostles' Creed. Observe the structural similarities between the terse affirmations in the Apostles' Creed and the thrice-repeated mantra: "I take refuge in the Buddha. I take refuge in the teachings. I take refuge in the community."

ISLAMIC CREEDS: SEVENTH CENTURY C.E. ◆

The primary Islamic creed is known as the *shahada*, or "profession of faith," and consists of two short statements: "There is no god but God" and "Muhammad is the Messenger of God." Both occur in the sacred Koran, but not combined.

Just as the Apostles' Creed is a baptismal formula for acceptance into the Christian faith, the shahada is recited by converts to Islam as part of the ceremony for becoming a Muslim. The shahada is the first of the so-called Five Pillars of Islam, which sum up the religious duties of all Muslims.

Since Christians, Jews, and Muslims all agree on the first expression of the shahada, "There is no god but God," it is the second credo that defines a Muslim; and the phrase "Muhammad is the Messenger of God" is intended to imply that Muhammad was the final and supreme prophet of all those in the three faiths God honored with prophecy.

The Koran's prologue or *Al-Fatihah* is a solemn prayer to the God of all three faiths:

All praise be to Allah, Lord of all the worlds,
Most beneficent, ever-merciful,
King of the Day of Judgment.
You alone we worship, and to You alone turn for help.
Guide us to the path that is straight,
The path of those You have blessed,
Not of those who have earned Your anger, not those who have gone astray.

JUDAISM ◆ *It is interesting that Judaism, from which both Christianity and Islam sprang, has, among world religions, a paucity of creeds. The reason is that Jewish identity and beliefs traditionally have been defined in terms of the observance of the commandments and of oral law, not by a tidy enumeration of doctrines summed up in a single creed.*

On the other hand, Christianity has over 150 officially recognized creeds (and confessions), since membership in the faith began through a profession of doctrinal beliefs; a bishop's baptismal interrogation of catechumens.

The essence of any religion's creed is summed up best in a classic phrase by the twelfth-century theologian Anselm: "Credo ut intelligam," "I believe in order that I may understand."

CONFITEOR: FOURTEENTH CENTURY C.E. ◆

The word "Confiteor" is from the Latin for "I confess." Just as it was customary at the time of baptism to make a credo, "I believe," at the time of the sacrifice of the Mass, it was customary for Christians to make a confession, with a prayer that began with the words "I confess."

This custom is ancient and grounded in the Israelites' practice of making a confession before sacrificing a burnt offering to the Lord.

The Catholic Confiteor opens with a Who's Who of the Heavens:

I confess to Almighty God, to Blessed Mary ever Virgin, to blessed Michael the Archangel, to blessed John the Baptist, to the holy Apostles Peter and Paul, and to all the saints, that I have sinned exceedingly in thought, word, and deed. . . .

Its wording has changed considerably over the centuries; and in different Christian countries, where locals substitute for the names of angels and saints their own national favorites.

In the earliest form of the confessional prayer, the sinner repented just before God the Father, Son, and Holy Spirit. The first litany of saints entered the Confiteor around the seventh century.

Not until the eleventh century did the prayer's most notable phrase—"through my fault, through my fault, through my most grievous fault [*mea culpa, mea culpa, mea maxima culpa*]"—begin to emerge. At that time, one *mea culpa* sufficed and the penitent struck his or her breast a single time. Five hundred years later, the sinner was required to strike the breast twice, uttering two *mea culpa*s. Another five hundred years, and a third *mea culpa* and third breast-beat became mandatory. One must conclude that people were sinning more. Or more grievously. In fact, by the fourteenth century, the Church had added the heavy adjective *maxima*: "through my most *grievous* fault." Since then, the prayer has changed not at all.

DE PROFUNDIS: BOOK OF PSALMS, TENTH CENTURY B.C.E. AND LATER ◆

Literally meaning "out of the depths," the De profundis originates with Psalm 130: "Out of the depths I have cried unto thee, O Lord. Lord, hear my voice . . ."

The penitential Psalm is a gasp of desperation and hope on the part of the penitent who is waiting for God's redemption. Christian churches have used the Psalm for centuries as a prayer to beg forgiveness of sin. Oscar Wilde borrowed the title for the intensely melodramatic memoir he composed while jailed on charges of homosexuality.

In about the tenth century, the prayer became one part of a priest's longer Office for the Dead; and then became a prayer principally for the dead. Its popularity in that regard remains a mystery to this day. One modern scholar has suggested that time constraints eventually forced priests to shorten the Office for the Dead, and the De profundis, which occurs early in the Office, became by default all that was read at a funeral service. Thus parishioners became acquainted with it as a prayer for the departed. Misled, perhaps, by the seemingly funereal phrase "out of the depths," when in fact *spiritual* depths is what the Psalm is about, not six feet under. Anyway, by the middle of the thirteenth century, families couldn't bury a loved one without chanting the De profundis.

AGNUS DEI: SEVENTH CENTURY C.E. ◆

Latin for "Lamb of God," Jesus Christ, the Agnus Dei is a short prayer of three invocations, each beginning with the phrase "Lamb of God." It is based on John the Baptist's exclamation on seeing Christ approach: "Behold, the Lamb of God, who takes away the sin of the world!" (John 1:29).

This reference is the source of the "lamb" symbol for Jesus Christ in Christian liturgy. The prayer goes on: "Lamb of God, who takes away the sin of the world, have mercy upon us! [recited twice] . . . Lamb of God, who takes away the sin of the world, grant us peace!"

The word "lamb" is common to Eastern liturgies, designating Christ and the consecrated bread of the Eucharist, and the Agnus Dei probably began in Syrian churches. It was introduced into the Roman rite in the seventh century, during the pontificate of Pope Sergius I (687–701), who was of Syrian descent.

In Roman Catholic services, the Agnus Dei is intoned between the Lord's Prayer and the Communion, and it sounds the theme of sacrifice. The sacrifice of Christ on the cross is juxtaposed with the Old Testament cult of sacrificing lambs in atonement for sin. In ancient times, the image of a lamb was associated with protection from disasters such as pestilence, flood, and fire, as well as the safekeeping of women in childbirth in an era when complications from labor could be deadly.

Anglican and Lutheran liturgies both include the Agnus Dei in their eucharistic rites, but this was not always the case. The popular Communion anthem was deleted from the 1552 Book of Common Prayer, as it was from most reformed liturgies of that religiously combative century.

WAX DISKS. In addition to being a thrice-chanted prayer, an *agnus dei* is also a devotional artifact: a disk of wax, embossed with the figure of a lamb, blessed by a pope. The practice began in the ninth century, and the wax used came from the drippings and remains of the previous year's paschal candles. The disks were cherished and used to invoke God's help against the dangers of fire, storm, plague, and childbirth.

The disks most likely derived from pagan amulets; many ancient lamb trinkets are extant. A lamb's innocence, purity, and helplessness made it an ideal sacrificial offering; whereas, its tender youth rendered it tasty "veal" (Old French *veel*, "little calf"). Popes blessed the disks on the Tuesday after Easter in the first and seventh years of their pontificates. Under the Reformation, the papal disks were melted down in England and turned back into candles. Waste not, want not.

MAGNIFICAT: NEW TESTAMENT, LUKE 1:46–55 ◆

This beautiful hymn of praise is spoken by the Blessed Virgin Mary, the mother of Jesus, in Luke's Gospel. What is most fascinating about its origin is that Mary is supposed to have composed it extemporaneously, in all of its abundant lyricism and with its numerous Old Testament references.

After the angel Gabriel startles Mary with news of her pregnancy, Mary visits Elizabeth, who is pregnant with Christ's cousin-to-be, John the Baptist. Elizabeth's reply makes clear that she realizes the Promised One is in Mary's womb: "Blessed are thou among women, and blessed is the fruit of thy womb! Why is this granted me, that the Mother of my Lord should come to me?"

Luke portrays Mary as bursting into song, a canticle (Latin *cantus*, "chant") called the Magnificat, deriving its name from its first line in Latin: *"Magnificat anima mea Dominum"*:

> *My soul magnifies the Lord, and my spirit rejoices in God my Savior, for he has regarded the low estate of his handmaiden.*
>
> *For behold, henceforth all generations will call me blessed; for he who is mighty has done great things to me, and holy is his name.*
>
> *And his mercy is on those who fear him from generation to generation. He has shown strength with his arm, he has scattered the proud in the imagination of their hearts, he has put down the mighty from their thrones, and exalted those of low degree; he has filled the hungry with good things, and the rich he has sent away empty.*
>
> *He has helped his servant Israel, in remembrance of his mercy, as he spoke to our fathers, to Abraham and to his posterity forever.*

It's certainly a spontaneous mouthful. Mary was quite a poet. And biblical scholar: for this canticle echoes the Psalms; and the triumphant song of Miriam; and, too, the long, lyrical speech of Hannah in 1 Samuel 2. Hannah, the mother of Samuel, the great eleventh-century B.C.E. judge of Israel, also burst into song upon learning she was to bear a son: "My heart rejoices in the Lord, and my strength is exalted in my God. . . ." Hannah goes on to say many of the things Mary would voice a thousand years later. Luke had read the Book of Samuel.

Some scholars contend that Mary's Magnificat originally was a song put into the mouth of Elizabeth, celebrating her own son-to-be, John the Baptist. However, most Greek and Latin texts attributed it to Mary.

Today, the hymn is incorporated, along with the burning of incense, into the liturgical services of the Western churches at Vespers, and of the Eastern Orthodox churches at the morning services.

BENEDICTUS ◆

At the birth of his son John the Baptist, Zechariah (or Zacharias, or Zachary) also burst into song, the canticle now known as the Benedictus. It is not unlike Hannah's song of thanksgiving or Mary's Magnificat. It begins: "Blessed be the Lord, the God of Israel, because he has visited and wrought redemption for his people" (Luke 1:68–79).

ANGELUS: POPE JOHN XXII, FOURTEENTH CENTURY ◆

Few popes write prayers that become church classics. One troubled pontiff did.

Second of the Avignon Popes, John XXII (1316–34) consolidated the stay of the papacy in France in spite of his many statements that he wished to move to Rome. Later, he was charged with heresy, provoked by four sermons he delivered in the winter of 1331–32. Whereas traditional Church doctrine held that the souls of the saints resided in Paradise enjoying the full vision of God, John insisted their arrival would be delayed until after the Final Judgment; until then, they could only contemplate the "humanity of Christ." In turn, French theologians insisted John was a heretic.

On his deathbed, to play it safe, John made a retraction, though he hedged. He agreed that the souls of saints see God face-to-face "as clearly as their condition allows."

Picking phrases he liked from the New Testament, he pieced together the devotional Angelus, to be recited three times a day, morning, noon, and evening, in honor of Christ and Mary. It became a Roman Catholic favorite. Phrases alternate between the priest (P) and the congregation (C).

Pope John XXII (1316–34) wrote the Angelus.

P: The angel of the Lord declared unto Mary.

C: And she conceived of the Holy Ghost. Hail, Mary . . . etc.

P: Behold the handmaid of the Lord.

C: Be it done unto me according to Thy word. Hail, Mary . . . etc.

P: And the Word was made flesh.

C: And dwelt among us. Hail, Mary . . . etc.

P: Pray for us, O holy Mother of God.

C: That we may be made worthy of the promises of Christ . . .

KYRIE ELEISON: PSALM 123, TENTH CENTURY B.C.E. ◆

The Greek invocation or cry for help, *eleison*, "have mercy," is found in numerous historical liturgies. In the Latin Mass, it occurs as a part of nine invocations, three addressed to God the Father, *Kyrie Eleison* ("Lord have mercy"); three addressed to God the Son, *Christe Eleison* ("Christ have mercy"); and three to the Holy Spirit, *Kyrie Eleison*.

Traditionally, it's said that the formula Kyrie-Christe-Kyrie was derived to symbolize the Trinitarian Godhead, but that is not so; the Christian prayer originally was addressed only to Jesus Christ. The phrase appears in Matthew 15:22, when the Canaanite woman beseeches Jesus: "O Lord, have mercy [pity] on me! . . . My daughter is sorely beset by the Devil."

But this cry for divine help was used by the Israelites as early as the tenth century B.C.E., and it's found in Psalm 123, a hymn of thanksgiving in which the people of Israel acknowledge that without the Lord's help, they would have been utterly destroyed by their enemies. In fact, so elemental is the cry of *eleison*, to any god, that it's safe to assume that a *kyrie* of some sort was among the earliest utterances of humankind.

In Latin, the cry "have mercy on us" is *misere nobis*, and it is common to many prayers, such as the Agnus Dei: "Lamb of God, who takes away the sin of the world, have mercy on us."

The Kyrie entered the Latin Mass in the fifth century, during the influential pontificate of Gelasius (492–96), an imperial pope renowned for his insistence on the supremacy of the See at Rome (*see* Papacy); he was the first pope to be saluted as "Vicar of Christ," at the Roman synod on May 13, 495. Gelasius's writings leave the impression of an arrogant, narrow-minded, harsh pontiff; he made considerable changes in the Roman liturgy.

KADDISH: JUDAISM, TALMUDIC PERIOD ◆

The Kaddish, part of Jewish doxology, is an Aramaic poem recited during synagogue services, in which the congregation responds: "May the greatness of His being be blessed from eternity to eternity." Its main theme, "Let us magnify and let us sanctify the great name of God," is echoed in the Christian Lord's Prayer in phrases such as "hallowed be Thy name."

Originally, the Kaddish (Aramaic *qaddish*, "holy") was recited in rabbinical academies by a preacher at the end of his discourse, or following the study of the nonlegal part of the Talmud, the Aggadah. The prayer contains a paragraph beginning with the words Al Yisrael, "for the sake of Israel," which is a petition for the welfare of scholars.

Aside from the final Hebrew verse, "May He who makes peace in the highest bring peace upon us and upon all Israel, Amen," the language of the Kaddish is Aramaic, the language used by Jews in Babylon and Palestine for nearly a thousand years, from the time of Ezra in the fifth century B.C.E. until well after the end of the Talmudic period.

MOURNER'S KADDISH: THIRTEENTH CENTURY C.E. ◆

Over time, the Kaddish also became a prayer for mourners, with modifications, and is known as the "Kaddish of the Orphan."

The earliest reference of a mourner's use of the Kaddish is in a thirteenth-century book, *Or Zarua*, by Rabbi Isaac ben Moses of Vienna. Human hearts filled with grief and sorrow, the prayer suggests, are to be laid in the lap of the Lord. Originally, only a son was obliged to recite the mourner's Kaddish for a deceased parent. Gradually, the practice was extended to include daughters; then brothers and sisters. At the conclusion of the prayer, the mourner terminates his "audience" with God and respectfully takes three steps backward, acknowledging God as the King of Kings.

There is no reference to the dead in the mourner's Kaddish. Rather, the prayer mitigates the grief of bereavement by a vision of the Kingdom of God triumphant. This because the highest test of a person's faith is his ability to praise God at the moment of deepest grief.

For deceased relatives, the Kaddish is recited for only thirty days after the death. For deceased parents, the prayer must be said daily for eleven months (minus one day), because, as the Talmud suggests, "The memory of the dead grows dim after twelve months." However, a duration of twelve months in Talmudic times was exactly the period a wicked sinner supposedly suffered the flames of Hell. Thus, to avoid people assuming that a deceased parent had sinned and was in Hell, sixteenth-century rabbi Moses ben Israel Isserles of Cracow knocked one month off the traditional twelve.

SALAT: ISLAM, SEVENTH CENTURY C.E. ◆

The prayer ritual *salat*, meaning "worship," is one of the so-called *Five Pillars of Islam*—along with *shahada* (profession of faith), *zakat* (almsgiving), *saum* (fasting), and *hajj* (pilgrimage)—and one of the earliest practices to arise in the faith revealed to Muhammad.

Initially, only Muhammad, who had studied Judaism and Christianity, recited the prayer, twice a day, at sunrise (*salat al-fajr*) and sunset (*al-maghrib*). Soon, though, the performance of the salat was required for all Muslims, and a third recitation was added, midday (*az-zuhr*), possibly influenced by the practice of Jews and early Christians, who performed their prayer rituals three times a day. And Muslims initially faced toward Jerusalem, a Jewish custom.

Quickly, though, came the so-called "break with the Jews," and Muslims rotated their direction of prayer (*qibla*) to face Mecca, the obligatory orientation for the salat ever since. By the time of the Prophet's death, there were five salats: sunrise, midday, afternoon (*al-'asr*), sunset, and evening (*al-'isha*); and the prayer ritual was distinctive in its bowing (*ruku'*) and prostration (*sujud*).

FACING MECCA. The salat is a richly complex ritual. Collective worship is prized over private praying in Islam, with worshipers preferably gathering in a mosque. With their faces turned in the direction of the sacred shrine, the Ka'bah, located in Mecca, worshipers align themselves in parallel rows behind the prayer leader, or imam, who directs them as they execute the physical postures and recitations. In an upright position, the worshiper proclaims "God is most great [*Allahu akbar*]." He then recites the opening chapter and passages from the sacred Koran.

The worshiper then bows from the waist and straightens up; and from a kneeling position, he lowers his face to the ground, rises up, then prostrates himself again. Having repeated the physical postures (*rak'ahs*) the prescribed number of times, he makes a profession of faith before reciting a prayer for the Prophet: "God bless him and grant him salvation." The salat ends when each person has said to the individual on his right and left: "Peace be to you." The ritual salat may be temporarily omitted in times of illness or war.

In total, the salat contains thirteen invariant essentials: six verbal utterances, six physical postures, and the mandate that these twelve be executed in the correct order. The bodily postures are said to express in a sacramental way the sense of the praise and prayer that accompany them.

BOOK OF PSALMS:
JUDAISM, TENTH TO THIRD CENTURIES B.C.E. ◆

The singing of Psalms by early Christians, called psalmody, gave rise to classical *Gregorian chant*, a musical form that experienced a resurgence of popularity in the early 1990s. For a time, music with roots two thousand years old topped contemporary best-seller charts. But psalmody originated among professional Hebrew singers who would turn to the Old Testament's Book of Psalms, the Psalter, for inspiration. Psalms could be secular in text, or sacred.

The Bible's 150 Psalms—which plead with God and praise him, appeal for forgiveness and for destruction of enemies, which offer wisdom and pose problems—express the entire range of human feelings and experience, from dark depression to exuberant joy. Although rooted in the era in which they were composed, the Old Testament's hymnal remains timeless. The Psalms are quite simply among the best-loved, most-read pages of the Bible. The final and magnificently climactic Psalm 150 forms a doxology to the sweep of the collection, and it is a choral symphony of praises. Psalms is the only book from the Old Testament that is regularly bound with the New Testament when only the New Testament is desired. It is as though the volume would not be a Bible without the Book of Psalms—testament to the Psalms' universal appeal.

Individual biblical Psalms cannot be dated. But manuscripts found at Qumran reveal that the entire collection as we have it may have been finalized before the Maccabean period of the second century B.C.E.

WHO WROTE THE PSALMS? Nearly half of the 150 are introduced by the suggestive phrase "A Psalm of David," David being the shepherd boy who became Israel's second king and founded the royal line from which the Messiah was foretold. This attribution, taken with the Bible's depiction of King David as "the sweet psalmist of Israel" (2 Sam. 23:1), has led many readers to the erroneous conclusion that David was their sole author.

King David wrote and collected a large number of Psalms, but the Book of Psalms—written in the style of David, and perhaps assembled in the memory of David—came together over a period of some six hundred years, the work of many skillful poets, some of them members of the Levitical guild of musicians. Some Psalms credited to David mention the Temple in

David and Goliath. As king, David wrote many—but not all—of the biblical Psalms.

Jerusalem, built after his death, or the Babylonian Exile, which occurred more than three centuries later.

PROSE TO POETRY. "The psalms are poems," wrote C. S. Lewis, "and poems intended to be sung." And poems that owe their form and meter to ancient Hebrew verse.

"We shall fight on the beaches, / We shall fight on the landing-grounds, / We shall fight in the fields and in the streets." That reiterative phraseology is, of course, Winston Churchill's, but it demonstrates perfectly how ancient Hebrew storytellers employed repetition and rhythm to elevate prose to poetry. In fact, the favorite Canaanite technique of composition was reiteration; that is, drive a point home by repetition: "Spoil of dyed stuffs for Sisera, / Spoil of dyed stuffs embroidered, / Two pieces of dyed work embroidered for my neck as spoil" (Judges 5:30).

The Book of Psalms, used by the Israelites centuries ago as we employ it today, is best thought of as an anthology of poetry, in the style of David.

The word "psalter," synonymous with "Book of Psalms," is from the Greek *psalterion*, which was a stringed, harplike instrument with a shallow sound box, played by plucking the strings with the fingers or a plectrum. Thus, the music of the Psalms is inherent in their name.

The Messiah is not mentioned by name in the Psalms, but phrases may be interpreted to foreshadow his coming. Certainly, the New Testament writers grabbed at such phrases to herald Jesus as the prophesied one: "Blessed is he who comes in the name of the Lord" (Old Testament, Psalm 118:26) became in the Christian Bible Matthew 21:9. And Matthew 27:46 has Jesus, crucified and expiring on the cross, quote Psalm 22: "My God, my God, why hast thou forsaken me?" The psalmists of old wrote words that took on a significance they could have hardly imagined. Good poetry is timeless.

CHAPTER

3

𝕬cts of 𝕯evotion

Rosary to Hajj

"DEVOTE"—LATIN *DEVOVERE,* "to dedicate by solemn vow."

"Devotion"—an act of piety, loyalty, or deep affection.

There are many ways to be devout, or to be orthodox, or unquestioning, or deferential, or dedicated, or sanctimonious, or obeisant, or pious, or narrow-minded, or holy. All are vows of sorts. Not all are to be aspired to. But in the history of religious devotion, all are well documented. Saint Rose of Lima, a beauty, it was said, rubbed chili pepper into her cheeks to deface her good looks and drive off suitors, saving her from temptation and preserving her virginity; the cause was noble, the act devout, but not to be emulated. (*See* Saints.) The point is, as we'll see, not all devotional practices have the purest of origins.

ROSARY, TRADITIONAL ORIGIN:
SAINT DOMINIC, THIRTEENTH CENTURY C.E. ♦

Today, the term "rosary" refers to the so-called abbreviated Dominican Rosary (five "decades" of beads instead of the original fifteen decades), a pious exercise of vocal and mental prayer. This popular form of Roman Catholic devotion consists in the recitation of five decades of Hail Marys, each preceded by an Our Father, followed by a Glory Be to the Father, and accompanied by a meditation on a mystery that is either joyous, sorrowful, or glorious.

The term "rosary" is from the Latin *rosarium,* "rose garden," a phrase that over time came to mean any grouping of similar things, such as beads on a string. Eventually, the terms "rosary" and "rose garden" became synonymous. For many centuries, the English referred to any planted bed of thorny rosebushes as their rosary. You pruned your rosary, fertilized and watered it,

41

shielded it from mites, and snipped off blossoms to arrange smartly in a vase. But the picturesque gardening phrase gradually fell into disuse.

KNOTS TO NUTS TO JEWELS. The practice of reciting prayers on a string of knots, or knotted string, goes back to the Indic priests of the Middle East prior to 500 B.C.E. It also developed in the Western world before the dawn of Christianity, and for a very practical reason.

In many early religions, the frequent repetition of a prayer was believed to increase its efficacy. A petition to a god droned one hundred times—say, for deliverance from a plague—stood a better chance of being answered than one recited only once. Quantity counted. Quality, too, most likely. Many religions prescribed the exact number of repetitions of a specific prayer, to achieve a desired end. For instance, the traveling Knights Templars, founded in the year 1119 to fight in the Crusades, could not attend church services regularly and were required to recite the Lord's Prayer exactly fifty-seven times a day; on the death of a fellow knight, the number jumped to a hundred times a day, for one week.

To keep tally *and* pray simultaneously, counting on one's fingers, was impossible; assistance was required. Knotted strings were a memory aid, a divine calculator. This device was referred to in Sanskrit as the "remembrancer," and in European languages as the *calculus* and the *numeralia*, both "counting" terms.

People in all cultures devised homegrown memory aids: stringed fruit pits, or dried berries, or fragments of bones of a beloved deceased. In the Pacific Islands, sharks' teeth were a favorite. Early monks tallied their numerous genuflections and signs of the cross with knotted cowhide cords, which also served as whips for penitent self-flagellation. Wealthy folk strung together precious stones, dazzling trinkets of glass, and gold nuggets.

Europeans even referred to an individual knot, berry, or pit as a "prayer." In fact, our word "prayer" comes from the Anglo-Saxon for "bead," *bede*, which in turn derives from *biddan*, "to beg"—a clear reference to the purpose of many prayers. As Saint Augustine said: "Man is a beggar before God." In a linguistic sense, prayer beads are made for begging, and the phrase itself, "prayer beads," is redundant.

In the eleventh century, the Anglo-Saxon gentlewoman Lady Godiva, remembered for her tax-protesting ride in the buff through Coventry, England, bequeathed to a monastery: "one circlet of gems which she had threaded on a string, in order that by fingering them one by one, as she successively recited her prayers, she might not fall short of the exact number."

No one person developed the Rosary, although traditionally Saint Dominic gets all the credit.

VIRGIN MARY APPEARS TO DOMINIC. It was in the twelfth century that the Rosary was popularized in the Catholic Church, supposedly by Saint Dominic (who died in 1221 at Bologna), founder of the Friars Preachers, which evolved into the Dominican order of priests. As tradition has it, the Blessed Virgin Mary appeared to Dominic while he was preaching to a group of heretics and presented him with a Rosary, instructing him to teach the Rosary "as a spiritual remedy against heresy and sin."

The only proof offered in support of this story is the fact that it was included in more than a dozen papal "Rosary bulls" in the following centuries. But the purpose of a papal bull is to foster devotion, not teach historical truth. Indeed, the tradition has never been made dogma. Furthermore, each Rosary bull contains a qualifying phrase like "it is piously believed" or "it is said to be true."

Did Saint Dominic, in fact, even promote the Rosary?

Probably not. In all the writings on Dominic's canonization as a saint (canonized in 1234; feast day, August 4), the Church is pointedly silent on his contribution to the Rosary. His early biographers, while even recounting sermons he preached, don't mention the Virgin's apparition; nor do Dominican chronicles attribute the Rosary to the order's founder. Most telling of all, perhaps, medieval art of the saint—carvings of his tomb, paintings by Fra Angelico—fail to depict beads in his hands. After the tradition of Dominic's vision took hold in the mid-fifteenth century, Dominic was never depicted without his beads. A pope, Pius V, a Dominican, embraced Dominic's Rosary as an act of devotion in 1569.

TRUE ORIGIN IN THE PSALMS. In fact, the Rosary evolved. Its strong association with Christian devotion arose in the twelfth century, when the then 150 beads (fifteen decades) came to symbolize the 150 biblical Psalms. Praying the 150-beaded Rosary, an Our Father on each bead, became an easy and convenient substitute for reading the full 150 Psalms. The Rosary was called the "poor man's breviary," since a poor man could not afford a Book of Psalms but could string 150 cherry pits. The pits or beads were called "paternosters," Latin for "Our Fathers," but over the next two hundred years, as devotion to Mary increased, Hail Marys gradually replaced Our Fathers.

By the time Mary appeared at Fátima in 1917, during World War I, she in-

The Presentation in the Temple, a "Joyous Mystery"; Simeon and Anna giving thanks to God for the baby Jesus.

troduced herself as the Lady of the Rosary, carried her own string of beads over her folded palms, scented the ambient air with intense rose fragrance, and cautioned the three children who claimed to see her: "Say the Rosary every day to obtain peace for the world and an end to the war." (*See* Fátima.)

MYSTERIES OF THE ROSARY: CHRISTIANITY, MIDDLE AGES ◆

While reciting the Rosary's Our Fathers and Hail Marys, a Christian, certainly a Roman Catholic, is suppose to meditate on the faith's fifteen greatest Mysteries.

These Mysteries evolved, replacing certain Psalms. For some time after Our Fathers and Hail Marys had replaced the 150 Psalms of the Old Testament, a few Psalms of Jewish origin had been retained as points of meditation between the Rosary's decades. But gradually these fifteen meditative Old Testament Psalms were replaced by the Christian Mysteries, transforming the circle of beads into the Christian Rosary devotion.

The fifteen Christian Mysteries:

JOYOUS MYSTERIES: The *Annunciation* that Mary was to be the Mother of God; her *Visitation* to Saint Elizabeth; Christ's *Nativity* and his *Presentation* in the Temple; and the *Finding of Jesus,* who was all the while preaching in the Temple.

SORROWFUL MYSTERIES: Christ's *Agony in the Garden;* his *Scourging* and *Crowning with Thorns;* his *Carrying the Cross,* and his *Crucifixion.*

GLORIOUS MYSTERIES: Christ's *Resurrection* from the dead; his *Ascension* into Heaven; *Pentecost;* Mary's *Assumption* into Heaven; and the *Coronation* of Mary as Queen of Heaven.

INDULGENCES FOR SAYING THE ROSARY. Pope Alexander VI, in his bull of July 13, 1495 (two decades before Martin Luther's revolt),

Saint Dominic (left). *Pope Alexander VI (1492–1503) granted indulgences for saying the Rosary.*

began the practice of granting indulgences for saying the Rosary, allowing a Christian to shorten his or her stay in Purgatory. A *Crosier Indulgence* grants five hundred days off for each Our Father or Hail Mary recited. The *Dominican* and *Brigittine Indulgences* grant fifty-five hundred days off for reciting all five decades of the Rosary. A plenary or an *Apostolic Indulgence* wipes away all time in Purgatory, and these are granted by a pope on special feasts of Our Lady, Saint Joseph, or the Apostles. (*See* Indulgences.)

BENEDICTION: OLD TESTAMENT TIMES ◆

A benediction is a verbal blessing—Latin *benedicere*, "to speak well of"—conferred upon a person, place, or thing. The words invoke God's name, and are spoken by a priest or minister. Later, in Christianity, benediction would become an elaborate devotional service in its own right.

In Judaism, there are numerous benedictions or blessings. The Hebrew word of "benediction," *berakhah*, derives from the same root as *berekh*, a word meaning "knee," since in Old Testament times "bowing the knee" was an accompaniment to worship and giving thanks or praise to God.

GRACE BEFORE AND AFTER MEALS. Jewish benedictions usually begin with the words "Blessed are You, O Lord," and as prayers, they celebrate many events.

For instance, *Ha-motzi* a blessing recited over bread—"He who brings forth bread from the earth . . ."—is the Jewish Grace Before Meals, which influenced the Christian custom of that name. The same is true for Grace After Meals, or the final Jewish benediction, *Birkat ha-Mazon*.

These benedictions of enjoyment are traced back to sources in the Bible that allude to expressions of thanksgiving before and after eating, notably: 1 Samuel 9:13, and Deuteronomy 8:10. The Talmud adds that "it is forbidden to taste anything before making a benediction," since the bounty of the earth belongs to the Lord, and not offering him thanks is tantamount to theft.

A major Jewish benediction is the *Amidah*, a collection of short sacred blessings, in the style of Scripture, that connects the Jew with spiritual and historical milestones. The act of devotion consists of three opening benedictions of *praise* (1–3), thirteen intermediate *petition* blessings (4–16), and three concluding benedictions of *thanksgiving* (17–19):

1. *Avot*: God of our father
2. *Gevurot*: the mighty God
3. *Qedushat Hashem*: the sanctification of God
4. *Binah*: for understanding
5. *Teshuvah*: for repentance
6. *Selihah*: for forgiveness
7. *Ge'ulah*: for redemption
8. *Refu'ah*: for healing
9. *Hashanim*: for natural abundance
10. *Qibbuts Galuyot*: for the ingathering of the Exile
11. *Mishpat*: for the establishment of justice
12. *Haminim*: for the destruction of oppression
13. *Tzaddikim*: for the righteous
14. *Yerushalayim*: for the rebuilding of Jerusalem
15. *David*: for the advent of the Messiah
16. *Tefilah*: that our prayer be heard
17. *Avodah*: for the restoration of the Temple
18. *Hoda'ah*: our expression of gratitude
19. *Kohanim*: the prayer for peace

When the Talmud speaks of "prayer," it always refers to the benediction of the Amidah, which was considered the devotion par excellence.

BENEDICTION OF THE BLESSED SACRAMENT: CHRISTIANITY, ITALY AND FRANCE, FOURTEENTH CENTURY ◆

The New Testament offers Christians many choices of blessings. The pious Pauline benediction found in 2 Corinthians 13:14 is preferred by some churches: "The grace of the Lord Jesus Christ, and the love of God, and the communion of the Holy Spirit, be with you all, Amen."

Martin Luther, for his German Mass, opted for the impressive dignity of the Aaronic benediction found in Numbers 6:24–26: "The Lord bless thee, and keep thee. The Lord make his face shine upon thee, and be gracious unto thee. The Lord lift up his countenance upon thee, and give thee peace."

MONSTRANCE AND THE WORD "MONSTER." By the fourteenth century, Christianity had developed a formal devotional service, called the Benediction of the Blessed Sacrament.

In the ceremony, the priest exposes the Holy Eucharist, encased in a monstrance—Latin *monstrare*, "to show off"—for public adoration. The origin of this display dates to the Stations of the Cross, discussed below, in which a Host, Christ himself in body and blood, was carried throughout the Passion reenactment.

For Catholics, the devotional benediction service was for a long time held on a Sunday, in late afternoon or early evening; a hymn, the *Tantum Ergo*, was sung, and the priest blessed the congregation by raising up the Host in the monstrance; a glass-faced vessel with disk-shaped head and chalicelike stem, often surrounded by a star burst of golden rays.

Interestingly, the term "monstrance" is related to our word "monster," through the Latin *monstrare*, "to show off," monsters being "showy" creatures hard to conceal. At one time, a monstrance, or Latin *monstrum*, was a divine portent of grave misfortune for a group of people; not unlike a threat from a monster.

The elevation of the Host itself, as a bare wafer of bread, which in Christian doctrine is Christ's body and blood, began in the late Middle Ages, during the Mass service and Passion procession. The act was immensely popular from the start, offering people a chance to "see" Jesus. Indeed, people clamored for additional viewings of Jesus, and there arose need for a church service devoted specifically to such a display: Benediction of the Blessed Sacrament.

Monstrance, from the Latin monstrare, *meaning "to show off," displays the Host during Benediction; the faithful sing the "Tantum Ergo," by Thomas Aquinas.*

In a very real sense, Benediction arose from public demand to see Jesus as a wafer held high in the air. Specifically, people at that time wanted to witness the wafer of bread transformed into Christ's body, as if by watching closely enough, they might catch a glimpse of the miracle. Theological dispute over the reality of the transubstantiation in those years had piqued everyone's curiosity. Here was a miracle any priest could conjure on demand. Was the transformation accompanied by a flash of light, a burst of heat, as some pious folk claimed to experience?

Processions through town, the Host held high in a glass-faced monstrance (the most popular procession being the Corpus Christi), became the rage in the fourteenth century, causing street congestion and considerable noise, as townsfolk rang bells of respect as Christ passed. By the sixteenth century, civil legislation had to be enacted throughout parts of Europe to limit the number of street exhibitions of the Eucharist.

TANTUM ERGO:
THOMAS AQUINAS, THIRTEENTH CENTURY C.E. ◆

So "showy" was Benediction that priests in time had to warn their congregations against affording the devotion greater respect than the Holy Mass itself.

The major hymn sung during Benediction is the Latin "Tantum Ergo," which is merely the last two stanzas of Thomas Aquinas's thirteenth-century Latin song "Pange Lingua," literally, "Sing with Tongue." The saint wrote the song to honor the Blessed Sacrament, and the opening verse of the Tantum Ergo reveals the majesty and fascination that was held by the Host:

> Down in adoration falling,
> Lo! the sacred Host we hail!
> Lo! o'er ancient forms departing,
> Newer rites of grace prevail;
> Faith for all defects supplying,
> Where the feeble senses fail.

Most older Catholics will find it hard to believe that not until 1958, in the *Instruction on Sacred Music and Liturgy*, did the Sacred Congregation of Rites explicitly affirm Benediction of the Blessed Sacrament a "true liturgical function" of the Church.

A second hymn sung at Benediction, "O Salutaris Hostia," "O Saving Victim," is taken from the last two stanzas of "Verbum Supernum," the hymn of lauds for the older Feast of Corpus Christi.

KIDDUSH: JUDAISM, FIFTH CENTURY B.C.E. ◆

Bread in the Catholic Benediction *is* Jesus Christ's real body. Bread in the popular Jewish blessing known as the *motzi* symbolizes manna, the biblical "gum resin" God miraculously showered on the hungry Israelites in the wilderness.

MANNA: WHAT KIND OF FOOD IS IT? The word "manna" is of uncertain origin, but in Exodus 16:15 it is given a popular etymology by Israelites who asked, incredulously, "What is it?"—asked in Hebrew, *man'hu*, it became "manna." This "bread of the mighty ones," as it's called, is the miraculous food supplied by the Lord during the forty years the Israelites wandered from Egypt to Canaan.

Manna rained down six days a week, every week. Each sunrise, when the dew had burned off, "there on the surface of the wilderness was a fine flaky substance, as fine as frost on the ground" (Exod. 16:14). Only one day's portion was to be parsimoniously gathered up, except on the sixth day, when a double portion could be collected to keep the Sabbath a day of rest.

We're told that the mysterious food was "like coriander seed, white, and the taste of it was like wafers made with honey" (Exod. 16:31). Its appearance was like "gum resin" (Num. 11:7). The thankful Israelites "ground it in mills or beat it in mortars, then boiled it in pots and made cakes of it; and the taste of it was like the taste of cakes baked with oil" (Num. 11:8).

What was it?

The answer might strike some as unappetizing, but it is nonetheless amazing. "Manna" may be the sweet, sticky excretion of two species of insects that live in the desert ("the wilderness") and thrive on the tamarisk bush's feathery flower clusters. Because the bush's carbohydrate-rich sap is poor in nitrogen, which the insects need, they must ingest large amounts of sap. The excess carbohydrate is then excreted as a "honeydew," rich in sugars and pectin. The bush is planted today in saltwater areas as a windbreak.

A solemn prayer recited during the Kiddush says: "This is the first day of holy gathering, a reminder of the exodus from Egypt. Blessed are You, Lord, who makes the Sabbath holy."

THE CEREMONY. This Jewish benediction and prayer, dating from about the fifth century B.C.E., is recited over a cup of wine immediately before the meal on the eve of the Sabbath or the eve of a festival. The ceremony, which according to the Talmud originated with the "Men of the

The full Kiddush cup symbolizes an abundance of life's goodness and God's blessing.

Great Assembly" and served to celebrate the Creation and the Exodus, acknowledges the sanctity of the day that has dawned.

The word "Kiddush" is a variation of the Hebrew *qiddush*, literally, "sanctification."

The recitation is often performed by the head of the household, but may involve family members, each of whom sips wine, the traditional Talmudic beverage, from a cup held in the right hand. Two covered loaves of bread, *challot* (or *hallot*), rest on the table as symbols of the "double portion" of manna, *lechem mishneh*, gathered by the Israelites on each sixth day. The loaves traditionally are made in a variety of shapes: plain round cakes, rectangular loaves studded with raisins or sprinkled with seeds, or rich white braided loaves called *challah*.

The wine drunk should be red and "strong" by ancient tradition, though white wine is not prohibited. And the cup should be brimmingly filled, implying an abundance of life's goodness and God's blessing.

In addition to reciting the Kiddush at home, some Jews chant the blessing at the end of the Friday-evening synagogue service. The custom has ancient associations. Following the destruction of the Second Temple in 70 C.E., hordes of Jews fleeing Roman persecution emigrated from Palestine to Babylon, swelling the Jewish community there and finding shelter in local synagogues. It was for these homeless itinerants that a synagogue observance of the Kiddush was introduced. In Palestine, however, which lacked a homeless population, the benediction was not recited in synagogues. To this day, synagogues in Israel do not recite the Kiddush at Friday-evening service.

NOVENA: ANCIENT GREECE ♦

This nine-day ritual, whose name derives from *novem*, the Latin for "nine," is an example of prayer as a form of dogged petition—nine days of asking for the same favor. For Christians, a nine-day period of praying is an exceptionally potent way to petition God.

Why nine days?

The Virgin Mary carried Jesus Christ in her womb for nine months; that's one popular answer. The Apostles spent nine days in Jerusalem at the command of the Lord as they awaited the coming of the gift of the Holy Spirit; that's another explanation that has been offered.

The truth is, the number nine was significant to both the ancient Greeks and Romans, who commemorated a person's death with nine consecutive days of mourning, the *novendialia*, capped with a feast on the ninth day after death or burial.

Early Christians adopted the number and attended nine daily Masses for their dead. Nine became something of a magic number, and throughout the Middle Ages, many religious devotions were performed nine times. For instance: If bitten by a dog, the victim said nine days of prayer to the eighth-century bishop Saint Hubert, patron of hunters and protector against rabies. (If possible, a victim traveled to Hubert's grave for a thread of his cloak, said to have been a gift from the Virgin Mary; the thread was placed in an incision in the patient's forehead and the person was forbidden to comb his hair for forty days, and ordered to eat only pork from a boar.)

The pagan origins of the novena are still apparent in what is called the Pope's Novena, or *Novendialia*, a nine-day period of mourning still observed after the death of a pontiff.

ASKING FAVORS. The Christian novena, asking for a favor from God, began in France and Spain in the early Middle Ages. Its origins are associated with a nine-day preparation of hymns and prayers for the feast of Christmas, commencing on December 17 and ending nine days later with gifts. The equation was set: nine days of prayer, then presents.

Making a novena, of course, did not mean that the faithful always got his or her wish. Thus, in the nineteenth century, a new practice arose in Catholicism. In return for nine consecutive days of prayer to Jesus, Mary, or a particular saint, the supplicant was guaranteed by the Church at least a spiritual favor: an indulgence of grace, credit against an accumulated punishment for sin.

In 1967, Pope Paul VI, in his Apostolic Constitution *Indulgentiarum Doctrina*, severely restricted the easy granting of indulgences. Today, the *Code of Canon Law* (sections 992–97) limits the power to grant indulgences to the pope, and those specially delegated by him.

STATIONS OF THE CROSS:
CHRISTIANITY, FIFTEENTH CENTURY ✦

Soon after Jesus Christ's death, Jerusalem Christians began the practice of visiting the scenes of the Passion, from the site of his condemnation to death by Pilate, to his Crucifixion on the hill called Golgotha, to the sepulcher that temporarily held his corpse.

The holy places were easily accessible for Jerusalem Christians, a stroll along their *Via dolorosa*, or "Street of Sorrow," but not for later Christians from distant lands. They, too, wished to tread the path Christ had walked on his way to Calvary. Thus arose the devotion known as the Stations of the Cross, or Way of the Cross, a series of fourteen depictions, each to be accompanied by a meditation.

"Calvary" and "Golgotha" refer to the same site, a rocky hill outside of Jerusalem where Christ was crucified. Calvary, or *Calvaria*, is the Latin form for the Aramaic Golgotha, both of which mean "skull." Scholars believe the hilly mound resembled a skull, hence its name.

EARLIEST REPLICA. The first Stations of the Cross, a combination of statues and paintings, were erected in the fifth century in Bologna, Italy, at the church of San Stefano. But the custom did not become widespread until the Crusaders of the thirteenth century returned home from Palestine and built tableaux of sites they'd visited in the Holy Land. The devotion was commonplace by the fifteenth century, promoted by the Friars Minor, who recommended it as a pilgrimage of spiritual renewal.

The fourteen Stations are:

1. Jesus Is Condemned to Death.
2. Jesus Is Made to Carry the Cross.

Jesus falls beneath the cross and
is helped by Simon.

Jesus is taken down from the cross.

3. Jesus Falls the First Time.
4. Jesus Meets His Grieving Mother.
5. Simon of Cyrene Is Made to Bear the Cross.
6. Veronica Wipes Jesus' Face.
7. Jesus Falls a Second Time.
8. The Women of Jerusalem Weep Over Jesus.
9. Jesus Falls a Third Time.
10. Jesus Is Stripped of His Garments.
11. Jesus Is Nailed to the Cross.
12. Jesus Dies on the Cross.
13. Jesus Is Taken Down from the Cross.
14. Jesus' Body Is Sealed in the Sepulcher.

The traditional fourteen Stations did not develop all at once. As late as the fourteenth century, only seven images along the Via dolorosa were vicariously visited, popularly known as the "seven travails." It was quite common for monks, priests, and members of guilds to construct small detailed replicas of the Stations, miniature models of Christ's Passion.

Since the Resurrection is the Mystery central to Christianity, some churches now celebrate an additional Station: (15) Jesus Rises from the Grave.

CONCESSIONS FOR THE HANDICAPPED. About the same time that the Stations of the Cross devotion appeared, popes began to promise plenary indulgences for Christians who made a *real* pilgrimage to the holy sites in Jerusalem. The Franciscan order, which was given custody of the sites in 1342, and especially Saint Leonard of Port Maurice (1676–1751), championed the Stations, and Leonard popularized them in more than six hundred towns in Italy.

In 1731, Pope Clement XII decreed that Christians who devoutly fol-

Pope Clement XII (1730–40)
granted a full indulgence for
making the Stations of
the Cross.

lowed *replicas* of the Stations in their own towns or churches also won
plenary indulgences. It is this papal decree more than anything else that elevated the Stations to wide popularity. Clement also fixed the number of
stations at fourteen; there had been as few as five, as many as thirty at one
time.

Today, following Vatican II (1962–65), a person devoutly performing the
Stations is still entitled a full indulgence. According to the official *Handbook
of Indulgences*: "A plenary indulgence is granted to the faithful who make the
pious exercise of the Way of the Cross."

One physical requirement is that the person actually move from one scene
to the next, on foot, or in a wheelchair, or hobble on crutches. Christ, after
all, trekked under a handicap. Severely handicapped individuals who cannot
execute the travel round a church, however, may still gain a full dispensation
from the temporal punishment of sin if, as the handbook states, "They spend
at least one half an hour in pious reading and meditation on the Passion and
Death of our Lord Jesus Christ." At home, or in a hospital bed.

Whereas Christians can ritually revisit the sites of Christ's Passion through
the Stations, Muslims must undertake an arduous pilgrimage to their holy
city of Mecca.

THE HAJJ ◆

The fifth of the Five Pillars of Islam is the Great Pilgrimage, or *hajj*, to the
sacred monuments in and near Mecca. The journey is mandatory for all
Muslims at least once in a lifetime, if they are physically able to hazard the
trek, and if the travel would not strap them financially. In recent years, more
than two million faithful have flowed annually into Mecca.

The term hajj, like its Hebrew cognate *hag*, reflects the ancient Semitic
notion of celebrating a deity at a sacred shrine. It implies a pilgrimage.

All hajj manuals open with a quotation from the Koran: "Truly, the first House of Worship established for man is the one at Mecca. . . . The *hajj* to the House is a duty man owes to God" (3:96–97).

IMPORTANCE OF THE KA'BAH. For Muslims, the shrine at Mecca embodies the core beliefs of their faith: (1) God's Creation began at Mecca; (2) Abraham (Ibrahim), father of all prophets, built the first house of worship, the Ka'bah, at Mecca; (3) the ancient pagan practices of Arabs at the Ka'bah were displayed by God's final revelation through the Prophet Muhammad.

It is the Ka'bah's locale that determines ritual prayer orientation for Muslims, as well as the orientation of the dead in their graves. Prayers recited before the Ka'bah are the most efficacious a Muslim can say.

Polytheistic Arabs, as we'll see later, had been worshiping at the Ka'bah, then a pagan shrine, centuries before the birth of Islam, when *al-Lah* was one of many gods in the Arabian pantheon. The Arabic word *hajj* and the Hebrew word *hag* both hark back to pagan days and sacrificial worship.

Muhammad did not destroy the pre-Islamic hajj rituals, but infused them with new symbols and meanings. In fact, Muhammad's Sermon on the Mount of Mercy, at Arfat, and his removal of all pagan idols from the Ka'bah at Mecca, are recollected annually during modern hajj ceremonies. The Prophet, near the end of his life (he died in 632 C.E.), is said to have made the first Muslim hajj.

THE CEREMONY. A pilgrim, before crossing the sacred territory (*haram*) surrounding Mecca, ritually purifies himself by performing an ablution and donning a white ceremonial robe (*ihram*). Now he is ready to walk around the sacred shrine, the Ka'bah, seven times; then he prays and walks along other prescribed paths.

In the course of the massive group ceremonies, which take place between the tenth month (Shawwal) and twelfth month (Dhu al-Hijjah) of the Muslim calendar, the pilgrim also visits holy places outside Mecca, and may sacrifice an animal in commemoration of Abraham's offering. The pilgrim's head is then usually shaved; he throws seven stones at each of the three pillars at Mina, on three successive days; then he returns to Mecca to perform the final circling of the Ka'bah before returning home. (Some pilgrims first visit Islam's second holy city, Medina.) Now he is entitled to affix to his name the title *hajji*.

CRITICAL MASSES ◆ *In the early 1990s, the two largest religions in the world are Christianity, with 1,870 million adherents, and Islam, with 1,014 million. These are also the two fastest-growing faiths.*

Judaism, which spawned both religions, is burgeoning in the state of Israel but actually shrinking in size worldwide, due to migration, marrying out of the faith, and general assimilation. Numerically, Jews have always been a small faith, but the impact of their teachings, and the influence of their sacred scriptures, have been immeasurable.

PART
II

Heavenly
Hosts

ngels

Messengers to Guardians

ANGELS IN AMERICA: THE MILLENNIUM APPROACHES ◆

"Do you believe in angels?"

Seventy percent of Americans in a recent poll answered with an unhesitant, unembarrassed, unequivocal yes.

"Do you believe you have a personal guardian angel?"

Fifty percent felt confident they did. And felt safer for it. In terms of popular orthodoxy, the heavenly host is upon us.

Perhaps this should come as no surprise. Belief in angels is an idea—and ideal—common to all religions and has been present in all cultures throughout the centuries. There are Jewish angels, Christian angels, Muslim angels. Haloed, white-robed angels populate Buddhism, Hinduism, Iranian Zoroastrianism. Winged messengers are chiseled in ancient Sumerian carvings, Egyptian tombs, and Assyrian reliefs.

As disembodied voices or full-bodied messengers, angels waft through more than *half* the books of the Bible, some anonymous, some named—

Lazarus carried to Heaven by angels.

Gabriel, Raphael, Michael. Michael is Israel's national guardian angel. Docile angels worship God, warrior angels battle Satan.

An angel told Abraham to spare his son from sacrifice. An angel saved David from the lion's den. An angel rolled the stone from Christ's tomb.

Archangel Gabriel announced to the Virgin Mary she was to bear the Son of God, then, six centuries later, Gabriel whispered to Muhammad his prophethood and the promise of the Koran.

Archangel Michael handed Moses the Ten Commandments, which turned Israelites toward a deeper piety. Thus it was two archangels, Gabriel and Michael, who heralded the birth of monotheistic Judaism, Messiah-based Christianity, and Koran-inspired Islam.

In the 1820s, in Palmyra, New York, the Mormon archangel Moroni inspired a teenager named Joseph Smith to found the Church of Jesus Christ of Latter-day Saints.

Guardian angels today are said to assist Roman Catholic children cross busy intersections, while Muslim angels sit in mosques and tally prayers of the faithful to present to God on Judgment Day.

How did this glorious chimera of a creature originate? How can you tell a Jewish angel from Christian angel? Why feathered wings?

BIBLICAL ORIGIN OF ANGELS:
GENESIS 1:1, 1800 TO 1400 B.C.E. ◆

Disappointingly, there is no explicit mention of the creation of angels in the Old Testament.

The heavenly hosts
of angels were created
before human beings.

Their origin is inferred, by Jews, Christians, and Muslims, in the opening clause of Genesis: "In the beginning God created the heavens . . ." Or as the Tanakh (Hebrew Bible) translates: "When God began to create heaven . . ."

Thus, in the creation of Heaven, God brought forth the heavenly hosts of angels, which therefore predate human beings.

Equally disappointing in the Old Testament is the fact that there is no mention of a battle between angels, or of fallen angels who become Satan and his minions. That is a New Testament revelation, occurring contemporaneously in the Second Epistle of Peter (c. 64 C.E.) and in the Gospel of Matthew (c. 65–75 C.E.):

God did not spare the angels when they sinned, but dragged them down by infernal ropes . . . to be tortured and kept in custody for judgment. (2 Pet. 2:4)

Then he [God] will say to those on his left hand, "Depart from me, accursed ones, into the everlasting fire that was prepared for the devil and his angels." (Matt. 25:41)

Most Catholics might not realize this, but they *must* believe in angels; the Fourth Lateran Council of 1215 declared the existence of the invisible spirits as dogma. Vatican Council I in 1870 backed this up (it also defined as dogma the doctrine of papal infallibility.) (*See* Infallibility.) Moreover, Pope Pius XII (1939–58) declared that angels must be regarded as "personal beings," not vague spiritual entities.

Also: Roman Catholics are supposed to invoke only three personal names for angels: Michael, Gabriel, and Raphael. These are the only archangels named in canonical Scriptures. (The Archangel Uriel is named in Judaic Apocryphal angelology; more on this to follow.)

JEWISH ANGELS: OLD TESTAMENT ◆

In the Old Testament, angels are portrayed as attendants of the heavenly court. Their role is to worship God first, then convey his divine will to earth; hence the appeal of flight wings.

In terms of imagery, the feathered appendage is a direct and sensible avian steal. What better way to fly Heaven-to-earth round-trip? Angel iconography throughout the ancient world, East and West, emphasizes oversized wings large enough to support a man-sized body. In fact, up until the time of the Wright brothers, virtually all man's mechanical attempts at flight mimicked birds' flapping wings.

ANGELS.
In Greek, angelos *are*
"messengers." They have
wings in mythology and
religion so that they can
carry petitions from earth
to the heavens.

The term "angel" enters our language through the Greek word *angelos*, which is equivalent to the Hebrew word *mal'akh*, meaning "messenger."

But the Israelites had other function-oriented words for angels: *avadim* = "servants," *mshar'tim* = "ministers," *tzavah* = "hosts," *k'doshim* = "holy ones set apart," and the Aramaic word *'ir* = "watchers." That about sums up the duties of an angel.

To the Israelites, angels were usually invisible, unapproachable, and unaffected by human needs. Jewish angels were never as popular—nor as numerous—as Christian angels would become. Christian theologians, starting in the fifth century, would erect a hierarchy of heavenly hosts, borrowing from Jewish angelology, Persian myth, and augmenting the roster with their own fertile imaginations.

First, angels from Hebrew Scriptures.

CHERUBIM, "PRAYING ANGELS": GENESIS 3:24 ◆

The singular is "cherub"—perhaps related to the Akkadian *karabu,* "to bless."

Cherubim, to the Israelites, were heavenly beings that supported God's throne, or chariot, and could also act as guardian spirits.

They first fly into the Old Testament pages in Genesis, brandishing fiery swords, protectors of Eden after the Fall and Adam's eviction from the Garden: "So he [God] drove out the man, and he placed at the east of Eden Cherubim" (Gen. 3:24).

The Israelites could not make up their minds as to a cherub's appearance.

For instance, in Exodus (25:20; written c. 1400 B.C.E.), two cherubim that guard the Tabernacle—the tent housing the Ark of the Covenant—each have two wings and one face. In Ezekiel (1:6 and 10; composed in the sixth century B.C.E.), four cherubim each have four wings and four faces—a man's, a lion's, an ox's, and an eagle's. Later in Ezekiel (chapter 41), the cherubim have only two faces—a man's and a lion's.

The Israelites did not dream up such bizarre imagery, but borrowed it from ancient Near Eastern mythology, where winged sphinxes, bulls, griffins, and humans were commonplace in art and sacred cults. Cherubim were hybrid cult chimeras long before they were sweet, chubby, rosy-cheeked Christian angels.

The Old Testament describes cherubim primarily as bearers of God's throne in the innermost sanctuary known as the Holy of Holies; they are known for their great mobility, but not mainly as message-bearers.

SERAPHIM, "FLAMING SPIRITS": ISAIAH 6:2,6 ◆

The singular is "seraph," from the Hebrew verb *saraph*; "to burn."

Seraphim were known to ancient Israelites as heavenly beings that surrounded God's throne, continually chanting his praises, in Hebrew, of course. The prophet Isaiah (6:2,6) tells us that seraphim each sport three pairs of wings, suggesting that a seraph could easily outfly a cherub.

In the Temple vision of the prophet, seraphim praise God in what is known in the Greek Orthodox Church as the *Trisagion* (meaning "thrice holy") and to Jews as the *Kedushah*:

> *Holy, holy, holy is the Lord of hosts; the whole earth is full of his glory.* (Isa. 6:3)

A cherub assures a product is gentle and pure. Seraphim trumpet the Kedushah, *or "Holy, holy, holy is the Lord."*

The exaltation is said to be the "song of creation," the "vibration of God's love" throughout the cosmos. Which some theology-minded modern cosmologists have posited as "background radiation."

Nor did the Jews dream up the seraph. It, too, originated as a chimera in ancient Near Eastern mythology. The English plural "seraphim" is from the Hebrew verb *serafim*, "to set fire to." In the Old Testament, seraphim often are referred to as "burning ones." Several prophets who glimpsed seraphim claimed they were "flaming spirits," and Saint Basil saw them as vaporous fireballs; like ball lightning.

The Israelites quite likely derived their multiwinged flaming seraph from the Egyptian god Serapis, who inhabited the lower realm, or burning circle, and whose cult spread to Greece and Rome.

Thus, angelology did not originate with Judaism, but was common in cults throughout the Near East. Many primitive peoples envisioned the spirits of dead relatives as winged and soaring into an afterlife. It seems possible—quite likely, in fact—that this notion of human spirits, hovering above family and interceding on behalf of loved ones, evolved into the concept of angels.

WARRIOR ANGELS: OLD TESTAMENT ◆

The ancient Israelites also viewed angels as fearless fighters in the army of the Lord, a warlike notion rooted in Near Eastern cults. Yahweh (God) in the Old Testament is called the Lord of hosts, or "Tzvaot," and the hosts are soldiers who battle evildoers and safeguard the righteous.

Warrior angels defeated the Assyrians (2 Kings 19:35), led the army of the Maccabees (2 Macc. 11:6–11), and they are guardians of countries (Dan. 4:10, 20).

Chief among the warrior angels is Michael, whose name means "Who is like God?," and who is the guardian of Israel. On the other hand, the chief messenger angel is Gabriel, "Man of God."

The Talmud (which means "the learning"), the collection of Jewish civil and religious laws compiled between the fourth and sixth centuries C.E., and second only to the Tanakh in authority, concentrates on angels much more than does the Old Testament. About one thousand years passed from the time the last book of the Hebrew Bible was admitted to the Jewish canon and the final editing of the Talmud was completed. Angel lore had expanded, influenced in large part by Christianity.

ANGELS ARE CREATED EVERY DAY:
TALMUD, 400 TO 600 c.e. ◆

With the advent of Jesus Christ and the Holy Spirit, angels, formerly God's chief messengers, assumed a lesser role.

Whereas Old Testament Law arrived through the ministry of angels—angels were even called "ministers," *mshar'tim*—new mediations came directly from "God the Son" and "God the Holy Spirit," who were superior to angels. Perhaps this is why the Talmud gives angels more prominence: the Christians had Christ and the Spirit; the Jews needed more powerful angels. And *more* angels.

DISPOSABLE ANGELS. Some rabbis of the Talmudic period claimed new angels were created every day; every time God opened his mouth to speak, winged angels flew out chaperoning his words.

Others conceived of disposable angels: each day's new supply, after singing God's praises, sank at heavenly sunset into a sea of fire, *nehar di-nur*.

The Talmud also claims that angels were created on either the second or the fifth day of Creation. They walk upright on feet, or fly, foretell the future, and speak only Hebrew.

Angels in the Talmud have human shape, but consist half of fire, half of water—which lends itself to the ethereal imagery of steam.

These new breeds of Jewish angels are free from evil inclination, have no personal needs, carry out only one mission at a time, cannot err, and specific angels control such matters as rain, hail, human pregnancy, and birth.

Early Christian writers claimed disparagingly that Jews had developed angel worship. In truth, only one Talmudic passage implies that angel worship was practiced by certain Jewish sects, and Talmudic sages took strong exception to this practice.

The rabbi and philosopher Maimonides, in his twelfth-century *Guide for the Perplexed*, challenges the concept of angels as corporeal beings with wings. Rather, he teaches that angels are "natural forces" placed in the world by God, and that these forces shape and control all the events in the universe.

Belief in angels has never been central to the Jewish faith. While some Jews with mystic leanings believe in angels as winged celestial beings with access to God's ear, most Jews today subscribe to Maimonides's view.

FALLEN ANGELS' REAL SIN: SIXTH CENTURY C.E. ◆

Pride, we say today, was the sin of the fallen angels. That, though, was a later interpretation favored by Church fathers Origen, Augustine, and John Chrysostom.

In the beginning, the sin of the fallen male angels was said to be their sexual copulation with human women, as interpreted through Genesis (author's emphasis):

> *When men began to multiply on earth, and had daughters born to them, the* sons of God *saw that the daughters of men were fair, and they took wives for themselves, as many as they wished. (Gen. 6:1–2)*

The term "sons of God" in Hebrew is *benei Elohim* and is an early phrase for angels, found in various places in the Tanakh (e.g., Job 1:6, 38:7).

That the fallen male angels' sin was sexual, and historically occurred just prior to the Great Flood, or Deluge, is an old Judaic belief. It is found in the *Book of Jubilees*, in *Enoch* (Enoch was a descendant of Adam, who lived to the age of 365), in the *Syriac Apocalypse of Baruch*, and was favored by first-century C.E. Jewish philosopher and theologian Philo in his *De gigantibus*.

In the book *The Birth of Noah*, the Qumran *Genesis Aprocryphon*, Noah himself is suspected of being the offspring of a disobedient male angel and a mortal woman.

Furthermore, many early Christian Church fathers—Clement of Alexandria, Tertullian, Ambrose, and others—sided with the sexual interpretation of Genesis 6:1–2.

Saint Michael evicting Lucifer and the fallen angels from Heaven is a New Testament revelation.

ANGEL RAPE. How scandalous all this sounds today. Angel seduction. Angel sex. But the concept of "fallen gods" is ancient and common to all Semitic peoples, and the major sin that caused a male god to be banished from the celestial pantheon was unauthorized copulation with a mortal female. Sometimes rape.

On the other hand, copulation authorized by the chief god produced "demigods" who were half-divine, half-human. The ancient Greeks claimed that all their great geniuses were demigods: Socrates, Plato, Aristotle, Alexander the Great. Roman emperors boasted of being offspring from male gods and mortal women.

SIN OF PRIDE TRIUMPHS. The belief that the fallen angels' sin was pride, and occurred prior to the creation of man, stems from the writings of Pope Gregory the Great, pontiff from 590 to 604. (Gregory I also said angels were absolutely spotless, sinless, sanctified by the Holy Spirit, blissfully happy always, and dwelt in blessed communion with God.)

Gregory, like Saint Augustine, reasoned that since Satan is already a seducer (of Eve) in the Garden of Paradise, he had to have sinned prior to the creation of Eve and Adam. Prior to the existence of "daughters of men." That is predicated, of course, on the interpretation of the seductive serpent as Satan, a fallen angel.

However, Hebrew scholars maintain that the depiction of fallen angels in Scripture was added after the Israelites' full acceptance of monotheism *and* "Persian dualism," that is, the strict good/bad dichotomy that entered Jewish thought after the sixth century B.C.E. Emboldened by the concept of pure good versus pure evil, as embodied by God versus Satan, Jewish scribes in effect reedited religious history, altering the words of earlier writings.

The term "sons of God," *benei Elohim*, in all likelihood did not originally mean "angels," but probably meant "heroes of days gone by," the famous men. It was only at a later date, when the dualistic belief in the existence of evil demons had become a firm component of popular religion, that attempts were made to find biblical authority for the concept of fallen angels.

The Catholic Church has never declared authoritatively the way in which the angels sinned and became the Devil and his demons. However, the Fourth Lateran Council of 1215 declared as dogma that the Devil and his demons do indeed exist and *must* be believed in.

CHRISTIAN ANGELS:
NEW TESTAMENT TIMES TO MIDDLE AGES ◆

In Christian theology, double-winged cherubim are ranked second to the more powerful multiwinged seraphim.

In early Christian art, the cherub is modestly draped in red cloth. A little later, its image is that of a chubby, rosy-cheeked tot with two dainty, downy wings. This is the Middle Ages imagery that allows us to affectionately call a pudgy human child with a sweet face "a cherub."

In later Christian art, cherubim sport four wings and are painted pale blue to symbolize the sky, whereas the six-winged seraphim are red to represent fire; they are the prophets' "flaming ones."

Christians did more than reinvent the look of angels. They stressed the meaning inherent in the term "angel"—"messenger," especially as heralds for the coming of Jesus Christ.

• Luke has the angel Gabriel visit the Virgin Mary in a waking vision (1:31): "You will conceive in your womb and bear a son, and you shall call him Jesus."

• Matthew employs an angel to assure Joseph that his betrothed, mysteriously pregnant, has not slept with a man (1:20): "An angel of the Lord appeared to him in a dream. . . . Do not fear to take Mary your wife, for that which is conceived in her is of the Holy Spirit."

• Jesus is born and an angel rushes to warn Joseph of King Herod's wicked designs: "Take the young child and his mother, and flee into Egypt, and be thou there until I bring thee word, for Herod will seek the young child to destroy him" (Matt. 2:13).

• Faithful to his promise, the angel reappears to Joseph in a dream: "Get

The angel announcing Christ's birth: "Behold, I bring you good news of a great joy."

up, take the child and his mother and go to the land of Israel, for those who were trying to take the child's life are dead" (Matt. 2:19–20).

Notice: Christian angels are directors. They move the actors around. Set the scene. Motivate the players. The play's script, the divine text, will be spoken by Jesus Christ.

CELESTIAL HIERARCHY: "DIONYSIUS THE AREOPAGITE," SIXTH CENTURY C.E. ◆

Early Christians borrowed the cherubim and the seraphim from the Old Testament, and also the notion of a hierarchy of heavenly hosts. Jews had been vague on ranking angels. Christians made a science of it.

One man more than any other labored hard at the task: a sixth-century Syrian monk (his real identity remains unknown) who wrote under the pseudonym "Dionysius the Areopagite"—scholars prefer to call him Pseudo-Dionysius because the first bishop of Athens, in the first century, was named Dionysius the Areopagite.

The Areopagus was a high Greek court of justice that met on a rocky hill northwest of the Acropolis; a member of the court was called an Areopagite. Maybe the sixth-century monk had once belonged to a high court. Or merely wanted to.

Pseudo-Dionysius penned a series of treatises attempting to unite Plato's philosophy with Christian theology and esoteric mystical experience; a huge undertaking, sort of a unified field theory of metaphysics. He scored his best successes in drawing up hierarchies: one for the Church at Rome, "On the Ecclesiastical Hierarchy," and one for the heavenly choir of angels, "On the Celestial Hierarchy." Whoever he was, Pseudo-Dionysius clearly was an organizer. Single-handedly, he established the nine classes of angels, grouped into three triads, that is the standard to this day.

FIRST TRIAD

SERAPHIM are the highest order. They most resemble God in nature, and continually sing his praises—"Holy, Holy, Holy"—through the Hebrew *Kadosh*.

CHERUBIM come next, and they, too, exist strictly to worship God. The cherub is thought to be the angel of knowledge because in Jewish mysticism the cherubim protect the Tree of Life, east of Eden—a tree with seven branches growing upward toward Heaven, and seven roots in the earth; seven was a sacred number in esoteric Judaism.

THRONES are next, and they are sometimes called ophanim, or wheels. Ezekiel (1:15–19) tells us that near the cherubim were many-colored wheel-like structures, "wheels within wheels." Cherubim seem to go nowhere without their wheels. They drive wheels "with many eyes and wings" through Ezekiel's heated visions, and Enoch—who "walked with God" and was taken into his presence without dying (Gen. 5:18–24)—made the contradictory claim that wheels resembled "fiery coals." Nonetheless, both Jews and Christians assumed the wheels to be a separate class of angels. The duty of thrones is to oversee justice in Heaven.

Angels in the first triad, called "the faithful," never wander far from God's throne. Thomas Aquinas, saint and theologian, taught that these three choirs have never—and will never—visit earth.

SECOND TRIAD

DOMINIONS are celestial housekeepers; they regulate life's hustle and bustle in Heaven. They keep track of the large celestial workforce, and assign duties to lesser angels.

VIRTUES are among the best-loved angels on earth, and for good reasons. They work miracles, like curing the sick. They provide moral support in hard times. And they dispense courage. And God's grace. It's said that two Virtues assisted Eve through the painful birth of Cain, the first labor. And two Virtues escorted Jesus to Heaven at the time of his glorious Resurrection.

POWERS protect humankind from evil, and on a personal level, too. They watch over each individual soul and try to shield it from Satan's influence. Powers battle evil head-on, and they're supposed to have lost legions of members in the heavenly war when Lucifer tried to seize control from God.

Members of this second triad are ministering angels, who guard both earth and Heaven. Paul, in his Epistle to the Colossians (c. 61 C.E.), names four groups in the same passage: thrones, dominions, powers, and principalities (Col. 1:16). Peter, the first pope, in his First Letter mentions Virtues (1 Pet. 3:22).

THIRD TRIAD

PRINCIPALITIES, which hover near earth, are preoccupied with the welfare of nations. Though their concerns are global, they also protect cities, as well as the world's religions.

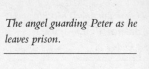

The angel guarding Peter as he leaves prison.

ARCHANGELS, as their name makes clear—*archos*, Greek for "chief"—served as the major guides and messengers for human beings. They are emissaries who work tirelessly between the Creator and his Creation (see next chapter).

ANGELS are a numerous and generic lot, resembling archangels in function but without the stature. Truly important messages *from* God are carried to earth by archangels; lesser messages are relayed to and from Heaven by angels. Of all celestial beings, angels hover closest to humans, always attentive and ready to carry off a prayer or petition. They comprise that special—and personal—class called guardian angels.

Members of this third triad have their ministry here on earth. Of all nine celestial groups in the hierarchy, only the last two—archangels and angels—should really be called angels since the word itself means "messengers."

This elaborate nine-tiered edifice held sway in the West from the time of Pope Gregory the Great. In the ninth century, it received wide scholarly attention following a Latin translation of the writings of Pseudo-Dionysius.

The celestial hierarchy obsessed Thomas Aquinas, who in the thirteenth century devoted a full one-twelfth of his hefty *Summa Theologica* to speculations on angels. What distinguishes one class of angels from another, the saint-theologian concluded, was nearness to God and intellect. Simply put, angels closest to the Lord are the smartest; those hovering in clouds above earth have minds like those they watch over: perplexed, limited, and gifted with free will. Unlike humans, said Thomas, angels are without lust or gender. Nonetheless, most angels have male names; males named them.

The Catholic Church has never officially spoken out on the hierarchy of angels. It has no hard-line stand on angel rankings.

Guardian angels watching over children; their feast day is October 2.

GUARDIAN ANGELS: EARLY JUDAISM ◆

One subset of the lowest rank of angels evolved into a cult. Guardian angels seem to be a religious concept common to the entire Semitic world. The Catholic Church has never defined as dogma that every human's soul has a guardian spirit or chaperon.

But the notion that each Christian child has his or her own guardian angel is posited in Matthew, when Jesus praises the innocence of children and warns:

> *Take heed that you despise not one of these little ones, for I say unto you, That in heaven their angels do always behold the face of my Father. (Matt. 18:10)*

In the early Church, theologians argued over whether *only* baptized individuals got guardian angels. What about pagans? The belief arose that at the moment of baptism—of a newborn or an adult convert—God assigned that person an angel, who had God's ear on that person's behalf.

The theologian Irenaeus declared that nations had guardian angels; the Jews had already laid claim to Archangel Michael as their national treasure.

Clement of Alexandria posited that individual cities had guardian angels. Angels had always been popular. Under Clement, they were nearly innumerable.

Tertullian, in *De anima*, declared that at the time of a person's death, his or her guardian angel would escort the soul into the "hereafter" (Heaven, Purgatory, and Limbo were not yet clearly conceived; each has a chapter in this book). In the same text, Tertullian suggested that angels assist God in creating new mortal infants.

For centuries, bishops petitioned Rome for a special feast day on which the faithful could thank guardian angels for their tireless vigilance. Thomas

Aquinas was in favor of such a day. Finally, in 1608, at the request of Ferdinand of Austria, guardian angels as a class were assigned October 2 as their own; popes Clement X and Leo XII both acknowledged the feast day as holy, but no pope has ever elevated it to the status of an obligatory holiday where attendance at Mass is mandatory.

Archangels and Demons

Michael to Metatron

ARCHANGELS: BOOK OF TOBIT, BOOKS OF ENOCH ◆

As we've seen in the last chapter, the Greek word *archos*, "chief," is the prefix that lifts common spirit messengers to the status of emissaries of major revelation.

Theologically speaking:

• *Jews* recognize three archangels as named in the Hebrew Bible: Michael, Gabriel, Raphael; plus perhaps Uriel from other Judaic writings.

• *Christians* tend to be equivocal on the number of archangels, as we'll see. Definitely the Old Testament three. Maybe Uriel. Perhaps three additional ones, for a grand total of seven.

• *Muslims* say the number is fixed at four. No more. No less.

Much of the original material on archangels comes from two sources:

1. The "Catholic" Book of Tobit (or Tobias; omitted in Protestant Bibles). This is a fanciful short story, taking place during the Captivity, and it depicts God's concern for humans. In the tale, the Archangel Raphael names six other angels of his own rank—which brings the total of archangels to seven. Seven, the sum of the days of Creation plus the day of rest, has always been a magical number.

2. The two Books of Enoch, from the Hebrew Apocrypha. Enoch is the seventh patriarch in the Book of Genesis, descendant of Adam's son Seth, who at age 365 was assumed into Heaven—the only other Old Testament figure to have cheated death is the prophet Elijah.

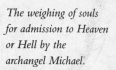

The weighing of souls for admission to Heaven or Hell by the archangel Michael.

The Books of Enoch, 1 and 2, perhaps compiled around the second century B.C.E., resemble biblical literature in content and style but are non-canonical, and are called pseudepigraphical works. They tell the story of how Enoch is chosen by God to be the world's greatest scribe. He gets a tour of Heaven, witnesses angels performing their daily chores, then compiles a Who's Who of heavenly hosts, in which he names seven archangels, the same seven who appear in the Book of Tobit.

Let's consider each:

MICHAEL, "WHO IS LIKE GOD?": PATRON OF ISRAEL ◆

The most famous, enduring, and busiest of all angels, Michael was called by the prophet Daniel "the great prince" who "standeth for the children of thy people." Thus, he became prince of Israel, its patron.

Michael gave Moses the Ten Commandments, twice, and stopped Abraham at the last minute from sacrificing his son Isaac.

Centuries later, Michael emboldened Joan of Arc to don male clothing and convince the dauphin he'd be crowned king of France if he'd allow her to do battle for him.

In the unearthed Dead Sea Scrolls, Michael emerges as the "Prince of Light," as the Essenes, a solitary Jewish sect, apparently knew him.

Catholics honor Michael with the title "saint," and have christened him "Defender of the Catholic Church." Thus, he is both patron of Israel *and* defender of Roman Catholicism.

In the Apocryphal gospel of Bartholomew, God creates man in his image using clay that Michael fetches from the four corners of the earth. Michael,

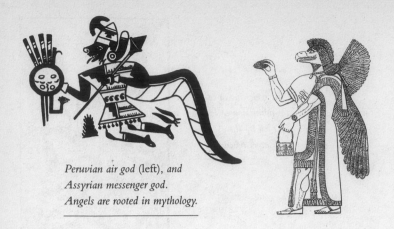

*Peruvian air god (left), and
Assyrian messenger god.
Angels are rooted in mythology.*

pointing to the man of clay, says to Lucifer: "This is God's image and we must pay homage to it." Lucifer, then God's most beloved, snaps back: "I, the first angel God ever made, should pay homage to that lump of clay? Never!" This haughty retort underscores the popular notion that the heavenly battle of angels was sparked by God's creation of man.

The name "Michael" is from the Hebrew *mikha'el: mi + khael* = "who is?" + "like God."

Michael, Heaven's mightiest defender, leads the battle against Lucifer and banishes the fallen angels to Hell. Thomas Aquinas forecasts: "At the end of the world [he will] destroy the Antichrist as he did Lucifer in the beginning."

Where did a creature so potent come from?

EGYPTIAN ROOTS. As to Michael's origin and angelic duties, it has been suggested that the ancient Israelites, during their bondage in Egypt, borrowed from Egyptian mythology; specifically, from their acquaintance with Anubis, the Egyptian hybrid god with the head of a jackal.

Anubis defends against evil, escorts souls to judgment, and weighs human justice. Michael, in ancient art, is often depicted as holding a pair of scales on which a man and woman are weighted for virtue. Anubis used a similar scale: on one pan rested the heart of the deceased, on the counterbalance lay a feather: a little virtue in life goes a long way in the afterlife.

Indeed, the Bible suggests (Prov. 21:1–2) that God weighs the goodness in each person's heart.

Michael was the first angel to merit a feast day. Michaelmas Day originated in fourth-century Rome not long after the emperor Constantine attributed his battle victories to the archangel; to honor Michael, the emperor built a church in Constantinople and christened it Michaelion.

In the Middle Ages, Michael became the patron saint of knights. Michael in medieval art usually is shown brandishing an unsheathed sword; he's youthful, strong, cloaked in full armor, bare-legged, wearing sandals.

Islam adopted Michael, as we'll see, but altered his appearance; he's depicted in Islamic art as having solid emerald wings of glistening green covered with a peach-fuzz patina of saffron hairs, each hair containing (supposedly) "a million faces and a million tongues."

Today, Roman Catholics and Anglicans celebrate Michaelmas on October 2; in the Greek and Armenian Churches, the feast day is November 8.

GABRIEL, "GOD IS MY STRENGTH":
PATRON OF TELECOMMUNICATIONS ◆

Second in importance to Michael, herald of good news, who sits at the left hand of God, is Gabriel, one of the most problematic of archangels—and not just because he's sometimes described as having 140 pairs of wings.

Four times he is mentioned in the Bible; never with the title "archangel"—that derived gradually from popular belief.

The name "Gabriel" is from the Hebrew *govri'el*, "God is [my] strength" —*gevurah* is "power" or "strength."

When it comes to miracles, Gabriel is credited with the most awesome in the Bible: the parting of the Red Sea (or perhaps, in fact, a smaller papyrus Reed Sea), which saved the Israelites from certain slaughter; Gabriel asked the favor of God. Angels themselves do not perform miracles.

By several medieval accounts, Gabriel is a female archangel, the only female. The question of her gender has caused controversy, and she has most often been described as male. The prophet Daniel, who received much of his news from Gabriel, favors the male pronoun: "His body also was like the beryl, and his face as the appearance of lightning . . . his eyes as lamps of fire . . . his arms and his feet like the color of polished brass" (Dan. 10:5–6).

A male Gabriel announces the birth of John the Baptist (Luke 1:11), and of Jesus Christ (Luke 1:26).

In Islam, it is a *male* Gabriel—named *Jibril*, angel of truth—who dictates the Koran to Muhammad.

Yet, in medieval art and legend, a female Gabriel, with long, flowing locks, jeweled tiara, a lily as her emblem, symbolizes conception and gestation. *She* foretells to Daniel the birth of a Messiah; *she* announces to Mary the conception of Jesus; *she* tells Zachariah his wife, Elizabeth, will bear John the Baptist; *she* broadcasts Jesus' birth to the shepherds of Bethlehem.

The archangel Gabriel appearing to Zechariah—a male or female angel?

Perhaps the gender confusion arose because of these conception duties, coupled with flowing locks, tiara, and long-stemmed lily. Catholic popular belief holds that Gabriel, as a male, watches over a fetus's soul during the nine months of gestation.

Catholics celebrate the Feast of Saint Gabriel on March 24. Pope Pius XII, on January 12, 1951, declared Gabriel, God's chief message-bearer, the patron of employees in the telecommunications industry. Telephones, telegraphs, television and radio, modems, faxes, the Internet, and cyberspace all come under his jurisdiction.

RAPHAEL, "GOD HAS HEALED": PATRON OF STIGMATICS ◆

Hebrew legend has it that when Adam, the first man, is evicted from Paradise, he begins to catch every earthly illness; even those yet to exist. An angel—unnamed, said to be Raphael (or Raziel, who is not an archangel)—presents Adam with a book of herbal cures, which lists every plant in creation and its medicinal wonders. The book has never been found, to the relief of the pharmaceutical industry.

The name "Raphael" is from the Hebrew *reaph'el*, "God hath healed." The archangel is regarded as God's chief healer on earth; all that is known about him is either from the Book of Tobit or Apocryphal works and legend.

His name is clearly stated in the Book of Tobit. Tobit is a man who was accidentally blinded. His son, Tobias, a troubled youth who contemplates suicide, meets up with a man named Azariah—who is the archangel Raphael in human disguise. They go fishing in the Tigris River, and the incognito angel tells Tobias to rub the gallbladder of a fish they've caught on his father's eyes. The son takes the stranger's advice and his father's sight is miraculously restored. (Other parts of the fish, its heart and liver, win Tobias a beautiful and wealthy wife.)

In the late Middle Ages, when a veritable epidemic of stigmata erupted among pious mystics—bleeding from the palms, feet, and side; Christ's five wounds (*see* Stigmata)—the angel Raphael became the patron of these sufferers.

CIRCUMCISION. To Jews, Raphael is the patron of circumcision, since he's supposed to have soothed the pain of Abraham's cut.

The biblical origin of the practice is Genesis 17:10, when "Abram" agrees to accept God as the national deity, and God strikes a bargain: "This is my covenant, which you shall keep. . . . Every man child among you shall be circumcised."

The Hebrew word for "covenant" is *bris* (sometimes *brit*), the name for the rite of circumcision, and "Abram" signs the deal by sacrificing foreskin, which allows him to be renamed Abraham, "father of a multitude." Raphael served as a spiritual anesthetic.

NOAH'S ARK. Traditionally, it is Raphael who presents Noah with the carpentry instructions for constructing the *tevah* or ark: 450 feet long, 75 feet wide, 45 feet high.

Confusingly, the Hebrew word *tevah* means "box" or "chest" and is used to designate both the papyrus basket in which Moses, as an infant, is left to float among the bulrushes of the Nile, *and* the huge ark Noah is to construct from "gopher wood"—a wood not mentioned elsewhere.

The ark, as Raphael instructs, is to have three decks and one door. An opening, about eighteen inches high, runs around its roof to allow light and air into the dark vessel. Interestingly, there is some resemblance between Raphael's ark for the Deluge and the gigantic boat in the flood story in the earlier Sumerian Gilgamesh epic.

In terms of prefigurements serving as origins—that is, prophecy serving as the origin of a later event, something we'll address in a subsequent chapter—the Old Testament Flood and Noah's salvation is taken in the New Testament (1 Pet. 3:20–21) as foreshadowing of the rite of baptism, salvation through water immersion. The Flood prefigures the sacrament.

URIEL, "LIGHT OF GOD": PATRON OF POETS ◆

The name "Uriel" comes from the Hebrew *uri'el—uri* is "light" or "fire." The name appears in Apocryphal Hebrew writings but not in Sacred Scripture.

The light that shines from Uriel usually is depicted as fire, for he is known popularly as the Angel of Repentance. In Christian art, the saint (all archangels merit that devout title of "saint" in Catholicism) is painted with one palm extended, cupping flames.

His equivalent in Islam is *Izra'il*, the Angel of Death. In fact, in both Christianity and Islam, this archangel has a kinder, gentler persona: he's the muse of music. And he's been adopted by poets as their patron. Popes have largely ignored Uriel.

In legend, it is Uriel who warns Noah of the coming Great Flood. And in Jewish mysticism, Uriel whispers, cants, and dictates the Kabbalah, a system of theoretical and practical wisdom that leads a believer to mental and spiritual growth. (*See* Kabbalah.)

The three lesser archangels—ancillary in their popularity and authenticity—which Islam does not recognize:

RAMIEL, meaning "God raises up," is the Angel of Hope. For faiths that believe in Limbo and Purgatory, Ramiel oversees those realms, supervising souls that one day will enter the Kingdom of God.

RAGUEL, meaning "friend of God," escorted Enoch in his assumption to Heaven; the Books of Enoch paint the angel as something of a warrior.

SARIEL, meaning "will of God," is described by Enoch as the heavenly keeper of the Lord's laws.

REFORMED ANGELS: SIXTEENTH CENTURY c.e. ◆

The Protestant reformers did not take kindly to angels. Men like Martin Luther and John Calvin rebelled against the notion of supreme beings doing God's work and lording it over hardworking folk. Luther's notion of salvation by faith alone, and Calvin's strict emphasis on predestination, did not leave angels with much to do.

And, too, by the sixteenth century, there were millions and millions of angels. Saint Albert the Great calculated there were exactly 399,920,004 angels. Which came remarkably close to the total arrived at by medieval Jewish Kabbalists: 301,655,722.

Also, the architectural excesses of the Renaissance—decadent, decorative winged creatures on cathedral friezes and stained-glass windows—impressed the reformers as pagan idolatry.

The cult of the guardian angel—it had reached cult status—was particularly irksome. In a mood for change, Protestants swept away not only the pope and papal bureaucracy, but the celestial hierarchy of angels as well. Man

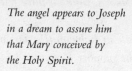

The angel appears to Joseph in a dream to assure him that Mary conceived by the Holy Spirit.

could communicate directly with his Maker without the intercession of soaring winged messengers.

Few Protestant theologians since have seriously addressed the subject of angels. The modern exception is Billy Graham, whose 1975 book *Angels: God's Secret Agents* was a national best-seller. In it, Graham argued that one cannot believe in the literal interpretation of Scripture and dismiss the role angels play in the Bible. Indeed. Here is a glimpse of angelic activity from Scriptures:

• Angels assist Abraham (Gen. 18), Lot (Gen. 19), Jacob (Gen. 28), Elias (2 Kings), Daniel (Dan. 6), Tobit (Tob. 5), the apostle Peter (Acts 10).

• The Law is given through angels (Heb. 2).

• Angels appear to Samson's mother (Judg. 13), Zechariah (Zech. 2), David (2 Kings), the carpenter Joseph (Matt. 1), the Virgin Mary (Luke 1), the shepherds tending their flocks (Luke 2), Jesus Christ in his Agony (Luke 22), the disciples after the Resurrection (Matt. 28), the disciples after the Ascension (Acts 1), the evangelist Paul (Acts 27).

• Angels reveal the Book of Revelation to John of Patmos.

• A woman must keep her head covered while in prayer, and in church, out of respect to angels (1 Cor. 11:10).

ISLAMIC ARCHANGELS: MIKAL, JIBRIL, IZRAIL, ISRAFIL ◆

Islamic cherubim, the *karubiyun*, continually praise God with the chant *tasbih*, "Glory to Allah." Existing in a state of eternal peace, the delicate Islamic cherubim dwell in a realm of Heaven that is inaccessible to vicious attacks from Iblis, the Devil.

Islam has adopted four archangels from Judaism, and modified them slightly:

ZOROASTER'S ANGELOLOGY ◆ *It is not surprising that there are so many similarities among Jewish, Christian, and Islamic angels, since all three faiths are indebted to Persian angelology of the sixth century* B.C.E.

It was during that time that the Jews were in exile in Babylon (Persia), and they fell under the influence of the teachings of the prophet Zoroaster, who'd developed a theology of angels. Consequently, angelology in Judaism became more highly developed during the Exile. A great deal of the angel lore that filtered into Christianity, and later Islam, came through Judaism from Zoroastrianism. (See Zoroaster.)

In truth, the most important source of angelology is not the Bible. That honor belongs to a library of extrabiblical texts—Jewish, Christian, and Gnostic—written between 200 B.C.E. *and 200* C.E. *These books, which present a cosmos teeming with angelic activity, were heavily influenced by Zoroastrian cosmology. The prophet Zoroaster recognized good angels, bad angels, and equivocating angels who straddled the moral fence. The latter came to be called genies.*

MICHAEL (MIKAL), warrior leader of the heavenly host—who in Islam also provides food and knowledge to mankind.

GABRIEL (JIBRIL), God's chief messenger, who announces Muhammad's prophethood, then dictates over a span of twenty years the divine Koran, God's own words.

URIEL (IZRAIL), who becomes the Islamic Angel of Death; he oversees the lower parts of Hell, keeping demons in tow. If a Muslim shivers, says folklore, Izrail is staring at him or her.

RAPHAEL (ISRAFIL), who places souls in human bodies and will sound the trumpets on Judgment Day. He is a healer.

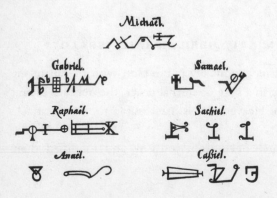

THE MAGIC SYMBOLS OF THE SEVEN ANGELS OF THE WEEKDAYS: Michael, Sunday; Gabriel, Monday; Samael, Tuesday; Raphael, Wednesday; Sachiel, Thursday; Anaël, Friday; Cassiel, Saturday.

ISLAMIC GENIES—AMBIVALENT ANGELS: POST–SIXTH CENTURY C.E. ◆

Islam's angelology (and demonology) differs in one curious way from that of Christianity. In general, Christians like their spirits to be polar opposites: angels/demons; good/evil; the legacy of Persian dualism.

Islam recognizes a third class of spirits, the *jinn*, or genies, who can go either way: be benevolent or malevolent.

According to Islamic legend, God created the genies two thousand years before Adam, and shaped them out of pure fire. Genies, if they wish, may be visible or invisible, can assume the shapes of animals or humans, be either a help or hindrance to humankind. They can act as the spirit moves them, so to speak.

Humans, in turn, using cunning or superior intellect, might be able to manipulate a genie for his or her own benefit—but we can never be sure of success. It's thought that genies are a holdover from Zoroastrianism.

ANGEL OF DEATH: PRE-BIBLICAL PERIOD ◆

That a specific angel is responsible for the occurrence of death on earth is a polytheistic concept, most likely a Canaanite idea related to their god Moth.

The ancient Israelites knew of Moth, and sometime after their conversion to monotheism, they seem to have had their own Angel of Death, *malakh ha-mavet*. Although Jewish monotheism would reject the notion, and

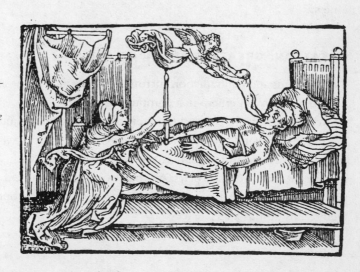

The Angel of Death taking the soul, in the form of a child, from a dying man.

come to view Yahweh/God as the master of life and death, there are passages in the Old Testament where "Death" is personified, and where "He" has angelic emissaries; notably in Proverbs 16:14 and Hos. 13:14. These allegorical notions are probably remnants of polytheism.

In monotheism, the origin of human death is man's own sin, as illustrated by Adam's punishment in Genesis. No supernatural force other than God himself takes human life. (*See* Monotheism; Polytheism.)

However, in postbiblical times, the title Angel of Death was reassigned to Satan. The Devil had no control over physical death, but he could cause a person's spiritual death. Thus, conceptually, there are really two Angels of Death: one, a primitive figure rooted in polytheism, snuffs out life; the second, postbiblical and dualistic, elicits sin.

APPEARANCE IN FOLKLORE. The diligent reaper's eyes are saucer-wide, since nothing escapes him. He's old, grim, nomadic, a beggar or a peddler, and he brandishes a sword to drip poison off its tip into the mouths of mortals.

In Jewish lore, there exists a plant, the "herb of life," that protects against stalking Death; this is a steal from the Gilgamesh epics of the Sumerians, c. 3000 B.C.E. In fact, many Jewish folk customs related to burial and mourning—breaking pots, the mourner's meal, the exchange of folktales—are attempts to drive away the Angel of Death.

Christianity and Judaism have rejected the Angel of Death, but Islam retains the concept, but in modified form: Izrail (or Azail) does not cause death but merely removes the soul, for God, after death has occurred. In Islamic folklore, Izrail is married, with children, and he can be the cause of human illness.

METATRON: GREATEST ANGEL OF ALL ◆

Conundrums and contradiction surround Metatron, whose name sounds like a contemporary superhero in a computer game.

Actually, his name is a combination of a Greek prefix and suffix: *meta + tron*. He is "beyond" (*meta*) ordinary angels. The suffix *tron* is affixed to a word to create an instrument, as physicists have done with "cyclotron," an instrument that cycles particles; or "betatron," an instrument that hurls beta particles. Thus, "metatron" is an instrument for "going beyond." Which perfectly sums up this angel's excesses.

Metatron is the greatest of angels in Jewish mysticism, especially in the

Kabbalah. He's also the tallest angel, measuring some eight to thirteen feet, depending on the legend.

His identity is every bit as shifty as his height. He is at times described as the "Prince of Angels" (superior even to the archangel Michael); as "The Presence" (an idolatrous-sounding name); as the "Lesser Yahweh" (a blasphemous title); as "Enoch Above"—that is, the scribe Enoch after his miraculous ascent into Heaven.

Jewish mysticism holds that Enoch was translated into the angel Metatron. Metatron is described as the "Lesser Yahweh."

To add to Metatron's identity crisis, he is elsewhere said to *be* the archangel Michael.

Even his functions shift from legend to legend. In some stories, he is described as the chief celestial scribe who records the sins and merits of humans. Elsewhere, he is the guardian of God's heavenly secrets. Or God's mediator with humans. Or he is the archetype of man, the blueprint God used to shape Adam from clay.

In Hebrew numerology, Metatron is called the one "whose name is like that of his master." That is, when the consonants that comprise the appellations "Metatron" and "Shaddai" (meaning "Almighty") are analyzed according to preassigned numerical values, each name totals 314—hence, "whose name is like his master's." This again has overtones of God the Father = God the Son.

Equally confusing is his appearance. Although he's supposed to be the prototypical man, at thirteen feet, he towers over most men, and in some stories he sports thirty-six wings, and in order to watch over all of Creation, he has "countless eyes."

Clearly, Metatron is a chimera rooted in pagan lore who has never been definitively—and decently—anthropomorphized.

LILITH, FIRST FEMINIST: ZOROASTRIAN DEMONOLOGY ♦

In Eastern European folklore, the Angel of Death is married to Lilith, a satanic female who seduces men, kills babies, harms pregnant women, and causes labor pains.

This female demon appears in Isaiah as one of the horrors of the Lord's day of vengeance:

> *Goat-demons shall greet each other; there too the lilith shall repose and find herself a resting place. (Isa. 34:14)*

Reform minister officiating at the marriage of the fool and the she-devil Lilith.

Lilith probably became known to the Israelites through Zoroastrian demonology, which is as rich and elaborate as its angelology. In medieval times, the *Alphabet of Ben Sira* elaborated on the tradition that Adam had a wife before Eve and she was named Lilith. It's Lilith who leaves Adam—she flies away, deserting her husband because he has rejected her demand that she be regarded as his equal. Lilith is independent, self-reliant, and she doesn't wish to bear children; the idea of motherhood bores her; she's obsessed with her career (which happens to be doing evil). She is the first feminist, predating Eve.

Male scribes created Lilith, probably as a literary balance to Eve, who is docile, obedient (except for the apple incident), dependent on her husband, Adam, careerless, and who begets children. The scribes made Lilith a bitch, who abandons her husband and spends aeons killing babies and causing miscarriages.

VULVA. The King James Bible translates "Lilith" as a "screech owl." The Douay Bible renders the character as a "lamia" (or "labia")—a bloodsucking female vampire; the word is from the Greek *lamos*, "a gaping mouth."

In fact, a gaping mouth is really a set of lips, and the Latin for "lips" is *labia*. In female anatomy, the labia majora (greater lips) are the outer folds of skin of the vulva, whereas the labia minora (lesser lips) are the two folds of mucous membrane within the labia majora. Hence, the name "Lilith" is intimately related to private female parts. Adam's "first wife" was, in short, a "gaping mouth" or vulva. Here we have a woman, the first woman, viewed not only as evil but also as a pure sex object. Sexism is ancient.

PART

III

Wise
Words

CHAPTER

6

𝔐oral 𝔗odes

Ten Commandments to Golden Rule

MORALITY SPLITS FROM RELIGION:
EUROPEAN ENLIGHTENMENT, EIGHTEENTH CENTURY ◆

For many people, the terms "morality" and "religion" are vaguely related yet distinctly different ideas.

Morality, we like to say, pertains to an individual's conduct and his or her relationships with other people. Morality involves *relationships between human beings*. Morality is concerned with conduct in the here and now.

Religion involves the *relationship between human beings and God*, or transcendent reality. Religion is concerned with how conduct in the here and now will influence one's standing in the hereafter. Whereas a "religious" person believes in an afterlife, a "moral" person need not believe there is anything after death except bodily decay.

The truth is, this distinction between morality and religion, often said to be a blight on our times, is rather recent in origin. No more than three hundred years old. And it came about for a very simple reason.

Although the Greek philosophers debated these two ideas, the popular modern notion that religion and morality are separate phenomena is rooted in the Enlightenment of eighteenth-century Europe, the philosophical movement characterized by aggressive rationalism, high-spirited skepticism, a love of learning, and a doggedness in thinking things through. Faith suffered. Blind belief was ridiculed. Religion and morality parted ways in the popular mind of the times. An "enlightened" person could say, "Oh, I'm not at all religious, but I'm highly moral," a distinction that was unheard of in earlier times.

The split between morality and religion was precipitated, ironically, *by* religion. European thinkers, weary of centuries of religious strife and holy wars—Crusades, Inquisitions, schisms, the sale of indulgences, hypocritical pontiffs, the Reformation, the Counter-Reformation—sought to elaborate ethical codes based not on divine revelation but on human reason, or at the very least on shared human sentiments.

By the early nineteenth century, it was possible to conceive of ways of thinking and acting morally that were not dependent upon religious revelation. Consequently, people began to question why throughout human history the ideas of religion and morality had been linked so closely.

Indeed, Sigmund Freud argued that religion must be abandoned because it undermines moral responsibility and encourages fantastical thinking and fanaticism: belief in miracles and in the superiority of one's own faith.

These views in our own century have been challenged most strongly by the comparative study of religions and their most revered moral codes. It is evident that all religions require strikingly similar codes of behavior. We'll examine the origins of religious precepts that mandate moral conduct—such as the Ten Commandments of Judaism; the Traditions of Muhammad in Islam; the Ten Precepts of Buddha; the Analects of Confucius; the Corporal and Spiritual Works of Mercy in Christianity.

TEN COMMANDMENTS: PRE-OLD TESTAMENT PERIOD ◆

This decalogue ("ten words") of moral law, inscribed on two stone tablets, traditionally was given by God through Moses to his Chosen People for guidance in conducting their lives in accord with the demands of the Covenant God established with them as a divine gift.

In fact, the laws were *twice* written on stone on Mount Sinai. The first tablets Moses smashed upon witnessing his people lapse into the old pleasures of idolatry: "He came into camp and saw the calf, and the dancing; and Moses' anger waxed hot, and he cast the tablets out of his hands and broke them" (Exod. 32:19). The second tablets were safely stored in the Ark of the Covenant (Exod. 40:18).

The Commandments appear in two places in the Hebrew Bible, in Exodus 20:1–14 and in Deuteronomy 5:6–18, and are alluded to or quoted in part in several other places, as well as in the New Testament. The differences between the Exodus and Deuteronomy listings are quite small, reflecting changes over time in the way the Israelites understood the code and applied it. Both the Books of Exodus and Deuteronomy were written sometime between the years 1400 to 1200 B.C.E.

Jews, Roman Catholics, and Protestants enumerate the Ten Command-

Moses breaking the Tablets of the Law: "He saw the calf, and the dancing, and . . . he cast the tablets out of his hands."

ments in different ways. For Jews, the First Commandment is "I am the Lord your God who brought you out of the land of Egypt, out of the house of bondage." Christianity, on the other hand, has deleted all reference to Jewish history, pruning the laws to their basic fiat.

ORIGIN. For scholars, it is clear that the legal materials of the Hebrew Bible developed over centuries, reaching one codification in Moses' time. Clearly, much of the substance of the Ten Commandments is unique to Moses' period of history. This is particularly true of the requirement of "one day in seven for rest," the day of the Sabbath, and the shunning of idolatry, two ideas without precedent in the ancient Near Eastern world. These *moral* codes determined how Israelites were to conduct their *religious* life; morality and religion then going hand in hand.

It is interesting to contrast the Judeo-Christian Decalogue with the moral codes, given below, of other faiths. Notice in particular how many are "positive" statements (Thou shall) versus the number that are "negative" (Thou shall NOT); reprimand of this sort is psychologically a more effective deterrent, more indelibly etched in memory.

1. I am the Lord thy God, thou shalt NOT have strange gods before Me.
2. Thou shalt NOT take the name of the Lord thy God in vain.
3. Remember to keep holy the Lord's Day.
4. Honor thy father and thy mother.
5. Thou shalt NOT kill.
6. Thou shalt NOT commit adultery.
7. Thou shalt NOT steal.
8. Thou shalt NOT bear false witness against thy neighbor.

9. Thou shalt NOT covet thy neighbor's wife.
10. Thou shalt NOT covet thy neighbor's goods.

The Commandments warned Israelites against conduct that would be ruinous to their survival as a community. Judaism, unlike Christianity, has always emphasized most strongly *this* life as opposed to life in the hereafter.

TEN PRECEPTS OF BUDDHA: SIXTH CENTURY B.C.E. ◆

In Buddhism, morality (*sila*) involves correct speech, correct actions, and correct livelihood. Moral conduct is a stage of development that leads an individual along the Eightfold Path of spiritual progress, culminating in wisdom or enlightenment.

Time is cyclical; reincarnation is unavoidable if a Buddhist has not become fully enlightened the first time around. Following the moral code eliminates the distractions to enlightenment. Ideally, the goal of a Buddhist is to extinguish the flame of human desire, achieve detachment from the self, such that rebirth does not occur, and the ultimate Nirvana is attained.

The Ten Precepts, or *dasa-sila*, recast in Judeo-Christian format for the sake of comparison:

1. Thou shalt NOT take another's life.
2. Thou shalt NOT take that which is not given.
3. Thou shalt NOT engage in sexual misconduct.
4. Thou shalt NOT engage in false speech.

Buddha. Buddhism has Ten Precepts—like the Ten Commandments.

5. Thou shalt NOT use intoxicants.
6. Thou shalt NOT eat after midday.
7. Thou shalt shun worldly amusements.
8. Thou shalt NOT adorn with ornaments and perfumes.
9. Thou shalt NOT sleep on high or luxurious beds.
10. Thou shalt NOT accept gold or silver.

The first five Precepts, the *panca-sila*, are to be observed by monks and laymen alike. As for number three, sexual misconduct is anything less than celibacy for a monk, and anything less than the accepted social norm, such as adultery, for everyone else. Normally, all Ten Precepts are followed only by Buddhist monks and nuns.

THE ANALECTS OF CONFUCIUS:
FIFTH CENTURY B.C.E. TO FIRST CENTURY C.E. ◆

The word "analects" means "selected sayings." These moral precepts were supposedly composed by Confucius himself, who was born around 551 B.C.E. and died in 479 B.C.E. However, Chinese scholars debate the authenticity of that claim the way Western scholars argue over the validity of Jesus' words in the Gospels, and Socrates' words in the dialogues of Plato. It is likely that these "selected sayings," *Lun yu* in Chinese, which occupy four books, came together gradually, over several hundred years.

The numerous Analects cover all the basic ethical concepts of Confucius. They discuss the importance of "benevolence," *jen*, toward one's fellow man. They lay out the concept of the "holy man" (the West's equivalent of saint), *chun-tzu*; the requirements to get into "Heaven," *T-ien*; as well as "proper conduct" in daily life, *li*.

Interestingly, the "sayings" are quite specific in that all phases of a person's life must be in perfect harmony with "names" that identify that particular aspect of life; for example, a marriage must be true to the word "marriage" and not be expanded to encompass such things as concubinage. This is the principle of *cheng ming*, or "adjustment to names." A couple cannot have an "open" marriage, or "modern" marriage; adjectives only taint the original purity of the concept of the noun.

The Analect closest to the Judeo-Christian "Honor thy father and thy mother" is the *hsiao*, or precept of "filial piety." *Hsiao* does not mean merely providing for one's elderly parents, for "even dogs and horses do that," said Confucius; filial piety is inseparable from a deep and genuine lifelong respect of children for their parents.

*Confucius, political and
ethical philosopher.*

The tone and format of the Analects can be appreciated in the opening lines of the First Book:

1. To learn, and in proper time to repeat what one has learned, is that not after all a pleasure?

   That friends should come to one from afar, is this not after all a delight?

   To remain unsoured even though one's merits are unrecognized by others, is that not after all what is expected of a gentleman?

2. Those who in private life behave well toward their parents and elder brothers, in public life seldom show a disposition to resist the authority of their superiors.

DECALOGUE OF THE KORAN: ISLAM, SEVENTH CENTURY C.E. ◆

Also called the Traditions of Muhammad, Islam's Decalogue, or Ten Laws, are, like the Hebrew Ten Commandments (in Exodus), found in Sacred Scripture: Koran, 17:22–39.

The chapter in which they're listed, number 17, is titled "The Children of Israel." The text makes clear that God "gave Moses the Book, and made it a guidance for the children of Israel" (17:2). However, God or Allah, through the intercession of the archangel Gabriel, revealed additional Sacred Scripture to Muhammad, starting in the year 610 C.E., and ending shortly before the Prophet's death. Thus, it should not be surprising that the Decalogue in Islam is very close to the Hebrew Ten Commandments.

Extracted from the Koran's long text and arranged with the negative emphasized for the sake of comparison:

1. Do NOT set up another god with God.
2. Be good to your parents, look after them with kindness and love.
3. Give to your relatives what is their due.
4. Do NOT be niggardly, nor so extravagant that you may later feel reprehensive and constrained.
5. Do NOT abandon your children out of fear of poverty.
6. Do NOT go near fornication, for it is an immoral and evil way.
7. Do NOT take a life, which God has forbidden, except in just cause.
8. Do NOT touch the property of others, except for bettering it.
9. Do NOT follow that of which you have no knowledge.
10. Do NOT strut about the land with insolence.

THE GOLDEN RULE: ALL FAITHS, ANTIQUITY ◆

The Hebrew Book of Leviticus, written between the years 1400 to 1200 B.C.E., served as a handbook for the ancient priests of Israel. Much of it is devoted to specific regulations concerning offerings, sacrifices, ritual purity, ordination, feasts, and festivals. But one line has withstood the passage of time: *"Thou shalt love thy neighbor as thyself"* (Lev. 19:18).

In rabbinic Judaism, it was recast as a negative statement by the sage Hillel: *"Do NOT do unto others, what is hateful to you."*

The origin of the Christian Golden Rule is Matthew 7:12 (King James Version): *"All things whatsoever ye would that men should do to you, do ye even so to them."*

The origin of the Chinese Golden Rule is the Analects of Confucius 12:2: *"Do NOT do to others what you would not like yourself."* The sage goes on to say: "Then there will be no feelings of opposition to you, whether it is the affairs of a state that you are handling or the affairs of a family."

The origin of the Golden Rule in Buddhism is the *Dhammapada*, 10:129–30: *"Having made oneself the example, one should neither slay nor cause to slay."* The text goes on to clarify the maxim: "As I am, so are other beings; thus let one not strike another, nor get another struck [by someone else]. That is the meaning."

The Golden Rule is so simple, so universal, and unfortunately so underused. To apply it in everyday life, round the world, would solve most problems. Treat others the way you want to be treated yourself.

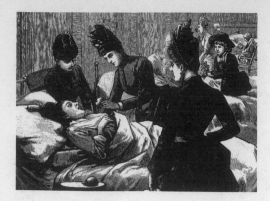

"Visit the sick"—a corporal work of mercy.

CORPORAL AND SPIRITUAL WORKS OF MERCY: CHRISTIANITY, MIDDLE AGES ◆

Roman Catholicism, reaching back to medieval times, has assembled two lists of moral actions that affect the bodies and souls of the faithful. (For the Eight Beatitudes of Jesus Christ, *see* Beatitudes.)

During the Middle Ages, when these lists were codified, they were often the subject of paintings and sculptures, many still extant. In today's frenetic and self-centered world, these simple precepts that are more than a thousand years old have undiminished relevance.

The corporal works of mercy that fortify one's body:

1. Feed the hungry.
2. Give drink to the thirsty.
3. Clothe the naked.
4. Visit the imprisoned.
5. Shelter the homeless.
6. Visit the sick.
7. Bury the dead.

The spiritual works of mercy that strengthen one's soul:

1. Admonish the sinner.
2. Instruct the ignorant.
3. Counsel the doubtful.
4. Comfort the sorrowful.
5. Bear wrongs patiently.
6. Forgive all injuries.
7. Pray for the living and the dead.

𝕭iblical 𝕻hrases

"Writing on the Wall" to "Eye to Eye"

THE BIBLE, a collection of volumes written under God's inspiration, has enriched our everyday language with countless phrases that through familiarity have become clichés on the tip of the tongue. Only the collective works of Shakespeare have been so thoroughly absorbed.

As the fundamental book and timeless best-seller of Western culture, the Bible offers wise and even witty one-liners on all aspects of life, secular as well as sacred. Daily, we use phrases from the Bible in conducting business, legislating laws, mourning our dead, reprimanding our children. Sometimes, a phrase still means today what it did to peoples in ancient eras; other times, a phrase's meaning has changed radically, either linguistically or socially. Translators of the Bible, bringing it from Hebrew or Greek or Latin into English, have used the words of their own era to best capture the intent of a biblical passage, and the usage of some of those words changed over time. There have also been some unforgettable Bible typos that perverted biblical intent, as we'll see.

First, though, the origins of the Bible itself.

BIBLE: C. 1800 B.C.E. TO 100 C.E. ◆

With God as its author and the Holy Spirit as its chief scribe, the Bible can contain no errors, typos aside.

Its highlights, which even illiterate peoples come to know by rote, involve the seminal episodes in Western spirituality:

The Creation Story, Genesis 1:1–2:7; The Fall of Man, Genesis 3:6–24; Noah and the Great Flood, Genesis 6:1–9:17; The Call of Abraham to Found Judaism, Genesis 12:1–9; The Ten Commandments, Exodus 20:1–17;

The Birth of Jesus Christ, Matthew 1:18–2:23; Luke 1:26–2:40; The Sermon on the Mount, Matthew 5–7; The Prodigal Son, Luke 15:11–32; The Good Samaritan, Luke 10:29–37; The Last Supper, Matthew 26:20–25; Mark 14:12–26; The Death of Christ, Luke 23:26–56; John 19:16–42; The Resurrection of Christ, Matthew 28, Luke 24, John 20; The Advent of the Holy Spirit, Acts 2:1–21.

ORIGINAL LANGUAGES. Three languages were used for the original texts of the Bible. The Old Testament was written in Hebrew, except for the Books of Wisdom and 2 Maccabees, which were first written in Greek. There are also a number of passages in Aramaic.

Of the New Testament books, all were written in Greek, except the Gospel of Matthew, which was originally in Aramaic.

The *Septuagint*, the first major Greek translation of the Old Testament, was made in Alexandria between 250 and 100 B.C.E., and was designed to be used by the large number of Jews in Egypt who had adopted the Greek language. The book derives its name from the Latin for "seventy," because of the legend that its first five books, the Pentateuch, were translated by seventy (or seventy-two) Jewish scholars.

The *Vulgate*, a major Latin translation of the Bible, was written by the Christian Saint Jerome in the late third and early fourth centuries C.E., at the request of Pope Damasus.

ENGLISH TRANSLATIONS. Scattered English translations of the Bible appeared from the seventh century to the time of the Norman Conquest in 1066 C.E., when various favorite books were rendered into Anglo-Saxon by such men as Caedmon, Guthlac, Aldhelm, and Aelfric. A partial English translation is attributed to Saint Bede (d. 735), but if it existed, it did not survive into modern times.

Translations into English and other European vernacular languages, plus the printing press, put the Bible in the hands of ordinary folk.

The Bible, the best-selling book of all times, has been translated in part into 2,062 languages.

The first complete translation into English was by John Wycliff (1320–84), an English priest and scholar who advanced one of the leading Reformation ideas nearly two hundred years before Martin Luther—that the Bible alone is the only authority people need for their faith. More on Wycliff later.

Following the Reformation of the sixteenth century, many Protestant Bibles were produced in English: Tyndale's Bible (1525), Coverdale's Bible (1535), the Great Bible (1539), the Geneva Bible (1560), and the Bishops' Bible (1568). The King James Version (1611), prepared at the command of James I, was a thorough revision of the English Bible, based particularly on the Bishops' Bible, but in vocabulary considerably influenced by the Catholic Douay New Testament.

The Douay Bible, the most famous English Catholic version, was published between 1582 and 1610. This translation, based mainly on the Latin Vulgate, was the work of Catholic scholars who had been driven from England by religious persecution. At Douay, in Flanders, they set up a Catholic college, then moved for a time to Rheims, France. They published the New Testament at Rheims in 1582, and the Old Testament in two volumes in 1609 and 1610 at Douay.

As of 1994, Sacred Scripture at least in part has been translated into 2,062 different languages. In 1993 alone, parts of the Bible were translated into forty-four new languages. Portions can now be read in 587 African tongues, 513 Asian dialects, 358 Central and Latin American languages, 341 Pacific Island languages, 189 European languages, and 71 different North American tongues.

Currently, the complete Bible, Old and New Testaments, is available in 337 of the world's approximately 6,000 languages.

Here's a rundown of the major books of the Bible, their dates of origin, their authors, and their principal themes:

GENESIS. Date: c. 1400 to 1200 B.C.E. Traditional "author," Moses. Themes: God's existence, his role in Creation, his concern at man's fall from grace, and his continued involvement in human affairs.

EXODUS. Date: c. 1400 to 1200 B.C.E. Traditional "author," Moses. Themes: God cares for his people, hears their cries, and rescues them from oppression. God has a master plan for humankind, which is not always apparent.

LEVITICUS. Date: c. 1400 to 1200 B.C.E. Traditional "author," Moses. Themes: Sin must be atoned for through ritual sacrifice and penance. Religion has its own laws and regulations. God watches.

NUMBERS. Date: c. 1400 to 1200 B.C.E. Traditional "author," Moses. Themes: Man wanders through life as through a "wilderness," and must constantly be on the alert for temptations. God will assist when he feels the time is appropriate; but he always demands total obedience.

DEUTERONOMY. Date: c. 1400 to 1200 B.C.E. Traditional "author," Moses. Themes: God gave laws not to hinder mankind, but to assist human beings from birth to death. All of the laws may not make sense all of the time, but they are part of God's mysterious master plan.

These five books are the oldest part of the Hebrew Bible, called the Pentateuch.

GOSPEL OF MATTHEW. Date: 65 to 75 C.E. Matthew was a Jew, a tax collector by profession, who allegedly died a martyr's death in Ethiopia. Themes: All of the events of Jesus' life were foreseen by the Old Testament prophets and predicted either straightforwardly or cryptically: Jesus' birth, healings, teachings, suffering, death, and Resurrection.

GOSPEL OF MARK. Date: 60 C.E. Mark was a Jew, occupation unknown, who allegedly died a martyr's death. His writings served as a basis for both Matthew and Luke. Themes: Jesus is the Son of God, who died for our sins. Salvation is possible only through the spiritual rebirth of baptism, and belief in Jesus Christ.

GOSPEL OF LUKE. Date: 65 C.E. Luke, a Greek physician, died a martyr's death in Greece. Themes: After tracing Jesus' ancestry back through David and Abraham to Adam and Eve, Luke shows particular concern for the role of women in Jesus' teachings; the good news, or "gospel," that Jesus preached was for men, women, slaves, Jews, and Gentiles. Luke also wrote the Acts of the Apostles, c. 65 C.E.

GOSPEL OF JOHN. Date: 95 C.E. John, a Jewish fisherman, believed to be banished to the island of Patmos, died a natural death. Themes: Jesus was both the Son of God *and* a human man; he was the Good Shepherd and we must be obedient sheep and follow Christ. Without Jesus' help, we can do nothing. John traditionally is taken to be the author of Revelation, c. 90 to 95 C.E., the most apocalyptic book of the Bible.

BIBLE BLOOPERS: ENGLISH TRANSLATIONS, FOURTEENTH TO TWENTIETH CENTURIES ◆

Despite the extreme care that goes into proofreading divine revelation, many embarrassing errors have crept into the Bible. In the Geneva Bible of 1560, Matthew's phrase "Blessed are the peacemakers" came off the presses as *"Blessed are the place makers."*

In Luke in the same edition, Christ *"condemns the poor widow,"* when, in fact, Jesus "commends" the woman. Most embarrassing, in John, the name "Jesus" is misspelled *"Judas."*

The Geneva Bible came to be best known as the "Breeches Bible" for the manner in which, by translating the Latin for "apron" as "breeches," it altered Adam and Eve's first venture into casual wear. In Genesis, the First Parents, sinless and naïvely naked, eat the forbidden fruit when suddenly: "The eyes of them both were opened, and they knew that they were naked, and they sewed fig leaves together, *and made themselves breeches"* (3:7).

In the 1612 version of the King James Bible, Psalm 119, which should have read, "Princes have persecuted me without cause," came off the press as *"Printers have persecuted me without cause,"* possibly a Freudian slip by the typesetter.

In another early English translation, Mark's phrase "Let the children first be filled" was printed *"Let the children first be killed"*—a serious typo in a world where many take Scripture literally.

A Bible issued in London in 1631 contains one of the most well-known typographical errors ever. The edition is known as the "Adulterous Bible" because the Commandment "Thou shalt not commit adultery" appeared as *"Thou shalt commit adultery."* The printer, Robert Barker, was heftily fined and forced to destroy the books before they could destroy the institution of marriage.

In a later printing, Barker went on to omit "no" in Revelation's phrase "And there was no more sea," creating a miracle of abundance with *"And there was more sea."*

The 1810 "Wife-Hater Bible," as it was subsequently labeled, misprinted Luke's "If any . . . hate not . . . his own life" as *"If any . . . hate not . . . his own wife."*

Our own century has witnessed some classic Bible bloopers. In a famous

1903 printing, Paul and Apollos, tentmakers by trade, are listed in the Acts of the Apostles as *"by profession landscape painters."*

In the 1966 Jerusalem Bible, Psalm 122 instructs its readers to *"Pay for peace."* And in the New English Bible of 1970, Paul the evangelist warns the Corinthian faithful against associating with fornicators with the line *"have nothing to do with loose livers."*

Phrases from the Great Book that have entered everyday language:

A DROP IN THE BUCKET: ISAIAH 40:15-17 ◆

BEHOLD, THE NATIONS ARE AS A DROP OF A BUCKET, AND ARE COUNTED AS THE SMALL DUST OF THE BALANCE . . . AND THEY ARE COUNTED TO HIM LESS THAN NOTHING, AND VANITY.

We mean by this phrase a quantity too small to be significant; skimpy; a smithereen. And that's exactly how the eighth-century-B.C.E. prophet Isaiah uses the phrase to remind the exiled Jews about God's sentiment toward hostile nations that treat them harshly. They're nothing: "not sufficient to burn, nor the beasts thereof sufficient for a burnt offering."

The metaphor first appeared in the English translation of the standard Latin Bible in 1382 by John Wycliff as a "drop *of* a bucket," and *of* gradually became *in*. Wycliff, a theologian and reformer, advocated that the Church at Rome relinquish its worldly possessions and return to evangelical poverty, a view popular with the English king and Parliament, but denounced by Pope Gregory XI, who had Wycliff arrested in 1377. After his death, Wycliff was declared a heretic, and his body was exhumed and burned for suggesting papal thrift among other things.

In the nineteenth century, Charles Dickens put a popular spin on the "bucket" phrase in *A Christmas Carol*. Says Scrooge to the ghost of his deceased partner, Marley: "The dealings of my trade were but a drop of water in the comprehensive ocean of my business."

The Book of Isaiah gives us many memorable phrases, sometimes with a slight twist from the original meaning. For instance, in coming to an agreement with someone we may *see eye to eye* with that person: *"For they shall see eye to eye, when the Lord shall bring again Zion"* (52:8).

We often describe purity with the words *as white as snow: "Though your sins be as scarlet, they shall be as white as snow"* (1:18).

A defenseless person approaches his cruel fate like *a lamb to the slaughter:* *"He is brought as a lamb to the slaughter, and as a sheep before her shearers is dumb, so he openeth not his mouth"* (53:7).

The Book of Isaiah, dating from about seven centuries before Christ's birth, is one of the best-known books of the Old Testament. In fact, it is the book most frequently quoted in the New Testament as an example of prophecy fulfilled, and the one used most often by Jesus himself. The reason for its high quotability is simple. It contains the clearest Old Testament presentation of issues such as the depiction of sin, the helplessness of the sinner, the marvelous love of God, his provision of a Savior, and the calls to repentance and to faith. For this comprehensive spectrum of Gospel issues, Isaiah is often called "the world's first evangelist."

In addition to phrases that have become popular clichés, we also borrow from Isaiah many religious expressions and picturesque figures of speech:

"Behold, a virgin shall conceive."

"For unto us a child is born."

"All we like sheep have gone astray."

"They shall mount up with wings as eagles."

On the other hand, for a putdown, we might use *holier than thou:* "Stand by thyself, come not near to me; for I am holier than thou" (65:5).

A person with a message that's going unheeded may lament that his is *a voice crying in the wilderness:* "The voice of him that crieth in the wilderness" (40:3).

MONEY IS THE ROOT OF ALL EVIL: 1 TIMOTHY 6:9–10 ◆

BUT THEY THAT WILL BE RICH FALL INTO TEMPTATION AND A SNARE, AND INTO MANY FOOLISH AND HURTFUL LUSTS. . . . FOR MONEY IS THE ROOT OF ALL EVIL.

The banker J. P. Morgan argued that Timothy, in quoting Saint Paul, should have been more specific; as Morgan clarified: "The *love* of money is the root of all evil."

Atheist George Bernard Shaw saw it still differently: "The lack of money is the root of all evil." Money has always been important to those who don't have it, and even more important to those who do.

Timothy, Paul's young companion and fellow missionary, with responsibilities for the church at Ephesus, went on to say that greedy people who actively go after wealth "have erred from the faith, and pierced themselves through with many sorrows." A prophesy once again fulfilled in the 1980s.

A secular cliché plucked from Timothy (1 Tim. 6:12): *fight the good fight.* Paul's friend, though, meant a very specific battle: "Fight the good fight of faith."

EYE FOR AN EYE, TOOTH FOR A TOOTH: EXODUS 21:23-24 ◆

*AND IF ANY MISCHIEF FOLLOW, THEN THOU SHALT GIVE LIFE FOR LIFE,
EYE FOR EYE, TOOTH FOR TOOTH, HAND FOR HAND, FOOT FOR FOOT.*

Tit for tat is the kind of hard-nosed law-and-order strategy that God imparted to Moses. Indeed, sections of the Old Testament portray a harsh, spiteful, vindictive Creator. The Israelites' penal code was indeed severe, for the above words are not meant figuratively. An eye meant a viscous orb of vision. The logical extension of the full Exodus passage, which continues in the same vein, seems to imply that a rapist must be raped, a molester himself molested.

The dramatic Book of Exodus, with its historical backdrop of slavery and oppression, shows God's people in a cruel foreign land, crying out for deliverance, which comes in the form of Moses, who leads the people into a wilderness, where God provides manna to live *on* and the Ten Commandments to live *by*.

Some Exodus phraseology that we might casually toss off in everyday conversation:

"I felt like a *stranger in a strange land*" (2:22).

"Her skin was like *milk and honey*" (3:8).

"The prize money was like *manna from heaven*" (16:14–15).

"Oh, how life has *hardened your heart*" (4:21).

Each of the Ten Commandments found in Exodus has entered our popular speech in its own abbreviated way: *Honor your father and your mother . . . don't steal . . . don't lie . . . don't cheat on your wife.* It's amazing how many times a day we unwittingly paraphrase the Commandments, which is the purpose of any moral code: to make moral behavior ingrained behavior.

TO SEE THE WRITING ON THE WALL: DANIEL 5:5-30 ◆

*IN THE SAME HOUR CAME FORTH FINGERS OF A MAN'S HAND, AND
WROTE OVER AGAINST THE CANDLESTICK UPON THE PLASTER OF THE
WALL OF THE KING'S PALACE.*

A mysterious hand is glimpsed writing on the wall during a feast hosted by Babylonian king Belshazzar, who, as it happens, is delighting over his subjugation of the Jews. As the distraught king watches the disembodied digits, he begs wise men to interpret the script—*Mene, mene, tekel, upharsin*—offering in exchange wealth and influence. But the royal assortment of soothsayers, numerologists, and astrologers are for once speechless. Out of desperation, the king summons the Jewish prophet Daniel, who breaks the news. The writing on the wall foretells of impending disaster: the downfall of the kingdom and death of the king himself. That night, Belshazzar is slain. Ever since, the meaning of "the writing on the wall" has been clear.

The prophet Daniel's name means "God is my judge," and the Book of Daniel, written in the sixth century B.C.E., consists primarily of a series of prophetic dreams and visions. We borrow from Daniel when, for instance, we say a person has *feet of clay* (2:33), meaning that the individual has no strong underlying foundation.

A WOLF IN SHEEP'S CLOTHING: MATTHEW 7:15 ◆

BEWARE OF FALSE PROPHETS, WHO COME TO YOU IN SHEEP'S CLOTHING, BUT INWARDLY THEY ARE RAVENING WOLVES.

Some five centuries before Christ issued that caveat, conveyed by Matthew, the famed Greek fabulist Aesop had penned a cautionary tale about a devious wolf with designs on a flock of unsuspecting sheep. To disguise himself and trick the ever-vigilant shepherd, the wolf slips into a simple sheepskin frock, and he appears so convincingly sheeplike, if not sheepish, that the master of the house, in the mood for mutton stew, slays the sinewy old wolf. Had Jesus read Aesop? Had Matthew? Aesop did enjoy a wide audience; he was a best-selling author of his day.

Today, when we caution, "Beware of a wolf in sheep's clothing," we tend to forget that in the original tale, Wolf gets his dastardly due.

Give up the ghost, a metaphor for death, is a cliché that's come down to us through a spin on Matthew 27:50, in which he wrote about Christ's death on the cross: *"Jesus, when he had cried again with a loud voice, yielded up the ghost."* Another clichéd image is *lilies of the field*. Jesus, celebrating divine providence, directed the attention of his disciples to the sweet flowers: *"Consider the lilies of the fields, how they grow; they toil not, neither do they spin, yet I say to you that not even Solomon in all his glory was arrayed like one of these."*

Then there's this familiar caution:

DON'T CAST PEARLS BEFORE SWINE: MATTHEW 7:6 ◆

GIVE NOT THAT WHICH IS HOLY UNTO THE DOGS, NEITHER CAST YE PEARLS BEFORE SWINE, LEST THEY TRAMPLE THEM UNDER THEIR FEET, AND TURN AGAIN AND REND YOU.

Jesus' words, from the Sermon on the Mount, suggest that we not offer something that is truly good or holy to a person who is unworthy of the gift. He'll trample on it, then turn on you.

English Bible translator John Wycliff gave his own explanation for the phrase in 1380, which a later wordsmith rendered as: "Grandma, don't bequeath your most treasured antiques to a daughter who likes only new things."

Matthew, it turns out, especially in relating Jesus' Sermon on the Mount, coined many phrases that appeal to us today:

Stay on the straight and narrow: "*Strait is the gate, and narrow is the way that leads into life*" (7:14). The word "strait" means "constricted," as we use it in "Strait of Gibraltar."

Seek, and you shall find: "*Ask, and it shall be given to you; seek, and you shall find; knock and it shall be opened unto you*" (7:7).

The salt of the earth: by which we imply that a person is dependable and steadfast and, therefore, as valuable to us as salt was to the ancients, is from Matthew 5:13.

Turn the other cheek: by which we mean, instead of seeking revenge, to follow Jesus' metaphorical advice: "*Whosoever shall smite you on the right cheek, turn to him the other also*" (5:39).

The right hand doesn't know what the left hand's doing is a phrase we use to

The Good Samaritan.

The return of the Prodigal Son.

describe confusion, befuddlement, or deception, even self-deception: Actually, Matthew tells us Jesus said, *"Let not your left hand know what your right hand does"* (6:3), meaning that, when performing good works like almsgiving, we should be *so* secretive that we ourselves barely take note of it (let alone tout the pious acts to our neighbors).

Another Gospel writer, John, in recording Jesus' words, gave us these memorable phrases:

Born again: "I say to you, except a man be born again, he cannot see the kingdom of God" (3:3).

To cast the first stone: "He that is without sin among you, let him first cast a stone" (8:7).

Greater love hath no man: "Greater love hath no man than this, that a man lay down his life for his friend" (15:13).

The truth shall make you free: "And you shall know the truth, and the truth shall make you free" (8:32).

The Gospels of John and Luke also present us with three individuals, whose names have come to refer to fundamental types of people:

A Doubting Thomas: John 20:24–25.

A Good Samaritan: Luke 10:30–34.

The Prodigal Son: Luke 15:11–14.

How often in the course of a day do we use Bible quotations or images and never consider the source?

EAT, DRINK, AND BE MERRY: ECCLESIASTES 8:15 ◆

A MAN HATH NO BETTER THING UNDER THE SUN, THAN TO EAT, AND TO DRINK, AND TO BE MERRY.

This pagan sentiment seems so worldly, self-centered, and hedonistic, without thought of God, the soul, or sin. In fact, the Old Testament phrase seems the equivalent of the 1980s hip maxim: "Don't worry, be happy."

The Book of Ecclesiastes dates from about the tenth century B.C.E. The word "ecclesiastes" is a translation of the Hebrew *qoheleth*, meaning "The Speaker" or "The Preacher," and it possibly makes reference to Solomon as the author.

Ecclesiastes is a difficult text to understand, mainly because it seems to offer two disparate sets of ideas. On the one hand, the book suggests, pessimistically, that we live life to the fullest, die, and pass into a state of eternal nonexistence where there is no feeling or consciousness, and from which there is no return.

Vanity of vanities! All is vanity, which opens Ecclesiastes (1:2), sets the cynical tone. "Vanity" is used here in the archaic sense of "futility" or "worthlessness." This remains a popular sigh of exasperation toward a person consumed with self-importance and worldly matters.

There is nothing new under the sun is also from Ecclesiastes (1:9), and sounds a further negative note; we use it today to suggest that no idea is really new and fresh, everything has been sequeled to death.

Interpreters who adopt this bleak view of the Book of Ecclesiastes—that human endeavor is vain and empty—go on to explain that the book's optimistic passages, those that imply a belief in God and in justice, are later additions.

An alternate interpretation is to view the Book of Ecclesiastes as a series of sermons, by "The Preacher," on the vanity of life *without God;* that is, only a life lived without God is a hopelessly dead-end affair. It's God's presence that spares life from being vain and empty, God's daily grace that makes everything under the sun new and interesting each day.

We also owe our expression *there's a fly in the ointment,* meaning "something we value has been slightly spoiled," or "a problem has cropped up in what seemed a fine arrangement," to a graphic line from Ecclesiastes: *"Dead flies cause the ointment of the apothecary to send forth a stinking savor; so doth a little folly in him that is in reputation for wisdom and honor"* (10:1).

SPARE THE ROD, SPOIL THE CHILD: PROVERBS 13:24 ◆

*HE THAT SPARES HIS ROD HATES HIS SON; BUT HE THAT LOVES HIM
CHASTISES HIM MANY TIMES.*

The Book of Proverbs embodies the collective wisdom of Israel, often dis-
tilled into short, sharp phrases; that is, a list of sayings, taught by sages, on
how one is to live life in the presence of God—the "fear of the Lord" being
the essence of all true wisdom.

The Bible tells us that King Solomon himself "spoke three thousand
proverbs." But did he compose the Book of Proverbs?

We know that Solomon, through marriage with Pharaoh's daughter, had
close links with Egypt, and it's conceivable that he was acquainted with the
Teaching of Amenemope, wisdom that is closely paralleled in Proverbs. Today,
scholars generally agree that the content of Proverbs belongs to the days of
Israel's first kings, though editing continued for centuries. King Hezekiah,
for instance, who organized some of the editorial work, reigned 250 years
after Solomon. The book as we enjoy it today was finalized, at the latest, by
the second century C.E.

Pride goes before the fall is from Proverbs: *"Pride goeth before destruction, and a
haughty spirit before a fall"* (16:18).

From the same ancient text come two other popular expressions: *apple of
my eye* (7:2; which makes more than one appearance in the Bible), which we
apply to someone we cherish, just as "The Preacher" of Proverbs cherished
his pupil; and a *double-edged sword* (5:4), or "two-edged sword," which means
something that "cuts both ways" and requires extra caution in embracing it.

The idea of wisdom epigrams is common in the Old Testament, as it is in
the Analects of Confucius, the Precepts of Buddha, and the Traditions of
Muhammad. In one place in the Old Testament, it is even said that wisdom is
the master craftsman along with God. The aphorisms in the Book of
Proverbs cover every aspect of life: spanking children, dealing with parents,
growing up, and old, resisting temptation, the folly of riches, the perfect wife.

A STUMBLING BLOCK: ROMANS 14:13 ◆

*JUDGE THIS RATHER, THAT NO MAN PUT A STUMBLING BLOCK OR AN
OCCASION TO FALL IN HIS BROTHER'S WAY.*

Our expression "to put a stumbling block in someone's way" means to im-
pede that person's actions, whereas the original quotation refers to a "stumbling block" more as a moral obstacle or temptation.

The term "stumbling block" dates from the sixteenth century English translation of the Bible by William Tyndale (the term also appears in 1 Corinthians 8:9). A Humanist and a Protestant martyr, Tyndale produced the English translation that became the basis for the King James Version of the Bible, though he himself was condemned for heresy and burned at the stake.

Romans is Paul's Gospel manifesto, written around the year 58 C.E. It is the fullest and most closely reasoned statement we have of the basic Christian truths of that time. The apostle Paul, though he had not visited the great city of Rome, sought to explain the nature of the new Christian movement to Romans via a letter. He wrote Romans in sweeping themes, spanning the Creation, Adam and Eve's disobedience, and on up until the end of the age.

The wages of sin is the phrase Paul gave us when he wrote to Christ's new followers in Rome: *"For the wages of sin is death; but the gift of God is eternal life through Jesus Christ our Lord"* (6:23). Rome, in Paul's day, was the rich, cosmopolitan capital of an empire that stretched from Britain to Arabia and was renowned for its love of pleasure and lack of principle. Paul knew in his heart the city and the people he was addressing.

The powers that be is a phrase Paul used in a discussion about the allegiances of Christians to God and to earthly emperors: *"The powers that be are ordained of God; let every soul be subject unto the higher powers"* (13:1).

Paul also gives us the phrase *a law unto themselves* (2:14), which we apply to people who act as if they're above the law, though that's not the passage's original intent. Here are Paul's words: *"For when the Gentiles, who have not the law, do by nature the things contained in the law, they, having not the law, are a law unto themselves."*

Another phrase from Paul in Romans is *Vengeance is mine!* We shout it as a personal triumph, but in Romans, the words make clear that God is asserting a prerogative: *"Vengeance is mine; I will repay, saith the Lord"* (12:19).

DEATH, WHERE IS THY STING?: 1 CORINTHIANS 15:55 ◆

O DEATH, WHERE IS THY STING? O GRAVE, WHERE IS THY VICTORY?

Paul traveled to Corinth on his second missionary journey, stayed eighteen months, founded a church, then wrote his letter in about the year 56 C.E. He'd encountered great opposition, for Corinth, a hustling seaport town that catered to all sorts of transients, was notorious as a city of superior wickedness. Indeed, crowning the town was the temple of Aphrodite, goddess of free love, which soldiers often paid for with war booty. The seaport was a haven for prostitutes and a synonym for sexual license: "to Corinthianize" was a popular euphemism of the day for fornication. Paul's task was a hard one, and a large part of 1 Corinthians is devoted to responding to questions put to him by locals.

If people could not resist sexual temptation, he advised, *"better to marry than to burn."* His full speech was: *"But if they cannot contain, let them marry; for it is better to marry than to burn"* (1 Cor. 7:9).

Addressing the seaport's licentiousness, he wrote, "It is reported commonly that there is fornication among you," and in the same passage, a little further along, he gives us: *absent in body, but present in spirit* (1 Cor. 5:3), which we say to a friend for moral support when we can't provide bodily comfort, or be present at an important time.

To *see through a glass darkly* is a popular expression, meaning not to see or comprehend well, like peering through sooty eyeglasses or a soiled windowpane. Paul's words are: *"For now we see through a glass, darkly"* (1 Cor. 13:12).

Then, in the next sentence of this passage, he strings together three little pearls we still find impossible to separate: *faith, hope, and charity* (1 Cor. 13:13); Paul omits the conjunction.

There *but for the grace of God go I* is something we say when we see someone far less fortunate than ourselves, and it is attributed to Paul in 1 Corinthians, but through common usage, we have somewhat modified the apostle's words: *"But by the grace of God I am what I am"* (1 Cor. 15:10).

In the twinkling of an eye (1 Cor. 15:52) is a phrase we use to emphasize the quick passage of time, though "wink" of an eye is what we really mean. Paul, when he uses the phrase, is referring to the speed with which we will be suddenly transformed by Christ's Second Coming from corporeal bodies to spiritual beings.

Elsewhere (Acts 20:34–35), we find him reminding Gentile followers: *"Remember the words of the Lord Jesus, how he said, It is more blessed to give than to receive."* When we give a gift to a friend and do not get one in return, we remind ourselves *it's better to give than to receive.*

A MAN AFTER MY OWN HEART: 1 SAMUEL 13:14 ◆

THE LORD HATH SOUGHT HIM A MAN AFTER HIS OWN HEART, AND THE LORD HATH COMMANDED HIM TO BE CAPTAIN OVER HIS PEOPLE.

The two books known as 1 and 2 Samuel, probably composed in the tenth century B.C.E. (though not by Samuel; authorship is unknown), were originally one volume in the Hebrew Bible. They provide a vivid history of Israel from the end of the Judges period to the last years of David, the nation's second and greatest king—roughly one hundred years.

Samuel gives his name to the books as the dominating figure of the early era, Israel's "kingmaker" under God's direction. It was Samuel who anointed as king first Saul—a strange fellow, alternately given to reasonable behavior and insane acts of violence—and then David: *"And Samuel said to Saul, thou hast done foolishly; thou hast not kept the commandment of the Lord . . . now thy kingdom shall not continue: the Lord hast sought him a man after his own heart"* (1 Sam. 13:13–14).

God save the King!, from 1 Samuel 10:24, is actually an English translation of the Hebrew phrase "Long live the king." This is the title of the British national anthem, which, with different words, is known in the United States as "My Country 'Tis of Thee."

Samuel was a born storyteller and a master of suspense, and in his tale of the battle between a feisty underdog and a towering Philistine, he gave us the memorable twosome *David and Goliath*, and a powerful metaphor for any battle between a righteous underdog and an outwardly more powerful foe.

There are several theological themes in Books 1 and 2 Samuel, foremost the fact that God is active in a nation's day-to-day history. God weaves his purpose through our acts. Although we possess free will, God never *puts words in one's mouth*, a phrase we take from 1 Samuel 14:3: *"So Joab put the words in her mouth."*

TO PUT ONE'S HOUSE IN ORDER: 2 KINGS 20:1 ◆

THUS SAITH THE LORD, SET THINE HOUSE IN ORDER; FOR THOU SHALT DIE, AND NOT LIVE.

The speaker is the prophet Isaiah, and he is warning the Judean king Hezekiah, who is "sick unto death." But the Lord hears the king's weeping and moaning and grants him another fifteen years of life.

Four centuries of Israel's history are recorded in the two Books of Kings, whose author may have been a prophet living in Babylon around 550 B.C.E., during the Exile. The story sweeps from the powerful reign of David, through the golden age of Solomon, to the fall of Samaria in 722 B.C.E. and the destruction of Jerusalem in 587 B.C.E. That is, from the highest heights to the deepest depths. And all with a moral: Goodness is rewarded, wickedness is punished. For when the nation and its leaders adhered to God's laws, they enjoyed peace and prosperity; and when their morals declined, so did everything else.

When Ahab marries Jezebel (16:31), who paints her face and worships the false idol Baal, language inherits one of its most colorful put-downs for an evil temptress: *a painted Jezebel*.

SKIN OF YOUR TEETH: JOB 19:19 ◆

MY BONE CLINGS TO MY SKIN AND TO MY FLESH, AND I HAVE ESCAPED WITH THE SKIN OF MY TEETH.

The title of a Thornton Wilder play, this phrase is learned early in life and adored by kids, who have ample opportunity to use it.

The Book of Job, of unknown authorship and dating from about the tenth century B.C.E., deals with a profound human theme: If God is in control, why do people continually suffer? The long answer is cast as a highly structured poem, about a man named Job who loses everything and becomes an outcast, awaiting death near a city dump. Several friends come by and attempt to explain why Job is being made to suffer; they represent different approaches to life.

One friend says Job sinned and was punished by a just God. Another says pride, the worst sin, overran Job's heart. Finally, God himself speaks and says they're all wrong. God is vague in his own explanation, but seems to suggest that when we have nothing in our life but God, only then do we appreciate that God is everything. Job grasps the lesson and his fortunes are restored.

The Lord giveth, and the Lord taketh away—that's our cliché today, and it aptly sums up Job's sad tale. As Job himself tells us: *"Naked came I out of my mother's womb, and naked shall I return: the Lord gave, and the Lord hath taken away; blessed be the name of the Lord"* (1:21).

Several self-explanatory expressions we use today originated in the Bible:

Fire and brimstone/Sodom and Gomorrah: "Then the Lord rained upon Sodom and upon Gomorrah brimstone and fire" (Gen. 19:24).

A pillar of salt: "But his wife [Lot's] looked back from behind him, and she became a pillar of salt" (Gen. 19:26).

A leopard can't change its spots: "Can the Ethiopian change his skin, or the leopard his spots?" (Jer. 13:23).

To fall from grace: "Ye are fallen from grace" (Gal. 5:4).

Wheels within wheels: "Their appearance and their work was as it were a wheel in the middle of a wheel" (Ezek. 1:16).

Am I my brother's keeper? "The Lord said unto Cain, Where is Abel . . . ? . . . And he said, I know not; Am I my brother's keeper?" (Gen. 4:9).

Render unto Caesar the things that are Caesar's, and unto God the things that are God's (Matt. 22:21).

To set one's teeth on edge: "Every man that eats the sour grape, his teeth shall be set on edge" (Jer. 31:30).

Out of the mouths of babes: "Out of the mouths of babes and sucklings hast thou ordained strength" (Ps. 8:2).

Be fruitful and multiply: "And God blessed them, saying, Be fruitful, and multiply, and fill the waters in the sea" (Gen. 1:22).

Whited sepulchers: "Woe unto you . . . hypocrites! for ye are like unto whited sepulchers, which indeed appear beautiful outward, but are within full of dead men's bones, and all uncleanness" (Matt. 23:27).

Tender mercies: "Remember, O Lord, thy tender mercies and thy loving kindness; for they have been ever of old" (Ps. 25:6).

The fat of the land: "I will give you the good of the land of Egypt, and you shall eat the fat of the land" (Gen. 45:18).

Dust to dust: "For dust thou art, and unto dust shalt thou return" (Gen. 3:19).

Rites and Rituals

$\mathcal{S}$acred $\mathcal{S}$ymbols

Halo to Star of David

SYMBOLS ARE POWERFUL. You can take two sticks, cross them, and convey the essence of Christianity. A swastika potently summons up vast atrocities and evil. A flag can represent centuries of people's aspirations and sacrifices, or their arrogance and folly. An eye wink is a symbol. So is a head nod, a handshake, a raised fist.

Symbols are secular, sacred, and everywhere.

Symbolism is so specific a language among a people that the sense or sentiment of a symbol is perfectly clear to all. Arrows piercing a saint's heart speak of sin and sorrow. A halo *is* holiness, no more need be said. A symbol strikes an immediate equation between two things, what a mathematician calls "one-to-one mapping." Lotus = Buddhism. Star of David = Judaism. Crucifix = Christianity.

Heraldry and family crests are elaborate symbols that speak for tribes and clans. An hexagonal benzene ring is a chemist's symbol. CD-ROM is a symbol, too, as is all computer language. All acronyms and abbreviations are symbols: RSVP embossed on an invitation. RIP chiseled on a tombstone. IHS *is* Christ. YHWH *is* God.

CHRISTIAN SYMBOLS:
I.N.R.I., "Jesus of Nazareth,
   King of the Jews";
Holy Spirit;
Lamb of God;
Sacred Heart;
Dove of Peace.

If you're told that the word "news" is an acronym for "north, east, west, south" (which it's not; it's from the Latin *novum,* "what is new"), the word becomes a vivid image for information flooding in from the four corners of the world.

Water is a symbol of life; fire of Hell; the phallus of fertility. For centuries, and across cultures, the color gold has stood for the sun, silver for the moon, blue for the sky, black for death, white for purity.

In short, symbols are among the most profound expressions of human nature. Carl Jung believed that certain images are universal and timeless, occurring in the East and West, in the ancient past and in our hurly-burly present. He argued that such universal images, or archetypes, carry dynamic, creative forces that move us deeply.

The word "symbol" is from the Greek *symbolon,* meaning "sign of identification."

Let's examine the origins, and the power, of humankind's most sacred symbols.

HALO: NEAR EAST, PRE-CHRISTIAN ERA ◆

The luminous circle of light used for centuries by artists to crown the heads of saints and spiritual leaders was originally not a Christian symbol but a pagan one, and is the origin of the *royal crown* worn by kings.

Early pre-Christian writings are replete with references to nimbuses of light around the heads of deities. In ancient Hindu, Indian, Greek, and Roman art, gods emit a celestial radiance upward from behind the skull. Greco-Roman mosaics depict disks behind the heads of Jupiter, Apollo, Venus, and lesser gods, and demigods that were half-human/half-divine.

Early kings, to stress both their special contact with a god and the divine authority invested in them, adopted crowns of gold, gems, and even feathers. The *crown of thorns* thrust upon Christ's head, a symbol in its own right, was intended as a public mockery of Jesus' heavenly kingship. (*See* Crown of Thorns; Relics.)

The halo was so pagan a symbol that early Christians discouraged artists from depicting a martyr's holiness with the nimbus image. Many bishops forbade writers to mention a celestial aura surrounding a martyr's head.

CHRISTIAN DISKS. The earliest examples of the halo in Christian usage are in paintings that survive in the Roman catacombs, where a disk emanating rays of light symbolized Christ. It was underground iconography.

Suddenly, in the seventh century, halos became commonplace on outdoor statuary in and around Rome, and with papal approval. Why?

The answer is surprisingly mundane. These halos were large, circular *horizontal* plates and, quite simply, they solved the nasty problem of bird droppings defiling a saint's face. A hatlike halo shielded a saint's pious features and kept them from becoming an unsightly mess. Mosaics of the time reveal that halos could also be rectangular. In many frescoes, a rectangle is reserved for a living holy man, a circle for a dead one.

From then on, the halo appears in the iconography of the apostles, the Virgin Mary, saints, and Christ. It generally disappeared from Western art during the Renaissance, when artists considered the halo too decorative; they wanted a saint's holiness to be conveyed by skillfully rendered facial features.

WORD ORIGIN. It's interesting to note that the word "halo," though it resembles "holy," has not a sacred root but an agricultural one. Millennia before Christ, farmers threshed grain by driving a team of oxen round and round over sheaves of wheat on the ground. The Greeks called the track a *halos*, meaning "circular threshing floor," which early astronomers adopted to describe the auras of refracted light around celestial bodies.

CRUCIFIXES AND CROSSES: PHOENICIA, PRE-CHRISTIAN ERA ◆

Of all Christian symbols, the cross is the most universally recognized, existing in some four hundred different configurations. Until the end of the sixth century, crosses were displayed *without* a figure of Christ upon them; depiction of his Agony was too painful. Besides, who would dare to recrucify Jesus Christ?

The Romans who crucified Jesus did not themselves dream up crucifixion on a cross as a cruel form of punishment. They adopted both the symbol and the torture from the Phoenicians, the ancient people who occupied the region that now is Lebanon and parts of Syria and Israel. The same people who gave us the alphabet gave us the crucifix.

Romans crucified Christ with arms outstretched on the T-shaped *Latin cross*, or *crux immissa*—a cross with a top that rises above the T-bar.

But at other times, they tied and nailed prisoners to a Y-shaped cross, feet together, arms apart. Or they used an X-shaped cross, all four arms and legs spread apart. This cross, known since the Middle Ages as *Saint Andrew's cross*, was called by the Romans the *crux decussata*, so named for the Roman numeral ten, X, the *decussis* symbol.

Criminals might also be crucified on a T-shaped cross (without the extended top), the so-called *tau cross*, from the Greek letter tau. Some legends claim that this was Christ's cross.

Any way you look at it, a man's two arms and two legs were an unfortunate match with the extended forks of crisscrossed planks.

Our noun "cross" is from the Latin for the word, *crux*, which itself is related to the Indo-European root *kreuk*, meaning "extension of the base."

Our noun "crucifix" is from the Latin verb *crucifigere*, "to hang on a cross."

SWASTIKA CROSS: MESOPOTAMIA, 2000 B.C.E. ◆

Although most people are unaware of it, the swastika now identified with Nazism is, in fact, an ancient cross known to the Greeks as the *crux gammata*, since each of its arms resembles the capital form of the Greek letter gamma. It is also known as the gammadion cross.

In early Christianity, the *swastika cross* became a coded symbol for Christ—one of the earliest—and it appears on numerous tombs of Christians as a veiled representation for the Latin cross on which Christ was crucified, which at the time was dangerous to use. Early Byzantine and Christian art is replete with sacred swastikas.

WORD ORIGIN. The word "swastika" is from the Sanskrit *svasitka*, meaning "conducive to well-being." It is composed of two Sanskrit words: *su + asti* = "well" + "it is."

The sacred swastika cross was a favorite symbol of the ancient Mesopotamians, and stood for prosperity and good fortune. Halfway around the world, the swastika cross was also used by the Maya in Central America and the Navajos of North America.

In India to this day, it is the most widely used symbol in Hinduism and Buddhism. To many peoples of the region, the swastika cross is a favorite symbol for a saint because its four arms bent at right angles reminds worshipers of the four possible places for rebirth: (1) in the animal or plant world, (2) in Hell, (3) back on earth as a human, or (4) in the spirit realm. Hindus use the sacred swastika cross over the doorways of their homes and on the title pages of their business accounting ledgers.

Most people have always distinguished between a clockwise or right-handed swastika and a counterclockwise or left-handed one. The right-handed symbol is considered a solar sign, the rotation of its arms imitating the course taken daily by the sun, which in the Northern Hemisphere appears to pass from east, then south, to west. The left-handed swastika, more accurately called the *sauvastika*, usually stands for night, magical practices, and in India represents the terrifying goddess Kali.

NAZI SWASTIKA. Guido von List, born in 1848 to a rich Viennese merchant, visited the catacombs of Saint Stefan's Cathedral in Vienna at the age of fourteen, and vowed before a dilapidated altar that he'd build a pagan temple to the god Wotan, said in ancient legend to have invented an old alphabet whose arrangement of letters invoked occult powers.

List imagined himself to be a descendant of an ancient race of Germanic priests and wise men called the Armanen. In 1908, he formed the secretive Armanen Society, whose members adopted the *Heil* (Hail) greeting (which harks back to paganism) and the holy emblem of the swastika cross. In Germanic myth, the swastika was a symbol for the "sun people" or "sun worshipers," a pure race of white-skinned people of innate superiority. Thus were laid the foundations for Hitler and his Aryan-Germanic ideals.

The roots of Nazism are deeply entangled with symbolism of all kinds, from the sacred swastika cross to the quest for the Holy Grail, the chalice from which Christ drank wine at the Last Supper. (*See* Holy Grail; Relics.) Hitler, in his youth, made an intense study of medieval occultism, ritual magic, and the power invested in symbols.

LATIN CROSS IN CHRISTIANITY: FOURTH CENTURY C.E. ◆

During the fourth-century reign of Constantine the Great, the Latin cross on which Christ was nailed was adopted as a sacred Christian symbol. However, at that time, no one dared to depict Jesus nailed to a cross in his utter humiliation.

As reported by Pope Eusebius (reigned 310 C.E.), Constantine "saw with his own eyes the trophy of the cross in the heavens, bearing this inscription, 'Conquer by this!'" On the strength of his mystical vision, Constantine painted his soldiers' shields with the letters chi rho, the first two letters of the Greek word for Christ. After defeating the tyrant Maxentius, whose army greatly outnumbered his own, Constantine in 326 dispatched his mother, Saint Helena, then age eighty, to Jerusalem in search of the True Cross. According to tradition, the old woman discovered it. (*See* True Cross; Relics.)

Because of his vision of the cross, the emperor abolished crucifixion as a legal form of Roman punishment.

In the fifth century, artists began to paint a lamb next to their rendering of a cross, for Jesus was the "Lamb of God," slain for the sins of the world.

The Crucifixion. For centuries, Christ's image was not shown on the cross.

CHRIST IS ADDED TO THE CROSS: LATE SIXTH CENTURY ◆

The practice of placing the figure of Jesus on the cross began near the end of the sixth century, but even then, no artist dared to show him in his pain and humiliation. Jesus wore a long royal tunic, sometimes a golden regal crown, and only his hands and feet were bare to show in a stylized fashion the nails that pinned him to the wood. The image was one of triumph. Jesus, whose kingdom would come, reigned open-eyed and smiling.

The first image of a *suffering* Christ on a cross, which appeared in the tenth century and was not at all popular, was condemned by the pope as blasphemy.

Over the next three hundred years, artists began putting a suffering Jesus on the cross, gradually deepening his hand wounds, adding a torturous crown of thorns, and liberal drippings of blood. Jesus' long tunic shrank in time to a skimpy loincloth, further revealing his body's torment.

CHRIST'S LOINCLOTH AND THE ISSUE OF CIRCUMCISION ◆

Interestingly, Jesus was never shown fully naked. Many art historians believe this had less to do with Middle Ages modesty, of which there was little, and everything to do with the fact that Jesus Christ, as a Jew, would have to be depicted as being circumcised. All European Christian men were *un*circumcised. A Jesus without his foreskin would be an unpleasant reminder that the God they worshiped had been a Jew—the very people Christians now blamed for Christ's arrest and death.

In fact, the Third and Fourth Lateran Councils of the Church (1179 and 1215) officially condemned Jews as "Christ killers," and suggested they be made to wear arm badges of shame—another form of symbol. Jews in Christian England were forced to wear a saffron-colored band; in France and

Germany, the color was yellow. In Italy, a Jew had to wear a small red hat of shame. As one modern-day author writes of the period:

> *Jews were forbidden all contact with Christians, barred from administration, deprived of lands, forbidden to own shops, herded into ghettos which were bolted at night. . . . A Jew who showed his nose on Good Friday was virtually committing suicide, even though the Man on the Cross had a Jewish nose. No system of apartheid was more rigorously enforced.*

By the thirteenth century, the Christ who hung on a cross was a gory nightmare, drenched in bright red blood, a face of agony. The vogue was to capture in art as much of Christ's torment as the artist was capable of rendering. Remarkably, at this time in history, specifically in the year 1224, Christian mystics, gazing at these gory crucifixes, began to experience the phenomenon of stigmata: spontaneous bleeding from the palms, feet, and one side; the locations of Christ's five wounds. Was this the power of suggestion at work? (*See* Stigmata.)

Christ on the cross became a widely popular symbol only during the Counter-Reformation, when the Roman Church sought to reestablish its holy reputation, and its original ties to Jesus Christ, and at the same time distance itself from nascent Protestantism. The crucified Savior, in all his suffering, became the new image of "reformed" Roman Catholicism.

CROSSES FOR ALL OCCASIONS: ANCIENT TO MODERN TIMES ◆

According to tradition, the symbol painted in blood on an Israelite's doorstep to spare the slaughter of the firstborn was in the form of the tau cross. In an instance of prophecy, this cross is also said to be the type Christ was nailed to, as suggested in the Gospel of John: "And as Moses lifted up the serpent in the wilderness, even so must the Son of man be lifted up" (John 3:14). This passage has led some to conclude that Christ must have been nailed to a tau cross and not a Latin cross.

There is a perfectly symmetrical cross, with four equal arms, that was known to the Greeks as the *crux quadrata*, because of its four equal quadrants; which became the geometers' X-axis/Y-axis graph. Known also as the *Greek cross*, it is the symbol of the modern Red Cross organization.

If you take the Latin T-shaped cross and mount it on three marble steps— symbols of faith, hope, and charity—you have the *Calvary cross*. Usually a statuette of Jesus does not appear on the Calvary cross, since it celebrates not

CROSSES:
Gammadion, tau (or Saint Anthony),
and Calvary (top, left to right).
Celtic, Greek (or Saint George), and
Latin (middle). Maltese, papal, and
patriarchal (bottom).

Christ's suffering and death, but the glory of his Resurrection and Ascension into Heaven.

The *crusader's cross*, also known as the *Jerusalem cross*, is a complex assemblage of five crosses: four tau crosses meet in the center to form a single large cross, and four Greek crosses occupy the four quadrants. The five crosses refer to the five wounds of Christ.

An emblem of John the Baptist is the *Maltese cross*. It has four arms of equal length, but each arm becomes progressively broader as it radiates outward from the center in slanting, rather than curved, lines. The cross has eight points in all, which are said to symbolize the Eight Beatitudes from Jesus' Sermon on the Mount.

The *papal cross*, scored with three unequal horizontal bars on the upper half, is used only to lead a procession in which the reigning pontiff plays a part.

The *Celtic cross*, which brings together a Latin cross and a circle in superposition, predates Christianity by many centuries. Its original symbolism was associated with fertility, the cross standing for male generative power and the circle for female receptivity. Within Christianity, it represents the union of Heaven and earth.

SAINT PETER'S CRUCIFIXION. The *inverted cross* comes from the legend of Saint Peter, the first pope, who supposedly was crucified upside down, feeling himself unworthy to be crucified on the upright cross of Christ. The inverted cross has come to symbolize humility.

In 1968, Pope Paul VI declared that the bones of his earliest predecessor, now in Rome, were authentically those of Peter. Vatican archaeologists who examined the mortal relics stated that the bones were those of a man between the ages of sixty-seven and seventy-two, which would make sense historically. However, Peter traditionally has been depicted as a toweringly tall, large-boned fisherman; the skeletal remains, now venerated relics and a huge tourist attraction, are those of a man five feet four inches tall.

"THE TWELVE DAYS OF CHRISTMAS":
ENGLAND, SIXTEENTH CENTURY ◆

Most Christmas hymns are straightforward carols containing no hidden imagery. One, though, is popularly believed to carry a cryptically coded message.

As the legend goes: Once Henry VIII broke with Rome over the issue of divorce, Catholics in England could not practice their faith openly. During this period, beginning in the sixteenth century, the carol "The Twelve Days of Christmas" was written. Tradition has it that the song was actually a secret catechism lesson for young Catholic children. In singing the song, children recited a creed of their faith's main tenets. The "partridge in a pear tree" is Jesus Christ, and the twelve gifts of Christmas are symbols for gifts from God:

> Two turtle doves—the Old and New Testament.
> Three French hens—Faith, Hope, and Charity.
> Four calling birds—the Four Gospels.
> Five golden rings—the Five Books of Moses.
> Six geese a-laying—the six days of Creation.
> Seven swans a-swimming—the seven gifts of the Holy Spirit: wisdom,
>   understanding, counsel, fortitude, knowledge, piety, and fear of the Lord.
> Eight maids a-milking—the Eight Beatitudes of Jesus.
> Nine ladies dancing—the nine classifications of angels.
> Ten lords a-leaping—the Ten Commandments.
> Eleven pipers piping—the eleven faithful apostles.
> Twelve drummers drumming—the twelve beliefs stated in the Apostles'
>   Creed.

However, the song probably predates the sixteenth century. It's believed that the original song, with slightly modified wording, derived from a "forfeits game" which was played on the Twelfth Night. Each player would have to remember and recite the objects named by the previous player and then add one more. The forfeits game played on the Twelfth Night is of Gallic origin.

"GOD THE FATHER" IMAGERY: OLD AND NEW TESTAMENTS ◆

One has only to glance up at the ceiling of the Vatican's Sistine Chapel to glimpse the most recognizable symbol of God: the outstretched *hand* with pointed finger, the hand that sculpted Creation and imparts life to bodies of "clay."

Hand imagery is commonplace in the Bible: "Thy right hand, O Lord, glorious in power" (Exod. 15:6); or "Thy right hand is filled with victory" (Ps. 48:10).

Early Christians like to depict God's hand emerging from a fluffy cloud against nighttime's starry backdrop. Or simply as a *cloud* studded with rays of light, nimbuslike. The cloud imagery is thought to originate with the story in Exodus, in which Mount Sinai was shrouded in clouds for six days.

Later Christians enriched the hand-cloud symbol by adding to the background a *circle*, which for most of the world's religions symbolizes unbroken continuity, eternity.

There is other hand imagery. Sometimes, God's hand, descending from a cloud, is cupped to cradle four or five human beings. The familiar picture comes straight from the Book of Psalms: "and thy right hand shall hold me" (Ps. 139:10).

Both the Greeks and Romans represented God with a single hand; sometimes, certain fingers were extended, while others were tucked inward toward the palm.

After the hand, the second most familiar symbol for God is a solitary eyeball, the *all-seeing eye*. God is omnipresent; everywhere; he misses nothing. Usually (as on the back of the one-dollar bill), God's eye is enclosed in a triangle, symbol of the Trinity. Again, the ocular imagery originates in the Bible: "Behold, the eye of the Lord is on those who fear him" (Ps. 33:18).

"GOD THE SON" IMAGERY: NEW TESTAMENT ◆

From the Hebrew practice of ritual sacrifice, the Christians borrowed the *lamb* as an image of Jesus. As John the Baptist declares: "Behold the Lamb of God, who takes away the sins of the world." In fact, the Bible contains several references to Christ as a pure, innocent lamb to be sacrificed for people's sins.

The image of Christ as a *fish* arose in the days when it was dangerous to be a Christian. Christ's followers, many fishermen by trade, needed a secret symbol that was recognizable by other Christians but not by their foes. With a stick, a man might silently sketch a fish in the sand, saying, in effect, "I'm a Christian, too," then quickly obliterate it.

Scholars claim that the Greek word for fish, *ichtys* (pronounced *ichtus*), was used as an acrostic by Greek-speaking Christians, for the phrase, in Greek, "Jesus Christ, Son of God, Savior." A single fish symbolized Jesus, and several fishes stood for his followers, imagery from the Bible: "And he said to them, 'Follow me, and I will make you fishers of men' " (Matt. 4:19).

The importance of the fish symbol also stems from the Gospels' miracles of multiplication, when Jesus fed five thousand people with five loaves and two fish, and the four thousand Christ fed with seven loaves and a few fish. The fish also became a favorite symbol for Christian baptism in catacomb art.

Many of the visual symbols for Christ have biblical sources:

Good shepherd: "I am the good shepherd; the good shepherd giveth his life for his sheep" (John 10:11).

Christ as a *vine* with branches representing his followers: "I am the true vine, and my Father is the husbandman" (John 15:1). Christ himself used the vine symbol when he spoke of his Church as a vineyard (Matt. 21:33–41). In the Old Testament, Isaiah spoke of the Israelites as the vine of Yahweh (5:1–7).

Christ is also pictured as a *door* that people must pass through for salvation: "I am the door; by me if any man enter in, he shall be saved" (John 10:9).

Candles on the altar are symbols to remind Christians that: "I am the light of the world" (John 8:12).

ALPHABETIC MONOGRAMS ◆

Aside from pictorials and sacramentals, Christ is symbolized by four alphabetic monograms:

ALPHA AND OMEGA. Church art depicting the Greek symbols for alpha and omega, the first and last letters of the Greek alphabet, derive from Scripture that defines Jesus as: "the first and the last, the beginning and the end" (Rev. 22:13).

Origins of the other three monograms:

IHS, "SON OF GOD." This monogram means "Son of God," and seven interpretations are given for its origin. Only the first is factual, but the

IHC (or S), monogram of "Jesus." X + P, called the
"Chrismon," appeared to Constantine. Chrismon
+ I + C, for "Jesus Christ, Savior."

others should not be entirely dismissed, as they came to be imbued with centuries of rich tradition. (The Council of Trent placed tradition on the same high ground as Scripture itself.)

1. A contraction derived from the Greek word for Jesus: *IHCOYC*; where C stands in for the Greek letter sigma. The symbol was initially IHC, but over time and through mistranscription, *C* became *S*. Since IHS are the first three letters of a word, they have no periods after them.

Later Christians confused the issue further, placing punctuation after the letters: I.H.S. The error of punctuation turned an abbreviation for the word "Jesus" into many possible phrases about him:

2. *Iesus Hominum Salvator,* Latin for "Jesus, Savior of Men."

3. *In Hoc Signo,* Latin for "In This Sign (of the cross) shalt thou conquer."

4. *In Hac Salus,* Latin for "In This Sign (of the cross) is Salvation."

5. *Iesus, Heiland, Seligmacher,* German for "Jesus, Lord, Savior."

6. Most recently in English: "I (Christ) Have Suffered."

This retroactive matching of phrases with initials can be seen as an instance where a symbol has an evolving life of its own, and continues to generate and inspire meaning.

**I.N.R.I., "JESUS OF NAZARETH, KING OF THE JEWS":
30 C.E.** The familiar symbol often stamped on Holy Communion wafers, I.N.R.I., refers to Jesus' Latin title: *Iesus Nazarenus Rex Iudaeorum.* John tells us: "Pilate wrote a title, and put it on the cross. And the writing was, JESUS OF NAZARETH, KING OF THE JEWS . . . and it was written in Hebrew, and Latin, and Greek" (19:19–20). Since the title derives from a phrase, the letters take periods after them.

The use of acronyms for gods was ancient, practiced by Greeks and Romans. I.O.M. was how the Latin-speaking populace spoke of "Jupiter, the Best, the Greatest"—*Iupiter Optimus Maximus.*

EASTERN SYMBOLS ♦ *Animal imagery has often been associated with holy men. Whereas Christ is a "lamb" or a "fish," in Buddhism, the Buddha himself is a white elephant. This is said to be the form he took when he entered his mother's womb. The animal symbolism stands for Buddha's patience, wisdom, and endless memory.*

An alphabetic symbol in both Hinduism and Buddhism is om *(pronounced a-u-m). It is not an acronym of a god's name, but supposedly the eternal, sacred sound that accompanies creation and still echoes throughout the universe; not unlike the physicist's concept of background radiation, the cosmic fingerprint of creation. Called a mantra, and possessing divine energy, it can be used for spiritual regeneration, either by being chanted aloud or sounded silently in the mind.*

XPICTOC. Another popular symbol for "God the Son" is a superposition of the Greek letters chi and rho, that is, *X* and *P*, which appear chiseled into altars and embossed on priest's stoles. The symbol derives from the first two letters of the Greek word *XPICTOC*, pronounced *Christos*, "Christ." The symbol is at least sixteen hundred years old, since it's known that the emperor Constantine had the monogram painted on the shields of his soldiers.

Xmas, meaning "Christmas" or "Christ's Mass," shows no disrespect for the Savior. *X* is not a pagan symbol in this case, nor a non-Christian slight. Simply, *X* is the first letter of the Greek word for Christ: *XPICTOC*.

"GOD THE HOLY SPIRIT" IMAGERY: NEW TESTAMENT ♦

A *descending dove*, often depicted with a three-ray nimbus round its head, is the most commonly used symbol for the third member of the Christian Godhead. The image is suggested in the Gospel of Mark (and elsewhere) in relating Jesus' baptism: "He saw the heavens open, and the Spirit like a dove descending upon him" (1:10).

The *dove and olive branch* symbolize the end of a period of strife and the imagery originates in the biblical story of Noah and the Flood:

He sent a dove out of the ark . . . and the dove came to him in the evening; and, lo, in her mouth was an olive leaf plucked off, so Noah knew that the waters were abated from off the earth (Gen. 8:10–11).

The dove was a very common bird in the Near East. Today, the ringdove dwells in immense numbers in the wooded districts of Palestine, the stock dove is common in the Jordan Valley, and the rock dove roosts along the highlands west of Jordan and in Lebanon. The bird is shy, gentle, monogamous, and was often used by Old Testament prophets as a symbol of peace and purity. The birds were not eaten, we learn in Leviticus, but used for sacrifice. (Today, the bird is eaten as a delicacy and its ritual sacrifice is deplored.) In the New Testament, Mary and Joseph offer two turtledoves at the Presentation of Jesus in the Temple. It's the dove's homing instinct that Noah was banking on.

Tongues of fire is perhaps the Holy Spirit's second most familiar pictorial. It, too, comes from the Bible: "And there appeared . . . tongues like as of fire. . . . And they were all filled with the Holy Spirit" (Acts 2:3–4).

In Christian theology, the Holy Spirit is "breathed forth" by the Father *and Son* for the purpose of performing works of love such as revelation, regeneration, and sanctification. At Jesus' baptism, the Spirit descends in the form of a dove (sanctification); at the Virgin Mary's conception, it's the Spirit that impregnates her (regeneration); after Christ's Resurrection, the Spirit descends upon the apostles to embolden them to preach the Gospel and harvest souls (revelation).

We might well ask: How did imagery of a pure ephemeral Spirit originate?

SPIRIT IMAGERY FOR THE THIRD MEMBER OF THE GODHEAD: GOSPEL OF JOHN ◆

There is no term for "spirit" in the languages of the Hebrew Bible. The concept was expressed metaphorically with the equivalent words "wind" or "breath," in Hebrew *ruah*, in Greek *pneuma* (origin of our word "pneumonia"). The study of the Holy Spirit is called pneumatology.

Our English word "spirit" is merely an Anglicized form of the Latin for breath, *spiritus*.

In the early books of the Old Testament, heavenly winds and breaths, exhalations from Yahweh, waft into prophets' ears, planting revelations or animating bodies. There is no personification of "wind" or "breath" as *the* Spirit. Indeed, none of the prophets of Israel prior to the Exile ascribe their vocation of prophecy to the intervention of the spirit or, for that matter, have much to say about wind/breath/spirit at all. There exists God in Heaven, and the prophecy for a Messiah on earth, but no mention of anyone else uniquely special. No Holy Spirit.

After the Exile, the vague concept of divine wind/breath/spirit comes into prominence, notably in the writings of the prophet Ezekiel, who was exiled to Babylon in 597 B.C.E. Ezekiel uses the word "breath" or *ruah* without its earlier qualification "of God"; for the first time, "breath" takes on a significance all its own, something of a personification.

However, the word "spirit" (lower case) becomes "Spirit" (upper case) only in the New Testament. It is the Fourth Gospel, John's, that truly develops the doctrine of the Spirit, called the "Paraclete," or "Advocate." The word "paraclete" is from the Greek verb *parakalein*, meaning "to summon from beyond." (I must confess that as a child I thought the Holy Spirit was called the "parakeet" of the Lord—only later did I learn that paraclete was a different breed of word.)

The function of the Spirit, after Jesus' return to Heaven, is to lead the community deeper into the truths espoused by Jesus himself. Thus, the New Testament "Spirit" is traced back to the Old Testament "breath" of God that served the dual functions of imparting revelation and life. The Holy Spirit in Christianity continues this tradition of revelation and the regeneration of spiritual life.

TRIANGLE REPRESENTS THE TRINITY: FOURTH CENTURY C.E. ◆

Three equal sides, three equal angles, no breaks anywhere; thus the equilateral triangle is the perfect symbol for the equality and unity of God the Father, Son, and Holy Spirit. Some Christians like to think of the sides as personages, others see the Three Members of the Godhead in the vertices of the angles. God is in geometry, said Einstein in a somewhat different context.

In the ancient world of magic, the triangle was a potent symbol. The uppermost vertex pointed toward Heaven and the chief god; the upward point also represented the phallus and male generative power. Flipped 180 degrees, the downward point represented gifts descending from Heaven, and female passivity.

Over the centuries, artists have depicted the Christian Trinitarian triangle in many diverse and complex forms: three fishes, heads touching tails. Or the Shield of the Trinity: a circle (the Godhead) inscribed in a triangle (the three members of the Trinity). This last figure is labeled with six phrases that sum up the mystery of coexistence and independence within the Trinity: "The Father is God," "The Son is God," "The Holy Spirit is God," and "The Father is not the Son," "The Son is not the Holy Spirit," "The Holy Spirit is not the Father." That says it all.

This kind of elaborate explanation was necessary in iconography and theology in order to fight against charges, leveled by Jews and later by Muslims, that Christianity, in worshiping Father, Son, and Spirit, was really a religion of tritheism and not monotheism. In truth, the word "Trinity" does not appear in the New Testament, or in early Church writings, and was not clearly defined until the Council of Nicaea in the fourth century C.E. (*See* Trinity.) It's said that a picture is worth a thousand words, and the symbol of an equilateral triangle helped Christians explain to their critics their three-in-one Godhead concept.

Indeed, this is exactly the function of the *shamrock* or three-leaf clover, a favorite preaching herb of Saint Patrick. As the legend goes, Patrick, while preaching to followers, was struggling with a way to convey the Trinity's threefold complexity. Holding up the herb, he asked his audience to imagine the three leaves as Father, Son, and Holy Ghost, and the stem as the single Godhead from which they spring. Whether or not the tale is true, the symbolism is effective and has endured.

"WORD OF GOD" IMAGERY: OLD TESTAMENT ◆

God's own words in the Old Testament are symbolized best by the *two tablets* containing the Ten Commandments. The tall rectangles with rounded tops, perhaps inscribed with nothing more than Roman numerals I through X, or Hebrew characters, sum up all God's fundamental rules for his children.

The tablets were sculpted from sapphire taken from God's throne, according to one Jewish tradition, although another school of thought has the tablets being rolled up as goatskin or parchment scrolls. Nonetheless, the tablets were so heavy that Moses was unable to carry them without God's helping hand. When the tablets came near the Golden Calf, the Hebrew letters took flight, God withdrew his helping hand, and Moses dropped the heavy weights, which shattered, so goes one tradition. Moses then spent forty days and nights on the mountain recopying the commandments. Thus, the first set of tablets was the work of God, the second set the work of man.

The ten laws or commandments, called *dibrot* in Hebrew, meaning "words" or "things," serve as a preamble to the so-called Book of the Covenant, the first major law collection of the Hebrew Bible. Later Jewish tradition came to maintain that the whole of the Pentateuchal law, in the form of the "613 Commandments," was given to Moses at Mount Sinai.

According to Jewish tradition, replicas of the two tablets contain five commandments on each panel, although some rabbis have preferred all ten commandments on each panel. The Hellenistic Jewish philosopher Philo drew a conceptual distinction between the first five and last five: the former teach religious and filial piety (honor God, the Sabbath, one's parents); the latter, in dealing with one's fellow human beings, teach probity (do not commit murder, adultery, don't steal, bear false witness, or covet).

The "word of God" is also symbolized by a *lamp and flame*, which represents the light of wisdom destroying the darkness of ignorance. An *open book* is also used as symbolism for "the word."

CHRISTIAN CHURCH AS A SHIP: FOURTH CENTURY C.E. ◆

Starting with Saint Ambrose's *De Noe et Arca*, Noah's wooden *ark*, often with a *rainbow* cresting above it, has been one of the most popular symbols for the Christian Church itself. The ark for Ambrose and writers of his day symbolized the "power to preserve all things and ensure their rebirth"—as the ark saved Creation to be born again after the Deluge. A popular image on stained-glass windows, the ark and rainbow are to remind Christians of the covenant God struck with Noah, and the new covenant God forged with his Church.

To the ancients, in virtually all religions, the appearance of a rainbow in the wake of a fierce storm signified the glowing presence of a benign god. And because it appeared to span from Heaven to earth, it was a particularly potent symbol. The rainbow was a major religious symbol for the Incas, and for the Greeks—it was the winged Greek goddess Iris ferrying messages from the gods on Mount Olympus to mortals on earth.

In Hindu and Buddhist traditions, the rainbow represents the highest state a person can evolve to symbolically. Having achieved the "rainbow body," the person realizes his or her earthly body is truly insubstantial.

In Christianity, the seven natural colors of the rainbow symbolize the Seven Gifts of the Holy Spirit to the Church: the *sacraments*, *doctrine*, *office*, *polity*, *prayer*, and the *powers to loose or bind sin*.

The image of the Church as a ship is reflected in the Old Testament and in late Judaic writings, which refer to the rough sea as a figure of eschatological trials. Indeed, the incident of Christ's calming the waters for the apostles on the lake of Tiberias had antecedents in the story of Noah's ark. Inherent in the symbolism is the battering the Church has taken from persecution, heresy, and schism while remaining on course.

Justin Martyr added to the ship symbolism the notion that Christ's cross was a mast: "One cannot sail the seas," he said, "unless the trophy that is called the sail is properly set on the ship." In other words, Christ had to die on the cross for his Church to sail through time.

In German churches, the nave of the building is called the *Schiff*, from the Latin *navis*, "ship."

A symbol not often used these days is the Church as a *beehive*. Ancient peoples, whose primary sweetener was honey, were well acquainted with the busy work of bees for the benefit of their community. Christ's followers, by analogy, work tirelessly for the benefit of his Church.

Jesus' words to Simon Peter suggest another symbol for the Church: "Thou art Peter, and upon this rock I will build my church" (Matt. 16:18). Indeed, a church perched securely on a *rock* has long been a Christian symbol. (*See* Papacy.)

SYMBOLS FOR THE BIBLE: OLD TESTAMENT ◆

Four symbols stand out from the many that pictorially represent Hebrew Scripture.

1. The *burning bush*, a symbol of the call of Moses to deliver the Israelites from Egyptian bondage, with God's voice emanating from an acacia bush.

2. The *multibranched candlestick* or Jewish menorah used in synagogue. (*See* Menorah.)

3. The *altar of sacrifice*, which represents the Jewish ritual of sacrificing clean, unblemished animals in atonement for sin, is richly detailed in the Book of Leviticus; the animal must be completely burned and God receives the gift as "a soothing aroma."

4. The *Ark of the Covenant*, adorned with cherubim, a symbol of God's relationship with the people of Israel. The two tablets bearing the Ten Commandments were deposited in the Ark of the Covenant, which went forth in battle in the front line of the Israelite army. Later, the Ark was housed in Solomon's Temple.

As the thorny acacia tree came to be a pictorial for the Old Testament itself, other plants took on symbolism for Jews or Christians:

Cedar of Lebanon, Christ; from the mystic reading of the Song of Songs: "his countenance is as Lebanon, excellent as the cedars."

Fig tree, lust; a reference to the fig leaves used by Adam and Eve to cover their nakedness after they'd sinned.

Clover, the Trinity; because of the herb's three leaves.

Olive branch, peace; since a dove carried an olive branch to Noah, signaling the safety of dry land after the Flood.

Red rose, martyrdom; because of its thorns and bloodred color, it's used in the iconography of saints to symbolize suffering.

Columbine, Holy Spirit; the plant, a member of the buttercup family, has flowers that are said to resemble a "flock of doves." Its name is from the Latin *columbinus*, meaning "dovelike."

Apple tree, wickedness; an obvious association from the corruption of Adam and Eve with an apple. But was the fruit actually an apple? (*See* Forbidden Fruit.)

STAR OF DAVID AS SYMBOL OF JUDAISM: EUROPE, SEVENTEENTH CENTURY ◆

The familiar six-pointed star, or equilateral hexagram, is known in Hebrew as *magen David*, literally, "Shield of David," but this paramount symbol of Judaism has been used explicitly in this way for only a few hundred years. It has gone by many names, and represented different concepts.

Mystery surrounds the origin of the Star of David. Almost certainly the symbol has nothing to do with the tenth century B.C.E. reign of King David. On this historians concur. If anything, it probably arose under a different name as the "Seal of Solomon," for such a six-sided star appears in the writings and practices of magicians of Solomon's day, and had strong associations with Hebrew mysticism. Mysticism imbues it with its first meaning.

The *Seal of Solomon* is composed of two intersecting equilateral triangles, hence, six apexes. The upward-pointing triangle of "fire and masculine energy" intersects with the downward-pointing triangle of "water and female energy," the two opposites merging in harmony. (The balancing of male/ female, good/evil, dark/light is common to the symbolism of all religions; the ancient Eastern symbol of balance is the *yin/yang*.) The base of each triangle bisects the other just under the apex, forming symbols for air and earth. The Seal of Solomon therefore portrays the four elements—fire, water, air, earth.

The star's earliest attested Jewish use, but not adoption for the faith, is as a seventh-century B.C.E. seal of one Joshua ben Asayahu of Sidon. It is found on a frieze in a second century C.E. Galilean synagogue, alongside a swastika cross, which then had overtones of paganism, not persecution.

IN CHRISTIANITY. Throughout the Middle Ages, the six-pointed star motif appears mostly in Christian and Muslim art and architecture: on royal seals, as a notary's stamp, on Byzantine and Spanish church friezes, carved into wooden church furnishings, and as decorative illustrations in Bibles produced in Christian and Muslim countries. Jews, living among Christians and Muslims, picked up the symbol in imitation.

It appeared in Jewish magical texts, alchemistry manuscripts, then decoratively on *mezuzot* (plural of *mezuzah*; *see* Mezuzah), between the tenth to fourteenth centuries. Mostly the symbol was magical, interchangeably referred to as the "Seal of Solomon" and "Star of David," and, in medieval Germany, it was the symbol for the superlative archangel Metatron. (*See* Metatron.)

The first known adoption of the symbol by a Jewish community occurred in Prague in 1354, when Charles IV granted Jews the right to bear a flag with the hexagram star. Its use in this nationalistic regard spread quickly.

In 1613, the symbol appeared on the tombstone of the astronomer and historian David Gans, author of a book titled *Magen David*.

JEWISH ANSWER TO CHRISTIAN CROSS. As European Christians in late medieval times erected stone crosses to fence off their lands, and keep out Jews, the Jews in turn erected wooden fences painted with Stars of David to define their small spaces. The symbol accompanied various movements for Jewish emancipation, and by the seventeenth century, it had become the Jewish counterpart of the Christian cross. The Jews had needed a symbol all their own.

The star became a Passover seder symbol around 1770, and in 1882, the Rothschild banking family adopted the Star of David as its coat of arms. In 1897, it was adopted by the First Zionist Congress as its symbol, and in 1948, it became the central figure in the flag of the new State of Israel. Although the symbol has no biblical or Talmudic authority, it is one of the major signs of Judaism.

The yellow badge in the form of the six-pointed star that Jews in occupied Europe were forced by Nazis to wear invested the *magen David* with symbolism for both martyrdom and heroism.

Today, the star's six points are said to symbolize: the six days of Creation;

Star of Bethlehem, Star of Creation, Star of David (or Seal of Solomon), and the Mystical Star (top, left to right).
Eight-pointed Star of Regeneration, Star of the Holy Spirit, Star of the Ten Disciples of Jesus, Star of the Twelve Tribes of Israel.

the six pairs of tribes of Israel; the 600,000 Israelites at Mount Sinai; reception of the Torah on the sixth day of the Hebrew month of Sivan (May/June); and the six million Jews martyred in the Holocaust. A potent symbol lends itself to ever-deepening interpretation; therein lies its power and its appeal.

STAR OF BETHLEHEM: NEW TESTAMENT, MATTHEW 2:1–12 ◆

In Christianity, this is the primary star symbol, which guided the Magi, the first Gentiles to worship Jesus, to his birthplace: "The Magi came from the East to Jerusalem, saying, 'Where is he that is born king of the Jews? For we have seen his star in the East and have come to worship him' " (Matt. 2:2).

This early symbol, the first connected with Jesus' birth, is of major importance to Christian theologians. Some half-century before Saint Paul would bring Christ's teachings to the Gentiles, a star prophetically had drawn three Gentiles to the new "king." As the Douay-Confraternity Bible makes clear in a footnote to the biblical text: "The first-fruits of the Gentiles seek the new-born king of the Jews, and pay Him honor as Christ and God." Thus the "star in the East" *is* the glow of Christianity on the horizon.

It is not coincidental that the word "magi" mirrors our word "magic." In Old Persian, *magi* (singular *magus*) were members of a priestly caste, magicians with occult powers. The Star of Bethlehem is correctly an occult symbol.

In truth, most of the details about the Magi are supplied by later tradition. For instance, they are assumed to be three in number only because three gifts are mentioned in the Bible: gold, frankincense, and myrrh. (In Eastern tradition, there are twelve Magi.) Their names—Balthasar, Melchior, and Caspar—were supplied later. The evidence for their wealth and kingship is based solely on the biblical reference that they conversed with King Herod, thus they are royal through association. It is perhaps ironic that the first symbol of Christianity, the Star of Bethlehem, is occult in nature, and the first Gentiles to recognize Jesus as a king are magicians fascinated by astrology.

MENORAH: OLD TESTAMENT, BOOK OF EXODUS ◆

This multibranched candelabrum used for centuries by Jews during the eight-day festival of Hanukkah has taken many forms. Yet its essential feature has been constant: it has eight receptacles for oil or candles; one is lit the first

JEWISH SYMBOLS:
Menorah, symbol of the Holy Temple
(top). Torah, the Law; the Ten
Commandments.

day, two the second, and so forth. There is a separate receptacle for the "servant" (*shammash*) light, set apart and used for kindling the other lights.

This familiar menorah is actually an imitation of the seven-branched golden candelabrum of Moses' Tabernacle, which signified to the Israelites, among other things, the six days of Creation plus the day of rest. The cup atop the central shaft, somewhat elevated to signify the Sabbath, was flanked by three lights on each side.

According to tradition, while the Israelites wandered in the wilderness, Moses and his Tabernacle architect Bezalel were commanded (Exod. 25:31–40, 37:17–24) to fashion a candelabrum consisting of three almond-shaped cups with a floral design, and the central shaft containing four others. Knobs adorned each cup and joined each branch at the central shaft. The whole work was shaped and hammered out of a single piece of pure gold, with accompanying lamps, lamp trays, and snuffers, also of pure gold. The tops of the branches and the central shaft were of the same height, according to one tradition: eighteen handbreadths.

The vessel was placed in front of the Ark curtain on the south side of the Tabernacle. It burned from evening to morning; it was lit at dusk, and trimmed by the high priest at dawn. It stood on a table symbolizing the delights of Paradise, and burned with a light symbolizing divine Presence. Supposedly, God gave Moses the blueprint for the Tabernacle menorah several times, but the old man kept forgetting the design; in frustration, God even sketched the design on his own palm.

It's the seven-branched menorah that is mentioned in the Talmud and that appears in Jewish art over the ages.

After the First and Second Temples in Jerusalem were destroyed, a tradition of respect developed such that no appurtenance of the Temple be duplicated. Thus, any number other than seven was acceptable. For a long time, six was a favored number.

The fate of the Second Temple menorah is uncertain. It was captured by the Romans, and a replica of it, shown being carried to Rome in a triumphal procession, appears on the famous Arch of Titus in the Roman Forum.

Today, many congregations install electric seven-branch *menorot* (Hebrew plural), arguing, reasonably, that an electric candelabrum is not a duplicate of the original.

KABBALAH, "RECEIVED LORE": FIRST CENTURY c.e. ◆

Rooted in Hebrew mysticism, the Kabbalah is an extraordinary system of wisdom designed to provide its students with a path to mental and spiritual growth, and a symbolic map of Creation itself. Though the Laws of Moses remained the basic tenet of Judaism, the Kabbalah provided a means of approaching God directly.

The word "kabbalah" is from the Hebrew *quabbalah*, meaning "received lore" or "tradition." The system is an occult religious philosophy, developed by certain rabbis, and based on a mystical interpretation of Scriptures.

The earliest form of Kabbalah, called *Merkava* ("chariot"), flourished in Palestine in the first century c.e. Its main concern then was the mystical contemplation of God's divine throne, or "chariot," seen in the vision of the prophet Ezekiel. Originally, the Kabbalah was an oral tradition. The earliest known Kabbalistic text is the third-century *Sefer Yetzira*, which had a strong influence on the then-burgeoning faith of Christianity. In Kabbalistic formulas, some mystics found "proof" of the Trinity.

Essentially, the Kabbalah is an esoteric system of symbols. The symbols are said to hold the mystery of God and the universe, and it is up to the Kabbalist (traditionally, a male) to find the unlocking key. The secrets may be revealed by decoding sacred Scripture through a system of numerical equivalences or *gematria*, in which each of the twenty-two letters of the Hebrew alphabet has a number associated with it; or can be permuted or abbreviated in certain ways.

For example:

Consider the brass serpent constructed by Moses and set on a pole so that "if a serpent had bitten any man, when he beheld the serpent of brass he lived" (Num. 21:9). This symbol is converted through *gematria* to the magic number 358, which is also the numerical equivalent of the word "Messiah." Thus, the brass serpent is held to be a prophecy of the coming of the Messiah, who will save all those bitten by the longing for spiritual truth.

Steeped in magic and mysticism, the belief system led Christian Kabbalists in the Middle Ages to adopt the symbol of the *serpent draped over the cross* as a representation of Jesus Christ.

WHY JEWS ARE ALWAYS ON THE MOVE. Following their expulsion from Spain in 1492, many Jews, seeking to understand their plight, turned to the Kabbalah with newfound reverence. By the sixteenth century, the center of Kabbalah was Safed, Galilee, home of one of the greatest of all Kabbalists, Isaac ben Solomon Luria.

Why were Jews repeatedly exiled, continually uprooted, and chased away by Gentiles? Luria claimed the answer was clearly stated in the Kabbalah. The dispersion or scattering throughout the cosmos of "divine light" that symbolized God presaged the scattering of the Jews throughout the world. It was the Jews' mission to disperse—they could no more come to rest than could a beam of light.

The complex belief system of symbols—which makes use of the Star of David—found its way into the doctrines of Hasidism, the social and religious movement that began in the eighteenth century and flourishes today in small but significant communities.

Many Jewish and Christian superstitions—such as the groom breaking a glass at the conclusion of the marriage toast—hark back to the Kabbalah. The Kabbalistic reason for loudly smashing a glass is that demons are intent on disrupting the happiness of the new couple and the evil spirits are best chased by loud noise.

When sixteenth-century Kabbalists decreed that it is essential for dead bodies to come in direct contact with the earth, burial in coffins was abandoned among many Jews. Burying the body, wrapped in a shroud, directly in the earth is a common practice in Israel today. The truth is, since the beginning of the Zionist revival in this century, Kabbalistic mysticism has been coming back into favor. The system has depths still unplumbed.

CHRISTIAN KABBALAH OFFERS PROOF OF THE TRINITY: FLORENCE, FIFTEENTH CENTURY ◆

Although the Roman Catholic Church plays down its mystical heritage, from the fifteenth century onward, many mystics of a theosophical persuasion developed a Christian Kabbalah. They were attempting to "prove" such profound mysteries as the Trinity and God's incarnation as the man Jesus Christ, and many saints shared this approach, which involved astrology and numerology.

"No science can better convince us of the divinity of Jesus Christ," wrote Christian Kabbalist Pico della Mirandola in 1486, "than magic and the [Hebrew] Kabbalah."

For instance: A central formula for proving the Trinitarian equivalency of the Father, Son, and Holy Spirit involves the various names through which the Lord revealed himself—*Shaddai* to the ancient patriarchs; *YHWH* to Moses; *Logos* to the Gospel writers, etc. Translate the letters in the appropriate languages into their numerical values, normalize the sums, and the conundrum of the Triune Godhead becomes, for believers in the numerological system, a tautology.

Christians claimed that the Jewish Kabbalistic teachings had direct bearing on Christianity because, like the Old Testament, the text was a prefigurement of developments in the Christian world. This incensed Jews of the period. First Christians had laid claim to the Hebrew Bible and brazenly renamed it the *Old* Testament, now Christians were laying claim to Jewish mysticism as well.

Christian Kabbalistic writings flourished in Florence's Platonic Academy, which was endowed by the Medici family. As the empirical sciences burgeoned in the Renaissance, quantitative theology was understandably attractive. The calculus of Christ appealed to many devout Christians wishing to be scientifically au courant. A seminal book on Christian Kabbalism is *De Verbo Mirifico*, "On the Science of Miracle-Working Names," published in 1494 by the German Humanist scholar Johannes Reuchlin. Kabbalism is a Christian fringe science just waiting to be reborn in our own soul-searching times.

𝔇ressed to 𝔎ill

Vestments to Vessels

DRESSING FOR SACRIFICE: JUDAISM TO CHRISTIANITY ◆

Fashion has always been central to religion, color a hallmark of rank, from the humble monk's dung-brown coarse-wool frock, the ecclesiastical equivalent of easy-wear, to the pontiff's royal silks in passion purple, topped with a gem-studded tiara.

The stunning cardinal, the crested bright-red songbird, was named after the magnificently red-plumed official of the Roman Catholic Church, and not vice versa; *cardinalis*, the songbird's ornithological designation, is Latin for "chief presbyter." A flock of such songbirds is called a "college of cardinals," as is the pope's privy council, though it distinguishes itself as a *Sacred* College of Cardinals.

In the Church, much attention has been paid to finery, despite Christ's caution: "Do not be anxious, asking, What are we to put on?"

Christ, of course, meant that one should not be excessively clothes conscious, and should avoid the trendy vogues of one's time. Certainly, the son of a poor carpenter could never have afforded the vestments worn by the priests who celebrate his sacrifice. But, then, men have always dressed up for war and religious ritual, their two primary fashion occasions.

Priests since ancient times have attired themselves in the finest duds of their day, mimicking the patrician styles of secular kings and nobility. High priests in religions around the world have painted their faces, tattooed their breasts, donned feathered headdresses, flowing fringe, and necklaces of shells, human bones, and teeth. Costume distinguishes the priest from the laity. Lay members of most faiths are forbidden to wear their priests' sacred garb.

Many vestments originated with the rite of sacrifice, an act central to most religions, from the burnt offerings of Israelites to Jesus Christ's sacrifice

*Bishops in their finery.
Christ's caution: "Do not
be anxious, asking, What
are we to put on?"*

on the cross, to the bloodless Eucharist that is the cornerstone of the Christian Mass. Sacrifice as atonement for sin has always been central to religion, whether it's the actual killing of innocent lambs and chaste virgins and helpless children, or ritualized sacrifices like the Mass.

JEWISH HIGH PRIEST: EARLY OLD TESTAMENT, 1800 B.C.E. ◆

God gave the first fashion instructions to priests. After he instructed Moses on the proper way to build an altar, he added:

> *These are the garments which they shall make: a breastplate, an ephod, a robe, a brocaded tunic, a miter and a sash. . . . They shall use gold, violet, purple and scarlet yarn and fine linen. (Exod. 28:4–5)*

The Levitical attire of the priestly class was richly decorative. While officiating, the priest wore a *me'il* or *mantle*, a sleeveless purple robe, whose lower hem bore a fringe of small gold bells alternating with pomegranate tassels in red, scarlet, purple, and violet.

The proudest object of his attire was the *hoshen* or *breastplate*, which was square in design and served as a pouch for sacred articles of service. Exodus 28:15–28 specifies that it was to be woven of golden and linen threads dyed blue, purple, and scarlet. On its face were twelve gems in four rows, representing the twelve tribes of Israel. These stones were: a sardius, a topaz, and a carbuncle in the first row; an emerald, a sapphire, and a diamond in the second; a jacinth, an agate, and an amethyst in the third; a beryl, an onyx, and a jasper in the fourth.

The richly embroidered breastplate was also called the "rational of judgment." It admonished both priest and people of their duties to God by carrying the symbols of all the tribes in God's presence. And it gave divine answers to life's problems, as well as revelation, as if it were rational and endowed with reason (Exod. 39:12).

On his head, the high priest placed a *mitznefet*, a "tiara" or *turban*. On the sacred Yom Kippur or "Day of Atonement," he wore only flowing white linen garments.

The *ephod* was a special garment similar to the later Christian chasuble. It was gold and violet and scarlet, with two onyxes on the shoulders on which were engraved the names of the twelve tribes of Israel.

Over the ephod was worn the "rational of judgment" breastplate, with the *Urim* and *Thummim*, Hebrew words of uncertain significance, which may represent either actual objects worn or words corresponding to abstract attributes. Many scholars maintain that these were two gems that, by changing from one color to another when the priest entered the Holy of Holies, signified God's judgment on the matter under consultation. The Protestant Authorized Bible leaves the two words untranslated, whereas the Latin Vulgate and its vernacular versions render the words as "doctrine" and "truth."

With the destruction of the Second Temple in 70 C.E., many religious vestments were destroyed and their design ultimately forgotten.

EARLY CHRISTIAN PRIESTS: PRE-313 C.E. ◆

Before the early fourth century, when the emperor Constantine embraced Christianity as the state religion and persecution of Christians ended, priests had no distinctive liturgical dress. They wore street clothes. They were on the run from Romans and sought to look as inconspicuous as possible. In celebrating Mass and the Eucharist, a priest wore the same clothes as lay members in attendance.

Ecclesiastical vestments, when they arose, had their origin in the ordinary secular dress of the Roman Empire: long, flowing tunics, abundant folds of fabric, materials often rich in texture and colors. After the fall of the Empire, fashion went into decline. With fabric scarce, ordinary folk adopted short, close-fitting apparel, and an abundance of cloth became the hallmark of the priest at the altar. This marks the beginning of vestments in Christian services.

LATER CHRISTIAN CLERICS: SIXTH CENTURY C.E. ◆

To begin with a nutshell overview.

Vestments worn at Mass in the *Latin rite* include the amice, alb, cincture, maniple, stole, chasuble, cope, dalmatic (deacon's outer garment), tunicle (subdeacon's outer garment), surplice, biretta, and zucchetto.

Vestments of the *Eastern rites* are quite similar.

Vestments worn by priests in the *Byzantine rite* include: the *sticharion*, corresponding to the alb; the *epitrakelion*, a broad stole joined in the front; the *zone* or cincture; the *epigonation*, a square piece of cloth suspended from the cincture (really proper to prelates, but commonly worn by priests); the *phelonion* or chasuble.

STOLE. This important garment, symbolic of the yoke of obedience, is a draped scarflike cloth, a few inches in width and about eighty inches long, worn like an untied necktie and originally a symbol of authority among Romans. A pope conferred a stole—red, green, violet, black, or white— upon archbishops, then later upon bishops, to symbolize their sharing in his papal power. The stole became commonplace in the sixth century and was greatly popularized during the ninth-century reign of the emperor Charlemagne. It is one of the Mass vestments, which a priest wears around his neck and crosses over his breast.

Reaching back into biblical history, the stole symbolizes the towel worn around the neck by townsmen who greeted weary travelers and washed their dust-covered feet. A sign of humility and servitude, the stole represents a pastor's responsibility to serve his congregation.

ALB. Celebrating Mass, a priest dons this garment (one of six), an ankle-length robe of linen with full-length sleeves, always white; the word is from the Latin *albus*, "white." In the early Church, the alb was a reminder of the robe that Herod draped over Jesus. The ecclesiastical alb derives directly from the *tunic alba* of classical times.

In antiquity, albs existed in two forms: long and short. The knee-length Greek *chiton* or alb was like a modern shirt, sometimes sleeveless. The long type, *chiton poderes* or *tunica talaris*, usually had sleeves.

In the New Testament, the word *chiton* is used in a maxim found in Matthew: "If a man wants to sue you for your shirt [*chiton*], let him have your coat [*himation*] also" (Matt. 5:40). The garment was worn by Jesus (John 19:23), and linguistically distinguished from his other garments (*himatia*), which at the time of the Crucifixion were shared by Roman soldiers. The long alb or *chiton poderes* is also found in Revelation in the description of the visionary personage who, we're told, is "robed to his feet" (Rev. 1:13). The simple garment is rich in history.

Sixth-century mosaic at Ravenna showing the emperor Justinian (left) *and Archbishop Maximianus.*

The long white tunic was standard dress for professional people until about the sixth century, when it became closely associated with Christian vestments. A mosaic in Ravenna, Italy, dating from this period, shows that bishops wore wide-sleeved tunics over narrow-sleeved albs.

CINCTURE. To hold the alb and stole in place, the priest ties a cincture or cord of linen, wool, or silk around his waist. It's a reminder of Christ's scourge ordered by Pilate, and symbolic of self-restraint and patient suffering. The word "cincture" is from the Latin *cinctura*, meaning "girdle."

CHASUBLE. The outer chasuble—Latin *casula*, "little house"—was a long, sleeveless mantlelike vestment, later lavishly embroidered, that had a hole for the priest's head and draped his torso. It is reminiscent of the purple garment worn by Jesus before Pontius Pilate. Later, the colors of chasubles— red, green, white—were adapted to a particular day's liturgy. The vestment derived from the commonplace and secular Roman cloak worn by both men and women.

If the sides were not sown together or held with clasps, the garment was called a cope, or *cappa*, meaning "topmost" article (see below). The so-called "overcoat" left by Saint Paul at Troas in 2 Timothy 4:13 is named a *phelones*, which is another word for chasuble.

AMICE. Around the priest's neck and shoulders hangs an oblong linen cloth, an amice, shaped like an apron but covering the back. The amice, once hooded, represents the helmet of salvation, symbolizing divine hope. For Mass, it is the first vestment the priest puts on, under the alb.

Its Latin name *amictus* is derived from *amicio*, meaning "wrap around," and as a neckerchief it was used to protect other vestments from sweat on hot days. Roman soldiers of the first century C.E. wore a similar garment, the *fo-*

cale, a scarf soaked in water and wrapped around the neck to cool down the body. Mosaics at Ravenna and elsewhere show that the amice was not worn before the sixth century.

MANIPLE. Over a priest's left forearm was a silk handkerchief-like band or maniple, which started out as a wipe to be used during altar services. It's said to symbolize the bands that held the wrists of Our Lord in Gethsemane, also when he was scourged, and later when he was dragged through the city of Jerusalem. It represents spiritual strength and endurance. First ordered for deacons by Pope Sylvester I in the early 300s, it's fallen into disuse since Vatican II.

There is no doubt that this vestment derives directly from the rank ornament of a Roman consul, the *mappa*, which he held in his right hand and waved as a signal for sporting games to begin. In fact, in later centuries, a pope would signal the pilgrimage of the Stations of the Cross to commence with a wave of his maniple.

The *mappa* itself originated as a simple folded personal handkerchief or table napkin draped over the arm in the days before clothing had pockets. You blew your nose in a *mappa* or used it to wipe gravy from your fingers. Thus, a purely practical rectangle of linen evolved into an ensign of rank and authority in the Empire and then in the Church. In the famous Bayeux tapestry, Archbishop Stigand is carrying a maniple in his hand.

The word "maniple" is from the Latin *manipulus*, meaning "handful"— *manus* + *plere* = "hand" + "to fill." Actually, this was the standard in which Romans measured out bundles of hay, in maniples or handfuls.

SURPLICE. This outer white robe with wide sleeves reaching to just below the hips entered the liturgical closet in the Middle Ages as a modifica-

Standard priestly garb: The outer white surplice, worn over the black cassock.

tion of the alb. Sometimes ornamented with lace, it evolved into standard dress for altar boys and nonclerical ministers. Christian teaching says the surplice is symbolic of righteousness, innocence, and purity.

In the twelfth century, the garment was adopted in cold northern countries for wear over fur-lined cassocks; hence its name, *superpelliceum*, meaning "over-fur alb." From this point onward, the surplice became the distinctive dress of the lower clergy and was worn by priests when they were not saying Mass. Today, it is commonly worn over the cassock by both clerics and laymen in choir or assisting in services.

CASSOCK. The popular black cassock worn daily by priests, sometimes beneath a surplice, has its origin in the barbarian *caracalla*, a robe or tunic favored by third-century Roman emperor Bassianus. Shunning all royal attire for his simple and comfortable black robe, Bassianus came to be known by his garment: the emperor Caracalla. In a sense, the emperor dressed like a peasant, like everyman, and that is precisely why the early Christian Church strongly promoted regular use of the cassock: so a priest and his flock were on equal footing.

In the fifth century, Pope Celestinus reprimanded bishops who wore anything fancier than a cassock. It became a standard for prelates and priests of all orders. Hierarchical rank eventually was conveyed by color: a purple cassock for bishops and archbishops; red for cardinals (hence the songbird's name); white for popes; black for everyone else.

Our English word "cassock" derives from the Italian for the garment, *cassaca*.

COPE. The cope is a variation of the chasuble, one that's open down the front and fastened at the chest with a large decorative button, called a morse or clasp. It's donned for all solemn functions except the Mass, and worn in place of the chasuble for baptism, marriage ceremonies, and processions. As mentioned, its name derives from the Latin *cappa*, "topmost."

The Reformation of the sixteenth century caused havoc with religious vestments. Reformers, such as those who rejected Rome's dogma of the transubstantiation—that the Eucharist *is* Christ's body and blood—also rejected dress that was for them *too* Catholic.

Lutherans kept the chasuble for Communion rites, and the surplice and alb for other services. And the cope was retained by both Lutheran and Anglican bishops, becoming for some the High Church liturgical vestment par excellence.

COLLAR. The familiar clerical collar stems not from a spiritual source but from a practice of Roman speakers at the Forum. To protect his voice and health on cold, wintry days, a speaker wrapped a white cloth around his neck for warmth. The cloth soon became a recognizable badge of the orator, and it was adopted by early Church clerics as a simple and inexpensive symbol of their ministry.

The word "collar" derives straightforwardly from the Latin for "neck," *collum*, which, in turn, is related to one of the early Indo-European words for the circular wheel, *kwel*. A stiff, starched collar rolls like a wheel.

MITER. The name is from the Greek *mitra*, meaning "headband" or "turban." This tall ornamental cap with peaks in front and back is worn by popes, bishops, and abbots as a mark of office. It has a stiff front and back, but soft sides, so that it may be folded when not in use. Two fanons or ribbons hang from the back of the miter and fall on the shoulders.

This was the official headdress of the ancient Jewish high priest. In Exodus, a tiara or turban is worn by Aaron, the high priest, and by successors to that office. The hat was ornamented with purple ribbon, to which a golden plate was fastened, bearing the words "Holy to the Lord" (Eccles. 45:14).

By the eleventh century, it was the preferred liturgical hat of bishops. By the thirteenth century, there were three kinds of miter used in Roman ceremonies. Depending on the solemnity of the occasion, a bishop would wear a *mitra pretiosa* (jeweled), *mitra aurifrigiata* (decorated with figures but without jewels), or a plain *mitra simplex*.

MONKS—DRESSING FOR SOLITUDE: SIXTH CENTURY C.E. ◆

WORD ORIGIN. Traditionally, a monk led a religious life in accordance with rules of strict asceticism, scant speech, and considerable isolation. The title is from the Greek *monachos*, "one who lives alone."

The word is first used in a Christian sense in the Apocryphal Gospel of Thomas (c. third century C.E.) to denote a "solitary, celibate person." By the middle of the fourth century, it referred to any member of a recognized ascetic group.

In the second half of the fourth century, due in large part to Athanasius's *Life of Antony* (an Egyptian hermit and perhaps the first real monk) and the writings of Saint Jerome, the word came to be restricted to ascetics who withdrew from the Christian community to do battle with the Devil and his demons, either alone as "hermits" or "anchorites" (literally, "ones who re-tire"), or in communities as "cenobites" (literally, "ones who live a common life"). All were monks or *monachos*.

Antony had withdrawn into the deserts of Egypt, where he stayed for twenty years in prayer and isolation. He converted to the ascetic life after reading what the Gospels had to say on the benefits of poverty. We're told that he finally emerged from isolation "as though from a shrine, having been led into divine mysteries and inspired by God." The perfected and trans-formed Antony "persuaded many to take up the solitary life," and was the inspirational source for the development of monasticism.

After Antony's death in 355 C.E., monasticism spread out of Egypt and Palestine and into Europe by the fifth century. There it took Western roots.

COSTUME. Monastic dress was first standardized in the sixth century by Saint Benedict (480–547), founder of Western monasticism and famous for his "how-to" book for monks, *Rule of Benedict*, which among other things laid out the simple attire: plain *black habit* with attached outdoor *hood* or cowl, *leather belt*, and *scapular*—a long, narrow, sleeveless outer cloth draped over the basic tunic. The monk's belt could also serve as a disciplinary aid used in self-flagellation. In iconography, Benedict is often depicted holding a rod of discipline. A monk began his day at 2:15 A.M. and retired at 6:30 P.M. Summers he stayed up an extra hour.

In *Rule*, Benedict, who was born to a wealthy family but preferred the simplicity and solitude of dwelling in caves, fused the concepts of long prayer, hard labor, and communal living into the blueprint for monastic de-velopments throughout Europe. Benedict conceptually transformed menial chores and manual labor into desirable acts filled with dignity and suitable as gifts to God. His philosophy had an understandable appeal to peasants. Since a monk's work was essentially the same as that of a peasant—plowing, plant-ing, and prayer—the simple dress of a Benedictine monk was also sensible.

Monastic clerics in dark-colored
"habit" and "hood" (or "cowl").
The belt was used as a
disciplinary aid.

MALE NUNS. In *Rule*, Benedict forbids monks from addressing each other simply by name; the names of elder monks take the prefix *pater*, "father," while those of younger monks take *nonnus*, the masculine form for "nun." Young monks are male nuns. This masculine usage eventually become obsolete. But the word *nonnus* did not become extinct, as we'll see.

It is said that Benedict died at his monastery at Monte Cassino on March 21, while kneeling in prayer, supported upright before an altar by two brethren. Six days earlier, he'd ordered his grave dug, having foreseen his death. His canny foreknowledge and calm acceptance of his fate is why Benedict became the patron saint of the dying. In art, the saint is pictured in his peaked hood or "monk's cowl"—from the Latin *cucullus*, meaning "pointed cap." Conservatism and sobriety have always been hallmarks of monastic garb, symbolizing a renunciation of luxury.

Later, reformed Benedictines, who eschewed any dyed material as being decorative, preferred natural off-white habits—which eventually they bleached white to symbolize chastity.

The Franciscans, founded by Saint Francis of Assisi, dressed in gray habits, and became known as the Gray Friars—a name that stayed with them even after the fifteenth century, when they traded in their gray dress for brown.

The Carmelites, an order founded in the twelfth century, became known for the color of their dress—they were the White Friars.

Dominicans, founded by Saint Dominic from Spain, introduced a black robe over a white gown.

NUNS, SIXTH CENTURY; SISTERS, NINETEENTH CENTURY ◆

A "nun" is not a "sister," although we use those two words interchangeably to say, for instance, "Sister Mary Catherine is a pious nun." A sister cannot be a nun, although a nun conceivably could be a religious sister.

Nuns originated in the sixth century C.E., the female counterparts of monks. They took private solemn vows, lived ascetic lives in cloisters, and prayed for all the sinners outside their high vine-draped walls. The life was one of "contemplation and mortification."

Sisters, on the other hand, did not receive legal recognition in the Church until the nineteenth century. Religious sisters make public vows of poverty, chastity, and obedience, and function in the outside world, teaching, ministering to the sick, and, today at least, raising their voices on social issues and Church reform, as well as a role for women in the priesthood. Sisters also engage in missionary work.

The order of sisters did not come into existence until 1841, when the sit-

With their heads covered, women served many roles, from church cleaner to nun to religious sister.

ting pope gave official status to the congregation of the Sisters of Mercy. Previously, groups of women living together had called themselves "sisters," the word referring to their chaste familylike living arrangements. Of course, consecrated virgins and holy women have sought perfection in the religious state since the beginning of Christianity, going by a variety of titles.

WORD ORIGINS. The word "nun" evolved from the Sanskrit *nana*, "mother," to the Greek *nanna*, "aunt," and finally to the Latin *nonna*, meaning "a child's nurse."

Though the masculine *nonnus*, for young monk, died out, the word lives on in Italian as *nonno*, where it means "grandfather," just as *nonna* means "grandmother." In a sense, a grandmother is a "child's nurse," which is the role Grandma often plays.

The word "cloister" is from the Latin *claustrum*, meaning "place shut in," and signifies that part of a religious house or outside garden strictly reserved for the use of monks or nuns.

A nun's costume has from the start been similar to that of a monk, the chief difference being the medieval replacement of the monk's hood or cowl by the nun's *wimple*, the stiff collar and bib that leaves only the face exposed. The word "wimple" has the same root as our word "wipe," a reference to the function a neck bib serves in protecting the chest and wiping the face. A medieval nun also wore a head veil, since she saw herself as a "bride" of Christ.

For centuries, nuns' habits were all white, all black, or mixed. But in the seventeenth century, the so-called Sisters (they were actually "Daughters") of Saint Vincent de Paul introduced blue, the only color relief ever. Habits retained their medieval look until reform was introduced by the Second Vatican Council in the 1960s.

VESTMENT COLORS:
CHRISTIANITY, PRE–TWELFTH CENTURY ♦

Color symbolism is universal, and has been consciously used in sacrifice rituals and liturgy, as well as in heraldry, alchemy, art, and literature. Even the most ancient religions have used colors to symbolize attributes and emotions. However, they have not done this with universal consistency.

Christian clerics mourn in black or violet, while Confucians prefer white. Buddhist priests wear yellow or saffron, while the Christian Church never adopted yellow garments, and only sparingly uses gold.

By studying the use of colors in various cultures, Carl Jung found a general pattern:

Red is associated with blood, wounds, death throes, and sublimation; *green* with vegetation and rebirth; *light blue* with the sky, day, and calm seas; *dark blue* with the night sky and stormy seas; *orange* with fire and unrest and revolt; *yellow* with sunlight and conceptual illumination and comprehension; *brown* and *ocher* with the earth and peasantry; *black* with fertile soil, death, and mourning; *gold* with the sun itself, and enlightenment; *silver* with moonlight.

IN LITURGY. Colored vestments began in the Christian Church rather late—and it was very late before a color scheme was finalized.

For at least two hundred years after Christ's death, his followers had no system of colors associated with seasonal liturgy. We know from Theodoret's *Ecclesiastical History* that early in the fourth century, the emperor Constantine gave a gift of a "sacred robe fashioned with golden threads" to Bishop Macarius of Jerusalem to be used for baptisms. And toward the end of the fourth century, textual references are made to priests wearing shining white garments to celebrate the sacrifice of the Eucharist. But the palette of hues was limited.

Saint Jerome, in 415, in a bitter dispute with Pelagius, who denied the doctrine of original sin, advocated white in commemorating Christ's sacrifice on the cross. For a time, white vestments had symbolic bloodred stripes, giving them a candy-cane pattern.

Inventories of Frankish churches in the ninth century reveal that a variety of colors were used for vestments, with no particular liturgical reason for their use. However, decades earlier, Saint Amand wrote that dark vestments—black and wine purple—were preferred over lighter colors for all major litanies. He doesn't say why. Perhaps this preference had more to do with the abundance of dark-colored grapes in the French wine-growing re-

*Pope Innocent III (1198–1216)
devised the color system of
liturgical dress.*

gions where Amand preached and established monasteries and convents. He
is today the patron saint of brewers, winemakers, hotelkeepers, and bar staff.

MODERN LITURGICAL COLORS: LATE TWELFTH CENTURY ◆

The modern color system of the Roman Church, with its accompanying
symbolism, was first outlined in Pope Innocent III's treatise *De sacro altaris
mysterio*, written before his election as pontiff in 1198.

Pope Innocent (1198–1216) based his symbolism on allegorical interpretations of colors and flowers mentioned in Scripture, especially in the Song
of Solomon. The book, written about the tenth century B.C.E., probably by
Solomon, deals candidly and passionately with human love, relating the story
of a Shulammite woman and her beloved; it even depicts their sexual love.
Colors play a large role in the narration. Innocent's recommendations were
made official in 1570 by Pius V.

Then and today:

Green symbolizes hope. To ancient peoples, green was spring, vegetation,
rebirth, hope for a bountiful harvest. Roman Catholic priests wear green
vestments on "ordinary" days, "ordinary" meaning nonspecial feast days; on
the Sundays after Epiphany and Pentecost. Green is worn on the first Sunday
after Trinity—though Lutherans prefer white.

The word "green" is from the Dutch *groen*, the root Indo-European word
for "grass."

White symbolizes purity and joy. Joyous white is reserved for the seasons
of Christmas and Easter, and feasts like the Ascension of Jesus into Heaven
and the Epiphany—events that don't commemorate Christ's suffering and
death. Pure white is also used on feasts of the Virgin Mary, of angels, and of
saints who were not martyred. In funeral services today, Christian clerics
who prefer to emphasize death as spiritual rebirth shun black vestments in
favor of white ones—as Confucius recommended.

The word "white" comes to us from the Old English *kwit*, which derived from the Indo-European *kweid*, meaning "to gleam brightly."

Black symbolizes solemnity and death. Black dress is preferred for Good Friday, and is optional for Masses of the dead—the alternate color is violet, the shade for mourning and penance. Black is also worn during the seasons of Advent and Lent. It's said, picturesquely, that a priest's daily black cassock symbolizes humankind's perpetual sinning ways, while his short white over-garment, the surplice, symbolizes God's forgiveness through grace. To gardeners ancient and modern, black is a sign of rich organic soil, ideal for sustaining new life.

The word "black" comes to us from the Old English *blaec*, which derived from the Indo-European *bhleg*, meaning "to burn." Hence the word's root connotes soot and dark smokiness.

Violet or *purple* symbolizes penance and mourning. Violet or purple is worn for Holy Week, on Sundays in Lent, and on the four Sundays in Advent. Violet was a favorite color for robes of ancient kings, the dye abundant in plants and shellfish. The word "purple" is from the Greek *porphyra*, a shellfish that yields a rich purple dye.

The word "violet" is from the Latin *viola*, the name of a bluish-purple plant that, like the African violet, belongs to the family *Violaceae*.

Red symbolizes fire and blood and royalty. Red can be seen during the feasts of the Passion, including Good Friday, and on days commemorating the deaths of martyrs, the apostles, and the Evangelists. The color of fire, red is a natural choice for Pentecost, symbolizing the fiery descent of the Holy Spirit.

The word "red" comes from the Old English *read*, which is from the Indo-European *reudh*, "to make red," as by rubbing.

Gold is a vestment color added later and used sparingly; it symbolizes virtue and the glory of God.

The word "gold" derives directly from the Old English and German word *gold*, and from the Indo-European *ghel*, "to shine."

Blue vestments, once worn briefly in the Late Middle Ages to celebrate feasts of the Virgin Mary, have never really come back into vogue, except in Spain and Latin America, where blue is the preferred color in celebrating the Feast of Mary's Immaculate Conception. The pope allows blue, but does not condone the use of any fabric that is multicolored; one shade must predominate.

The word "blue" derives from the Middle English and Old French *bleu*, which comes from the Indo-European *bhle-wos*, "light-colored sky."

In the sixteenth century, the Reformed Churches generally rejected color as an adjunct to worship. Calvinists did away with all variety in color and texture, opting for black preaching gowns worn over dark-colored street clothes. Many Protestants, especially Lutherans and Anglicans, eventually reintroduced color, sometimes preferring their own schemes; yellow, for instance, could be substituted for green.

ISLAMIC DRESS: POST-SEVENTH CENTURY ◆

Islam has always attached less importance to liturgical vestments and colors than most other religions. Rather, all devotees who enter a mosque remove their footwear—so as not to defile the floor with impure debris—and all pilgrims to Mecca don the same *white seamless habit*, the *ihram*, arriving at the sacred place in the guise of humble beggars. Observant women wear a *veil*.

Islam recognizes no Roman-like priesthood set apart by its power to confer sacraments on the laity. Clerical functions are carried out by the *ulama*, the one "learned in the Law," whose most notable insignia is the head scarf or *turban*. "What differentiates us [in appearance] from the polytheists," said the Prophet Muhammad, "is the turban."

The garb of the *ulama*, aside from the turban, varies from region to region. All Muslim males, clerical or lay, are strictly forbidden by the Prophet from wearing gold or silk.

In general, Muslim garb is: the *jubbah*, a *long, wide-sleeved gown*—blue, gray, brown, or black—reaching to the feet and buttoned halfway down its total length over a *striped caftan*. Headgear might include a *soft collapsible cap*, a *qalansuwah*, of red felt with blue tassels, round which is wound a white muslin turban. A green turban usually denotes a descendant of the Prophet. Though turbans have long been worn in India by non-Muslims, the Muslim

---

WHIRLING DERVISHES ◆ *The mystical Islamic Sufi order known in the West as the* whirling dervishes *has its own distinctive and highly symbolic attire: a* black outer robe (khirqah) *that symbolizes the grave, and a high* camel's hair hat (sikke) *that represents the grave's tall tombstone. Underneath the black robe are white "dancing" robes with a* wide pleated frock (tannur), *over which fits a* short, snug jacket (destegul). *Whirling, the dervish casts off the blackness of the grave and shines radiant in the white shroud of resurrection.*

turban is distinguished by the use of a skullcap at its foundation.

THE MASS AS SACRIFICE:
TRADITIONALLY, THE LAST SUPPER ◆

The Mass is at the very heart of Christianity, for as Pope Pius XII said: "The mystery of the most Holy Eucharist is the culmination and center of the Christian religion; it is the crowning act of the sacred liturgy."

The Douay Bible defines the Mass as:

> *The* Sacrifice *of the New Law, in which the* Sacrifice *of Calvary is represented and renewed in the* unbloody *manner, the Divine* Victim *offering Himself under the appearance of bread and wine as He did at the Last Supper, when He instituted the Eucharist* Sacrifice *and celebrated Mass for the first time [author's emphasis].*

We glean two facts from this definition:

1. Jesus Christ originated the Christian Mass around the year 30 C.E., shortly before his death. After giving his apostles his body and blood to eat and drink, he told them: "Do this in memory of me" (Luke 22:19).

2. The rite is unequivocally one of sacrifice; in fact, the definition uses that word three times, refers to Christ as a "Victim," and acknowledges that what distinguishes the New Law from older forms of sacrifice is that it shall be "unbloody."

Theologically, the Mass is a "sacrificial meal": sacrifice is its primary internal reality; the eating ritual is its primary external form.

Cannibalism, one of humankind's most ancient rituals, underlies the "Sacrifice" of the Mass.

CANNIBALISM. The Christian Church has never made an attempt to conceal the Mass's sacrificial and cannibalistic overtones. (*See* Eucharist.) Church father Tertullian preferred to call the rite a "Sacrifice," and much of early Church theology centered on arguments over Christ's real presence in the bread and wine. The Second Vatican Council (1962–65) declared:

> *On the night he was betrayed, Our Savior instituted the Eucharistic Sacrifice of his Body and Blood. He did this in order to perpetuate the Sacrifice of the Cross. . . . As long as the Sacrifice of the Cross is celebrated on an altar, the work of our redemption is carried on.*

Although Catholics receiving Holy Communion may not wish to imagine that they are ingesting Christ's real flesh and blood, the belief that they are is central to the faith. One of Thomas Aquinas's beautiful antiphons, written for the Feast of Corpus Christi, begins: "O sacrificial banquet, in which Christ is eaten."

Cannibalism, as we'll see when we look at the Sacrament of the Eucharist, is one of man's most ancient rituals. Since earliest times, one person has eaten the flesh of another to share in the "victim's" strength, goodness, and wisdom. Cannibalism, symbolic or in the flesh, has existed in all cultures, over all times. And priests in all cultures have dressed in their finest attire for the sacrifice.

Indeed, as we've seen, ritual sacrifice is the real origin of religious vestments.

WORD ORIGIN. The word "Mass" came into popular favor in the sixth century. Previously, the rite had gone by many names, such as "sacrifice," "banquet," "the Lord's Supper," "Passover meal," and "Eucharist," the latter deriving from the Greek *eucharistia*, meaning "gratitude."

"Mass" derives from the Latin *missa*, meaning "dismissal." Historically, it occurs in an early phrase used by the priest to "dismiss" the congregation at the end of any religious service: *Ite, missa est (contio)*, meaning "Go, (the meeting) is dismissed."

Acts 2:42, 46 suggests that the apostles celebrated Christ's Sacrifice of the Mass daily. In the fifth century, Mass was celebrated in some places every day, in others on Saturdays and Sundays, or on Sundays only. In the Middle Ages, priests were paid a stipend for performing the ritual. This practice got out of hand, and offering numerous Masses became a way for a priest to increase his income. Indeed, the situation got so bad that in 1061, Pope Alexander II forbade any priest to say more than one Mass a day for a stipend.

The original language of the Mass was Greek, but Latin became the official language of the Roman rite in the third century. In recent times, Latin was replaced by English in an attempt to make the Mass more meaningful, though it now seems to be making a comeback in some parishes.

VESSELS. As is befitting a sacrifice, many vessels accompany the Mass service:

The *paten* holds the bread wafer that is Christ's body; the *chalice* holds the wine that is Christ's blood. Traditionally, both items should be made of the purest metal, preferably gold, and be unbreakable and "incorruptible," so they will not contaminate the bread and wine.

The *monstrance*, as we saw earlier in the section on Benediction of the Blessed Sacrament, is the receptacle that displays Christ's body. The *ciborium* (*cibus* is Latin for "food") is the vessel used to hold Hosts, both those for distribution to the faithful and those to be reserved in the Tabernacle.

The *finger towel* is a small white napkin used by the priest to dry his fingers after cleansing them following the sacrifice. The *cruets* contain the wine that will be consecrated and the water that will be used to wash or purify. *Candles* symbolize Christ as the light of life, and also the "burnt offerings" of past sacrifices. Of course, no sacrifice can be performed without an altar.

ALTAR: OLD TESTAMENT TIMES ◆

The rite of the Eucharist takes place on a raised platform, the preferred site for sacrifice since ancient times. "Altar" derives from the Latin *altare*, "high place," and in Hebrew, "altar" is related to the verb meaning "to slaughter."

Since sacrifice was the central act of worship for the Israelites and their Near Eastern neighbors, altars are often mentioned when the Bible speaks of paying homage to God. The first altar explicitly referred to in the Old Testa-

The altar appears in most cultures. The word is rooted in the Latin for "high place" (altare) and may also be related to adolere, *"to burn up."*

ment is the one Noah constructs for thanksgiving following the ruinous Flood:

> *Noah built an altar to the Lord, and took of every clean beast and every clean fowl, and offered burnt offerings on the altar. And the Lord smelled a sweet savor . . . and the Lord said in his heart, I will not again curse the ground any more for man's sake. (Gen. 8:20–21)*

Abraham also builds an altar when he is about to sacrifice his son (Gen. 22:9). The earlier tale of Cain and Abel implies that the first brothers made their sacrifices on an altar. On Mount Sinai, God commands Moses to build an altar and gives him two directions: (1) the altar is not to be built of hewn stones, and (2) there are to be no steps leading up to the sacrificial table (Exod. 20:22–23).

Archaeological excavations have uncovered the remains of numerous ancient altars in the Holy Land and the Middle East. They range from a simple pile of rough stones of the sort that served Elijah on Mount Carmel—twelve stones for the twelve tribes of Israel—to fragments of gold-covered wooden altars from the inner sanctums of houses of worship.

In primitive religious observances, a natural rock, heap of stones, or mound of earth sufficed as an altar—blood of the sacrifice staining the structure. With the rise of sanctuaries and temples, the altar moved from outdoors to indoors, and blood from sacrifice was neatly channeled off along hewed brick troughs.

In the Middle Ages, it became popular in the West for churches to have many altars, each associated with a different guild or fraternity, each funded perhaps by that organization. Each of ten altars, say, could have a Mass in progress simultaneously. The Eastern Orthodox Church never went in for this multiplicity, and stuck with one altar and only one Eucharist on a given day.

ALTARPIECE: EARLY CHRISTIANITY ◆

It was indoor altars that made possible—and popularized—the altarpiece, that structure above an altar table adorned with holy personages, saints, and biblical themes.

After bloody sacrifice became merely a symbolic enactment, elaborate altarpieces emerged, composed of some of the finest paintings, reliefs, and sculptures of religious art: such things as the diptych altar scene (two panels), the triptych (three panels), and the polyptych (four or more panels).

One of the earliest known painted panels, dating from the eleventh century, is the magnificent triptych the *Savior between the Virgin and St. John* in the cathedral at Tivoli, Italy. One of the most famous is in the Cathedral of Saint-Bavon, in Ghent: *The Adoration of the Lamb*, also known as the *Ghent Altarpiece*, a polyptych in twelve panels painted by Hubert and Jan van Eyck, completed in 1432.

CHRIST'S TABLE AND CUP. As early as the third century, Christians had already applied the word "altar" to their ritual table used by a priest to prepare Holy Communion.

Traditionally, the first Christian altar was the long wooden table at which Christ, at the Last Supper, instituted the Mass. Relics believed to be portions of that altar table are preserved and reverently regarded in the Lateran Basilica in Rome.

Two chalices, each believed by some to be the Holy Grail from which Christ drank wine at the Last Supper, are held by New York Metropolitan Museum of Art (which occasionally displays their cups at the Cloisters Museum) and the Cathedral of Valencia, Spain. Both cups date from the early Roman period. (*See* Holy Grail; Relics.)

CHAPTER

1 0

Sacraments

Godparents to Seven Deadly Sins

"SACRAMENT"—WORD ORIGIN:
CHRISTIANITY, THIRD CENTURY c.e. ◆

A sacred secret rite.

That's what Christians in the third century meant by their special coinage of the term "sacrament." They combined the Latin word for "sacred" or "holy," *sacer*, with the Greek for "secret rite" or "mystery," *mysterion*, arriving at *sacramentum*: a holy secret mystery. All Christian rites had to be secret then, when being identified as a Christian meant being persecuted.

The word "mystery," which to us today suggests an uncertainty we strive to resolve, originally referred to the baffling mode by which a sacrament works its spiritual magic and is always beyond human comprehension. To the ancients, mysteries were sacred, impenetrable truths, to be cherished and not exposed and explained away.

Actually, Roman soldiers already used *sacramentum* in another, legal sense: a "sacrament" was a soldier's binding oath of allegiance to his commander, sworn when embarking on a new campaign. A soldier would die for his general, just as Christians would die for their faith in Christ.

Early Christians believed that through a sacramental ceremony, Jesus Christ mysteriously came into intimate contact with them, infusing their soul with grace. Saint Augustine coined a durable definition of a sacrament: "The visible form of an invisible grace." Today, the Anglican catechism sharpens Augustine's phrase to "an outward and visible sign of an inward and spiritual grace."

In the early Church, a formulaic representation would have read: Sacrament = Element + Word. In the thirteenth century, through the philosophy of Italian theologian Thomas Aquinas (1225–74), the formula was altered to read: Sacrament = Matter + Form. (In baptism, for instance, the matter is the water, whereas the form are the words intoned.) Today, the formula is: Sacrament = Outward Sign + Inward Grace.

SEVEN SACRAMENTS IN NUMBER: TWELFTH CENTURY ◆

In Roman Catholic and Eastern Orthodox Churches, there are seven "sacred secret rites," which these days are performed quite publicly: *baptism*, *Holy Communion* (the Lord's Supper or the Eucharist), *confirmation*, *penance*, *extreme unction* ("anointing" those near death), *ordination* (or holy orders), and last but not least, *matrimony*. The latter, because of its historical complexity, and the accompanying phenomena of divorce and annulment, merits a later chapter all its own. The same is true for holy orders, which involves the origins of priestly celibacy and the controversial subject of the ordination of women.

Seven became the official number of sacred rites only in the twelfth century, through the theological persuasion of Bishop Peter Lombard. Lombard "proved" to the Church's satisfaction that Christ himself instituted seven sacraments, citing evidence for each, explicit or implied in the New Testament.

Not everyone agreed, but Thomas Aquinas, called the Church's Angelic Doctor, did wholeheartedly. He wrote about the powers of such "sacramentals" as holy water and oil, incense, candles, vestments, making the sign of the cross, plus fasting and abstinence. So did the powerful Council of Florence agree in 1439.

THREE SACRAMENTS? Protestant Reformers of the sixteenth century whittled the number of sacraments from seven down to two—maybe three.

To this day most Protestants contend that Jesus Christ authorized only two sacraments—baptism and Holy Communion. Some will admit penance,

THE BAPTISM OF JESUS: "*And a voice from heaven said, 'This is my beloved Son, in whom I am well pleased.'* "

too. They reject as having no biblical basis the rites of confirmation, ordination, matrimony, and the anointing of the sick. Not that these acts are without merit; it's just that they have no explicit biblical sanction.

In truth, Christ most explicitly instituted only baptism and the Eucharist. He himself was baptized, and he passed around bread and wine at the Last Supper. With the other five sacraments, it becomes an issue of interpretation.

Catholics say seven. Protestants say two, maybe three. Jews say none. Judaism does not recognize the concept of a "secret sacred rite" that confers "sanctifying grace." A Jewish marriage, for instance, is a sacred but secular affair. (*See* Matrimony.)

PRE-CHRISTIAN TIMES. It is incorrect to imagine that Christians conceived the idea of sacraments. Pagan peoples and preliterate societies all had sacred secret rites in which a god or goddess conferred power to humans through ceremony. As we'll see later in this chapter, a sacrament like Holy Communion—partaking of the body and blood of Christ through bread and wine—was once practiced through eating the real flesh of a sacrificial victim, or by consuming the so-called cereal image of a crop deity, both of which were enjoyed by the Aztecs in ancient Mexico. The modern Communion wafer made of starch and stamped with Christ's initials is not unlike the Aztec's cereal image.

Before examining the origins of the individual sacraments, it's essential to consider what makes a sacrament such a special rite. As Thomas Aquinas said: "A Sacrament is a sign of a sacred thing in as much as it *sanctifies* men." (He meant women, too.) That sanctification is accomplished by a phenomenon unique to Christian thought: grace.

GRACE—A GIFT FROM GOD:
SAINT AUGUSTINE, FOURTH CENTURY ◆

A sacrament is defined in Catholicism as a "sacred outward sign or rite instituted by Christ to confer grace upon the soul." Each sacrament consists of a visible external ceremony, and an invisible confirmation of sanctifying grace.

The word "grace" is from the Latin *gratia*, meaning "favor" or "thanks." It's related to the Sanskrit *grnati*, meaning "he sings" or "he praises." It is this gift of grace from God that is a cornerstone of Christian revelation. God does not have to give humans grace, but he chooses to do so under specific conditions.

The purpose of grace in a sacrament is to assist the participants in carrying out the requirements of that sacrament. The grace received through the rite of matrimony, for instance, is supposed to guide the couple through the difficulties of sharing a life together—all smooth sailing at first but later perhaps stormy weather.

The grace is given not because of the sanctity of the officiating priest, but solely through the power of the sacramental rite. This confirmation of grace is what makes the rite a sacred sacrament and elevates it above being a secular ceremony. The technical term for describing the manner in which the rite confers grace is *ex opere operato*, literally, "from the effect of the rite."

As mentioned, the notion of grace is central to Christian thought, and is one of the thorniest aspects of Catholic doctrine. It took centuries for the concept to be definitively defined, yet the theology of grace clearly can be tracked back to Saint Augustine, who in the Western Church is called the Doctor of Grace.

IN SACRED SCRIPTURE. In the Bible, grace may mean "acceptability," as when Noah "found grace before the Lord" (Gen. 6:8). Or grace may mean, as it often does in the New Testament, a gift from God to assist human behavior, as when Saint Paul says: "By the grace of God I am what I am" (1 Cor. 15:10). It is this Pauline formula on which Augustine built his theology of grace.

In terms of quality, grace comes in two basic varieties, with one refinement:

ACTUAL GRACE. A passing or transitory gift bestowed upon the soul. It is an enlightening of the mind or a strengthening of the will to do good or avoid evil. It is a divine impulse helping one to perform vital actions above the power of his or her nature. Saying a prayer, for instance, confers actual grace. So does attending Mass. In fact, a "good mother," a "good Christian home," a "good Christian book"—all these things traditionally are called "graces" because they help a Catholic lead a good life.

SANCTIFYING GRACE. A permanent or abiding glow given to the soul; it remains in the soul unless destroyed by a mortal sin. A sacrament confers sanctifying grace. This luminous gift transforms the person's soul and elevates it to a supernatural plane, so that the soul is holy and pleasing to God, a temple of the Holy Spirit, and has the right to enter Heaven.

Sanctifying grace is a new life given to the soul by God. Since this new life is a created share in the life of God, the soul in sanctifying grace is said to be a "partaker of the divine nature." It is the special gift of sanctifying grace that a Roman Catholic receives in the seven rites—baptism, confirmation, Communion, penance, matrimony, holy order, and extreme unction—that makes sacraments out of these rites.

SACRAMENTAL GRACE. This is a refinement of sanctifying grace. It is the unique spiritual uplift one receives from each specific sacrament. This is what Saint Paul hints at, what Saint Augustine develops, what Saint Thomas refines. How Christians benefit from sacramental grace:

In *baptism*, it enables the infant to begin a new spiritual life, and later to carry out his or her baptismal vows.

In *confirmation*, it helps a boy or girl keep the faith and defend it with martyrdom if necessary.

In the *Eucharist*, it nourishes the life of the soul and unites it to God through charity.

In *penance*, it enables the sinner to expiate past offenses and avoid future pitfalls.

In *extreme unction*, it overcomes the temptations of the last hours of life— despair and suicide—and prepares the soul for immediate entrance into Heaven.

In *holy orders*, it helps a priest to perform divine worship, to administer the sacraments to his flock, and to honor his vow of chastity.

In *matrimony*, it helps a husband and wife remain faithful to each other, assists them in conceiving children and overcoming the temptation of birth control, and aids them in all the duties of the married state. The Catholic Church bases its discomfort with civil marriages on the fact that a couple thus united does not receive the extra spiritual support of sacramental grace to help them negotiate the many hazards of married life.

BAPTISM: NEW TESTAMENT, MATTHEW 28:19 ◆

GO YOU THEREFORE, AND TEACH ALL NATIONS, BAPTIZING THEM IN THE NAME OF THE FATHER, AND THE SON, AND THE HOLY SPIRIT.

That, of course, is the Christian origin of baptism; Jesus' words to his apostles. Nothing could be more explicit.

But the rite Jesus preached was in his time already some three thousand years old. It had been practiced by the ancient Sumerians, the people who invented the first system of writing, at their temple city of Eridu, where they worshiped the water god Ea, literally, "God of the House of Water." The god's symbol was the tenth sign of the zodiac, Capricorn: a composite beast with the foreparts of a goat and the body of a fish. This is the astrological sign in which the sun enters at the winter solstice in late December for its "rebirth"—that is, the days get longer with the promise of spring and vegetation.

What is quite curious is this:

In the Hellenistic period, the water god Ea was called *Oannes*, which in Greek is *Ioannes*, which in Hebrew is *Yohanan*, which in Latin is *Johannes*, and in English is *John*. It is interesting that John the Baptist, who institutes the water rite of baptism around the year 27 C.E., bears the same name as the Sumerian water god of 3000 B.C.E. Is this coincidence?

Several scholars have suggested that John the Baptist never existed, only the legend of a pagan water god and an old pagan rite, given a new Christian spin. However, the chronicle of the Jewish historian Josephus (c. 85 C.E.) seems to confirm John's existence as an historical figure. As Joseph Campbell concludes in *Occidental Mythology*: "I shall leave it to the reader to imagine how he [John the Baptist] came both by the god's name and by his rite."

For Christians, John the Baptist and the sacrament of baptism are prophesied in the Old Testament, in Malachi 3:1, with the promise: "Behold, I will send my messenger, and he shall prepare the way before me."

For John the Baptist, every Israelite needed rebirth through a water baptism. Donning a hair shirt, a prophet's proud badge since the time of Elijah, John preached that it was no longer enough for a Jew to claim descent from Abraham. The end was near, God's judgment imminent, and to avoid fiery death and destruction, a person had to confess his or her sins and be plunged into the waters of the river Jordan. It's not surprising that early Christians, believing God's judgment imminent, spoke in the same breath of baptism and repentance.

Baptismal references in the Bible are many. John the Baptist spoke of "the baptism of repentance" (Mark 1:4); Jesus advised Nicodemus: "Unless one is born of water and the Spirit, he cannot enter the kingdom of God" (John 3:5).

In the sermon preached by Peter on Pentecost, he charged those present: "Repent, and be baptized every one of you in the Name of Jesus Christ for the forgiveness of your sins" (Acts 2:38). Some three thousand people waded into the water and were spiritually reborn, and since that time, for some Christians, the feast of Pentecost is a favored time for the rite of baptism. All branches of Christianity acknowledge baptism as a sacred rite.

WATER AND EXORCISM. It's vital for the life of the body. It's essential for salvation of the soul. And, too, the "rebirth" sacrament of baptism—Latin *baptisma*, "a dipping under"—is necessary in order to receive any of the other six sacraments.

In Christianity, there are three kinds of baptism. *Baptism of water*, as practiced in Christ's time by John the Dipper, cousin of Jesus. *Baptism of blood*, the spiritual salvation hard won through martyrdom. *Baptism of desire*, a person's wish, explicit or implicit, to be initiated into the faith when the formal ritual itself, for one reason or another, cannot be performed; most often due to imminent death in the absence of a priest.

Technically, baptism is an exorcism, in which Satan is renounced; after all, it was Satan who tempted Adam and Eve and made spiritual "rebirth" necessary. In the Roman rite, the priest breathes three times on the infant's face, saying: "Depart from him, thou unclean spirit, and give place to the Holy Spirit, the Paraclete!" (*See* Exorcism.)

CIRCUMCISION OF THE HEART. Little known is the fact that the benign practice of baptism replaced the traumatic ritual of circumcision in the early days of the Christian faith.

For Jews, circumcision had long been an initiation rite, the forfeited foreskin sealing a pact with God. The new priests of Christianity retained the custom, requiring that grown Gentile men wishing to convert to the new faith submit to circumcision. Well, to non-Semitic peoples, the practice was foreign and repugnant, as well as agonizing and dangerous in an era that could not offer anesthetic or sterilization. The insistence on circumcision was impeding the spread of the new religion.

Saint Paul, who was attempting to convert Gentile men, grasped the magnitude of the problem and proposed a solution. All that was required to convert, he wrote, was a circumcision "of the heart, in the spirit," not in the flesh. Sort of a circumcision by desire. In 50 C.E., the Apostolic Council ruled that Gentile proselytes could retain their foreskins, and thus the rituals of baptism and circumcision went their separate ways.

Paul saw in baptism added symbolism: passing beneath water, then rising above the surface, recalled the burial and Resurrection of Jesus. Baptism was rebirth. The sacrament became a great symbolic entrance to the Christian community.

Today, when we automatically baptize infants, we tend to forget that in centuries past, it was adults who were baptized, seldom newborns.

INFANT BAPTISM: EARLY THIRD CENTURY c.e. ◆

It's not clear exactly when the baptizing of newborns first arose. Of course, the only stain on a newborn's soul is the inheritance of original sin. Church father Tertullian in *On Baptism* asked why an infant "in the innocent period of life" should be made to undergo a ritual for the "remission of sins." At that time, the concept of original sin was still embryonic. (*See* Original Sin.)

In the early years of the Church, only adult converts were baptized. But by the time Christianity became the state religion of Rome in 313 c.e., families routinely were being baptized together, something of a family event. At some point in that century, baptism of infants became customary. Although the earliest explicit mention of infant baptism occurs in the second century, its chief promoter only arrived two hundred years later in the voice of Saint Augustine. Through Augustine's persuasive writings, baptism of infants became obligatory in most Christian Churches.

For some theologians, however, Christ himself instituted infant baptism when he rebuked the disciples for "hindering" the little children from coming to him:

> *They brought young children to him, that he should touch them, and his disciples rebuked those that brought them . . . and Jesus said, "Suffer the little children to come unto me, and forbid them not, for such is the kingdom of God." (Mark 10:13–14)*

BAPTISTS. The act of infant baptism, ironically, stripped the sacrament of its active profession of faith, since a baby was in no position to proclaim its belief in Jesus Christ as Savior. This troubled theologians for some time.

Some sixteenth-century Reformers sought to abandon infant baptism, to restore full-body immersion in water, and to perform the sacrament only on people of a responsible age who could actively profess belief in the faith. They were called the Baptists, and they heralded a new branch of Christianity.

Today, the majority of Christian denominations—including Roman Catholic, Methodist, Presbyterian, Anglican, Lutheran, Congregationalist, and Eastern Orthodox—baptize infants. On the other hand, Baptists, Assemblies of God, and the Brethren believe that an initiate must be able to speak his or her own mind; that is, a "believer's baptism." What's more, he or she should demonstrate some evidence of spiritual conversion, usually through a marked improvement in social behavior.

Thus, the ancient notion of adult baptism, accompanied by an explicit statement of faith, survives throughout many parts of the world. Adults are "born again" as only adults once were. And what is the fate of infants who die unbaptized, or of fetuses who die in the womb? (*See* Limbo.)

Not surprisingly, Churches that continued to practice infant baptism long ago adopted another sacrament, confirmation, as an active expression of one's faith.

GODPARENTS: EARLY THIRD CENTURY c.e. ✦

Why, when a baptized infant has biological parents, does it need godparents at the sacred rite?

An infant's parents, at the time of baptism, pledge to instruct their child in the Ten Commandments, the Lord's Prayer, and the Apostles' Creed. All well and good if the parents survive long enough to carry out their promises. But they often did not in the early days of persecution in the Church.

With persecution widespread, children needed a surrogate set of parents—godparents—to take over the teaching pledge. This notion of spiritual foster parents was commonplace by the third century, with godparents taking a vow to raise the child as a Christian. Interestingly, Tertullian argued strongly against godparents; what if, he said, the child grows up and fails to honor his baptismal vows? Are the godparents then not to be held responsible?

Technically, today, the obligation of godparents ends when the child receives the rite of confirmation—the child's own statement of his or her intent to practice in the faith.

CONFIRMATION: EARLY THIRD CENTURY c.e. ✦

What water is to baptism, oil is to confirmation; the word is from the Latin *confirmatio*, meaning "corroboration" or "ratification." Traditionally, oil was the preferred sacramental used to anoint divinely appointed prophets, priests, and kings.

As we've seen, the emergence of infant baptism as commonplace led to a need for another ceremony marking the transition to full and active participation in the Church. The rite of "confirmation of faith" began as a charismatic and apostolic *laying on of hands*. This ancient Jewish practice became for Christians something of a dispatch of grace through the Holy Spirit: "Then they laid their hands on them, and they received the Holy Spirit" (Acts 8:14–17).

The earliest evidence of a formal ceremony of confirmation is found in the baptismal rites of Tertullian's treatise *De Baptismo* (198 C.E.) and Hippolytus's *Apostolic Tradition* (215 C.E.). Both works mention a prayer said by a bishop, a laying on of hands, and an anointing on the forehead of the candidate. There is evidence that when infants were baptized, often they were simultaneously anointed with confirmation oil. In 1533, England's future Queen Elizabeth I was baptized and confirmed when she was only a three-day-old princess.

Not until late in the sixteenth century did all branches of Christianity permanently separate baptism from confirmation. The latter sacrament is administered at (or after) the age of reason, which can vary with sects from seven to fourteen. In 1566, the Council of Trent declared seven to twelve years old to be the appropriate ages, favoring the latter.

Some theologians argue that confirmation confers a new and distinct gift of grace from the Holy Spirit, others view the rite as a reinforcement, or bolstering, of the grace bestowed in baptism.

BAR MITZVAH AND BAT MITZVAH ♦

Christianity is not the only faith that celebrates a moral coming-of-age for both boys and girls. In Judaism, a child is considered a Jew if his or her mother is Jewish (irrespective of the father's faith). A boy is circumcised on the eighth day after his birth, and remains a minor until age thirteen—then assumes full moral and legal responsibilities of an adult, and is officially indoctrinated through the ceremony of becoming a *bar mitzvah*, literally, "son of the commandment." The custom of celebrating a bar mitzvah was unknown before the fourteenth century; though records from the second century mention thirteen as the age of religious manhood.

The age of moral reason for a girl is twelve, and her ceremony is a *bat mitzvah*, "daughter of the commandment." The custom of celebrating a girl's moral coming-of-age dates only to the nineteenth century—and the prac-

*Bar mitzvah—
the moral and
legal coming-of-age.*

tice did not catch on until after 1922, when it was promoted by the Reconstructionist Movement, or Society for the Advancement of Judaism. The female celebration has been encouraged over the years specifically to establish an equality between the sexes.

Contrary to popular belief, all Jewish children automatically become morally responsible—become "children of the commandment"—without a formal ceremony; even without an adolescent's conscious awareness of his or her coming-of-age.

In ancient times, both Abraham and Jacob, at age thirteen, made crucial decisions that altered the rest of their lives: Abraham abandoned the worship of idols, and Jacob parted from his brother Esau. These events underscore the origin of a moral coming-of-age ritual for all Jews.

The bar mitzvah ceremony, as it has developed, centers on the boy's obligations as a man. Traditionally, on the Monday or Thursday following his thirteenth birthday (in the Jewish calendar), he attends morning service in the synagogue. He dons *tefillin* for the first time, and reads directly from the Torah. This, in traditional Jewish communities, *was* the bar mitzvah ceremony. Any lavish party with family and friends, in which the boy receives gifts, is, so to speak, icing on the cake. Now most ceremonies take place on Saturday morning. It's customary for the boy to deliver a scholarly lecture, *drashah*, during the festive meal—or he may choose to deliver a speech of thanks to gathered family and friends.

One form for a girl's becoming bat mitzvah is for her to deliver, in synagogue, a short discourse on a section of the Torah. Or the girl might read Psalms or prayers from the Bible. Modern-day emphasis on the equality of the sexes often means that a bat mitzvah may be as extravagantly celebrated as a bar mitzvah.

In the nineteenth century, Reform congregations in Germany replaced the bar mitzvah with a ceremony called confirmation—and they upped a boy's age of moral responsibility to sixteen. In the United States, confirmation is held in Reform and many Conservative congregations, in addition to celebrating *b'nai* (Hebrew plural) *mitzvah*. Confirmation is held generally on Shavuot, the holiday associated with the giving of the Torah on Mount Sinai.

SPEAKING IN TONGUES ◆

The Holy Spirit was for early Christians also a tonic for heightened consciousness through the "gift of tongues": to utter with fluency a range of sounds outside normal speech—and sense. The phenomenon, known as

The Holy Spirit descending on the disciples on Pentecost with the gift of tongues.

"glossolalia" (Greek *glossa*, "tongue" + *lalein*, "to prattle"), experienced a vogue during the apostolic age, though Saint Paul doubted its value.

The gift of tongues is mentioned in the New Testament in the Acts of the Apostles, and it has occasioned a great deal of hand-wringing and soul-searching. What happened on the first Pentecost, when the apostles were understood by listeners of many different languages, is clearly a miracle of some sort. An apostle would speak in his own language of, say, Aramaic, but miraculously he would seem to be speaking in Greek to a listener who understood only that language. This is a miracle that the Church has never been comfortable with.

By mid-second century, speaking in tongues already was frowned upon, ascribed to the hysteria of demonic possession. In our own century, it has made a resurgence both in America and in Europe, spawning new Pentecostal faiths, a burgeoning form of Latin American Protestanism, and believers who call themselves "charismatics," from the Greek for "gift of God's grace."

HOLY COMMUNION: NEW TESTAMENT, MATTHEW 26:26-28 ◆

Along with baptism, the Eucharist—Greek *eucharistia*, "gratitude"—is the most cherished of Christian rites, viewed as a true Bible-based sacrament by all denominations. Despite the solemnity of its precedent—Christ's Last Supper and subsequent suffering—the sacrament is approached with gratitude and rapturous joy. Christ died for humankind's redemption.

Although Holy Communion is held in high esteem by Christians, there is precious little written about it in the New Testament. Of this we are certain: During the Last Supper, actually a Passover seder, Jesus broke unleavened bread and drank wine, intoning: "Take, eat; this is my body"; "Drink of it, all of you; for this is my blood of the covenant" (Matt. 26:26–28).

What did Jesus mean?

The answers over the centuries, hotly argued among theologians, fall into three categories.

TRANSUBSTANTIATION. Jesus meant that the bread and wine mysteriously—inscrutably—become his actual body and blood, the so-called transubstantiation, a dogma of Roman Catholicism. The bread *is* flesh. The wine *is* blood. The appearance of "bread" and "wine" is illusory. This interpretation carries the strongest cannibalistic overtones, a feature that has troubled many religious authorities who see paganism in the concept.

MEMORIAL. Jesus spoke metaphorically; the bread and wine are merely remembrances of his bodily suffering and death. The symbols are to prompt us to meditate on the events surrounding the Last Supper and Crucifixion.

REAL PRESENCE. This doctrine states that the bread and wine at Mass do not change; bread is flour, wine is grape juice. But, miraculously, the flesh and blood of Jesus commingle with the earthly substances and are truly present, coexisting with them.

These views have evolved out of deep philosophical differences, not just denominational nit-picking.

The transubstantiation is believed by Roman Catholics, Eastern Orthodox, and some Lutherans and Anglicans. Thomas Aquinas in his impressive *Summa Theologica* attempted to explain the mystery: the "accidents" of the bread and wine—that is, their surface appearances: shape, color, texture, taste—do not change. What changes are their "substances"—their base elemental structure, which, the Church assumes today, is even more elemental than molecules and atoms, particles unknown to Saint Thomas.

Many Baptists, Presbyterians, Methodists, and some Anglicans believe the bread and wine are symbols of Jesus' body and blood. In support of their belief, they cite Jesus' words to his disciples, reported by Paul: "Do this in remembrance of me" (1 Cor. 11:23–26). The word "remembrance," they argue, means that the bread and wine are "memorials" only, reminders of the Last Supper.

On the other hand, the majority of Lutherans, many Anglicans, and some other Protestants adhere to the theory of the Real Presence. First advanced in the sixteenth century by Martin Luther, the Real Presence dogma maintains that bread is flour, wine is grape juice, but Jesus is "in with, and under the bread and wine," as Luther put it.

CHRIST IN CANDIED YAMS ◆ *A few Christian communities have made substitutions for bread and wine, drawing on their own local fare. For instance, more than three million Christians in Central Africa receive the Eucharist in the form of sweet potatoes and honey. Jesus is "in with, and under" honeyed yams.*

Plants were sacred in primitive vegetation rites. About six centuries before Christ's birth, Persian mystic Zoroaster founded a cult, Zoroastrianism—the religious system of Persia before its conversion to Islam—which evolved a communion and liturgy that was a remarkable anticipation of the Christian Eucharistic Mass; even early Christians acknowledged the similarities.

To Zoroaster, the Creator's son was Haoma, believed to be incarnate in a sacred yellow plant, the haoma, that was pounded "to death" during "mass" in order to extract its life-giving sacramental juice, which imparted the grace of immortality. Haoma was the "son of god" and the mass's sacrificial victim. As the rite evolved in the Near East, haoma juice was replaced by red wine, and, too, sacred bread was eaten at the sacramental banquet. Many early Christian writers commented on the similarities between their Mass as a Eucharistic Sacrifice and the Zoroastrian haoma ceremony.

WHY BREAD, WHY WINE? Bread and wine were the daily fare of first-century Palestinians. They were commonplace and inexpensive. Christ used them at the Last Supper. In Old Testament times, wine was poured on the ground as a sacrifice for the worship of God and for repentance of sin (Exod. 29:40).

Up until the sixth century, women were forbidden to receive the consecrated bread in their naked hands because of possible menstrual contamination, long an abomination feared by Jewish and Christian males. (*See* Prohibitions.) Men, their lips still moist with communal Communion wine,

All Christian denominations recognize the Eucharist as biblically ordained in the story of the Last Supper.

were told to "touch it with your hands and hallow both your eyes and brow and other senses."

By the thirteenth century, the communal cup of wine had been dispensed with in many Western Churches. This was not out of fear of transmitting disease, since the concepts of bacteria and communicability were nonexistent, but because clothing fabrics were getting costlier and spilled wine stained permanently. The Hussites, followers of John Huss, in Bohemia, retained the cup and cautioned care.

CANNIBALISM. Martin Luther and Catholic popes promoted the Eucharist—as consumption of real flesh and real blood—as a form of cannibalism, one of humankind's most ancient rituals. Since earliest times, one person ate a small piece of flesh of another—or drank drops of blood—to share in that person's strength, holiness, wisdom, or courage; the list of attributes is long and noble.

Eskimos and Africans nibbled, preferring the corpses of fallen warriors, medicine men, and virgins, to gain, respectively, bravery, knowledge, and purity. Slavonic children ate of their deceased parents, in token bites, to maintain blood ties. All deceased blood relatives (not in-laws) were enjoyed by the early settlers of Ireland. And, today, elders in tribes along the Orinoco River in Venezuela request as a last wish whom they'd like to be consumed by. A mouthful is all that is bitten off.

All these peoples, through cannibalism, feel they commune in a holy way—Holy Communion—with the deceased.

Unfortunately for early Christians, the Romans abhorred cannibalism, condemning it as savage, and reports that Christ's followers were "eating his body" and "drinking his blood" only intensified their hatred for the fledgling faith.

WHY IS THE EUCHARIST BREAD CALLED A "HOST"? It serves as a containment vehicle, or Host, for Christ's body. That's the standard line. But there is a deeper linguistic reason. The Latin verb *hostire* means "to recompense," and the noun *hostia*, origin of the word "host," means "sacrifice."

WHY IS THE EUCHARIST WINE ALWAYS RED? In a theology that attempts to equate wine with blood, a chablis in the chalice would be needlessly antagonistic to unbelievers. Technically, though, white wine can be used; but not soured wine, which is "invalid matter" to undergo transubstantiation.

Biblically, Noah made the world's first wine, and suffered the first hang-over: "And he drank of the wine and was drunken; and he was uncovered within his tent" (Gen. 9:21). Historically, the Egyptians made the first wine about two thousand years before Noah's time, from the wild grape species *Vitis sylvestris*, which grew from the Nile to Gibraltar, and which they domesticated.

WHY DURING THE ROMAN CATHOLIC MASS IS WATER OFTEN ADDED TO THE WINE? Not to keep the priest from getting tipsy. The commingling is symbolic and suggested by a biblical passage: "One of the soldiers with a spear pierced his side, and forthwith came out blood and water" (John 19:34).

WHY IS PSALM 34 CALLED THE COMMUNION PSALM? According to Saint Cyril (376–444), archbishop of Alexandria, it was customary to sing this Psalm in Jerusalem churches in the fourth century. Furthermore, both the *Apostolic Constitutions* and Saint Augustine recommend the practice, since the psalmist sings his grateful praise of God for having rescued him from danger, and concludes with an admonition to fear the Lord and keep his commandments.

WHY ARE BELLS RUNG AT MASS BEFORE THE CONSECRATION? As early as the fourth century, the priest kept a small altar bell handy, and rang it at important parts of the service. The intention has always been to alert the faithful, particularly the unschooled, that something significant is about to take place in an otherwise abstruse and secretive ceremony. This was certainly true for English-speaking people attending a Latin Mass. In the Roman Mass, the bell would ring at the *Sanctus*, at the elevations of the Host and chalice, and just before the priest's Communion at the *Domine, non sum dignus*, "Lord, I am not worthy."

In the Roman Catholic Church, the English Mass was introduced on November 29, 1964.

PENANCE: NEW TESTAMENT, MATTHEW 16:19 ◆

Ancient Semites who sinned repented by suffering under the scratch of a hair shirt and the humiliation of ashes marring their foreheads—like Christians on Ash Wednesday. From this outward expression of contrition arose the Christian concept of confession—of whispering embarrassments

For Catholics, the origin of the sacrament of penance is in Jesus' command to the apostles: "Whose sins you remit, they are remitted unto them; and whose sins you retain, they are retained."

and moral failures (often of a sexual nature) into the ear of a (celibate) priest.

To Jews (and early Christians), an inward, private sorrow for one's sins was necessary but inadequate for forgiveness. Humiliation in some public form—and forum—was mandatory. In Deuteronomy, chapter 30, God promises mercy for the repentant, and he seems to say that forgiveness for sin is strictly between the sinner and God. Not mediated through a priest. Or a rabbi; Jews don't believe in this kind of mediated contrition.

Christians, on the other hand, and especially Roman Catholics, find the biblical basis for the sacrament of penance in Christ's words to the apostle Peter:

And I will give thee the keys to the kingdom of heaven; and whatever thou shall bind on earth shall be bound in heaven, and whatever thou shall loose on earth shall be loosed in heaven. (Matt. 16:19)

Read: Peter and his priest successors can grant absolution for sin, or withhold it. (Matthew says the same thing in 18:18.)

The Gospel writer John repeats the formula:

Whose sins you remit, they are remitted unto them; and whose sins you retain, they are retained. (John 20:23)

It is from these biblical passages that a Roman Catholic priest takes his authority to hear one's private indiscretions on God's behalf. To be a proper sacrament, penance must be administered by a priest *with proper jurisdiction*, a territorial imperative. A priest can't cross parish lines, without a bishop's permission, to forgive sin in another priest's district. For centuries, this has been a technical fine point of the sacrament.

IRISH JUSTICE. Although the concept of repentance dates from the foundation of the Christian Church, the forms penance took for centuries varied from lenient to brutal. Early on, certainly in the second century,

Christians put up great resistance to the idea of confessing their sins to a priest. Priests often were very ordinary folk, married, with children of their own.

In the third century, it became the practice to confess directly to a bishop concerning apostasy, homicide, and adultery, as if superior authority were needed to forgive serious sins.

In the seventh century, Irish Penitentials began to appear, advocating what is called "tariffed penance," in which punishment is made to fit the crime. A murderer is murdered. A rapist is gang raped. (By whom?) This eye-for-an-eye justice spread to the Anglo-Saxons and as far east as the Byzantine province.

Only around the twelfth century did it become standard for penance to be private, between the sinner and a priest, with absolution granted sometimes only *after* the prescribed penance had been carried out. In 1215, the sacrament of penance received the stamp of approval from the Fourth Lateran Council, and confessing to a priest became *obligatory at least once a year*—at Eastertime. Unfortunately, the Church's system of penance included winning grace through "indulgences," which eventually led to scandalous abuses. By Luther's era, Christians with cash could simply purchase penance from priests. Luther's revolt was in large part against this penitential system, which was reformed by the Council of Trent in the middle of the sixteenth century. (*See* Indulgences.)

IN JUDAISM. Jews have a special period of contrition, the so-called *Ten Days of Repentance*, which occurs between Rosh Hashanah and Yom Kippur and offers the opportunity to make an "atonement for the children of Israel for all their sins once a year" (Lev. 16:29–34).

In this penitential window in the Jewish calendar, it's believed that God passes judgment on each and every individual, reserving his verdict until Yom Kippur, Hebrew for "Day of Atonement." (*See* Feasts.)

SEVEN DEADLY SINS:
POPE GREGORY THE GREAT, 590–604 C.E. ◆

"Sin" is the twenty-first letter of the Hebrew alphabet, sometimes spelled "shin." But the English lowercase "sin" derives from the Old English *synne*, meaning "offense." In the early Church, Christians used the Greek and Latin words for sin: *hamartia* and *peccatum*, respectively.

In theology, sin is the free and deliberate transgression of the law of God. The essential nature of sin is rebellion; harking back to the archangel Lu-

THE SEVEN DEADLY SINS:
Pride, Envy, Anger, Sloth,
Avarice, Gluttony, and Lust;
1510 German woodcut.

cifer's rebellion in Heaven, the first sin. Adam and Eve's rebellion in the Garden was the first sin on earth.

Catholicism recognizes two kinds of sin, based on the seriousness of the transgression, and the degree of willfulness and deliberation:

Venial sin is a slight offense, which does not annihilate the friendship of the soul with God. It is a disease of the soul, not its death, and sanctifying grace remains in the soul.

Mortal sin is a grievous offense, committed with full knowledge and consent. It kills the supernatural life of the soul, hence destroying sanctifying grace. To die in the state of mortal sin guarantees one will go to Hell. Murder has always been a mortal offense; for centuries, blasphemy was as well.

The Greek monastic theologian Evagrius of Pontus laid the groundwork for categorizing sin when he drew up his list of eight offenses and wicked human passions: *gluttony, lust, avarice, sadness, anger, acedia* ("spiritual sloth"), *vainglory,* and *pride.* The ascending ordering was significant in that it represented progressively greater fixation with self, pride being the worst offense.

The word "acedia" is from the Greek *akedeia,* meaning "not to care": *a + kedos* = "not" + "care."

Late in the sixth century, Pope Gregory the Great reduced the list to seven. First he folded *vainglory* into *pride;* then he folded *acedia* into *sadness.* And he added *envy.* Then he inverted the ordering, producing what for centuries served as the seven deadly sins: *pride, envy, anger, sadness, avarice, gluttony, lust.* During the seventeenth century, the Church replaced the vague sin of *sadness* with the more specific sin of *sloth.*

EXTREME UNCTION: NINTH CENTURY c.e. ◆

As a mortuary rite of passage into the next life, anointing the sick with holy oil did not officially become a sacrament in the Roman Catholic Church until around the ninth century. Luther and other Reformers saw no biblical basis to justify the rite, an ancient tradition, being elevated to the sacred status of sacrament. Rome could find only one, an injunction in the Epistle of James, half-brother of Jesus.

James had been uncertain of Jesus' unique prophethood until after the Resurrection, when he prayed so devoutly that he callused his knees and was nicknamed "camel-knees," since the cud-chewing beasts of burden spend much time resting on their haunches. He wrote his small but forceful Epistle some time between the years 45 to 48 C.E., in the style of his half-brother, and near the end, he suggests the benefits of anointing the sick:

> *Is any among you sick? Let him call for the elders of the church, and let them pray over him, anointing him with oil in the name of the Lord. And the prayer of faith shall be forgiven him. (James 5:14–15)*

Of course, not every devout injunction found in the New Testament is made into a sacred sacrament. To justify its decision, the Roman Church called also upon tradition, which is more than mere custom, but custom fortified by revealed truth.

The tradition of anointing with pure olive oil predates Christianity. Pressed from beaten olives free of all foreign debris, olive oil was used centuries before Christ's time to anoint high priests and kings into their sacred offices. Oil of unction was so important to the Israelites that the Book of Exodus (29:7, 21; 30:23–31) gives several rules for its preparation and use. It was made aromatic by adding balsam, incense, and myrrh.

In Catholicism, aromatic oils or chrisms are used for sacramental anointing in baptism, confirmation, and holy orders. Only pure olive oil, blessed by a bishop on Holy Thursday before the Pater Noster of the Mass—called the Mass of the Chrism—is used in extreme unction.

OIL-SECRETING SAINTS. Mystics and saints claim to have witnessed oil miraculously oozing from venerated relics. In fact, the relics of three major saints—Saint Andrew (d. first century), gift-giver Saint Nicholas (d. fourth century; the model for "Santa Claus"), and Saint Walburga (d. eighth century)—are said to still occasionally exude a mysterious oil with curative powers. The relics of at least a dozen other saints are cherished today

Peter and John, and the "laying on of hands"—a rite that could convey power or health, or exorcise demons.

for their oily excretions (which seem never to have been scientifically tested). Saint Sharbel Makholouf, who died in 1898, secreted up until the time of his beatification in 1965, then he seems to have dried up. (*See* Relics.) For centuries, it was customary to pour oil over relics of martyrs and collect the blessed runoff, called *oleum martyris*.

In Eastern Christendom, extreme unction was never confined to people near death, *in extremis*, but was liberally administered, by anywhere from three to seven bishops, as a spiritual boost to the physical recovery from illness. Nor did holy oil have to be smeared in small crosses on the person's forehead, palms, and feet.

Historically, extreme unction was coupled with a rare and potent rite that Christians borrowed from Jews: exorcism. Although today's horror movies depict a sprinkle of holy water as Satan's searing nemesis, traditionally, blessed oil was applied to body parts of the possessed to drive the Devil out. Mental illness was long misconstrued as evil possession and in the Eastern Orthodox Church, mental disease is still spiritually treated with blessed chrism. (The subject of exorcism merits its own chapter.)

𝔙ows 𝔗hat 𝔅ind

Celibate Priests to Ordained Women

ORDINATION IS THE act of conferring holy orders upon men, and sometimes upon women, such that the candidate becomes a minister of the Church.

The candidate can be a happily married man with children, in some Churches, whereas in other Churches, he must swear that he'll never marry, and certainly never have sex with a woman (or a man). He must live a life that is "celibate" (from the Latin *caelebs*, "unmarried"—which itself is from the Indo-European phrase *kaiwelo libs*, "living alone") as well as chaste (from the Latin *castus*, "pure," implying "no sex of any kind").

In some Churches, a woman candidate for the priesthood can be a wife and a mother, even a lesbian, whereas in other Churches, her gender is an insurmountable obstacle to ordination. Although in ancient times, certainly before the year 2000 B.C.E. in the West, women were high priestesses who dominated religions. We'll examine how the priestess was eclipsed by the priest, and how sexism entered religion.

Pope John Paul II recently assured the faithful that the all-male priesthood in Roman Catholicism does not represent discrimination against women, merely fidelity to Christ's plan for the Church. "I declare," said the supreme pontiff in 1994, "that the Church has no authority whatsoever to confer priestly ordination on women." He issued this brief apostolic certitude "in order that all doubt may be removed" on the issue.

In this chapter, we'll also examine the tangled origins of priestly celibacy, a cautionary tale of good intentions gone awry, as well as the origin of the "glass door" that allows Catholic women to peer into the inner sanctum of the Roman Church but not enter into its hierarchy.

Are the origins of priestly celibacy and the prohibition against women priests rooted in Sacred Scripture or in Church tradition? We'll begin with the origins of the Christian priesthood.

Jesus calls Peter and Andrew to the "priesthood."

SACRAMENT OF HOLY ORDERS: LATE SECOND CENTURY ♦

The Christian Church in general claims that its ministry of bishops, priests, and deacons derives its sacred authority straight from Jesus Christ himself. At the Last Supper, Jesus ordered Peter: "When you have converted, confirm your brethren" (Luke 22:32). And: "Upon this rock I will build my church. . . ." (Matt. 16:18–19).

In the Roman Catholic Church, bishops ordain new priests through a laying on of hands, a symbolic transferal of "the power of orders"—a power to confirm, absolve, bless, consecrate the Eucharist, and ordain more priests. One popular biblical reference for this laying-on-of-hands tradition is the story of the seven men who wished to become ministers of the Gospel shortly after Jesus' Ascension into Heaven:

> *These they set before the apostles, and after they prayed they laid their hands upon them. And the word of the Lord continued to spread, and the number of disciples increased rapidly in Jerusalem. (Acts 6:6–7)*

Claims of inherited power and direct lineage from gods predate Christianity and Judaism by thousands of years. In ancient Sumer, in the Lower Valley of the Euphrates River, high priests around 3500 B.C.E. claimed kinship with the gods, with authority passing along family lines.

For Judaism, though, in the time of the patriarchs, there was no formal priesthood. Abraham, Isaac, and Jacob each built altars and offered sacrifices, but the major function of early holy men was to receive revelations from God and shoot queries back: "inquire of the Lord" (Gen. 25:22).

Not until after the Exodus from Egypt, when Israel became a nation, was the profession of the priesthood assigned to a specific tribe, and clan within that tribe: the tribe of Levi. Moses and his brother Aaron, who had led the Exodus, were both of the tribe of Levi, and the Lord commanded them and their offspring "to serve me as priests" (Exod. 28:1). (Elsewhere in the Bible, it says that priests do not have to be in the line of Aaron.)

FIRST ANTIPOPE. The earliest-known rite for ordination of Christian clergymen is found in the *Apostolic Tradition* of Saint Hippolytus of Rome (b. 170, d. 235), a martyr and brilliant theologian with the dubious distinction of being the Church's first antipope; he reigned from the year 217 until shortly before his death.

Hippolytus was the first Roman priest to write a theological work on Christian dogma and the rites of baptism, the Eucharist, and ordination. In another work, *Chronicle*, he records world history from Adam to the year 234 C.E. His view of the Trinity—which he argued was composed of three distinct Gods (Father, Son, and Holy Spirit), coexisting and indivisible—was deemed heretical by the previous pontiff, Saint Zephyrinus, who maintained that the names Father, Son, and Holy Spirit were only different titles for the same deity. Hippolytus split with Rome and headed a dissident group, becoming the first antipope in history. Eventually, he reconciled with Rome and soon after was martyred.

Most Christians, and all Roman Catholics, believe in "apostolic succession" for valid ordination; that is, that power has been passed down from the apostles to priests. But some denominations, especially Fundamentalist Protestants, feel that the only necessary criterion for a valid ministry is an inward call—a calling—that compels the individual to preach the faith. To support this belief, they point to biblical prophets such as Isaiah, whose ministry began with God's call and Isaiah's personal pledge: "Here I am! Send me!" Furthermore, nowhere does the Bible explicitly say that ordination without apostolic succession is invalid. (*Also see* Papacy.)

MARRIED PRIESTS:
FIRST CENTURY TO TWELFTH CENTURY C.E. ◆

Celibacy has existed in some form or another throughout the history of religions. Its basic function is to hold up as a symbol of holiness a human life freed of sexual wants and dedicated to sacred worship. A priest, a monk, a nun, Jesus Christ, the Buddha, is ideally an hermaphrodite expounding on gender-neutral spirituality. The concept looks good in theory, but is scarred by a long history of abuses, from the sexual shenanigans of priests to cross-pollination between cloistered monks and nuns. Some people have always found sexual abstinence easier than others.

What is the origin behind priestly celibacy in the Roman Catholic Church? Is there any prohibition in Scripture or tradition that would prevent married men from holy ordination? And how did the concepts of celibacy (no marriage) and chastity (no sex) take such iron-strong hold of the Roman Catholic Church, a grip so absolute and unconditional that today it stands as a major obstacle between the reconciliation of Rome with other Christian denominations?

THE FIRST POPE WAS A HAPPILY MARRIED MAN. Let's begin with this fact: The apostle Peter, the Church's first priest—and first pope—was married. The "big fisherman" from the shores of Galilee, whom Jesus hand-selected to head his disciples, was wed at the time to a local woman named Perpetua, and they lived at Capernaum with Perpetua's mother. Jesus was well aware of this. Jesus could have picked a single man, but he didn't. It is amazing how many Catholic treatments of the life of Peter fail to mention that he lived a married life.

Few facts are known, but we're told that Peter left his wife for about three years, during which time he followed Christ. But after Jesus' death, tradition has Peter returning to Perpetua as a husband in good standing. There is no evidence one way or another that they did not live a sexually loving married life together.

One tradition has Peter bringing his wife with him to Rome, where he set up the first Roman See. According to French Catholic scholar Abbé Constant Fouard, Perpetua was active in evangelical work. She preached. She led prayer meetings. And Fouard claims that Perpetua even baptized converts.

Since there was no formal priesthood in these early years of the Church, such claims are not at all outlandish. The new faith needed every evangelist it could get, male or female. In a very real sense, Perpetua was a priest in the

Christ chose Peter to lead the Church, knowing he was a married man.

days before ordination had any formality whatsoever. Peter and Perpetua were husband-and-wife priests. She was Mrs. Pope.

SCRIPTURE FAVORS MARRIED PRIESTS. The truth is, throughout its early years, the Church welcomed married men into the priesthood. Indeed, it preferred married men for their stability, sense of responsibility, and greater age. The only limitation was that a man wishing to be a priest or a bishop could be married only once, a requirement noted in New Testament Scripture, in the First Epistle of Saint Paul to Timothy, written in 64 C.E.:

> *If anyone is eager for the office of bishop . . . he must be blameless, married but once, reserved, prudent, of good conduct, hospitable, a teacher, not a drinker or a brawler. (1 Tim. 3:1–3)*

Timothy was a convert of Saint Paul's and bishop of Ephesus. In the above-quoted letter, Saint Paul, who was responsible more than any other single individual for the blossoming of Christianity, goes on to explain the benefits of married men as clergy:

> *He should rule his own household, keeping his children under control and perfectly respectful. For if a man cannot rule his own household, how is he to take care of the church of God. (1 Tim. 3:4–5)*

MISOGYNISTIC CELIBATES. Many early clergy chose celibacy after the example of Jesus Christ. It was not mandatory at first, but a personal choice. In fact, several popes were themselves married, with children. Others had mistresses.

The sad truth is, a virulent wave of misogyny and antisex swept through the Church in the second, third, and fourth centuries, stirred up by celibate Church fathers such as:

Saint Ambrose, bishop of Milan: "I consider chastity higher than marriage." Ambrose glorified virginity. "I do not condemn marriage," he conceded, "only I consider chastity higher. The former is permissible, the latter I admire." He went so far as to argue that only by remaining a virgin could a woman redeem the sin her parents had committed in conceiving her.

Saint Jerome, a solitary monk and a scholar: "Virginity is natural, marriage came after the Fall." Jerome wrote in a manual for priests, the *Penitential*, that "those joined together in matrimony should abstain from cohabitation three nights before receiving communion," so polluting was sex, even in marriage.

Tertullian, Church father from Carthage, labeled woman "a temple built

*Saint Ambrose, bishop of Milan:
"I consider chastity higher than
marriage."*

over a sewer." Himself a sworn celibate who continually fought sexual temptation, he wrote: "Woman! You are the devil's doorway! You lead astray one whom the devil would not dare attack directly."

Saint Augustine was nearly as bad; he had a pathological dread of intercourse. Augustine wrote about "passionless procreation," that is, copulation to conceive children but devoid of pleasure; sex without arousal. Impossible? Augustine thought not.

Even Saint Paul had been hard on marriage: "Better to marry than to burn," he preached, meaning that if a man can't be chaste, the preferred state, then the next best thing was marriage.

IN JUDAISM. Contrast these views with those found in Judaism. For instance, the Semitic word for "prostitute," *k'deshah*, has the same root as the word for "holy," underscoring the era when sacred prostitutes practiced their trade in temples.

The Talmud sings the praise of the human libido: "Were it not for the sexual instinct, no man would build a house, marry a wife or beget children." Indeed, the Creation accounts in Genesis present marriage as a good and natural state. "Any Jew who has no wife is no man," taught third-century rabbi Eleazar. (*See* Marriage.)

WHY EARLY CHRISTIAN PRIESTS ABHORRED SEX. In the centuries following Christ's death, Christians genuinely believed the world was about to end any day; God's Judgment was due with the next sunrise. Faced with earthly annihilation and heavenly rebirth, procreation became unimportant, children pointless, salvation of the soul paramount. This meant refraining from sin, especially sexual sin, and the major Church fathers exhorted unmarried men to remain celibate and married men to practice chastity.

Indeed, celibacy was deemed a higher human calling than marriage.

Woman, once indispensable as wife and mother, lost her raison d'être in society and came to be viewed as man's greatest obstacle to salvation. Men, acknowledging their weakness for women, cursed women for it.

Paul taught that at the time of the Last Judgment, virgins would rise to Heaven's uppermost echelon. In fact, he preached, lifelong virgins would be the first to be saved, followed by convert celibates like himself; last would be folk who married. (Hell was reserved for those who had sex outside of marriage.)

Clearly, celibacy was *the* state to aspire to. And because "The End" was near. Soon, in the Kingdom of God, all good Christians would be sexless angels. Many male followers of Jesus abandoned their wives and children. The most extreme actually castrated themselves to cut off the source of their lust.

Thus, celibacy first appears in Christianity out of apocalyptic expectations. And as decades passed, then centuries passed, and no Apocalypse arrived, the Church was in a doctrinal bind; its dim view of intercourse, and exalted stand on virginity, was solidly entrenched. Still, at this time in history, no official law yet forbade priests, bishops, and even popes from marrying and fathering children. Many did.

CELIBACY BECOMES LAW:
SECOND LATERAN COUNCIL, 1139 C.E. ◆

Wrangling within the Church over the issue of priestly celibacy began early in the fourth century. We'll follow it step by step.

306 C.E., THE SYNOD OF ELVIRA. This regional council in Spain decreed that all clerics, even those already married, were to live in continence;

Woman locked into a "chastity belt" slips the key to a lover as her husband bids her good-bye.

that is, a man could continue to cohabit with his wife, but they could no longer copulate. The "continent marriage" idea was largely ignored from the start. The council also stated that bishops in particular should not be married men, thus ignoring Saint Paul's Epistle to Timothy. In turn, most priests ignored the regional decree altogether.

325 C.E., THE ECUMENICAL COUNCIL OF NICAEA. This council disagreed with the Synod of Elvira; it declined to make any prohibition against married priests. However, the council did condemn the practice in which supposedly celibate priests harbored young women in their households in order to "test their sexual restraint and prove their moral strength." It seems unlikely that all such priests sincerely intended to resist temptation.

419 C.E., THE COUNCIL OF CARTHAGE. This council came down hard on the side of celibacy, extending it to include subdeacons, as well as bishops, deacons, and ministers. But the ruling was not universally binding. Furthermore, the breakup of the Roman Empire at the end of the century tossed the wrench of chaos into the workings of the Church hierarchy. Communication all but broke down.

567 C.E., THE SECOND COUNCIL OF TOURS. This Church body decreed that any cleric found guilty of having sex with his wife would be excommunicated for one year. So many clerics were discovered to be sleeping with their wives that instead of losing hundreds of priests through excommunication, the Church decided to punish the wives with excommunication. The later Italian bishop Rathurio said that if he excommunicated unchaste priests, there would be no males left but young boys to administer the sacraments.

580 C.E. Pope Pelagius II tolerated married clerics as long as they did not give Church property and money to wives and children. And as long as married priests bequeathed their deathbed estates to the Church.

In truth, for the next 550 years, the Church in Rome did not officially forbid priests from marrying (proscriptions occasionally were made against bishops marrying), but continued to insist that priestly marriage be continent. However, priests, bishops, and popes fathered children, making a mockery of the continent marriage.

1012–24 C.E. Pope Benedict VIII promulgated drastic canons prohibiting marriage—and concubinage, since priests forbidden to marry were taking mistresses. The pope even forbade subdeacons from marrying, and he labeled all offspring from priestly marriages illegitimate, thus condemning them to a life of serfdom.

Still, these statutes were not universal, nor did they nullify the marriages of major clerics who defied the prohibitions. And there were many. No married priest could understand how having sex with his wife was adultery; nor could unmarried priests see what was wrong with partaking of the sacrament of matrimony.

Though it is no doubt an exaggeration, it's been said that during the Middle Ages, in certain metropolitan cities like Milan, *all* priests had wives and were themselves good husbands and proud fathers.

FIRST BINDING LAWS. In response to this situation, the Second Lateran Council of 1139 enacted the first written and binding laws making holy orders incompatible with marriage for the universal Christian Church. The Second Lateran Council also put an end to the sham of continent marriages for priests.

However, the plague of the Black Death, the Hundred Years' War, and the Western Schism within the Church brought about a general decline in clerical morality. As did the rise of the secular spirit that ushered in the Renaissance. Most historians of this later period point to clerical marriage as again being commonplace, and to the sons of priests who were legitimated, and, as in the case of the educator Erasmus, even ordained to the priesthood with a dispensation from the Roman Curia.

LUTHER CHAMPIONS MARRIED CLERGY. This laxity in priestly celibacy played into the hands of Martin Luther. In his *Commentary on the Galatians*, Luther boasts that his reform movement would have made little headway against the papacy at Rome if clerical celibacy then had been as highly regarded as it was back in the time of Jerome, Ambrose, and Augustine; then "celibacy was something remarkable in the eyes of the world, a thing that makes a man angelic."

Martin Luther claimed that clerical celibacy in the Roman Church helped the spread of his reform movement.

When Martin Luther and other Reformers opted for a married clergy, the Council of Trent in 1563 passed stronger-worded legislation demanding celibacy of its priests. Basically, this is when the Roman Catholic Church formulated its intransigent position on the matter.

In 1920, Benedict XV (1914–22) roundly condemned a Christian organization that championed the abolition of clerical celibacy, declaring that the Church "never would abrogate or mitigate the law of priestly celibacy"; which is the stand of the current pope.

The Church's stand was firmly bolstered by Pope Paul VI's 1967 encyclical on the sacredness of celibacy, *Sacerdotalis Caelibatus,* "On Priestly Celibacy." In this view, a priest, for the honor of Christ and the coming of his Kingdom of Heaven, must be totally available to his congregation and free of domestic responsibilities.

Thus, the pontiff was saying, the law of clerical celibacy is not of biblical or divine origin. It is strictly of ecclesiastical design. Consequently, it is not an infallible doctrine and theoretically can be overturned by any pope at any time.

In general, today, celibacy is considered the preferred state of spiritual leaders in Roman Catholicism, Eastern Orthodoxy, Hinduism, Buddhism, and Taoism. On the other hand, celibacy falls short of marriage, which conveys greater honor, in the religions of Judaism, Islam, Confucianism, and Protestantism.

WHEN GOD WAS A WOMAN: PRE-ELEVENTH CENTURY B.C.E. ◆

It is impossible to understand the resistance to women becoming priests without some background.

In the ancient past, women were high priestesses. This was quite standard throughout the Near East in the centuries when goddesses such as Astarte, Isis, and Ishtar reigned supreme. When, in fact, for many peoples, god was a woman.

A goddess was worshiped for her fertility, and also revered as the wise creator and source of universal order. At this time, women bought and sold property and traded in the marketplace, and the inheritance of title and property was passed from mother to daughter.

What happened? How did men take over religion? Take over everything?

Clues, believe it or not, are in the Old Testament; and the answer has to do with the battle between Hebrew monotheism and the Israelites' lapses into pagan worship of "false gods and goddesses." Particularly the goddess Ashtoreth, a Queen of Heaven to the Canaanites, and her male consort, Baal.

The Canaanites had a flourishing civilization in Palestine and southern Syria in the second millennium B.C.E. But the Old Testament supporters of monotheism were highly critical of the Canaanites' "corrupt religion."

Harsh references to the Israelites worshiping Ashtoreth (also called Asherah) appear in Judges and Samuel:

Judges 2:13—"And they forsook the Lord and worshiped Baal and Ashtoreths."

Judges 3:7—"And the people did what was evil in the sight of the Lord, forgetting the Lord their God, and served the Baals and Asherahs."

1 Samuel 7:3, 4—"Samuel spoke to the house of Israel, saying . . . put away the strange gods and Ashtoreths from among you and prepare your hearts for the Lord . . . and he will deliver you out of the hands of the Philistines."

The time frame of Judges and Samuel is about the eleventh century B.C.E. And it is here in Hebrew Scriptures that men, particularly Levite priests, destroyed the worship of goddesses and restricted the role of women as priests. With this came the final destruction of the matrilineal system, and the subsequent triumph of monotheism of a single male God, and of the all-male priesthood.

Hebrew priests, by portraying goddesses as wanton, depraved, and pagan, took control of religion. The story of Eve—her wickedness, her tempting of Adam, and the consequent curse on the human race—provides a basis for this hostile coup.

ALL-MALE CLUB OF CIRCUMCISION. Historian Merlin Stone, in *When God Was a Woman*, claims that the Adam and Eve legend was concocted by Levite priests to justify the suppression of women. Thus, the Bible opens with one woman, the first woman, sinning and causing centuries of grief for all of humanity. Men masterminded a takeover, says Stone, stripping women of power and blaming them for everything bad that occurs in the world.

Furthermore, men made the initiation into their all-male club the rite of circumcision, which became the covenant or contract between the new God of Abraham and humankind. How could women possibly take back power? In Genesis 17:7–10, Abraham merits his name change from "Abram" once he agrees to undergo circumcision as his "signature" on the new pact with God. In return, God promises Abraham divine right to the land of Canaan. Thus, not only does man snatch away the reins of religion from the goddess, man claims divine right to the goddess's home turf. The takeover is total.

Writing about the early chapters of Genesis, Stone notes: "We may indeed find that the seemingly innocent myth of Paradise and how the world

FALL OF THE GODDESS (left to right):
Athena, wisdom and the arts;
Hera, marriage and birth;
Aphrodite, love and beauty;
Artemis, the moon and the hunt.

began was actually carefully constructed and propagated to 'keep women in their place,' the place assigned to them by the Levite tribe of biblical Canaan." Moses, traditional "author" of Genesis, belonged to the Levite clan.

GODDESSES' LAST STAND. Ashtoreth, as well as other goddesses, was still worshiped by some peoples as late as the third century C.E. Saint Clement of Alexandria (150–215), the Greek theologian, reproduces a saying from *The Gospel According to the Egyptians* that puts these words into the mouth of Jesus Christ: "I have come to destroy the works of the female." Historians say the reference here is to the goddess Isis, popular in Christ's day.

Goddesses fall fast in the Christian era:

• In 300 C.E., the "Christian" emperor Constantine (as yet unbaptized) closed the ancient sanctuary of *Ashtoreth* at Aphaca and thus put an end to her worship throughout Canaan, claiming it was "immoral." The emperor himself was in the process of converting to Christianity.

• In 380 C.E., the Christian emperor Theodosius closed the temple of the goddess known as *Artemis* (or *Diana*) at Ephesus in western Anatolia; he despised "the religion of women." He also closed goddess temples in Eleusis and several in Rome.

• In 450 C.E., the Christian emperor Justinian converted the several remaining temples of the goddess *Isis* into Christian Churches.

• In the same period, in Athens, the Parthenon of the Acropolis, a sacred site of goddesses since the Mycenaean times, was converted into a Christian church.

• In Arabia, in the seventh century, Muhammad put an end to the national worship of the sun goddess *Al-Lat* (the same deity as Ashtoreth in Arabic paganism) and the goddess *Al-Uzza*. *Al-Lah* means God, *Al-Lat* means "goddess."

Coming full circle, Muhammad picked up the thematic thread of the Levite priests when he wove into the Koran:

Men have authority over women because God has made the one superior to the other and because they spend their wealth to maintain them. So good women are obedient, guarding the unseen parts as God has guarded them. (Koran 4:34)

Muhammad stated: "When Eve was created, Satan rejoiced."

The Old Testament, which greatly influenced the development of Christianity and Islam, came together during the very centuries that male priests worked hard to stamp out the pagan worship of goddesses. Indeed, many of its authors were the ones stamping hardest.

It must be said that in early Judaism, women still could become prophets through whom God spoke, and there were several, but a woman's primary role became that of wife and mother. In the temple, and later in the synagogue, women were not allowed to lead services or to teach from the Torah. To this day, many Jewish men are taught to offer the daily prayer: "Blessed art Thou O Lord our God, King of the Universe, who has not made me a woman."

By the time Christianity began to flower in the West, the goddess was dead and women were, in a sense, confined to the kitchen, veiled, aproned, and on their knees.

ORDINATION OF WOMEN:
PROTESTANTISM, TWENTIETH CENTURY ◆

In 1994, the Church of England joined more than ten other provinces of the Anglican Communion in carrying out the ordination of women to the priesthood. Both Parliament and the queen of England ratified the decision. The ordinations of thirty-two women took place on March 12, in the cathedral at Bristol. Additional ordinations that one year alone raised the number of women priests in the Church of England to more than twelve hundred.

This was the same year that Pope John Paul II, while seeking reconciliation with the Anglican Church, said: "I declare that the Church has no authority whatsoever to confer priestly ordination on women, and that this judgment is to be definitively held by all the Church's faithful."

How can two faiths that spring from the same roots and worship the same God and lay claim to the same Scriptures espouse such antithetical views? Can they ever reconcile their differences?

WHAT CHRISTIAN SCRIPTURE SAYS. In the New Testament, Jesus welcomes women into his new church. They become local leaders and traveling evangelists. Baptism, not circumcision, becomes the sign of Christ's calling of men and women into service.

Yet gender contradictions plague the New Testament. In the Fourth Gospel, for instance, in the story "Jesus Meets the Samaritan Woman" (4:1–42), John elevates women to an equal status with men; John clearly liked women.

Paul, on the other hand, once a notorious womanizer, would limit women to childbearing. In his Epistles, he blames woman for the Fall. He claims a woman's salvation lies in giving birth. In Paul's words, we can see the roots of the Roman Catholic attitude toward the "fairer sex":

> Let women learn in silence with all submission. For I do not allow a woman to teach, or to exercise authority over men; but she is to keep quiet. For Adam was formed first, then Eve. And Adam was not deceived, but the woman was deceived and was in sin. Yet women will be saved by childbearing, if they continue in faith and love and holiness with modesty. (1 Tim. 2:11–15)

Yet, in other parts of the Pastoral Epistles, Paul mentions women as his missionary coworkers, using the same terms for women and men who evangelize. Paul, once a Jew, even takes for granted that God might call on women to be prophets, as women were in Judaism. (It's wrong to speak of the exclusion of women as priests in the New Testament, since no formal ministry existed in the years that the Gospels were written.) In truth, women played a large role in the early Church.

In Paul's Letter to the Ephesians, we read:

> Wives, submit yourselves to your own husbands as to the Lord. For the husband is the head of the wife even as Christ is the head of the Church. . . . Therefore the Church is subject to Christ, so let the wives be to their own husbands in everything. (Eph. 5:22–24)

The downfall of women as active players in the Church really arrives in the third and fourth centuries, when, as we've seen, a new breed of celibate

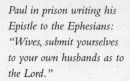

Paul in prison writing his Epistle to the Ephesians: "Wives, submit yourselves to your own husbands as to the Lord."

priests views women as temptresses, as occasions for their own sins. All sorts of proscription manifest. Women can't teach. Women cannot enter the church sanctuary. Women must remain silent in church. Women must cover their heads in church.

Saint John Chrysostom, a teacher in the fifth century, warned: "The woman taught once and ruined everything. On this account . . . let her not teach."

Saint Augustine in the same period claimed that man, but not woman, was made in the image of God. Woman was made *from* man and therefore a woman is not complete without a man.

If there is a major theme throughout these centuries, it is this: Women are the Daughters of Eve. As the later theologian Hubmaier wrote: "Adam knew very well that the words of the serpent were contrary to the words of God. Yet Adam willed to eat the fruit against his own conscience so as not to anger his rib, his flesh, Eve. He would have preferred not to do it." In other words, without woman, man would follow his natural inclination toward virtue. Women lead men into sin.

THE SINGULAR REASON FOR ORDAINING MEN ONLY. Pope Paul VI (1963–78) said: "The Church does not consider herself authorized to admit women to priestly ordination." Why?

Pope Paul explained: "The real reason is that, in giving the Church her fundamental constitution, her theological anthropology, Christ established things this way." That is, Christ chose only men as his apostles. This is the primary argument of the Catholic Church. And yet Christ's first choice for an apostle was a married man—who went on to become pope. The inherent contradictions are hard to overlook.

In truth, there is no Scriptural prohibition against the ordination of women. Other Christian denominations have come to realize this. As one contemporary author writes: "Today, married men have no objection to their wives being presidents, prime ministers, leading politicians, judges, lawyers, doctors and so on. But celibate priests cannot bear the thought of women, whom they have renounced, being on a par with them."

Many denominations now ordain women. By 1995, for instance, there were more than twenty-two hundred female Anglican priests; four women were bishops. That same year, Pope John Paul reiterated the stand of his predecessors: Never will there be a female Roman Catholic priest. The supreme pontiff did make one concession: Women can now assist a priest in serving Mass.

Any pope, at any time, can open ordination to women. With the dwindling numbers of new priests entering the Church, perhaps ordaining women would provide the kind of spiritual rejuvenation the priesthood so clearly needs. But perhaps women would take holy orders in such large numbers that within a few decades, they'd predominate as priests, bishops, archbishops, and cardinals. There might even be a woman pope. Women would be in charge of religion again, as they were three thousand years ago. Maybe this is the supreme pontiff's real fear: women taking back the reins of religion. But how bad could that be? It might be just what Christianity needs.

Feasts and Festivals

CHAPTER

1 2

Christian Feasts

Ash Wednesday to Palm Sunday

THROUGHOUT THE HISTORY of human culture, certain days—holy days—have been set aside to celebrate or reenact religious events. A religion's followers may feast or fast, gorge themselves with food and drink or purify their bodies through days of abstinence.

The Romans, who seem to have partied continually, did in fact do so: more than one hundred days each year were spent in celebration of various gods and goddesses. Days not considered sacred, called *dies vacantes*, "vacant days," the Romans set aside for work. Our word "vacation," a time for rest and relaxation, derives from the Latin for "vacant days."

Ancient customs could be comical by today's standards (and vice versa). Among the pre-Columbian Maya, the first month of the New Year, called Pop, was a time for renewal in a figurative and literal sense: last year's pottery, fiber mats, and clothes were destroyed, and new pots were cast, new mats woven, new clothes sewn.

People reenforce their identity with certain feasts—like Jewish Passover and Christian Easter. The Jew understands his or her status as a member of the "people of God," so chosen during the Exodus of the Hebrews from Egypt in the thirteenth century B.C.E. to be witness to the liberating love of Yahweh. Passover commemorates the Exodus. Jewish feasts are considered in the next chapter.

On the other hand, the Christian understands his or her status as a member of the "new people of God," so chosen by Christ, who was crucified and resurrected by God. Easter commemorates the Resurrection.

Birth, puberty, marriage, and death—all have merited special days of celebration. And new holy days—and holidays—are continually added to the calendar.

In America, the pilgrims, having survived a harsh winter, added Thanksgiving Day; the colonists freed from the British crown penciled in Independence Day; blacks added a commemoration to Martin Luther King. In Israel, Holocaust Day, commemorating the systematic destruction of European Jews by Nazi Germany, has been placed on the national calendar. Today, in America at least, there's been a strong tendency to confuse the sacred with the secular, to shop for bargains at malls and cheer football teams in front of television sets when meditation is the appropriate activity of the day.

In this chapter, we'll examine the origins of Christianity's most profound holy days and the events they commemorate. First, though, it's important to understand a religion's ecclesiastical calendar and how that definition of a year came to be. For instance, the Jewish religious year is grounded in the divinely revealed Law of the Old Testament. But the Christian cycle of feasts and fasts has never been based on divine revelation.

CHRISTIAN RELIGIOUS YEAR: POST–FOURTH CENTURY c.e. ◆

The Christian liturgical year is an annual cycle of seasons and days that commemorates the life, death, and Resurrection of Jesus Christ and the virtuous lives of his major followers. It is certainly not the calendar Jesus himself followed.

Jesus, in his early life, was bound by the Hebrew calendar to the law of the Sabbath and to observing feasts and fasts prescribed in the Old Testament. Although as his ministry developed he became less concerned with outward conformity to Jewish legal sanctions—"The sabbath was made for man," he said, "and not man for the sabbath" (Mark 2:27)—his Last Supper was nonetheless a Passover feast. This was the chief springtime feast, under a lunar-month calendar of the ancient nomadic Hebrews, celebrated at the first full moon of the vernal equinox.

The basic concept of a liturgical year—Christian, Jewish, or other—is deeply rooted in primitive man's impulse and need to follow Creation's own two linked cycles: (1) the cosmic phases of the moon and the solar equinoxes and (2) nature's periodic seasons for sowing and reaping. Cosmic laws impose a calendar upon us. Divine Law, as we'll see, adheres closely to this calendar.

For the first three centuries of Christianity, the only real festal observance was Easter (Christ's glorious Resurrection), and to a lesser extent Pentecost (the Descent of the Holy Spirit upon the apostles).

From the fourth century onward, the liturgical calendar began to grow more complex. One of the first developments was that of Holy Week: the

The Resurrection, start of the Catholic liturgical calendar. Mary Magdalene, Salome, and Mary, the mother of James, at the empty tomb.

feast days leading up to Easter Sunday, a period in which Christ is betrayed, suffers, is crucified, and dies. We'll examine each one of these feast days.

The full calendar, we'll see, expanded around Easter and Holy Week, with Lent and Ash Wednesday added on. Only somewhat later came the Christmas-Epiphany cycle, centered around Christ's birth. This cycle then served as a second nucleus that itself expanded to include the preparatory season of Advent.

In summary: The Christian liturgical calendar began with the Resurrection, the primary feast in Christianity; it then expanded to include events pertaining to Christ's death—the *paschal cycle*; then to events connected with Christ's birth—the *Nativity cycle*. Death, in Christianity, was always viewed as more significant than birth. Much later came feast days of the Blessed Virgin Mary: her Immaculate Conception (made dogma in 1854), and her Assumption into Heaven (made dogma in 1950).

SUNDAY AS THE LORD'S DAY: LATE FIRST CENTURY C.E. ◆

The Hebrews had long observed a seven-day week, of which the last day, Saturday or the Sabbath, was a holiday given over to rest—a reminder of God's day of rest after completing his Creation.

By Jesus' time, the Sabbath had been consecrated to the Hebrew Yahweh and was highly sacred, replete with restrictions as to what activities one could or could not engage in. A principal hallmark of Judaism was "keeping holy the Sabbath."

After Christ's death, his followers retained the Jewish seven-day week, but by the end of the apostolic age—the first century C.E.—as the Church became predominantly Gentile in membership, the first day of the week, Sunday, become holy to Christians. Sunday, no longer Saturday, was the proper time when Christians assembled to worship.

The biblical origin of Sunday as the "first" day of the week is found in Mark 16:2, when he speaks of the Lordship of Jesus Christ made manifest in the Resurrection, which occurred "very early in the morning on the first day of the week."

Named "the Lord's Day," Sunday became a symbol by which Christians differentiated themselves from Jews. The first unmistakable reference in Christian literature to Sunday as a special day bearing the word "Lord" appears to be in John's Book of Revelation, written about 95 C.E. John explains how his lengthy vision of the world's final Apocalypse came to him (1:10): "I was in the Spirit on the Lord's day."

However, it was not until Christianity became the official religion of the Roman Empire in the early decades of the fourth century that the Lord's Day took over the full significance of the Sabbath, and that the observance of the seventh day was dropped by Christians and left entirely to the Jews. By that time, each Sunday was regarded as a weekly celebration of the paschal mystery of Christ's Resurrection. In other words, each Sunday was a mini-Easter.

The astrological origin of the word *Sunday* is revealed in its Latin name, *dies solis*, literally "sun's day," for the Roman god of the sun. It entered English through the Anglo-Saxon equivalent, *sunnandaeg*.

The astrological origin of the word *Saturday* is revealed in its Latin name, *Saturni dies*, literally "Saturn's day," for the Roman god Saturn, thought to be the father of Jove. It entered English through the Anglo-Saxon equivalent, *Saeternesdaeg*. All of our weekdays are named after pagan gods, as we'll see.

EASTER SUNDAY:
EARLIEST OBSERVANCE, SECOND CENTURY c.e. ◆

> WHEN OBSERVED: *ON THE SUNDAY FOLLOWING THE FIRST FULL MOON*
> *AFTER THE VERNAL EQUINOX, FALLING BETWEEN MARCH 22 AND*
> *APRIL 25.*
> COMMEMORATES: *JESUS CHRIST'S RESURRECTION FROM THE DEAD.*

In the Christian faith, Easter is the most sacred of holy days because it commemorates the cornerstone miracle of the faith—had Christ not risen, Christianity could never have flourished, since the man Jesus would not have been proved to be the Son-of-God Jesus. But the holy day's name derives from an ancient pagan festival and is the name of the Saxon goddess of spring and offspring, Eastre.

How did a raucous pagan ritual evolve into a solemn Christian service?

Second-century Christian missionaries, spreading out among Teutonic tribes north of Rome, encountered numerous "heathen" religious observances. Whenever possible, the missionaries tried not to interfere too strongly with entrenched and popular customs. Rather, quietly—and often ingeniously—they attempted to transform pagan practices into ceremonies that harmonized with Christian doctrine.

There was a very special reason for this. Converts publicly partaking in a Christian ceremony, and on a day when no one else of their clan was celebrating, stood out like the proverbial sore thumb, easy targets for persecution. But if a Christian rite was staged on the same day as a long-observed pagan celebration, and if the two modes of worship were not glaringly different, then the new converts might live to make other converts.

The Christian missionaries astutely observed that the centuries-old festival to Eastre, commemorated at the start of spring, coincided with the time of year of their own observance of the miracle of Christ's Resurrection. Thus, the Resurrection was subsumed under the protective rubric Eastre—later spelled Easter—saving the lives of countless Christians.

It just so happened that Eastre, a fertility goddess (the ancient word *eastre* means "spring"), had as her earthly symbol the prolific hare, or rabbit. Hence, the origin of the *Easter bunny*.

At the feast to Eastre, an ox was sacrificed and the image of his horns carved into ritual bread—which evolved into the twice-scored Easter biscuits we call *hot cross buns*. In fact, the word "bun" derives from the Saxon for "sacred ox," *boun*.

For several decades, Easter was variously celebrated on a Friday, Saturday, or Sunday. Finally, in 325, the Council of Nicaea, convened by the emperor Constantine, issued the so-called Easter Rule: Easter should be celebrated on "the first Sunday after the first full moon on or after the vernal equinox." Consequently, Easter is astronomically bound never to fall earlier than March 22 or later than April 25.

At this same council, Constantine decreed that the cross be adopted as the official symbol of the young faith.

The high significance of Easter as the feast of Christ's Resurrection led early Christians to believe that the celebration could not be undertaken without spiritual preparation. Their souls needed conditioning through days—eventually, forty days—of fasting, penance, and prayer. That became the function of Lent.

It is interesting that the holiest day of the liturgical Christian year, Easter Sunday, bears the name of the pagan sex goddess Eastre and the pagan sun god Solis.

LENT: EARLIEST OBSERVANCE, FOURTH CENTURY ◆

WHEN OBSERVED: FOR FORTY DAYS PRIOR TO EASTER SUNDAY.
PURPOSE: PENITENTIAL PREPARATION FOR THE FEAST OF THE
RESURRECTION.

As the Church moved away from the fervor of apostolic times, people's piety began to wan, and bishops cast about for some celebration that would deepen the devotional approach to Easter, climax of the spiritual year.

Many Christians had already reserved a period prior to Easter for fasting, confession, and schooling candidates for baptism on Easter Eve. But the time frame was never fixed, rules never formalized. Different groups of Christians followed different customs—some fasted several days, others several weeks. Some observed a total fast for exactly forty days (minus the Lord's day, Sunday), a feast called *Quadragesima*, which would evolve into Lent.

The number forty certainly carried much religious significance: Jesus fasted for forty days in the desert after his baptism and before beginning his public ministry; in the Old Testament, Moses and Elias spent forty days in the wilderness; the Jews wandered forty years in search of the Promised Land; Jonah gave the city of Nineveh forty days' grace in which to repent.

Thus, by mid–fourth century, the duration of Lent—the word itself means "lengthening spring days," from the Indo-European *langat-tin*, "long" + "day"—became more or less fixed at forty days, less Sundays; the time frame did not become official, though, until the eighth century.

What constituted a fast varied: no meat for forty days; no milk and eggs; or only one light meal a day.

In the Western Church today, Lent begins six and a half weeks before Easter, providing forty fast days when Sundays are excluded. In the Eastern Church, however, Lent begins eight weeks before Easter, since fasting is excluded on Saturdays and Sundays. Today, too, a fast can be as slight an inconvenience as abstaining from chocolate or ice cream for the duration. A token fast.

ASH WEDNESDAY: SIXTH CENTURY C.E. ◆

The first day of Lent, a Wednesday, was always special, and it came to be called Ash Wednesday from a custom involving ashes, long a symbol for repentance. Early Christians approached the church altar to have the ashes of blessed palm leaves scored on their forehead in the shape of a cross—which more often than not resembled a smudge.

Today, as then, the priest applies the ashes and intones, "Thou art dust and unto dust shalt thou return" (Gen. 3:19). A worshiper wears the mark on his forehead throughout the day as a symbol of his sorrow for his sins. The blessed palm leaves that are burned to make the ashes are, in fact, "leftovers" from the previous year's Palm Sunday. This Lenten custom originated in the sixth century, during the papacy of Gregory the Great.

The astrological origin of the word *Wednesday* is revealed in its Latin name, *Mercurii dies*, literally, "Mercury's day." It entered English through the Anglo-Saxon equivalent, *Wodnes daeg*. Mercury, in Roman mythology, was the messenger of the gods, usually depicted with winged feet; he is not unlike a Christian angel. Woden was the Saxon god of war and victory.

PALM SUNDAY:
EARLIEST OBSERVANCE, FOURTH CENTURY c.e. ◆

WHEN OBSERVED: *THE SUNDAY BEFORE EASTER.*
COMMEMORATES: *JESUS' TRIUMPHANT ENTRY INTO JERUSALEM.*

In the Christian Church, the entire week prior to Jesus' death and Resurrection is considered holy and observed on a daily basis. On the Sunday before his Resurrection, Jesus rode victoriously into Jerusalem, cheered by crowds, fanned by palm branches. As Matthew (21:8–9) records:

Most of the crowd spread their garments on the road, and others cut branches from the trees and . . . shouted, "Hosanna to the Son of David! Blessed is he who comes in the name of the Lord!"

Palm Sunday observance is thought to have begun with the Christian Passover, or Pascha, a celebration of Christ's death *and* Resurrection. A Palm Sunday procession, replete with palm branches, is first mentioned in the

*The entry into Jerusalem—
Palm Sunday.*

travel writings of the Spanish nun Etheria. Rome itself did not stage regular Palm Sunday processions until late in the eleventh century.

As the custom of blessing palm branches spread, countries lacking the tree were forced to make substitutions. Hence, Palm Sunday became known in other lands as: Olive Sunday, Willow Bough Sunday, Blossom Sunday, and simply the generic Branch Sunday—any branch would do—as the day was known for a time in England.

As mentioned, "leftover" leaves are burned to make ashes for the next Ash Wednesday's smudge.

Palm Sunday begins *Holy Week*, which follows Jesus' activities day by day through his death. By the late fourth century all of the following feasts, major and minor, were being celebrated.

HOLY MONDAY. Twenty-four hours after Jesus rode triumphantly into Jerusalem, he's thought to have cleansed the temple by chasing out money changers: "My house shall be called a house of prayer, but you make it a den of robbers" (Matt. 21:13). Then he preached and healed the sick. Events, though, were about to escalate. Holy Monday is commemorated with private meditation and Mass.

The astrological origin of the word *Monday* is revealed in its Latin name, *Lunae dies*, literally, "moon's day." It entered English through the Anglo-Saxon equivalent, *Monandaeg*.

HOLY TUESDAY. Jesus addressed his disciples on the Mount of Olives, speaking about the sad destruction of Jerusalem and the signs of the last day. This is also the day when the plotting Pharisees attempted to trap Jesus into making a blasphemous statement: "Then went the Pharisees, and took counsel how they might entangle him in his talk" (Matt. 22:15–21). It is also from this day, through Luke (20:22–25), that we get the familiar quotation: "Render unto Caesar the things which are Caesar's, and unto God the things which are God's." Holy Tuesday is commemorated with private meditation and Mass.

The astrological origin of the word *Tuesday* is revealed in its Latin name, *dies Martis*, literally, "Mars's day." It entered English through the Anglo-Saxon equivalent, *Tiwesdaeg*. Mars was the Roman god of war; Tyr was the Saxon name for him.

HOLY WEDNESDAY. Once widely known as "Spy Wednesday," this is the day Judas Iscariot agreed, for thirty pieces of silver, to show Jesus' enemies where they could capture him easily without arousing the populace. Holy Wednesday is commemorated with private meditation and Mass.

MAUNDY THURSDAY. This is associated with three tragic and closely spaced events near the end of Jesus' life: his Last Supper with the apostles, his Agony in the Garden, and his arrest.

The strange word "maundy" is thought to be a corruption of the Latin *mandatum*, "commandment of God," and borrowed from Jesus' words (as they appear in the Latin Vulgate) at the Last Supper: "A new commandment I give to you [*Mandatum novum do vobis*], that you love one another; even as I have loved you" (John 13:34–35). Thus, traditionally, Thursday has been the day of "brotherly love."

At the Last Supper, Jesus washed the feet of his disciples, an ancient act of humility that has appealed to the imaginations of people down through the ages. Kings washed the feet of the poor. Feudal lords washed the feet of serfs. Popes washed the feet of cardinals. During the Middle Ages, a ceremony in which a priest washed the feet of the indigent was called a *maunde*—the term deriving from Christ's "mandatum" statement.

Maundy Thursday services have been varied and deeply symbolic of Christ's arrest and predicament: altar candles are extinguished to symbolize the victory of the forces of darkness; the altar is stripped bare and washed in preparation for Christ's Resurrection; Hosts or wafers are consecrated in commemoration of Christ's initiation of the Sacrament of the Eucharist at the Last Supper.

The astrological origin of the word *Thursday* is revealed in its Latin name, *dies Jovis*, literally, "Jove's day." (Jove was another name of the Roman god, Jupiter.) It entered English through the Anglo-Saxon equivalent, *Thunresdaeg*, or "Thor's day." Jove and Thor were gods of thunder.

GOOD FRIDAY. Scourged and forced to carry his own cross, Christ is crucified on "Good" Friday, the blackest day in Christian history.

The origin of the word "good" is a perplexing mystery. Some scholars argue that "good" is a corruption of "God" and that early Christians commemorating the sad event called it God's Friday. Others claim that "good"

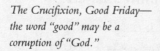

*The Crucifixion, Good Friday—
the word "good" may be a
corruption of "God."*

signifies the bounty of blessings—indeed, salvation—Christ won for humankind by his sacrifice.

Tre Ore, "Three Hours," is the name of the solemn service—from noon to 3:00 P.M.—that has represented over the ages Christ's three hours on the cross. During this time, Christians meditate on the Seven Last Words of Christ, the seven utterances Jesus delivered from the cross, culled from the Four Gospels:

1. "Father, forgive them, for they know not what they do" (Luke 23:34).
2. "Truly I say to you, today you will be with me in Paradise" (Luke 23:43).
3. "Woman, behold, your son! . . . Behold, your Mother!" (John 19:26–27).
4. "My God, my God, why hast thou forsaken me?" (Matt. 27:46; Mark 15:34).
5. "I thirst" (John 19:28).
6. "It is finished" (John 19:30).
7. "Father, into Thy hands I commend my spirit" (Luke 23:46).

The astrological origin of the word *Friday* is revealed in its Latin name, *dies Veneris*, literally, "Venus's day." It entered English through the Anglo-Saxon equivalent, *frigedaeg*, or "Frigg's day." Frigg was the wife of Woden, chief of the Saxon gods.

HOLY SATURDAY. This brings both Holy Week and the forty-day season of Lent to a close. It was the day for baptisms in the early Church. Also, a tall "Paschal candle" was lit, placed on the altar, and embedded with five grains of incense, representing Christ's five wounds. The candle remained on the altar for forty days, a living presence of the risen Christ, until the feast of his Ascension into Heaven. Holy Saturday is also called Easter Eve. Thus, the period from Ash Wednesday through Easter Sunday is the most profound duration in the Christian calendar.

ASCENSION OF JESUS CHRIST:
EARLIEST OBSERVANCE, PERHAPS 68 C.E. ◆

WHEN OBSERVED: *FORTY DAYS AFTER EASTER.*
COMMEMORATES: *JESUS CHRIST'S ASCENT INTO HEAVEN.*

After Jesus' Resurrection from the dead, we read in the Acts of the Apostles that "he presented himself alive after his passion by many proofs" and appeared to his disciples during a period of forty days, speaking to them "of the Kingdom of God." On the fortieth day, after promising them, "You shall receive power when the Holy Spirit has come upon you," he ascended into Heaven—"a cloud received him out of their sight."

For this reason, the fortieth day after Easter (always a Thursday) has since early times been observed as the Feast of the Ascension in the Christian Church. However, in the Gospel according to John, the glorification described by the Ascension story seems to have taken place immediately after the Resurrection. And while the imagery of the account in Luke is similar to that of Acts, there is no mention of a period of forty days.

Tradition holds that the day was first celebrated in 68 C.E., and three hundred years later, Saint Augustine claimed it originated with the apostles. However, it did not enter the liturgical calendar until late in the third century, nor become a major theme of Christian art for another hundred years. Indeed, at one time, the Church felt it was theologically redundant to say that Jesus, a member of the Godhead and omniscient, ascended into Heaven; he *was* Heaven.

One of the earliest depictions of the Ascension in the West shows Jesus climbing to the top of a hill and grasping the hand of God, which emerges from a cloud to pull him heavenward. The apostles, assembled, watch.

Today, for American Roman Catholics, the Ascension is a "holy day of obligation," that is, a Catholic must attend Mass on that day.

The site of Christ's Ascension has always been taken to be Mount Olivet (Acts 1:1–12), near Jerusalem. A legend arose that a stone on the hill bore Christ's footprints, plainly visible, and pilgrimages to the spot—to kiss the stone—became commonplace. Jewish historian Josephus is said to have been impressed by the footprints, as were others, especially since repeated trampling by Roman soldiers failed to wear them away. Saint Helena, Constantine's mother, had a church built over the Ascension rock in the fourth century, but the Persians destroyed it. A second church on the site was razed by Moslems, who left standing only a small octagonal structure that was incorporated into the present church as an oratory. The stone of the Ascension is said to be in the oratory. (*See* Relics.)

Ten days after Christ ascended, his promise to empower the apostles was kept by a visitation from the Holy Spirit—the Pentecost.

PENTECOST:

EARLIEST OBSERVANCE, EARLY THIRD CENTURY c.e. ◆

WHEN OBSERVED: *FIFTY DAYS AFTER EASTER.*
COMMEMORATES: *THE DESCENT OF THE HOLY SPIRIT UPON THE
APOSTLES.*

Since the Holy Spirit conveyed power and authority to the apostles, transforming them from twelve frightened followers into a band of bold evangelists, the Pentecost is known as "the birthday of the Church." And its details
are dramatically set down in the Acts of the Apostles (2:1–6):

> *When the day of Pentecost had come, they were all together in one place. And
> suddenly a sound came from heaven like the rush of a mighty wind, and it filled
> all the house where they were sitting. And there appeared to them tongues as of
> fire, distributed and resting on each one of them. And they were all filled with
> the Holy Spirit and began to speak in other tongues.*

So empowered were the apostles that they are said to have almost immediately baptized three thousand people.

As it happens, the Holy Spirit visited the apostles on the Jewish feast of
Pentecost, a long-established festival of thanksgiving for the firstfruits of the
wheat harvest. The Church's transformation of this Jewish feast into a Christian festival was, in a way, related to the belief that the gift of the Holy Spirit
to the apostles was the firstfruits of a new harvesting—of souls.

When the Christian Pentecost was first celebrated is uncertain. It was
mentioned in a second-century Church book, *Epistola Apostolorum*, and in
the next century by theologians Origen of Alexandria and Tertullian of
Carthage. By the third century, it was certainly a well-recognized feast.

The word "Pentecost" is from the Greek *pentecoste*, meaning "fiftieth day,"
but the early Christians often referred to the entire fifty-day period prior to
Easter as Pentecost.

In England, in *The First Prayer Book of Edward VI* (1549), the feast was officially titled "Whitsunday," or White Sunday, for the color of vestment then
worn during services. Today, in the Roman and Anglican Churches, the
color red is worn, symbolizing the tongues of fire in which the Holy Spirit
appeared.

PENTECOSTAL CHURCHES. This group of Protestant churches
originated in the nineteenth century, teaching that all Christians should seek
a postconversion, or second religious experience, called "Baptism with the

Holy Spirit." Pentecostals maintain that a Spirit-baptized believer can miraculously receive some of the supernatural gifts that were once known in the early Church: the power to prophetize, to heal, to "speak in tongues," and to understand the language of someone else speaking in tongues. Later Pentecostals split off in a "Jesus Only" movement, maintaining that only the "name of Jesus" could confer a postconversion religious experience.

ASSUMPTION OF MARY:
EARLIEST OBSERVANCE, POST–431 C.E. ◆

WHEN OBSERVED: *AUGUST 15.*
COMMEMORATES: *THE ASSUMPTION INTO HEAVEN OF THE BLESSED VIRGIN MARY, BODY AND SOUL, AT THE MOMENT OF HER "DEATH" OR "DORMITION" (A FALLING ASLEEP).*

It is only since November 1, 1950, that Roman Catholics are compelled to believe as dogma that Christ's mother, Mary, was assumed into Heaven, body and soul, at the time of her death, thus avoiding any physical decay. The imagery of Mary's Assumption clearly parallels that of Christ's Ascension.

Mary's Assumption had been observed in the Church since the fifth century, but no pontiff before Pope Pius XII had elevated it to dogma: an article of faith that must be believed. Although the Assumption is not explicitly mentioned in the New Testament, popes before Pius XII had located passages that could support such a doctrine—a glorification of Mary's personality; and, too, a glimpse of God's Judgment Day promise for the rest of humankind.

Pius elevated the event to dogma also because belief in the Assumption was widespread and popular with both the clergy and laity. But the Assumption is not considered a revealed doctrine among the Eastern Orthodox and has been an obstacle to ecumenical dialogue between Rome and many Protestant Churches.

The feast, which originated in the Byzantine Empire, and did not get its title "Assumption" until the 630 C.E., once spoke of Mary's "dormition" or "falling asleep" at the end of her life, opening much debate as to whether she actually died, or was spared real bodily death. According to one popular legend, at the time of Mary's passing, her body was transported by a cloud to Jerusalem, and while the apostles watched, the archangel Gabriel took her soul to Heaven.

Saint John himself told the most popular version of Mary's Assumption. When Christ's mother was seventy-three years old and dying, news of her condition reached the apostles, who had scattered across the globe to preach the Gospel. Hurrying back, all but Saint Thomas (who'd also missed the risen Christ's first appearance to the apostles) witnessed Mary's peaceful passing. When Thomas finally arrived, he asked to see Mary's body, but when the tomb was opened, she was gone—the Assumption had already taken place.

It should be pointed out that Pius XII's dogma of 1950, expressed in the apostolic constitution *Munificentissimus Deus*, is not based on legend; theologians used various New Testament texts to adduce the appropriateness of the doctrine. For a full discussion of the origin of this dogma, see the chapter "Virginity of the Virgin."

IMMACULATE CONCEPTION OF MARY: EARLIEST OBSERVANCE, POST–431 C.E. ◆

WHEN OBSERVED: *DECEMBER 8.*
COMMEMORATES: *THE BIRTH OF CHRIST'S MOTHER WITHOUT ORIGINAL SIN ON HER SOUL.*

This Roman Catholic dogma states that Mary, the mother of Jesus, is unique among all human beings in that she was the only person ever conceived without the stain of Adam's sin on her soul. Born without concupiscence, Mary was never inclined to sin.

Although various texts in both the Old and New Testament have been cited in defense of the doctrine, it arose in the Eastern Church only after Mary had been solemnly declared the Mother of God at the Council of Ephesus in 431 C.E. Most theologians, who readily acknowledged Mary's great holiness, felt that a person so close to God could never have committed a single sinful act.

Not everyone agreed. In the Middle Ages, such eminent theologians as Saint Thomas Aquinas and Saint Bonaventure rejected the concept of Mary's innate sinlessness, basing their opposition on the text of the Epistle of Paul to the Romans, where it is declared that all human beings sinned in Adam. Not long after, their views were strongly countered by the Franciscan theologian John Duns Scotus, who argued that Christ's redemptive grace was applied to Mary to prevent sin from reaching her soul and that this special intervention resulted in perfect redemption in her case, and hers alone. Thus, Mary's privilege was the result of God's grace and not of any intrinsic merit on her part.

Gradually, this view was accepted by several popes, especially Sixtus IV in the late fifteenth century. It was not, however, until December 8, 1854, that Pius IX, urged by the majority of Catholic bishops throughout the world, solemnly declared in the bull *Ineffabilis Deus* that the doctrine was revealed by God and hence was to be firmly believed as dogma by all Roman Catholics. For a full discussion of the origin of the dogma of the Immaculate Conception, see the chapter "Virginity of the Virgin."

A few years later, in the summer of 1870, this same pope, Pius IX, would issue the infamous and highly controversial bull decreeing papal infallibility. In fact, Pius IX used the dogma of the Immaculate Conception to "test the waters," so to speak, for acceptance of the bolder issues of papal inerrancy. For a full discussion of the origin of this concept, see the chapter "Papal Infallibility."

ORIGIN OF MARIOLOGY ◆ *It should be pointed out that all the major feasts in honor of the Virgin Mary, related to her "incarnation" cycle, developed in the East after the third ecumenical Council of Ephesus in 431 C.E., where Mary was declared to be* Theotokos, *"God-bearer."*

The study of the Blessed Virgin, known as Mariology, originated with this council. It is from this point in Church history that the Mother of God, now officially recognized as "God-bearer," began to play a larger and larger role in the Church—a role that eventually would contribute to the gulf between Protestants and Roman Catholics. Mariology is discussed in detail in two chapters: "Virginity of the Virgin" and "Visions of the Virgin."

The Mary liturgical cycle includes: her Nativity (September 8); the Purification of the Blessed Virgin (February 2, with a procession of candles—hence its name, Candlemas*); the Annunciation (March 25); and her Assumption (August 15).*

CHRISTMAS:
EARLIEST OBSERVANCE, FOURTH CENTURY C.E. ◆

WHEN OBSERVED: *DECEMBER 25.*
COMMEMORATES: *FEAST OF THE NATIVITY; CHRIST'S BIRTH.*

The biblical narrative of Jesus' birth gives no date for the event, though it more likely occurred in spring than in winter. Saint Luke tells us that shepherds were "abiding in the field, keeping watch over their flocks by night"— shepherds guarded their flocks day and night only at lambing time, in the spring; in winter, the animals were kept in corrals, unwatched.

The idea of celebrating the Nativity on December 25 was first suggested early in the fourth century, a clever move on the part of Church fathers, who wished to eclipse the December 25 festivities of a rival pagan religion, Mithraism, that threatened the existence of Christianity.

It is important to note that for two centuries after Christ's birth, no one knew, and few people cared, exactly when he was born. Birthdays were unimportant; death days counted. Besides, Christ was divine and his natural birth was deliberately played down. In fact, the Church even announced at one point that it was sinful to contemplate observing Christ's birthday "as though He were a King Pharaoh."

On December 25, pagan Romans, still in the majority, celebrated *Natalis Solis Invicti*, "Birthday of the Invincible Sun God," Mithras. The Mithras cult originated in Persia and rooted itself in the Roman world in the first century B.C.E. By the year 274 C.E., Mithraism was so popular with the masses that Emperor Aurelian proclaimed it the official state religion. In the early 300s, the cult seriously threatened Christianity, and for a time, it was unclear which faith would emerge victorious.

Church fathers debated their options.

It was well known that Roman patricians and plebeians alike enjoyed festivals of a protracted nature. The Church, then, needed a December celebration.

Thus, to offer converts an occasion in which to be pridefully celebratory, the Church officially recognized Christ's birth. And to offer head-on competition to the sun worshipers' popular feast, the Church located the Nativity on December 25. The mode of observance would be characteristically prayerful: a Mass; in fact, Christ's Mass. As one theologian wrote in the 320s: "We hold this day holy, not like the pagans because of the birth of the sun, but because of him who made it." Although centuries later, social scientists would write of the psychological power of group celebrations—the unification of ranks, the solidification of collective identity, the reinforcement of common objectives—the principle had long been intuitively obvious.

Christian Christmas began as a feast
to compete with a pagan solar festival.

The celebration of Christmas took permanent hold in the Western world in 337, when the Roman emperor Constantine was baptized, uniting for the first time the Crown and the Church. Christianity had become the official state religion in 313. And in 354, Bishop Liberius of Rome reiterated the importance of celebrating not only Christ's death but also his birth.

Saint Francis of Assisi popularized the Christmas *crib* or *crèche* in his celebration of the Nativity in Greccio, Italy, in 1223. Francis used wooden figures of Mary, Joseph, the infant, sheep and shepherds, starting a tradition still popular to this day.

The period of time leading up to Christmas—from the Sunday nearest November 30 until Christmas Eve—is known as *Advent*, Latin *adventus*, "coming," and was first celebrated in the late fourth century. At one time, Advent was observed by strict fasting, prayer, and meditation, but now it must compete with Christmas parties and shopping.

EPIPHANY: EARLIEST OBSERVANCE, SECOND CENTURY c.e. ◆

WHEN OBSERVED: *JANUARY 6.*
COMMEMORATES: *THE FIRST MANIFESTATION OF JESUS TO*
THE GENTILES.

From the Greek word *epiphaneia*, meaning "manifestation," the Epiphany is one of the three oldest and most important festival days of the Christian Church—including Easter and Christmas. Its prominence lies in the fact that it symbolizes three "firsts" in Christ's life. His three major epiphanies—Visit of the Magi, Baptism in the River Jordan, Miracle at Cana—were said to have two remarkable things in common: all involved divine intercession, and all three occurred on the same day, January 6, though in different years.

VISIT OF THE MAGI. The Epiphany commemorates the first manifestation of Jesus Christ as God to the Gentiles, when he was revealed to the Magi who visited his manger at Bethlehem. According to Matthew (2:9–11): "When they saw the star, they rejoiced. . . . Then, opening their treasures, they offered him gifts." In the Western Church, the Epiphany is devoted primarily to this visit of the three Wise Men, a practice that seems to have originated in either Spain or Gaul.

By showing himself to the Wise Men, the infant Jesus affirmed the inclusion of the Gentiles in the divine redemption. The Bible never tells us their names, nor that there were three "kings"; textual references indicate there may have been as few as two or as many as twelve. The number three seems

*The Wise Men guided
by the star they saw
in the East.*

to have taken hold because three gifts were presented to the infant—gold, frankincense and myrrh—symbolic traditionally of tribute (Christ the King), worship (Christ the God), and death (Christ as the sacrificial Victim).

As for their names, around the ninth century, custom designated them as Caspar, King of Tarsus; Melchior, King of Arabia; and Balthazar, King of Sheba.

BAPTISM. The Epiphany also commemorates the first manifestation of Christ's divinity, as it occurred at his baptism in the Jordan River. After Jesus received the sacrament from John the Baptist, the heavens opened "and he saw the Spirit of God descending like a dove, and alighting on him; and lo, a voice from heaven, saying, 'This is my beloved Son, with whom I am well pleased' " (Matt. 3:6–17).

The feast of the Epiphany originated in the East, where at first it commemorated Christ's birth; later, it came to commemorate primarily his baptism, and to be called the Feast of the Jordan. Or the Feast of the Lights, from a belief that preternatural lights appeared at the time of Christ's baptism.

MIRACLE AT CANA. The Epiphany celebrates the manifestation of Christ's first miracle—changing water to wine—at the marriage feast of Cana in Galilee. This was the first public display of his heavenly power.

These three events, or epiphanies, were long assumed to have occurred on the same day, January 6, although none of the four biblical accounts of the life of Jesus mentions the dates on which these events took place.

How did January 6 take hold?

The first reference to the Epiphany is in the *Stomata* of Clement of

Alexandria, written near the end of the second century C.E. He tells us that certain Christians in Alexandria, Egypt, celebrated the baptism of Jesus on the sixth, which, perhaps significantly, was the date of an ancient Egyptian solstice, and had long been the date of a major pagan festival in Alexandria and its environs, one with striking similarities to the Nativity: the birth of a new god (Aeon, or "age"), from the loins of "a maiden" or virgin (Kore), at the time of a rising star in the sky.

Whereas the solstice caused the banks of the Nile to overflow, the sacred birth caused water in royal and public fountains to miraculously turn into wine. As we've seen, it was quite common for the dates of ancient pagan festivals to be usurped by converts to Christianity in celebrating their new feasts.

REFORMATION SUNDAY:
EARLIEST OBSERVANCE, EARLY SIXTEENTH CENTURY c.e. ◆

WHEN OBSERVED: *SUNDAY NEAREST OCTOBER 31.*
COMMEMORATES: *MARTIN LUTHER'S SPLIT WITH
THE ROMAN CHURCH.*

Reformation Sunday commemorates the daring challenge Martin Luther issued on October 31, 1517. On that day, the German monk, an ordained Roman Catholic priest and lecturer on philosophy and theology at the University of Wittenberg, nailed his "ninety-five theses" up on a church door— and unexpectedly touched off a reform movement that swept like a bushfire all across Europe.

Luther did not intend to break with Rome, but was disgusted with some of the practices prevalent in the sixteenth-century Church, especially the sale of indulgences by which people thought they were buying reprieve from the wages of sin for cash or crops. Pope Leo X's large-scale sale of indulgences to raise money for an enlargement of Saint Peter's Church in Rome finally drove Luther to outraged protest, forcing him to draw up a list of ninety-five grievances.

Luther posted the grievances on October 31 for a reason. At the end of October, his town, Wittenberg, like all towns, would be filling up with pilgrims arriving for *All Saints' Day* (November 1), and Luther expected to get some worthy opponents for debate and a good-sized audience for his grievances.

The result was beyond the monk's expectations. Nobody in Wittenberg argued with Luther. Instead, so many people agreed wholeheartedly that his

Pope Leo X (1513–21)
sold indulgences to finance
the expansion of Saint
Peter's Church in Rome.

reform ideas spread rapidly over all of northern Europe. Half the continent was soon involved in violent controversy.

Other leaders arose—John Calvin in France, Ulrich Zwingli in Switzerland, John Knox in Scotland—and in many cases, Christians broke their centuries-old allegiance with the Roman Catholic Church and established new independent Churches of their own.

Not that this was the first split in the unity of Christianity. Five centuries earlier, in 1054, the bishops of Rome and Constantinople had come to a parting of ways, and when Antioch, Alexandria, and Jerusalem sided with Constantinople, the result was a complete separation between East and West. But the Protestant Reformation started by Luther was more than a high-level theological argument among Church leaders. It was a groundswell, a rising up of the worshipers who filled the church pews across Europe, and it shook the Church to its foundations.

CHAPTER

13

𝔍ewish 𝔍easts

Passover to Hanukkah

JEWISH RELIGIOUS YEAR: OLD TESTAMENT TIMES ◆

Our seven-day week, and our respectful nod to one weekly day of rest, as well as numerous Christian and Islamic holiday observances, owe their origins to the Jewish religious calendar.

The Jewish calendar is "lunisolar"—that is, times are regulated by the positions of both the moon and the sun. Consequently, the days of the week upon which an annual Jewish festival falls vary from year to year—movable feasts—despite a given festival's fixed position in the Jewish month. The months, and their approximate equivalents in the Western Gregorian calendar, are:

1. Tishri, seventh Hebrew month, September/October, including Rosh Hashanah (on the first), Yom Kippur (on the tenth), and Sukkot (between the fifteenth and the twenty-first).

2. Heshvan, eighth Hebrew month, October/November.

3. Kislev, ninth Hebrew month, November/December, including Hanukkah (on the twenty-fifth).

4. Tevet, tenth Hebrew month, December/January, Hanukkah ends.

5. Shevat, eleventh Hebrew month, January/February.

6. Adar, twelfth Hebrew month, February/March, including Purim (fourteenth).

7. Nisan, first Hebrew month, March/April, including Passover (fifteenth through twenty-second).

8. Iyyar, second Hebrew month, April/May.

9. Sivan, third Hebrew month, May/June, including Shavout or the Jewish Pentecost (sixth).

10. Tammuz, fourth Hebrew month, June/July.

11. Av, fifth Hebrew month, July/August, destruction of the Temple (ninth).

12. Elul, sixth Hebrew month, August/September.

The Jews had an optional thirteenth month, called Adar Sheni or the intercalary month—from the Latin *intercalare*, "to insert." Since the fourth century C.E., this month occurs on a fixed regular cycle: seven times in nineteen years.

SABBATH—DAY OF REST:
BOOK OF EXODUS, C. 1400 B.C.E. ◆

The Jewish Sabbath—from the Hebrew *shavat*, "to rest"—is observed throughout the year on the seventh day of the week, Saturday. It commemorates the original seventh day on which God rested after completing the Creation.

The Sabbath is the only Jewish holiday whose observance is mandated in the Ten Commandments, its biblical origin in Exodus: "Remember to keep holy the Sabbath." At the beginning of Genesis, God had blessed the seventh day and sanctified it.

Interestingly, scholars have not been able to find among other cultures the notion of a sacred "day of rest." It appears that the idea of a holy day of relaxation, linking God to his people and recurring every seventh day, was unique to ancient Israel. Other days of rest, such as the Christian Sunday and the Islamic Friday, are direct steals from this Jewish weekly luxury.

The sacred significance of the Sabbath for Judaism is apparent throughout both Talmudic literature and popular legend: "If you wish to destroy the Jewish people, abolish their Sabbath first," or "More than Israel kept the Sabbath, the Sabbath kept Israel."

It's argued that the day of rest from *all work*—and Talmudic rabbis listed thirty-nine categories of prohibited work; from agriculture, to manufacturing, to construction—forced the Jewish people, at least once a week, to concentrate their efforts on intellectual activity and spiritual regeneration. The day of rest was not a time for idle leisure but, under the rabbis' strict rules, a time for inner growth. Thus, a tradition of learning and meditation was established, and passed on. A tradition that has proved invaluable.

The Sabbath is a "female" day, since it is personified as a bride, whose groom, according to Genesis, is "the Community of Israel." The Sabbath, a fresh and new bride each week awaiting her groom, commences one hour before sunset each Friday evening. Interestingly, when in the fourth century Christians designated Sunday as their day of rest, the day began just before sunset on Saturday evening, the Semitic concept rather than the Roman notion of a day starting at midnight.

PASSOVER:
EARLIEST OBSERVANCE, TRADITIONALLY C. 1400 B.C.E. ◆

WHEN OBSERVED: *SEVEN DAYS (FOR REFORM AND ISRAELI JEWS) OR EIGHT DAYS (FOR ORTHODOX AND CONSERVATIVE JEWS), BEGINNING WITH THE EVE OF THE FIFTEENTH DAY OF THE LUNAR MONTH OF NISAN, MARCH/APRIL.*
COMMEMORATES: *THE EXODUS OF ISRAELITES FROM EGYPTIAN BONDAGE.*

The Jewish Passover has been known as the Festival of Freedom ever since the Jews escaped from slavery in Egypt more than three thousand years ago. The event, also called the Independence Day of the Israelites, is regarded as the true beginning of Israel as a nation and a religious community.

The name Passover, or Pesach, comes from the time when God sent an angel to slay the firstborn son in every Egyptian household, "passing over" homes of Jews—that is, families that had marked their doorposts and the lintels of their homes with the blood of a lamb. The people were then to eat the lamb (*pesach*) roasted, along with bitter herbs (*maror*), and unleavened bread (*matzah*). Any leftover flesh was to be burned, not consumed. This was to be the Israelites' last meal in Egypt before their redemption from slavery. Each family symbolically reenacts the first Passover as they eat their own Passover meal.

Although Passover, which the Israelites were instructed to commemorate as a "memorial day," is a joyous celebration, strict dietary laws, especially against leaven, must be observed, and (as for all holy days) special prohibitions restrict work at the beginning and end of the celebration.

As the Resurrection is regarded as the cornerstone event in Christianity—without it, the faith would not have flourished—Passover is celebrated as the key event in Jewish history—without the escape from slavery, the Jews would not have become the people they did. Symbolically, the two events are linked in that Jesus Christ's Last Supper was a Passover meal.

ANCIENT ROOTS. Even before their deliverance from Egypt, while they were nomadic shepherds in the desert, the Jews had a spring festival. In celebration of the rebirth of the agricultural cycle, they sacrificed a lamb (or goat) and ate only unleavened bread and bitter herbs. This may be the real and more ancient origin of the festival that came to be called Passover. For the biblical account in Exodus, with all of its drama and detail, was cast into sacred text centuries after the events took place. Thus, an ancient rite was later given new meaning. Jews altered the significance of the ancient agricultural rite—as many faiths have done—to coincide with their saga of the Exodus from Egypt.

For many centuries after the Exodus, until King Josiah of Israel instituted reforms, Passover was not celebrated as prescribed in the Torah. After the establishment of the Second Temple in the sixth century B.C.E., the rite was revived and given new meaning from the words in Exodus (13:8): "And you shall instruct your son" about the meaning of the Exodus. This instruction was to take place through the Seder.

SEDER. It is the function of the Seder—Hebrew for "order"—to keep alive the story of the Exodus from Egypt. This exchange between generations, detailed in a book called the *Haggadah* (Hebrew for "narrative"), takes place at the dinner table, in words, mood, and food. This home ritual is held on the first night of Passover (and repeated on the second night by those who observe the second day of the festival as a full holiday).

Traditionally, the youngest child at the table asks four questions, prefaced by a query, which the leader of the Seder answers:

QUERY: Why is this night different from all other nights?
FOUR QUESTIONS: (1) Why do we eat only unleavened bread? (2) Why do we eat bitter herbs? (3) Why do we perform a ceremonial dipping twice? (4) Why do we dine in a reclining position?

It's not clear when the first "modern" formal Seder was conducted, but it is believed that Rabbi Gamaliel II, at the end of the first century C.E., may have begun the tradition. It was he who admonished: "Anyone who has not explained these three words on Passover has not done his duty: *pesach, matzah, maror*"—"lamb, unleavened bread, bitter herbs." Passover is one of the most significant and complex festivals of the Jewish year.

And along with Shavuot (Feast of Weeks, the Jewish Pentecost) and Sukkot (Feast of Tabernacles), Passover is one of the three so-called pilgrim festivals, occasions on which male Israelites were required to go to Jerusalem to offer sacrifice at the Temple and bring offerings of their produce from the fields. In synagogue liturgy, special Scriptures are read: the Song of Solomon on Passover; the Book of Ruth on Shavuot; Ecclesiastes on Sukkot.

The biblical origin of Passover is taken to be Leviticus 23:4–8.

כשר לפסח

The Seder plate—the word means "order." Passover commemorates the Jews' Exodus from Egypt.

SHAVUOT—PENTECOST: OLD TESTAMENT TIMES ◆

This is the only biblical festival whose date of observance is not specified in biblical law.

It's observed for one day (for Reform and Israeli Jews) or two days (for Orthodox and Conservative Jews), beginning on the fiftieth day after Passover, that is, on the sixth day of the lunar month of Sivan (May/June). Its start on the "fiftieth" day caused it for some time to be called "Pentecost," which derives from the Greek word for "fifty."

The Israelite farmer was expected to dedicate a portion of the firstfruits of his grain to the Lord as a token of recognition that it is God who protects the crops. Sometime after King Solomon built the Temple in Jerusalem, the offering shifted from the countryside shrines to the capital city—hence, it became a pilgrimage feast.

Then, early in the Christian era, a confusing notion arose, based on shaky biblical fact, that on Shavuot, Israel received the Ten Commandments and thus sealed its covenant with God. Thus, a feast with an agricultural motif became something much more sacred.

Perhaps this transformation is not surprising. After the Jews lost their homeland and stopped being farmers, they could not continue celebrating an agricultural feast in which homegrown crops had to be presented. Thus, Shavuot, instead of dying out entirely, resurfaced with a different significance. To this day, Shavuot is called "the season of the giving of the Law."

Today, Shavuot commemorates the covenant between God and the people of Israel, and their willing acceptance of God's Law and protection. The Book of Ruth (author unknown; written around the eleventh century B.C.E.) is read for its symbolism: it is the story of a Moabite woman who tends the fields of the man who is later to become her husband, whose God and covenant she voluntarily accepts.

Reform Jews have instituted on Shavuot an important ceremony dealing

Shavuot, a time to gather branches and fruits.

with acceptance of the Law: the ritual of confirmation, supplementing (formerly supplanting) the ritual of bar mitzvah. (*See* Bar Mitzvah.)

Sometimes, a biblical basis for Pentecost is given as Leviticus 23:9–22.

SUKKOT—ISRAEL'S WANDERINGS IN THE WILDERNESS: BOOK OF LEVITICUS 23:33-43 ◆

Meaning "tabernacles" or "booths," Sukkot is an autumn festival featuring the memory of the tentlike structures in which the early Israelites lived during their forty years wandering in the wilderness under Moses after their dramatic exile from Egypt and slavery. Indeed, one of the principal activities of Sukkot for a long time was dwelling for days in "booths" constructed of branches and boughs and hung with fruit.

A *sukkah* (singular) had to be precisely constructed. The hut had to be no lower than five feet, no higher than thirty feet. The roof had to be of leaves or straw, allowing some exposure to the sky above. And each sukkah had to be constructed anew each year. In all likelihood, the ancient Israelites wandering in the desert did not possess the materials to construct *sukkot* of the kind celebrants later built. Today, many observant Jews still build sukkot for the feast day.

A biblical injunction from Leviticus, to gather branches and fruits from four species of trees and rejoice, remains essential to the Sukkot ritual. The custom, as it developed, is to assemble a branch from a *citron* tree, a *palm* branch, a sprig of *myrtle*, and a *willow* branch, and to shake them in four directions, plus upward and downward. Some authorities claim the four tree species symbolize the patriarchs Abraham, Isaac, Jacob, and Joseph.

As Sukkot evolved, it became increasingly rich in themes and symbolism. Scriptural readings from Leviticus, Ezekiel, and Ecclesiastes strike notes of the sacredness of seasonal feasts; of the importance of rain; of the Lord's

apocalyptic war with monsters Gog and Magog; and of the fragility of life.

Sukkot, with a traditional procession and chanting, is set in the month of Tishri (September/October), the seventh month of the Jewish ecclesiastical calendar. Beginning with a day of rest and ceremony on the fifteenth day of Tishri, Sukkot lasts eight days.

ROSH HASHANAH:
EARLIEST OBSERVANCE, SECOND MILLENNIUM B.C.E. ◆

WHEN OBSERVED: *ONE DAY (REFORM AND ISRAELI JEWS) OR TWO DAYS (ORTHODOX AND CONSERVATIVE JEWS), BEGINNING ON THE FIRST DAY OF THE LUNAR MONTH OF TISHRI (SEPTEMBER/OCTOBER).*
COMMEMORATES: *THE INAUGURATION OF THE RELIGIOUS NEW YEAR.*

The High Holy Days, the most solemn season for Jews, are the first ten days of the New Year, opening with Rosh Hashanah ("head of the year") and ending ten days later with Yom Kippur. Since the New Year ushers in a ten-day period of self-examination and penitence—in which each Jew reviews his or her relationship with God, the Supreme Judge—it is also called the annual Day of Judgment.

During the ten-day period, each person's fate is sealed in Heaven for another year. Ancient tradition says that on Rosh Hashanah, God opens three books: one for the wicked, one for the righteous, and one for straddlers in between. The righteous are immediately inscribed and sealed in the Book of Life; the wicked are inscribed for death. But judgment on the in-between group is suspended until Yom Kippur, giving them ten days in which to attain merit. Thus, the typical New Year's greeting is: "May you be inscribed and sealed for a good year."

A distinctive feature of the liturgy for Rosh Hashanah is the blowing of the ram's horn, or *shofar*, as prescribed in Numbers: "It is a day of blowing the trumpets unto you" (29:1). The notes of the horn call the Jewish people to a spiritual awakening associated with the revelation on Mount Sinai.

Rosh Hashanah is also known as the Day of Remembrance, for on this day, Jews commemorate the Creation of the world, and just as God is mindful of the good works of his creatures, so on its part the Jewish nation recalls its responsibilities as God's chosen people.

Rosh Hashanah is notable as being one of the few Jewish holidays—along with Yom Kippur—whose observance is more public than domestic. With the exception of festive meals at home on Rosh Hashanah, the main activity

Rosh Hashanah, "head of the year," inaugurates the New Year for Jews. The blowing of the ram's horn marks the spiritual awakening associated with the revelation on Mount Sinai.

takes place in the synagogue, where the service is lengthy and richly elaborate.

ANCIENT ROOTS. Creation beliefs of the ancient Babylonians and Canaanites contributed to the feast that became known as Rosh Hashanah. For instance, the Babylonians' New Year feast celebrated a time when their god Marduk defeated the forces of Chaos to create Heaven and earth; and the Canaanites possessed a similar legend about their god Baal. Such ideas subtly wound their way into Hebrew Scriptures and contributed to Rosh Hashanah the theme of Creation; indeed, it came to be called "birthday of the world."

Actually, the Jewish calendar of ancient times contained not one but *four* beginnings of the year, each having to do with some aspect of the agricultural cycle. And, in fact, the one that fell on the first day of the autumn month of Tishri (September/October), the time of an important new moon, was originally one of the most obscure. The Bible never calls it a "beginning of the year" but rather a "memorial" or "day of blowing the horn." Only over time did the day come to be regarded as *the* beginning of the year, or Rosh Hashanah, ranked with the Day of Atonement as the most solemn and important of Jewish holidays.

By the time the Mishnah ("text")—a collection of Jewish legal traditions that make up the basic half of the Talmud—was compiled about 200 C.E., Rosh Hashanah was important enough to merit an entire legal treatise. The rabbis called it the day on which "all who come into the world pass before Him like flocks of sheep." It was a time when, it was believed, all men were judged for their sins, and their destinies inscribed in the Book of Life.

The biblical origin of Rosh Hashanah is taken to be Leviticus 23:24–25.

YOM KIPPUR:
EARLIEST OBSERVANCE, SECOND MILLENNIUM B.C.E. ◆

WHEN OBSERVED: *TENTH DAY OF THE LUNAR MONTH OF TISHRI
(SEPTEMBER/OCTOBER).*
COMMEMORATES: *PEOPLE REESTABLISHING THEIR AMICABLE RELATION-
SHIP WITH GOD THROUGH PENANCE.*

Yom Kipper, the Day of Atonement set by Moses nearly thirty centuries
ago, brings to an end the Jews' High Holidays. On Rosh Hashanah, the Book
of Life was opened in Heaven and God prepared to write in it the names of
those who were worthy of a good year. But in his Mercy he did not make
the final decision then, but allowed ten more days in which those who fell
short might repent and attain merit. On Yom Kippur, that extension runs out
and every Jew's fate is finally sealed. Little wonder that Yom Kippur is the
holiest, most solemn day of the Jewish year.

The Bible calls Yom Kippur the "Sabbath of Solemn Rest," for on this
day, solemnity and cessation from work are most complete—even though
Yom Kippur may fall on some other day of the week.

The Day of Atonement is marked by abstention from food, drink, and sex
and forbids anointing with oil and the wearing of leather shoes. Confession
of sins is accompanied by prayers of supplication for forgiveness; friends mutually request and accept forgiveness for offenses, since God's forgiveness is
signified by the obtaining of forgiveness of one's fellow men. The efficacy of
Yom Kippur depends on one's sincerity or repentance.

It is a day to be spent largely in a synagogue. No Jew should work or
transact business. The fast is absolute; not even water may be taken from sundown to sundown. The only persons excused from this severe fasting are the
sick (and only if they ask to be excused) and children less than nine years
old. And, as mentioned, it is a day for reconciliation between friends who
during the past year may have done insult or injury to each other, for no
man (or woman) can expect forgiveness from God if he hardens his heart
against his fellow man.

And, too, it is a day of charity, of satisfying the needs of those less fortunate. Traditionally, Yom Kippur is the time of appeals for funds for the synagogue, for Jewish institutions, and for organized charities.

SCAPEGOAT. In ancient times, the high priest performed an elaborate
sacrificial ceremony in the Temple, successively confessing his own sins, the
sins of other priests, and the sins of all Israel. Clothed in white linen, he then

entered the Holy of Holies (the only time of the year when this was allowed) to sprinkle the blood of the sacrifice—a bull and a goat—and to offer
incense.

The ceremony concluded when a second sacrificial goat, the "scapegoat,"
symbolically carrying the sins of the nation, was "driven to his death in the
wilderness." Actually, the priest led the scapegoat along a secret causeway,
one designed to guard the procession from sabotage by heathens and rival
sects, while the congregants chanted, "Hurry! Go!" The priest ushered the
scapegoat to the end of a precipice, from which it was pushed to its death—
symbolically carrying with it the sins of the nation.

All of these brutal but picturesque rituals ceased with the destruction of
the Second Temple in 70 C.E. The rituals and sacrifices were replaced with
prayer, supplication, and penitence. It was then that the personal character of
the Day of Atonement achieved primary importance. The focus of the holiday shifted from the high priest and the Temple to the synagogue, and the
principal performers were the members of the community itself.

Most important, the concept of repentance, the actual mending of one's
behavior, took precedence over all other acts of atonement. The ritual of the
Day of Atonement was insufficient to clear a person of his or her sins without a change in one's actions.

The biblical origin of Yom Kippur is taken to be Leviticus 23:26–32.

HANUKKAH:
EARLIEST OBSERVANCE, PALESTINE, 165 B.C.E. ◆

WHEN OBSERVED: *FOR EIGHT DAYS, BEGINNING ON THE TWENTY-FIFTH
DAY OF THE LUNAR MONTH OF KISLEV (NOVEMBER/DECEMBER).*
COMMEMORATES: *THE REDEDICATION OF THE SECOND TEMPLE OF
JERUSALEM.*

Also called Feast of Lights, or Feast of the Maccabees, Hanukkah commemorates the rededication in 165 B.C.E. of the Second Temple of Jerusalem, which had been desecrated three years earlier by Syrian king Antiochus
IV Epiphanes in his efforts to wipe out the Jewish religion.

One of the chief sources of information about this period is the collection of Jewish writings known as the Apocrypha, containing the Books
of the Maccabees, which recount some of the historical background of
Hanukkah.

Antiochus IV was an ambitious monarch, who sought to establish political
and religious uniformity within his vast empire, which included Palestine. In

short, he wanted to "Hellenize" the Jews totally, from their attire and customs to their religious beliefs to outlawing circumcision. Many Jews caved in under pressure.

The most outrageous violation of Jewish custom occurred when Antiochus decreed that the Temple of Jerusalem was to become a temple of the Greek god Zeus—outright desecration. Altar statues of that deity were erected, bearing the likeness of the emperor himself, who, adopting the surname Epiphanes ("God manifest"), proclaimed himself the incarnation of the god. A band of rebellious Jews, lead by Judas Maccabeus, eventually won the so-called Maccabean War against Antiochus, and saved the Jewish religion from extinction.

The story of the Maccabees stresses that the Syrian king was able to get as far as he did in his Hellenization campaign because of laxity and neglect on the part of the Jewish community; and because of a desire of many Jews to assimilate. Thus, Hanukkah stands for the *continual* dedication of the people to the practices and ideals that bind them together as a distinctive community.

Although modern Israel tends to emphasize the military victory of Judas Maccabeus, the solemn ritual of lighting the multibranched candelabrum—the menorah—has a spiritual meaning and represents the inextinguishable faith in God.

The ceremony also recalls the Talmudic story of how a small, one-day supply of nondesecrated oil miraculously burned in the Temple for eight full days until new oil could be obtained.

The customs of Hanukkah have become like those of the Christian Christmas, which falls in the same season: giving gifts, lighting candles, decorating the home, and enjoying a festive meal. Whereas Christians hang up a Star of Bethlehem and decorate in red and green, Jews hang a Star of David and wrap their gifts in paper of blue and white. (*See* Star of Bethlehem; Star of David.)

One special symbol of Hanukkah is the elephant, because of the trained elephants used by the Syrian armies. Another is the hammer, in commemoration of the dogged leader Judas Maccabeus, called "Judah the Hammerer."

PART

VI

Saints and Their Bones

$\mathscr{S}$aints

Abused Virgins to Celibate Clerics

SAINT TRIVIA ◆

• Number of Roman Catholic saints: there are forty-five hundred listed in the *Roman Martyrology*.

• First Christian saint: the Greek-speaking Jew named Stephen, martyred in 35 C.E.; what we know of him comes from the Acts of the Apostles, chapters six and seven.

• First officially canonized saint: Ulrich, canonized by Pope John XV in 993.

• First American saint canonized: Mother Frances Xavier Cabrini (1850–1917). Born in Sant'Angelo, Italy, youngest of thirteen children, she founded the Missionary Sisters of the Sacred Heart (1880), and moved to the United States in 1889 to work with Italian immigrants; canonized by Pope Pius XII in 1946; declared patron of immigrants by Pius XII on November 13, 1950.

• First American-born saint canonized: Elizabeth Ann Seton (1774–1821). Born in New York City, she founded the Sisters of Charity, pioneered the American parochial school system, and was canonized by Pope Paul VI on September 14, 1975.

• Most popular saint suppressed by the Church in the 1960s: Saint Christopher, patron of travelers; after nearly two thousand years of veneration, he is no longer a saint. More on suppression later.

• Fastest canonization after death: Saint Anthony of Padua, one year between death and sainthood. Runner-up: Saint Francis of Assisi, two years. Third place: Saint Thomas of Canterbury, three years.

• First female saint to be a victim of rape: Agatha (d. 251); to keep her adolescent vow of chastity, she fought off the local governor of her region,

Saint Maria Goretti (d. 1902),
killed by a would-be rapist;
patron of teenage girls.

who overpowered her, then killed her. Most recent: Maria Goretti (1890–1902); canonized by Pope Pius XII in 1950 as a model of purity to youth; she was killed by her would-be rapist, whom she forgave moments before she died.

• First female saint physically abused by her husband: Monica (331–87), mother of Saint Augustine, Church father and bishop of Hippo; married to a pagan with a violent temper and taste for the bottle, named Patricius; he taunted her about her Christian piety, and it's said that only her Christian virtue saved her from serious harm. She is the patron of victims of physical abuse.

• Total number of beatifications and canonizations in the twentieth century: 1,396. The record number in one pontiff's reign: 555; held by Pope John Paul II.

• Approximate cost of a modern canonization: one million dollars per case.

• Number of popes made saints by later popes: eighty; from Saint Peter (d. 64 C.E.) through Saint Pius X (1903–14).

WORD ORIGINS: WHAT A SAINT IS ◆

Contrary to popular belief, Christianity, and the Roman Catholic Church in particular, does not have a monopoly on saints. It just seems that way. Primarily because of saints like Patrick and his feast day revelry, and Nicholas (aka Santa Claus) and the associated seasonal debt incurred. In the pantheon of popularity piety such saints eclipse other contenders; especially those from other faiths.

Word origins:

SEER: A person who predicts the future, or who is gifted with profound moral or spiritual insight. The word translates the Latin *videns*, which is from *videre* "to see." In English, the plural for seer (male) is "sir," and the plural for seeress is "siris"—terms today more or less reserved for esoteric literature. (A business letter that begins with the salutation "Dear Sir" does not imply oracular powers in the receiver; that "sir" derives from the Latin *senior*, meaning a "senior" or "man of rank.")

PROPHET: A man or woman who proclaims a revelation directly from God, perhaps through an angel. It's from the Greek *prophetes*, "one who interprets a god's will."

SAVIOR: Someone who liberates people from oppression or, ideally, redeems their souls for salvation. It's from the Latin *salvator*, "one who saves."

PRIEST: Conducts the rites and services of the faith. "Priest" is from the Latin *presbyter*, "an elder." "Pastor" is identical with the Latin *pastor*, "shepherd."

RABBI: A teacher of Jewish law and a spiritual head of a congregation. The word is Hebrew for "my master"; *rabb + i* = "master" + "my."

MYSTIC: A person who professes to undergo enigmatic experiences, occult or parasensory, not always pleasant, often unpredictable, by which he or she intuitively comprehends truths that lie beyond ordinary human understanding. The moniker is from the Greek *mystes*, "one who is initiated." Mystics have always been regarded with a certain degree of suspicion.

SAINT: May be any of the above; or come from among ordinary folk. A saint is a person who is connected in a special way with the sacred realm of God, gods, spiritual powers, or mystical planes.

The word "saint" is from the Latin *sanctus*, "holy." The study of saints' lives is called hagiography; the word's prefix is from the Greek *hagios*, "holy."

All world religions embrace the concept of sainthood; that is, the personal attribute of holiness spilling over into a special relationship with the sacred sphere. Many religions, East and West, venerate individual saints, as well as their mortal remains or relics.

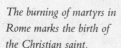

The burning of martyrs in Rome marks the birth of the Christian saint.

CULTUS OF SAINTS ✦

Some religions, like the Roman Catholic Church, have been accused of promoting a cultus (Latin for a religious cult) of saints, since the faith's pantheon of canonized martyrs, mystics, and visionaries is so densely populated—and so popular.

Among Latin American Catholics, for instance, spiritual relationships are not so much with God or Jesus as with the Virgin Mary and patron saints: saints for whom individuals are named. Local calendars list favorite saints for each day of the year, and a saint's "birthday"—which is actually the saint's day of death, the day he or she was spiritually reborn—is often celebrated with more pomp, pageantry, and enthusiasm than a living local's own natal day. It is to saints, or the Virgin Mary, that Latin Americans most often direct their prayers.

The notion of a saint as an intermediary to God—which can easily escalate into unwitting idolatry, and at times has—deeply disturbed reformers like Martin Luther and John Calvin.

In fact, for centuries, Muslims argued that Roman Catholicism—with its Trinitarian doctrine of three Gods in One, its near-deification of the Blessed Virgin Mary, its veneration of a cult of saints, and its hierarchy ruled by an infallible pontiff—was really a pantheistic religion in form and function, masquerading as monotheism.

Officially, Judaism and Islam have rejected cults of saints—more on that later.

GREEK HERO AS MODEL FOR CHRISTIAN SAINT:
FIFTH CENTURY B.C.E. ✦

Centuries before Christianity revered martyrs of the faith as saints, the ancient Greeks worshiped a cult of heroes in which each deceased model of goodliness and greatness was thought to be an active spiritual helper of mankind. Hero worship is the name of the game, and the concept really predates the Greeks and is found in all primitive cultures.

For the Greeks, however, heroic deeds, especially victorious battle, was what "canonized" a man after his death as a "saint." A prime example is Hercules, who masterfully pulled off so many "herculean" tasks. In death, he was the full-fledged equivalent of the later Christian saint. The active spirit of a dead hero like Hercules could not only intercede between humans and various gods, but he could also become the mythical progenitor of a genetic stock of heroes. And, too, he could perform miracles.

Indeed, the hero Apollonius of Tyana, who lived in Christ's century, was revered as a saint endowed with supernatural powers, particularly that of raising the dead. He was, in fact, often contrasted with Jesus as a miracle worker. Thus, early Christians were well acquainted with the religious concept of hero worship. They got it from several sources, in fact.

One source was the Persian religion of Zoroastrianism, founded in the sixth century B.C.E. by the Persian prophet Zoroaster. According to that faith, a humble human being is caught up in the relentless battle between the forces good and bad (embodied by the cosmic deities Wise Lord and Evil Spirit), as well as between the tendencies toward truth and falsehood (represented by the gods Asha and Druj). Struggling man is aided in these battles by an entire cult of "saints" called *Fravashis*.

The spirit Fravashis prefigure the Christian saint. They are called upon in times of trouble, in moments of temptation, and they intercede with greater gods. The liturgy of Zoroastrianism contains hymns called *Yashts* devoted to more than three hundred male and female Fravashis. Or saints. There are even saints who are patrons of certain causes. Zoroaster's own wife became a saint after her death.

JEWISH SAINTS—"PIOUS ONES" OR HASIDIM: 300 B.C.E. ◆

Early Christians also found a model for sainthood in Judaism. Technically, there aren't any Jewish saints. A cultus of popularly venerated saints never caught on in the religion of Israel, even though the ancient Israelites during their exile in Babylon came under the strong influence of Zoroastrianism. And yet the Jewish notion of "saintliness" influenced Christian thinking on sainthood.

Saintliness, or holiness, was an attribute possessed in abundance by Jewish prophets, seers, and kings; and later by rabbis. It was a state to which many pious folk aspired. The model of the perfect Jewish "saint" was the so-called "righteous one" who's often depicted in the Psalms: "he delights in the law of the Lord, and on his law he meditates day and night." Abraham, Moses, Joshua, Samuel, David, Elijah, Isaiah—they are not called saints but they are examples of saintliness.

During the Hellenistic period, from about 300 B.C.E. to 300 C.E., Jews came under many foreign influences that threatened to alter their religion. To preserve the purity of their faith, many Jews, calling themselves "pious ones," *Hasidim* in Hebrew—which in the eighteenth century became the modern movement called *Hasidism*—segregated themselves from other Jews. Although many edifying legends were told about these "saints" after their deaths, a cult of saints as found in Christianity never took hold.

Before examining how—and why—Christianity transformed a "pious person" in life into a "beatified" idol in death, then into a "canonized" saint, it's of interest to see how other faiths originated their concepts of saints.

CHINESE SAINTS—"TRUE MEN" OR CHEN JEN: POST-SIXTH CENTURY B.C.E. ◆

TAOISM. "True men" or *chen jen* is the title for saints in Taoism, the second major religion native to China (after Confucianism). Taoism was founded in the sixth century B.C.E. by the sage Lao-tzu, or Master Lao, and it celebrates a pantheon of saints.

The main criterion for sainthood in Taoism is the attainment of a passionless unity with the divine Absolute. An ancient text sums up the simple traits of "true men": "They do not forget where they come from, they do not care about where they pass to; readily they accept what is allotted to them, peacefully they await their decease." This is consciously passive sainthood, unlike the highly active variety typified by courageous, defiant Christian martyrs.

Not surprisingly, "true men" were usually recluses who lived close to nature and who submitted totally to the Way (Tao) of nature. The Christian counterpart would be the hermit or monk, whose passive, peaceful lifestyle could qualify him as a saint.

CONFUCIANISM. In this Chinese religion named after its sixth century B.C.E. founder, Confucius (K'ung Fu-tzu, or Master Kung), saintliness is achieved more through ideal ethical conduct. Confucius taught that correct conduct in life was a means of achieving ideal harmony with the Way of Heaven; the Tao of Heaven. Saints, or "pure men," as they are called, are those who seek wisdom and scrupulously observe the ethical precepts of the faith. Thus, they become "more than human."

JAPANESE SAINTS—"GREAT ONES" OR KAMI: POST–FIFTH CENTURY B.C.E. ◆

The native religion of Japan is Shinto, and it is concerned with ancestor worship, a concept not unlike Greek hero worship. Qualification is not victorious battle but bloodline.

Shinto does not have saints based on the Christian concept of holiness, or the Confucian notion of ethical perfection, or the Taoist ideal of passive, harmonious submission to nature. Rather, each person after his or her death becomes a supernatural being, a *kami*, who continues to enjoy life in the family, the community, and the nation. Good men and women in life become good *kami*; great men and women become great *kami*. And so forth and so on.

The *kami* are like Christian saints but with a difference: wicked, unconscionable men and women upon death become evil *kami*—demonic saints. In effect, sainthood is denied no one, mystic or murderer; however, the life you lead determines the kind of saint you become—one who's worshiped by the living, or despised.

Shinto also has the concept of patron saints. A dwarf deity called Sukumabikona is the patron saint of brewing rice beverages; and Okuninushi, or Master of the Great Land, is the patron saint of medicine and magic.

BUDDHIST SAINTS—"BUDDHAS-TO-BE" OR BODHISATTVAS: SECOND CENTURY B.C.E. ◆

In early Buddhism (called Theravada, "Way of the Elders"), saints, called *arhats*, are individuals who, through their own pious efforts, attain Nirvana, the state of bliss, and hence salvation from the compulsory circle of rebirth. Saints are souls who no longer need to be reborn into the world to attain further perfection. A saint is a soul at rest.

The Buddha, or Enlightened One, who was named Siddharta Gautama, founded the religion about 530 B.C.E. and became its first saint. He declared his own sainthood when he said of himself: "I am the holy One in this world, I am the highest teacher, I alone am the completely enlightened One; I have gained peacefulness and have obtained Nirvana."

In one later form of Buddhism (Mahayana, "Greater Vehicle," originating at the start of the Christian era), saints, or Bodhisattvas (Buddhas-to-be), serve functions very close to those of Christian saints. They forgo their own final realization to help struggling human beings who are not in a position to give up worldly possessions and live a hermit's life.

The Bodhisattva saint as a helper is markedly different from the do-it-on-your-own *arhat* saint of earlier Buddhism. The dying Buddha's last words had been: "Seek *your own* salvation with diligence."

Yet another form of Buddhism (Vajrayana, "Vehicle of the Thunderbolt") recognizes *living saints* (a phrase that in the West is merely a metaphor for extraordinarily patient souls). Living saints who walk the earth are actually incarnations, or *tulku*, of past scholars or holy men. The Dalai Lamas, the heads of the Tibetan hierarchy, are viewed as saintly reincarnations of the beloved Bodhisattva of Mercy, Avalokitesvara. Thus, the current Dalai Lama is a living saint. Christianity has no counterpart.

HINDU SAINTS—"HOLY ONES" OR SADHUS: POST–400 B.C.E. ◆

A *sadhu*, a Hindu saint or "holy one" is an individual who adheres to the Vedic motto, found in the philosophical commentary known as the Upanishads: "If a man is without desire, free of desires, his vital spirits will not depart; Brahman he is and unto Brahman he goes." Brahman is the "Universal Soul," and the state is best achieved by living the life of an ascetic.

The Upanishads, a group of late Vedic metaphysical treatises dealing with humans and their relationship with the universe, date from about 400 B.C.E. and form the basis of much of later Indian philosophy. In fact, Hinduism, the predominant religion of India, is mystical in character, and mysticism in general starts with ascetic practices as a means of eliminating base desire. Hindu ascetics, like Christian monks, are highly honored.

AVATAR ◆ *In Hinduism, a living saint who walks the earth, called an* avatara, *is actually thought to be a deity incarnated. Hence our word "avatar" for an incarnation of a god; the word is from the Sanskirt* avatara, *literally, "he passes beyond."*

In Hinduism, the Jewish-born Jesus Christ, the eponym of Christianity, is regarded as an avatar of the cosmic god Vishnu. And the great Hindu saint Ramakrishna is considered to be an avatar of the god Shiva.

ISLAMIC SAINTS—"FRIENDS OF ALLAH" OR WALI:
POST–SIXTH CENTURY B.C.E. ◆

Islam is a rigorously monotheistic faith that forbids any consortship to Allah; in holiness, Allah has no competitors. Thus, in the early years of the religion, its followers flatly rejected a cult of saints.

And, yet, due to popular demand, saints slowly came into existence in Islam—people came to need people to inspire them. While stressing Allah's supreme powers, religious leaders made room for saintly men as intermediaries. These saints, or *wali*, "friends" of Allah, were believed to be endowed with charismatic powers that allowed them to go miraculously and instantaneously from one place to a distant other.

The *wali* in time came to wield supernatural power over plants and animals and clouds and weather. Whereas the Prophet Muhammad had decried the Christian concept of saints, years after his death, Muslims venerated holy men and even "canonized" some men while they were still living. After such "canonized" men died, their graves became the sites of pilgrimages, and cults of devotion arose in their memory. Friends of Allah were thought to have access to God's ear. A miracle could be requested by the *wali* on an individual's behalf, but it was Allah who wrought the stunning effect.

In Islamic mysticism or Sufism, the *wali* are merely men who live a life of service and obedience to Allah, and they are viewed in their lifetime as living saints. In fact, the entire world is thought to owe its daily continuance to the frequent intercession of these living, praying Friends of Allah. As a Sufi text of the eleventh century reads: "God has saints whom he had distinguished especially through his friendship, and whom he has chosen to represent his kingship. . . . He has especially favored them with manifold miracles."

Sacred Arab burial site; Islamic saints and relics arose out of popular demand.

Muslims believe that any saint should be remembered for his deeds rather than for details of his person. Thus, biographies of Islamic saints are short on personal specifics.

CHRISTIAN SAINTS—MARTYRS: FIRST CENTURY C.E. ◆

As we've seen in the above survey of cultures, saints grow out of two needs: the spiritual yearning to have a "superhuman" being living among us, and the desire to witness miraculous events that inspire awe and fortify our faith.

These very human longings, especially in monotheistic religions, present a dilemma: Is God's divinity denigrated when we honor, venerate, or even worship deceased human beings? Is a cult of saints not a form of polytheism? As mentioned, sixteenth-century Protestant Reformers thought so. And so did eighteenth-century Islamic reformers in the so-called Wahhabiyah movement. Reformers like to go back to the basics.

The Roman Catholic Church has attempted to skirt the dilemma posed by a popular cult of saints through semantics.

Church doctrine draws a distinction between adoration and veneration. God, and God alone, is *adored*; Latin *adorare*, "to worship." Saints are *venerated*; Latin *venerari*, "to show deep respect and reverence." Thus, theologically, the dilemma is resolved; though in popular practice, it's hardly perceived. Who, when petitioning a patron saint, thinks, "I must not cross the line from veneration into adoration?" Indeed, local saints—say, a holy man from a particular Latin American or Polish town who has been canonized—are often worshiped: their graves become shrines; their bones are saved as relics that work miracles; their humble homes are transformed into chapels.

Several studies have shown that the supplications directed at saints in the various religions around the world are often indistinguishable, word for word, from prayers made to gods or to God.

That said, in Roman Catholicism in particular, and in Christianity in general, there are several categories of saints.

PROPHET SAINT. Saint Paul is a prime example of the prophet-made-saint. He is honored by Roman Catholics, Eastern Orthodox, and Protestants as the chief prophet of early Christianity. Indeed, he is credited with the evolution of Christianity from a fledgling Jewish sect—perhaps on the verge of extinction, with somewhere between two hundred to two thousand followers—to a full-fledged world religion. For his hard work and foresight, he was granted the title "saint." He did not have to work miracles for it, or be

The conversion of Paul,
a "prophet-made-saint."

martyred, although one tradition has Paul being beheaded in Rome on orders of Nero around 68 C.E.

Other honorary prophet saints: Matthew, Mark, Luke, and John.

MYSTIC SAINT. Saint Teresa of Ávila is a major mystic saint. She was born in 1515 in Castile, Spain. As a very young girl, she read the *Lives of Saints* and ran away from home, resolved to be gloriously martyred by the Moors. Her dogged efforts to this end (as it turned out, she died a natural death) are recounted elsewhere in this book (*see* Patron Saints); suffice it to say for now that Teresa gained the title of saint through her many mystical experiences, which included auditory hallucinations and bodily levitation while in states of ecstasy.

TEACHER SAINT. Thomas Aquinas is perhaps the best known of the teacher saints. He was neither a mystic nor a prophet, but a scholar par excellence. The Church venerates him not for any miracles he directly performed, but for his intellectual achievements, specifically for the theological and philosophical system he developed—which reconciles the often seemingly disparate views of Plato, Aristotle, and the early Latin doctors of Christianity on such issues as knowledge through faith, the existence of the soul, and the power of grace. He was proclaimed a saint in 1323.

MARTYR SAINT. Christianity's first casualties for the faith automatically became its first recognized saints.

Stephen, who was stoned to death in 35 C.E., is traditionally held to be the first Christian saint. Not one of the original apostles, he was one of the seventy-two original disciples of Christ, and was accused by pious Jews of preaching blasphemy. Taken before a hostile court, he preached a fiery sermon of astonishing power (as it is recorded in Acts), ending with a vision of

*The stoning of Stephen,
the first Christian martyr.*

Jesus standing at the right hand of God in Heaven. This so inflamed the court that all formalities of a trial were forgotten and his accusers drove him outside the city and stoned him to death. He is the patron saint of stone-workers and bricklayers, a patronage hard won.

His supposed grave was discovered in 415 at Kafa Gamala and his relics—including stones used in his murder (*see* Relics)—were transferred to Constantinople, then to Rome. Technically, he is called a protomartyr, one who set the pattern for martyrdom.

The word "martyr" is from the Greek *martus*, meaning "witness," and the verb form, *marturein*, means "to testify."

CANONIZATION BY A PONTIFF: TENTH CENTURY c.e. ♦

The first saint canonized by a pope was Ulrich, bishop of Augsburg, who died in 973. During his fifty years as bishop, Ulrich assumed a highly visible role in Church and public affairs. The only taint on his exemplary character was a letter he supposedly penned arguing against clerical celibacy, a letter that was shown to be a slanderous forgery.

Ulrich was elevated officially to the status of saint by Pope John XV at the Lateran Council on January 31, 993. Thus, the first pope to make a saint did not reach back into the colorful history of martyrdom for a dramatic candidate, rather he chose a popular, well-known holy priest from his own era; Ulrich and John were contemporaries.

It's ironic that today Ulrich is remembered not for miraculous deeds or exceptional holiness but merely as the first pope-made-saint. Why was Pope John's first choice for canonization the holy but unspectacular Bishop Ulrich?

The official reason is straightforward: By public demand, local bishops had been making local saints for centuries—ever since the bones of the second-century martyr Polycarp had been salvaged from his ashes and venerated.

There was growing sentiment in the Church to have popes, in virtue of their supreme authority, do the honors. After all, the cult of a pope-made-saint would carry more cachet and receive recognition far beyond local communities.

But Pope John's decision to make a saint at the time he did, and chose the man he did, also may have been political: a show of his own spiritual authority in turbulent times. The antipope Boniface VII had recently died and Church leadership was in turmoil. The Papal States were ruled by John Crecentius, titled "patrician" and head of the powerful Crecentii family. Pope John's powers were restricted to ecclesiastical affairs. Making a saint would be a bold move and would strengthen and enhance his position.

But another seven centuries passed before all the paperwork was done. After much haggling over fine points, the complex process of canonization was set in stone. Canonization confers seven privileges on the chosen.

1. The man or woman is listed in the catalog of saints.

2. The person's name may be invoked in public prayers of the Church.

3. Churches may be named in honor of the saint—like Saint Patrick's in Manhattan, Saint Peter's in Rome—but they are dedicated to God.

4. Masses may be offered to God in the name of the saint.

5. A day is set aside in the Church calendar to honor the memory of the saint.

6. Pictures of the saint may be surrounded by a glow of light that suggests his or her new celestial status in Heaven. The process of canonization shifts the saint's soul from Purgatory—where one school of thought teaches it is awaiting God's Final Judgment—directly to Heaven.

7. Relics of the saint may be publicly honored.

BEATIFICATION. Before being canonized, a candidate must be beatified. And before being beatified, a candidate must be scrutinized; that is, the life of the deceased is investigated for evidence of exceptional holiness, heroic virtue, and any miracles associated with his or her name, occurring either before or after death.

In fact, a kind of court trial ensues, involving both a defense and prosecution. The person chosen by a bishop to be the defender for the candidate is called the "postulator of the cause," and he puts forward all of the candidate's saintly assets. "Your Honor, the deceased displayed extraordinary virtue and healed five hopelessly ill townfolk." That kind of advocacy.

On the other hand, the prosecutor is known as the "Devil's advocate," and it's his duty to challenge every shred of evidence. "Medical science cured the illness, Your Honor, and the candidate's published writings reflect discord with doctrine on many issues." Of course, the purpose of the trial is to get at the truth, the whole truth if it's available. In effect, the judge and jury is the sitting pope. If he orders beatification, the honor comes in the form of a solemn papal proclamation, accompanied by a Solemn Mass. The candidate for sainthood may now enjoy "limited veneration," confined to his or her hometown locale—a local saint-to-be.

MIRACLES. The canonization process—which may take place years or decades later, and is essentially the same—cannot begin until, traditionally, at least two authentic miracles have occurred in the candidate's name since beatification. However, judging miracles today, in light of medical knowledge and the physiological aspects of disease, is quite a different process than in the past. In fact, it is so difficult to authenticate a "healing" miracle today, that a pope may decide to modify greatly—or suspend entirely—that requirement for sainthood.

It was not until the seventeenth and eighteenth centuries, under popes Urban VIII and Benedict XIV, that the processes of beatification and canonization were formalized. And a special process called "equivalent canonization" was invoked to grant persons already venerated for centuries the status of official sainthood.

SUPPRESSING A SAINT ◆

Just as a pope through an "annulment" can dissolve an undissolvable marriage between a man and a woman—after many years of the husband and wife sleeping together and rearing children—so, too, can a pope "suppress" a saint after that saint has enjoyed decades of public veneration and papal approval.

Why would a saint long venerated suddenly be suppressed?

Further historical research may cast serious doubts on a saint's holiness, virtue, or miracles associated with his or her name. However, just as a legal prosecutor is loath to reopen a criminal case, viewing the action as an admission of error, so, too, is the Vatican disinclined to retry a saint and evidence of miracles.

Most saints are suppressed because historical sleuthing reveals that a particular saint never existed in the flesh, only in popular imagination. Pope Paul VI, in 1968, for instance, abolished forty saints' feast days from the Church calendar.

Among the suppressed:

SAINT BARBARA, fourth-century virgin martyr; patron of gunners, artillery men, firefighters, fireworks makers, miners, fire and lightning, and sudden death. In short, explosives. Former feast day, December 4.

Barbara, a great beauty, youthful virgin, and secret Christian, was locked in a tower by her father, Dioscurus, for her own good, he said. Dioscurus commissioned a bathing pool to be built for his own use near the tower. The construction worker glimpsed the chaste beauty, who asked him to add a third window to her tower—symbolizing the Trinity. The father, certain the window was not the only thing the worker had erected, drew his sword to slay his daughter, who leaped from her new window.

Father and daughter then fought; he demanded she renounce her faith, as she had given up her virginity; she declined. He stripped her naked, flogged her bloody, cut off her head. From Heaven came a mighty bolt of lightning that instantly rendered the father cinders. Hence, Barbara became the patron of explosives.

Venerated in Italy throughout the Middle Ages, Saint Barbara was suppressed by the modern Church, which could find only fanciful legend as the basis for her existence.

SAINT CHRISTOPHER, third-century bachelor martyr; patron of travelers, motorists, pilgrims, bus drivers, truck drivers, skiers; anyone on the move. Former feast day, July 25. One of the best known and most loved of all the patron saints, Christopher was suppressed in 1969 after centuries of veneration. The act was inevitable. Still, it troubled many Catholics at the time.

At twenty-four feet tall, with the face of a dog (some legends say he had the full head of a dog), Christopher was the most feared man in his native Palestine. He intimidated Satan himself. One stormy night, he ferried a small child on his shoulders through raging floodwaters. The child grew mysteriously heavier and heavier, but the giant Christopher never collapsed. Upon reaching the safety of shore, the child revealed himself to be Christ; the name "Christopher" is from the Greek *Christophoros*, "one who carries Christ," and its original connotation was spiritual, not shoulder-bearing physical.

Christopher planted his staff in the floodwaters and it instantly became a palm tree. Then he set off on a campaign of preaching and brothel-closing. His cult soared during the Middle Ages, and with the advent of the automobile, Saint Christopher medallions dangled from many a rearview mirror. By then, his visage was that of a handsome man, if overly large.

The suppression of no other saint in modern times—his status was reduced to that of a "local cult"—has caused such disappointment among believers. Many Roman Catholics continue to carry Saint Christopher medals.

SAINT EUSTACE, martyr of the early Church; patron of hunters, people in difficult situations, families in turmoil. Former feast day, September 20.

One of the most popular saints of the Middle Ages, Eustace was a wealthy Roman, perhaps captain of the guards under the emperor Trajan. While hunting one day in the woods near Tivoli, Italy, he encountered a stag with a luminous crucifix between its antlers. "Thou shalt suffer many things for My sake," said a mysterious voice. And right it was. The huntsman converted to Christianity, was kicked out of the army and reduced to abject poverty. Pirates kidnapped his wife. Wild boars carried off his son.

Years later, his wife miraculously reappeared, none the worse for wear; then the son reappeared, intact. As the family celebrated their good fortune, the emperor ordered them to worship idols. When lions would not consume them in the arena, the family was stuffed into the belly of a large brass bull and roasted to death. Hence, Eustace became the patron of families in trouble. The legend did not hold up under modern scrutiny.

EXPEDITUS, Armenian martyr; patron of emergencies and hospital emergency rooms—most likely because of the word play between his name and the term "expeditious." Former feast day, April 19.

Amazingly little is known about the saint; that's the problem. His name was long invoked in Germany and Sicily in cases of pressing emergency. He seems to have come into existence through a misunderstanding.

As the tale goes: Bishops in Rome once mailed a crate containing the bones of an anonymous saint to a convent in Paris for safekeeping. The crate was labeled in Italian SPEDITO, "Express" or "Special delivery." The well-intentioned nuns, schooled in Latin, took "spedito" to be the martyr's name and christened him with the Latin equivalent, *Expeditus*. With so flimsy a legend, it's surprising the saint was not suppressed more expediently.

SAINT MARGARET, virgin martyr; patroness of childbirth; former feast day, July 20. Hers was one of the "voices" that spoke to Joan of Arc.

One of the most popular female saints of the Middle Ages, Margaret is yet another example of a stunning beauty who sought lifelong virginity but was sexually harassed by overbearing men; one threw her in jail. In her cell, she was visited by Satan in the form of a dragon, who swallowed her. A crucifix around her neck elongated into a sword, and she sliced her way out of Satan's belly. Hence she became the patron of C-sections.

Another spurned suitor had her beheaded. Her many mortal relics were highly prized in the Middle Ages, and were stolen from churches on more than one occasion. Later research revealed that her life was pure fiction, something of a "romance novel," written by a man who called himself

Theotimus. Whether it was fact or fiction, the tale of a beautiful virgin forced into sexual submission and then slaughtered by her oppressor riveted common folk, for whom it obviously rang true.

SAINT PHILOMENA, virgin martyr; former feast day, August 11. In 1802, the bones of an adolescent girl were unearthed in the catacomb of Priscilla in Rome. Turned over to a parish priest of Mugnano, near Naples, they were enshrined in his church as relics of the legendary Saint Philomena. Local veneration escalated into near worship; miraculous cures were reported at the shrine; pilgrimages to Mugnano multiplied; new churches were dedicated in the name of Saint Philomena. Her feast day was set.

In this century, the science of archaeology proved that the bones could not have belonged to a centuries-old virgin martyr. The facts precipitated a scandal, for Philomena was no obscure, half-forgotten saint, but one actively venerated throughout Italy. Still, in 1961, the pope declared Saint Philomena "suppressed." The shrine at Mugnano was dismantled, and her name was stricken from the Church calendar.

$\mathfrak{R}$ elics

Buddha's Tooth to Christ's Cross

MORTAL RELICS AND SACRED ARTIFACTS: ALL FAITHS ♦

Buddha's tooth, canine, left side, is honored at the Tooth Shrine at Kandy, Sri Lanka. His two collarbones and three other canine teeth are the focus of widespread devotion in other Asian temples. His alms bowl, with which he solicited donations, is venerated in Peshawar, India.

In Buddhism, in fact, relics play a greater role than in any other of the major non-Christian religions. A follower circles a *stupa,* or shrine, several times, offering food and flowers while meditating on doctrines taught by the Buddha, a devotion called "circumambulation."

In Christianity, there are *Saint Paul's handkerchiefs,* which he used to swab the sick. The hankies aren't extant, but they are significant in that they represent the very first Christian reference to relics—those personal artifacts or mortal remains of holy men and women. Items that spawn miracles still. The New Testament mentions these first Christian relics. Gospel writer Luke, a physician, writing in 65 C.E., tells us:

> *God worked extraordinary miracles at the hands of Paul. When handkerchiefs or cloths which had touched his skin were applied to the sick, their diseases were cured and evil spirits departed from them. (Acts 19:11–12)*

There is the *heart of Saint Teresa* (d. 1582), patron of heart disease, at the convent in Ávila. In life, she claimed to have experienced God's deep love "like a lance driven into the heart," and today her heart is displayed under glass, wearing a small decorative crown. According to tradition, a slice of the heart is venerated in Milan. An arm in Lisbon. A breast in Rome at the Church of Saint Pancras—himself the patron of headaches; he was beheaded at age fourteen and is best known today for the London railway station that bears his name. Saint Teresa's remains are said to be miraculously incorrupt, still emitting "a fragrance of roses that is overpowering."

Then there are innumerable splinters from Christ's bloodied cross; plus the nails that held Jesus to the wood; plus the vinegar-soaked sponge on which he sucked, and the lance that pierced his side, as well as the cotton shroud, now at Turin, which swaddled Christ's body and became stained with his crown-of-thorns likeness. All of which we'll examine.

What to believe, though? What is authentic?

At least it can be said with certainty that the word "relic" is from the Latin plural *relinquiae*, "remains." Equally trustworthy, the Latin verb form of the word, *relinquere*, gives us our English verb "to relinquish."

Let's start at the beginning, with the Jews.

JEWISH SACRED OBJECTS:
OLD TESTAMENT, 2 KINGS 13:20–21 ◆

Jews do not recognize saints, and they do not venerate relics.

Jews do recognize certain religious articles as being sacred, such as a Torah, a *mezuzah*, and *tefillin*. In Hebrew, such items are called *tashmishay kodesh*, "appurtenances of holiness," and they must be treated with respect; buried or stored away when no longer in use.

The Talmud details how sacred articles are to be disposed of, or converted into other uses. For instance, an eternal light or menorah can be sold in order to earn money to commission a scribe to write a Torah, but a Torah cannot be sold to buy a menorah because the latter is of lesser sanctity. The hierarchy of worth is not unlike the Catholic concept of relics of three different classes, which we'll get to.

Hebrew Scriptures suggest that some people believed relics of holy prophets retain miraculous powers. Elisha, for instance, is long dead and buried when the body of a second man is tossed into the prophet's grave:

> *When the man came in contact with the bones of Elisha, he came back to life and rose to his feet. (2 Kings 13:21)*

CHRISTIAN RELICS: SECOND CENTURY c.e. ◆

Devotion to relics started early in the Christian Church. Not surprisingly, the mortal remains and personal artifacts of martyrs were among the earliest

> **HINDUISM** ◆ *Hinduism, like Judaism, does not recognize relics. This is undoubtedly the result of two facts. Hinduism has no historical founder like Judaism's Abraham, Christianity's Christ, Islam's Muhammad, or Buddhism's Buddha. Then, too, Hinduism regards the physical world, and existence itself, as illusory. Thus, it is somewhat pointless to venerate the corporeal remains and earthly possessions of holy men.*

venerated objects. They were abundant, and their authenticity was probably genuine, due to the propinquities of time and place.

During the second century C.E., in the *Martyrdom of Polycarp*, the bones of the martyred bishop of Smyrna in Asia Minor, collected out of his cremation ashes, are described as "more valuable than precious gems, more costly than gold." Already a cultus had begun.

Saint Polycarp (c. 65 to c. 151) preached the Gospel throughout Greece. When he was in his eighties, he attended a festival held in Smyrna, attended by Statius Quadratus, a proconsul of Caesar. In the public arena, Statius demanded three times that Polycarp deny Christ and embrace Caesar. Thrice Polycarp refused, finally saying: "For eighty-six years I have served Christ, and he has done me no injustice. How, then, can I blaspheme my king and Savior? Hear me declare with boldness, 'I am a Christian.' "

Incensed, Statius ordered that the bishop be burned at the stake alive. As flames licked his robes, Polycarp was heard to pray: "I thank thee, Heavenly Father, that thou hast thought me worthy of this day and hour, that I should have a part in the number of thy martyrs in the cup of Christ." The feast day of Saint Polycarp is February 23, the date, according to tradition, of his martyrdom.

Every new Christian congregation sought relics of martyred saints to seal into its church altar. By the sixth century, side altars were being built specifically to honor certain saints and their mortal remains. Three classes of relics developed.

• First-class relics are corporeal parts of saints—hair, bones, teeth, and "incorruptible" flesh, blood, and hearts; as well as artifacts from Christ's Passion and death.

• Second-class relics are articles of clothing and household artifacts touched by saints, as well as instruments of a martyr's torture.

• Third-class relics stretch the definition of *reliquiae* as "remains," for they are merely items that have touched second-class or first-class relics. Holy by

ISLAMIC RELICS ♦ *Like Christians, Muslims have hoarded and honored mortal remains and personal artifacts of their many saints, and of their Prophet Muhammad: two hairs from Muhammad's head are kept in a domed reliquary in Jerusalem, which itself rests beside the huge limestone rock from which the Prophet is said to have ascended into Heaven. This is known as the Dome of the Rock. The rock itself is also a relic, since it touched the Prophet.*

Unlike Christianity, Islam has never officially sanctioned the veneration of relics; or for that matter homage paid at the tombs of saints. In fact, as we've seen earlier, saints themselves were only grudgingly due to the devotions of the faithful. The reason for the official resistance is simple. Muhammad, unlike Christ, insisted that his nature was purely human, nondivine; not a bone in his body was more than a bone. Only Allah was to be worshiped, all idolatry condemned.

association. Their ability to work miracles is, by the logic of hagiolatry, less impressive than that of higher-class relics.

CHURCH APPROVAL. The veneration of relics grew rapidly in Christianity. Saint Augustine found that soil from the Holy Land worked miracles (and grew better plants; the Miracle-Gro of its day), and Saint Jerome early on distinguished between the worship of God and the veneration of relics: "We do not worship [relics] . . . but we venerate the relics of the martyrs in order to better adore Him whose martyrs they are."

The Council of Gangra in 340 C.E. decreed excommunication of Christians who did not believe wholeheartedly in relics. The Second Council of Nicaea in 787 was equally harsh in its condemnation of those suspicious of relics. This stand was backed by the Council of Constantinople in 1084.

HOW MIRACLES HAPPEN. Although miracles were associated with relics from the beginning, it was during the hardships of the Dark Ages that relics acquired an almost fierce magical potency. And dubious authenticity. There was, in short, a suspicious glut of saintly remains coming from all parts of Europe and Asia. The bloody Crusades of the late Middle Ages produced countless questionable relics and brought into suspicion the ethical means of procurement.

There was, of course, no concept of scientific testing for authenticity. Tradition was the sole measure of a relic's value; if the legend surrounding a

*Five planks from the wooden
manger that held the Infant
Jesus were brought to Rome
during the pontificate of
Theodore I (642–49).*

relic was old enough, believed devoutly enough, and the relic produced miracles—a major criterion—the item was deemed genuine.

Master theologian Thomas Aquinas championed the veneration of the
relics of saints, and reasoned that God would indeed work miracles in the
presence of a relic. How did a relic work? A relic served as a magnifying lens,
said Thomas, which concentrated the glorious rays of God's grace. A saint's
bone fragment served as a kind of home base from which the Holy Spirit
worked.

Today, many relics in shrines around the world stretch credulity. Their
"authenticity" is based largely if not solely on legend and lore. That they are
still working miracles, and drawing pilgrimages, says less about the relics
themselves and more about the role of belief in the phenomenon of healing.
The Church itself acknowledges this.

Major relics from Christ's birth:

BABY JESUS' MANGER AT BETHLEHEM. Five wood planks from
the cradle that held the infant Jesus, darkened with the patina of age, are kept
in an elaborate gold-and-silver reliquary in the Basilica of Saint Mary Major
in Rome. The boards (from a sycamore tree, as a later study revealed) that
once touched Christ's body are said to have been brought from Palestine
during the pontificate of Pope Theodore I (642–49). The crib fragments are
encased in glass and viewed through several windows. One board bears
Greek graffiti from a later date.

CHRIST'S SWADDLING CLOTH. At the shrine built by the emperor Charlemagne in Aachen, Germany, is a fabric venerated as the Baby
Jesus' swaddling garment, preserved in a golden reliquary. Art surrounding
this early diaper depicts the Presentation of the young Jesus in the Temple.

Pope Gregory I (590–604) climbed the stairs from Pilate's palace for spiritual rejuvenation.

Seldom exhibited for public veneration before the late Middle Ages, the cloth now is shown once every seven years, and prompts great pilgrimages to Aachen.

Major relics from Christ's Passion:

STAIRS FROM PILATE'S PALACE. Near the Lateran Basilica in Rome are twenty-eight worn marble steps, called the Scala Sancta or "Holy Stairs," believed to have been scaled by Christ on the night Pilate condemned him to death. Tradition claims they were moved to Rome in the fourth century under the watchful eye of Saint Helena, mother of the emperor Constantine; the emperor had sent his aged mother to Palestine in search of the true cross.

Pilgrims kiss the glass panes protectively covering the spots on the stairs bloodied by Christ's feet. Pope Gregory the Great (590–604) liked to climb the steps for spiritual rejuvenation, and seventy-eight-year-old Pope Pius IX (1846–78), on the eve of the invasion of Rome by the troops of Victor Emmanuel, scaled the steps on his knees.

(For the current whereabouts of the cup Christ drank wine from at the Last Supper *see* Holy Grail.)

CHRIST'S SCOURGING POST. A portion of the post to which Jesus was tied and whipped is on display at the Church of Santa Prassede in Rome. It is said that in the year 1223 Cardinal John Colonna transported the relic from Constantinople to Rome; its previous whereabouts remain unknown. The column, not of wood but of Oriental jasper, is viewed from the main floor of the church through an iron grille.

CHRIST'S CROWN OF THORNS. Today, the crown is but a bare circlet of woven vines stripped of their prickly thorns, which were distributed over the centuries as individual relics. Various chapels throughout Europe claim to hold the thorns; the crown itself rests in a magnificent reliquary at the Cathedral of Notre Dame in Paris. It is displayed once a year, during Good Friday services, on the day Christ wore the crown.

The relic is said to have been found in the sixth century on the floor of the Holy Sepulcher. It was moved to Constantinople in the eleventh century, and later given as a peace offering to King Louis of France, who, barefoot and wearing a humble tunic, carried it through the streets for public veneration. Napoleon, too, venerated the crown.

The vines still bore their thorns in 590 C.E., when Saint Gregory of Tours commented that the thorns were fresh and green, "miraculously renewed each day." The thorns made excellent gifts, for we're told that the emperor Justinian impressed Saint Germanus, bishop of Paris, with the presentation of a single thorn in a gold box. Charlemagne, first of the Holy Roman emperors, was gifted with eight thorns, which today are in the cathedral in Aachen, Germany (along with the holy swaddling cloth). Mary Queen of Scots cherished the thorns she owned, which are in the Stanbrook Abbey, in England.

Unfortunately, the sum total of thorns in chapels and museums around the world—more than seventy to which must be added the scores of thorns that have been reported lost—could not have come from a single twist of botanical vines; the plant is now named *Zizyphus spina-christi*. It is said that these extra thorns are actually third-class relics, that is, they are thorns that were later touched to the crown and acquired some degree of holiness through association.

CHRIST'S CROSS. In the fourth century, the emperor Constantine sent his eighty-year-old mother, Saint Helena, to Palestine in search of the true

The crown of thorns is in France;
a piece of the cross is in Spain;
nails from the cross are in Italy.

cross. (*See* Latin Cross.) Led by divine inspiration, the aged empress interviewed local Jews and Christians, and ultimately discovered a wooden crucifix that had been hidden under dirt in the Holy Sepulcher—over which her son then erected a magnificent basilica with a vaulted atrium directly above the precious find.

Legend has it that actually three crosses had been hidden in the grave by Jews who wished to thwart Christian worship of the true artifact. The true cross was identified only when it was touched to the body of a dead man, who immediately rallied back to life; the other crosses had been tried but hadn't worked. Another legend claims the man was not dead but merely sick, and the cross healed him.

Considerable portions of the true cross (too many to come from one cross) have circulated Europe over the centuries, each serving as the focal point for a new church, such as the Holy Cross Basilica in Rome.

As Catholic historian Joan Carroll Cruz reports in *Relics*: "Relics of the cross of a notable size are claimed by the Cathedral of Trier, Notre Dame in Paris, the Cathedral of Ghent in Brussels, Oviedo Cathedral [in Spain] and the Monastery of St. Toribio of Liebana. A sizable piece of the relic is in the Vatican and is enclosed in one of the four huge piers that face the high altar. The pier is readily identified by a monumental statue of St. Helena that stands before it." Microscopic analysis of the Vatican relic indicates that it is pine.

CHRIST'S NAIL FROM THE CROSS. Each of Christ's wrists bore a nail, and one nail in each of his feet (the crossed-feet imagery was a later artist's conception). Four nails total. At least that is the standard count. Yet at least thirty churches in Europe claim to have one or more nails apiece. Notre Dame has three (in addition to the crown of thorns and a large chunk of the true cross), as does the Cathedral of Florence. Santa Croce claims its nails are the only authentic ones. All of the nails are in fact old, dating from the Roman period.

The standard argument on any suspicious abundance of relics is that the inauthentic ones touched the original ones and became third-class relics. It has been suggested that the classification of "third-class relic" was specifically devised to make it possible to create more relics so that they could be widely disseminated and venerated.

CHRIST'S SPONGE. The natural sea sponge that was dipped in vinegar and offered to Christ when he thirsted has been divided up and pieces passed around. A large fragment is in France, other crumblings are in reliquaries in the cathedrals of Saint John Lateran, Saint Mary Major, Saint Mary in Trastevere, as well as in the cathedral in Aachen, Germany.

Even the long reed on which the sponge was offered up to Christ's lips has also been broken into parts—now to be found in Florence, Bavaria, and Greece.

LANCE THAT PIERCED CHRIST'S SIDE. Used by the Roman soldier Longinus, the lance first turned up late in the sixth century, said to have been discovered in the Holy Sepulcher, along with the crown of thorns and true cross. The lance, and especially its blade (which was eventually removed), has been venerated in cities all over Europe, as the item has changed hands many times since its discovery. Though the blade seems to have been lost—it was the most prized part, and perhaps was stolen—the staff today resides in Saint Peter's Basilica in Rome.

To the above first-class relics of Christ's Passion, Joan Carroll Cruz gives us an up-to-date history on the much-studied *Shroud of Turin*, Christ's burial cloth, as well as on the lesser-known *Veil of Veronica* (it's at Saint Peter's Basilica), used to wipe the face of Jesus on his way to Calvary; and the *Grave Cloth*, a piece of fabric tied under Jesus' chin and above his head to keep his mouth closed for burial, which is displayed at the Cathedral of Oviedo in Spain. (A blank strip on the Shroud of Turin suggests that there may have been a tie under the figure's chin.)

Most American Christians do not realize that major chapels throughout Europe and the Near East claim to have, in part or in whole, mortal remains or personal artifacts of Gospel writers Matthew, Mark, Luke, and John; of the evangelist Paul; of the apostles Peter, Andrew, James, and Thomas; of Mary Magdalene; of Lazarus; and of hundreds of saints.

AUTHENTICITY. The Catholic Church does not like to call into question the authenticity of these venerated relics—sometimes whole bodies preserved, other times blood still liquefied—since they prompt so much pious devotion.

An official stand was taken in 1563. The Council of Trent sanctioned the veneration of relics and laid down rules by which bishops were to authenticate a saint's remains. The job has never been easy. At one time tradition sufficed. Today, with the availability of DNA testing, no relic wants to offer itself up for close scrutiny. What was thought to be the heart of a learned saint may turn out to be that of a boar.

Around the same time the Council of Trent was approving the veneration of relics, Protestant Reformers denounced relics—a stand that remains in effect to this day in much of Protestantism.

Eastern Orthodox Churches tend to venerate icons over relics, those gem-studded lavishly wrought silver-framed paintings of saints.

Relics of specific patron saints are discussed in the next chapter, which deals with the origins of saintly patronage of various diseases and occupations. How does a saint, for instance, come to be the patron of hemorrhoid sufferers? Or the patron of cybersurfers?

𝔓atron 𝔖aints

AIDS to Cyberspace

SAINTLY PATRONAGE ◆

A relationship with a patron saint can come about in a variety of ways. By Christian Church tradition, every child baptized is "christened" with the name of a saint, who becomes the child's patron or heavenly helper. Or a person might choose to pray to the saint whose feast day coincides with his or her own birthday.

A saint who in life was a bricklayer may become the patron of masons.

Adam, the first man, who toiled in the first garden, is the patron of gardeners.

Epistle writer Saint Paul, a tentmaker by trade, is the patron of tentmakers and upholsterers. One tradition has Paul being beheaded in Rome on order of Nero in 68 C.E. At the supposed site today stands the Church of San Paolo alle Tre Fontane, "Saint Paul of the Three Fountains," so named because his head rolled and bounced three times on the ground, each time miraculously producing a wellspring of water; now three marble fountains that draw tourists. Paul's head (tradition says it's his) is enshrined, along with that of Saint Peter, in a golden urn set in the papal altar of the Lateran.

Saint Francis of Assisi, who loved birds and bees and nature, has long been the patron of animals, and now, by obvious extension, of the science of ecology. His remains are in a reliquary atop an altar in the chapel of the Basilica of Saint Francis in Italy. Two of the habits he wore in life—one gray and coarse, the other white and less coarse—hang in the basilica.

A similar extrapolation occurred with Saint Gabriel. The archangel, God's chief message-bearer, was declared in 1951, by Pope Pius XII, as the patron of telecommunications. Now he also watches over cyberspace, that meta-realm in which, say, a human telephone voice hovers once it has left the speaker's mouth and before it has arrived at the listener's ear. (The word "cybernetics" was coined in 1948 by mathematician Norbert Wiener—from the Greek *kybernetes*, meaning "helmsman"—for the comparative science of computers and the human nervous system. Wiener envisioned a day when the human nervous system, via electrodes, would be the "helmsman" of a computer operation—man wedded to a machine.)

Sometimes, these designations of patronage are official and come from the Church. In other instances, they derive from popular devotion.

The martyr Sebastian, whose body in art is depicted as being pierced painfully with arrows (a more accurate tradition has him being clubbed to death), is the patron of archers, and, with perverse charm, of pinmakers. Many churches in Spain and Italy have parts of the saint, and Sebastian's head is allegedly preserved in a reliquary in the Church of Santi Quattro Incoroati, "Four Crowned Martyrs."

The third-century spinster Saint Apollonia of Alexandria is the patron of dentists—and her name is invoked against toothaches—since in the course of her protracted martyrdom a pagan mob bashed in her teeth and yanked out others. Her crest or emblem is a tooth gripped by a forceps, and fragments of her jawbone and numerous teeth are claimed as relics by at least five cathedrals of Europe.

Following are the origins of several ethnic and regional saints:

FIRST PATRON OF AFRICAN-AMERICANS: BENEDICT THE BLACK ◆

A FREED SLAVE; BORN IN SICILY, 1526; DIED AT PALERMO, 1589; CANONIZED IN 1807; FEAST DAY, APRIL 4.

The illiterate son of African slaves on an estate near Messina, Benedict was granted his freedom by his benevolent master at age eighteen. About three years later, a mob of youths hurled racial slurs at Benedict, and his calm and dignified bearing on the occasion impressed several Franciscan hermits—who invited him to join their ragtag group. They lived in the woods and dressed only in palm leaves. In time, he became their leader.

The group disbanded about 1564, when Pope Pius IV ordered all solitary hermits to join recognized religious orders, and Benedict became a lay brother, dishwasher, and cook at the Franciscan friary at Palermo. His culinary skills impressed the brothers, as did his seemingly miraculous ability to stretch meals—not unlike the multiplying of "loaves and fishes." His piety earned him the moniker Il Santo Moro, "The Holy Negro," and he acquired a reputation for healing the sick. People flocked to the friary and many claimed to witness a glowing halo surrounding Benedict when he prayed.

When offered the rank of "superior" of the order, he reluctantly accepted, yet his inability to read or write in no way hindered his success as an administrator. Eventually, he returned to his first love, cooking, and spent his later years working in the kitchen. On his deathbed, he was visited by the Virgin Mary, who allowed him to cradle in his arms the Christ Child.

It's believed that Benedict was actually Nubian, that is, a mixture of Negroid and Caucasoid races. Nubia, the region and former kingdom, is in northeastern Africa, between the Red Sea and the Sahara, now in Egypt and Sudan.

SECOND PATRON OF AFRICAN-AMERICANS: PETER CLAVER ◆

A JESUIT MISSIONARY; BORN 1580 IN VERDU, CATALONIA, IN SPAIN; DIED 1654 AT CARTAGENA (MODERN COLOMBIA); CANONIZED IN 1888; FEAST DAY, SEPTEMBER 9.

Peter Claver studied at the University of Barcelona, and at age twenty enrolled with the Jesuits, continuing his theological studies in Majorca, at the Montesione College. There he came under the influence of Alphonsus Rodriguez (later made a saint himself), who impressed upon Peter the need for missionaries in the Americas.

He arrived in the New World in Cartagena in 1610, and five years later was ordained. The city that would become part of modern Colombia was then the center of slave trade. Blacks from West Africa were shipped to the port under appalling conditions—caged like animals—then sold at auction. Peter would visit slaves in the holding pens, bringing them food and luxuries like brandy and tobacco, and administer medical care. Through interpreters, he preached the Gospels; redemption, he taught, comes through Christ.

When slaves were sold to mines and plantations, Peter would regularly check on their status, ensuring that the few humane laws on the books were enforced. He ministered to slaves in city jails and hospitals and became a thorn in the side of slave traders. Many locals, however, acknowledged Peter's unselfishness, fortitude, and holiness. His care for the sick, both blacks and whites, impressed his contemporaries—who were astonished by Peter's many "miraculous" cures.

Myth began to accrue around him. When an arrogant nobleman struck a slave girl, spilling eggs from her basket, Peter touched the oozing yokes and scattered shells with his staff and the eggs were made whole again. It was said that he could read sin in people's hearts and prophetize. In his forty-year ministry, he supposedly baptized hundreds of thousands of converts—some twice, it was rumored, which led to his right to perform the sacrament being taken away. But his influence remained undiminished.

In old age—stricken by plague, partially paralyzed, and in constant pain—he was ignored by his fellow priests, confined to a small cell with a Negro servant, Manuel, to look after him. Ironically, Manuel treated his fellow black unkindly: Manuel ate most of Peter's food and tossed the scraps into Peter's mouth. Peter didn't complain. "My sins deserve more punishment than this," he said. He referred to himself as "the slave of the Negroes forever."

Peter died alone. His friends extolled his extraordinary virtue, and Spanish officials honored him with a civil funeral and Solemn Mass. Slaves held a second Mass for him. Peter was canonized in 1888, and in 1896 was named by Pope Leo XIII as patron of "all missionary activities among Negroes."

PATRON OF HISPANICS AND LATIN AMERICANS: ROSE OF LIMA ◆

A VIRGIN MYSTIC; BORN 1586, LIMA, PERU; DIED THERE IN 1617; CANONIZED IN 1671; FEAST DAY, AUGUST 30.

Born Isabel de Santa Maria de Flores y del Oliva, she preferred to be called by her confirmation name, Rose, and she was the first native of the New World to be declared a Roman Catholic saint. Of mixed Hispanic and Incan descent, she liked her religion passionate and gory.

She supported her aged and indigent parents by selling flowers—hence her popular title, "the flower of Lima." Extraordinarily devout, at an early age, she underwent an agonizing surgical procedure (its nature is unknown)

Rose of Lima, first native saint of the New World.

that awoke in her an appetite for suffering. Her self-inflicted tortures, which the Church has since come to view as pathological rather than pious, are chilling: to deface her beauty and repel suitors, she'd cut her cheeks and rub pepper into the wounds, causing inflammation and unsightly pustules. Once when a man complimented the smoothness of the skin of her hands, she soaked them in lime, disabling herself for months.

At twenty, Rose shunned a marriage proposal to become a Dominican nun. She donned a chastity belt and is said to have thrown away the key. She's been called the founder of the School of Aggressive Chastity. Her self-inflicted penances became increasingly cruel. There were daily scourgings; she continually chewed bitter herbs that blistered her gums; and she fasted until her appearance was skeletal. She slept in a shed on cold bricks, wearing gloves full of nettles. During the day, she wore a hair shirt and a skull crown studded on the *inside* with spikes symbolizing Christ's thorns. Whenever she walked more than a few feet, she insisted on dragging a heavy wooden crucifix over her shoulder.

Family, friends, and fellow nuns criticized her penances. After all, she'd never sinned. But Rose claimed that the pain induced mystical experiences. An ecclesiastical inquiry concluded that she was visited regularly by the Devil and the tortures were necessary to keep Satan at bay. The mystical recluse won wide popular acclaim when she announced that through her prayers, Lima had been spared a devastating earthquake. And, indeed, there had been no earthquake.

So great was the devotion of the people of Peru to Rose that Pope Clement X—who had a considerable devotion to her himself—proclaimed her patron of that country in 1670, almost two years before she was canonized; and he extended the patronage to the whole of Central and South America, and the Philippine Islands.

Today, Rome honors Rose for her many charitable works among Lima's poor, and overlooks her pathologies, or, when pressed, views her harsh lifestyle as an attempt on her part to redress the corruption of the era in which she lived. Her sanctuary in Lima is a place of annual pilgrimage. Its greatest treasure, pictured on postcards and photographed by devout visitors, is the deep well into which the young Rose threw the key to her chastity belt.

PATRON OF THE UNITED STATES OF AMERICA:
MARY OF THE IMMACULATE CONCEPTION ◆

MOTHER OF JESUS; FEAST DAY, DECEMBER 8.

First, some interesting chronology:

February 7, 1847: Pope Pius IX declares the Blessed Virgin Mary patron of the United States under her title of the Immaculate Conception—born without original sin on her soul.

December 8, 1854: In the papal bull *Ineffabilis Deus*, Pius IX, by an exercise of his supreme pontifical power of infallible teaching, declares Mary's Immaculate Conception church dogma. Thus, Mary of the Immaculate Conception had already been patron saint of the United States for some seven years before Rome recognized as dogma the miracle of the Immaculate Conception:

> . . . *a doctrine revealed by God and therefore to be believed firmly and constantly by all the faithful that the Blessed Virgin Mary in the first instant of her conception was, by a unique grace and privilege of Almighty God in view of the merits of Jesus Christ the Savior of the human race, preserved exempt from all stain of original sin.*

If that sequence of events seems backward, consider this: In 1854, when Pius IX issued his infallible teaching on the Immaculate Conception, he hadn't yet declared himself infallible. It was not until 1870—sixteen years later—that the First Vatican Council, after much acrimonious debate and a near mutiny, permitted Pius IX to declare himself and all future popes infallible when they speak *ex cathedra*, "from the chair" or "throne," as supreme teachers of the faith. In the Roman Catholic Church, tradition has always preceded dogma—if not dictated it. (*See* Infallibility.)

After Mary of the Immaculate Conception was made patron of the United States, many other countries beseeched Rome for her official patronage.

July 1891: Leo XIII names Mary the patron of Zaire, because of the devotion to her of Belgian missionaries who were evangelizing the Congo.

November 1914: Rome makes Mary of the Immaculate Conception patron of Inner Mongolia.

May 1942: Amidst war, Mary is named patron saint of American Catholic soldiers.

July 1958: In an Apostolic Letter of Pius XII, Mary is recognized as patron of the Philippines.

July 1962: Mary becomes patron saint of Spain; and of the country's infantry and high command.

November 1984: John Paul II names Mary patron saint of Tanzania.

May 1986: Mary of the Immaculate Conception is made patron of Equatorial Guinea in West Africa.

Today, Miriam (to use her Hebrew birth name) is the only patron saint whose patronage—under her many titles—includes the entire human race, according to Roman Catholic teaching.

PATRON OF JAPAN: PETER BAPTIST ◆

A FRANCISCAN MISSIONARY; DIED AT NAGASAKI, 1597; CANONIZED IN 1862; FEAST DAY, FEBRUARY 5.

When Christian missionaries first arrived in Japan in the sixteenth century, they found the country a hotbed of feuding shoguns—military governors who constituted quasi-dynasties, exercised absolute rule, and relegated emperors to nominal positions. The Spaniard Peter Baptist, a Franciscan, preached the Gospel and tried to preserve some of the people's old folkways, those that were not blatantly pagan from Peter's point of view.

Within a few decades, Christianity had begun to take root. Many military men feared they'd soon lose power over the people, and that Japan would lose its unique identity. In 1585, the shogun Hideyosi assumed absolute power and set out to unify his country and purge it of what he saw as predatory priests. He moved quickly to outlaw Christianity.

On a day in 1597, the shogun ordered the mass torture of twenty-six Christians—among them were Peter Baptist; a Japanese Jesuit priest, Paul Miki; a Korean layman, Leo Karasuma; and several young boys. The martyrs' ears were cut off, their private parts mutilated, and they were raised up on

A sixteenth-century shogun ordered the mass torture of twenty-six Christians.

crosses, then stabbed through with spears. All twenty-six eventually were canonized as saints, and named patrons of Japan.

PATRON OF IRELAND: PATRICK ◆

A MISSIONARY BISHOP; BORN 385 C.E.; DIED IN SOUL, COUNTY DOWN, IN 461; FEAST DAY, MARCH 17.

Patrick, apostle of Ireland, is a perfect example of a folklore saint, one whose legend as hero eclipses his real life. For a patron saint of his popularity, Patrick is a figure mired in contradictions.

For starters, he was born in either Scotland, England, Wales, or France, but definitely not in Ireland. His given name was not Patrick, but Maewyn. Or Succat. Or something else. Barely did he become bishop of Ireland; his superiors felt he lacked the finesse and scholarship for the post.

As best as can be determined:

He was born about 385 C.E., most likely in a small village near the mouth of the Severn River in what is now Wales. By his own admission, he was until age sixteen covetous, licentious, and materialistic; very much a heathen.

When he was sixteen, a band of Irish marauders raided his village and carried off Patrick and hundreds of other men and women to be sold into slavery. For six years, he toiled as a sheepherder in County Antrim, Ireland, and it was during this spell of slavery and solitude that he found God. In *Confession,* one of his two published works, he renounces his heathen bent, beginning: "I, Patrick, a sinner, the most rustic and the least of all the faithful . . ."

Escaping Ireland and slavery, he spent a dozen idyllic, studious years at a monastery in Gaul. As a priest, he planned to return to pagan Ireland as its first bishop. But his superiors felt the position should go to someone of more tact and learning. They chose Saint Palladius. Patrick importuned for two years, Palladius transferred to Scotland, and Patrick became Ireland's second bishop. By this time, he'd chosen the name "Patrick."

His imposing presence (he was handsome), unaffected manner (he was coarse), and immensely winning personality (he liked to drink) won him many converts—which irked the ruling Celtic Druid priests. A dozen times they arrested him, and each time he escaped. Eventually, he traveled throughout Ireland, founding monasteries, schools, and churches, which would in time transform the non-Christian country into the Church's proud "Isle of Saints."

He liked to use a three-leaved shamrock to elucidate the mystery of the

Trinity: three distinct Godheads sprouting out of a single substantive stem. It became his trademark, and Ireland's.

After thirty years of missionary work, Patrick retired to Soul in County Down, where he died on March 17, his commemorated "death day," in or about the year 461. He is believed to be buried in Downpatrick, and many pilgrims each year visit a local tombstone, chiseled with a *P*, which may or may not be his grave.

PATRON OF FRANCE: JOAN OF ARC ◆

MYSTIC OF ORLEANS; BORN AT DOMREMY, 1412; DIED AT ROUEN, 1431; CANONIZED IN 1920; FEAST DAY, MAY 30.

It is difficult to separate the life and brutal death of Jeanne la Pucelle, "Joan the Maid," from what George Bernard Shaw called "the whitewash which disfigures her beyond recognition."

Joan was the youngest of five children born to well-to-do peasant parents at Domremy in the French duchy of Bar. She received no formal education, could neither read nor write, and worked as a housemaid and a shepherdess. Intensely pious and patriotic, she was disturbed by the seemingly endless Hundred Years' War between her homeland and England.

At age thirteen, something miraculous—or at least medically significant— happened to the religious teenager. She heard voices and saw visions of Saint Michael, dressed as a knight, attended by saints Margaret and Catherine. For three years, the numina whispered in her ears—eventually persuading her to go to the dauphin, Charles VII, and reveal she had a divine mission: to drive the English and Burgundians from his country, to dedicate the cleansed kingdom to the service of God, and to see the dauphin's coronation; something that had been impossible since the traditional consecration site, Rheims, was deep within English-held territory.

Joan of Arc's visions were accompanied by vomiting and vertigo.

The dauphin liked what he heard. He entrusted the fervent teen—who by now dressed like a man and wore her hair cropped close to her head—with his troops.

On May 22, 1430, the eighteen-year-old Joan was captured and imprisoned by the English—whom she had helped to defeat; the dauphin had already been crowned. Twelve serious charges were leveled against her, including the "abomination" of cross-dressing, the shedding of British blood, and refusal to disavow her saintly voices.

Were the voices and visions real or imaginary?

At her trial in 1431, Joan gave some telling specifics. The saintly apparitions, she said, were accompanied by a "pleasant odor" and they brought her to her knees. "I heard the voice on the right-hand side," she told the court, "and rarely do I hear it without a brightness . . . [that] comes from the same side."

Joan's jailers, who observed her over many weeks, claimed that her rapturous attacks often prompted fits of vomiting.

The current medical opinion is of two minds. One, Joan suffered from severe intermittent tinnitus, a disorienting ringing in the ear that sufferers often translate into speech, and which can be accompanied by visual phenomena, profound dizziness, and vomiting. Two, Joan suffered from a type of brain tumor called a tuberculoma, which can produce her whole spectrum of symptoms.

Her inquisitors ordered: "Death, by burning at the stake."

At 9:00 A.M. on May 30, 1431, Joan stepped into the prison cart and was drawn to the marketplace in Rouen. The square was packed with soldiers, Church dignitaries, nobles, and townfolk. As she was being dragged to the stake, Joan pleaded that a crucifix be brought from the church so she might fix her gaze on it until the end. This was done. She was tied to the stake, and the miter of the Inquisition—a headband bearing the familiar slogan "Heretic, Relapse, Apostate, Idolatress"—was slipped over her hair. The fire was lit.

A monk held the cross she had requested high in the air, forcing her to stare upward, away from the crackling flames. As the smoke rose, she coughed, and, licked by the first flames, she screamed. The rambunctious crowd froze. A deathly silence hung over the square, broken only by the sizzling of timbers. As her clothes were engulfed, she cried, *Jesus! Jesus!*

When her clothes were entirely seared off—but her flesh not yet consumed—the burning wood was yanked away so that spectators could gawk. "They saw her quite naked," said one account, "revealing all the secrets of a woman, and when this vision had lasted long enough, the executioners rekindled the fire high around the poor corpse." The executioners knew how to give a crowd its money's worth.

"WE MADE A TERRIBLE MISTAKE." A quarter-century after her death, the Church that had condemned Joan posthumously retried her.

It concluded that Joan of Arc was, in fact, a good Catholic, privy to saintly apparitions, and had been unjustly burned by hasty but well-intentioned clerics. There were political reasons for this new verdict: exonerating Joan removed the shadow that hung over the dauphin's holy consecration as king at Joan's behest. Besides which, a growing number of Catholics were beginning to view Joan's death as martyrdom.

For centuries, the issue remained a delicate one for the Church. Finally, in 1909, the Vatican officially declared Joan "blessed," and in 1920, Pope Benedict XV canonized her a saint.

With an important proviso: Joan of Arc is not a martyred saint of the Church because her death was brought about by a properly constituted court of the Church that had simply erred. In other words, the Church can make a mistake but cannot make a martyr.

Benedict's successor, Pius XI, named Joan the patron saint of France in an Apostolic Letter of March 2, 1922.

PATRON SAINTS OF ILLNESSES ◆

There is a heavenly patron to pray to for almost every human ill. Most of the saints are not that well known—until perhaps a person comes down with an ailment and feels a need to seek out a patron as an alternate form of treatment.

What follows are several modern complaints and the saints who watch lovingly or disapprovingly over them. Sometimes, it is a pope, in an Apostolic Letter, who designates a saint's patronage. Other times, it's tradition and popular legend.

ABORTION—CATHERINE OF SWEDEN; FEAST DAY, MARCH 24. Patroness to be invoked against abortion, Catherine was born about 1331 to Saint Bridget and her husband, Ulf Gudmarsson. As an infant, she instinctively refused breast milk "as if it were absinthe" for days after her mother had been forced to have sex with her husband. At age fourteen, she married at her father's command, but remained a virgin. Her husband walked out; she joined a convent, founded by her mother; fought off a rapist in Rome—her attacker was distracted by the miraculous appearance of a shining white doe. She died a virgin on March 24, 1381, and earned her patronage for a lifetime of chastity.

ALCOHOLISM—JOHN OF GOD; FEAST DAY, MARCH 8. This serious Portuguese sinner and soldier of fortune till the age of forty underwent a "conversion through lunacy" in the 1530s when he heard a stirring sermon by a traveling preacher. His flailing, seizures, and fits of insanity were interpreted as penance for his past sins. In an asylum, he was subjected to the standard tortures that then passed for treatment. Later, when he gained his senses, and freedom, he opened a hostel for the sick, destitute, and for alcoholics. He's also patron of hospitals; confirmed as such by Pope Leo XIII in 1886. Canonized: 1690.

ARTHRITIS—JAMES THE GREATER; FEAST DAY, JULY 25. One of the twelve original apostles, brother of Saint John the Evangelist, possibly a cousin of Christ, James was the first apostle to be martyred; he was run through by a sword at the command of King Herod Agrippa I to appease Jewish opponents of Christianity. He died in Jerusalem in the year 44. His mortal remains were discovered in the 800s and transported to Spain, where the relics worked miraculous cures of joint diseases like arthritis and rheumatism. They remain at the shrine of Santiago, given the stamp of authenticity in a bull of Pope Leo XIII in 1884.

BLADDER DISEASE AND PROSTATE CANCER—COSMAS AND DAMIAN; FEAST DAY, SEPTEMBER 26. These twin brothers, born in Arabia, became barbers and doctors, not an uncommon joint occupation throughout the Middle Ages. Never charging a fee, they soon become known as "the moneyless ones." For a miraculous cure, they advised patients to sleep in a church overnight. At their martyrdom, Cosmas and Damian caused a hail of arrows to turn midair and pierce the archers themselves. When, miraculously, their persons could not be set afire, or drowned, the twins were beheaded—something that worked.

Modern historians believe the doctor twins might actually have been the reinvention of Greek mythological twins Castor and Pollux. Nonetheless, mortal remains in churches in Constantinople and Rome have performed aptly as relics, meriting the doctors' role as patrons of druggists, surgeons, barbers, and hairdressers.

BREAST CANCER—AGATHA; FEAST DAY, FEBRUARY 5. Born at either Palermo or Catania, Sicily, Agatha dedicated herself and her virginity to God. Around the year 250 C.E., she rejected the advances of the Roman senator Quintianus, who accused her of being a Christian, the worst crime of the day. Her first torture was to work in a brothel, where she fought off repeated attempts of rape. (She is also the patron of victims of rape.)

After a month, Quintianus ordered her stretched on a rack, then seared with red-hot steel spikes. Her cheerfulness throughout all of this enraged the senator, who ordered her breasts cut off. Indeed, her iconography depicts her carrying her shorn breasts on a silver tray. After a stint in prison, with neither food nor medical care, Agatha was visited by Saint Peter, who appeared to her in a heavenly light. Her breasts grew back. Now truly incensed, the senator ordered her to be rolled naked over burning coals—hence her role as patron against fires and volcanic eruptions. To put an end to her cheerfulness, the senator had her beheaded.

Saint Agatha is also the patron of bell founders, for one of two reasons. Bells tolled in Sicily, warning of eruptions of Etna; or Christians in the Middle Ages mistook the two strange cones on her silver tray for bells.

CHILDBIRTH—FORMERLY, MARGARET, NOW RAYMOND NONNATUS; FEAST DAY, AUGUST 31. Saint Margaret, an imprisoned princess of Antioch, was long considered the patron of childbirth, midwives, and pregnant women. This because when in her jail cell she was swallowed by Satan disguised as a dragon, the crucifix around her neck conveniently elongated into a sword and allowed her to cut herself from his belly. In recent times, her sainthood has been papally "suppressed." (*See* Suppression.)

The current patron saint of childbirth is Raymond Nonnatus, whose curious surname means "not born," *non natus.* In 1204, he was surgically cut from his mother's womb after she died in labor. He became a monk in Spain, and later in Algeria sold himself into slavery to free another man who was being sold on the auction block. His attempts to convert Muslims to Christianity met with the swift hand of Islam; though standard punishment was impalement through the groin, Raymond merely had his preaching lips pierced with a hot spoke, then padlocked. Only his jailer, who brought him bread and water, had the key.

Legend has it that after his stint in the Tunisian dungeon, he made it back to Rome, where he was made a cardinal in 1239. He died the next year.

DEPRESSION—COLUMBAN; FEAST DAY, NOVEMBER 23. Perhaps the most influential of Irish monks in Gaul, and founder of several monasteries, was Columban, born in 540 C.E., in Leinster. In France, his proud Celtic ways, and his belief that in Ireland Christianity was practiced in its purest form, put him in constant conflict with French bishops and the pope at Rome. For instance, he refused to calculate the movable feast of Easter by the Roman calendar, preferring the Celtic method.

Respectful of papal authority, he nonetheless warned popes Gregory the Great and Boniface against abusing their high office. He made powerful enemies when he denounced Theoderic II of Burgundy for his sexual dalliances, and he refused to baptize the king's numerous illegitimate children. He died at the ripe old age of seventy-five, leaving behind a wealth of poetry, sermons, a treatise against the Arian heresy, and rules for monastic life that were punishingly harsh. It's possible, judging from his fierce emotional highs and lows—his public rantings followed by hermitlike retreats—that Columban was a bipolar manic depressive.

DRUG ADDICTION—MAXIMILIAN KOLBE; FEAST DAY, AUGUST 14. Following in the footsteps of Christ, this Polish Franciscan priest, who died in 1941 of a lethal injection administered to him in a cell in Auschwitz, laid down his life for a friend: Kolbe volunteered to die in the stead of a fellow Nazi prisoner. "There is no greater love than this," preached Jesus, "that a man should lay down his life for his friends."

The facts of Father Kolbe's heroic gesture are well documented. "At 6:00 P.M. on July 30, 1941," writes Kenneth Woodward in his eye-opening behind-the-scenes book *Making Saints*, "the prisoners of Cell Block 14 were ordered outside and to stand at attention for Kommandant Fritsch. A prisoner from the cell block had escaped and because of this ten men would be chosen to starve to death. Among the chosen was Francis Gajowniczek, who began to weep. 'My poor wife and children,' he sobbed. When the ten were chosen, Kolbe stepped forward and asked that he be chosen in Gajowniczek's place."

Stripped and jailed in basement cells in Bunker II, the ten men were gradually executed over a period of sixteen days. On August 14, the final four, including Kolbe, received a lethal drug in their veins. Kolbe's act did not qualify as martyrdom, the Vatican concluded after his beatification in 1971, but Pope Paul VI asked a delegation to Rome—which included Archbishop Karol Wojtyla, who would become pope—to allow Father Kolbe to be recognized as a "martyr of charity," a new category of sainthood.

On November 9, 1982, before 250,000 faithful at Saint Peter's Basilica, one of the largest crowds ever assembled for a canonization, John Paul II proclaimed: "And so, in virtue of my apostolic authority I have decreed that Maximilian Maria Kolbe, who, after his beatification was venerated as a confessor, shall henceforward be venerated also as a Martyr!"

HANGOVER—VIVIANA; FEAST DAY, DECEMBER 2. In the fifth century, there was a church dedicated to this virgin martyr on the Esquiline Hill in Rome. Her relics were supposedly entombed there, but actual historical knowledge of Viviana is slight. She may be no more than legend. She supposedly suffered under the despotic emperor Julian the Apostate and was arrested and scourged to death.

Her popularity as patron of alcoholics, and the invocation of her name against hangovers, is also steeped in legend. Her Italian name is the equivalent of the English "Vivian," which derives from the Latin feminine *Vivianus*, meaning "to live a full life"—the Latin *vivus* means "alive." In the Mediterranean world, the letters *V* and *B* have often been used interchangeably. Thus, the name Saint Viviana also appeared in print as Saint Bibiana—a word hazardously close to the Latin *bibulus*, "full of drink," from the Latin verb *bibere*, "to drink." As legend has it, this female martyr was rather fond of her drink, perhaps too fond.

HEMORRHOIDS—FIACRE; FEAST DAY, SEPTEMBER 1. The name of this seventh-century hermit was probably Fiachra, a name once known in Ireland, the place of his birth. In legend, he is portrayed as a rabid misogynist. In France, the hospice he built for travelers—now the site of the town of Saint-Fiacre-en-Brie—excluded women, and stories were told of the appalling misfortunes that befell any woman who trespassed there, even after his death. His dislike of women also has made him one of several patron saints of victims of venereal disease.

Oddly, Fiacre is also the patron of cabdrivers. This because the first place in France to offer horse-drawn coaches for hire, in 1620, was situated in front of the Hotel Saint-Fiacre in Paris, and the vehicles became known as fiacres.

Because of the miraculous vegetable garden he maintained behind his hospice—a vast tract of land he plowed with only his walking staff, and which was remarkably productive—Fiacre is also the patron saint of horticulturists.

His association with hemorrhoids—which he may or may not have suffered from—developed only after cabdrivers, who often suffer from the ailment, began to pray to the saint for relief.

After his death, his corporeal relics were installed in a shrine in the cathedral at Meaux, which became a popular center for pilgrimages. Of the many

healing miracles reported to have taken place at the shrine, the most efficacious have been cures of hemorrhoids and fistulas.

IMPOTENCE—GUIGNOLE; FEAST DAY, MARCH 3. The
French called him Guignole and venerated his relics; to the English, he was
Winwaloe, a sixth-century abbot and founder of the great monastery at Lan-
devennec. Little is known of him—a ninth-century biography is notoriously
untrustworthy.

For dress, he preferred prickly hair shirts. For penance, he enjoyed physical self-mortifications. As to his patronage of impotence and infertility . . . well, in a church in the city of Brest is a curious statue of Guignole
sporting a rigidly erect male member; exactly the kind of phallus-worship
statue used in ancient Greek and Roman fertility rites. Its significance in a
Christian church remains unclear.

In the Middle Ages, Guignole became the name of the star puppet in a
violent, sex-oriented French Punch-and-Judy-style show. The character was
hilarious, outrageous, and lewd, and to this day, bawdy grotesque theater in
Paris lovingly dubs itself le Grand Guignol.

INFERTILITY—ANNE; FEAST DAY, JULY 26. Devotion to
Anne as the patroness of childless women dates back to the Middle Ages, and
is rooted in the legend that Anne gave birth to Mary, the future mother of
Christ, only after many years of marriage.

For a person of Mary's historical significance, it's quite shocking that
nothing is known about her parents, Anne and Joachim. Actually, even the
name of Christ's grandmother is unreliable, since it comes from the Apocryphal *Protevangelium* of James. According to this dubious second-century
document, Joachim, publicly ridiculed over his wife's barrenness, retreated to
the desert for forty days of prayer and fasting. Anne, while praying herself,

Saint Anne, mother of Mary,
patroness of childless women,
was told by an angel of
Mary's Immaculate
Conception.

was visited by an angel who promised her a child as long as the child would be dedicated to God.

Anne answered: "If I beget either male or female I will bring it as a gift to the Lord my God, and it shall minister to Him in holy things all the days of its life."

She turned out to be carrying a female fetus, conceived free of original sin, later named Mary. Interestingly, the tale bears relationship to an earlier myth: the Old Testament conception and birth of Samuel, to a woman who thought she was barren, and whose name was Anne—Hannah, in Hebrew. Anne/Hannah means "grace."

Although nothing is known about Christ's grandmother, her relics somehow materialized in the Middle Ages—numerous churches claimed to have her bones. In England, her feast was made obligatory in 1382 by Pope Urban VI; probably more of a political move on the pontiff's part, since the occasion coincided with the marriage of King Richard II to Anne of Bohemia. In fact, the pope acknowledged that he'd been requested to make Anne a saint by certain "English petitioners." It made a nice wedding gift to Anne of Bohemia.

INFERTILITY AND WIFE ABUSE—RITA; FEAST DAY, MAY 22.

Born near Spoleto, Italy, in 1381, Rita is the patron of childless women, and of abused and battered women. Battered women have several patronesses, all themselves victims.

Rita's patronage of infertility is due to the fact that she was born to a seemingly sterile couple who desperately wanted children; the wife miraculously conceived late in life, well beyond childbearing years, and bore Rita.

Rita's second patronage stems from her own abusive marriage. Her brute of a husband—a bully given to violence, alcoholism, and infidelity—grossly mistreated Rita for eighteen years of married life. One day, in a drunken brawl, he was fatally stabbed, and his body was carried home to Rita. When their two sons swore to avenge their father's death by killing his murderer, Rita prayed that God would take her boys before they committed the sinful act. The sons were struck violently ill, and Rita tenderly nursed them—though not back to health; in their final words, they forgave their mother, as well as forgiving their father's murderer.

Free of her husband and children, Rita joined an Augustinian convent in Cascia—after three rejections on the grounds that the nunnery accepted only virgins. As a nun, she displayed the same submission to authority she'd shown as a wife. And whatever the convent lacked in punishments, Rita supplemented with her own self-mortifications.

While in chapel one day, listening to a sermon on Christ's crown of thorns, she experienced a sharp pain on her forehead and "saw" a thorn pierce the spot. The gaping wound suppurated, and the smell became so offensive that she had to be secluded from the other nuns. Unhealed, the injury tortured her for the last fifteen years of her life.

Rita died on May 22, 1457, and her body, supposedly incorrupt to this day, is entombed in the Basilica at Cascia, Italy—a country where her cult remains immensely popular. In art, she's usually depicted as wounded by a flying thorn from Christ's crown as she prays before a crucifix, or as receiving a crown of thorny roses from the Virgin Mary. It's said that the air in the chapel housing her mortal remains is perpetually suffused with the fragrance of roses. Rita was beatified in 1626, and canonized in 1900.

MISCARRIAGE—BRIDGET OF SWEDEN; FEAST DAY, JULY 23. Bridget, a married Swedish mystic with a brood of children, lived a more or less normal life for a saint of the Middle Ages. That is, she was not a raped or martyred virgin, or a maiden coerced into a sadistic marriage.

Born in Sweden in 1303, daughter of the governor of Upland, Bridget at age fourteen married the eighteen-year-old nobleman Ulf Gudmarsson. With time spent at court, at home, and on pilgrimages, she enjoyed a happily married life, which lasted twenty-eight years. She experienced one or more miscarriages, and bore eight children—including the future Saint Catherine of Vadstena.

Appointed lady-in-waiting at the palace, Bridget zealously endeavored to get Queen Blanche and King Magnus II to adopt a less hedonistic lifestyle—her voices and visions had prompted her to undertake this risky task. Although the royals liked Bridget and respected her piety—even believing in her visions—they liked their pleasure-oriented lifestyle even more.

After her husband's death, and with a generous endowment from King Magnus, Bridget founded the Order of the Most Holy Savior, the Bridgettines, at Vadstena by Lake Vattern. Her monastery became a center of Swedish spirituality, with an emphasis on simplicity of lifestyle and the importance of religious study. After a pilgrimage to the Holy Land, she died in Rome at age seventy on July 23, 1373. She was canonized in 1391.

RABIES—HUBERT; FEAST DAY, NOVEMBER 3. Little is reliably known of Hubert's early life. Born around 656 C.E., he may have been the son of a duke, as well as a hedonistic courtier under Pepin of Heristal. Legend claims that on Good Friday, instead of worshiping in church, the young

Hubert was hunting when a stag confronted him with the glowing emblem of a cross between its antlers. A voice advised him to repent.

Hubert became a priest, and later the first bishop of Liège, working tirelessly to evangelize the pagans of his region. In addition to preaching Christ's Gospels, he'd smash pagan idols whenever he could. Hubert is said to have had a vision of his own death—a peaceful passing due to illness—a year before it happened. He died near Brussels on May 30, 727, after six days of fever. His relics were enshrined at Liège.

Devotion to Hubert as a patron saint of hunting, huntsmen, and against rabies appears to stem from the time of his conversion experience. He hunted, kept dogs, and therefore ran the risk of rabies; but his patronage in these areas is popular, not papal. According to legend, he was once given a stole of white silk and golden thread by the Blessed Virgin Mary. Starting in the twelfth century, a treatment for those suffering rabies delirium was to make a small incision in the forehead and lay in it a thread from the miraculous stole.

SKIN CANCER, MELANOMA IN PARTICULAR, ALL CANCERS IN GENERAL—PEREGRINE LAZIOSI; FEAST DAY, MAY 1.
The choice of this fourteenth-century saint as the patron of cancer has not been officially confirmed by the Church, but derives from his own miraculous cure of a foot lesion that may well have been a melanoma.

The only son of well-to-do parents, Peregrine Laziosi was born in 1260 at Forli, in Romagna. As a young man, he took an active part in the politics of his day, aligning himself with the so-called antipapal party. One day, the Blessed Virgin appeared to him with a quite specific instruction: "Go to Siena. There you will find the devout men who call themselves my servants. Attach yourself to them."

After arriving in Siena, Peregrine received the Servite habit. For thirty years, the pious priest observed silence and solitude whenever he could, and as a form of penance, he never sat down. Standing became a problem, however, when he developed a foul-smelling cancerous lesion on his foot, which caused him excruciating pain and made him an object of repulsion in his town. Doctors recommended amputation of the foot.

The night before the surgery, Peregrine prayed, then sank into a light slumber. He awoke in the morning to find no trace of the lesion—to the amazement of his doctors. From that day on, his reputation as a holy man grew. He lived to age eighty, and was canonized in 1726.

**SYPHILIS, OTHER SEXUALLY TRANSMITTED DISEASES, IN-
CLUDING AIDS—GEORGE; FEAST DAY, APRIL 23.** Little is
known historically about this third-century martyr, legendary dragon-slayer
and patron saint of England, knights, equestrians, archers, and Boy Scouts.

It is known that George was a Palestinian soldier who was martyred during the persecutions of Diocletian; his cult flourished during the Crusades of
the Middle Ages. It's the dragon myth that made George popular, and that
accounts for most of the above-mentioned patronages.

As the story is told:

A fierce, fire-breathing serpent lived in a swamp near a city called Sylene.
The town residents kept the dragon at bay by feeding it two sheep a day.
When they ran out of sheep, a human victim was selected by lot. As it happened, the king's own virgin daughter was chosen. Dressed as a bride to
meet her doom, she was about to enter the swamp when George—a knight
in shining armor—rode up on his steed, mesmerized the serpent by swaying
his lance, then wrapped round its neck the virgin's own girdle and guided
the dragon into town. The hero told the terrified townfolk they had nothing
to fear: if they converted to Christianity, he'd slay the beast on the spot. The
people were baptized, the dragon killed, and its carcass drawn away on four
carts. By the time of the Crusades, George, the fearless warrior, was something of a quasi god.

In art, George is often depicted with the hot-breathed serpent skewered
on his spear. The saint's patronage of sexually transmitted diseases seems to
stem from this image combined with a widespread British colloquialism,
"riding Saint George." The phrase implies sexual intercourse with the
woman on top, kneeling above the man. A woman who copulated by "riding Saint George" was believed to bear a boy who'd grow up to be a bishop.
In England, George became the patron of all sexually transmitted diseases.

**TUBERCULOSIS—TERESA OF LISIEUX; FEAST DAY, OCTO-
BER 1.** Canonized a saint in 1925, Teresa was born in 1873, the youngest
of five sisters, all of whom became nuns. Her father, Louis Martin, was a
watchmaker and son of an officer in the armies of Napoleon I; her mother
was Zelie Guerin. In 1888, Teresa entered the Carmelite convent of Lisieux
in Normandy, where two of her sisters were already nuns.

The nine years of life that remained to her were ordinary for a virgin who
would soon be venerated as a saint. The most traumatic event in her life was
her beloved father's plunge into insanity and confinement for three years in
an asylum. "The three years of my father's martyrdom," Teresa wrote, always

looking on the bright side, "seem to me the dearest and most fruitful of our life. I would not exchange them for the most sublime ecstasies."

Soon tuberculosis struck. Contemplating her own death, she wrote that after it, "I will let fall a shower of roses"—meaning miracles through her intercession. The remark, taken literally, made her the patroness of flowers, florists, and gardeners, indeed, the delicate Teresa is most often referred to as "The Little Flower."

In June of 1897, hemorrhaging from her TB, she was moved into the convent's infirmary and never left it. Problems with swallowing, nausea, and spitting up blood prevented her from receiving Holy Communion. Finally, she succumbed to the scourge of her era, dying at the age of twenty-four. She was beatified by Pope Pius XI in 1923, and canonized by him two years later.

After her death, her simple autobiography, *The Story of a Soul*—heavily edited if not entirely reworked by her sister, Mother Agnes—became an international sensation, spreading Teresa's popularity and leading many to pray to her for help.

Along with Joan of Arc, Teresa is also patron of France. Scores of relics from her personal life are kept in shrines in France: locks of hair, a toy tambourine from her childhood, a hand-drawn map of the United States annotated by the saint at age twelve.

ULCERS—CHARLES BORROMEO; FEAST DAY, NOVEMBER 4.

Charles Borromeo was aristocratic by birth: his mother was a Medici, and his uncle was Pope Pius IV.

Born in 1538 at the family castle of Arona on Lake Maggiore, Italy, the wealthy Charles, who suffered a speech impediment, was educated in the finest schools of Paris and Milan. By the age of twenty-two, holding a doctorate in civil and canon law, he was appointed papal secretary of state, administrator of Milan, and summarily elevated to the rank of cardinal-deacon by his pontiff uncle—even though Charles had never been ordained a priest.

This nepotism came to good ends. Charles used his immense power, intelligence, and wealth to build schools and hospitals, and he played a major role in the final sessions of the reforming Council of Trent, which had been suspended in 1552.

He entered the priesthood in 1563, and two months later was consecrated bishop, then quickly named archbishop of Milan. He established "Sunday schools" to hold catechism classes, founded several seminaries, and often distributed his wealth to the poor. When a plague struck Italy in the 1570s,

Charles worked tirelessly with the sick and dying, and in relief efforts, he exhausted his family fortune. Essentially, his commitment wore him down—stress may have brought on ulcers—and he died on November 3, 1584, at age forty-six. A popular cult immediately sprang up around him and he was canonized in 1610.

"The body of the saint is incorrupt," writes Joan Carroll Cruz of Borromeo in *Relics*, "but this is due to the embalming it received soon after death. The face is covered with a silver mask, while the body is clothed in gem-studded vestments." This whole-body relic is kept in the Cathedral of Milan, Italy.

Celestial Personae

od

Appearance to Existence

god. GOD.

The lower-case word summons images of paganism and humankind's primitive past: warring male and female powers, worship based on fear, bacchanalia, and the sacrifice of animals.

The upper-case word invokes the single unifying being or oneness who triumphed over polytheism, evicting numerous pantheons of deities. One God. A personal God.

Names tell us a lot. There is much information to be mined in the origin of a word. By looking at the various names of God, it is possible to trace his roots, construct his family tree, and witness his troubled gestation and painful birth in the Near East, a labor that was long but ultimately joyous.

"I am the Lord thy God," he made clear early on, perhaps as early as 1400 B.C.E., "thou shalt have no other gods before Me" (Exod. 20:2–3).

Let's start with God's earliest name.

YAHWEH: NEAR EAST, C. 1400 TO C. 1200 B.C.E. ✦

He's *Allah* to Muslims, a word that in Arabic translates as "God."

He's *God the Father* to Christians, who distinguish him from two other Trinitarian Godheads, the Son, and the Holy Ghost. ("Ghost" sufficed for centuries, but in this age of horror films and haunted houses, "Spirit" has become the norm.)

To the ancient Israelites, however, he was *Yahweh*. A personal name.

On Mount Sinai, c. 1400 B.C.E., from out of a burning bush, God called to Moses (whose name means "drawn out of water"), ordering the prophet to free the Israelites from bondage in Egypt. Startled, Moses asked:

"If I come to the people of Israel and say to them, 'The God of your fathers has sent me to you,' and they ask me, 'What is his name?' what shall I say to them?" (Exod. 3:13)

God answered cryptically, cloaking his name in four Hebrew consonants: *YHWH*—called the *tetragrammaton*, meaning "four things written." It is pronounced *Yahweh*, which has various translations: "I am who I am," or "I shall be what I shall be," or, as some linguists argue, "He who brings into existence whatever exists."

All three meanings demonstrate how the word "Yahweh" is related to the Hebrew verb "to be," which reaches beyond "to exist" to encompass "to be actively present in." This connotation of "active presence" implies that God is with us and active in daily events.

UNSPOKEN AND UNWRITTEN. Up until the destruction of the First Temple in 586 B.C.E., people freely invoked the name "Yahweh" aloud. It was around the third century B.C.E. that a prohibition arose against speaking God's personal name. Only the high priest, on Yom Kippur (Day of Atonement), inside the Temple's Holy of Holies, would be permitted to recite the name and thereby help expiate the sins of all Israel.

The name "Yahweh" appears in the Hebrew Bible starting with the Creation story of Genesis.

That day on Mount Sinai, around 1400 B.C.E., God also gave Moses Ten Commandments. The First Commandment, as we've seen, demands singular devotion: "Thou shalt have no other gods before me."

The Second Commandment, "Thou shalt not take the name of the Lord thy God in vain," suggested to third-century B.C.E. high priests that God didn't want his personal name spoken aloud. Thus, out of reverence, the Jews shied away from saying "Yahweh," referring instead to God by the Hebrew word *Adonai*, meaning "Sovereign" or "Lord."

Centuries later, the Greek-speaking Jews who produced the first Greek translation of Hebrew Scriptures, the *Septuagint*, rendered *Adonai* as *Kyrios*, their own word for "Lord." Later still, early Christian Church fathers, speaking Latin, used *Dominus*. Interestingly, our English spelling l-o-r-d derives from the Old English word *hlaford*, which literally means "loaf-keeper," or "one who feeds dependents." The Lord provides.

It was not by coincidence that the Gospel writer Luke (his name means "light-giver") and the evangelist Paul (his name means "little") appropriated the name *Kyrios* as their primary designation for Jesus Christ. The Jews had called God (the Father) *Kyrios*, now the Christians called God the Son by the same title. *Kyrios* became something of a family name, linking Son to Father.

Today, strict Jews will not write the name of God even in the vernacular; for "God" they pen "G-d."

"JEHOVAH" AS A CORRUPTION OF YAHWEH: SIXTEENTH CENTURY C.E. ◆

Jehovah is a much later name for God, and a false rendering of Moses' original tongue twister, YHWH.

The Jewish Masorete scribes, who labored from the sixth to the tenth centuries C.E. to reproduce the correct Hebrew text of their Bible, the Tanakh (which has the same material as the Christian Old Testament but presents it in a slightly different order), combined the unpronounceable YHWH with vowels from two popular old Hebrew terms for God: *Adonai* and *Elohim*—arriving at YeHoWah, which Renaissance Christians rendered as Jehovah. This form made its way into the King James Bible.

Had the word "Yahweh" been spoken before Moses heard it on Mount Sinai?

Linguists tell us that Yahweh was one of many names for a primary pagan "god" known to all ancient Semitic peoples before the birth of monotheism. The tribe of Levi, to which Moses belonged, knew the word and was aware that it often was voiced in a shortened form as a sacred invocation—*Yo!*, or *Yah!*, or *Yahu!*—like a mantra. Curiously, the name of Moses' mother was Jochebed—or Yokheved—a word that is derived from Yahweh. Was there an echo of a more ancient matriarchal era in God's spoken name to Moses?

THE YAHWIST: GERMANY, 1800s C.E. ◆

Today, scholars use the word "Yahweh" in a different context entirely: the "Yahwist" is the mysterious author who actually wrote much of early Hebrew Scriptures.

Moses, it's now believed, did not write the first five books of the Hebrew Bible, the Pentateuch or Torah: Genesis, Exodus, Leviticus, Numbers, and Deuteronomy. Scholars agree that it is a composite work, consisting of texts by several different authors, cleverly woven together around 500 B.C.E. by a master editor known as the redactor—from the English verb "redact," meaning "to arrange in proper form for publication."

(The redactor's work paid off. The Bible has been a best-seller ever since.

Today, at least one book of the Bible can be read in 2,062 different world languages—there are 6,000 known world languages total. The entire Bible, Old and New Testaments, exists in 337 different languages.)

The oldest of these texts, running through Genesis, Exodus, Leviticus, and Numbers, was written by the author whom scholars call the Yahwist—to German biblical scholars of the last century, the Jahwist, or "J." The Yahwist is the oldest-known author of biblical scripture.

Historically, who might the Yahwist have been? Do we have any hints to his actual identity?

In his fascinating 1990 work *The Book of J*—an audacious effort of literary restoration—Harold Bloom argues that J was a woman, a brilliant female of the stature of a Homer or Shakespeare, who lived in the royal house at King Solomon's court, mid–tenth century B.C.E. Bloom's argument is based in part on the vivid, forceful, and unforgettable portraits of Old Testament women like Eve, Sarai, Rebecca, Tamar, and Zipporah. Bloom feels these portraits display a woman's point of view that would have been unlikely in a male writer of that time.

GOD'S APPEARANCE:
BOOK OF DANIEL, C. SIXTH CENTURY B.C.E. ◆

What does God look like?

The Bible provides no clear physical description of the Almighty. And yet the narrative is primarily about God. At least the Old Testament books are.

The writers of the Old Testament anthropomorphize God by giving him hands, ears, and eyes; feet so he can walk in the Garden at Eden; the sense of smell so he can sniff at Noah's burnt offerings.

Jews and Muslims are forbidden to illustrate Yahweh and Allah, respectively, viewing any image as a form of idolatry; as Exodus 20:4 warns: "You shall not make for yourself a graven image." One description in particular has influenced countless illustrators of the Christian "God the Father." It occurs in the Book of Daniel, in Daniel's own vision:

> *Thrones were set in place, and the Ancient of Days took his seat. His clothing was as white as snow; the hair of his head was white like wool. His throne was flaming with fire. (Dan. 7:9)*

This simple passage is the origin of our most familiar and grandfatherly image of the Almighty.

Daniel's name means "God is my judge," and the book that Daniel wrote, some time in the sixth century B.C.E., consists primarily of prophetic dreams and visions, with actual history serving merely as backdrop.

Daniel was either of royal descent or from a distinguished family of Jerusalem. In the government of Babylon, he was made third chief governor after interpreting some mysterious handwriting on the wall during a banquet. This, and the fact that he was protected by God in many miraculous ways, put him in a position to write a book of forecasts and foreshadowings. About his later years and death, we know nothing. It would, of course, have been helpful if Daniel had described God in more detail.

Several people in the Bible saw God, but notice how little was revealed:

• Moses saw the back of God (Exod. 33:23).

• Jacob dreamed of "a stairway resting on the earth, with its top reaching to heaven, and the angels of God . . . ascending and descending on it" (Gen. 28:12–13). Above the ladder stood the Lord, but he's not described at all.

• Micaiah saw "the Lord sitting on this throne with all the host of heaven standing on his right and on his left" (2 Chron. 18:18).

Many saw thrones:

• Isaiah saw "the Lord seated on a throne, high and exalted" (Isa. 6:1).

• Ezekiel saw "what looked like a throne of sapphire, and high above on the throne . . . a figure like that of a man" (Ezek. 1:26).

• In the New Testament, John is as vague: "I was in the Spirit, and there before me was a throne in heaven with someone sitting on it" (Rev. 4:2).

Even Jesus, in the course of four detailed Gospels, never describes his Father.

METAPHORS FOR GOD ◆ *To the Jews, God was many things, even if they had trouble picturing him. He was the personal God of each individual Israelite and took on many images:*

Rock (Exod. 17:1–7), Shepherd (Ps. 23:1), Shield (Ps. 18:2), Light (Ps. 27:1), Sun (Ps. 84:11), Father (Ps. 89:26), Mother-Bird (Ps. 91:4), Shade (Ps. 121:5), Song (Isa. 12:2), Redeemer (Isa. 41:14), Warrior (Isa. 42:13), Potter (Isa. 45:9), Husband (Isa. 54:5), Fountain (Jer. 2:13), Dew (Hos. 14:5), Lion, Leopard, Bear (Hos. 13:7–8).

None of these metaphors tells us what God looked like. For that, we must be thankful to Daniel for the glimpse he gave us.

GODS TO GOD: NEAR EAST, C. 1800 TO 1400 B.C.E. ◆

The God of the Hebrew Bible, or *Tanakh*, suffers from a bad case of divine multiple personality disorder. As well as from intense paranoia, lack of self-esteem, dark rage, vengefulness, and a morbid love of war. He vacillates between his role as gentle liberator and stern lawgiver, as tender arbiter of disputes and genocidal warrior against unbelievers.

He's certainly not the all-good, all-compassionate, Almighty monotheist of more recent times.

There is a reason for the God of the Israelites' multiple personalities. In the Near East, monotheism gradually emerged from polytheism. Furthermore, the Old Testament is not a single book, but an anthology of tales composed by different authors living in various countries over a period of more than a millennium.

If God in the Book of Genesis, in particular, appears at times to be two different people . . . well, he was.

On the one hand, he was the lofty, self-assured Creator of the universe who made man in his image. On the other hand, he was a brooding, indecisive, volatile, punishing curmudgeon. Many scholars believe that remnants of polytheism, of God's plurality, were never completely purged from Hebrew Scriptures.

For instance, after Adam disobeys the divine injunction not to eat of the tree of knowledge, God says (author's emphasis):

Behold, the man is become as one of us, *to know good and evil. (Gen. 3:22)*

*The Tower of Babel and
the Confusion of Tongues:
"Let us go down, and
there confound their
language."*

Later on, when arrogant men try to build a tower that would reach up to Heaven, the Tower of Babel, God, glancing down from Heaven, says (author's emphasis):

Let us *go down, and there confound their language. (Gen. 11:7)*

The use of "us" suggests traces of the polytheism of the ancient Near East.

EL TO ELOHIM: THE EVOLUTION OF GOD'S NAME ◆

Let's further pursue the way in which the word "God" emerged from the word "gods." The popular Hebrew word for God, *Elohim*, which appears more than two thousand times in Hebrew writings in reference to the God of Israel, is plural and translates in its oldest usage as "gods." (Later, it's used as "divinity.") The singular, *eloha*, is relatively rare in the Bible outside of Job, where it is found about forty times.

In the Near East, the plural *elohim* was used to address pagan gods, a single god, and also female deities. Some biblical scholars, who see no traces of polytheism in the Old Testament, argue that *elohim* invests in the One God all the attributes once possessed by many pagan gods. That's why the Bible uses the plural.

Elohim is believed to be an elongation of the very first Semitic word for god, *El.* And El was the chief god in the Canaanite pantheon of deities in ancient Near Eastern myths.

Why did ancient peoples call their chief god El?

"Power" is the answer. The etymology of the word "El" is obscure. It's commonly thought that the term derived from a root *yl*, meaning "to be powerful."

Notice in the Old Testament how this divine pagan word "El" is pivotal to arriving at God's many titles as known to the patriarchs:

- *El Elohei Yisrael:* "El, the God of Israel" (Gen. 33:20).
- *El Elyon:* "God Most High," *elyon* being the Hebrew adjective for "higher" or "upper" (Gen. 14:18).
- *El Olam:* "God Everlasting," the word *olam* literally meaning "an indefinitely long time" (Gen. 21:33).
- *El Shaddai:* "God Almighty," (numerous references in Genesis). Later Greek-speaking Jews writing the Septuagint rendered *Shaddai* as the Greek *Pantokrator*, meaning "All-powerful"; the later Latin Vulgate uses *Omnipotens*,

meaning "Omnipotent." Through shadings in translations, the image of God evolved.

- *El Roi:* "God who sees me" (Gen. 16:13).
- *El Brit:* "God of the Covenant" (Gen. 31:13).

It is true that in the Bible, the article *ha* often is attached to *elohim*: *ha-elohim*, meaning "the [true] God." But whereas many biblical scholars claim that *el* and its elongation *elohim* to the Israelites simply meant "the Divinity," singular, many linguists aren't so sure. It is possible that in the very earliest oral traditions on which the Bible is based, the creation story detailed in Genesis was indeed the work of a plurality of gods. As are creation stories in many ancient myths.

As God in the Bible settles into having one benevolent personality, the terms used to describe him become more purely monotheistic. To express that another way: As the books of the Old Testament were continually edited and reedited, God matures and monotheism becomes the Bible's principal theme.

A VENGEFUL GOD IS SILENCED:
THE BOOK OF JOB, C. TENTH CENTURY B.C.E. ◆

The Jews arrange their Bible, or Tanakh, differently from the way Christians arrange their inheritance of the Old Testament from the Jews. In fact, Tanakh is not really a word, but an acronym that brings together the initial Hebrew terms for the three principal parts of Jewish Scripture:

PENTATEUCH—*Torah.* Also known as the Five Books of Moses, it consists of Genesis, Exodus, Leviticus, Numbers, Deuteronomy.

PROPHETS—*Nevi'im.* It includes several of the historical books (Joshua, Judges, 1 and 2 Samuel, 1 and 2 Kings), the three major prophets (Isaiah, Jeremiah, Ezekiel), and the twelve minor prophets (Hosea, Joel, Amos, Obadiah, Jonah, Micah, Nahum, Habakkuk, Zephaniah, Haggai, Zechariah, Malachi).

THE WRITINGS—*Ketuvim.* This comprises the Psalms, Proverbs, Job, Song of Songs, Ruth, Lamentations, Ecclesiastes, Esther, Daniel, Ezra, Nehemiah, 1 and 2 Chronicles.

TORAH + NEVI'IM + KETUVIM = TANAKH. This Jewish arrangement of Scripture reveals a fascinating pattern. From Genesis through Second Kings, *God acts.* From later Prophets to Job, *God speaks* but does not act himself. After Job, *God falls utterly silent.*

"From the end of the Book of Job to the end of the Tanakh," writes Jack

Miles in *God: A Biography* (1995), "God never speaks again. His speech from the whirlwind is, in effect, his last will and testament." God's earlier speeches will be repeated, miracles will still be attributed to him, he'll be glimpsed, but God gradually recedes from view, abandoning the stage he created, giving over the spotlight to the Chosen People of his covenant.

Why?

The author of the Book of Job is unknown. The work is complex and profound in that it poses, but can't adequately answer, one of humanity's most perplexing questions: If God is in complete control, and all-wise, why does he allow innocent people to suffer?

Job asks this of God. In fact, Job challenges God as to why he punished an innocent man. God is embarrassed, backs down, and makes amends. From then on, God is silent. Miles and others claim that through the Jewish arrangement of the Scriptures, we witness a previously wrathful, vengeful God—the God of Abraham and Moses—being muted into a Presence of compassion who then stays in the background of his own narrative. The sequence of God the Doer, God the Speechmaker, and the Silent God is fascinating to ponder.

𝕮hrist

Son to Trinity

GOD THE FATHER, God the Son, God the Holy Spirit. Three Gods in One. The Trinitarian formula. This concept is known only to Christians. In this chapter, we'll examine its convoluted origin.

Pure, unadulterated monotheism is, of course, the Jews' great legacy to Christianity and Islam. To religion, in general. The Jews posited monotheism. That concept, though, was a long time in coming. Its origins, however, are clear.

In brief: Jews developed monotheism, Greeks refined it, Christians elaborated upon it (with the Trinitarian Godhead), and Muslims centuries later went back to the basics. What Christians did with monotheism—adding to God the Father, the Son and the Spirit—offended Jews, and later incensed Muslims.

PROPHECY AS THE ULTIMATE ORIGIN:
INTERPRETING THE OLD TESTAMENT, FIRST CENTURY C.E. ◆

For Christians of all denominations, the origin of Jesus Christ as the *Son of God* is foretold through messianic prophecy in Hebrew Scriptures. Let us juxtapose several prophecies and their subsequent fulfillment:

PROPHECY: A new ruler would come from the town of Bethlehem: "Out of thee [Bethlehem] shall he come forth unto me that is to be the ruler in Israel: and his going forth is from the beginning" (Mic. 5:2). The Jewish prophet Micah (whose name means "who is like God?") penned that prediction in the eighth century B.C.E.

FULFILLMENT: "And Joseph went . . . unto the city of David, which is called Bethlehem. . . . To be taxed with Mary his espoused wife, being great with child" (Luke 2:4–5). Jesus Christ is born around 6 to 3 C.E.; Luke recorded the events around 65 C.E.

PROPHECY: Date c. 1400 B.C.E. Author: Moses. "A prophet like me will the Lord, your God, raise up for you from among your own kinsmen; to him you shall listen" (Deut. 18:15). The forecast in Deuteronomy was written about 1400 B.C.E., allegedly by Moses.

FULFILLMENT: "Now it came to pass . . . Jesus also having been baptized and being in prayer, that heaven was opened, and the Holy Spirit descended upon him in bodily form as a dove, and a voice came from heaven, 'Thou art my beloved Son, in thee I am well pleased' " (Luke 4:21–22). Jesus was baptized at the start of his ministry, around 24 to 27 C.E.; Luke wrote of the messianic event around 65 C.E.

For many Christians (all Roman Catholics, at least), even the *virgin birth of Christ* is foretold.

PROPHECY: "Behold a virgin shall conceive and bear a son, and his name shall be called Immanuel" (Isa. 7:14). Date of prophecy: eighth century B.C.E. Author: Isaiah.

FULFILLMENT: "Do not be afraid, Mary . . . thou shall conceive in thy womb and bring forth a son, and his name shall be Jesus" (Luke 1:30–31). Luke writing about 65 C.E. of the angel Gabriel's visit to the Virgin Mary. The name "Immanuel" means "God with us." (For more on the virgin birth, see the chapter "Virginity of the Virgin.")

For all Christians, even *Christ's death on the cross* is foretold.

PROPHECY: "He shall be led as a sheep to the slaughter, and shall be dumb as a lamb before his shearer, and he shall not open his mouth" (Isa. 53:7). Date: eighth century B.C.E. Author: Isaiah, relating how a servant of the Lord would be rejected by his people and suffer.

FULFILLMENT: "They crucified him there, and the robbers, one on his right hand and the other on his left. And Jesus said, 'Father, forgive them, for they know not what they do' " (Luke 23:33–34).

These are the biblical "origins" (or roots) for key events in Christianity. In religion, a divine prophecy is the ultimate origin for a later event.

For Christians, the Book of Isaiah, written in the eighth century B.C.E., forecasts (or is the origin of) most of the Christian faith's highlights. Isaiah's theological message has to do with the coming of the Messiah, and the Jewish prophet's words are quoted frequently by the New Testament authors of the first century C.E., often attributed to Jesus Christ himself.

The Jewish Book of Psalms, written between the tenth to the fourth centuries B.C.E., was used by Christian Gospel writers of the first century C.E. as the "origins" of Christ's agonies and humiliations on the cross, as well as his glorious Resurrection:

PROPHECY: The Messiah would be mocked and insulted (Ps. 22:7–8).

FULFILLMENT: Bystanders sneer at Christ on the cross (Luke 23:25).

PROPHECY: The Messiah would be given gall and vinegar (Ps 69:21).

FULFILLMENT: To quench his thirst, Christ is given vinegar mixed with gall (Matt. 27:34).

PROPHECY: The Messiah's clothing would be divided up by lot (Ps. 22:18).

FULFILLMENT: As Christ hangs on the cross, the Roman soldiers divided up his clothes by casting lots (Matt. 27:35).

PROPHECY: God would raise the Messiah from the grave; his body would not decay (Ps. 16:10, 49:15).

FULFILLMENT: Jesus' Resurrection becomes the pivotal event in Christianity (Mark 16:6–7).

The writers of the Four Gospels—Matthew ("gift of Jehovah"), Mark ("polite"), Luke ("light-giver"), and John ("grace")—were well acquainted with old Hebrew Scriptures and scoured the scrolls for prefigurements of Christ as the Messiah.

On the hill at Golgotha, a Roman soldier pierces Christ's side with a sword, and John, writing of the event around 95 C.E., finds in the Book of Zechariah (12:10), written some six centuries earlier, a prediction that the Messiah's body would be pierced.

As we'll see, it was this kind of interpretation of old texts that allowed Christian theologians in the third and fourth centuries C.E. to discern in the Gospels evidence of the Trinitarian Godhead.

But before the doctrine of the Trinity could be declared—indeed, before Christ could be prophesied as the Messiah; before Christianity itself could be born—monotheism had to emerge.

Let's go back to the beginning.

MONOTHEISM TO POLYTHEISM: NEAR EAST, C. 1800 TO C. 1400 B.C.E. ◆

The history of religion is a progression of ever-narrowing "isms": animism to polytheism to monotheism.

Bacchus, Roman god
(left). *Poseidon, Greek*
god. Kali, Hindu god.

Animism, in its broadest sense, is the belief that all things possess spirits or soul: babbling brooks, yellow maize, sturdy oaks, sly cats, sagacious humans. Innumerable spiritual beings are the *animating* forces that gave life to living things. As well as meddle in human affairs, for better or worse.

Animistic religions probably dominated the world in prehistoric times; they were the first religions; they are still found among tribal peoples. The word "animism" has its roots in the Latin *anima*, "soul."

Polytheism established a pantheon of named gods—male, female, or a gender hybrid. Most significantly, these deities often existed "elsewhere"—high up in the heavens, on Mount Olympus, or in some other remote and sacred place. Often one sky god dominated all the others. Scholars call this *primitive monotheism*.

Origin of the word "polytheism": Greek *polys*, "many" + *theos*, "god."

As we'll see, even the Islamic Allah once was a high sky deity who ruled over a host of lower gods, until the Prophet Muhammad identified him as the One and Only and banished other gods to oblivion.

Thus, it was only one step from a multiplicity of celestial gods to one exclusive heavenly Creator—but it was a giant step.

How did one monotheistic God—*exclusive monotheism*—come to be the center of worship for Jews, Christians, and Muslims?

The answer has to do with the *Zeitgeist*, or spirit of the times, that existed in the Near and Middle East some three thousand years ago.

MONOTHEISM TRIUMPHS DURING THE BABYLONIAN EXILE: BABYLON, SIXTH CENTURY B.C.E. ◆

In ancient Babylon, there was no such thing as monotheism. A Babylonian could pick from among a pantheon of gods one deity to worship above all others—could ignore the others, in fact. This is known as *henotheism*, from the Greek words *hen*, "one," and *theos*, "god." It is the worship of one God without denying the existence of others. Hints of it can be found in the Old Testament, though in the Hebrew Bible, these other gods are usually classified as false gods.

Molech was the national god of the country of Ammon (Zeph. 1:5). *Marduk* was the chief god of Babylon (Jer. 50:2). *Baal* was a main storm god of Canaan (1 Kings 16:31–32). *El*, as we saw in the previous chapter, was the head of the pantheon of Canaan.

Hence, henotheism was not unknown to the ancient Israelites. In fact, some biblical scholars speak of the Old Testament conception of God as "monolatry"—worship of one among many—rather than pure monotheism. They claim that the God of Abraham (c. 1800 B.C.E.) was not yet the exclusive God or Yahweh of Moses (c. 1400 B.C.E.).

EGYPTIANS ALMOST TRY MONOTHEISM. In ancient Egypt, under religious reform initiated by the pharaoh Akhenaton in the fourteenth century B.C.E., we see the *Zeitgeist* of henotheism again. From a celestial multitude of gods—so many they were hard to keep track of—the pharaoh singled out Aton, the sun god, to be revered above all others.

As time passed, Egyptians became intolerant of the lesser gods—those less mighty than Aton—and their names were deleted from the registry of deities. Egypt was on the verge of exclusive monotheism: one god, Aton.

But for some reason, the tide turned, and Egyptian rulers eventually reinstated many of the lesser gods. Their religion backtracked to polytheism.

But the idea of exclusive monotheism was in the air.

JEWS BECOME A MONOTHEISTIC PEOPLE. The God of Israel, Moses' Yahweh, could not have been more explicit in his demand for exclusive monotheism. "I, the Lord thy God, am a jealous God, visiting the iniquity of the fathers upon the children . . . of them that hate me" (Exod. 20:5).

It was the Israelites under Moses who embraced the concept of pure monotheism. Their passionate rejection of other gods became the Judaic affirmation of faith: "Hear, O Israel: the Lord is our God, the Lord is one." (Deut. 6:4).

In their pledge to monotheism, the Israelites did occasionally slip into idolatry, from the time they made the golden calf until the Babylonian Exile. Old ways die hard.

For Jews, however, strict monotheism can be dated from the time of their Exile in Babylon in the sixth century B.C.E.; from 586 to 539 B.C.E., when their nation was lost. The once-glorious Temple and capital city of Jerusalem now lay in ruins. But the spiritual catharsis of the Exile forever exorcised the impulse toward idolatry from the Jewish people. Paradoxically, it was the painful Exile that led to the final victory of monotheism over pagan worship. In its monotheism, Israel was utterly unique.

As the eminent Old Testament scholar Theodorus Vriezen observes: "It is striking how the whole life of the people is seen as dominated by Yahweh and by Yahweh alone. Faith in Yahweh is the foundation of the life for the Israelite."

This is the legacy that Jews would pass on to Christians.

MONOTHEISM CATCHES THE GREEK FANCY:
GREECE, FOURTH CENTURY B.C.E. ◆

The Jews really practiced what's called *ethnic monotheism*—there is One God, and that God belongs only to his Chosen People. The Greeks saw this as limited.

Greek philosophers, beginning in the sixth century B.C.E., broadened Judaic ethnic monotheism in a direction that would influence Christianity, and later Islam. Basically, the Greeks said: If there is only One God, *He* then must be the Creator of everybody. And belong to everybody. It was a democratic notion.

The Greeks previously had been pure polytheists. But monotheism impressed them as a sophisticated idea. And philosophically they had been moving toward the idea of "the unity of all things."

The single best-known document to express the Greek shift toward monotheism is the fourth century B.C.E. hymn to Zeus, by the Stoic philosopher Cleanthes. It praises Zeus as the essence of divinity, creator and ruler of the cosmos, omnipotent, the giver of every gift, father of all mankind. Monotheism was taking hold.

"ISMS." It's interesting to note that in the East, no local form of monotheism evolved; any notion of a single, exclusive god was an import from the West. Although in many cases one god eclipsed others in importance—Shiva or Vishnu, for instance—the emphasis never negated other deities.

Two basic "isms" have offered differing views of God for centuries:

DEISM, posited by the Greeks, claims God created the world, set it in motion, and stepped back to watch passively—perhaps bemused. This view would deny all claims of divine providence, miracles, and God's intervention in human affairs.

Furthermore, deism (from the Latin *deus*, "god") claims that the laws of nature and moral laws are discoverable by man, through the use of man's own rational powers; revelation from God is unnecessary.

THEISM is the basis for the religions of Judaism, Christianity, and Islam. It regards God as the Creator of the world, who continues to work with his power in the world.

But the Greeks did not buy the idea of God's absolute dominion over nature and over man. Yes, monotheism was clever as a concept, good for consolidating the many gods in a pantheon, but the One God could not be all-powerful, all-knowing, all-present.

For the Greeks, the monotheistic God served as a unifying principle, in the abstract, satisfying their love for "the unity of all things." The Jewish God was a personal, knowable Lord, but in Hellenized monotheism, God is absolutely unknown: *deus absconditus*, "god concealed."

The word "theism" is rooted in the Greek *theos*, "god."

PANTHEISM, an entirely different "ism," is found in the East. Pantheism holds that God *is* the world, identical to it and indistinguishable from it. Its essence is found in Hinduism, where God—or Brahman—is the sole reality; the world of human sense experience is mere appearance. Illusion.

Origin of the word "pantheism": Greek *pan*, "all" + *theos*, "god." The word was coined in 1705 by English deist J. Toland. Its roots lie in the much older word "pantheon," home of "all of the gods."

Early Christians, as we're about to see, borrowed aspects of monotheism from the Jews and from the Greeks and gave it a unique triple twist.

TRINITY—THREE GODS IN ONE:
CHRISTIANITY, SECOND CENTURY C.E. ◆

Christianity borrowed not only the Jewish concept of monotheism, but the Hebrew Bible as well. Christians referred to the Testament of the prophets as "the Old Testament" to acknowledge God's "old" covenant with the Jews, as opposed to God's "new" covenant with the followers of Jesus Christ. Thus, the new Scripture became known as "the New Testament."

But among the three great monotheistic religions, only Christianity embraces the *Trinitarian Creed*: the coexistence of God the Father, God the Son, and God the Holy Spirit in a single Godhead, distinctly different, yet one

*The Holy Trinity—
Father, Son, and
Holy Spirit.*

and the same. Little wonder that Romans eavesdropping on early Christians suspected them of idolatry; how many gods did these people worship?

One might ask—as Jews and Muslims repeatedly have—isn't it cheating for a religion to claim to be monotheistic if it recognizes three distinctly different Gods? Three Gods; three different names; three different functions: the Creator, the Redeemer, the Sanctifier. Should, Muslims suggested, this not be called "tritheism"?

How did Christians come to develop the Trinitarian creed?

Significantly, the Christian books of the Bible—the Gospels, Acts, Epistles (or letters), Revelation, and the Apocrypha ("things that are hidden")—make no explicit reference to a threefold Godhead.

Nor did Jesus, a Jew, perhaps with rabbinical training, violate the Judaic motto—"Hear, O Israel: The Lord our God is one Lord"—in his teachings.

God the Father does mention God the Son in the New Testament, and the Son in turn mentions the Father *and* the Holy Spirit. The outline of a trinity is there, but it is never clearly delineated.

A LAWYER STEPS IN. The task of delineation fell to Church father Tertullian. Born in Carthage about the year 160 C.E., he was educated in Rome as a jurist. Upon converting to Christianity, he gave up law to devote himself to theology, writing texts that would influence the faith for the next thousand years.

With his legal background, Tertullian scoured the Gospels for passages that alluded to the Trinity. Or, better yet, linked the three Persons in a single sentence. Unearthing several examples, he zeroed in on Matthew 28:19, where Jesus gives his apostles the formula for baptism (author's emphasis):

Go, therefore, and make disciples of all nations, baptizing them in the name of
the Father *and of the* Son *and of the* Holy Spirit.

Tertullian's legal eye also liked Luke 1:35, when the angel Gabriel announces the conception of Jesus in Mary's womb (author's emphasis):

The Holy Spirit *will come upon you, and the power of the* Most High *will*
overshadow you; therefore the child to be born will be called holy, the Son
of God.

These passages that invoke Father, Son, and Spirit proved the Trinity's
validity to Tertullian. And to preserve the essential notion of exclusive
monotheism, he concluded that three Persons had to exist as "one substance"—*homoousious*, literally, "made of the same stuff."

But the biblical passages that seem to suggest a Triune God did not convince all theologians of the time. For many decades, Church fathers bitterly
argued fine points among themselves. Some viewed the Son as secondary to
the Father. No one was quite sure how to rank the Spirit.

Some viewed the Trinity as consisting of *God,* his *Word*, and his *Wisdom*;
the Son being the Father's Word incarnate, the Spirit being the Father's Wisdom revealed.

Critics of Christianity, Romans and Jews alike, charged that the fledgling
two-hundred-year-old religion had merely given a new spin to pagan polytheism. Christians, they argued, clearly worshiped three gods. The new
Church had to do something decisive.

ARIAN CONTROVERSY AND THE TRINITARIAN FORMULA: NICAEA, 325 C.E. ◆

Early in the fourth century, the Trinitarian controversy heated to the high
point of heresy, pitting two theologians, Athanasius and Arius, against each
other and drawing concern from the Roman emperor Constantine himself,
who had warmed up to Christianity and would eventually convert.

Today, Arius's name is a byword for heresy: the Arian Heresy.

Back in 320, Arius, who knew Scripture inside out—and was a skilled
propagandist and musician—insisted that Christ, the Word, Logos, could only
be a creature like ourselves, *created by God.* When he put his ideas to music
and sang songs of Christ's second-rank status to God, thousands of ordinary
Christians, once content in their monotheism, became aware of the passionate debate raging among bishops.

Arius, from his arsenal of textural ammunition, fired off passages to theologians proving Christ was not part of the Godhead. Passages he also put to music. A key weapon—and a key song—was a passage in Proverbs that describes divine Wisdom, and states explicitly that God had created Wisdom—the Word, Logos, Christ—at the very beginning. Thus, asserted Arius, Christ, the Word, had been with God for a long time indeed, since the beginning, and was undeniably of high holy status, but because the Word had been created *by* God, Logos was essentially different and distinct from God; certainly, Jesus Christ was not God's equal.

Constantine, troubled by the growing split among theologians, demanded resolution of the conundrum. Was God's divinity singular and unique, or shared equally by the Son and the Spirit?

BISHOPS PUT THEIR HEADS TOGETHER. Christian bishops gathered at Nicaea on May 20, 325, convening the Council of Nicaea, which, after much acrimonious contention, decided upon the crucial formula for the Trinitarian doctrine, setting it forth in a credo, the Nicene Creed. The Son, it declared, is "of the same essence [*homoousious*] as the Father." The creed said troublingly little about the Holy Spirit.

In fact, the entire lengthy creed, as first written, wrestles with logic and common sense to equate Father and Son, giving nod to the Holy Spirit *only* in the last passing line: "And we believe in the Holy Ghost."

That's it. One line. "And we believe in the Holy Ghost." An afterthought. Three hundred years after Christ's Resurrection the Latin doctors of Christ's Church still didn't know what to make of the Spirit who could be a peaceful dove or licking tongues of fire.

Nonetheless, the bishops' apparent agreement on the equality of God the Father and God the Son pleased the emperor.

THE NICENE CREED IS REWRITTEN. In truth, theologians had not comfortably agreed, and the Arian crisis raged on for the next fifty years.

Various Church fathers repeatedly worked and reworked the Nicene Creed, attempting to give equal emphasis to the *three* Persons in God, slighting none. Finally, under the leadership of Basil, bishop of Caesarea (d. 379), the doctrine of the Trinity—and the Nicene Creed—took the form it has maintained ever since. In part:

> *We believe in one God, the Father,*
> *The Almighty, maker of heaven and earth . . .*
> *We believe in one Lord, Jesus Christ,*
> *the only Son of God,*

eternally begotten of the Father . . .
We believe in the Holy Spirit, the Lord,
   the giver of life,
   who proceeds from the Father . . .

The Nicene Creed is professed by the majority of Christians, although some, such as the Baptists, the Disciples of Christ, and the United Church of Christ, refuse to endorse it—or any other creed for that matter. They hold that no human-made credo of faith is necessary since the Bible reveals all one needs to know.

Thus, the concept of the Trinity did not take its present form until some four hundred years after Christ's death.

NAMES OF JESUS: FIRST CENTURY C.E. ✦ *Jews had lavished metaphors on God the Father, but early Christian writers gave us many indelible names and images of God the Son. The terms and their biblical origins:*

ALPHA AND OMEGA (Rev. 1:8), BRIGHT MORNING STAR (Rev. 22:16), CHRIST (Matt. 1:16), DAYSTAR (2 Pet. 1:19), GATE (John 10:9), GOOD SHEPHERD (John 10:14), KING OF KINGS (Rev. 19:16), LAMB (Rev. 5:6–13), LAMB OF GOD (John 1:29), LORD OF LORDS (Rev. 19:16), NAZARENE (Matt. 2:23), RABBI (John 1:38), ROOT OF DAVID (Rev. 5:5), SON OF DAVID (Matt. 15:22), SON OF GOD (Mark 1:1), TRUE VINE (John 15:1), WORD (John 1:1), WORD OF GOD (Rev. 19:13).

𝒜llah

Abraham to Koran

god. GOD. In an earlier chapter, we saw the difference a capital letter can make.

al-Lah. Allah. In this chapter, we'll see the difference that removing a hyphen can make.

ALLAH, ISLAM'S OWN YAHWEH:
ARABIAN PENINSULA, SEVENTH CENTURY C.E. ◆

No religion has embraced monotheism more literally than Islam. The first of the so-called Five Pillars of Islam—the basic beliefs of Muslims—states unambiguously that "there is no God but Allah."

How did the Arab people come to recognize their own monotheistic God, who is, theologically, one and the same with the Jewish Yahweh and Christian God the Father?

In Muhammad's time, the seventh century C.E., Jewish and Christian monotheism was well known on the Arabian Peninsula. Arabs, though, were still polytheistic. And in a state of crisis. Trade with the East and West had made the city of Mecca wealthy and cosmopolitan in its temptations. Arabs, long a humble and nomadic people, were losing their sense of identity, adopting alien and elitist lifestyles. Old Arab customs were being abandoned, and the wealthy distanced themselves from the poor—scandalous behavior under past customs.

Many Arabs sought to take charge of their people's destiny and revive old values. They succeeded because of Muhammad, founder of Islam, who did for the Arabs what Moses did for the enslaved Israelites in Egypt: through divine revelation from God established the identity of a chosen people.

For Moses, it was Yahweh, God of the Israelites, who revealed himself in the divine books of the Torah.

For Muhammad, born in Mecca (now in Saudi Arabia) in 570 C.E., it was Allah, God of all Arabs, who revealed himself in the divine Koran.

The *Koran* is the Divine Word of God, disclosed to Muhammad piecemeal, beginning in the year 610 and continuing until near the end of the Prophet's life in 632 (he died on June 8, in Mecca).

The popular English spelling "Koran," more correctly transliterated from Arabic as "Qur'an," means "the recitation."

The preferred transliteration of the Prophet's Arabic name is "Muhammad," not "Mohammed," as once was widely used.

The preferred transliteration of the Prophet's followers is "Muslim," no longer "Moslem."

The word "Islam" means "submission" to God, and the word "Muslim" means "one who submits."

Linguistically, the name for a follower of Islam, "Muslim," is related to the word "muslin," the sheer cotton of simple weave slept on in sheets and pillowcases. The fabric, first woven in the city of Mosul, Iraq, and known eponymously to locals in Arabic as *mosul*, came to us through the Italian name for the cloth, *mussolo*.

FROM AL-LAH TO ALLAH: MECCA, 610 C.E. ◆

Much can be learned from a name, as we've seen. In the Semitic tongue, *El* was elongated into *Elohim*, and thus a pagan chief god of "power," El, became "the Divinity" of monotheism, God. People don't like to discard terms with which they are familiar and comfortable. They tend to keep them and let their meaning evolve.

Something quite similar happened on the Arabian Peninsula several centuries later. In parts of the peninsula, there already existed a familiar and popular pagan god named *al-Lah*, literally "the-god."

By Muhammad's time, Arabs were beginning to think quite seriously about monotheism, but were reluctant to convert to Judaism or Christianity; that would only further muddy their identity as a people.

And, too, Arabs felt a strong sense of religious inferiority. Jews and Christians living on the peninsula mocked Arab polytheism as primitive pagan idolatry. Arabs, they joked, had not caught up with the times. There was only one God.

Indeed, many Arabs—like earlier Greeks—thought of monotheism as a more highly developed and sophisticated faith. One group of Arabs, whom the pagan establishment called *hanifs* or infidels, sought a solution.

In the old pagan pantheon, the chief god was *al-Lah*. In the old myths, he had never exerted much influence over lesser gods, but now the *hanifs* decided to worship "Allah" alone, and they claimed that he was the same God as that of the Jewish-Christian tradition.

In fact, they developed beliefs which confirmed that the Arab people ever since Abraham's own time, c. 1800 B.C.E., had been essential to Yahweh's master plan for humankind. The Jews and the Christians of Muhammad's time would have been shocked to hear that the Muslim faith is clearly prefigured in the Book of Genesis.

THE CLEVER CONCEPT IS THIS. Abraham was the founding father of Judaism. And Jewish Scripture tells us that Abraham's wife, Sarah, was barren. To ensure Abraham had descendants, she encouraged him to take her Egyptian slave girl Hagar as his concubine, a common practice at that time.

Hagar bore Abraham a son called Ishmael—meaning "God has heard"—and thereafter she had no peace with Sarah, who was, despite her best intentions, wildly jealous. But God promised Hagar that he would protect her child.

Sarah one day discovered she was pregnant, and she bore her own son, Isaac, now forcing Abraham to drive Hagar and Ishmael away. Abraham grieved, and was consoled by God himself—in a biblical passage dear to the hearts of the *hanifs* (author's emphasis):

> *Do not distress yourself on account of the boy and your slave girl. Grant Sarah all that she asks of you, for it is through Isaac that your name will be carried on.* But the slave girl's son I will also make into a nation, for he is your child too. *(Gen. 21:12)*

Hagar and Ishmael in the wilderness:
". . . the slave girl's son I will also make into a nation."

That single last sentence, claimed Muhammad, prophesied the Islamic faith. In God's promise is the true origin of Islam.

The Bible goes on to say that God watched over Hagar and Ishmael in the desert, preserved their lives, and repeated his promise that Ishmael would be the father of a mighty nation. The Arab *hanifs*, seizing on this passage and promise, claimed that Ishmael (c. 1800 B.C.E.) had lived in the deserts of Mecca, and that his descendants were the Arabs.

Thus, Arabs, through a different but equally direct lineage with Abraham, were also God's Chosen People.

ABRAHAM VISITS MECCA. A story circulated the peninsula that when Ishmael (whose name means "whom God hears") had grown up, his father, Abraham (whose name means "father of a multitude"), now an old man, visited him in the deserts around Mecca. Together, father and son built the sacred Black Stone Shrine called the Kaaba, the first shrine to Allah in Arabia—and to this day the principal site of Muslim worship.

In fact, the Black Stone Shrine, with a meteorite set in its wall, had existed for some time. It belonged to the pagan god Hubal, and was venerated by polytheistic peoples who hazarded desert pilgrimages to the site.

Thus, the holy Kaaba had existed previously as a pagan shrine, and the monotheistic Allah had existed previously, in name at least, as the chief pagan god *al-Lah*. People don't like to discard things they are familiar with.

The English word "Kaaba" is from the Arabic *Ka'bah*, which itself literally means a "square building," since it is built on the unit *ka'b*, meaning "a cube."

ALLAHU AKBAR!, "GOD IS MOST GREAT!": MECCA, 610 TO 632 C.E. ◆

Monotheism reached the Arabian Peninsula in the year 610 when one of the *hanifs*—named Muhammad ibn Abdullah—began to have revelations that he believed came from Allah.

And like Moses' Yahweh, whose early words were "I am the Lord thy God, Thou shalt have no other gods before me," Allah's early messages to the forty-year-old Muhammad were:

- "Muhammad is the Messenger of God."
- "There is no god but God."

The two statements, found in the Koran (though in different places), comprise the simple Islamic creed called the *shahada*, or "confession." It is one of the Five Pillars of the Islamic faith.

RAMADAN: EARLIEST OBSERVANCE, MID–600S C.E ◆

WHEN OBSERVED: *THE ENTIRE NINTH MONTH OF THE MUSLIM YEAR, ROUGHLY FEBRUARY.*
COMMEMORATES: *THE MUSLIM VICTORY AT THE BATTLE OF BADR IN RAMADAN.*

In Islam, Ramadan is a holy month of fasting, similar to the Jewish Yom Kippur in that both constitute a period of atonement. It's believed that the month-long fast was modeled on the Christian forty-day period of Lent, which should not come as a surprise since Islam, the third great monotheistic religion, was heavily influenced by its predecessors, Judaism and Christianity.

The bloody Battle of Badr in Ramadan on March 15, 624, pitted a small clan of Muhammad's followers against their enemies, a caravan of wealthy Meccans who wished to annihilate the fledgling faith. Against all odds, the clan routed the caravan, and the Prophet interpreted the victory as divine vindication of his priesthood. The victory marked a turning-point in the influence of Islam on the Arab world. In the short period of ten years—the final decade of Muhammad's life—the religious leader of a small band of loyalists rose to become political leader of virtually all of central and western Arabia.

Two years before the battle of Badr, threatened by an assassination plot, Muhammad had fled Mecca for the city of Medina, arriving secretly and safely on September 24, 622. This escape became celebrated as the great hijra, *meaning "emigration," and is the starting point of Islamic history. The Islamic new year begins on the day the* hijra *began—in the Western calendar, July 16.*

Traditionally, the twenty-seventh day of Ramadan is called the "Night of the Decree" and is identified as the day the Prophet Muhammad began receiving the divine revelations that would become the Islamic Bible or Koran. Muslim law forbids food, drink, and sexual intercourse from dawn until dusk throughout the sacred month.

The basic requirements of the fast are found in two verses of the holy Koran. The first verse states that the fast applies throughout the thirty days of Ramadan. Sexual intercourse is addressed in the second verse:

You are permitted during the night of the fast to go in to your wives . . . and eat and drink until so much of the dawn appears that a white thread can be distinguished from a black one. Then keep the fast completely until night and do not lie with them when you should remain in the mosques.

> By tradition, the beginning and end of Ramadan are announced when one trustworthy witness testifies before authorities that he has sighted the new moon in the sky; thus, an overcast night sky can delay the start of the feast or prolong its completion. The obligatory month-long fasting—the saum—is one of the five sacred Pillars of Islam.

Like many of the Jewish prophets, Muhammad was sometimes wary of the Voice and the Presence that came to him with increasing frequency. Was it really God, or hallucination?

The Voice—later identified as that of God's angelic messenger Gabriel—promised to reveal Allah to all mankind in a great book, the Koran, which would be dictated to Muhammad, much like the first five books of the Hebrew Bible were transmitted to Moses.

Muhammad, as mentioned, called his religion *Islam*, "submission," and his followers *Muslims*, "those who submit."

TRACING ROOTS ◆

Was Muhammad himself the first Muslim?

No. Abraham was the first Muslim, reasoned Muhammad, because the father of the Jewish people had submitted so perfectly to God.

In fact, Muhammad argued that Abraham had not been Jewish because he'd lived long before God gave the Torah to Moses on Mount Sinai. Abraham was a Muslim.

Muhammad acknowledged that Jesus was a prophet, and that the New Testament was a divine work, but Christ was no God; this seemed as blasphemous a claim to Muslims as it always had seemed to Jews. The Koran refuses to imagine God would "beget" a son. Let alone a third member of a Trinity.

In Islam, there is no deity but Allah, Creator of Heaven and earth: "He begets not, and neither is he begotten."

The call that summons Muslims to their prayful salat—*Allahu Akbar!*, "God is most great!"—reaffirms God's uniqueness and superiority.

Like Jesus, Muhammad himself was a prophet, but with a distinction: he was to be the last in the line of great prophets. God would reveal no more divine messages after the completion of the Koran.

Though Islam regards itself as the final and supreme revelation, the Koran teaches Muslims to respect Jews and Christians, the "People of the Book"—the Bible, that is, Testaments Old and New:

Be courteous when you argue with the People of the Book, except with those who do evil. Say "We believe in that which is revealed to us and that which is revealed to you. Our God and your God is one." (Koran 29:46)

END NOTE ◆

By the close of the seventh century C.E., monotheism, in the form of Judaism, Christianity, and Islam, had all but wiped out the polytheism of the past. One God had replaced many.

The Hebrew "Yahweh," the Christian "God the Father," and the Muslim "Allah" were deemed one and the same Almighty Creator, yet each was distinctly different, went by a different name, and favored a different ethnic group.

It is not hard to imagine the three—Yahweh, God the Father, Allah—as an ethnic Trinity in itself, a Triune Godhead that struggles to unite three disparate peoples, Jews, Gentiles, and Arabs. Sometimes, in reading newspaper headlines, it's hard to believe that all three groups worship the same God.

PART
VIII

I Do

CHAPTER

20

Marriage

Mazal Tov *to Diamond Ring*

MARRIAGE, DIVORCE, ANNULMENT—DEFINING JOY, HEARTBREAK, AND REPRIEVE ♦

"What God has joined together, let no man put asunder"—except by divorce or annulment.

Marriages are made in Heaven. Divorces are often made in the United States, which has the highest divorce rate in the civilized world. Prior to the American Revolution, there were *no* divorces in the United States. A marriage could not be dissolved. After two hundred years, it seems as if the idea of "independence" has been taken too far.

In this chapter, and the next two, we will examine:

• The origins of the institution of marriage and the sacrament of matrimony.

• The first inklings of the concept of divorce—was it a husband or wife who filed first?

• The curious Roman Catholic custom called annulment, in which a husband and wife, married in a church, by a priest, and after having sired several children, can, with sufficient cash and modest cause, petition the Vatican to recognize that their marriage never existed—and be granted the wish. Each of the parties is then free to be remarried in a Catholic Church, by an ordained priest, and to sire more children. Does an annulment make the earlier children bastards?

Some interesting word origins first:

MARRIAGE—from the Latin *maritus*, meaning "a male partner." The word itself sides with the man, as do earlier variations. *Meryo*, an Indo-European root, means "young man," and *marya* in Sanskrit means "suitor." No doubt this is because men drew up the first rules for couples.

DIVORCE—from the Latin verb *divertere*, which means "to turn different ways." Implying, of course, to turn at a later crossroad in life and try a road not taken. Perhaps with a younger partner. The Latin is also the root of our word "diverse"—a divorce presupposes diversity.

ANNULMENT—from the Latin verb *annullare*, meaning "to reduce to nothing." Thus, the Vatican will reduce a man-woman relationship of many years and numerous children "to nothing." Notice that linguistically "annulment" renders a union null and void, whereas "divorce" says nothing about negation of all that has gone before; rather, "divorce" suggests the richness of future diversity heaped on top of past experience.

FIRST MARRIAGE CEREMONY:
GARDEN OF EDEN, C. 4000 B.C.E. ◆

The first couple to wed was Adam and Eve, and the marriage ceremony was officiated, so to speak, by God himself. The place: The verdant garden in the Valley of Eden—probably the land between the Tigris and Euphrates rivers known as Sumer.

The time: Late October in the year 3761 B.C.E. (as Jews date the nuptial). Or early September in the year 4004 B.C.E. (as Bishop Ussher concluded). The affair was small; as yet, there were no relatives. The bride and groom wore nothing, and they had met under unusual circumstances. She hailed not from a nearby town, but from the groom's rib.

Let's consider several origins.

After placing Adam in the Garden, God says: "It is not good that the man is alone; I will make him a helper like himself" (Gen. 2:18).

The term "like himself" has linguistic significance: "man" and "woman" (wo + man) are a deliberate play on words. Woman is like man in many ways, even in the spelling. The writer of Genesis intended this equivalence. The Hebrew play on words is: "man" = *ish*; "woman" = *ishah*. In English, the play is in the prefix; in Hebrew, it's in the suffix.

Our English words "man" and "woman" are from Old English, which gives the terms a sexist slant. "Woman" is *wifmann* (*wif* + *mann*), where *wif* means "female" and *mann* means "man." Thus, a woman is a female man. This is seen in the biblical derivation of Eve from Adam's rib:

> *The Lord God cast the man [ish] into a deep sleep and, while he slept, took one of his ribs and closed up its place with flesh. And the rib . . . he made into a woman [ishah]. (Gen. 2:21–22)*

God wakes Adam, introduces him to an unfamiliar creature, and asks Adam to come up with a name. Adam says:

She now is bone of my bone, and flesh of my flesh; She shall be called Woman [ishah], for from Man [ish] she has been taken. (Gen. 2:23)

The writer of Genesis was deliberately causing words to carry the weight of imagery here.

WHO MARRIES WHOM? ◆

God may have introduced the couple, but he did not marry them; he merely blessed the union. This concept is at the heart of both Jewish and Christian marriages. The bride and groom marry *each other*; the rite or liturgical act is not the essence of the union; rather, it is a blessing to the contract entered into by the couple, in front of witnesses.

In the Old Testament, the marriage contract is so sacred that it is considered a covenant to which God himself is the witness.

According to Roman law—on which the Christian marriage contract is based—consent, not living in common, created a valid marriage. Today, when a priest says, "I now *pronounce* you man and wife," he is not creating the holy bond, but merely *announcing* that it has just come into existence.

The words that actually create the bond are: "I do"—delivered in response to the priest's question: "Do you take [name] as your lawful wife . . . till death do you part?" And then: "Do you take [name] as your lawful husband . . . till death do you part?"

I do. I do. Two little words, spoken twice. No contract is simpler.

CHRISTIAN BETROTHAL: SECOND CENTURY c.e.

In early Christianity, betrothal was every bit as binding as actual marriage. In fact, the rite of betrothal evolved into the now familiar marriage ceremony.

According to early Church fathers Ignatius and Tertullian, a betrothal had to take place in front of a bishop. It involved the exchange of "earnest money," *arrhae*, as a pledge that the marriage would actually take place. A ring was given to symbolize that the wife would be "bound to" (or "in charge of") the home. A dowry was promised, and the woman was veiled—the veil, in the Near East, being a standard part of daily dress for an engaged or a married woman. The couple joined hands, and exchanged a kiss.

In the course of time, many of these elements of the betrothal were transferred to the marriage ceremony itself.

MEANING OF "NUPTIAL" ◆

There are three parts to getting married.

A "betrothal" is a promise or mutual pledge to marry. The word's Middle English origin means "at truth"—*betreuthe* (*be* + *treuthe*, at + truth).

The "marriage" itself marks the time from which the man and woman may start living together, sharing the same bed. "Marry," from the Latin *maritare*, means "to become a husband."

The "nuptial" is the ceremony or rite surrounding the marriage. The word derives from the Latin *nubere*, meaning "to veil oneself"—which is the origin of our word "nubile." Today, when we call a girl "nubile," we refer more to her youthful glow and tender limbs—which characterized a bride of the past whose age was fourteen or fifteen. "Nubile" and "nymph" share the same root; and same overtones.

Tertullian tells us that the Christian nuptial included the couple receiving the Holy Eucharist and the presiding bishop's blessing. In Eastern Christianity, the man wore a crown during the nuptial rite, which Saint John Chrysostom says was "a symbol of victory"—meaning, innocently enough, that the man approached the marriage bed a prince of purity, a virgin, unconquered by pleasure.

OUTLAWING THE AGAPE ◆ *After the nuptial, the two families engaged in an* agape *or "love feast." This is a meal that early Christians ate together as a symbol of affection and brotherhood. The word "agape" is Greek, meaning "love," and is found in verse 12 of Saint Jude's Epistle.*

The earliest Christian agapes, unrelated to a marriage, consisted of a banquet, prayers, and the reading of Psalms, at which the rich and poor ate at the same table, the "haves" providing what the "have-nots" lacked.

All Christian agapes were banned in the seventh century because their partylike atmosphere had gotten wildly out of hand. In fact, the Christian agape had regressed to precisely the wild pagan lovefest it was for the Greeks.

HEBREW BETROTHAL—KIDDUSHIN: GENESIS TO TALMUD ◆

In olden times, a Hebrew wedding ceremony was a social occasion rather than a religious or legal one. That's because the bridal couple was formally united in matrimony at the time of the betrothal (*erusin* in Hebrew) when the marriage contract, the *ketubah*, was sealed, and the bridal price handed over.

In biblical and Talmudic times, marriage was a two-stage process. It began with the betrothal, and concluded with the marriage, or *nissu'in*; the word means "nuptial." First came the *erusin*, which is the commitment by the couple to marry at some future date. Then came the *kiddushin*, the wedding ceremony—which alone allows the consummation of the marriage.

The word *kiddushin* means "sanctification" and reveals that Jews viewed marriage as sacred, an institution with cosmic significance, integral to the divine plan.

LOOKING OUT FOR THE WIFE'S INTERESTS. Created by Simeon ben Shetach in 80 B.C.E., the *ketubah* was written in Aramaic, language of the masses, and it spelled out the legal obligations of the husband to the wife should he die or divorce her. For a long while, the obligations of the wife to her husband were unenumerated and considered numerous and obvious to all.

A father chose a wife for his son from girls within their clan who were as young as twelve. In fact, in Jewish law, a male of thirteen and a female of twelve are regarded as adults and fit for marriage.

(The Hasidim regard eighteen as the ideal age for marriage and try to have their children marry as close to that age as possible.)

The father of the bride received cash, the *mohar*, commonly fifty shekels of silver for his daughter, and he intoned Saul's words to David: "You shall now be my son-in-law." The origin of the exchange of money for marriage, as well as the Hebrew term *mohar*, are found in Genesis, chapter 34.

By Talmudic times, the term *mohar* had fallen into disuse. The Talmud rephrases the negotiations between the respective parents into haggling one-upmanship: "How much are you giving to your son? . . . How much are you giving to your daughter?" The terms agreed upon were written in a binding document called a *shetar*. The sum given to the son was called *nedunyah*, meaning "dowry," which later became common parlance for money given with a daughter.

The betrothed couple were technically husband and wife, and expected to be faithful to each other, despite the fact that the wedding might take place a full year later.

Christ's Jewish parents, Miriam (Mary) and Joseph, were betrothed at the time of Jesus' birth, and Matthew acknowledges them as husband and wife. A betrothal could be broken only by a formal divorce. And in Judaism divorce was possible. More on this later.

A major change eventually occurred in the custom of the *mohar.* Since the money could be used up by the father of the bride—as indeed happened in the case of Rachel and Leah (Gen. 31:13)—a wife could remain penniless if her husband divorced her or predeceased her. Thus, the *ketubah* was rewritten to provide for widows.

JEWISH MARRIAGE CUSTOMS: PAST AND PRESENT ♦

Monogamy was the Hebrew ideal. Why? Because One God was married to One People, the Chosen Jews. The equation balanced. One on one. Fidelity was expected. All around.

Polygamy was tolerated for many centuries. Why? Because before the birth of monotheism, many gods were married to a loose confederation of tribes and clans. Polygamy was a holdover from the Jews' ancient, prebiblical past, a time when the people's worshiping of gods was as promiscuous as the men's bedding of wives.

The patriarchs still took more than one wife, and the kings of Israel and Judah boasted of their harems. Solomon's was most notorious: "He had seven hundred wives, princesses, and three hundred concubines" (1 Kings 11:3).

As is the case with liberal customs, they are enjoyed most by the elite and upper classes. Nonetheless, by the Roman period, monogamy appeared to have been the common practice in Judaism, and seemed to best symbolize the monogamous union of God and the Chosen People.

The following several customs pertain to unions that are *mono + gamy,* "one" + "marriage."

DAYS WHEN WEDDINGS ARE CELEBRATED. No weddings are to be held on the Sabbath or festivals, including the intermediate days of Passover and Sukkot—this because of the rabbinical injunction that Jews not mix one joy with another.

By custom, weddings generally do not take place on the day before a festival, or on Purim if at all possible—but weddings are permissible on Hanukkah. In Judaism, it became popular to hold weddings on Tuesdays, regarded a lucky day because on that day of Creation God twice said, "It was good" (Gen. 1:10, 12).

Tuesday is the third day of the Jewish week, the Creation day on which God "called the dry land Earth; and gathering together of the waters called the Seas." And it was good. Also on Tuesday "the Earth brought forth grass, and herb yielding seed . . . and the tree yielding fruit . . . and God saw that it was good."

SECURING A BRIDE WITH A RING. In early Judaism, there were three ways for a man to get a wife: by money, by deed, or by intercourse. The first two speak for themselves; the third needs clarification. The first man who had sex with a virgin was entitled to marry her. If a virgin submitted to a man, she was saying, in effect, "I'm marrying you." The man, of course, did not have to accept her proposal. By Talmudic times, sages had already begun to frown on men who used sex as the means for contracting marriage.

A man wishing to marry a young girl lifted her index finger and slipped it through the hole of a simple, unadorned ring. The ring (which could be a nose ring) was part of the purchase price.

At this early ring ceremony, the groom-to-be said: "Behold, you are consecrated [*mekuddeshet*] unto me with this ring according to the law of Moses and of Israel."

This was followed by a blessing over wine: "Blessed are You, O Lord our God . . . who has hallowed us by Your commandments . . . who has forbidden unto us those who are betrothed to others."

After the wedding ceremony, even today, the bride and groom were led into a private room for *yihud*, "seclusion"—this action symbolizes the consummation of the marriage. The word originally meant "union" or "joining" and it referred to a time when the bride was chaperoned into the groom's house and laid upon his bed.

Thus, securing a virgin wife by intercourse eventually evolved into slipping a ring on her finger and joining her for a moment of seclusion.

SMASHING A GLASS. At an actual wedding ceremony today, the *nissu'in*, the couple recite Seven Blessings over another cup of wine, and the affair ends with the smashing of a glass—an act that has been interpreted in many ways.

Some scholars say the glass is smashed to commemorate the destruction of the Temple in Jerusalem. "The shattering noise of the glass is a stark reminder of the loss of Jewish national independence suffered at the hands of the Romans in 70 C.E.," writes one modern rabbi.

Others maintain it's a superstitious custom to scare off evil spirits. Noise in ancient times was the best remedy against evil spirits.

In Jewish mysticism, the Kabbalists also explain the smashing of a glass as a superstitious action. They believe that demons are bent on destroying the couple's happiness and that the chaos of broken crystal appeases the demons' passion for disorder.

Today, the glass is not thrown but crushed under foot. Some rabbis prefer smashing a lightbulb, since its vacuum makes for a louder pop and more dispersed glass fragments. Presumably, the chaos-loving demons prefer this, too.

SHOUTING "MAZAL TOV." According to biblical law, a man may take a second wife. This alone could be reason for toasting *mazal tov*, "good luck." The practice of polygamy, common among the great prophets, was banned in Ashkenazi communities with the decree of Rabbi Gershom Meor Ha-Golah in the year 1000 C.E. (Married women were never allowed to take a second husband.) Today, almost all Jewish communities, Sephardi as well as Ashkenazi, follow the ban.

In the Middle Ages, both the Ashkenazim and the Sephardim congratulated a bride and groom at the conclusion of the wedding ceremony. Ashkenazim shouted *mazal tov*; the Sephardim cheered *siman tov*, "good omen."

Throughout biblical and Talmudic times, the word *mazal* variously represented a star, a full constellation of the zodiac, and also a planet. This was the period in which people believed that a person's fate depended on the favorable alignment of the heavens. Literally meaning "good star," *mazal tov* only later came to mean "good luck."

In some Ashkenazi communities, the *bride circles around the groom* a number of times, often seven. The notion is that the bridegroom is like a king, circled by his loving followers. Seven, the number of days in a week, and the length of time of God's Creation plus the day of rest, is a magical number in Judaism and its branch of mysticism.

Some Jews have the bride *circle three times*. This practice originated from

Toasting "Mazal Tov,"
"Good luck."

Hosea 2:21–22, in which God (the groom) speaks to Israel (the bride): "And I will *betroth* you unto Me forever; and I will *betroth* you unto Me in righteousness . . . ; I will *betroth* you unto Me in faithfulness." Each "betroth" is enacted as a circling.

In some services, the couple's escorts *carry lighted candles*—a symbol, it is said, of the "marriage" on Mount Sinai, when the bridegroom (God) gave the bride (Israel) a gift of the Ten Commandments amidst thunder and lightning: "There were voices and lightning and a thick cloud on the mountain" (Exod. 19:15).

This same chapter of Scripture can be quoted to explain why *the groom stands under the marriage canopy before the bride*: God (the bridegroom) received Israel (the bride), just as the groom under the canopy receives the bride as she walks down the aisle.

JEWISH MARRIAGE PROHIBITIONS: PAST TO PRESENT ◆

A marriage in Judaism is forbidden if it violates either biblical or rabbinic law. Temporary prohibitions include: a widow or divorcée may not remarry for ninety days after the death of her husband, or after receiving the *get*—the bill of divorce; this to avoid confusion over the paternity of any child.

A man may not marry a pregnant woman, or a nursing mother, until the child has reached the age of twenty-four months—the prevailing length of time for nursing. Once the child is weaned, the couple may wed.

The origins of *permanent* prohibitions:

• Mixed marriage is forbidden—since the Bible forbade the Israelites to marry the Canaanites for fear of idolatry and assimilation: "For they shall turn your children away from Me to worship other gods" (Deut. 7:3–4).

Indeed, Isaac's father, Abraham, forbade his son to marry a local Canaanite, and ordered a trusted servant to travel some four hundred miles to select a bride from the region of Haran, where Abraham's clan had settled.

This prohibition was later extended to include all non-Jews.

• If a man divorces his wife and she remarries and her second husband subsequently dies, the first husband may not remarry the woman. It doesn't look good—it may cast suspicion on the second husband's death.

• A wife who commits adultery may no longer have sex with her husband; and if he divorces her, she cannot marry the man with whom she'd committed adultery. As punishment.

• A woman may not marry any man who represented her in her divorce case; or who witnessed her husband's death—all to avoid the suspicion of collusion.

• Leviticus 18 and 20 prohibit a man from marrying his daughter-in-law, his sister-in-law, his stepdaughter, stepgranddaughter, or his wife's sister during the wife's lifetime. In regard to such unions, the Bible uses words like "depravity," "reproach," and "indecency," but does not explain. According to Maimonides, these restrictions served to preserve chastity and morality within the family.

• A priest may not marry a divorcée, according to Leviticus 21:14—or even remarry his own wife if he had divorced her. Nor may a priest marry a widow. And because of his sanctity, he may not marry a harlot (Lev. 21:7).

• A *mamzer*—a "bastard," defined as the offspring of an adulterous or incestuous relationship—may not marry a Jewish man or woman. Maimonides explains that this prohibition creates "a horror of illicit marriages . . . the adulterer and adulteress were thus taught that by their act they bring upon their seed irreparable injury"—the so-called sins of the father.

CHRISTIAN MATRIMONY AS A SACRAMENT: MIDDLE AGES ◆

There is no detailed teaching about marriage in the Gospels. From passages that make reference to divorce, we can infer that Jesus, chaste and celibate himself, viewed marriage in a positive light—with monogamy the ideal.

The most detailed discussion is in 1 Corinthians 7, where Paul, the disciple of self-denial, argues that marriage is an antidote to sexual immorality, though not as effective as chastity.

In the Roman Catholic Church, it was only in medieval times that the institution of marriage was elevated to the status of a holy sacrament, for two reasons:

1. It was assumed to be of divine origin, hence sacred. Christ himself instituted the Christian marriage, with its bond of indissolubility, when he said: "What therefore God hath joined together, let no man put asunder" (Matt. 19:6; Mark 10:9).

2. The irrevocable bond between husband and wife was said to typify the indissoluble union of Christ with his Church: "For this cause a man shall leave his father and mother, and cleave to his wife, and the two shall become one flesh. This is a great mystery—I speak concerning Christ and his Church" (Eph. 5:31–32). Thus, no divorce, ever, since Christ will never divorce himself from the Church. This reasoning is behind the Vatican's steadfast refusal to grant divorce. More on this later.

A PEOPLE MARRIED TO THEIR FAITH ◆

A similar equation is found in Judaism. Early rabbis regarded marriage as so sacred an institution that they spoke of it by way of analogy: God is "married" to the Jewish people; the Jews contract a "marriage" with their Torah, and in this symbolic marriage the Sabbath is regarded as the "bride" of the Chosen People—as expressed in a hymn heralding the holy day: "Come my beloved to meet the bride; let us welcome the presence of the Sabbath."

The Christian and Jewish equations:

Christ (as groom) + Church (as bride).
Chosen People (as groom) + Sabbath (as bride).

As early as the eighth century B.C.E., the covenantal relationship between Yahweh and Israel is likened to a covenanted marriage. Use of this analogy begins in Hosea 1–3, and continues in later material, such as Jeremiah 3:1–5. It is not surprising that the Christians borrowed the equation, substituting as their own variables, "Christ" and "His Church."

SEX IN MARRIAGE: JUDAISM VERSUS CHRISTIANITY ◆

When it comes to sex in marriage, Jews and Christians have parted ways, like the proverbial waters of the Jordan.

The early Church fathers of Christianity revered celibacy over marriage, and chastity over copulation, because they believed the end of the world was near. Traditional Judaism strongly discouraged celibacy.

A folk Jewish saying: *"A man is not even called a man until united with a woman."*

Whereas saints Jerome, Ambrose, and Augustine taught that fulfillment was to be found in chastity, rabbis taught that a Jew was not fulfilled until he married.

Another Jewish saying: *"Any man who has no wife is not a complete human being."*

In fact, a rabbinic aphorism dares to go even further: *"Marriage takes precedence over the study of the Torah."* A healthy sex life in marriage was considered God's will. God, after all, created the ideally compatible sexual organs.

The celibate Church fathers viewed chastity as superior to marriage, and advised Christians that if they couldn't abstain from sex, they should marry in order to cope with sexual temptation. Jews, on the other hand, rather than seeing sex as something to transcend, viewed the promise of sex through marriage as motivation.

A verse from the Talmud notes: *"Were it not for the sexual instinct, no man would build a house, marry a wife, or beget children."* A man was forbidden sex outside of marriage.

In biblical law, the groom was excused from military service for a full year "for the sake of his household, to give happiness to the woman he has married" (Deut. 24:5). According to the Talmud, among the chief duties a father has to his son is to find him a wife. As a saying predicts: *"Whoever spends his days without a wife has no joy, no blessing, and no good life."*

It is only fair to reiterate that the prudish antimarriage, anti-sex-in-marriage sentiments of early Christian fathers were in large measure due to their belief in the imminent Second Coming of Christ and the Day of Judgment. Why breed when all life on earth would soon end?

One final word of Jewish wisdom: *"When an old man marries a young wife, the man becomes young and the woman old."*

CHRISTIAN MARRIAGE CUSTOMS: PAST AND PRESENT ◆

Just as the Christian agape began as a pagan rite, so, too, did many of the most cherished marriage practices.

The *best man* at a Christian service is a witness, and he carries the ring. But in earlier times, when young women within a tribe were in short supply, the best man was the groom's closest friend, who assisted in the capture of the bride-to-be from a neighboring village.

Capture of a bride-to-be from a neighboring town.

From this practice of abduction, which literally swept a bride off her feet, also sprang the later symbolic act of *carrying a bride over the threshold* of her new home. A captured bride was carried to her new home by force.

The tradition that *the bride stand to the left of the groom* is not mere etiquette. Among the northern European barbarians (so named by the Greeks; *barbaros*, which meant "non-Greek-speaking stranger," came to connote "rude, uncivilized"), a groom placed his captured damsel in distress on his left to free his right hand, the sword hand, against sudden surprise attack by the girl's father and brothers.

GOLD WEDDING RING. A finger ring was first used in a marriage ceremony in the Third Dynasty of the Old Kingdom of Egypt, around 2800 B.C.E.—hundreds of years before the first Hebrew patriarchs. To the Egyptians, a circle, having no beginning or end, signified eternity—for which marriage was binding.

Not surprisingly, the endless circle of a ring became the perfect symbolic embodiment of Christ's words on the indissolubility of marriage: "What therefore God hath joined together, let no man put asunder."

Tertullian, writing in the second century C.E., tells us that Christian men of modest financial means went for broke when it came to buying a ring. Gold rings were favored, and the Church father says: "Most women know nothing of gold except the single marriage ring placed on one finger." That was the only gold she saw in her entire lifetime. In fact, in public, she "wore a ring of iron," writes Tertullian, for her gold ring was kept at home. This could mark the origin of costume jewelry.

DIAMOND ENGAGEMENT RING. This expensive custom began in the 1500s. A Venetian wedding document dated 1503 lists "one marrying ring having diamond." The ring belonged to one Mary of Modina, and is among the earliest betrothal rings that featured a diamond setting. Thus began a tradition that may last forever.

Henry VIII, who broke with Rome over the issue of divorce and began the Church of England, owned the most famous diamond engagement ring of the 1500s. The king ordered the ring made for the betrothal of his two-year-old daughter, Princess Mary, to the newly born dauphin of France, son of King Francis I. The male infant and female toddler were engaged as a matter of state policy, to assure a more intimate alliance between France and England.

In 1553, Mary became the first queen to rule England in her own right. A year later, she married King Phillip II of Spain, and soon became infamous

*Pope Nicholas I (858–67)
made the engagement ring
a standard custom.*

as "Bloody Mary" for her persecution of Protestants in an attempt to restore Roman Catholicism to England.

In the Anglican Church (founded by Mary's father), and the Roman Catholic Church in England, the marriage ceremony is based on text from the ancient *Sarum use rite*—named after the city of Salisbury (its Latin name, *Sarisberia*), England, seat of the bishopric from 1075 to 1220. The groom gives the bride gold and silver with the ring, and says: "With this ring I thee wed; this gold and silver I thee give; with my body I thee worship; and with all my worldly goods I thee endow."

In the ninth century, Pope Nicholas I (858–67) decreed that an engagement ring become a required statement of nuptial intent; previously, it had been only a tradition.

In that century, two other marriage customs were established: *forfeiture of the ring by a man who reneged on a marriage pledge and surrender of the ring by a woman who broke off an engagement.*

The Roman Catholic Church became unbending regarding the seriousness of a marriage promise and the punishment if broken. The Council of Elvira condemned the parents of a man who terminated an engagement to excommunication for three years. And if a woman backed out for reasons unacceptable to the Church, her parish priest had the authority to order her into a nunnery for life. For a time, "till death do us part" began weeks or months before a bride and groom knelt at the altar.

RING FINGER. The early Hebrews placed the wedding ring on the index finger, the finger that an illiterate person used to score his *X* on a legal contract.

The Christian custom of placing a wedding ring on the "third" finger (not counting the thumb) began with the Greeks, through carelessness in cataloging human anatomy. Greek physicians in the third century B.C.E. believed that a certain vein, the "vein of love," ran from the "third finger" directly to the heart. It became the logical digit to carry a ring symbolizing an affair of the heart.

The Romans, copying Greek anatomy charts, adopted the ring practice unquestioningly. The "third" finger also became the "healing finger" with which Roman physicians stirred mixtures of drugs.

Early Christians continued this ring-finger practice, but worked their way across the hand to the vein of love. In what is named the Trinitarian formula, a groom first placed the ring on the tip of the bride's index finger, praying with the words "In the name of the Father." Saying, "In the name of the Son," he moved the ring to her middle finger, and, finally, with the words "of the Holy Spirit, Amen," he slipped the ring down onto the "third" finger.

MARRIAGE BANNS. Church law in Catholicism requires that a pastor publicly announce the names of a man and woman who intend to wed. The announcement must be made during services on three successive Sundays or holy days; or posted in the church for eight days. The purpose of the banns is to discover any existing impediments to the marriage. Maybe the man already has a wife. Maybe the woman is a non-Catholic.

These, though, were not the primary concerns of Charlemagne, king of the Franks, when he instituted marriage banns in the eighth century.

On Christmas Day in 800 C.E., Charlemagne was crowned emperor of the Romans, marking the birth of the *Holy* Roman Empire—sort of a marriage between the pope and the emperor. In those days, among rich and poor alike, a child's parentage was not always clear; an extramarital indiscretion could lead to a half-brother and half-sister marrying, and frequently did.

Charlemagne, alarmed by the high rate of sibling marriages, and the subsequent imbecility among offspring, issued an edict throughout his unified kingdom: all marriages were to be publicly proclaimed at least seven days

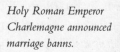

*Holy Roman Emperor
Charlemagne announced
marriage banns.*

prior to the ceremony. To avoid consanguinity between bride and groom, any person with information that the man and woman were related was ordered to come forth.

In Rome, the pope's additional concern was preventing mixed marriages with non-Catholics, for which the banns served equally well.

REFORMATION MARRIAGES: POST-SIXTEENTH CENTURY ◆

Marriage underwent many changes in the sixteenth century due to the Protestant Reformation. Virginity, for instance, was no longer regarded as a near prerequisite in Reformation Churches. Furthermore, priests could officially marry. The first record of the sanctioned marriage of a priest is found in a document from Augsburg dated 1523. (*See* Celibacy.)

For Lutherans, the rite of marriage was prescribed in Martin Luther's *Traubuchlein*, "Little Wedding Book," of 1529, and mixed local German customs with traditional Christian rites. The Lutheran service consists of three parts: public announcement, betrothal, and blessing. The publication of banns is also a public summons to prayer for the couple. If no one objects to the union, the betrothal, or *copulatio*, comes next; this is staged in front of the church door, called the "bridal door." Luther provides the wording the priest is to read: "Hans, will you have Greta as your wedded wife? Greta, will you have Hans as your wedded husband?"

After the exchange of rings, and the joining of right hands, Matthew 19:6 is read *in the present tense:* "What therefore God now joins together, no man will put asunder."

The priest says, "I pronounce them joined," and the "confirmation" of the union takes place inside the church, consisting of Scripture readings and prayers. In Luther's view, marriage is a "divine state" but not a sacrament, as it is in Roman Catholicism. He rejected the need to receive the Holy Eucharist in a Nuptial Mass. Today, according to the *Lutheran Book of Worship* (1978), the marriage rite may be inserted within the celebration of Holy Communion.

METHODIST COMMON SENSE. The basis for Methodist marriage services is John Wesley's 1662 edition of the *Book of Common Prayer*, which appeared in 1784 as *The Sunday Service of the Methodists in North America*.

For unexplained reasons, Wesley edited out the part of the service in which the father of the bride gives away his daughter. He also altered the phrase "plight thee my troth," adding a spiritual twist by changing it to "plight thee my Faith." He dropped the Psalms. And he removed the reference to the exchange of rings.

In America, in 1854, the banns were dropped—but the giving away of the bride was reinstated in 1916 (then dropped again in 1979, as part of a modernization campaign). The promise on the woman's part "to obey" was already out by the mid-1860s—by which time the exchange of rings was back in the service.

Unlike Roman Catholics, Methodists seem fearless when it comes to making changes. Since publication of *A Service of Christian Marriage* in 1979, provisions now exist for the Church blessing of a civil marriage, celebration of the anniversaries of a marriage, and Church renewal of wedding vows.

Seventh-Day Adventists, while regarding marriage as a divine institution, grant it no sacramental value. In fact, all Reformed churches reject the medieval Catholic idea that marriage is a sacrament. For them, the essence of marriage lies wholly in the couple's mutual declaration and promise of fidelity before witnesses.

WORD ORIGINS: "MARRIAGE" VERSUS "MATRIMONY" ◆

It is of interest to compare the words "marriage" and "matrimony."

"Marriage" (or "marry") derives, as we've seen, from the Latin *maritare*, meaning "to become a husband." It's a masculine-sided word.

"Matrimony," on the other hand, which is the sacrament of marriage, derives from the Latin *mater*, "mother."

The Catholic Church, in elevating marriage to the sacramental status of matrimony, did more than confer sanctifying grace upon it; it shifted the emphasis to the feminine. Secular "marriage" sides with the father. Sacred "matrimony" favors the mother.

An interesting aside: In botany, the plant known as the "marriage vine" is of the genus *Lycium*, belonging to the nightshade family. It has small, delicate flowers and red berries that are deadly poisonous.

EVOLUTION OF A SACRAMENT—"MARRIAGE" TO "MATRIMONY": MIDDLE AGES ◆

A sacrament is defined in Catholicism as a "sacred outward sign or rite instituted by Christ to confer grace upon the soul."

Each sacrament—and there are seven in Catholicism, as we saw in a previous chapter—consists of a visible external ceremony, and an invisible confirmation of sanctifying grace, that luminous gift from God that imparts an abiding glow to the soul and elevates the person to participation in divine nature.

Today, the Catholic Church claims that marriage was *always* a sacrament, from the first service performed. That is retrospective reasoning. In truth, centuries would pass before the Church recognized the sanctifying status of matrimony. The theology of marriage, and its elevation to the supreme status of a sacrament, was a long time in gestation.

In the early centuries of the Christian Church, marriage liturgy was neither fixed nor obligatory. Priests and bishops quoted pertinent Scripture on the subject, of course, but they had great latitude with what they said—and where they said it; a marriage did not have to take place in a church. There weren't all that many churches.

Marriage was sacred, but not a sacrament. The early Church then recognized only two rites as sacredly ordained: baptism and the Eucharist—events Jesus himself had a hand in originating.

At best, there were hints about the sacramentality of marriage, and as to how a ceremony should be conducted. Saint Ignatius of Antioch said: "It is proper for those who marry to be united with the consent of the bishop, so that the marriage may be according to the Lord and not according to lust."

Church father Tertullian spoke about "the happiness of a marriage which the Church unites," and "at which angels are present as witnesses," and "which the Father ratifies." But, surprisingly, references to matrimony in the first three centuries of the Church are sparse.

HOW MARRIAGE BECAME A DIVINE VOCATION—WHOSE PRIMARY FUNCTION IS TO BEAR OFFSPRING. With the breakdown of social order in the Dark Ages, it was wise to formalize rules and rites whenever possible. Civilization had collapsed. Bastards roamed the countryside. Half-brothers were marrying their half-sisters. Marital banns, as we've seen, had to be instituted.

Hence, the Church instituted the rite of marriage *in facie ecclesiae*, literally, "in front of the doors of the church." Previously, people could be married in a tavern, at any time of day or night. Now the couple had to come to a church—at least to the front door of a church.

This new strictness is first recorded in Normandy in the early twelfth century. In essence, this is the origin of the *church wedding*.

GET ME TO THE CHURCH ON TIME. A couple now could look forward to an organized ceremony.

The priest questioned the bride and groom at the church door. Did they freely consent to marriage? The bride was "given away" by a member of her family. The dowry was read aloud for all to hear. The ring was blessed by the priest and placed on the bride's "third" finger.

If a Nuptial Mass was to take place—if the couple was so lucky, was so highly connected in the community—the spouses entered the church carrying candles. They made an offering at the offertory (the redundancy implies the word's origin). The priest quoted Scripture. The couple recited prayers. A veil was laid on the bride's head, scalloping over to the groom's shoulders.

The *veil* originated in the earlier Christian rite of *velatio virginis*, the practice of compelling virgins to wear veils. In Church art, virgin saints are always draped in veils; the "veil of the virgin."

It is during this period of formalization that the Sarum use rite of marriage originated in England. The bishops of Salisbury, in setting up the so-called Sarum rites, compiled missals, breviaries, and liturgical books of canonical hours.

And it is during this period in Catholicism that the secular rite of marriage began to evolve into the sacred ritual of a sacrament.

Marriage was beginning to be viewed as a sacred vocation, in which the man and woman hear a "call to holiness"—as a priest hears a special "holy calling" to ordination. Still, though, marriage was not yet on the solid sanctifying footing of matrimony.

Until as late as the tenth century, the Church's blessing was not obligatory in consecrating a marriage. Pope Innocent III (1198–1216) wrote of matrimony as a "Sacrament of the faith . . . both true and ratified." Over the next one hundred years, Rome gave many a nod to matrimony as a sacrament, but stated no details about its sacramentality.

During this period, Thomas Aquinas gave the first real definition of a sacrament: "A Sacrament is a sign of a sacred thing in as much as it sanctifies men." It imparts grace to the soul.

The Council of Florence (1438–45) finally decreed: "Seventh is the Sacrament of Matrimony, which is the sign of unity between Christ and His Church." A couple married not only each other, but entered into a supernatural union with the Mystical Body of Christ.

LUTHER AND CALVIN—FAITH SUFFICES. It was not until the Council of Trent in 1563, which devoted its entire twenty-fourth session to the doctrine, that the form and status of matrimony was finalized. From then on, a marriage was no longer valid unless a couple exchanged consent before their parish priest (or his delegate) and two witnesses, and received his blessing.

Martin Luther rejected Rome's view of the unique sacramentality of matrimony. For Luther, marriage was indeed a sacred state—though merely a rite that fortified the couple's faith. Faith, for Luther, calls forth its own grace; the Holy Spirit did not have to attend the couple's wedding.

John Calvin placed somewhat more emphasis on the presence of the Holy Spirit in a marriage ceremony, but because of his strong view on predestination (which implies a passivity in human nature), he did not go so far as the Catholic Church—which now viewed the married couple, who had heard a "holy calling" from the Holy Spirit, as partaking in divine nature. The couple had stepped on to a new and high spiritual plane. Not through their faith alone, as Luther would have it, but through the intercession of God's sanctifying grace, delivered by the Holy Spirit.

Confronted with the new theology of the Reformation, the Catholic Church looked back into its long history and "found evidence" that matrimony had *always* been a sacrament, even if it had not been clearly recognized as such. Whereas Jesus Christ had unequivocally instituted the sacraments of baptism (at the River Jordan) and Holy Eucharist (at the Last Supper), Christ had, concluded the Church, "generically instituted" the other five sacraments, so subtly that they only later were given substance and significance. Past quotations from popes and saints were appropriately reinterpreted to support this latest doctrine.

Even Saint Augustine, who had made so many harsh condemnations on sexuality, was reevaluated with a focus on the few positive asides he had made on the benefits of the married state. Most notable was his belief that marriage conferred three advantages: *proles, fides, sacramentum*—"offspring," "mutual fidelity" (marriage diminished sexual promiscuity), and the "oath" that the couple would remain together forever—the indissolubility of the rite. (*Sacramentum* here means neither "sacred" nor "mystery," that is not how Augustine used it; rather, it has its Roman definition of "oath of allegiance"—as was typically sworn by military men.)

SECRETS NON-CATHOLIC CHRISTIANS DON'T KNOW: EARLY TO MODERN TIMES ◆

The Catholic pope in Rome has something to say about non-Catholic Christian marriages. A lot, in fact. Non-Catholic Christian marriages were for centuries governed by the laws of the Catholic Church—which may come as something of a surprise to non-Catholic Christians.

Since the pope views himself as the leader of *all* Christians, of every denomination—under the so-called primacy of the papacy—the pope regards marriage between two baptized non-Catholic Christians as a sacrament, even if the new husband and wife don't realize they've entered into a sacrament. Sacramental status, in the Catholic view, is conferred by God.

The union is still a sacrament even if no religious rite is observed by the couple. When the non-Catholic Christian couple first copulates, consummating their marriage, the sacred bond between them becomes absolutely indissoluble in the eyes of Rome. It cannot be terminated except by the death of one of the parties. Thus, a non-Catholic Christian couple that divorces in their own Church, or by civil law, is still sacredly bound in the eyes of the Roman Catholic pope.

If each party remarries . . . Well, he or she shouldn't, because, according to Rome, they are still spiritually married to each other.

Further, if two unbaptized persons marry, their marriage cannot be a sacrament, says Rome, because baptism (through one faith or another) is required to remove the stain of original sin from the soul before any Roman Catholic sacrament can be received. However, if either or both parties are later baptized in their own faith or faiths, their marriage instantly turns into a sacrament in the eyes of Rome, even if the couple is totally unaware of the fact.

The Catholic Church insists that marriages in which one party is a Catholic must take place before a priest or deacon, and two witnesses. If both parties are non-Catholic Christians, each baptized in his or her own faith, the pope views their marriage as a sacrament, but he does not insist on the form in which the ceremony takes place. The pope may have a long spiritual arm, but he recognizes its physical limitations.

Today, at least, the Catholic Church freely acknowledges that its own Code of Canon Law no longer applies to non-Catholic Christians. These ecclesiastical laws aside, a non-Catholic Christian couple still receives the sacramental grace of matrimony, even if the parties don't believe in such a gift from the Holy Spirit. Certain spiritual truths, in the Catholic view, are binding to every baptized individual. The pope does not see this as meddling, but as taking care of his flock, as that flock is, for him, divinely defined.

Things have softened in recent years. For example: A few decades ago, two Catholics who married before a Protestant minister were automatically excommunicated from the faith. This harsh ban was lifted on March 18, 1966, in a decree issued by the Sacred Congregation for the Doctrine of the Faith.

Furthermore, as a result of Pope Paul VI's 1970 letter *Matrimonia Mixta,* "On Mixed Marriages," it is somewhat easier for a Catholic and a non-Catholic Christian to come together in marriage. At least now a mixed marriage can take place with a Nuptial Mass, or, with a bishop's special dispensation, the Catholic party can marry his or her spouse in a non-Catholic church service. Also, a Catholic priest can now be present at the ceremony, and he can even bless the couple. No longer must the Catholic spouse swear to raise all children of the union in the faith, only to "do all in his (her) power to share" the faith with the children. Such concessions were a long time in the making.

The special Roman Catholic sacramental status of matrimony is obvious in the standing prohibition: "It is not permitted to have two religious services or to have a single service in which both the Catholic marriage ritual and a non-Catholic marriage ritual are celebrated jointly or successively."

The sacrament of matrimony can be received only once.

𝔇ivorce

Get *to Jackie Kennedy Onassis*

**BIBLICAL ORIGIN: OLD TESTAMENT,
DEUTERONOMY 24:1–4** ◆

Get is the Hebrew word for "divorce document."

This is how simple divorce was in the early days of Jewish biblical tradition:

> *When a man takes a wife and possesses her, if she fails to please him because he finds something obnoxious about her, then he writes her a bill of divorcement [get], hands it to her, and sends her away from his house. (Deut. 24:1)*

It's clear from these words that the power of divorce rests exclusively with the husband; further, the act of divorce must be in a written document. The pain of divorce seems exclusively the woman's.

If the wife remarries, which she's allowed to do, then gets a *get* from her second husband, she's considered "defiled"—"for this an abomination before the Lord"—and her first husband may not take her back.

Marriage is forever. Circle, clasped
hands, wheat, and pomegranate—
symbols for eternal union,
friendship, fertility, and posterity.

Deuteronomy, of course, was written by a man; if not Moses, some other male, or males.

Much scrutiny has been given to the phrase "something obnoxious." What did Moses, the traditional author, have in mind?

Three answers from religious scholars are standard:

1. According to the School of Shammai, named after its first century B.C.E. Palestinian-born founder, a wife's "obnoxious" behavior refers to adultery. A serious offense. She might be carrying another man's child.

2. The School of Hillel, founded by the contemporaneous Babylonian-born Hillel the Elder, argues that the wife could do as little as burn her husband's dinner. This gives the husband considerable leeway.

3. Rabbi Akiva, a successor to Shammai, claims a man can divorce his wife if he finds a prettier woman. Her looks are "obnoxious" to him. If *his* looks become obnoxious to *her*, she has no recourse.

The Hebrew word *get* derives from an Akkadian term meaning "court writ." Inherent in the word's root is the fact that a divorce must be a written document. Our English word "writ," for a legal document, comes from the Old English *writan*, meaning "to write," which in turn derives from the Indo-European root *wer*, "to scratch." The original divorce documents were handwritten, literally scratched on parchment or goatskin.

A WIFE'S DIVORCE: FIRST CENTURY c.e. ◆

Biblical interpretation flourished in the first centuries of the common era, especially among the rival schools of Shammai and Hillel, eventually producing a body of literature called the *Mishnah*, which became the authoritative source of Jewish law, second only to the Bible.

Cruel as the second and third reasons above for a husband's divorce sound, provisions in the marriage contract, the *ketubah*, assured the woman financial protection against homelessness and destitution. She was out, but not down. In fact, new laws of divorce early in the common era favored the wife with an astonishing degree of modernity. A wife, in court, could compel a husband to grant her a divorce:

1. If he physically abused her after having been warned by the court to halt the behavior (this is something of a "restraining order").

2. If he contracted a venereal disease, or some other loathsome condition like leprosy.

3. If he withheld money for household expenses—or if he became destitute and could no longer support her and the children.

4. If he denied her sex on a regular basis. Indeed, Deuteronomy 24:5 stipulates that a new husband "shall not go out with the army or be assigned to it for any purpose; he shall be exempt one year for the sake of his household, to give happiness to the woman he has married."

5. If *she* remained childless after ten years of married life—which seems to suggest that the onus of sterility might be on the husband.

SENDING A HUSBAND TO JAIL: SECOND CENTURY C.E. ◆

The biblical law laid out in Deuteronomy clearly grants the husband exclusive power of divorce. How, then, could contradictory laws that shifted some of the power to the wife be legitimized in later times?

The Talmud resolves the problem by demanding that the Jewish court continually badger, coerce, and imprison the husband if necessary until he screams, "I *want* a divorce." A cry of "uncle." Today, in Israel, rabbinical courts, though reluctant to use coercion, will hold a husband in contempt, even turn him over to secular authorities for imprisonment, if he refuses a court order to grant his wife a divorce. The husband remains in prison until he abides by biblical law and issues his wife a *get*.

MUTUAL DIVORCE: TENTH CENTURY C.E. ◆

The concept of divorce by mutual consent—*takana*, when both parties feel they have grown apart—arose in the tenth century C.E. under the authorship of Rabbenu Gershom, and was accepted as binding by European Jewry.

It also stipulated that a husband could not divorce his wife without first getting her consent, putting the husband and wife on equal footing. A husband could get an "emergency" unilateral divorce in one instance only: if his wife apostatized and abandoned the Jewish community. The husband had merely to submit a *get* to the rabbinical court.

Today, a husband is still obliged to give the *get* to his wife, even if she initiates the idea of divorce. This presents an insuperable problem if the husband's whereabouts are unknown. The wife remains a "chained woman," *agunah*, and may not remarry under Jewish law.

JEWISH ANNULMENT. There is one way that a "chained woman" can wriggle free. The Conservative Rabbinical Assembly, in 1953, inserted a clause in the marriage contract whereby, in instances of extreme hardship, both parties agree to abide by the decision of the religious court, the *bet din*. In a test case in the United States, the enforceability of the agreement was upheld by the Superior Court of New York.

If a husband cannot appear before the *bet din* (if, for instance, his where-abouts are unknown), the court invokes the Talmudic principle of annul-ment, *hafka'at kiddushin*, in effect saying that the sanctification (*kiddushin*) of the union never took place. Thus, no bill of divorce is required.

Annulments are rare, and not countenanced by certain Orthodox rabbis. In the Roman Catholic Church, on the other hand, annulments are on the rise (see next chapter), whereas "divorce," technically, is not countenanced under any circumstance.

It must be said that Jews have always discouraged divorce, for the institu-tion of marriage was and is sacred. God "sheds tears" at news of a divorce; and the Talmud tells us that even "the altar sheds tears for the man who di-vorces his wife."

The interesting fact is that Jews—unlike Christians, who copied so much from Judaism—never regarded marriage as indissoluble; a Jewish divorce, one way or another, has always been available.

The Christian historian Tertullian, at the end of the second century, looked back over six hundred years of Roman customs and observed that "there was not a single divorce," and lamented that in his own time, women "long for divorce as though it were the natural consequence of marriage." The quotation is enlightening when juxtaposed with modern statistics: Today, the majority of divorces are instituted by women; men tend to stay in a bad marriage and cheat, enjoying the benefits of having both a wife/mother and a mistress. While the laws governing divorce have changed over the centuries, human behavior hasn't.

CHRISTIAN DIVORCE: SIXTEENTH CENTURY ◆

Jesus Christ was asked to comment on the Deuteronomic law that opens this chapter ("When a man takes a wife . . . if she fails to please him because he finds something obnoxious about her, then he writes her a bill of divorce-ment . . . and sends her away from his house"), according to Matthew (chap-ter 19) and Mark (chapter 10). At the time, debate raged among the Pharisees: What did the Old Testament divorce laws mean by vague phrases like "if she fails to please him," and if he finds "something obnoxious about her"?

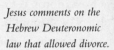

Jesus comments on the Hebrew Deuteronomic law that allowed divorce.

In reply, Jesus dismissed the Mosaic divorce law, calling it a sinful convenience, a concession to human weakness (Mark 10:2–12):

> *Some Pharisees coming up asked him, testing him, "Is it lawful for a man to put away his wife?"*
>
> *Jesus answered them, "What did Moses command you?"*
>
> *They said, "Moses permitted us to write a notice of dismissal, and to put her away."*
>
> *Jesus said to them, "By reason of the hardness of your heart he wrote you that commandment. But from the beginning of creation God made them male and female. "For this cause a man shall leave his father and mother, and cleave to his wife, and the two shall become one flesh. . . ." What therefore God has joined together, let no man put asunder.*

This is the origin of Christian, and later Roman Catholic, opposition to divorce.

According to Mark, Jesus opposed divorce more vigorously than any of the Pharisees: "Whoever divorces his wife and marries another commits adultery against her" (10:11). This was a revolutionary statement at the time, for it put wives on an equal basis with husbands within marriage.

Of course, it was Henry VIII (d. 1547) who broke with Roman Christianity over the issue of divorce. The king divorced his first wife, Catherine of Aragon, who had had a series of miscarriages, in order to marry Anne Boleyn. Pope Clement VII (1523–34), on July 11, 1533, excommunicated the king and pronounced his divorce and remarriage void. Christianity was split by a major schism.

ROMAN CATHOLIC DIVORCE: EARLY MIDDLE AGES ◆

Catholic divorce. That sounds like an oxymoron—from the Greek *oyxmoros*, "shrewdly foolish" (*oxys* + *moros*, "sharp" + "stupid").

Contrary to popular opinion, the Vatican does grant divorces, and has for centuries—it just doesn't call them by that name. Rather, it uses the kinder, gentler words "dissolution" and "separation." It is essential to distinguish between two terms: "dissolution" and "annulment." They are not the same thing.

A *dissolution*, technically, breaks the bond of a marriage that was valid in the eyes of the Church. The Vatican has been quietly granting this kind of "divorce" for most of its two-thousand-year history. For several centuries, it actually kept such documents hidden from public view.

For instance: A valid but unconsummated marriage of baptized persons (the claim of "no sex" is not always easy to disprove) is granted if one spouse wishes to enter the religious orders. The pope gives his blessing, and the marriage is automatically dissolved when the individual takes religious vows. The other party is free to marry again. The pope also has the discretion to grant a dissolution to a valid but unconsummated marriage for "grave reasons" that are determined on a case-by-case basis. Dissolutions are granted for the "spiritual welfare" of the concerned persons. They are discouraged, today as in the past, but issued.

An *annulment*, on the other hand—of the kind granted to Frank Sinatra—declares that no valid bond ever existed between the parties; thus, they were never really married. Despite appearances. And children. Annulments today are actually encouraged for the several million U.S. Roman Catholics who've been divorced through civil law. For if their past marriages can be annulled, they can return to the Church in good standing. Annulments are getting easier to win. More on this in the next chapter.

WORD ORIGINS. Annul—Latin *annullare*, "to bring to nothing."

Dissolve—Latin *dissolvere*, "to pull part."

Divorce—Latin *divertere*, "to turn different ways."

Interestingly, that last word has inherent in its origin a sense of freedom and a future, which is not evident in the first two words. "To turn different ways" seems to imply that the ex-spouses will go off and remarry. On the other hand, "to pull apart" and "to bring to nothing" say nothing about any future plans. The meaning of "annul" and "dissolve" concerns actions confined to the present. The meaning of "divorce" suggests there's a future.

LOOPHOLES IN THE MARRIAGE BOND. In Jesus' time, a pervasive male chauvinism blamed women for adultery and divorce. Matthew's account of Jesus' teaching on divorce reveals this. A man may commit adultery in his heart by looking lustfully at a woman, but by divorcing a faithful wife, the man causes *her* to commit adultery (5:28–32).

Later, Matthew includes an exception clause that seems to modify Jesus' total rejection of divorce (author's italics): "whoever divorces his wife, *except for unchastity*, and marries another commits adultery" (19:9).

Just as the Old Testament phrase "something obnoxious about her" baffled Hebrew scholars, the New Testament phrase "except for unchastity" bedeviled Christian scholars. What constitutes "unchastity"? Does divorce on this basis allow a man to remarry?

Three interpretations became popular:

1. The early Church, up to about 500 C.E., took "unchastity" to mean some grievous sexual sin like adultery. Still, though, the wronged husband, freed from his wife, could not remarry.

2. In the sixteenth century, following the lead of the scholar Erasmus, Protestants defined "unchastity" as adultery and allowed the innocent husband to remarry.

3. Still later, scholars took "unchastity" to mean something as simple as premarital sex on the part of the wife; she'd entered into marriage not a virgin. And a liar. Her secret uncovered, the marriage could be annulled. The deceived husband could remarry. Woe unto the wife.

PAULINE PRIVILEGE:

NEW TESTAMENT, 1 CORINTHIANS 7:12–15 ◆

Saint Paul poked a loophole in Jesus' teaching on the indissolvability of marriage. It's called the Pauline privilege, and its purpose is to protect the faith of Christian converts.

Under the privilege, a marriage between *unbaptized* persons may be dissolved, even if the couple consummated the union, as long as one spouse receives baptism and converts to Christianity. It is divorce in "favor of the faith." It says, in effect, "If you want to become a Christian, we'll get you out of your pagan marriage."

In the United States, with its large Christian population, it would seem that the Pauline loophole is virtually useless. After all, Rome recognizes all Christian baptisms as valid, regardless of denomination, and some Christians, those "born again," are even baptized twice. Even Jews are baptized—in a

Paul, in his letter to the Corinthians, allows divorce in "favor of the faith."

ritual bath, *mikva*, and ritually circumcised as well, *brit mila*. In America, true "pagans" are hard to find; a married pair of unbaptized spouses is even rarer. Two Buddhist immigrants, say.

Nonetheless, each year in the United States some five hundred unbaptized individuals convert to Christianity, get baptized, and are granted dissolutions of their marriages to pagan spouses. The grounds: "disparity of worship."

HOW IT STARTED. In Paul's time, the privilege was a wise move. Romans slaughtered Christians. A pagan woman might convert to the new faith, but her husband might not wish to take the risk himself. Furthermore, he might become openly hostile to his wife's new Christian ideas about sex and children.

Saint Paul, to his credit, encouraged converts to remain with their pagan spouses whenever possible. But he gave them a way out "in favor of the faith" in 1 Corinthians 7:15.

If the unbeliever wishes to separate, however, let him do so. The believing husband or wife is not bound in such cases. God has called you to live in peace.

Refusal of the unbaptized person to "live in peace" with the convert, and without interfering with his or her freedom to practice the Christian faith, merits a dissolution of a valid consummated marriage.

DIVORCE IN FAVOR OF THE PRIESTHOOD:
TWELFTH TO SIXTEENTH CENTURIES C.E. ◆

The origins of this practice are not clearly etched in time. Events evolved. Protestantism intruded. One pope, perhaps more than any other, is central to the story.

Pope Alexander III (1159–81) declared, officially, that a marriage in which two baptized people do not have sex is a real sacrament, but a dissoluble union. Not attempting to conceive children undermines the primary purpose of marriage—or so came later reasoning. A couple can get out of such a marriage through a pontifical dispensation: *quod Papa facit, potest facere.* "Papa" is the pope.

This convenience appears not to have been used much until the papacy of Martin V (1417–31)—thereafter, such dispensation records are extant—but Pope Alexander III invoked it in a case that set precedent regarding priests. A particularly thorny situation was presented to him by the English bishop of Exeter. A nobleman of great wealth and influence had sworn a betrothal oath to marry his fiancée. Shortly before the wedding, he heard a calling to the religious life. Instead of wanting to be a husband, now he wanted to be a monk.

The pope advised the nobleman to marry the woman, but not to copulate with her. After all, a betrothal oath was binding. The marriage would be valid, Alexander said, in much the way that Mary and Joseph's chaste marriage was valid.

The nobleman married, then headed straight for the monastery, abandoning his frustrated bride practically at the altar. Alexander then decreed that the bond between husband and wife automatically dissolved when the husband took his religious vows. (As a theological aside: In such cases, couples get to keep the sanctifying grace bestowed on them through the sacrament of matrimony.)

This event set a precedent and extended the pope's power. In 1563, the Council of Trent went further and decreed that the call to the religious profession was valid grounds to dissolve a marriage—even if the couple *had* consummated their marriage.

On what grounds?

Metaphorical death. When a man passes into the priesthood, his previous

Pope Alexander III (1159–81) said a sexless marriage—like Mary and Joseph's—is still a sacrament.

life "dies" as he takes up a new spiritual existence. Thus, he has not really divorced his wife; he has "died" and left her. Consequently, it is not the pope who dissolves the marriage, but the man's own "death."

This policy indicates that the sacrament of holy orders is superior to that of matrimony. Priests can't marry, but a married man can desert his wife to become a priest.

THE DECEITFUL WIFE. A man marries, but before consummating the union, he discovers his wife is pregnant by another man. Popes in the past set such men free. Virginity and honesty—on the part of the woman—were highly valued.

In the twelfth century, Pope Celestine III argued that certain other consummated marriages can be dissolved. For instance: If a wife is abandoned by her husband, who then marries a pagan, the wife is free to marry again in the Church. If the husband tires of the pagan and beseeches his first wife to take him back, she doesn't have to.

ILLNESS. In 726, Pope Gregory II was petitioned by Saint Boniface, the apostle of Germany, on behalf of a local man whose wife was so seriously ill she could not live with him. The pope allowed the man to remarry, but the somewhat inexplicable ruling did not set a precedent. Illness of a spouse would not normally seem to be grounds for divorce. The unusual details that would perhaps explain this exceptional case were spelled out in a papal letter, long hidden, from the pope to the saint, dated November 22, 726. All sorts of rationale have been offered to explain the pope's decision. "It is reasonable to suppose," wrote a later Jesuit priest, that "previous to consummation, the bride had been attacked by a disease which made conjugal life impossible."

The papacy took a giant step on divorce/dissolution in consummated marriages in 1585. Pope Gregory XIII granted blanket dispensation to mar-

Pope Gregory II (715–31) handled an exceptional case of Catholic divorce.

Pope Gregory XIII (1572–85) allowed any married pagan slave who converted to Catholicism to take a new, Catholic spouse in marriage.

ried slaves who converted to Catholicism to remarry into the faith. Divorce was granted, that is, "in favor of the faith."

MODERN GROUNDS FOR DISSOLUTION OF A MARRIAGE: TWENTIETH CENTURY ◆

In this century, the pope's power to dissolve the bonds of marriage has been extended.

Many canonists over the years have maintained that God granted to Saint Paul and the apostles wide powers to dissolve marriages and that these powers are not restricted to the Pauline privilege. Pius XI, on November 8, 1924, settled the dispute when he dissolved a natural bond of marriage "in favor of the faith."

The American case, submitted to Rome by the bishop of Helena, Montana, involved an unbaptized man who had married a baptized woman (an Anglican). The man later divorced the woman, and converted to the Catholic faith. So that he could remarry, he petitioned the pope to dissolve the natural bond of his first marriage as a privilege for his embracing of the "true faith." Pius XI granted the man's wish, and this extension of the Pauline privilege has been used many times since, and is known as:

THE PETRINE PRIVILEGE. The word "Petrine" implies that the authority emanates from the "office of Saint Peter"—the Vatican, that is. Pope Pius XI (1922–39) declared that he possessed the power to dissolve a valid *consummated* marriage between a Christian (baptized) and a non-Christian (unbaptized). Saint Paul had said "two unbaptized persons."

The pontiff offered no scriptural basis for this extension of power—indeed, there is none. He was Christ's authority on earth, said Pius XI, and this was Christ's new teaching, issued under the title: "Norms for the Dissolution of Marriage in Favor of the Faith by the Supreme Authority of the Sovereign Pontiff."

The key phrase is "in favor of the faith." To encourage more people to take up the faith, the pope held out a carrot to non-Christians: "If you get baptized into the faith, I'll let you out of your consummated marriage. You can take a new wife." This violated hundreds of years of papal teaching.

The condition for a papal divorce under the Petrine privilege is this: The unbaptized spouse cannot have had sex with his or her partner *after* he or she is baptized.

So shockingly bold is the Petrine privilege—which really renders the Pauline privilege redundant—that the Vatican did not make the new norms public. Cases were brought to the pope through local bishops. Marriages were quietly dissolved with no publicity—and continue to be.

EXPANDING PAPAL POWER. Quietly, and without publicity, papal power in regard to divorce has expanded greatly in this century. This would not be so shocking—quite the contrary, Church policy seems to be moving in the same direction as civil divorce laws—if the Vatican did not so vociferously insist that divorce is impossible.

Roman Catholic popes have also extended their authority to venture into other faiths:

• In 1957, Pius XII (1939–58) dissolved a valid consummated marriage between two Muslims; the husband wanted to leave his Muslim wife and marry a Catholic woman; the man himself would convert to Christianity. In "favor of the faith," Pius dared to go where no pope had gone before: he dissolved the consummated marriage of two members of the Islamic faith, invoking the Petrine privilege.

Pius XII then went on to dissolve five other marriages involving members of other faiths. Clergy of those faiths were understandably irked.

• On February 7, 1964, Pope Paul VI (1963–78), while penning his encyclical on the sanctity of human life, *Humanae Vitae,* took time off to grant a divorce to two Jews from Chicago. The husband had divorced his wife and remarried a Catholic woman. The Catholic wife did not feel comfortable with her husband's Jewish divorce. To put the wife's mind at ease, to reassure her that she was validly married in the Catholic Church, Pope Paul retroactively divorced the Jewish man from his Jewish wife, citing the Petrine privilege—even though the man clearly stated that he had no intention of converting to Catholicism. Rabbis were not pleased.

• The most scandalous U.S. case involved millionairess Consuela Vanderbilt, who wed Charles Spencer, duke of Marlborough in 1916. Both were baptized Christians. They'd married in a Protestant Church, before a Protestant bishop. Nonetheless, Pope Pius XI, at Consuela's behest, *annulled* her marriage of ten years—with two children—on the grounds that her mother had pressured her into the union. Protestant bishops were incensed. The Episcopal bishop of New York condemned the Vatican's action as an "amazing and incredible" attack on the "sacredness and permanence of marriage."

The awesome concept of annulment allows virtually any marriage to be discarded. (See next chapter.)

"EXCOMMUNICATION" OF JACQUELINE KENNEDY ONASSIS, OCTOBER 1968 ◆

In the past, a Catholic who divorced and remarried was automatically ex-communicated—tossed out of the active Church, and, if ultimately unrepen-tant, condemned to the fires of Hell. The remarried divorced person lived in a state of perpetual mortal sin—each sex act with the new spouse further blackened the stain on his or her soul.

The most widely debated case for excommunication in this century was that of First Lady Jacqueline Kennedy, the then thirty-nine-year-old widow of America's thirty-fifth president. In the fall of 1968, she married divorced shipping tycoon Aristotle Onassis and became "Jackie O." Onassis, age sixty-two and a Greek Orthodox, had civilly divorced his first wife, the mar-chioness of Blandford, but remained a married man in the eyes of Rome. Jackie O now lived in a state of permanent adultery and would, if she died suddenly and unrepentant, go straight to Hell.

Technically, the widow of the first Roman Catholic president of the United States was excommunicated, and numerous bishops backed that stand. The authoritative Vatican weekly, *L'Osservatore della Domenica*, printed that the former First Lady was in "a state of spiritual degradation, a public sinner." However, to publicly excommunicate an icon as popular as Jackie Kennedy would incur the wrath of millions of American Catholics. Just the loss in Sunday service contributions from angry Americans could by itself have a serious impact. What ensued was pure ecclesiastical farce.

The former First Lady's close friend, Richard Cardinal Cushing, the arch-bishop of Boston, rebuked Jackie's critics, saying to the press: "This idea of saying she's excommunicated, she's a public sinner, what a lot of nonsense. Only God knows who is a sinner, and who is not." For this, the cardinal was himself rebuked by the Vatican in a public statement: "Whoever contravenes the law of the Church incurs her sanctions." An angry Cardinal Cushing snapped: "I've had it!" and threatened to resign as archbishop by year's end.

Behind closed doors, the Roman Rota, the Church's supreme marriage tribunal, decided that Mrs. Kennedy Onassis was in an "irregular position" with the Church, and that she could not receive the sacraments until Rome studied the circumstances surrounding Mr. Onassis's marriage to the mar-chioness of Blandford, examining it, said one bishop, for "possible irregulari-ties." He meant looking for technical loopholes that might get Rome out of its embarrassing bind. A long silence ensued, then Aristotle Onassis conveniently died and the case was automatically closed. The marital bond between Jackie and Onassis had been broken by his death.

Excommunication is also practiced by the Lutheran, Anglican, and Eastern Orthodox Churches, as well as some Protestant denominations. Catholics call the practice "the capital punishment of church crime."

At least they used to.

BAN LIFTED: NOVEMBER 10, 1977 ◆

In 1977, the Catholic bishops of the United States lifted the penalty of excommunication for Catholics who divorce and remarry. Jacqueline Onassis may or may not have sighed in relief.

Many Catholics still don't know the ban no longer exists. The bishops felt that since they were the ones who imposed the sentence in the year 1884, they had the power to remove it. In Rome, Pope Paul VI, after painful consultation with his advisers, had approved the action.

There had been many opponents to lifting the ban. They felt that the only way to get Catholics who divorced to buckle under and not remarry—or prevent them from divorcing in the first place—was with severest discipline and the threat of Hell. Those who favored lifting the ban argued that American Catholics were beyond intimidation, and were bent on doing what they pleased, regardless of the Church's threats.

One can't help but wonder about the fate of those remarried who died in mortal sin during the century when the ban of excommunication was in effect. Were they released from Hell? Or did the Lord, foreseeing that one day the ban would be lifted, not send them there at all?

GOOD CONSCIENCE PROCEDURE ◆

Though no longer subject to excommunication and doomed to Hell, a divorced and remarried Catholic still cannot receive the sacraments, technically. In practice, it depends on one's parish; some local bishops are very flexible and follow a "good conscience procedure," which allows administration of the sacraments of penance and the Eucharist to divorced and remarried Catholics who are unable to obtain, or are waiting for, a decree of nullity of their first marriage, and who are living in their subsequent marriage "in good faith." Though many parish priests champion the "good conscience procedure," the Roman Rota, the court of appeal for marriage, declares that the kindness has no standing or recognition in Church law. Protestant faiths are also wrestling with this dilemma.

The general belief of most Christian denominations is that Holy Communion should not be received *for the person's own sake,* as Saint Paul warned:

Whoever . . . eats the bread or drinks the cup of the Lord in an unworthy manner will be guilty of profaning the body and blood of the Lord . . . [and brings] judgment upon himself. (1 Cor. 11:27–29)

He or she may attend Mass. Pray. And petition for an annulment.

𝔄nnulment

Impotency to Senator Edward Kennedy

NULLITY—MARRIAGE NEVER EXISTED: AUGUST 15, 1936 ◆

In America, about eight million living Roman Catholics have gone through the heartbreak of divorce. Civil divorce, that is. The number increases by about a quarter-million each year. Not one from this multitude is allowed to remarry in the Catholic Church so long as the divorced spouse is still alive. The wait can be long.

There is a way out.

It's called an annulment. It means that the marriage never existed, *ab initio* ("from the beginning"), as a sacramental union under canon law. The couple may have *thought* they were married for, say, two decades or more; they may have produced a family of children; but if one party can prove that there existed "from the beginning" some defect in the union, or defect in his or her spouse, then the marriage can be annulled. Both parties are then free to remarry—since the first marriage never really happened.

To Catholics wishing to get out of a marriage, an annulment sounds almost too good to be true. To non-Catholics, an annulment has a surreal quality about it; how can a long-standing marriage with children be declared to not have existed?

In the past, grounds for an annulment could be as substantial as the physical impotency of the husband, or the unwillingness of the wife to have children. Nowadays, as we'll see, grounds vary, from the alcoholism of one party to the emotional immaturity of the couple at the time they wed.

The rules by which a Church tribunal decides on nullity of a marriage were issued by the Congregation of the Sacraments on August 15, 1936 (under Pius XI), and further delineated to tribunal members of the Roman Rota by Pius XII on October 2, 1944.

American Roman Catholics have drifted further and further away from Rome. The pill, abortion, and civil divorce have been the modern-day *Niña, Pinta,* and *Santa María* that have carried them. The eight million civilly divorced U.S. Roman Catholics technically cannot receive the sacraments. Rome would like to welcome these folk back into the fold. Consequently, annulments are getting easier to come by.

A Church official for a tribunal that grants annulments recently said: "There is no marriage which, given a little time for investigation, we cannot declare invalid." That quotation is given by Joseph Zwack in his rigorously complete how-to manual, *Annulment.*

VATICAN'S BEST-KEPT SECRET ◆

"The church has given every sign of being willing to grant annulments far more readily than in the past," writes Zwack. "The clearest indication of this has been the overwhelming increase in annulments over the past decade."

How overwhelming?

Enough to notice. In 1968, only 338 annulments were granted to American Catholics. In 1978, the number was up to 27,670. In 1992, in the United States alone, 59,030 couples received nullification of their marriages; worldwide that year the Catholic Church granted 76,829 couples annulments. This from a Church that insists marriage is indissolvable, divorce is impossible. As Zwack writes, this flood of annulments is "one of the best-kept secrets in the Church today."

It's also noteworthy that in 1968, only 25 percent of the cases the tribunal investigated were granted annulments. By the late 1980s, in many jurisdictions, at least 95 percent of the cases submitted were granted annulments. Rome wants its adrift flock back. "Your chances for success in many Tribunals," writes Zwack, "have increased from one-in-four to about nine-in-ten." (Statistical figures are from the annual *Statistical Yearbook of the Church.*)

Still, fewer than one out of ten divorced Catholics seeks an annulment. Why? Lack of information. Although Rome seems almost eager to grant annulments to fallen-away Catholics, it doesn't want to publicize the fact. It looks hypocritical to say: "You can't have a divorce. And your marriage doesn't qualify for a dissolution. But we can grant you an annulment."

MODERN GROUNDS FOR ANNULMENT: 1995 ◆

It caused a ruckus in Roman Catholic circles when, in 1995, Senator Edward Kennedy received Holy Communion at his mother Rose's funeral Mass.

Senator Kennedy was on the outs with the Church. In 1982, he had divorced his first wife, Joan, after twenty-two years of marriage, and in 1992, he married Victoria Reggie in a civil ceremony, witnessed by a federal judge.

At the time, Kennedy's archbishop, Cardinal Bernard Law of Boston, scolded him, noting: "Senator Kennedy, in the eyes of the church, is married, and, as long as he is married, is not free to enter into another marriage."

The senator's press secretary explained that his reception of the Eucharist at his mother's funeral Mass was not a sin, since his marriage to Victoria Reggie "had been blessed by the church." There was no elaboration. Had his marriage to Joan been annulled?

The grounds for nullity today are far broader than ever before. The most frequently cited reason is psychological problems in one spouse. The Old Canon Code of 1917 did not speak directly about psychological hurdles; psychology was a new science then. The modern code of the 1970s is as liberal spiritually as the decade was socially.

In fact, the development of the modern annulment parallels the development of modern psychology. The latter is the underpinning of the former.

Acceptable psychological grounds for getting out of a Catholic marriage include:

ALCOHOLISM. If one spouse took to the bottle shortly after the wedding—ideally, even before the ceremony—the marriage may qualify for nullity under the article "lack of due competence."

The tribunal is willing to accept evidence from shortly *after* the wedding as proof of an existing problem *before* the ceremony.

INTOXICATION. If one spouse was soused at the time of the wedding, the marriage could qualify for nullification under the article "lack of due discretion," or "lack of due competence."

DRUG ADDICTION. If one spouse at the time of the wedding was "high" on drugs, or "down" on tranquilizers, this could qualify the couple for a later annulment. The burden of proof always rests on the spouse who impugns the validity of the marriage.

HOMOSEXUALITY. If one spouse late in a marriage reveals having had gay inclinations—either desire or action—this can be regarded as proof of that party's "invalid consent" at the time of the ceremony. A wife who discovers her husband is bisexual qualifies. A husband who learns that his wife has lesbian feelings has a case.

IMMATURITY. This is a broad category. A sixteen-year-old boy, say, who marries his pregnant teenage girlfriend "to do the right thing" can later seek nullification if he can prove that he was immature when they wed.

Other grounds:

A woman whose husband shows *financial irresponsibility*—he bets at the track, abuses the state lottery, doesn't earn enough to support the family—has grounds.

So has any spouse who can prove that he or she married as a *rebellious act* against his or her parents.

So has a man who can prove his wife refuses *to care for the house and children*.

A wife can challenge a husband on the grounds of *infidelity*. Especially if his fooling around with an old girlfriend predates the marriage. She can then charge him with "intention against infidelity," claiming that at the time of their wedding, he gave only "simulation of consent" to his vows. In his heart, he never terminated his previous affair.

Co-dependency now has been added to the list.

So has *peer pressure*: If a couple marries because of excessive reliance on the approval of their peers, they may later be allowed to back out.

Victimhood seems to be the common theme. No one is responsible for a failed marriage anymore.

THE NOVEL CASE OF FEMALE "IMPOTENCY," 1989—AND OTHER EXCUSES ◆

Contraception, too, is now justification for annulment. Since children are the primary purpose of a Catholic marriage—the only real excuse for sex—if either spouse *permanently* thwarts that intention with condoms, sponges, IUDs, pills, spermicides, onanism, and the like, that's "intention against conception." If the spouse never wants children, that's grounds for annulment.

There are many nonpsychological grounds for annulment. Too many to list them all. Two, however, seem particularly cruel.

MALE IMPOTENCY. As mentioned earlier, if a husband is permanently impotent, that's grounds of nullity, since he can't produce children. He should never have entered into marriage in the first place.

If the impotency occurs well into the marriage, due, say, to an accident, it is more complex. He many remain married, but he must refrain from all sexual techniques that are not procreative in nature—which in his case is everything. He may hug and kiss his wife, caress and console her, but he mustn't sexually arouse her, since foreplay is a step toward copulation, which he cannot participate in.

FEMALE IMPOTENCY. The Church considers a woman "impotent" (not sterile; that's a different matter) if due to some malformation of the cervix, vagina, or Fallopian tubes semen cannot freely swim up to an egg and implant. This unfortunate woman, who has enough heartache, can be abandoned by her husband through an annulment.

One is reminded of the days when a man could not qualify for the priesthood if he lacked a thumb or index finger—the two fingers Christ used, presumably, to elevate the bread and wine at the Last Supper; the two fingers a priest uses to consecrate the Eucharist.

Cruelest of all, the Church definition of female "impotency" extends beyond physical impediments to psychological and organic ones as well. If, due to the trauma of rape, a woman cannot ever again bear to have intercourse with her husband, that's grounds. If she contracts a permanent vaginal disease (like cancer) that discourages her husband from entering her, that's grounds. A medical hysterectomy presents several avenues for a husband to one day annul his marriage in order to remarry.

Of course, the above impediments can also be grounds for a civil divorce. And it must be pointed out that the Church does not grant an annulment until *after* the couple wins a civil divorce.

THE STRANGE CASE FOR STERILITY. Sterility, in the husband or the wife, is *not* grounds for an annulment; nor is it an impediment to marriage in the first place. Why not, since the couple can't conceive and satisfy the primary condition of marriage?

The answer lies in the medical uncertainties surrounding sterility itself; at least as those uncertainties have been understood up until now. Is the infertility due to the wife's eggs? To her husband's sperm? Could the problem be temporary?

The important thing is that the couple's primary intent in copulating is the ardent wish to have children. Maybe one day she'll conceive. Miracles happen.

PERFORATED CONDOMS, OR TRICKING GOD. In the 1960s, when doctors turned to examining a husband's sperm to determine the cause of a couple's infertility, the Vatican was in a dilemma. The pope wanted couples to be fertile and fruitful, but how was the husband supposed to turn over a sample of his sperm for evaluation? Masturbation was a grievous sin.

One theologian recommended that doctors siphon sperm directly from a husband's testicles with a needle and syringe. Rome said no, that was still "spilling seed," the equivalent of masturbation. A man's ejaculate can only be deposited in one place: his wife's vagina.

Another theologian suggested that the infertile couple copulate just before they leave their front door for the doctor's office. The physician would then spoon out a sample of sperm from the wife's vaginal tract. This appealed to the pope, but not to doctors.

Rome opted for the idea of a couple using a mildly perforated condom. The man slips on a condom that he's first punctured with needle holes. The presence of holes allows for the *possibility* of conception, hence fulfilling the theological imperative. After this trick sex act, the husband carefully slips off the condom with its residual sperm and rushes it to the doctor's lab. Thus, no sin is committed.

HOW-TO ◆

The rules for annulments are made in Rome, though marriage tribunals exist in every major diocese. Some dioceses are strict in granting annulments; others are favored for their laxity. A few marriage cases are so conceptually difficult that Rome is consulted, and there may even be a solemn ecclesiastical trial. But this is rare these days. Most of the time, local bishops have the power to annul and use it.

The cost for an annulment is coming down as the volume of cases goes up; in the United States, annulments now cost less than civil divorces. No lawyer is needed. The process takes six to eighteen months; two years if the case is tricky. The forms one must file can be found in many parish rectories.

Indeed, annulments have come to look very much like divorces by a different name. Given the multiplicity of grounds on which to base an annulment, tribunal officials have hinted that any broken marriage, if sufficiently scrutinized, can be rendered null and void.

It's been reported that some clever couples (perhaps too clever)—most notably in the Catholic countries of Spain and Italy—write and notarize letters before their wedding, declaring their insincerity to spend a lifetime together. These pieces of paper can then be pulled out of mothballs and mailed to the Roman Rota when times get tough and one party, or both, wants out. The grounds: "intention against indissolubility." The certain verdict: free to remarry.

> **ARE THE CHILDREN OF ANNULLED MARRIAGES BASTARDS?** ◆ *Technically,*
> *yes. No marriage ever existed.*
>
> *But that answer is inadequate. Unfair. And unappealing. Decades ago,*
> *Church canon law came up with a humane solution. The children of an an-*
> *nulled marriage are legitimate as long as one parent entered into the marriage*
> *with sincerity and without impediment. Thus, a wife, for instance, who has*
> *children, then later discovers her husband is a homosexual and gets an annul-*
> *ment, legitimizes her kids through her honesty and good intentions.*

HOW HARD IS IT TO PROVE THAT A SPOUSE SUFFERS FROM PSYCHOLOGICAL PROBLEMS? ◆

The presumption of law favors the validity of a couple's marriage. Hence, as mentioned, the burden of proof rests on the spouse who impugns that validity. At least in theory.

"Psychological cases," writes Joseph Zwack, "rely heavily on testimony from psychological experts." Just as in a criminal trial, the two parties might well present experts in the same field who espouse antithetical points of view.

At a civil trial, the defense may cross-examine the prosecution's witnesses, and vice versa. Not so in a tribunal case. "If an expert says that one of the parties was incapable of making or keeping a marriage vow," writes Zwack, "the Tribunal is unlikely to question his or her opinion. That opinion, when received as evidence in the annulment case, becomes nearly unchallengeable proof of an invalid union."

As mentioned, in 1992, U.S. tribunals granted 59,030 civilly divorced couples annulments. The breakdown of reasons was: 39,753 for "invalid consent," 4 for "impotency," 15,944 for "defect of form" (e.g., the newly-weds-to-be were not counseled by a priest), 3,329 for "other impediments" (e.g., emotional immaturity).

The harsh truth is that the Roman Catholic Church does indeed grant divorces, but since historically it has taken such an absolute stand against divorce, it is now forced to call its divorces annulments.

PART
──────
IX

𝕰xtraordinary
𝕰vil

$\mathfrak{S}$atan

Lucifer to Genies

BEELZEBUB. DEVIL. Lucifer. Baal. Prince of Darkness. Evil One. Enemy of God. Tempter of Eve. Abaddon. Apollyon. Mephistopheles. Antichrist.

He is the Western world's most powerful symbol of evil. He answers to many chilling names and incantations, seeds our darkest private thoughts, and he's sufficiently sly to slip into something sexy when appropriate.

To the pure and virginal Eve at Eden, Satan slithered up in the phallic guise of a serpent. And was irresistible. To celibate medieval monks, Satan appeared as the apparition of a seductive buck-naked wench.

Sex and the Devil have always gone hand in hand.

Sex *is* the Devil in early Christian teachings.

Surprisingly, Satan as God's archenemy, a fallen archangel hell-bent on destroying Creation, first surfaces in the New Testament, late in religious history. The Satan we fear is a Christian construct.

Satan's origins are revealed in the evolution of his various names—from the luminous "Lucifer" to his cryptic calling card "666," the area code of Hell.

The story begins in Heaven.

LUCIFER: CHRISTENDOM, FIRST CENTURY C.E. ◆

Lucifer is the name Christians, late in the first century C.E., conferred on Satan prior to the archangel's fall from the celestial sphere, when he was still a glorious white-robed, feather-winged splendor in God's good graces.

The word "Lucifer," though, was not always associated with images of disobedience and wrongdoing.

In classical mythology, Lucifer is the bright Morning Star, the visible planet Venus that glows above the horizon in the eastern predawn sky. Per-

Lucifer beginning to reign over the souls of sinners.

sonified as a muscular male bearing a lighted torch, Lucifer has scant legend associated with his lustrous name; merely the poetic connotation that he heralds daybreak.

Indeed, his name proclaims "light-bearer," from the Latin *lux*, "light" + *ferre*, "to bear."

How did Christians come to stigmatize the name "Lucifer"?

MIXING METAPHORS. The Christian origin of Lucifer comes from combining two biblical lines, written nine centuries apart, on the surface having nothing to do with each other:

"I beheld Satan fall as lightning from heaven" (Luke 10:18).

"How art thou fallen from heaven, O Lucifer, son of the morning!" (Isa. 14:12).

Luke, writing in 65 C.E., is reporting Jesus' comment on the fallen archangel's blinding luminosity. Christians in Luke's day already believed in the heavenly war waged between obedient and defiant angels.

Isaiah, writing in the eighth century B.C.E., metaphorically used "Lucifer" (he actually used the Hebrew word *helel*, meaning "Shining One" or "Morning Star") as sarcastic contempt for the mighty Babylonian monarchy that recently had fallen, vanished as does Venus from the daytime sky.

In translating the Hebrew Bible into the Latin Vulgate, the language in which Christians read their Scripture, *helel* was rendered as "Lucifer." Isaiah's metaphorical usage of the Morning Star was read by Christians as the fall of the disobedient archangel.

Revelation is rich and allows for more than one interpretation. Church fathers later saw in Isaiah's statement a prefigurement to Jesus' comment (in Luke) on Satan. Maybe Isaiah was sarcastically poking fun at the fallen Babylon, but the Holy Spirit, through divine revelation, had packed the prophet's line with double intent: the literal meaning of words, and the figurative puzzle of prophecy. So Church fathers said.

FRICTION MATCH. The Hebrew word *helel*, "Shining One," gives us *two* origins. Translated in Latin Bibles as "Lucifer," it gave Christians a proper name for God's disobedient archangel.

In Greek Bibles, *helel* was translated as *Phosphoros*, the name of the Morning Star in Greek mythology. Centuries later, in 1680, British physicist Robert Boyle discovered a new element that ignited from friction and he named it "phosphorus." When smeared on the end of a small splinter of wood and scratched, it produced the first friction match, which was called a "Lucifer." A modern-day light-bearer.

MILTON'S PARADISE LOST:
ENGLAND, SEVENTEENTH CENTURY ◆

The appellation "Lucifer" gained wide popularity in the Middle Ages, and achieved literary status in John Milton's *Paradise Lost*.

In Milton's masterpiece, one-third of the heavenly host of angels assemble under Satan's banner for a three-day battle before they are defeated and flung into Hell—where Satan resolves to build a new, alternative empire. Hence, Satan is the first empire builder, the first imperialist.

Arrogantly, the fallen archangel embraces his brave new world with Milton's meter: "Better to reign in hell, than serve in heaven."

In leaving Heaven, Satan becomes the first explorer: "Farewell happy fields / Where joy forever dwells; hail horrors, hail / Infernal world, and thou profoundest hell / Receive thy new possessor."

For Milton, Satan was the archetypical antihero.

Traditionally, Satan's sin, the cause of his expulsion from Heaven, is said to be pride, chief among the deadly sins. Today, Satan's sin would be called rebellion, or political ambition, for he dared to question authority, claiming equality with his superior.

The cliché "as proud as Lucifer" is two thousand years old and denotes the haughty pride that precedes an almost certain comeuppance.

BEELZEBUB: NEAR EAST, PRE-SIXTH CENTURY B.C.E. ◆

"Go, enquire of Baal'zebub, the god of Ekron, whether I shall recover of this disease" (2 Kings 1:2).

The speaker is the king of Ahaziah, who's fallen mysteriously ill, and he's dispatching a messenger.

The unknown author of 2 Kings, probably a Jewish prophet in Babylon during the sixth century B.C.E. Exile, does not use Baal'zebub in reference to Satan; it's merely the title of the Phoenician pagan god at Ekron.

The Hebrew phrase *Baal' zebub* literally means "god of flies," or "lord of dung." (It's a corruption of the older *Baal'zebul*.) Among several Semitic peoples, Baal was a fertility god, who in some cultures accepted the sacrifice of children to ensure a bounty of more children. A firstborn was burnt as an offering to Baal so the parents could be assured a large family.

The early Israelites, scorning idolatry and human sacrifice, linked the name "Baal"—which at an earlier time may have meant "Master of the heavenly house"—with the word "dung" to create a nasty slur, which they hurled at their enemies, and at unbelievers.

Both the Greeks and the Romans adopted "Beelzebub" to characterize a master of evil.

Christians identified Beelzebub with Satan on the basis of three virtually identical passages from the Synoptic Gospels of Mark (c. 60 C.E.), Luke (c. 65 C.E.), and Matthew (c. 65–75 C.E.); called Synoptic because they provide similar synopses of Christ's life. (John, c. 95 C.E., offers a different perspective.) One passage suffices:

> He has Beelzebub, and by the prince of the devils he casts out devils. (Mark 3:22)

The generic word "devil" is from the Greek *diabolos*, meaning "slanderer."

Beelzebub, literally,
"god of flies."

ISRAELITE SATAN: PRE-SIXTH CENTURY B.C.E. ✦

satan. Satan.

The first word was known to the early Jews, but not the second.

The Hebrew noun *satan* means merely "enemy," and as a verb it means "to plot against." Nothing more sinister than that. Both the noun and verb are scattered thorough Hebrew Scriptures with these relatively benign connotations.

The noun *satan* is believed to have evolved from an older verb infinitive *liston*, meaning "to oppose or obstruct."

Almost nowhere in the Hebrew Bible is the word *satan* used as a proper name referring to a demonic being, or to God's archrival.

Rather, in Hebrew Scriptures, *satan* refers to: (1) any human who plays the role of accuser or enemy, (2) a divine messenger sent to earth to stir up trouble, (3) legitimate members of God's heavenly court who object to his decisions, such as the appointment of Joshua as chief priest.

It should not be surprising that the ancient Israelites recognized no single archenemy of God who dwelt in the netherworld, for as a people they had yet to articulate a clear concept of Hell. (*See* Hell.)

Nor did the ancient Israelites need a Satan to dispatch plagues, pestilence, famine, and heartache; their God of Abraham, a wrathful Lord, worked all this on his own.

For the Hebrew people, not until around the third century B.C.E. does a character emerge as the archvillain of Yahweh and humankind. However, even then, figures variously named vie for the notoriety: Mastemah, Semyaz, Beliyaal, the Devil.

JEWISH SATAN: BOOK OF ZECHARIAH, C. 520 B.C.E. ✦

As an appellation of a particular angel, a legal prosecutor in God's celestial court, Satan first appears around 520 B.C.E. in the Book of Zechariah:

> *The Lord rebukes thee, O Satan; even the Lord that has chosen Jerusalem rebukes thee. (Zech. 3:2)*

God and the angel Satan are deep in disagreement, but are not yet archadversaries.

Next, Satan as a particular angel appears in the Book of Job (1,2), but here he is merely a divine troublemaker who questions Job's integrity and suggests God torturously test the prophet. Nonetheless, Satan is clearly subordinate to God, unable to act without God's permission, and a member-in-good-standing in the celestial court: *bene ha-elohim*, "one of God's own."

In 1 Chronicles 21:1, Satan appears as a proper name. Satan is said to incite King David to take a census of Israel, which results in the death of seventy thousand Israelites. Hebrew scholars say that the term "Satan" was a later substitution for the phrase "the Lord," who played a part in the massacre. In other words, to theologically clean up the wrathful God's image, Satan was made to take the rap.

Here we see the beginnings of the polarization that was to come: God will be all-good; Satan will be all-evil. It's called dualism.

SATAN GETS WICKED DURING THE EXILE: BABYLON, 586 TO 539 B.C.E. ◆

The Jews, during their traumatic sixth-century B.C.E. Exile in Babylon, came under the influence of "Persian dualism"—belief in the continuous battle between the forces of good and evil. Persian philosophers summed up the never-ending war with two archetypes:

• Ahriman, the Destructive Spirit and Fiend hell-bent on defiling Creation, and

• Ormazd, or Virtuous Man, who is isolated, alone, frightened, and forever struggling to remain righteous.

The chief Persian philosopher, Zoroaster, taught that a divine being could never do evil. Evil and good are disparate concepts. Oil and water. The two never mix. Evil flows solely from an inherently polluted source.

The troubled Jews listened and learned. God, they heard, cannot be vicious, vindictive, vengeful. God does not cause plagues, earthquakes, and torment for mankind. Someone fundamentally villainous does these wicked things—and does them with pleasure.

The Jews in Exile took this Persian dualism to heart. Their God was good. That's undoubtedly why some Jewish scribe went back to the massacre scene in 1 Chronicles 21:1–14 and deleted "the Lord," substituting "Satan." O, wicked Satan!

Compare 2 Samuel 24:1, where *God* incites King David to take a census of the people with the later 1 Chronicles 21:1, where the king is provoked by Satan:

Satan, from a fifteenth-century manuscript.

The anger of the Lord was kindled against Israel, and he moved David against them to say, Go number Israel. (2 Sam. 24:1)

And Satan rose up against Israel, and provoked David to number Israel. (1 Chron. 21:1)

We may never know how much revision of this sort was done, but in a short time all evil doings were attributed to Satan. In the later Jewish Talmud, a collection of civil and religious laws, Satan assumes a much larger role. He incites humans to disobey the will of God.

Thus, *satan*, "an adversary," had evolved into Satan, God's archenemy and humankind's chief tempter.

Christians adored dualism. Good/bad. Black/white. Virtue/sin. God/Satan. Celibacy/sex. It would become the basis for their early theology.

Indeed, Christian writers would eventually thumb back to the early pages of Genesis and recognize in the nameless serpent "more cunning than any beast of the field," the one who destroyed Paradise for everyone: Satan.

CHRISTIAN SATAN: NEW TESTAMENT, FIRST CENTURY C.E. ◆

In the New Testament, Satan truly blooms into his unique function as *the* Evildoer—if not yet into his singular form as horned, hairy, and cloven-hoofed, with trident in hand. That imagery would come after the inventory of his duties.

Saint Paul, writing about two decades after Christ's death, nails down the dualist view that had been emerging in late Old Testament writings. We are told that God's forces are clothed in an "armor of *light*," whereas Satan rules "the dominion of *darkness*." Dualism: light/dark. Cool/hot. Above/below. In other words, Heaven/Hell.

Clearly *the* villain of Matthew, Mark, Luke, John, and the Book of Revelation is Satan, God's chief adversary, the personification of evil. The Devil, we're told, can imitate an "angel of light" and command the air, or troll the earth as a fire-breathing "dragon." This last image derives from ancient myths of the Near East in which gigantic primordial beasts wreak havoc on Creation. Satan is:

- Author of all evil (Luke 10:19).
- Personal tempter of Jesus Christ (Matt. 4).
- "That old serpent who is called the devil" (Rev. 12:9).

Jews who refuse to accept Christ as the Messiah are referred to as "the synagogue of Satan" (Rev. 2:9, 3:9).

In the Middle Ages, the Church used New Testament passages such as "Ye are of your father and the devil" (John 8:44) to propound the doctrine that Jews were the "spawn of Satan," possessing even his repulsive visage. Regarded as less than human beings—as sorcerers, magicians, and evildoers—Jews were persecuted because in rejecting Christ, they'd sided with Satan.

SATAN AND SALVATION THEOLOGY: FIRST CENTURY c.e. ◆

The earliest Christian theologians embraced dualism. Man is trapped between God and Satan, they said, between good and evil.

The Gospel writers drove home the point that evil may dominate good for a time, but ultimately God will destroy Satan and create a New World. They took the crucifixion and Resurrection of Jesus Christ as a sign that Satan's defeat was at hand.

In Christian theology, Adam and Eve were tempted into sin, as we are, and such failures are pardonable.

But Lucifer and his maverick angels were not tempted, they chose sin out of untrammeled free will. For their disobedience, there is no redemption. Milton's Satan moans: "Which way I fly is hell; myself am hell."

MILTON'S SOURCE. *Paradise Lost* is the most comprehensive account of the fall of Lucifer, and of his subsequent machinations in Hell as Satan. It's believed that Milton gleaned some of his information on Satan from an old Anglo-Saxon poem called *Genesis B*, or *The Fall of Angels*. The unknown Anglo-Saxon poet was clearly bent on fleshing out events he felt the Bible had given short shrift.

The poem shows Satan's haughty, proud, rebellious nature: "I can work just as many marvels with my hands. I have plenty of power to furnish a

Satan as a sorcerer, exchanging the New Testament for a book of black magic.

goodlier throne, one more exalted in heaven. Why must I wait upon *His* favor and defer to *Him* in such fealty?" (*Genesis B* 11:246–91).

ISLAMIC SHAYTAN AND GENIES: PRE-BATTLE OF BADR, 624 C.E. ◆

Islamic theology is rich in references to the Devil. Although he answers to many names, his chief appellation is *Shaytan*, a word obviously related to "Satan."

As in Judeo-Christian tradition, he is called *aduw Allah*, or "Enemy of God."

His personal name, though, is *Iblis*, thought to be an Arabic derivation of the Greek *diabolos*, "devil." The prophet Muhammad makes clear that Iblis *is* the fallen Judeo-Christian archangel, the vainglorious Lucifer. Thus, the Islamic-Christian equations are: Shaytan = Satan; Iblis = Lucifer.

Furthermore, the sacred Koran states (the Torah does not) that the fallen Iblis was the serpent, the tempter of Eve at Eden.

However, in Islamic legend, Iblis is also the ringleader of the *jinn*, or genies, a band of spirits that can behave either like helpful angels or harmful devils. Christianity has no counterpart of these ambivalent spirits.

Iblis, the story goes, believed himself to be superior to the other angels, and amassed a following of celestial discontents. Because of his pride, he and his horde were cast out of Heaven by Allah, banished to the punishment of hellfire. Until the Last Judgment, Iblis, or Shaytan, will continually try to tempt souls away from Allah.

DEMONS TO ANGELS. Muhammad began to receive divine revelations in the year 610. It is significant that the evil Shaytan, as well as the unpredictable jinn, are no longer mentioned in parts of the Koran that date from *after* the establishment of distinctly Islamic beliefs and practices—at about the time of the victorious Battle of Badr in 624. This bloody scrimmage was a definitive turning point in the advancement of the new and struggling Islamic faith, which flourished after the victory at Badr throughout the Arabian Peninsula. The Prophet Muhammad was now in supreme control, and no longer received revelations about Shaytan and other evildoers.

In fact, the Koran goes on to replace detestable demons with an exalted view of angels. The victory for Islam, in effect, tosses out devils and ushers in angels.

The angels in the Koran are presented as invisible, abstract symbols of God's power. Satan in the Koran becomes an abstract symbol for evil and unbelief.

Over the decades, as Muslim beliefs continued to downplay the Devil, they simultaneously exalted God to unparalleled heights—as the One Creator, Sustainer of Life, Judge at the end of time; ninety-nine titles in all. In truth, as mentioned, early parts of the Koran are striking for their lack of statements about God and angels.

In a sense, early and late Koran are not unlike early and late Hebrew Scriptures. Ideas evolve. Dualism surfaces. God matures and takes center stage. Evil retreats to its own dark corner.

Subsequent Islamic creeds do not expand on the Koran's statements about Shaytan, the jinn, or angels. But popular Islam has maintained belief in the Devil and the rest of the spirit world, and added to its ranks angels and demons that touch all aspects of life in this world and in the hereafter.

CHAPTER

24

ℭxorcism

Satan to Dybbuk

SATAN WAS FRIGHTENINGLY real to early Christians. He could enter the human body and force it into evil acts. He could jump from one body into another. Demonic possession was feared by the ancient Assyrians, the Babylonians, and the Egyptians; all prescribed rites of exorcism.

Jesus Christ himself, on at least six occasions, cast out demons.

The first century C.E. Gospels of Matthew and Luke provide the biblical origin for the Roman Catholic Church's belief in demonic possession, and its charismatic gift of priestly exorcism.

SATAN'S APPEARANCE: MIDDLE AGES ◆

What does Satan look like?

The Bible offers many contemptuous epithets for Satan. Liar. Father of Lies. Angel of the Bottomless Pit. Accuser of Our Brethren. Great Dragon. Only the last conveys straightforward imagery.

In truth, for a long time, Christians were in the dark as to Satan's face and form.

As late as the sixth century C.E., a mosaic in Ravenna, Italy, which depicts the Last Judgment, portrays Satan wearing a glorious halo—a symbol that was the due of every celestial being.

In addition, the Ravenna Satan has feathered wings, and is standing at the left hand of Christ. The single artistic nod to Satan's wickedness is the hue of his robe—it's blue, not red. Red was the color worn by angels nearest to God; blue cloaked angels that hovered above earth as messengers-at-the-ready.

The iconography of this period still had not permanently condemned the former archangel Lucifer to the sinister imagery of a vile beast basking in a fiery Hell.

By the Middle Ages, however, Satan had become a monster, a brute, an ogre. Now he had horns, hoofs, and a hirsute body. The once-luminous "light-bearer" was a hybrid beast, half-man, half-goat; Christian artists took the goat imagery from the Greek god Pan.

Artists over the next several centuries glanced back to the ancient iconography of pagan demons in order to supply additional features: a long serpentine tail with a heart-shaped tip, long clawlike fingernails, the leathery wings of bats, and a trident. Satan had become a collage of past chimeras. Even heretical sects that worshiped the Devil favored repulsive imagery. Lucifer's halo and white downy wings had been packed away for good.

In virtually all cultures, the Devil is male. He is inarguably male in the great monotheistic faiths.

CHRISTIAN RITE OF EXORCISM: MATTHEW 10:1, C. 70 C.E. ◆

The term "exorcism" originated in Greek paganism and derives from the Greek *exorkizein*, "to secure an oath" or "to adjure." It was a solemn, intense address to a demon—or to a god—requesting immediate action.

Luke makes clear that Satan can take over a human body for purposes of evil. He employs demonic possession to account for Judas's betrayal of Christ:

> Satan entered into Judas surnamed Iscariot, one of the Twelve, and he discussed with the high priests how he might betray him. . . . He sought out an opportunity to betray him without a disturbance. (Luke 22:3–6)

Thus, Judas was not himself, and not responsible for his actions.

The idea is expressed in the modern phrase: "The Devil made me do it."

Exorcising demons originated with the ancient Greeks; "to exorcise" means "to adjure" in Greek.

Cookie-stealers and murderers alike have used this defense. Perhaps Luke 22:3–6 is the origin of that plea.

God's charismatic gift to the Church that allows priests to exorcise demons is recounted in Matthew:

Having summoned his twelve disciples, he gave them power over unclean spirits, to cast them out, and to cure every kind of disease and infirmity. (Matt. 10:1)

In Luke (11:14), Jesus suggests that the name of the Holy Spirit be invoked to cast out demons. Jesus expelled demons by command, and claimed his success at doing so was a sign of the coming of the Kingdom of God.

Early Christians were convinced that Satan ruled their age, and that his reign heralded the coming of the Kingdom of God. Demonic possession was commonplace, and the gift of exorcism was freely granted to laymen and clergy alike. The slightest aberrant behavior merited exorcism; an insane person was taken to be hopelessly possessed. Church fathers such as Justin Martyr, Tertullian, and Origen all expelled evil spirits from the bodies of demented Christians.

Too often, though, Satan leaped from the body of the possessed into that of the exorcist. Hair-raising tales, both frightening and entertaining, were common.

BAPTISM AND EXORCISM GO HAND IN HAND. Around the year 250, the Church instituted a new order of priests, the exorcistate. It was a minor order, made up of low-ranking clergy (presumably, dispensable). To them was entrusted the dangerous rite. If an exorcist succeeded, he'd go on to become a full-fledged priest. If he failed . . .

About that time, exorcism was made one of the ceremonies preparatory to baptism, and remnants of the rite have remained a part of the Roman Catholic baptismal service.

Why the need to automatically exorcise newborns?

They're vulnerable. They possess no free will and bear the stain of original sin on their souls.

In fact, the water, salt, and oil used in the rite of exorcism are themselves exorcised before being used. Why? Satan might be in the sacramentals.

MODERN METHOD. In 1972, the Catholic Church disbanded the office of exorcist; today, any priest, with the permission of his bishop, can cast out demons. Although antipsychotic drugs and an understanding of schizophrenia have reduced claims of possession to nearly nil, the rite is still strictly prescribed by canon law and occasionally called upon.

The chief command of the sacred rite, issued with equal parts holiness and conviction:

Hear, accursed Satan! I adjure you by the name of the eternal God and of our Savior Jesus Christ, depart with your envy, conquered, trembling, and groaning. May you have no part in this servant of God [insert name] who already has thoughts of heaven and who is about to renounce you and your world and achieve a blessed immortality.

In the Catholic Church today, the preferred practice in exorcism is not to address the Devil directly, which is seen as giving Satan too much importance. This breaks with centuries of tradition. Instead, the priest performing the rite addresses God, begging for divine intercession. Satan may be addressed, as long as the comments are few, and brief.

Furthermore, sacramentals like holy water, oil, and crucifixes are no longer first exorcised themselves. This, too, is to play down the emphasis on Satan's presence.

DEMON TOTS ◆ *Exorcism as part of an infant's baptismal rite was abandoned by the Church of England shortly after its founding in the sixteenth century. Anglican bishops argued that it implied all prebaptized infants were "demoniacs."*

The Catholic Church still exorcises infants as part of the baptismal rite. The action is subtle, consisting of two soft-spoken prayers that mention either Satan or "the Devil." The first prayer sets the infant free from original sin (which could be a window of opportunity for Satan to enter); the second asks God to lift the infant above the power of darkness.

One Church manual suggests: "Three times the priest breathes gently upon the face of the child [symbolic of the Triune God] saying, 'Depart from him, thou unclean spirit, and give place to the Holy Spirit.'" The manual explains that "the enemy" has "been ousted to make room for a new Guest."

JEWISH EXORCISM: POST-BIBLICAL PERIOD ◆

In the Hebrew Bible, there are no clear examples of exorcism.

True, David employs music to soothe Saul, who's troubled by "an evil spirit from Yahweh" (1 Sam. 16:14). But a careful reading of the incident suggests Saul really suffers from severe manic-depressive psychosis, with paranoid delusions that prompt episodes of impulsive homicidal violence. At least that's today's interpretation.

It was only after the Jews became enamored with Persian dualism, relegating good to God, evil to Satan, that they adopted exorcism as a respected rite, with the professional exorcist receiving special status. Manuals from the early centuries C.E. give practical advice on avoiding and appeasing *shedim* (demons) and *mazikim* (spirits).

Later rabbinic literature names individual demons who are responsible for specific human illnesses.

An incantation to exorcise a demon was effective only when recited in Hebrew, due to "the subtleties of vocalization"—the rhyme of vowels, sometimes seven vowels per line, soothed out the evil spirit. *"Hafkaid alov rasha v'satan"* would not work in translation.

The exorcist searched for five traits that would confirm that a person was possessed: (1) hallucinations (interestingly called "fascination with the senses"), (2) body sores or blisters, (3) frequent masturbation ("corruption of the organ"), (4) "contraction of the limbs," and (5) epileptic thrashing.

It is no exaggeration to say that the Jews gave Christians "God" and the Christians gave Jews "Satan." As the personification of evil, Satan is a New Testament development, one that greatly influenced Jewish notions of exorcism. "For do not all the books found in the Christian language," sighed an early rabbi, "call for exorcism and give accounts of possession."

DYBBUK: MIDDLE EAST, 1752 ◆

Today a "dybbuk"—the spirit of a dead person that enters the body of a living person and takes it over—is part of Jewish folklore, more amusing than sinister. The word is relatively new.

The original "evil spirit" in Judaism was called *ruach ra'ah*. This spirit was

Jewish scholars, in pointed hats, suck "evil" from the Devil disguised as a pig. From the earliest anti-Semitic broadside, Germany, 1475.

said to "cling" or "cleave" to the body of its host, like a barnacle to a boat. A cleaving spirit. The Hebrew word for "cleaving" is *mitdabake*, and, in the suffix, we can see the origin of "dybbuk."

The root "dabake" was not used as a noun or spirit title until 1752, when the mystic scholar (Kabbalist) Jacob Emden spoke of a certain Jew being possessed of a dybbuk. From then on, "dybbuk" was part of popular jargon.

DEMONIC MANIA ◆

For reasons that have never been clearly explained, the last quarter of the sixteenth century witnessed a veritable plague of possessions—both Christian and Jewish. Manuals on exorcism in Latin, Italian, and Hebrew were bestsellers. *A Practica of Exorcists*, published in Padua in 1587, gave Catholic priests a checklist:

> *Things to be learned from the demon: His name, that it may be written on paper and burned. Names of his associates and their number. Holy words he especially abhors so they may be repeated. Beware of curious digressions. Shut him off if he volunteers too much information.*

To exorcise one possessed woman, Rabbi Menashe ben Israel, in 1571, put smoke, fire, and sulfur to her nostrils. "The demon should leave by means of her big toe," he said. He goes on: "All the spectators decided to hush up the story because of the danger that Gentiles would want to burn the woman for witchcraft."

A contemporary Jewish scholar claims that the rash of exorcisms in the late 1500s "was a pan-cultural phenomenon, shared by Jews and Christians, and Jewish authorities borrowed liberally from Christian sources, both live and literary."

What was going on?

Perhaps it was a backlash to the birth of the empirical sciences. Physics, chemistry, astronomy, and medicine were challenging religion and superstition with reason and logic. Poor, illiterate folk were afraid of the new. The shock of science. Spirit possession was perhaps an attempt to hold on to a familiar past. Whatever the reason for the onslaught, it passed. By 1650, new cases of demonic possession had slowed to a trickle.

"LETTERS FROM THE DEVIL": EUROPE, LATE MIDDLE AGES ◆

This popular genre of literature, which presaged the sixteenth-century Reformation, consisted of letters written by scholars and clerics with a three-

An envoy of Satan carrying "Letters from the Devil."

fold purpose: (1) to satirize the corruption in the Roman Catholic Church at the time (such offenses as the sale of indulgences); (2) to amuse the public; and (3) to point out the need for Church reform.

Popes, cardinals, and bishops had amassed great wealth and become highly materialistic. The form of these popular critiques "from Satan" was that of a legal charter in which Satan bestowed rewards for services rendered. Typically, he'd thank the clergy for their greed, drunkenness, and worldly ambition, all of which, he'd say, brought him many welcomed recruits to Hell.

One opening salutation read: "Satan, Emperor of all the realms of hell, King of shadows, Duke of the damned, to his most faithful servant John Dominici, Archbishop of Ragusa and Abettor of all our works, sends good health and eternal pride." The archbishop was notoriously materialistic.

The most popular example, widely circulated, was the "The Letter of Lucifer," composed mid–fourteenth century. After the salutation to "all the Members of our kingdom, the Sons of pride, particularly the Princes of the modern church," it goes on to needle, "we are sending some of the eminent demons and nobles of hell to counsel and aid you. Your cleverness knows very well how to acquiesce in their suggestions and add to their treacherous inventions."

After a long satire on the sad state of the Church in Rome, the letter concludes: "Dated at the center of the Earth in our shadowy kingdom, in the presence of hordes of demons specially summoned for this purpose in our treacherous consistory."

Today, of course, the media openly report on religious leaders, and key issues are debated in public. At the time, the "Letters from the Devil" served as both a public venting of frustration and a call for Church reform—which would arrive as the Protestant Revolt.

CHAPTER

2 5

$\mathscr{A}$ntichrist

"666" to Apocalypse Now

"ANTICHRIST" DEFINED: GOSPEL OF JOHN, C. 95 C.E. ◆

Satan is the archenemy of God.

Antichrist is the archenemy of Jesus Christ; from the Greek *anti,* "against."

Is Satan the Antichrist? Yes and no. The Devil is certainly *an* Antichrist. But there are others. Many. An Antichrist is anyone in Satan's employment.

The concept of Antichrist was formulated in the first century C.E., a period of intense religious persecution and political upheaval throughout the Roman Empire. A compelling combination of myth, history, and legend commingled in that era to explain the persistence of evil in everyday life. For, by late in the first century, Jerusalem had fallen, the Second Temple lay in ruins, and Christians were being slaughtered as sport by Roman soldiers. Evil seemed to lurk everywhere. People prayed that the next sunrise would usher in Christ's Second Coming and their release from misery.

The earliest mention of the term "anti-christ" appears in the Epistles of John, composed near the close of the first century. In his Gospel, John writes with the purpose of winning converts to the new faith; in his Epistles, he addresses Christians whose faith has been shaken by "false teachers" or "anti-christs." He coins the word to convey a message. And he uses the word in three self-defining passages, including:

Dear children, it is the last time: and as you have heard that anti-christ is coming, so now many anti-christs have arisen; whereby we know that it is the last hour. (1 John 2:18)

"Anti-christ" here takes on its full eschatological overtones. False prophets are many and their presence heralds total destruction.

The word "eschatology" is from the Greek *eschatos*, meaning "furthest out," and it's the name of the branch of theology that deals with death, resurrection, judgment, and immortality. The "furthest out" things.

A few lines later, we're told:

Who is a liar but he who denies that Jesus is the Christ? He is anti-christ who denies the Father and the Son. (1 John 2:22)

Here anyone who does not believe in Jesus as the Messiah is lambasted an "anti-christ." The word is used in the same way in the Second Epistle:

For many deceivers have gone forth into the world who do not confess that Jesus is the Christ coming in the flesh. This is a deceiver and an anti-christ. (2 John 7)

John never names names. We don't know which Antichrists he had in mind. But we do know the historical figure the Jews had in mind when they thought of their own faith's archvillain, and laid the groundwork for the Christian Antichrist concept.

JEWISH MODEL FOR "ANTICHRIST":
SYRIAN KINGDOM, SECOND CENTURY B.C.E. ◆

Jewish eschatology had been influenced by Persian and Babylonian myths, in which battles between gods and demons would mark the end of earthly time. In the Old Testament, the Jewish conception of such a struggle is found in the prophecy of Daniel.

The historical figure who served as the model for the Antichrist in the second century B.C.E. was King Antiochus IV Epiphanes, who persecuted Jews.

Antiochus "the Mad," as he was called, was Seleucid king of the Hellenistic Syrian kingdom from 175 to 164 B.C.E. A popular ruler among his people, he promoted Greek culture and, in expanding his domain, conquered the Jewish stronghold of Jerusalem and attempted to Hellenize the city— that is, to paganize it from the point of view of the Jews.

In response, Judas Maccabeus raised the Jewish rebellion that eventually led to the formation of the independent Judean state of the Maccabees.

Antiochus (whose name only coincidentally begins with the prefix "anti") left a lasting impression upon the Jews. In attempting to wipe out their religion, he came to symbolize any Great Ruler who battles God's Will (God's People) and consequently presages the end of time.

Early Christians borrowed this concept, dubbed the villain "Antichrist," and applied the notion (if not always the name) to a succession of persecuting rulers: Caligula (who attempted to have himself worshiped as a god in the decades before the word "Antichrist" was coined), Nero, Domitian, Decius, Diocletian. A people persecuted see Antichrists everywhere.

ANTICHRIST CONCEPT: PAUL, CORINTH, C. 50 C.E. ◆

A thoroughly Christian view of Antichrist first appears some twenty years after Christ's Crucifixion; that is, nearly forty years before John employs the term "anti-christ" in his letters.

The concept is found in the Second Epistle of Paul the Apostle to the Thessalonians. Epistles 1 and 2, circa 50 C.E. (written a few months apart), are among Paul's earliest surviving writings; he wrote the two letters to the Thessalonians from Corinth a short time after preaching there on his second missionary journey:

> Let no one deceive you in any way, for the day of the Lord will not come unless the apostasy comes first, and the man of sin is revealed, the son of perdition. (2 Paul 2:3)

In this Epistle, Antichrist ("the man of sin") appears as a tempter who works his devious ways by magic and wonders, seeking divine honors. We're told this "man of lawlessness" will easily win over the Jews, since they have rejected Christ and his teachings.

Christians bought into this notion. And what more devout followers could this "man of sin" have than the Jews who'd scorned Jesus. John, in his Gospel, written around the same time as his Epistles, has Jesus predict: "I have come in the name of my Father, and you do not receive me; if another come in his own name, him you will receive" (5:43).

In summary: Paul posits an Antichrist concept circa 50 C.E.; John uses the term "anti-christ" circa 95 C.E. Drop the hyphen and the generic villain becomes the full-fledged fiend, Antichrist.

OVER EVIL, JEWS AND CHRISTIANS PART WAYS: FIRST CENTURY C.E. ◆

Ironically, while Christians late in the first century were honing their concept of Satan, giving the Devil his due, so to speak, Jews were beginning to view evil in a more abstract manner.

When Jerusalem fell to the Romans in 70 C.E., the Second Temple was destroyed and the Jews were exiled from Palestine. In the Diaspora, or "scattering," they settled throughout the Mediterranean and Europe. With its geographic center gone, the Jewish religion entered a new stage.

The center of Jewish religious life was now the synagogue rather than the Temple; its leaders were the rabbis or "teachers" rather than the old priests and prophets.

Both Judaism and Christianity had inherited Persian dualism from sixth century B.C.E. Zoroastrianism. Rabbinic Judaism now began to reject the dualistic concept of Prime Good (God) versus Prime Evil (Satan).

Rather, said rabbis, evil results from the imperfect state of the created world (metaphysical evil) and from the human misuse of free will (moral evil), not from the fiendish machinations of a cosmic Satan.

Most rabbis rejected the concept of a personified being leading the forces of evil and preferred to speak of the Devil only as a symbol of the tendency toward evil within humans. The Lord created both the inclination toward good (*yetser ha-tov*) and the inclination toward evil (*yetser ha-ra*), but God gave humankind the Law so that people might overcome evil *yetser* by following the Torah.

For Christians, however, evil was being personified more vividly with each written text. Christians were ever vigilant to identify any Antichrist among them—because arrival of Antichrist heralded Jesus' Second Coming.

APOCALYPSE NOW: BOOK OF REVELATION, C. 95 C.E. ◆

The origin of the Christian belief in a spectacular end-of-time Apocalypse—a monstrous final finale before the curtain falls—is easy to pin down.

The word "apocalypse" is from the Greek verb *apokalyptein*, "to reveal."

There are apocalyptic passages in the Old Testament; for instance, in Isaiah (c. eighth century B.C.E.), and especially in Daniel (c. sixth century B.C.E.). But no book of the canonical Old Testament is entirely apocalyptic.

Starting around 200 B.C.E., a new literary genre began to flourish in both Judaism and Christianity. Apocalyptic literature was written primarily to give hope to peoples undergoing persecution and the stress of cultural upheaval. Its language was cryptic, but desperate Jews and Christians understood what the codes and symbols meant: the sudden and dramatic intervention of God in human affairs on behalf of believers, heralded by cataclysmic events of cosmic proportions—famines, plagues, wars, earthquakes—and temporary rule of the world by the Prince of Evil.

Inarguably, the most bizarre dramatic work to appear was the Book of Revelation, written about 95 C.E., perhaps by a man named John. Perhaps he was John the Apostle, though probably not.

This text has shaped the Western imagination as it envisions the Last Days. At the close of the first millennium C.E., Christians turned to John's text for a glimpse of what was in store. As we near the close of the second millennium, John's book is still a primary text consulted by those seeking to imagine the end of the world.

THE AUTHOR. The book—which was only accepted into the Christian Bible after much debate—was written on the island of Patmos in the Aegean Sea by a man who identifies his name as John: "I, John, who also am your brother . . . was on the isle that is called Patmos" (Rev. 1:9). Tradition suggests that John the Apostle was in exile there, though many historians doubt that. In any case, the language, style, and vocabulary of Revelation seem to rule out John the Apostle, Christ's beloved disciple who composed the Fourth Gospel.

The King James Version of the Bible is cautious regarding the authorship and names the book "The Revelation of St. John the Divine" (not "the Beloved"). The Revised Standard Version is more noncommittal, calling it "The Revelation of John." The Jerusalem Bible simply says, "The Book of Revelation." The Douay-Confraternity Bible calls it "The Apocalypse," with a footnote that the book was written by "St. John, while a prisoner on Patmos."

Historically, the dire event that prompted John to put pen to parchment, perhaps while in prison, and create "The Apocalypse" was most likely the bloody persecution of Christians under the emperor Domitian, which swept misery across Asia Minor, John's evangelizing territory. Domitian was assassinated in 96 C.E.; Revelation is thought to have been written between 90 to 95 C.E.

Saint John on the island of Patmos composing the Book of Revelation.

THE NIGHTMARE. The book is a bewildering kaleidoscope of scenes, punctuated by voices and bursts of heavenly hymnody, fracturing grammatical rules to create fireworks.

John seems to have scoured the Old Testament for its most harrowing images and idioms, plagues and pestilences, maledictions and misfortunes—then spun them all into his own hallucinogenic vision.

The end of the world, in brief, according to Revelation:

John is summoned to Heaven. He sees God enthroned, brandishing a seven-sealed scroll no man can open. Standing by the throne is a Lamb scarred by sacrificial slaughter. The Lamb (a symbol of the Messiah already familiar to Christians) breaks the seals and unleashes a series of disasters, representing God's wrath against an idolatrous and unpenitent world.

Each of the broken first four seals releases a horse and rider: the *Four Horsemen of the Apocalypse.* The white horse and rider represent foreign invasion. The red horse and rider signify civil war and insurrection. The black horse and rider symbolize famine. The pale horse and rider are death by disease. Hence, the four horsemen are: *War, Revolution, Famine, Pestilence.*

Seven seals broken; *seven* trumpets blast; *seven* bowls of God's wrath pour out; the Antichrist, Satan's emissary, is a *seven*-headed beast. The beast's city,

---

THE MAGIC OF "SEVEN" ◆ *The Book of Revelation is poetic and visionary. And wild. It expresses serious ideas through phantasmagoric imagery and symbols. To take John's picturesque language literally, or treat the book as a practical timetable for eternal salvation, is to misread its spirit.*

The book is rich in numerology. The number "seven" is given great weight. In addition to the seven seals, seven trumpets, and seven bowls, John lists seven churches in Asia that will receive seven apocalyptic letters of warning.

In fact, so frequent is the number "seven" used in Revelation that scholars suspect "seven" churches were selected not because they actually existed in the province of Asia but because of the number's mystic qualities. In Genesis, the six days of Creation are followed by a seventh day of rest. Ancient Sumerian and Babylonian Creation stories ran on for seven-day lengths; a fact known to the ancient Israelites, which influenced adoption of their seven-day week. It is no coincidence that our week has six workdays and one day of rest.

But it is another number in Revelation that for centuries has captured people's imagination: "The Number of the Beast—666." The coded name of Antichrist.

Allegorical representation of the Four Horsemen of the Apocalypse: War, Revolution, Famine, and Pestilence.

Babylon, the "great whore," is destroyed, the beast defeated, Satan bound; the saints reign for a millennium; Satan is released for his final assault and farewell. God then judges the world, and a new Heaven and earth replace the old.

The holy city, Jerusalem, the bride, descends from Heaven, and all earth's splendor is gathered into it.

"666"—HELL'S AREA CODE ◆

No passage in Revelation has generated as much superstition and hysteria as chapter 13, verse 18:

> *Here is wisdom. He who has understanding, let him calculate the number of the beast: for it is the number of a man; and his number is six hundred and sixty-six.*

The evil empire in John's time was Rome, with its oppression of Jews and Christians. The city was ruled by a "beast," an Antichrist John is reluctant to name—perhaps to spare himself the charge of treason and subsequent execution. In the above passage, he codes the man's name in such a way that his more knowledgeable readers will be able to decode the puzzle and yet the law of Rome will not be able to touch him.

To decode John's "666" reference, we must realize that for many centuries, Jews, Greeks, and Romans assigned numerical values to letters of the alphabet; something we don't do with our own alphabet. The most familiar example to us today is that of Roman numerals: $I = 1, V = 5, X = 10, L = 50,$

*The magic number "seven":
seven angels, with seven
plagues.*

C = 100, D = 500, M = 1000. Words constructed from these letters then not only have word meaning but also numerical value.

Mystics in John's time (and well into the Middle Ages) assumed that God-inspired words in the Bible had hidden numerical significance in addition to their literal meanings. Mystics spent considerable time analyzing the number values of biblical words and passages, a tedious endeavor called "gematria," a corruption of the Greek word *geometria*, mathematics (cf. our "geometry").

The "Number of the Beast," 666, is the most significant example of the game of gematria in the Bible.

Scholars have considered countless personages from John's time as possible candidates for the beast, and two stand out among the many—both were harassing, immoral, unethical Roman emperors.

NERO. Nero's name in Greek is *Neron*; his title "Caesar" in Greek is *Kaisar. Kaiser Neron* written in Hebrew letters is *qsr nrwn*. Hebrew letters also function as numbers with the following assigned values: q = 60, s = 100, r = 200, n = 50, w = 6. Therefore, *qsr nrwn* adds up to 666.

Nero had been dead for about a quarter-century when John, on Patmos, wrote Revelation. Nero had stabbed himself in the throat, and popular legend had him either returning from the dead one day, or still alive and exiled in the East—from which he'd return with a crushing army. So perhaps Nero was John's Antichrist.

To many modern-day scholars, "666" is Nero, who claimed divine authority and whose power seemed invincible. John wanted his readers to understand that the Roman state and its rulers were neither divine nor invincible. They were human and carried the seed of their own destruction; and their number is a sequence of sixes that never reaches the mystical perfection of "seven."

DOMITIAN. At the time John was writing Revelation, Domitian sat on the throne of Rome, and his persecution of Christians was in high gear. He was far meaner than Nero. It would be logical to refer elliptically to the living, punishing emperor in a code, as John does. But does Domitian's name— perhaps combined with one of his many titles—sum up to 666? For many historians prefer Domitian over Nero.

To date, his name doesn't work out as making him the Antichrist. It may be that he bore a nickname commonly known to Christians in John's time, and it's the nickname that sums to 666.

POPES AS ANTICHRISTS: MARTIN LUTHER, 1519 ◆

By the Middle Ages, the code "666" and the concept of Antichrist had become potent political weapons. At the outbreak of every civil crisis, people hurled the number and name at the villainous ruler in charge.

In the twelfth century, for instance, the emperor Frederick II was called Antichrist, and the Apocalypse was seen as being just around the corner.

Later, Church popes Boniface VII (974, 984–85) and John XXII (1316–34) were dubbed Antichrists. A politically appointed pope, Boniface took part in the murder of Count Sicco, who sought to restore the legal pope; when the populace turned against him, Boniface absconded with the papal treasury, settling comfortably for a time in the south of Italy. On July 20, 985, he is thought to have been assassinated by an angry mob.

John XXII was the second of the so-called Avignon popes; he kept the papacy captive in sunny France, while giving lip service to his wish to return to politically strife-torn Rome.

The pope as the Devil, "Ego sum Papa" ("I am the Pope"). From a Reformation handbill against Pope Alexander VI.

Martin Luther triumphs over the
Roman Catholic demon monk.
From a Reformation pamphlet,
Germany, 1521.

Reformer Martin Luther, two years after he nailed his ninety-five theses (1517) to the church door at Wittenberg, denied that the papacy had a scriptural foundation, and cursed *all* popes as Antichrists.

In fact, it became common for any two opponents—two politicians, two kings, two popes (and there were simultaneously two popes for a number of years, one in Avignon, one in Rome)—to call each other Antichrists. Oppressive regimes of any sort were seen to herald Christ's Second Coming.

Natural catastrophes like earthquakes and volcanic eruptions were viewed as signs that the Antichrist had arrived, and that Jesus Christ was about to make his Second Coming.

A popular ruse in the fifteenth century was for preachers to spread warnings of the imminent coming of the Antichrist to get people to repent. And contribute. It's still done by televangelists today. Many hype the Apocalypse—seemingly foreshadowed in the moral laxity of our times—to maximize viewer donations.

Not long ago, a major soap manufacturer was pressured to redesign its logo when customers claimed the seal contained a coded "666" and thus promoted a satanic product.

The Book of Revelation continues to capture the popular imagination.

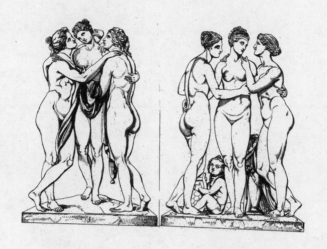

Divine Dos and Don'ts

Forbidden Foods

Pork Chops to Meatless Fridays

FORBIDDEN FRUIT ◆

The first forbidden food—the first forbidden anything on earth—was an apple. Or was it?

After Adam is comfortably settled in the lush garden in Eden (the Bible never actually assigns the garden a name: "God planted a garden eastward in Eden"—Gen. 2:8), God grants him the right to full enjoyment of the garden's earthly delights, with one exception:

> From every tree of the garden you may eat; but from the tree of the knowledge of good and evil you must not eat; for the day you eat of it, you must die. (Gen. 2:16–17)

The species of tree is never identified. What might humankind's first forbidden morsel have been?

POMEGRANATE. This is the preference of Hebrew scholars. They point to the love song Solomon sang: "You are fair, my love. Your cheeks are [red] like the halves of pomegranate" (4:3). The fruit adorned the robes of the high priests. A famous pomegranate tree was a landmark in the outskirts of the town of Gibeah, and several biblical towns are named after the pomegranate: Rimmon (which is Hebrew for "pomegranate"), Rimmon-Peretz ("Pomegranate of the Wellspring"), Sela-Rimmon ("Pomegranate Rock"), Eyn-Rimmon ("Pomegranate Fountain"), and Gath-Rimmon ("Pomegranate Press").

The round fruit, with red, leathery rind, an abundance of seeds, and red, juicy, edible flesh, had been cultivated in Egypt long before the time of Moses. The Jews wandering through the wilderness remembered with longing the pomegranates of Egypt, and were heartened when the scouts they sent into Cananna brought the fruit back from that "land of wheat, and barley, and vines, and fig trees, and pomegranates."

King Solomon maintained a large grove of pomegranates. Carbonized pomegranates were found in a tomb at Jericho dating from the Bronze Age. A pomegranate tree could have grown in Eden.

The English word "pomegranate" is from the Latin *pomum granatum*, "fruit full of seeds."

APPLE. This is the preference of Christian scholars. The apple was one of the early fruits cultivated in Asia Minor, as early as 1200 B.C.E.; carbonized apples, rock-hard, soot-black, and resembling chunks of coal, have been unearthed and dated to 6500 B.C.E.

But the apple entered the competition for the tree at Eden late, only after Christian artists began to graphically depict the biblical tale. By then, the Greeks had mythologized the "golden fruit," belonging to the family *Rosaceae* (which includes the queen of flowers, the rose): an apple was given to the goddess Hera from the Garden of the Hesperides as a wedding present when she married Zeus.

Our word "apple" is from the Old English *aeppel*, which stood not only for the fruit, but also for anything round, and was, in addition, the common name for an eyeball.

The Old English *aeppel* in turn derives from the Latin *Abella*, the name of a Campanian town renowned for its orchards.

BANANA. The Islamic Koran claims that the forbidden fruit was a banana—which botanically isn't a fruit, but an herb. Bananas were prized in the Indus Valley at least four thousand years ago.

The Koran was compiled in the seventh century C.E., dictated by the

Adam and Eve driven out of Eden for eating . . . an apple? a banana? or a pomegranate?

angel Gabriel to the Prophet Muhammad, and this is precisely the period in which Arab traders enjoyed a thriving export business in bananas. In fact, it was Arabs who introduced the banana to the Near East and into northern Egypt—all in the seventh century. The fruit was popular in Muhammad's day, and profitable, and its name was inserted into the Old Testament story.

Pomegranate? Apple? Banana?

The point is, food, and dietary laws in general, have always been used by a people to stake claim to their own version of events. As we're about to see.

EATING AS A FORM OF SOCIAL EXCLUSION: BIBLICAL TIMES TO THE PRESENT ◆

Food, in the past, expressed social relationships. In fact, "eating together" still does. Family or friends, village or tribe, clan or kinsmen who eat together stay together; or at least they are stating a current friendship.

In olden days, for men to be gluttonous together was the highest form of fraternity. Perhaps it still is. Gluttony was and is a kind of binding glue.

In Old Testament times, almost every secular pact or sacred covenant was sealed with a common meal. Sharing salt, a highly savory seasoning, expressed the deepest loyalty among friends.

Conversely, refusal to eat with someone was a put-down, an insult, a denunciation perhaps of a former friendship. It can still be—and can be highly effective. *Not* to invite someone to a chic dinner party, wedding banquet, or bar mitzvah speaks louder than words. Food and drink are universally associated with good health, happy times, and hospitality.

Alcohol was essential to ancient religious life. Beer in Mesopotamia was drunk in temple services by high priests to help them communicate with gods. The ancient Greeks preferred wine, and believed their intellectual superiority was due to the use of wine and olive oil. One can assume they had low cholesterol counts.

Wine in the Old and New Testaments is both praised and condemned. When Samson's birth is foretold, an angel of the Lord cautions the mother-to-be: "You will conceive and bear a son. Now, then, be careful to take no wine or strong drink" (Judges 13:3–4). This sounds surprisingly like the prenatal warning to pregnant women that now appears on modern alcoholic beverages.

In fact, the Israelites made an art of food taboos.

*Dietary laws developed
as a form of social
exclusion.*

JEWISH DIETARY LAWS:
LEVITICUS 11, DEUTERONOMY 14, C. 1400 B.C.E. ◆

In *Purity and Danger*, British anthropologist Mary Douglas argues that religiously sanctioned food taboos—of the kind that abound in Leviticus, chapter 11, and Deuteronomy, chapter 14—are the means by which ancient societies maintained their separateness from others, their cohesiveness as a clan, and the exclusivity of their religious beliefs.

Gastronomic concepts of pollution and defilement did not have to make rational sense, or even offer health protections. They merely had to be a social code known and adhered to by a clan. "*We* do this, and *you* don't."

To join that clan, you adopted their gastronomic dos and don'ts. Americans, mid–twentieth century, were still separating themselves from foreigners by shunning ethnic and exotic foods; it was Chef Boyardee, with his canned meatballs and spaghetti, who removed the onus from Italian cuisine. Previously, only folk of Italian ancestry ate Italian. Today, of course, eating ethnic is a sign of sophistication; multiculturalism is a reality.

DISPELLING A POPULAR MISCONCEPTION. Perhaps the greatest misconception concerning Jewish dietary laws (the laws of *kashrut*) is that they were instituted for health reasons—because certain foods spoil easily, because one can get trichinosis from pork. Though the myth is prevalent, this is not so.

Leviticus explains the real reason behind dietary laws in simple, straightforward language—one has only to realize that by the word "holy" the God of the Jews is instructing his people to preserve their separateness and religious identity:

Passover meal. "Kosher" means "fit" or "proper."

For I am the Lord your God! Therefore, sanctify yourselves and be holy, for I am holy. . . . For I am the Lord that brought you up out of the land of Egypt to be your God. You shall therefore be holy. (Lev. 11:44–45)

Simply put, God said: "Eat from this menu I give you, and you will always recognize yourselves as Jews, and others will always know you are Jews." God knew what he was doing; strict dietary laws kept Jews from easily socializing with people of other faiths. Less socializing meant less intermarriage. "Holiness" meant separateness.

KOSHER MEANS "FIT" OR "PROPER." "Holiness" in Hebrew is *kedushah*, from the Hebrew *kadosh*, meaning "separated." What was "proper" or "kosher" (read "Jewish") was separate from everything else; from everybody else.

The word "kosher" did not originally apply to food. It is first used in the Bible (Esther 8:5 and Ecclesiastes 11:6) to mean "proper" or "good"—and it may also mean "fit" in the sense of mental competency; as in "fit to testify."

In later rabbinic literature, it refers to holy objects "fit for ritual use." It can be argued that the Jews' extreme separateness as imposed by strict dietary laws often brought them much grief from their enemies.

The rabbis of Talmudic times came right out and said to their flock, in effect, "Don't try to understand these mandatory statutes, or *chukim*, they don't have a rational basis, just obey them."

Maimonides, on the other hand, in his twelfth-century philosophical work *Guide for the Perplexed*, sought some additional meaning for the laws of *kashrut*: They "train us to master our appetites; to accustom us to restrain our desires; and to avoid considering the pleasure of eating and drinking as the goal of man's existence."

DIETARY DOS AND DON'TS: OLD TESTAMENT ◆

The Jews more than any other Western people formalized food dos and don'ts. Their dietary laws and customs, as spelled out in the Mosaic Law of the Old Testament books of Leviticus and Deuteronomy, are prime examples of Jewish separateness and religious discipline.

Foods that are nonkosher as proscribed in the Bible:

• *All animals (and their products) that do not chew the cud* and *do not have cloven hoofs, such as pigs, horses, camels, are nonkosher.*

Foods that are neither meat (*fleishig*, in Yiddish) nor dairy (*milchig*) products, nor derivatives of such products, are called *pareve*, meaning "neutral." Technically, most pareve products made up of a single ingredient—such as salt, sugar, and coffee—do not require kosher certification.

The ancient Hebrews were shepherds, tending animals like sheep and goats, thus cloven-hoofed and cud-chewing hoofed animals are standard food for such pastoralists. The animals were domesticated and eaten. Pigs, on the other hand, are distinctly unsuited to the life of nomadic herders.

These are the animals you may eat: the ox, the sheep, the goat, the deer, the gazelle, the roe deer, the wild goat, the ibex, the antelope, and the mountain sheep. (Deut. 14:4–5)

But you shall not eat any of the following that only chew the cud or only have cloven hoofs: the camel, the hare and the rock badger . . . the pig, which indeed has hoofs and is cloven-footed, but does not chew the cud and is therefore unclean for you. Their flesh you shall not eat, and their bodies you shall not touch. (Deut. 14:7–8)

• *Fish without fins and scales are nonkosher.* "Whatsoever has fins and scales may you eat; and whatsoever has no fins and scales, you may not eat; it is unclean to you" (Deut. 14:9–10).

Some fish with fins and scales eventually shed them; for example, swordfish and sturgeon. Strict Orthodoxy makes these fish nonkosher, but some Conservative rabbis allow them to be consumed.

• *Blood from any animal is forbidden.* The Bible is emphatic that blood not be consumed, because blood symbolizes the essence of life. "This shall be a perpetual ordinance for your descendants where ever they may dwell. You shall not partake of any fat or any blood" (Lev. 3:17).

Based on this, the rabbis of the Talmud concluded that when an animal is slaughtered for its meat, as much blood as possible must be drained off. The jugular vein is severed. The man who performs the butchery is called a *shochet*—he uses a wickedly sharp knife called a *challef*, and he's thoroughly versed in the laws of kosher slaughtering, the laws of *shechitah*.

- *Mollusks are nonkosher:* clams, scallops, oysters.
- *Crustaceans are nonkosher:* shrimp, crab, lobster.
- *All living creatures that creep are nonkosher:* such as snakes.
- *Fowl specifically named in the Bible are nonkosher:*

You shall not eat the following: the eagle, the vulture, the osprey, the various kites and falcons, all the various species of crows, species of hawks, the owl, the screech owl, the ibis, the desert owl, the buzzard, the cormorant, the stork, the ostrich, the nightjar, the gull, the various species of herons, the hoopoe, and the bat. (Deut. 14:12–18)

HUNTING IS FORBIDDEN IN JUDAISM: BOOK OF EXODUS AND TALMUD ◆

When a man hunts, he shoots and kills an animal in the wild. That animal is usually dead long before he butchers it. Its blood has not been immediately let. Therein lies the hunting prohibition in Jewish tradition.

Any food that is nonkosher is called *trefah* (*trefe* in Yiddish), a Hebrew word which means "torn." Exodus (22:31) states: "Neither shall you eat any flesh that is torn of beasts in the field; you shall cast it to the dogs." The interpretation is that any animal killed by a hunter (or killed by another animal in the wild)—even a kosher animal that has split hooves and chews its cud—becomes nonkosher because the laws of kosher slaughtering cannot be observed.

If, however, a kosher animal such as a deer is rescued from a trap before it dies, the animal can be eaten so long as it's slaughtered by a *shochet* in the prescribed ritual manner.

Judaism, for animal lovers, is a comforting faith. Not only does its ancient Scripture exalt a prohibition against hunting such creatures as deer, but its later writings such as the Talmud emphatically discourage hunting as sport, and place the pursuit in the same category as willful cruelty to animals—something that is condemned by the Bible.

Rabbi Akiva, martyred in the first century by Romans, went so far as to suggest, with figurative intent, that no animal should be slaughtered without first giving it a lawful trial before a court of twenty-three judges to determine a valid need for its death. By putting an animal's life on the level of human life, the rabbi was confirming the sanctity of all God's creatures.

JEWS DON'T EAT MEAT AND MILK AT THE SAME MEAL: TALMUD ◆

Talmudic scholars drew this prohibition from the Books of Deuteronomy and Exodus, which say, in essence, "You shall not cook a kid in its mother's milk." This biblical command was later extended to set a number of hours between completing a meat meal and commencing a dairy meal.

The length of the wait varies from one to six hours, depending on a community's rabbis. Eastern European Jews traditionally waited six hours. Western European Jews waited half that time. Strict Dutch Jews wait exactly seventy-two minutes.

Jewish dietary laws can seem to be quite nit-picking. Since hard cheeses (dairy) tend to stick to the teeth, some rabbis, who do not require an hour's wait or more between consuming meat and dairy, do discourage chewing meat immediately after chewing cheese, lest the meat come in contact with the cheese.

At one time, the process of cheesemaking involved the use of rennet, an extract of the enzyme rennin, found in the lining of mammals' stomachs. Rennet hastens the coagulation of milk. Thus, Orthodox Jews shunned all

---

DILEMMA WITH LIVER ◆ *Today, Jews are encouraged to wash even kosher meat with water to remove as much residual blood as possible.*

Technically, meat should be soaked in water and salt to let as much blood into the solution, then it should be drained on a tilted, grooved board to maximize runoff. A further salting, and subsequent washing (twice), make the meat pretty bloodless. Officially kashered or rendered fully kosher, it is then fit for consumption.

Liver, saturated through with blood, defies kashering. A strict Jew who wants to eat liver is supposed to first broil the organ over an open fire so heat evaporates a good amount of blood. Then the liver can be fried or sautéed, or prepared to taste.

Meat should never be frozen before it is kashered. The cold temperature causes blood to congeal, so that even thawing and washing may not then remove it sufficiently.

---

commercially-processed cheeses, believing they were contaminated with the blood of an animal.

It should be remembered that all Jewish dietary laws originated solely to segregate Jews from other cultures and faiths, to prevent a contamination of Judaism with foreign ideas, and to prevent intermarriages. A strict Jew who adhered to every biblical and Talmudic proscription could not easily sit down at the dinner table with Gentiles, or even socialize for long with them.

To be "kosher" results in being separate. In fact, the writers of the Talmud went so far as to prohibit Jews from drinking any wine *touched* by a Gentile; even wine whose grapes were picked by Gentile hands. Clearly, Jews were not to mix socially with the enemy faith; the faith that had stolen their Hebrew Scripture and renamed it *Old* Testament.

HIGH HASIDIC STANDARDS:
POLAND, EIGHTEENTH CENTURY ◆

As a final illustration of the idea that dietary laws are intended to separate a group from the mainstream, consider the strict sect of Judaism that today calls itself Hasidism.

The Hasidim (Hebrew plural, "Pious Ones"), like other ultra-Orthodox Jewish groups, live in self-contained enclaves. Not only do they consider Gentiles as nonreligious, but they also regard non-Hasidic Jews as nonreligious. And they base these arguments partly on food.

The Hasidim assert that the larger Jewish community, especially in America, does not maintain adequate dietary standards in the manufacture, preparation, handling, and sale of foods. Hence, many kosher products are not kosher enough for the Hasidim.

Even so-called neutral foods like vegetables become nonkosher once touched by the hands of a non-Hasid. Not that the hands of a Gentile or "lax" Jew are themselves vile, but there is always the suspicion that the vegetable might have touched some contaminated, proscribed meat or blood.

For instance, a Hasidic housewife can only cook with noodles made by someone in the Hasidic community. This is because noodles are made with eggs, and eggs sometimes contain drops of blood, which must be avoided, whether it is in menstruating women or egg yolks.

A Hasidic housewife must even be careful of the paper bag in which she carries her groceries—not only might the bag have been contaminated by meat and blood, but also the glue holding its seams may have come from a cloven-hoofed animal that does not chew its cud.

Why such severe restrictions?

The Hasidim regard the growing secularization of Jewish life in the United States as a major threat to the preservation of ancient traditions of Judaism. Extremism becomes a high wall to stave off an assault under the banner of assimilation.

CHRISTIANITY ADOPTS THE OLD TESTAMENT BUT NOT ITS DIETARY LAWS: MID–FIRST CENTURY C.E. ◆

Just as Jews, and later the Hasidim, erected dietary laws to delineate and preserve their identity, Christians, wishing to distance themselves as much as possible from Jews, dropped the dietary don'ts defined in the Books of Leviticus and Deuteronomy.

The apostle Paul, who is credited with catapulting a small band of Jewish Christ-followers into the religion of Christianity itself, said point-blank: "Nothing is unclean in itself." Paul knew exactly what he was doing.

The New Testament repudiates the entire body of Hebrew purity laws—especially those pertaining to food. Although none of Jesus' words were written down in his lifetime, he's later credited with the declaration that defilement cannot be caused by an external agent. Blood, for instance, cannot contaminate a food—or make a woman "unclean" in the Old Testament sense.

The apostle Peter—the first pope—drove home the theme. Peter's vision of a sheet lowered from Heaven, which contained all types of animals, pronounced by God to be clean and fit for consumption, gave the Church a mandate to abandon the Old Testament dietary laws. It was important that Christianity not too strongly resemble Judaism; the new faith needed its own new identity, its own set of dos and don'ts.

One faith's food becomes another faith's forbidden meal, emphasizing separateness.

WINE INTO BLOOD, BREAD INTO FLESH ◆

While the consumption of blood in any amount was an abomination to Jews, Christians made it a part of their most revered sacrament, the Eucharist.

And though Jews could not eat meat unless from a cloven-hoofed, cud-chewing mammal, Christians joyously partook of the flesh of Christ.

What did Christ, a Jew acquainted with the Mosaic food laws, fully intend by his actions at the Last Supper? Giving his apostles a piece of bread, he says: "Take, this is my body." Then passing around a cup of wine, he says: "Drink, this is my blood." In addition to establishing the Eucharist (*see* Eucharist; the word means "the giving of thanks"), was he symbolically suggesting that his followers drop the old Hebrew dietary proscriptions in order to "separate" themselves from other Jews?

CHRISTIAN MEATLESS FRIDAYS: ENGLAND, 1548 ◆

There is nothing sacred or profound about the tradition of meatless Friday. Its origins are purely economic.

For a period of four hundred years, many Christians were prohibited from eating meat on Friday, particularly on Good Friday. Willful violation of this proscription was a mortal sin; the most grievous kind, punishable by damnation in Hell if one died with the sin unconfessed.

This act of private devotion began in England during the second year of the reign of King Edward VI, and its function initially was more economic than spiritual.

With a meat shortage in the country, and a struggling fish industry, Parliament, with backing from the Church of England, ordered people to replace meat meals on Fridays with a fish dish. Roman Catholics adopted the personal sacrifice—in memory of Christ's supreme sacrifice—and made it mandatory; to consciously eat meat on Friday, the weekday on which Christ died, was henceforth a mortal sin to be confessed as quickly as possible.

Roman Catholics continued the fast until the 1960s, when the Church declared it optional—except for the Fridays of Lent. The ban was lifted as part of the modernization of Roman Catholicism begun under the reign of Pope John XXIII (1958–63).

ISLAMIC DIETARY LAWS: SEVENTH CENTURY c.e. ◆

If the ancient Israelites established strict dietary laws to define and protect their identity, and Christians dropped those laws in order to define their differentness, what were Muslims to do to separate themselves from both Jews and Christians?

Islamic dietary laws are spelled out in the Koran—as is nearly everything else in the religion. These dietary laws clearly illustrate how the proscriptions were intended to separate Muslims from Christians, and, more specifically, from Jews.

In welding a nation out of warring Arabian tribes, Islam's founder, Muhammad, needed to give these disparate peoples a sense of common identity, as well as a sense of differentness from all non-Arabs. Muhammad derived his main theological tenets from both Judaism and Christianity, and he borrowed heavily from Jewish Mosaic food laws—the ones that Christians had abandoned. He instructed his followers:

- Not to eat the flesh of animals found dead—carrion, that is;
- Not to consume blood in any form;
- To stay away from swine at all costs;
- Not to eat food that had been previously offered or sacrificed to idols.

These rules separated Muhammad's followers from non-Muslim Arabs, and from Christians.

Then, to separate his own Arab followers from Jews, he departed radically from Hebrew Scripture in the area of alcoholic beverages. Although Jews frowned upon intoxicating spirits, they did not forbid them, and wine was an important sacramental in many of their rituals. Christians did not even frown on moderate drink. Muhammad, however, utterly forbade beverages with the power to inebriate. Thus, through dietary laws, the Prophet delineated his followers as distinctly different from Jews and Christians.

HINDUISM—FOOD DEFINES SOCIAL CLASS: 1500 b.c.e. ◆

Islam's sharpest contrast in food dos and don'ts is with the Hindu religion of India. Muhammad, as we'll see, by rejecting the Hindu caste system, tailored Islam in a way that made it very appealing to the peoples of India.

In Hinduism, Indians follow a caste system. "Caste" derives from the Latin *castus*, meaning "pure," and in its earlier Indo-European sense, it meant "cut off" or "separated from" and is the basis for our word "castrate." Certainly, a castrated man is "pure" and "separated from" the rest of society—in a caste by himself.

In India, higher castes do not eat or socialize with lower castes. In fact, food observances help define social rank. Brahmins, for instance, are the highest caste *because* they eat only those foods prepared in the finest manner—called *pakka* foods. Everyone else eats inferior food, called *kacca*—a most unfortunate pronunciation.

Pakka foods are offered to gods, and given to guests of the highest status. *Pakka* foods contain clarified butter, or "ghee"—*ghi* in Hindi. This is the liquid butter remaining when butter from cow's milk—the cow is a sacred animal in India—is first melted, then boiled, and finally strained. Ghee is a costly fat, from a sacred mammal, and believed to promote health and vitality.

Kacca, on the other hand, is defined as inferior food because it does not contain ghee. For instance, bread baked without ghee is drier.

The lowest class of food, enjoyed (one hopes) by the lowest caste, is called *jutha*, or "garbage." This is any *kacca* food left on the plate after eating; *jutha* is *kacca* leftovers; considered to have been polluted by the eater's saliva. The eater himself cannot touch the leftovers; only someone of lower status may scrape off the plate—someone like a wife. "Garbage" can be fed to either domestic animals or such members of the lowest caste as street sweepers, called "untouchables."

UPWARD SOCIAL MOBILITY THROUGH SWAPPING FOOD. The highest Brahmins do not eat foods cooked by members of lower castes. Nor will such Brahmins accept water handed across caste lines. They shun onions and garlic, since the smell is unbecoming to their status. Alcohol is prohibited since it threatens the Brahmins' sense of self-control. The lower castes may drink alcohol, and they do.

Under the rules of Hindu religious castes, status is immutable in the short

Upward social mobility, and distinction of the classes, is expressed through food.

run; but a family's lowly station can rise over many generations—if they are clever, maybe faster. Because food is an index of rank, it can be used to assist in upward mobility.

For instance, if a higher family accepts food from a slightly lower family, the lower family moves stepwise up the social ladder to the status of the higher family. This doesn't happen often. And there is no way to force a higher family to accept a lowly offering. But a lower family might withhold a service from a higher family until the latter accepts a gift of food.

Needless to say, under Hinduism, not everyone gets a place at the same table.

In stark contrast, Muhammad allowed Muslims of all social strata to sit together and enjoy a common meal, the same foods for all. And he allowed people of all ranks to worship in the same mosques. This breakdown of class walls made the religion of Islam particularly appealing to the lower castes or "untouchables" of India. By adopting the new faith, one was immediately elevated to equal social status with that of other Muslims.

NATION OF ISLAM DIETARY DON'TS: AMERICA, TWENTIETH CENTURY ◆

Formerly known as the Black Muslims, now known as the Nation of Islam, this U.S. group has sought to develop a separate social identity for itself by adopting Islamic names, as well as food and beverage proscriptions, and by the nature of their worship itself. Not only does a follower of the Nation of Islam assume a new name upon conversion, but he avoids all alcohol *and tobacco*—the latter a prohibition not found in Judaism, Christianity, or traditional Islam.

Forbidden foods include those listed in the Koran, but, significantly, also more than a dozen vegetables that were staples in the black American slave diet. This "separateness" statement says, in effect, "We'll no longer be slaves, or be thought of as descendants of slaves. We are our own people."

BUDDHIST CODES—THE SIN IS ON THE SLAYER: 534 B.C.E. ◆

Buddhism is perhaps the most complex of religions in terms of sacred dietary customs. The lowest caste of people in general have the dirty job of butchering animals for the supply of meat.

However, a Buddhist is allowed to eat animal flesh only if the meat has not been intentionally procured for that purpose; or if the eater believes the animal died for some other reason than to satisfy his hunger. Whereas in Judaism and Islam the sin is in eating certain meats, in Buddhism, the sin is committed by the animal's slayer; not necessarily by the eater.

In China, a different set of dietary codes symbolized status. While the early rabbis of Judaism were refining the Mosaic food codes, Chinese at that time allowed beef, mutton, and pork to be eaten only by an emperor; beef by feudal lords; mutton by high-ranking state ministers; pork by lower ministers; fish by generals; vegetables by commoners. In fact, the Chinese term for public officials was "meat-eaters." Once again, we see food being used to separate and define a group; exactly the purpose of Judaism's dietary code.

FISH ENTERS THE JAPANESE DIET: EIGHTH CENTURY C.E. ◆

In Japan, where Shinto was the indigenous religion, deer, rabbit, and pig were acceptable foods. The flesh of ox, horse, dog, monkey, and fowl were prohibited. Fish was not particularly popular in these ancient days.

However, around the eighth century C.E., the Japanese people began to rely more heavily on plants, ricegrass, and vegetables than on meats. This had to do with the limited grazing territory of the island county. It was more economical to use cattle to plow soil for vegetables than to breed the animals for slaughter.

The Shinto religion began to stress dietary concepts of uncleanliness in terms of scarce meats and the blood from those animals—and also in terms of menstrual blood, bloody wounds, and blood in general. In fact, the belief developed that contamination by blood could darken a man's life, and his misfortunes could be passed on to his descendants.

It is at this time, during the eighth century, that fish, especially raw fish— the food we associate most strongly with Japanese cuisine—began to play a major role in the Japanese diet, contributing a large portion to a person's daily protein intake.

Judaism treats fish as if it contains no blood, which is not true. Wounded fish do not bleed copiously since they are cold-blooded and not dependent on a circulatory system for maintaining bodily heat. Like snakes and other cold-blooded creatures, fish control their temperature by movement. A fish wanting to warm itself swims into warmer water; to cool down, it descends into colder depths.

Pomegranate? Apple? Banana? Which is the forbidden fruit? Pig? Cow? Eel? Which is the forbidden meat? Judaism? Christianity? Islam? Which is the true faith? Abraham? Jesus? Muhammad? Who is the true prophet?

Your answers depend on the table you sit at.

CHAPTER

27

𝔉orbidden 𝔖ex

Gay to Lesbian

IN THE PREVIOUS chapter, we examined the prevalent misconception that biblical dietary laws were instituted for health and sanitary reasons.

In this chapter, we examine the origins of the religious prohibitions against homosexuality, and the common belief that Christianity has always been intolerant of homosexual behavior. As the late historian John Boswell pointed out in *Christianity, Social Tolerance and Homosexuality*, intolerance of homosexuals was not initially an essential feature of the faith, but only became the dominant attitude around the twelfth century—the same point at which the Roman Catholic Church formalized its stand on celibacy in the priesthood. (*See* Celibacy.)

Monasteries of unmarried men living in close quarters apparently led to the need for harsh condemnations of homosexual activity. This is clear from the frequency with which Saint John Chrysostom, fourth-century archbishop of Constantinople, attacked homosexual dalliances among monks.

In tracing the origins of proscriptions against homosexuality, we'll look at nine biblical references. But we'll begin with a curious omission.

LESBIANISM—WHAT THE BIBLE DOESN'T SAY ♦

The Bible, written by men virtually without exception, says nothing about female homosexuality.

We may infer from this either that lesbianism was not widely practiced in ancient times, or that if it was, it was not considered significant or a problem. (To a degree, men have always found female same-sexuality erotic and perhaps have never wished to stamp it out.)

There is one line of the New Testament, found in Paul's Letter to the Romans, which some interpret as a statement against lesbianism: "Their women

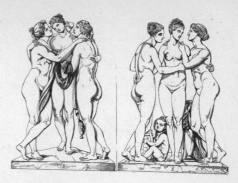

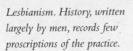

Lesbianism. History, written largely by men, records few proscriptions of the practice.

have exchanged the natural use for that which is against nature" (Rom. 1:26). Paul may well have been referring to heterosexual females who engage in nonprocreative sex with males. And, of course, any means of birth control would qualify.

In Jewish law, lesbianism was treated as a minor offense, and still is. The Talmud discourages female homosexual behavior, but allows a lesbian to marry a priest in a valid and sacred union. This general leniency toward lesbianism, and its lack of mention in the Bible, led twelfth-century rabbi Moses Maimonides to state that female homosexuality is not so bad since it does not involve "wasting the seed"—the biblical sin of onanism.

This suggests that the prohibitions against male homosexuality have to do in part at least with the "spilling of semen," considered by the Jews a sacred fluid, vital for the spreading of the Jewish people.

Furthermore, the men who wrote the Bible presumably were heterosexual, since most men are. It seems safe to assume that straight men have always been queasy about male-to-male intimacy.

The Talmud, also written by males, states emphatically that Jewish men never engage in homosexual behavior, that it is unknown among Jews. Maimonides, who was also a physician, noted: "Jews are not suspected of practicing homosexuality." Not suspected is different from not doing.

What follows throughout the remainder of this chapter pertains to male homosexuality.

OLD TESTAMENT STAND ON HOMOSEXUALITY: BOOK OF LEVITICUS, C. 1400 B.C.E. ◆

Two of the most often-quoted proscriptions against homosexual behavior appear in Leviticus, which served as a handbook for the ancient priests of Israel. Much of the book is devoted to specific regulations concerning offerings, sacrifices, ritual purity, ordination, feasts, and festivals.

First we find:

You shall not lie with a male as with a woman; such a thing is an abomination. (Lev. 18:22)

It is worth noting that that unambiguous sentence is surrounded by hundreds of equally clear don'ts, including Don't eat pork, Don't touch any item touched by a menstruating woman, and Don't sit in a chair that a menstruating woman sat in.

Indeed, if merely the injunctions regarding menstruating women were followed to the letter, every husband and child who believed in a literal reading of the Bible would have to move out of the house for seven days each month.

The second quotation is blunt and carries a death sentence:

If a man lies with a male as with a woman, both of them shall be put to death for their abominable deed. (Lev. 20:13)

That is quite an explicit condemnation and punishment. But the lines of text that immediately precede and follow the death sentence for homosexuality condemn heterosexuals of many varieties:

Anyone who curses his father or mother shall be put to death. (Lev. 20:9)

If a man commits adultery with his neighbor's wife, both the adulterer and the adulteress shall be put to death. (Lev. 20:10)

If a man disgraces his father by lying with his father's wife, both the man and his stepmother shall be put to death. (Lev. 20:11)

If a man lies with his daughter-in-law, both of them shall be put to death. (Lev. 20:12)

If a man marries a woman and her mother also, the man and the two women as well shall be burned to death. (Lev. 20:14)

If a man lies in sexual intercourse with a woman during her menstrual period, both of them shall be cut off from their people. (Lev. 20:18)

If a man marries his brother's wife and thus disgraces his brother, they shall be childless. (Lev. 20:21)

The list of penalties is long and brutal. Many otherwise decent men and women of modern times would be put to death if the Bible were taken literally. The so-called Holiness Code of Scripture, which includes the bans on homosexuality, also strictly prohibits:

- Eating raw meat (no big loss here except for the somewhat passé steak tartare);
- Planting two different kinds of seeds in the same bed (no more herbaceous borders);
- Wearing clothes made of two different kinds of yarn (this could ruin Donna Karan and Calvin Klein, and outlaw the fancier vestments of the pope);
- Body tattoos (there go the bikers, the sailors, and a significant number of musicians and teenagers).

Anyone claiming to read the Bible literally must of necessity be applying a "pick-and-choose" mind-set.

Biblical quotations selectively plucked out of context and given narrow literal readings can encourage people to act upon their fears rather than their virtues. The Bible was misused for centuries by the advocates of slavery to "prove" blacks were inferior. Until modern times, the same Scriptures were used to keep women silent in church and subservient at home.

Fundamentalists and literalists fear that if Scripture is "wrongly interpreted," it will deprive them of values they dearly cherish. But that fear is really grounded in the realization that such values often are not explicitly spelled out in Scripture; rather, one's values are derived from how Scripture is understood.

Just as the U.S. Constitution, written some two hundred years ago, has had to be continually interpreted to address issues and situations the Founding Fathers could not foresee, so, too, everyone has to *interpret* Scripture to some degree. No one, despite his or her intent, could possibly be a true literalist. Peter Gomes, professor of Christian morals at Harvard and himself a Baptist minister, asks the relevant questions concerning biblical text: "By what principle of interpretation do we proceed, and by what means do we reconcile 'what it meant then' to 'what it means now'?"

SODOM AND GOMORRAH: BOOK OF GENESIS 19 ◆

The story of Sodom and Gomorrah plays a pivotal role in the religious view of homosexuality. The name of the city of Sodom, and the name of its people, Sodomites, became synonymous with homosexuals and with taboo sexual practices both homosexual and heterosexual.

Most countries have sodomy laws relating to: (1) gay sex, (2) anal intercourse between any two people, (3) bestiality, and (4) a number of sexual activities ranging from hand-genital contact with minors to mouth-genital contact between a husband and wife.

How did a poor small town on the banks of the Dead Sea come to lend its name to such a range of activities?

THE HISTORY. The infamous cities of Sodom and Gomorrah are believed to lie beneath the shallow waters south of al-Lisan, a peninsula near the southern end of the Dead Sea in Israel. Along with the cities of Admah, Zeboiim, and Zoar, Sodom and Gomorrah constituted the five biblical "cities of the plain."

Supposedly destroyed by "brimstone and fire" because of their wickedness, Sodom and Gomorrah actually were devastated around 1900 B.C.E. by an earthquake that struck the Great Rift Valley, an extensive rift extending from the Jordan River Valley in Israel to the Zambezi River system in East Africa. The quake occurred at most five hundred years before the biblical tale of Sodom was written down, that is, during the time of Abraham.

Archaeological evidence indicates that the soil in this area was richly fertile during the Middle Bronze Age, about 2000 B.C.E., and would have supported agriculture—which is probably what made the land appeal to Lot, the nephew of Hebrew patriarch Abraham, who settled in the region.

The spectacle of "brimstone and fire" most likely came from an ignition of petroleum and gases beneath the rift, released by the catastrophic quake. It is not surprising that the upheaval and destruction of the region during the period of the Hebrew patriarchs certainly would be remembered in story.

The flight of Lot, his wife, and daughters: "The Lord rained brimstone and fire upon Sodom and Gomorrah."

THE STORY. Genesis, chapter 19, spins the bizarre saga of the town of Sodom, itself named for Mount Sodom (*Har Sedom* in Hebrew) at the southwest end of the Dead Sea.

In Sodom, a mob of men demand sex with two males who have visited the humble home of Lot. The visitors, who are actually angels of the Lord, strike the mob blind and God destroys the town with fire and brimstone.

According to three prominent biblical figures—the prophet Ezekiel, the Gospel writer Luke, and Jesus Christ—the story of Sodom is *not* about sexual perversion and homosexuality. It is about two other issues entirely: *inhospitality*, as Luke tells us (Luke 10:10–13), and *failure to care for the poor*, as Ezekiel makes clear:

> *Behold, this was the iniquity of thy sister Sodom, pride, fullness of bread, and abundance of idleness within her and in her daughters, neither did she strengthen the hand of the poor and needy. (Ezek. 16:49–50)*

As professor and minister Peter Gomes writes: "To suggest that Sodom and Gomorrah is about homosexual sex is an analysis of about as much worth as suggesting that the story of Jonah and the whale is a treatise on fishing." We'll shortly get to Christ's own interpretation of the story.

THE EVIDENCE. There are many disturbing elements to the story that have nothing to do with homosexuality. The two angels enter Lot's house and the rowdy townsmen surround the place demanding:

> *"Bring them out that we may abuse them." Lot went out to the men, and shut the door behind him, and said, "I entreat you, brethren, do not act wickedly. I have two daughters who have not known man. Let me bring them out to you; do as you please with them." (Gen. 19:5–8)*

A father offers his virgin daughters to a horny pack of heavy breathers—is this not a sin in itself? A worse sin perhaps than male-on-male rape? If indeed that is what the townsmen were about to do to the angels.

What did the angry mob want from the visitors?

The Douay Bible says the men wanted to "abuse them." The King James Version says: "Bring them out that we may *know them*." Linguistically, the evidence is that "know them" refers to "know who the two strangers are." Know their identity.

WORD ORIGIN. Contrary to popular opinion, the Hebrew verb "to know" is very rarely used in the sexual sense in the Bible. In fact, in only 10 of its 943 occurrences in the Old Testament does it carry the meaning of "carnal knowledge." Furthermore, the passage on Sodom is the only place in the Old Testament where the verb "to know" has been given a gay sex spin.

And, too, one cannot overlook Jesus' own interpretation of the story: Christ, speaking some two thousand years after the earthquake that devastated Sodom, claims that the city was destroyed for the sin of inhospitality:

> And whoever does not receive you, or listen to your words—go forth outside that house or town, and shake off the dust from your feet. Amen I say to you, it will be more tolerable for the land of Sodom and Gomorrah in the day of judgment than for that town. (Matt. 10:14–15; also in Luke 10:11–12)

God had sent two angels to investigate the general wickedness of the town of Sodom and the angels are rudely, inhospitably received. To appease the rowdy mob, Lot tries to bribe the men by offering his virgin daughters—and begs of them: "Only do nothing to these men [the angels], for they have come under the shelter of my roof."

PROSTITUTION AND INCEST—THE TALE CONTINUES. Lot, his wife, and two daughters flee Sodom before its destruction, but Lot's curious spouse glances back and is "sodiumized"—turned into a pillar of sodium chloride, or salt. The destitute father and his virgin daughters visit the city of Zoar, but are unable to afford lodging there, and take up residence in a cave, where the teenage girls soon grow restless.

The older complains to the younger: "There is no man in the land to marry us as is the custom everywhere. Let us give our father wine to drink, then lie with him, that we may have offspring by our father."

They seduce their father. The older daughter gives birth to a son, Moab, who becomes progenitor of the *Moabites*. The younger daughter produces a son named Ben-ammi, who sires the *Ammonites*. Thus, these clans, both enemies of the Jews, were allegedly conceived (according to the Jews) through the crime of incest.

The origins of the words "Moab" and "Ben-ammi" are uncertain. "Moab" may mean "from [my own] father," whereas "Ben-ammi" may mean "son of my [own] people." So linguists conjecture. It makes sense historically: for centuries after the Israelite conquest of Canaan, the Moabites and the Ammonites remained perennial enemies of the Jews. Thus, the writers of Genesis were only too pleased to pen the folktale of their enemies' scandalous origins through incest.

No careful reader of the Hebrew text can see this bizarre Sodom and Go-morrah escapade—involving two angels in the night, a man offering up his virgin daughters, and subsequent conniving daughter-father incest—as a seminal condemnation of homosexuality. Homosexuality, in fact, is not even directly implied—while heterosexual prostitution and incest are stated explicitly.

Yet, today, many Christians overlook Lot's offering of his daughters to the mob, conveniently forget the daughters' seduction of their father, and see the destruction of Sodom as punishment for homosexual conduct.

Some argue that the girls, believing the world had ended, seduced their father only to continue the species. But the girls had visited Zoar, and knew the city had been spared; furthermore, the wine used to get their father drunk had to have come from somewhere; they'd left Sodom empty-handed.

EARLY CHRISTIANS REINTERPRET THE STORY. The inter-pretation of the story of Sodom as the inhospitality of Sodomites to messen-gers from the Lord persisted in some circles well into the Middle Ages.

The homosexual spin to the story originated with early Christian moralists who were bent on sexual purity—for heterosexuals as well as homosexuals—and only centuries later emerged as the predominant theme.

To give this story an even more bizarre twist: according to one Jewish legend, both the men and women of Sodom were sexually licentious, and it was the *women*, in a worshipful wanton frenzy, who demanded sex with the two male angels at Lot's house—and got it.

No one for a long time seriously believed the story of Sodom, written about 1400 B.C.E., had anything to do with homosexuality; not the ancient Jews; not even Jesus Christ himself. The people who developed that belief were early Christians. In Judaism, it is *post*-biblical literature that sees a homosexual element in the Sodomites' attitude toward Lot's male guests.

Not surprisingly, once Christianity became the predominant religion of

NO DRAG ◆ *One of the early official pronouncements against male cross-dressing was issued by Saint Asterius, the fourth-century bishop of Amasia, in what is now Italy, when he condemned the men in his diocese who celebrated New Year's Eve by dressing in female attire. He called their drag an "abomina-tion to the Lord." He meant their sex acts, too.*

the Mediterranean region, the homosexual version of the story became prevalent, and "sodom" and "sodomite" became synonymous with homosexuals and their behavior.

HOMOSEXUALITY AND THE NEW TESTAMENT: ROMANS, CORINTHIANS, TIMOTHY; FIRST CENTURY C.E. ◆

There is no mention of homosexual sex in the four Gospels. Not a word. The moral teachings of Jesus are not concerned with the subject. Apparently, homosexual sex never crossed Christ's mind. Or if it did, the subject didn't trouble him. At least not enough to comment upon.

In fact, Jesus showed a special love and concern for outcasts; he enjoyed being in their company, even when he was despised for it. As one contemporary author writes: "Jesus was surrounded, day and night, by publicans and prostitutes, the lame, the sick, the lepers; and he touched them all with his healing hands. His closeness to these marginal people was the great parable of his mission."

Paul, though, does have something to say on the matter of homosexual conduct. Writing in the decades after Christ's death, Paul becomes the primary source of New Testament homosexual proscriptions. Three references are usually cited.

ROMANS 1, C. 58 C.E. Here Paul scolds homosexuals, but he's equally harsh on idolaters, which is to say all non-Christians who worship their own religions' god or gods. This summary condemnation lumps homosexuals into the same category as Buddhists, Hindus, Taoists, and the like. All are equally wicked in God's eyes, says Paul.

Of homosexual coupling, he says:

Paul scolds adulterers, thieves, drunkards, gossips, effeminate men, and sodomites.

Having abandoned the natural use of women, [men] have burned in their lusts one towards another, men with men doing shameless things and receiving in themselves the fitting recompense of their perversity. (1:27)

1 CORINTHIANS 6:9–11, C. 56 C.E. Here Paul slips homosexuals into a fairly comprehensive list of undesirables:

Neither fornicators, nor idolaters, nor adulterers, nor the effeminate, nor sodomites, nor thieves, nor the covetous, nor drunkards, nor the evil-tongued, nor the greedy will possess the kingdom of God.

Many Christian Churches selectively extract from the above the word "sodomites" to condemn homosexuality. Clearly, though, the quotation would ban from Heaven much of modern society: evil-tongued gossips, greedy Wall Street brokers, any covetous neighbor, all effeminate priests, every cheating husband and wife.

Some biblical scholars contend that by the word "sodomites" Paul was condemning not adult homosexuality but pederasty—from the Greek *paiderastes*, meaning "lover of boys" (*paid-*, "boy" + *erasthai*, "to love"). Because in the first-century Greco-Roman world, it was quite common for an older, wealthy, educated married man—often a scholar or military man—to take a prepubescent boy under his wing. The boy received gifts, a free education, and was expected to submit passively to further education of a carnal nature, though not typically anal sex, as is often assumed, but rather rubbing of the man's penis between the boy's thighs.

The third often-used reference to condemn homosexuality:

1 TIMOTHY 1:10, C. 64 C.E. This is where Paul discusses the role of law in everyday life:

We know that the Law is good, if a man uses it rightly . . . for the unjust and rebellious . . . for parricides and matricides [for killing Dad and Mom], for murderers, for immoral people, for sodomites, for kidnappers, for liars, for perjurers . . .

CONSIDER THE SOURCE. Saint Paul was, before his Damascus conversion, a sexually sinning Jew named Saul from Tarsus. Saul, once he changed his name and cleaned up his immoral ways, was against lust, sensuality, and sexuality in everyone—both heterosexual and homosexual. For Paul, anyone who put himself or his desires ahead of God was condemned.

After Christ's death, Paul expected the world to end in a short time. Thus, he advocated celibacy for everyone, since continuation of the species was moot. As for those hot-blooded men and women who could not abstain, Paul issued his famous epigram: "Better to marry than to burn."

The full quotation is found in the seventh chapter of Paul's First Letter to the Corinthians:

> *It is good for a man not to touch a woman. . . . I say therefore to the unmarried and widows, It is good for them if they abide even as I [chaste]. But if they cannot contain, let them marry: for it is better to marry than to burn.*

Paul viewed Heaven as a hierarchy. At the time of the Last Judgment, as we saw in an earlier chapter, Heaven's upper echelon would be for virgins. In fact, lifelong virgins would be the first saved, followed by convert celibates like himself; last would be the folk who had succumbed to the temptation of marriage.

Paul believed Ecclesiastes: "Woman is the origin of all sin and it is through her that we all die."

Paul's real problem with homosexuality was this: in Greco-Roman culture, homosexuality represented a purely secular sensuality, which was contrary to his Jewish-Christian spiritual idealism. With the end of the world imminent, if husbands and wives were to strive for chastity in marriage, certainly anyone outside of marriage should remain chaste.

For Saint Paul, and Saint Augustine, two of the most powerful figures in early Christianity, the body was a beast to be tamed.

SAINT AUGUSTINE'S PROSCRIPTION:
HOMOSEXUALS CAN'T PROCREATE, FOURTH CENTURY ◆

The fourth-century bishop of Hippo (modern Annaba, Algeria) came to Christianity late in life, after a period of dissolute pagan living, which he chronicled in his *Confessions*.

He calls the Carthage of his day a "cauldron of dissolute loves," and confesses that he "fell in love with loving."

Before his conversion, Augustine was a member of the Manichean Church, whose elect were celibate monks, although Augustine chose to be "unelected," since he refused to give up a young concubine. "Lord," he bargained, "give me chastity and continency, but do not give them yet."

To use a cliché by way of analogy, the great saint was saying, "I want to have my cake, and eat it, too." The full quotation is worthy of attention. Looking back at his younger self, he's confiding to God:

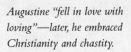

Augustine "fell in love with loving"—later, he embraced Christianity and chastity.

"I had prayed to you for chastity and said, 'Give me chastity and continence, but not yet.' For I was afraid that you would answer my prayer at once and cure me too soon of the disease of lust, which I wanted satisfied, not quelled."

Although his mother, Monica, was a devout Christian, Augustine was not baptized until age thirty-three, when he met Bishop Ambrose in Rome, who performed the service in 387 C.E. Augustine told Ambrose that his release from the clutches of women, temptresses one and all, came when a child's voice whispered in his ear, "Take up and read." A book beside his bed miraculously fell open to Saint Paul's warning three centuries earlier to the Romans: "Make no provisions for the flesh, to fulfill the lust."

Guilt-ridden for his sinful past, Augustine converted to Christianity that very day, vowing celibacy. Indeed, henceforth he tried to impose chastity on everyone else; even married couples.

His primary objection to homosexuality was this: homosexual sex is evil because gays can't procreate, thus they violate God's intent for human sexuality. For Augustine, the *only* valid reason for even heterosexuals to engage in sex was to produce offspring.

BREEDING CHILDREN THROUGH PASSIONLESS SEX. As we saw elsewhere in this book, Augustine postulated that human conception could conceivably take place through "passionless procreation"—a husband and wife, without any sensation of lust, by sheer dint of will, could copulate and conceive a child.

"The human organ," he wrote, "without the excitement of lust, could [obey] the human will for all the purposes of parenthood."

How could the penis perform without excitation?

By way of analogy, Augustine gives several examples of how the human will accomplishes other equally extraordinary feats. Here are two:

- "Some people can make their ears move, either one at a time or both together."
- "There are individuals who can make musical notes issue from the rear of their anatomy, so that you would think they were singing."

As he grew older, Augustine became an extreme opponent of sexual intercourse. He begged married men to practice self-denial, as he did. The more he meditated on the fact that God created Adam *without sex*, and the Virgin Mary conceived Jesus Christ *without sex*, the more he condemned the act of sexual intercourse—between heterosexuals—as unnatural. Little wonder that he condemned homosexual coupling as well.

Today, all that is spoken of are the great saint's few harsh asides on homosexuality. But a thorough and honest reading of Augustine makes abundantly clear that he had infinitely more to say against heterosexual sex than homosexual sex. He had nothing good to say about sex, period.

THOMAS AQUINAS'S OBJECTION: NO HOMOSEXUAL ANIMALS IN NATURE, TWELFTH CENTURY ◆

The Christian secular world did not enact serious legislation against homosexual behavior until the reign of the Byzantine emperor Justinian I, between the years 527 and 565. Previously, homosexuality had been something of a misdemeanor. Under Justinian's sweeping codification of Roman Law, called the Justinian Code, homosexual conduct was made a capital offense, like adultery.

Yet, Justinian's new laws on homosexual behavior were more hortatory than harshly condemnatory.

Throughout the Middle Ages, various Church councils condemned homosexual behavior, but—and this is a crucial point—there are many indications that the Church's real concern was not homosexual intimacy among the general population, but within cloistered orders of monks and nuns. Lay homosexuals were not really of much concern to the Church; but it was troubled by sexual activity among its clergy, which had taken vows of chastity and celibacy.

Indeed, cloistered same-sex living, male and female, was far more conducive to homosexual conduct than life in the outside world, where even a male with gay inclinations usually went ahead and married. This was true right up until the modern era of gay liberation and out-of-the-closet openness. No longer do gay young Catholic men feel they have only two options: marriage or the priesthood.

By the thirteenth century, the Church's condemnation of homosexual conduct had become part of canon law, buttressed by the writing of Thomas Aquinas.

Perhaps the greatest theologian of the faith, Aquinas argued that homosexuality violates natural law because in part it is not found in lower animals. One is reminded of Maimonides's boast that Jewish men are not suspected of practicing homosexuality. Had Thomas left his desk and wandered through the pastoral countryside, he'd have had to come up with a new argument. Thomas may have been a great theologian, but he was no animal behaviorist.

Today, we know that homosexuality exists throughout the animal kingdom, occurring naturally, and under particular social conditions. For instance, we know that males deprived of females—monkeys in zoos; mice in pens; men in prisons—all resort to homosexual sex.

ORDAINING GAYS AND LESBIANS ◆

With modern medical research suggesting that homosexuality is rooted in genetics and brain wiring, many Churches have softened their stands.

In a 1976 pastoral letter, U.S. Roman Catholic bishops drew a moral distinction between homosexual sex and homosexual orientation—and drew the praise of Pope John Paul II. It was the first time a pope ventured so far as to say that to be gay is not a sin but merely "a propensity toward sinfulness that presents a constant struggle."

The pope advised gays to practice self-denial; what Saint Augustine in his day advised heterosexuals to do.

Southern Baptists, who take a hard line on homosexuality, now express their Christian compassion this way: "God hates the sin, not the sinner."

Resolutions to approve homosexual ministers in Protestant Churches are hotly debated today. However, the Roman Catholic pope won't even listen to a debate on the matter; there will be no homosexual priests in the Roman Catholic Church. (Except, one feels compelled to add, those who are exposed through their acts and transferred to another parish.) Some Episcopal bishops have ordained sexually active homosexuals despite Church resolutions.

In England, in 1995, a group of militant gays "outed" David Hope, the bishop of London, then the Church of England's third most senior cleric. Bishop Hope, who hoped to become the Church's second most senior cleric, archbishop of York (and he did), conceded that his sexual orientation was at worst "ambiguous."

So what does the Bible really say about homosexuality? Very little, really.

The Bible contains far more condemnations of heterosexual license—from premarital sex, to adultery, to divorce, to remarriage; the entire modern progression.

Assuming, for the sake of argument, that one took all of the biblical don'ts mentioned in this chapter literally, then, certainly, the most abominable individual imaginable would have to be a male homosexual with a body tattoo, who ate steak tartare, wore blended fabrics, and hoed an herbaceous border.

Contraction

Condoms to Crushed Testicles

ORIGIN OF "EDEN": SUMER, 3500 B.C.E. ◆

God's first command to the earth's first parents—"Be fruitful and multiply" (Gen. 1:28)—has for many faiths an implicit prohibition of contraception, suggesting a subsequent right to overpopulate the planet.

Nevertheless, human beings have attempted to control pregnancy and family size at least as far back as recorded history goes, which is some fifty-five hundred years.

The origin of the written word is traced to the Sumerians of the Mesopotamian region of the Near East. Sumer, in fact, may have been the biblical Paradise: "And the Lord God planted a garden eastward in Eden" (Gen. 2:8). In the Sumerian language, which has been extensively decoded, and is related to no other known tongue, the word for "fertile land" or "plain" is *eden*. To the Israelites who later settled in the region, the word *eden* came to mean "delight" or "enjoyment," which seems appropriate for a fer-

*"Be fruitful and multiply"—
the biblical passage cited
against contraception.*

tile garden. A "garden of delight." Thus, linguistically, the word *eden* embodies a sense of fertility and fun, if not frivolity.

The most extensive surviving texts on contraception are about four thousand years old and come from Egypt: the Petri Papyrus was written about 1850 B.C.E. the Eber Papyrus three hundred years later. Egyptian couples were quite ingenious when it came to pleasure without risk of pregnancy. It is, coincidentally, around this time that the biblical Book of Genesis was written.

Let's begin with what the Bible says about contraception, as well as masturbation.

ONAN'S STORY—COITUS INTERRUPTUS: GENESIS 38:6–10 ◆

We must assume that for tens of thousands of years the primary means of contraception was coitus interruptus: the man withdraws to ejaculate outside the woman's body. This is the so-called biblical sin of Onan, second son of Judah, who was married to a Canaanite woman named Bath-shua.

In Christianity, the story is cited as the first biblical prohibition of masturbation.

Judah had three grown sons: Er, Onan, and Shelah. God, for some mysterious reason, slew the wicked and childless Er (the nature of his wickedness is not specified). Judah then ordered Onan, elder of the two remaining brothers, to impregnate Er's wife, Tamar, but the young man "spilled his seed on the ground"—and was put to death by God.

Onan's attempt to avoid impregnating his sister-in-law gave rise to the term *onanism*, which, in time, became synonymous with masturbation. The passage, though, has nothing to do with the rightness or wrongness of self-stimulation, though many faiths interpret the story as a divine condemnation of autoeroticism.

Why did God kill Onan?

THE FACTS. Onan's sin was not sexual in the least. Rather, it was his refusal to fulfill the obligation of the levirate marriage contract (Deut. 25:5–10), which stipulated that a man was obliged to impregnate the wife of his brother if his brother died without an heir—thus ensuring the continuation of his brother's line and inheritance.

Levirate marriage—or *yibum*, as it is called in Hebrew—was an ancient practice followed by many people in the Near East in prebiblical times. It was introduced into the region by Indo-European tribes as early as 2000 B.C.E.

Thus, Onan's sexual act, most likely coitus interruptus, Genesis isn't very specific—"It came to pass when he went into his brother's wife that he spilled it [his seed] on the ground, lest he should give seed to his brother"—was the means by which Onan avoided his fraternal duty. Furthermore, he gave the appearance of fulfilling that duty by cohabiting with Tamar. It was for this grand deception, on top of his deliberate disobedience, that Onan was punished: "God slew him." Nowhere does the notion of masturbation enter the story.

CHRISTIAN PROHIBITION OF MASTURBATION: FIRST CENTURY c.e. ◆

That early Christians misconstrued Onan's punishment from God as a condemnation of masturbation is apparent from rabbinic interpretations of the story.

It is true that early rabbis condemned any man who "brings forth seed for no purpose." Semen was considered a holy fluid primarily because the Jewish people wished to be fruitful and multiply.

The notion of "wasting the seed" (*hashchatat zera* in Hebrew), many scholars say, is the true reason behind ancient prohibitions against male homosexuality but not female homosexuality, as we saw in the previous chapter. Two women engaged in sex do not waste their eggs; two males reaching climax together spill a lot of seed.

Later rabbis stressed that Onan's sin was his violation of the levirate marriage laws. Modern rabbis (some Orthodox ones included) side with the medical profession's view that masturbation is normal, harmless, and a healthy form of release.

For Roman Catholics, masturbation remains an abominable vice, condemned in papal encyclicals up to the present day. It must be confessed, and in each confession, the sinner must swear he will spill no more. Female masturbation is seldom discussed in theological circles (of male clergy), as if the practice, and pleasure, didn't exist. Theologically, masturbation is a greater vice than adultery, since the former is less in accord with natural law than the latter.

JEWISH FAMILY SIZE—TWO IS ENOUGH: FIRST CENTURY b.c.e. ◆

Adam was told by God to "be fruitful and multiply," but the rabbis of the Talmudic era differed among themselves as to just how far a couple should go to fulfill that command. The binding view finally adopted in Jewish law, *Halakhah*, was expressed in the first century B.C.E. by the scholar Hillel:

Parents' duty to procreate is satisfied after the birth of one male child and one female child.

The opposing school of thought, under the scholar Shammai, defined the basic family unit as two boys.

Consequently, in Judaism, contraception is allowed in a wide variety of cases. Some rabbis are more lenient than others. Most permit the use of birth control techniques—preferably after the birth of one male and one female child—in order to space out the births of future children. If pregnancy would threaten a woman's health, she may use contraceptives at all times.

Unlike Catholicism, Judaism does not promote abstention from sexual intercourse in hardship cases; abstinence, in fact, is regarded as abnormal in a marriage.

The use of mechanical means to prevent pregnancy was permitted in part due to a reference in the Talmud to "three kinds of women" who could use a *moch*—a tuft of wool or wad of cotton inserted into the vagina—a minor who feared being raped; a pregnant woman; and a nursing mother.

Jewish women of earlier days inherited a wide array of surprisingly effective contraceptive devices. Birth control then (and to a lesser extent now) was the responsibility of the woman.

SPERMICIDES, SPONGES, CERVICAL CAPS: ANCIENT TO MODERN ◆

Spermicide from crocodile dung. This method is described in the Petri and Eber papyri. Before intercourse, a woman prepares a viscous mixture of fresh crocodile dung and honey and inserts it into her vagina. Not only does the compound physically prevent sperm from colliding with an egg, but dung is sharply acidic, altering the pH of the vaginal canal enough to kill off sperm. It is history's first spermicide.

Spermicides were surprisingly popular in biblical times. In the Middle East, women soaked natural sea sponges in a variety of liquids that we now know effectively kill sperm: alcohol, iodine, quinine, and carbolic acid. Syrian sponges, from local waters, were highly prized for their absorbency; soaked in perfumed vinegar, they were inserted into the vagina before intercourse. This is history's first recorded use of a *contraceptive sponge*.

(The papyri also mention how women handled menstruation: a woman used a homemade tampon-shaped device composed of shredded linen and crushed acacia branch powder, later known as gum arabic.)

Cervical caps are first mentioned in the sixth century B.C.E. by Greek physicians. Ironically, the preferred cap was made by scooping the seeds out of half a pomegranate—the same fruit Hebrew scholars believe Eve and Adam ate from, condemning woman to labor pains and the travail of birth.

Centuries later, Casanova, the celebrated Italian lover, would present his mistresses with cervical caps made from partially squeezed lemon halves; the acid juice was also an ideal spermicide.

It is unclear whether women in biblical times used IUDs. They were commonly used throughout Saudi Arabia to prevent female camels from becoming pregnant on long journeys. Using a tube, an Arab herder slid a small stone or glass bead into a camel's uterus. The body—animal or human—attacks a foreign object by producing white blood cells, which secrete the antiviral compound interferon, an effective spermicide. The physiological way an IUD works was not understood until the 1970s.

JEWISH WOMEN AND MALE PLEASURE: MODERN JUDAISM ◆

Today, an approved means of birth control in Judaism is the pill. Oral means have superseded mechanical devices, and not merely because the pill is convenient. Though seldom stated, one reason has to do with the fact that males make the rules, often with their own pleasure in mind. Also, the rabbis prefer that women take the responsibility for birth control in order not to have "semen spilled in vain."

In the Middle Ages, Jewish rabbis, quite unlike Christian priests of the period, held the view that sex in marriage went beyond the purpose of procreation; the sexual gratification of the husband and wife took on a significant role. Mutual pleasure from intercourse became a legitimate pursuit in itself.

By the thirteenth century, rabbis in parts of Europe and the Middle East allowed liberal use of the *moch* after a couple had produced their basic boy-girl unit (or two boys). With one stipulation, said the rabbis: the mechanical means of birth control must allow for complete male penetration, full physical contact during intercourse. The male rabbis seem to have been thinking of their own gratification: the *moch* should not be too big or too interfering.

Today, most rabbis allow women to use the pill. Many discourage the use of mechanical devices that interfere with full physical sensation during intercourse. Often it is said that the pill, in allowing semen to flow along its natural course unimpeded, is more biblically acceptable.

MALE CONTRACEPTION—CONDOMS AND VASECTOMIES: ANCIENT TO MODERN ◆

Strict Jewish law prohibits a *male* from using contraceptive devices, even after he's produced the basic boy-girl (or boy-boy) family. This is because the biblical precept to "be fruitful and multiply" is interpreted in the Talmud as being addressed by God to males exclusively. (God seldom spoke to females.)

Technically, a Jewish man cannot wear a condom; in practice, many rabbis are sensibly lenient.

The origin of the proscription is curious. Contraceptive methods that diminish male pleasure have never been popular. The original condoms in biblical times all but deadened sensation: these were penile sheaths made from oiled animal bladders and lengths of intestines. They were used primarily to prevent venereal disease.

In the mid-1500s, Italian anatomist Gabriel Fallopius (who described the Fallopian tubes) designed a linen sheath that tied to the base of the penis. The first rubber condoms appeared in the 1870s, and allowed for about the same degree of sensitivity as would a garden hose. They were not all that different from the "rubber fingers" bank tellers use to count paper bills. Sheer latex was a breakthrough and godsend of the 1930s. Perhaps rabbis of old condemned prelatex condoms because they had to wear the cumbersome contraptions.

CRUSHED TESTICLES. Unlike Christianity, especially Roman Catholicism, Judaism has few rigid rules on birth control.

Still, Judaism frowns on the operation called a vasectomy—the severing, or tying off, of a man's tubes. Disapproval of vasectomy is based on Deuteronomy 23:2: "He whose testes are crushed, or whose male organ is cut off, may not be admitted to the congregation of the Lord." Vasectomy in biblical times was not yet an option, but crushed testes were taken to be the scriptural equivalent.

Today, with the development of reversible vasectomies, many rabbis allow the operation. On what grounds? That the mere possibility of reversal lifts the vasectomy above the permanency of crushed testicles or castration—a small but significant triumph of science over Scripture.

CHRISTIAN TURNING POINT: 1930 ◆

Saint Augustine was the first Christian theologian to condemn birth control, calling it "the poisons of sterility." The fourth-century bishop of Hippo, who had by then given up his concubine in favor of lifelong chastity, wrote in *Marriage and Concupiscence* that a husband and wife who engage in "the evil" are "married in name only."

And, prior to 1930, virtually all Christian denominations interpreted Onan's sad fate as a primary biblical condemnation of birth control.

That year, on December 31, Pope Pius XI, who, as we have seen, was expanding the papal power to divorce Christians and non-Christians alike, released his encyclical *Casti connubii*, "On Christian Marriage." The literal translation of the title is actually more telling and truthful: *casti*, "chaste" or "pious"; *connubii*, "marriages":

> *Any use whatsoever of matrimony exercised in such a way that the act is deliberately frustrated in its natural power to generate life is an offense against the law of God and of nature, and those who indulge in such are branded with the guilt of a grave sin.*

The pope certainly didn't change the Catholic Church's position on birth control, but he did break with centuries of tradition to say that sex in marriage can be "good and holy" in itself. It was a daring and, to many, long-overdue recognition.

In England that year, the Lambeth Conference of the Anglican Church sanctioned birth control outright. This was the first official Protestant acceptance of contraception. While the bishops of the Church of England maintained that abstinence was still *the* way to limit a family, in certain instances, they allowed condoms, caps, and IUDs.

The timing was perfect. Latex condoms had just been perfected. The cervical cap, engineered in Germany in the 1860s as a rubber hemisphere with a watch spring round the head to secure it in place, was now 98 percent effective; as good as today's diaphragms. And the first modern IUDs, the coiled "silver loop" designed in Germany, was just two years old.

The next year, 1931, the U.S. Committee on Marriage and the Home of the Federal Council of Churches approved of the "careful and restrained" use of contraceptives. This established a precedent that was gradually followed by all major Protestant denominations.

The *Zeitgeist* was ready for birth control in the 1930s. At the start of the decade, the Central Conference of American Rabbis (Reform) approved contraception for social and economic reasons, as well as health reasons. Mid-decade, the Rabbinical Assembly of America (Conservative) followed suit.

In Rome, the pope felt the heat. Protestants now were wearing condoms. Jews, too. (So were a great many Catholics, polls showed.)

Yet condoms seemed to the Church to thwart the sex act so unnaturally that theologically, from Rome's point of view, a rapist who wore a condom committed a greater offense than one who did not.

In fact, if a husband approached his wife wearing a condom, she was required to resist him, said a Church manual, "as a virgin would a rapist." If the husband threatened her with physical violence, the wife was allowed to "passively" submit, but she must take no pleasure in the rape, and she must hold her body stiffly rigid to display her disapproval.

Pius XII (1939–58), the new pope, did made a slight concession to the times: grudgingly, he gave his nihil obstat (official sanction) to the so-called rhythm method or safe period of contraception: a wife, with the aid of a thermometer, plots her infertile periods, and the couple then enjoys sex during that "safe" time, and abstains at all other times.

So unsafe was the method—measuring the infertile period can be thrown off by a case of the flu; by lactation (when menstruation ceases but conception is possible); and by the approach of menopause, when a woman's cycle gets hopelessly wobbly—that the pope's concession spawned jokes among liberal-minded priests. "Papa allows the safe method because he knows it's not safe." Or "A wife's only safe period is after age sixty." Obstetricians called the method "Vatican roulette."

MUTUAL MASTURBATION. In fact, accepting the rhythm method, this small papal compromise, grossly violated prior Church teachings on birth control. Turned them on their head.

For centuries, the *only* morally correct reason to copulate was to conceive children. But Pius XII, following up on Pius XI, who'd just said that sex in marriage was "good and holy," felt confident that he, too, could reverse Church teaching. In 1951, he addressed the midwives of Italy, instructing them on the cautious use of the rhythm method.

Actually, his predecessor, Pius XI, had condemned birth control pioneer Margaret Sanger (who coined the term "birth control") for suggesting that Christian couples who wanted to limit the size of their family might try the "safe period" method. Indeed, this method was scowled upon in Rome as a form of mutual masturbation—as was all intercourse without the intent to conceive.

Pius XII could not have misunderstood his predecessor. No one could have. Pius XI had called *all* methods of contraception "criminal abuse." In his 1930 encyclical *Casti connubii*, he stated that couples who attempt not to conceive—*all* Christians, not just Roman Catholics—"sin against nature and commit a deed which is shameful and intrinsically vicious." God, warned the pope, "detests this unspeakable crime with the deepest hatred and has sometimes punished it with death."

Death for using a condom. Death for a husband and wife having sex during the safe period. Now Pius XI's successor had lifted the death penalty and the burden of guilt in regard to the safe period.

Major change was underway. In viewing sex in itself as "good and holy," Pius XI had broken with centuries of tradition. In allowing the rhythm method, Pius XII had boldly contradicted centuries of doctrine—the words of Saint Augustine, Thomas Aquinas, and scores of past popes, including his immediate predecessor.

On the horizon was a new method of contraception, which was to prove very appealing.

THE PILL—THEOLOGY'S "GREATEST THREAT": 1960 ◆

No event in the long and clever history of contraception has had a greater impact than the development of the birth control pill. Oral contraception had been predicted as far back as the mid-nineteenth century. Doctors knew then that chemicals in the bloodstream could disrupt the production of ova and ovulation. In 1958, Pius XII saw that the pill was just around the corner and cursed it as "illicit sterilization."

That year, researchers tested a yam-derived ovulation inhibitor, norethynodrel, on 1,308 volunteers in Puerto Rico—a Catholic island. It established menstrual regularity and was an effective contraceptive. Searle Pharmaceuticals moved quickly to apply for FDA approval to market "the pill."

A new pope had just taken office: John XXIII (1958–63). He, and many other religious leaders around the world, condemned the pill as the evil of the century. They forecast that it would socially and sexually change the world. They were right.

In 1960, women across America began buying Enovid, history's first chemically manufactured oral contraceptive.

By the end of 1961, a half-million American women were on the pill, and that number more than doubled the following year. Catholic wives had ignored Rome's instructions.

Many parish priests and local bishops were beginning to take a liberal view toward contraception.

Many rabbis, as we've seen, actually preferred the pill over mechanical methods of birth control.

There was the sense that in the Vatican, the compassionate, modern-minded Pope John XXIII was about to make sweeping changes in regards to human sexuality. Those who would have been opposed might like to think that is why God called him immediately to Heaven before he could act on this subject.

The moderate-minded pope was gone, and his successor, Paul VI (1963–78), did something that would alienate more Roman Catholics than any prior papal action in history.

HUMANAE VITAE—THE SECOND "GALILEO AFFAIR": JULY 25, 1968 ◆

As if he could single-handedly stop the use of modern methods of contraception, Pope Paul VI moved quickly and took a firm, dogmatic stand, penning a harshly worded encyclical.

He withdrew all matters of contraception from discussion within the Church's General Council. There would be no further discussion, no debate, no public airing of dissent. In fact, a commission of bishops, physicians, and lay folk convened by Paul in 1964 had voted four to one that the Church should liberalize its teaching on birth control. Liberal-minded bishops were begging the pontiff not to condemn good couples who wanted to limit the size of their families.

Cardinal Suenens of Belgium pleaded with the clergy who sided with the

Pope Urban VIII (1623–44) condemned Galileo for saying the sun, not the earth, was at the center of the universe.

pope: "I beg you, my brother bishops, let us avoid a new 'Galileo Affair.' One is enough for the church." In 1633, during the Inquisition, Pope Urban VIII had condemned Galileo for saying that the sun, not the earth, is at the center of the universe and ordered the scientist tortured if he did not conform to Church teaching on cosmology.

On July 25, 1968, *Humanae Vitae* ("On the Regulation of Birth") was released. The encyclical fiercely banned all artificial methods of contraception. And it banned all bishops and priests from allowing laxity in their own congregations. Christ's vicar on earth had declared the following:

ALL WIVES ARE LIKE MARY. "For Us," Pope Paul VI told an audience of obstetricians and gynecologists,

> *Woman is a vision of virginal purity which restores the highest moral and emotional sentiments of the human heart. . . . For Us, she is the creature most docile . . . singing, praying, yearning, weeping, she seems to converge naturally towards a unique and supreme figure, immaculate and sorrowful, which a privileged Woman, blessed among all, was destined to become the Virgin Mother of Christ, Mary.*

No gynecologist snickered. No obstetrician laughed when the pope bid them farewell: "You see, gentlemen, this is the plane on which We must meet Woman." To doctors who had to deal with women who wanted to limit family size, who had medical conditions that a pregnancy would compound, the pope left them with a promise: "[My words] will provide you with food for new, noble and good thoughts and you will add dignity and merit to your profession."

Millions of wives wanted compassion, and the supreme pontiff held up the Virgin Mary as the epitome of womanhood. If a couple with five children could afford no more, they would be forced to lead a sexless life, for if the rhythm method failed, abortion was not an option.

Did Paul VI really think that a married man and woman in, say, their thirties, and with four children, could enjoy a happily married sexless life? Indeed, he did. God, he said, through the sanctifying grace bestowed in the sacrament of matrimony, had provided for just that kind of chaste discipline, should it be called for. Papa knows best.

Interestingly, *Humanae Vitae* offers no specific scriptural references in support of its many condemnations of artificial conception—and of abortion and sterilization. Nor, significantly, did the pope dare stamp the document *ex cathedra*, making its demands infallible dogma. To do such would have bound the hands of his successors forever—and summarily cut millions of married couples off from participation in the Church.

For, indeed, Catholics *were* practicing birth control, with a passion unequaled in the past. A poll of the day revealed that 49 percent of American Catholics (the most openly defiant breed of Catholic) used the pill or some other means of artificial birth control; 89 percent of Protestants did; 96 percent of Jews.

In terms of birth control, Roman Catholicism had become one of the most punitive of the major religions.

GREAT SCHISM OF MODERN TIMES: 1968 TO THE PRESENT ◆

Near the end of *Humanae Vitae*, the pope warns priests to give "that sincere obedience, inward as well as outward, which is due to the magisterium of the Church." Due the papacy. He knew priests would defy him, as couples were doing.

The harshly worded encyclical only exacerbated dissent among liberal and conservative priests, and publicly damaged the status of the papacy itself.

Humanae Vitae had a surprise effect. The unreasonableness of the encyclical forced many priests to rethink their own sexuality, that is, their vow of celibacy. If Holy Mother Church could be so wrong-spirited about sex in marriage, might the Church also be wrongheaded in its demand of celibacy for priests? *Humanae Vitae* set off a trickle, than an exodus, of priests from the priesthood.

MEDIA REACTION TO THE ENCYCLICAL. The response from newspapers and magazines around the world was predictable. A major daily called Paul's encyclical "one of the most fateful blunders of modern times." A Catholic weekly, *The Tablet*, demanded of the pope: "Where is the new and deeper reflection the church had been promised?" A group of U.S. Catholic bishops pleaded they be allowed to makes decisions in their own dioceses. They, after all, dealt directly with the problems of married couples.

In open defiance of Rome, 172 American teaching theologians asserted that Catholics should follow their consciences—even though the pope had spoken loudly and unequivocally, he had not spoken infallibly.

Paul's rigid encyclical, following on the heels of his successor John's promise to modernize Catholicism, had devastating consequences among the laity. Especially in America, where the pill and other birth control devices were dispensed at local drugstores. American Catholics in large measure simply went their own way, often with the blessings of their priests.

Today, Roman Catholic missionaries to overpopulated Third World countries forbid the use of contraceptives, whereas Lutheran, Presbyterian, Methodist, and Baptist missionaries sponsor free clinics and pass out free condoms to young mothers wanting to know how to limit the size of their families. Birth control splits Roman Catholics from many other Christian denominations.

AMERICAN CATHOLIC CHURCH ◆

It is no exaggeration to say that today *Roman* Catholicism is not *American* Catholicism. There are two distinctly different branches of the Catholic faith, two Churches, one headed by an archconservative pope, the other presided over by a college of reasonably moderate bishops, though the schism has never been formally acknowledged and is seldom discussed openly. Poll after poll reveals that virtually no American Catholic couple adheres to the letter of Rome's many laws, especially on birth control.

Theologically, this means that virtually no American Catholic couple is in good standing with Roman Catholicism. After all, the papacy is not a democracy but a dictatorship when it comes to hard-worded doctrine and infallible dogma. When the pope makes an unequivocal pronouncement, *all* Catholics (*all* Christians, in fact, from his point of view) must do as they are ordered. A good-standing Catholic cannot pick and choose from among dogmatic teachings; and the Church's teachings on birth control, abortion, and sterilization are not open to compromise.

One cardinal, Leger of Montreal, had implored Pope Paul VI prior to publication of *Humanae Vitae* to reconsider his position, lest "this fear with

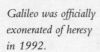

Galileo was officially exonerated of heresy in 1992.

regard to conjugal love which has paralyzed our theology for such a long time might persist."

END NOTE ◆

In 1992, 359 years after Galileo was condemned for heresy and nearly stretched on the rack, he was exonerated by Pope John Paul II. The pontiff, conceding that the earth revolves around the sun, and has for some time, closed the case in Galileo's favor.

PART

X I

Religious
Realms

CHAPTER

2 9

𝕳eaven

Soul to Immortality

HEAVEN IS THE abode of God or gods; the eternal haven for the immortal souls of the elect; the celestial afterlife that is endless, though never tedious, we're assured. But the paramount quandary always has been: What does Heaven look like?

To the medieval visionary Gerardesca (d. 1269), Heaven was a sacred city-state, surrounded by tall castles and crenellated fortresses; a feudal ideal.

To Renaissance Humanist Francesco Colonna (d. 1527), Heaven was an idyllic countryside, dotted with gushing fountains, where gorgeous maidens and beardless lovers frolicked in sunlit fields and shadowy groves; a Tuscan ideal.

To Swedish mystic Emanuel Swedenborg, Heaven was positively cosmopolitan, with matrixed numbered streets and named squares, where angels lived in elegant abodes with grassy lawns that never needed mowing; a modern-day ideal.

To nineteenth-century spiritualists, Heaven was a sprawling college campus for self-improvers, where the souls of perpetual students sat raptly through seminars and studied in libraries; a self-improver's ideal.

The point is: every philosopher, every saint, every mystic has offered a view of the hereafter that is tellingly influenced by the tenor—or terror—of the times. Heaven is always, it would seem, whatever people need it to be. Perhaps that's how it should be.

How did the very concept of Heaven, which is more or less universally embraced, originate?

*Images of Heaven have
varied over the ages
and in different faiths.*

TWO MAJOR MODELS OF HEAVEN ◆

Of the numerous and diverse views of Heaven that have been recorded, in the West and in the East, two major models emerge. The "theocentric" model stresses an individual's relationship with God and has always been favored by theologians. The "anthropocentric" model appeals to ordinary folk, for the emphasis is on human ties between family and friends in the presence of God.

In other words, there exists the Heaven of my Maker, and the Heaven composed of my contemporaries, colleagues, and cohorts; though the two are not mutually exclusive, our popular conception of them tends to be.

Contrary to popular opinion, throughout history, a religion's theology has not influenced its view of Heaven; the converse is true: more often than not, how a people come to view Heaven sets the parameters for their theological concepts. Also, cultural and social shifts over the centuries revamp a religion's attitude toward the afterlife; for instance, the persecution of early Christians under Roman yoke dramatically shaped their image of what they wanted— and needed—Heaven to be. Heaven's evolving imagery mirrors the unfolding of human history.

Let's begin our tour of Heaven with the Jews as our guide.

HEBREW HEAVEN—RESTRICTED AND EXCLUSIVE ◆

Most Christians may not be aware of the fact that the ancient Israelites had no Heaven for themselves. No personal hereafter. In sacred Scriptures, Heaven is the exclusive abode of Yahweh, God of the Israelites.

The Israelites believed that because Yahweh created the sun and stars, his abode had to be higher up in the celestial sphere, a vantage from where he could glance down on Creation. The Hebrew Bible makes no direct reference to a postmortem Heaven for the righteous. Heaven is Yahweh's home, and its gates never open for mere mortals.

The Israelites believed that after bodily death, all men and women—good and wicked—slept forever in *Sheol*, the underworld, a neutral place of neither pain nor pleasure, neither punishment nor reward. Saul in the Bible communicates with the deceased Samuel (1 Sam. 28)—who continues to exist after death in Sheol. The Israelites adopted this notion from Assyrian and Babylonian cultures; Sheol, for many pagan Semites, was ruled by a benevolent deity called Mot, "Death"—a toned-down version of the Canaanite god of death, Moth.

POSTEXILIC PROGRESS ♦

It was only after the destruction of the First Temple in 586 B.C.E. and the subsequent Exile of Jews to Babylon that the Jewish people began to seriously consider Heaven as the postmortem destination of the righteous, who would be resurrected to live with God. Why this reversal?

The answer lies in the fact that Babylon was conquered by Persia, and the Jews in Exile came under the strong influence of Persian Zoroastrian teachings. Zoroaster, the sixth-century B.C.E. prophet, taught that four days after death, a person is judged by his deeds in life. If good outweighs evil, the person crosses a bridge into Heaven (if evil outweighs good, the person falls from the bridge into a freezing, foul-smelling Hell). For the Jews suffering in Exile, the idea of spending an eternity with God, in his own well-appointed abode, was understandably appealing. Certainly more appealing than spending eternity in a numbing sleep in Sheol. Under the influence of Zoroastrianism, the Jews had begun to question the justice of a God who demands strict obedience in life but delivers both the wicked and the faithful to inert oblivion. Was there no reward for virtue?

It is during this postexilic period that Jewish devotional literature posits a clear dualism: *olam ha-ba* is "the world to come," while *olam ha-zeh* is "this world." Heaven, as Christians would come to know it, was beginning to take shape.

DAILY LIFE IN HEBREW HEAVEN ♦

The concept of reward for living a virtuous life greatly shaped Heaven's evolution.

The doctrine of reward and punishment, as applied to life after death, developed during the times of the Maccabees (c. 170–160 B.C.E.,). As Jewish martyrs were persecuted for the faith, the concept of the resurrection of the righteous came into full flower. "For if he had not hoped that they that were slain would rise again, it would have been superfluous and vain to pray for the dead" (2 Macc. 12:44). The Second Book of Maccabees, the last book of the Apocrypha, details the religious persecution of the Jews during those nightmarish years.

Later, during the Roman persecutions of the early centuries C.E., the concept of a personal Heaven took even deeper root, and belief in corporeal resurrection of the dead became an essential part of rabbinic eschatology. "All Israel has a portion in the world to come," the Talmud taught, except "one who says, 'There is no resurrection of the dead.' " The fifth-century Babylonian Talmud offers three hundred arguments for the resurrection of the dead.

Rabbis scoured the Hebrew Bible to support their newfound belief in the immortality of the soul and the existence of a personal hereafter. They found little, reinterpreted what lent itself to prefiguration and prophecy, and argued bitterly among themselves over what life in Heaven would be like, as well as where Heaven was located. All agreed that the just, like the prophet Elijah, would be restored to the bosom of the Lord and that the wicked would feel the flames of an everlasting Hell.

Some rabbis believed that the deceased would reside in God's celestial palace. The third-century Babylonian scholar Rav taught that in "the world to come," there would be "no eating, no drinking, no begetting of children, no business dealings, no jealousy or hatred or competition. The righteous will sit with crowns on their heads, enjoying the glory of God's radiance." This sounds like the Heaven early Christians pined for; in fact, Christian Heaven, as we'll see, grew out of these Jewish beliefs.

Other rabbis felt the resurrected dead would spend eternity in a terrestrial Paradise, an earthly Heaven. In fact, this latter view equated postmortem Paradise with the Garden of Eden, *Gan Ayden*. Adam and Eve's homeland was considered the place where the righteous would go after death to enjoy the fruits of the good life they had merited. Like Adam and Eve, the inhabitants of Eden would be blissful and sexless.

The Talmud says that the illustrious rabbi Yochanan ben Zakkai wept just before his death out of fear that he might not go to Paradise. And many Talmudic passages point to Paradise as an actual terrestrial place.

Today, most Jews—Orthodox and non-Orthodox—believe in the immortality of the soul, but not all believe in a physical resurrection of the dead and a celestial Paradise. In general, the tendency in Judaism is to stress the obligations in this world, *olam ha-zeh*, which if addressed justly lead inexorably to reward in the hereafter. The afterlife in Judaism is a far more marginal concept than in Christianity and Islam.

EARLY CHRISTIAN HEAVEN: OLD TESTAMENT EVIDENCE ♦

The first Christians craved knowledge of Heaven and they turned to the Hebrew Bible for their first glimpses of God's Paradise—which for Christians had its gates opened wide to believers in Jesus Christ.

From Moses' vision, they gleaned that God's throne rested on a "pavement of sapphire" (Exod. 24:10). From Ezekiel's dramatic tale, they saw God's throne shaped like a chariot, with gleaming wheels within wheels driven by four cherubim.

And, too, they knew God was not alone in Heaven. Like any king, he was surrounded by a court. One breathtaking vision of the celestial court is described by Isaiah:

> *I saw the Lord sitting upon a throne, high and lifted up; and his train filled the temple. Above him stood the seraphim; each had six wings; with two he covered his face, and with two he covered his feet, and with two he flew. (Isa. 6:1)*

Genesis 1:6–8 stated that God created the firmament ("dome") and "called the firmament Heaven." Christians regarded this dome as an overarching vault held up on great pillars at the ends of the earth, supporting a celestial ocean. Windows round the dome allowed in trickles of celestial ocean that descended as rain. God dwelled above this ocean in Heaven (the Hebrew Bible uses the plural *samayim*, "heavens").

But early Christians wanted to know more. They were being martyred in large numbers for the faith, and the Hebrew Bible was short on specifics, leaving much to individual imagination.

For Christians, Christ's Ascension opened the gates of Heaven to mortals' souls.

Why, we might ask, does the Hebrew Bible, which contains only hints of an afterlife, express no clear concept of immortality as related to human destiny and divine justice? Well, for the Israelites, their sacred Scripture was a national document of a people and its covenant with God. Thus, the Hebrew Bible concentrates on earthly rewards and punishments: peace and prosperity versus destruction and dispersion. The Hebrew Bible's concerns are with events that pertain to the fate of a nation, not the immortality of individual souls in Heaven.

CHRISTIAN HEAVEN:
BOOK OF REVELATION, FIRST CENTURY c.e. ◆

With the New Testament, Heaven really developed into the abode of God, elders, angels, and the blessed, especially through the vivid, kaleidoscopic imagery in the Book of Revelation (c. 95 C.E.).

Many traditional Christian images of Heaven derive from John's heated description of a city built of "pure gold, clear as glass," with walls of jasper, foundations adorned with jewels, gates of pearl . . .

> *Immediately I saw a throne . . . and He who sat was in appearance like a jasper-stone . . . round the throne was a rainbow like an emerald . . . sitting upon seats were twenty-four elders, clothed in white garments and on their heads crowns of gold. . . . From the throne issued flashes of lightning and voices and peals of thunder . . . and before the throne is a sea of glass like crystal . . . four living creatures having each six wings do not cease day and night chanting, Holy, Holy, Holy, the Lord God Almighty. (Rev. 4:2–8)*

Precious and semiprecious stones play a large part in Heaven's decor.

From John, early Christians also gleaned what they could expect once they made it to Heaven: the blessed will eat from the tree of life, and God himself "will wipe away every tear from their eyes, and death shall be no more, neither shall there be mourning nor crying nor pain any more, for the former things have passed away" (Rev. 21:4).

The Book of Revelation was written during a time of great persecution. Many Christians already had been martyred, others imprisoned for their faith. Worse was to come. Worship of Roman emperors soon would be obligatory. No wonder Christians lived in eager expectancy of Christ's promised return, and John's book was tailored to these desperate people's needs. Indeed, John himself, as we've seen, may have been imprisoned on the island of Patmos when he wrote Revelation.

John bore reassuring messages: No matter how bad life gets, God is in control. Remember that Christ, not the emperor, is Lord. Jesus *is* coming to execute justice. There will be a glorious afterlife, a peaceful, pain-free Paradise for faithful believers—especially for those who lay down their lives for Christ. Christian Heaven is reward for suffering.

By contrast, Jewish Heaven is reward for executing life's obligations.

ROMAN CATHOLIC HEAVEN: LATE FOURTH CENTURY c.e. ◆

When John wrote Revelation, the Blessed Virgin Mary was not yet Queen of Heaven; indeed, her glorious Assumption, body and soul, into Heaven would not become Catholic dogma until 1950.

Also, in John's day, the Church still had not decided on the heavenly roles of Jesus Christ and the Holy Spirit; the Triune Godhead, as we've seen, was not clearly stated until completion of the Nicene Creed late in the fourth century.

The Gospels present a glimpse of Heaven, and for early Christians, there was no better architect of the new imagery than Jesus Christ himself; as the Son of God he should know. Although Christ left no written commentary, his views were committed to paper decades after his death, by Matthew, Mark, Luke, and John.

In Luke, Christ explains that there will be no marriage in the afterlife; men and women will be spiritual, pure, asexual, like angels. He makes it clear that he soon will be joining the celestial community, which includes Abraham and the patriarchs, he says, plus Old Testament saints like Elijah and Moses (figures Jesus communicated with in mystical rapture), plus common folk like Lazarus. Christ's Heaven is open to all. Church fathers, though, soon would close the gates to certain unelected.

Dying on the cross, Jesus assures the repentant thief crucified beside him that "today" the scoundrel would be with him in Paradise. And in a farewell speech to the apostles, Christ assures them of ample space in Heaven: "There are many rooms in my Father's house."

The Roman Catholic Church would later stratify Heaven into tiers of desirability based on the concept of sanctifying grace. (*See* Grace.) As the doctrine decrees, not everyone who makes it into Heaven gets an equal share of bliss, for each person's capacity for eternal happiness depends on the degree of sanctifying grace he or she has in his soul at the moment of death. Strictly speaking, a lifetime of virtue can be snuffed out with one final serious sin unconfessed. Modern theologians are more liberal in their teaching.

MODERN HEAVEN: 1994 POLL ♦

Today, some two thousand years after the basic imagery of Heaven was established, how do Americans view the afterlife?

From a recent poll:

• Seventy-seven percent believe Heaven exists.

• Seventy-six percent think they have an excellent chance of getting there one day.

• Many respondents (91 percent) believe Heaven is a place of consummate peace and ample leisure time; stress-free.

• Many (83 percent) think they will be in God's eternal presence.

• Fewer (77 percent) believe they will meet up with their children, relatives, and friends.

• A surprising number (74 percent) believe Heaven is a celestial home full of humor and frequent laughter.

• About a third of the respondents think they'll spend eternity at exactly the age they died. Interestingly, decades ago, the predominate belief was that one spent eternity in one's prime, everyone twentysomething. As the crest of society has aged, and as old age has become a less fearsome concept, people seem more willing to spend eternity in their final earthly form. As we saw at the opening of this chapter, Heaven has always been what people of an era need it to be.

WORD ORIGIN. Our English word "Heaven" is from the Old English *heofon*, meaning "to cover," and related to the Old High German *himil*. The origin implies Heaven's location: it hovers overhead. The oldest root of the verb "to cover" is the Indo-European *kem*, which is the basis for the Latin for "shirt," *camisia*. Also a covering. A kind-hearted person who'd give you the "shirt off his back" is offering you a little taste of Heaven.

ISLAMIC HEAVEN: SEVENTH CENTURY c.e. ♦

Visions of traditional Islamic Heaven draw on imagery borrowed from Judaism, Christianity, Zoroastrianism (the faith of the Persian prophet Zoroaster), and Arab elements.

The celestial Paradise is a place of consummate joy and bliss, consisting of seven grades of pleasure (a sensuous-sounding word Christians do not associate with Heaven), and where admission is granted only by the will of Allah, God.

The bodies of the dead remain in their graves until the end of the world, when everyone will be resurrected to stand before Allah at the Final Judgment. Allah will require each person to walk the Path, which is the Zoroastrian-like bridge that stretches over Hell and ultimately ascends to the heights of Heaven. The righteous will walk the full length of the bridge, but the damned will fall off along the way, plunging into the fiery pits of Hell, where they'll be roasted, boiled, and afflicted with pus. (In Zoroastrianism, the fall is into a freezing, foul-smelling Hell; the image of fire comes from Christianity.)

As in early Judaism, the Islamic Heaven physically resembles the Garden of Eden, though it is no longer populated with only one man and one woman. There are many available young maidens in this male-oriented Paradise, which brims with an abundance of fresh figs, dates, and sweet libations. But the greatest delight, stressed the Prophet Muhammad, is spiritual: one glimpses the glory of God, which dwarfs all the pleasures of the body "as an ocean surpasses a drop of sweat."

MORMON HEAVEN: PALMYRA, NEW YORK, 1820 ◆

In recent times, the most dramatic revamping of Christian Heaven's imagery has come from the Church of Jesus Christ of Latter-day Saints, whose members are called Mormons. This made-in-America vision of the afterlife posits a Paradise not unlike an idealized United States itself: bustling with family, dedicated to social progress, with full-time employment for all.

According to Mormon doctrine, God, once a man, married a "heavenly mother" and fathered "spirit children" who assumed bodily shapes and populated the earth. Like their heavenly parents, Mormons are expected to marry in a Mormon temple "for time and eternity." Marriage for Mormons is the first step—after baptism—toward becoming godlike themselves.

Mormon Heaven comes complete with lakes, forests, cities with towering buildings, but this Paradise is no place for idle hands. Mormons in Heaven continue to labor nonstop for the Church, converting the souls of deceased nonbelievers through a practice called *baptism of the dead*; this is the only faith in which proselytizing spills into the afterlife. In 1995, Jews asked Mormons to stop "converting" dead Jewish Holocaust victims into the Mormon faith; the Church agreed to remove the names of an estimated 380,000 Jewish Holocaust victims, who had already received Mormon baptism of the dead, from its International Genealogical Index. This practice of baptizing the dead of other faiths originated decades ago in order to swell the ranks of the new religion.

The practice continues. The more deceased nonbelievers a Mormon collects into the "body of the faithful"—which now totals 147 million members—the greater his own progress toward his ultimate exaltation as a god.

Furthermore, only married, faithful couples can progress to full Godhead. And the theology is male-oriented: a wife achieves exaltation by participating in her husband's eternal priesthood.

Eventually, all righteous people receive glorified bodies, and exalted couples spend eternity in painless—and perhaps pleasurable—procreation. Their spirit children, in turn, assume physical bodies, and inhabit other planets in the galaxy, spreading the Mormon faith to places no man has gone before. All Mormons, on all planets, worship the original Heavenly Father and Mother.

This scenario is very modern, very American (very *Star Trek*, in fact), and unlike any earlier conception of Heaven in history. How did it originate?

MORMONS LIVED IN CHRIST'S TIME. All faiths posit their roots retrospectively, glancing back to earlier times to anchor their origins in tradition. Christianity, we've seen, finds itself prefigured in Jewish Sacred Scriptures. Islam reasons that the Jewish prophet Abraham was, in fact, the first Muslim; that Islam predates Judaism. Mormonism, most people might be surprised to learn, traces its roots to an alternate Church Jesus Christ himself founded.

According to Latter-day Saint theology, Jesus, in his lifetime, established a Church on earth called the Church of Jesus Christ, whose members were called saints. After his Resurrection, Jesus visited the continents of the Americas and established his Church there as well. Then he ascended into Heaven and the trouble started. The original followers were persecuted mercilessly, their Church leaders died off, and evil in many forms caused the Church to vanish from the earth, resulting in a period known as the "Great Apostasy." Jesus, though, promised that one day he'd restore the Church.

In the year 1820, Joseph Smith (1805–44), a fifteen-year-old youth from Upstate New York, received a divine vision. He was warned by Christ, through the angel Moroni, not to join any Church, since the one, true Church did not yet exist. Over the next decade, he received a series of revelations that marked him as the first prophet of the new Church, the Church of Jesus Christ of Latter-day Saints. (As opposed to the Earlier-day Saints, who'd been persecuted into extinction.)

POLYGAMY: "JACOB'S BLESSING." Whereas Joseph Smith liked to describe himself as an unschooled, pious youth who grew up at a time of intense religious revivalism, his neighbors in Palmyra, New York, remembered him as a hot-blooded teenager, a self-styled ladies' man, who once confessed to a friend: "Whenever I see a pretty woman, I have to pray for grace." Now he instituted polygamy, took as many as fifty wives himself, and gave the practice the biblical sanction of "Jacob's blessing." Polygamy, preached Joseph Smith, was the ultimate solution to the evils of adultery and prostitution.

America, though tolerant of diverse religious beliefs, would not stand for polygamy. The Republican presidential platform of 1856 called for the end of Mormon plural marriages. Congress enacted laws against the practice, and between 1885 and 1890, more than one thousand Mormon men were convicted. In 1890, the U.S. Supreme Court agreed that polygamy was illegal and, coincidentally, the head of the Mormon Church at the time, Wilford Woodruff, received a "divine command" that the practice of multiple wives must stop.

Polygamy is a chapter in Mormon history that the religion's devout followers would like to close and forget—much the way the Roman Catholic Church feels about the era in which indulgences were sold for cash, cattle, and crops.

MORMON BIBLE: U.S.A., 1827–44 ◆

All religions have their sacred literature. For Judaism, it's the *Tanakh* (which Christians call the Old Testament); for Christianity, it's the New Testament and the Apocrypha ("Things that are hidden"); for Islam, it's the Koran ("The Recitation"); for Confucianism, it's the Analects of Confucius ("Selected Sayings" of Confucius); for Hinduism, it's the Vedas ("The Wisdom"); for Buddhism, it's the Tipitaka (the Three Baskets); for Mormonism, it's the Book of Mormon.

*Mormon Temple,
Salt Lake City.*

Joseph Smith, in his short lifetime, received from the angel Moroni "golden plates" (they've since vanished), which he translated into the Mormon Bible. This records the faith's sacred history and cherished beliefs. The Book of Mormon holds that God is a real person with a tangible body of flesh and bones, and that all people existed in a premortal life as spirit children of God.

In style and themes, the Book of Mormon resembles the Old Testament. It recounts the history of the virtuous, industrious, fair-skinned Nephites, who were eventually exterminated by the sinful, red-skinned Lamanites. God's good people are first prosperous, then prideful, then decadent; finally, they're punished and they repent—this moral cycle is common to sacred literatures.

Another of Joseph Smith's revealed Scriptures was the *Book of Abraham*. But facsimiles published by Smith were later declared by experts to be segments of common Egyptian funerary texts; the original papyri exist in the Metropolitan Museum of Art in New York City. In Smith's translation, persons with "black skin" were cursed "as pertaining to the priesthood," which led to decades of racial strife, as African-Americans were excluded from office in the Mormon Church.

The Book of Mormon denies the existence of original sin, and Mormons believe that family relationships can be eternal. Less theocentric, more anthropocentric, the Mormon faith is perhaps the most family-oriented religion practiced today, extending the maxim "the family that prays together stays together" into the afterlife.

SOUL AS THE "BREATH OF LIFE": OLD TESTAMENT ◆

The Israelites did not have souls. They didn't realize this, of course; the concept hadn't yet come into existence. They did not speak of a spiritual component of the human body that survives death, is eternal, and ascends upward, being lighter-than-air. A dead Israelite *descended* into the neutral underworld that was Sheol for a long, numbing sleep. For eternity.

The Hebrew Bible speaks of a "breath of life," *nishmat hayyim:*

> *Then God formed man out of the dust of the ground and breathed into his nostrils the breath of life, and man became a living being. (Gen. 2:7)*

But at the time Genesis was written, around 1400 to 1200 B.C.E., and for a long time thereafter, "breath of life" was not conceived of as an immortal soul, only as an animating force. Further, the words from early Hebrew

Egyptian symbol of the soul, "Ba."

Scriptures translated as "spirit" or "soul" also refer to the personality of the individual.

Later books, however, begin to make references to a spirit that can separate from the body. One of the clearest glimpses of the concept of the soul in development is Ecclesiastes:

> *All are of the dust and return to the dust. Who knows if the spirit of man goes upward and if the spirit of the beast goes downward to the earth? (Eccl. 4:20–21)*

But the true origin of the soul would come about only after the "breath of life" was viewed as a independent spirit entity that survives death, retains the individual's personality, and returns to God, who'd breathed it into creation. And it would be the Greeks, not the Jews, who made this leap of faith.

SOUL AND IMMORTALITY:
GREECE, FOURTH CENTURY B.C.E. ◆

Greek views on the soul made a vivid and lasting impression on Jews, and eventually on Christians.

Plato, the fourth-century B.C.E. Greek philosopher, laid the groundwork. He reasoned that the soul contained the vital essence of a person, which, once released from its imprisonment in the body, grew strong, more powerful, more rarefied and refined—more godlike—and thus it floated upward. The soul of the righteous ascended high above the stars to a haven Plato called the Isle of the Blest.

For Plato, the soul had three parts: *desire* and *action* were mortal and perished with the body; *intellect* was superior, eternal, forever incorruptible.

Plato called the totality of a person's vital essence his *psyche*, a noun related to the Greek verb *psychein*, meaning "to blow." Thus, we see that the soul is the breath of life as well as the embodiment of personality: desire, action, reason.

SEXLESS SOULS ◆

Another philosopher, Philo of Alexandria, born about two decades before Christ, elaborated on Plato's ideas and paved the way for centuries of Christian thinkers. Philo, a Greek-speaking Jew and theologian, created a unique synthesis of Platonic philosophy and Hebrew biblical tradition.

For Philo, death restores the soul to its original, prebirth state; that is, a person's spirit exists before his or her body does, and death is simply the soul returning home to God. Since the soul belongs inherently to the spiritual realm, its brief tenure in the body, taught Philo, is nothing but unfortunate travail: life is insignificant; the afterlife is the end-all be-all.

Philo acknowledged that many human souls lose their virtuous way in the pleasurable labyrinth of the material world, but the soul of the righteous eventually assumes "a higher existence, immortal and incorporeal." He went a step further: in addition to being immortal and immaterial, the soul is asexual—neither male nor female. It ascends to Heaven, joins a chorus of angels, and may even move higher up to reside near God himself. The soul, in concept and destiny, had arrived.

Rabbinic Judaism also refined the ancient and vague "breath of life" into the unambiguous concept of "soul." The doctrine was recited in morning liturgy as a prayer from the Talmud, with wording that could apply to many faiths:

> *My God, the soul which You gave me is pure. You did create it. You did form it. You did breathe it into me. You preserve it within and You will take it from me, but will restore it to me hereafter. . . . Blessed are You O Lord, Who restores souls unto the dead.*

IS THE SOUL INFUSED AT CONCEPTION? ◆

The original teaching of the Catholic Church for centuries was that the immortal soul enters a fetus weeks *after* conception. In fact, throughout the Middle Ages, all Catholics, and popes, believed that the soul enters the fetus at different times, depending on the child's sex. Male babies got their souls sooner than females. This meant in theory that females could be morally aborted at a later date than males.

These long-held notions stem from the incorrect embryology of Aristotle and early physicians. Greek doctors, as well as early Church fathers, believed that an embryo from some time after conception remained a nonhuman speck of cells that was only gradually animated with life and given a soul.

Shortly after the Council of Nicaea (325 C.E.), at which the Trinitarian Godhead was defined, the Roman emperor Flavius Gratianus (375–83) stated to physicians the view of the day: "He is not a murderer who brings about abortion before the soul is in the body."

And when exactly did the soul enter the body?

A male fetus became human and got his soul forty days after conception. A female fetus became human and got her soul eighty days after conception. Her worth was only half his worth, at least till day eighty.

This sexist view was based on another misconception. Up until the invention of the microscope in seventeenth-century Holland, doctors and theologians believed that a man's sperm alone made a baby; a woman's uterus merely housed that sperm for nine months of gestation. If a child looked like its mother, that was thought to be the "influence" of the uterus. The microscope proved that the mother makes a contribution that is substantial: an egg.

Thomas Aquinas in the thirteenth century taught that all perfect sperm produces male babies; defective seed from the father yields a female child. There were other reasons that contributed to female fetuses: illness of the mother during early gestation, or the couple copulated in cold, damp weather.

POPES OKAY ABORTIONS ♦

Misconceptions about human embryology have made for some historical embarrassments within the Catholic Church.

Shortly before the microscope was perfected in the Netherlands by Anton van Leeuwenhoek (1632–1723), in Rome, Pope Gregory XIII (1572–85), whose background was in Church law, declared that it was not homicide to kill an embryo of less than forty days since it was not yet human. Interestingly, at this time, the pope helped persuade the Netherlands to remain Roman Catholic, while countries like Sweden had just broken with Rome to follow Martin Luther into Protestantism.

Gregory's successor, Pope Sixtus V (1585–90), in his bull of 1588, *Effraena-*

Pope Gregory XIV (1590–91) said that not all abortions are homicides.

tum, declared all abortions were homicides, carrying the penalty of excommunication for parents and doctors. But shortly thereafter, Pope Gregory XIV (1590–91), in an uncharacteristically blunt reversal, announced that Sixtus's view was too severe and censured the bull as if it had never been written.

Confusion and contradiction continued. In 1621, Roman physician Paulo Zacchia, revered in the papal court, proclaimed that Aristotle's views on embryology were nonsense and that life began at the moment of conception. Still, though, the Vatican did not make mandatory baptism of spontaneously aborted fetuses of less than forty days; the decision was up to the grieving parents if they wished to have the soul of their unborn cleansed of original sin. A fetus spontaneously aborted after forty days was deemed to clearly have a soul and baptism was expected before burial of the body.

As late as the eighteenth century, the Church's greatest moral theologian, Alfonsus Liguori, later canonized a saint, still denied that God gave a fetus a soul before forty days of gestation. Abortion was morally wrong in general, said Liguori, but because of uncertainty as to when the soul entered the fetus, there were circumstances, such as when a mother's life was at stake, when abortion was acceptable.

In 1869, Pope Pius IX (1846–78), a year before he signed as dogma the doctrine of papal infallibility (*see* Infallibility), repeated the Church's general belief that any destruction of an embryo, even to save a mother's life, was a mortal sin that merited excommunication. Earlier, in 1854, the pope had elevated to dogma the Virgin Mary's Immaculate Conception, the belief that as Christ's mother, Mary was born without original sin on her soul. Mary, once a female fetus, had not gotten her spotless soul on day eighty of gestation, but on day one.

In 1930, Pope Pius XI (1922–39), in his stern encyclical *Casti connubii*, "On Chaste Marriages," invoked the Commandment "Thou shalt not kill" to protect fetuses from the moment of conception, when the soul enters the flesh.

Thus, the true origin of the Church's current stand on abortion, and the sanctity of life from the moment of conception, dates from the development of the microscope and a more accurate understanding of embryology.

Is the soul infused at conception?

Now it is.

𝕳ell

Hot to Hotter

WITH A LOWER-CASE *h*, "hell" is slang, a curse word, one of the notorious four-letter profanities that, if uttered too frequently in puritanical times, could send you straight to "Hell" with an upper-case *H*. Which goes to show, sins aren't what they used to be.

Once the transgressions worthy of postmortem punishment were divorce, premarital sex, adultery, and homosexuality; now who can say?

Just as the offenses that merit eternal damnation have changed over time—a Catholic in the 1950s who willfully ate beef on a meatless Friday went to the great barbecue below—so, too, have changed the concepts of what Hell is, and where it is.

Today more than 60 percent of Americans say they believe in Hell, but fewer than 4 percent think it is a state of mind or place in their own personal future. Hell is for others.

But which Hell?—for there is no single torrid smelly netherworld to receive the wicked, but different Hells depending on one's beliefs:

*Hades, Greek god of
the netherworld.*

• The ancient Greeks had a distant island called *Hades*, where abandonment and social isolation were sheer torture.

• The Israelites who wandered the desert had a relatively tame site called *Sheol*, a dusty, dry underworld in which good and evil souls commingled in a state of continual thirst.

• The Norse netherworld of *Niflheimr* was wracked by gale-force winds, bitter cold, and shrouded in impenetrable dark.

• Christian *Hell*, as we'll see, underwent many modifications to become the severest hellhole of all, a kingdom of cruelty, an eternal furnace of physical torture and emotional torment. The followers of Christ raised the dark art of damnation to heights that prompted artists and poets to create visionary masterpieces: the paintings of Bosch, the prose of Goethe, the poetry of Blake, the *Inferno* of Dante, to name a few.

A tour:

"VALLEY OF GEHINNOM" BECOMES "HELL": FIRST CENTURY c.e. ◆

An infamous ravine south of Jerusalem, the Valley of Gehinnom, gave Hell its name. And a pagan cult of child sacrifice conducted there, on a stone hearth back in the days when the highest offering a man could send up to a god was the body of an innocent, gave Hell its fiery imagery.

The Israelites were horrified by the child sacrifices practiced by their neighbors, especially those offered up to the greedy god Moloch. We are told in the Bible (2 Kings 3:26–27) that when the king of Moab "saw that the battle was going against him," he proposed his eldest son as a burnt offering, much to the disgust of the Israelites, who gave up their almost certain victory and "withdrew from him and returned to their own land."

There is an exceptional instance in the Bible of a child being sacrificed to the God of Israel. In Judges 11:30, Jephthah kills his only daughter as a burnt offering in fulfillment of a vow he had made to God in return for victorious battle against the Ammonites in 1143 B.C.E. The story is told without comment or condemnation.

Clearly, though, the laws of Moses condemned child sacrifice. And in the seventh century B.C.E., King Josiah destroyed the stone shrine in the Valley of Gehinnom. The charred stretch of earth had become a local dumping ground, a town garbage heap for sundry refuse as well as for the bodies of slain animals and executed criminals. For sanitary reasons, carcasses and corpses were routinely burned, and the valley's reputation remained that of a hellhole.

Indeed, Jewish prophets continued to denounce the old-time abominations of Gehinnom, such that, in time, the fiery place would become a metaphor for the site where God punishes the evil for eternity.

WORD ORIGIN. The Hebrew word "Gehinnom" was translated into the Greek Bible, the Septuagint, as *Gehenna*, which was translated into the New Testament as "Hell." Actually, the spelling h-e-l-l comes from an Old Norse verb *helan*, "to hide": in Norse mythology, which predates Christianity, Hel was the goddess of death and the underworld.

As an aside: Hel's father was Loki, who gate-crashed a party of twelve gods, in which the favorite god was killed. Thus, in Norse mythology, the number thirteen is unlucky, which is the origin of triskaidekaphobia, or "fear of thirteen." The word "hell" and fear of the number thirteen derive from the same mythological family, daughter and dad.

The "Valley of *Ben* Hinnom" means the "Valley of the *Son* of Hinnom." The actual valley south of Jerusalem rested between the territories of Judah and *Benjamin*: "*son* of the right hand," as the proper name translates.

HEBREW HELL—SHEOL: OLD TESTAMENT ◆

For the ancient Israelites, the Valley of Gehinnom was a hellhole, but not their Hell. Another word occurs sixty-five times in the Old Testament: *Sheol*. Sometimes it has been translated as "Hell," other times as "grave" or "pit," which are more accurate, since Sheol is a dark region in the lower world

---

TARTAR SAUCE ◆ *Thus, the Hebrews called Hell "Sheol," the early Christians used the word "Gehenna," and the Norse used "Hel."*

The Greeks used "Hades" as the general home for the dead, and Tartarus was the infernal abyss below Hades where in mythology Zeus hurls the rebel Titans. Tartarus was Greek Hell. The spicy condiment "tartar sauce," and the meat dish "steak tartare," derive their names from Tartarus, which was used to label the colorless crystalline acid, tartaric acid. The chemical tartar, potassium bitartrate, is also that pesky hard deposit that forms around the teeth and leads to gingivitis. Flossing, in a sense, can ward off Hell.

where both good and evil souls exist as ghosts, or shades, in a state of continual thirst.

The Jews of the Old Testament, like their Mesopotamian neighbors, had no morbid fascination with the concept of eternal punishment and suffering. After death, a person's shade—from the Greek *skotos*, "darkness"—passed into a dry, dusty, vague sort of desert. There was no fire, no Lucifer, no pitchfork and red embers, just thirst.

The Old Testament makes no direct reference to a postmortem Hell—or to a Heaven, for that matter, as we've seen. Like Heaven, Hell enters Jewish lore after the destruction of the First Temple in 586 B.C.E. and the subsequent Exile of Jews to Babylon, at which time they fell under the influence of Persian dualism and Zoroastrianism—which made a profound impression on Jews, Christians, and Muslims.

Today, most Jews—Orthodox and non-Orthodox—believe in the immortality of the soul, but not all believe in a Hell, certainly not in the torturous Christian Hell.

ISLAMIC HELL—"JAHANNAM" OR "HELLFIRE" ◆

Zoroaster, the sixth-century B.C.E. Iranian prophet, taught that the soul at death waits three nights to be judged and on the fourth day ascends to the Bridge of the Requiter, where one's deeds in life are weighed. If good outweighs evil, the soul crosses the bridge, which widens and welcomes one straight into Heaven. If, however, one's evil deeds are heavy, the bridge sags and narrows and the soul plunges into a freezing and foul-smelling Hell, where it's treated to all kinds of devious torments and chastisements until the Resurrection.

The Jews borrowed from Zoroaster's teachings, and in Talmudic times, especially during the period of Jewish persecution by the Romans in the early centuries C.E., the Jewish notion of Hell as fire-and-brimstone began to take root. At this point, Hell was also a reference to the notorious torrid Valley of Gehinnom.

Christians also borrowed from Zoroaster—"Zarathustra" in Persian—who taught that a person whose good and evil deeds in life are equal in number will, after death, travel to a location called *hamestagan*, "the place of the mixed," and there suffer alternating hot and cold climes until the Resurrection. (*See* Purgatory; Limbo.)

Islam adopted Zoroaster's view of Hell, modifying it with concepts from Judaism and Christianity. *Jahannam* is the name of Islamic Hell, literally "hellfire," a straightforward derivation from the Greek *Gehenna* and Hebrew

Gehinnom. Islamic Hell is a huge crater of fire beneath a narrow bridge that all souls must pass over to enter into Paradise. The damned, however, fall from the bridge and suffer torments, unless Allah wills otherwise and intercedes.

Islamic Hell is ambiguously described in the sacred Koran, and was never clearly spoken of by Muhammad. At one point, Hell seems to be a fantastic monster that God can summon at will to torture sinners. In another description, Hell is a fiery pit located on the underside of earth.

The Muslim theologian and philosopher al-Ghazali considers the bridge in strictly metaphoric terms: it is the straight and narrow path a believer must walk to God. Punishment in Hell is not necessarily eternal; any sinner can be released when Allah wills it.

Still another Muslim picture of Hell is a place where the soul retains the body's intense sexual lust but suffers because it possesses no organ for acting on it. Hell as eternal horniness.

CHRISTIAN HELL: LUKE, 65 c.e. ◆

The nightmare of Christian Hell, exceptional for its explicitness, did not originate with the first Christian writer to put pen to paper—Paul, the Jew from Tarsus who'd changed his name from Saul.

Paul never met Jesus, but his letters in the New Testament predate the first Gospel, Mark's. Paul condemned fornicators, drunkards, thieves, homosexuals, and many others, but not to a fiery Hell; rather, "the wages of sin is death" (Rom. 5:6), by which Paul meant destruction and oblivion. Not eternal suffering.

Mark, the next Christian recorder, does speak of "eternal damnation," but for those who slander the Holy Spirit. He mentions Hell once, when Jesus warns his disciples against slander: "It is better for thee to enter into life maimed, than, having two hands, to go into hell, into the unquenchable fire" (Mark 9:42).

The first significant Christian story of Hell is found in Luke, the traveling companion of Paul, who penned his Gospel more than three decades after Christ's death. Jesus, Luke tells us, employed Hell in his parable of the rich man who ignores the beggar Lazarus at his gates—only to witness after his death the same Lazarus cradled in "Abraham's bosom." Presumably, Abraham, the father of the faith, is in the company of the Lord. The rich man, crying desperately for deliverance from "the fire of torment," pleads with Abraham to allow Lazarus to visit him so that Lazarus may "dip the end of his finger in water and cool my tongue, for I am in anguish in this flame" (Luke 16:22–24).

Lazarus at the rich man's gate—the first significant Christian story of Hell.

The lesson here: Good souls go to the bosom of Abraham, wicked souls go into flames. Still, though, Luke is never graphic in his description of Hell.

MATTHEW AND JOHN. It is Matthew, who wrote his Gospel perhaps a decade after Luke's, who gives Christian Hell its dastardly due, in language at least.

Matthew argues, again and again, that Hell exists, is sheer torture, and is reserved for the damned who will be cast "into the furnace of fire; there will be wailing and gnashing of teeth" (Matt. 13:42); or "Serpents, generations of vipers, how can you escape the damnation of hell?" (Matt. 23:33); or sinners shall be cast into the "everlasting fire that was prepared for the Devil and his angels" (Matt. 25:41).

Hell gets painted more vividly in the intensely apocalyptic Book of Revelation. John presents, as we've seen earlier, a dramatic struggle between the cosmic forces of good and evil, between the domains of Heaven and Hell. Hell unleashes dragons, serpents, armies of sinister angels, plagues of locusts, earthquakes, and hailstorms, and Satan and his demons are responsible for the slaughter of two-thirds of mankind.

ETERNAL DAMNATION:
COUNCIL OF CONSTANTINOPLE, 553 c.e. ◆

Is damnation eternal?

Early Church writers weren't sure. Clement of Alexandria expressed reservations about the idea of everlasting chastisement. In the *Miscellanies*, he argues that God does not punish, God corrects—through a little torture if necessary. For Clement, the fires of Hell were remedial in nature.

Other writers, such as Justin Martyr, Irenaeus, and Arnobius, seem to sug-

RELIGIOUS REALMS

gest that Hell's greatest agony is the sinner's alienation from God. Indeed, this tends to be a popular modern view; Hell is not full of crispy critters but of sad folk weeping and gnashing their teeth over loss of the Beatific Vision.

What troubled many early theologians, like Origen, was the fact that everlasting punishment meant the sinner had thwarted God's will that all be saved and come to truth. If Hell was eternal, and sinners were not redeemed after some suffering, God's will would be frustrated. The notion arose that the time spent in Hell was directly proportional to the degree of sin on the soul. A soul lightly tainted would be purified in an instant; a soul blackened from vice could take weeks or years to clean up. Hell was a blast furnace that seared off sin.

Origen, though he didn't know it at the time, was laying the groundwork of the Christian concept of Purgatory, the subject of our next chapter.

The fiercest exponent of eternal damnation was Augustine, fourth-century bishop of Hippo. Hell was forever. This became the predominant view. The Council of Constantinople in 553 denounced the notion of universal salvation and embraced the concept of eternal damnation. Case closed.

The 1995 *Catechism of the Catholic Church* states that the souls of those who die in a state of mortal sin descend "immediately into the furnace of fire," and "the chief punishment of hell is eternal separation from God." The Church "affirms the existence of hell and its eternity."

In Origen's view, Hell eventually would empty out; even Satan would return to God as an obedient servant. In the predominant Christian view, Hell, not unlike our criminal penitentiaries, gets increasingly crowded with offenders.

DOES GOD PREDESTINE ANYONE FOR HELL?: COUNCIL OF ORANGE, 529 C.E. ◆

Is it cruel of an all-merciful, all-just Creator to blueprint certain of his creatures for eternal damnation? That issue was not resolved until five centuries after Christ's death.

The biblical basis for the doctrine of predestination stems from the God of Abraham's schizophrenic nature and is twofold in origin:

1. The Old Testament portrays a vengeful God who punishes indiscriminately, raining plagues and heartbreak on the virtuous as well as the wicked. Capriciously, God sides sometimes with the bad guys. "The Lord works in strange ways" is the cliché that sums up the confusion.

2. God in Scriptures oversees actions that seem to contravene his best in-

tentions. For instance, the Pharaoh's *resistance* to Moses advances God's plan to establish the Jewish faith; Judas' *betrayal* of Jesus advances God's plan for the Crucifixion and establishment of Christianity. God sets up roadblocks, then skirts round them to get his way.

Thus, early Christians concluded that God had it in for some people; some were created to be roadblocks to others. It seemed that God determined the ultimate destiny of an individual, then led the person into the trap. Saint Paul felt this way (Rom. 8–11); so did Matthew (20:23), and John (6:44–45, 66).

Only in the fourth century did Christian apologists attack this theme; and even then, Saint Augustine counterattacked.

Augustine said that God elects certain people for conversion, grants them the power to believe, guarantees them the performance of good works, and shepherds them to glory. The person can claim no credit for his or her salvation, since after Adam's fall, salvation can be achieved only through God's mercy. This idea got Augustine into a lot of trouble.

The Council of Orange in 529 settled the issue. It stated that God does indeed elect certain individuals for the Christian faith, and without regard for their intrinsic merits; some may be scoundrels. Thereafter, it's up to each individual to save himself. Each person has free will. God assists in salvation, but he'll not walk the elected through the gates of Heaven.

The Council of Trent in 1547 supported the view that God does not predestine anyone to go to Hell. Through prayer, the faithful implore the mercy of God, a Lord who does not want "any to perish, but all to come to repentance" (2 Pet. 3:9).

PUBLISHED TOURS OF HELL: EARLY CENTURIES c.e. ◆

Horror stories sell today, and they did in the past. Everyone likes a good scare.

A major feature in early Christianity was the boom in bogus apocalyptic literature. Texts mysteriously appeared, purportedly written by Old Testament prophets or by Christ's apostles, that hyped the horrors of damnation. Christians were being persecuted and someone had to remind them of worse tortures that lay ahead if they buckled under and abandoned the faith.

The *Apocalypse of St. Paul* read one tract, though the text was freshly written three hundred years after Paul's death. Or the *Apocalypse of the Virgin*, which Mary didn't pen. A later story has the Virgin interceding on behalf of a lesbian in Hell; the deviant woman is returned to life to try again. A feature common to all these tracts was a gory tour of Hades; what Satan's place was really like. Hell was hellish. Better to be martyred for the faith and go straight to Heaven.

This was not the first wave of such dire literature. A valid literary genre known as *apocalyptic literature* flourished from about 200 B.C.E. to 200 C.E. In truth, much of it was written to give hope to Jews and Christians suffering Roman persecution. The authors, for their own safety, often hid behind pseudonyms.

The word "apocalypse" is from the Greek *apokalypsis*, meaning "disclosure" or "unveiling," and for believers, it connotes the dramatic sudden intervention of God in human affairs, heralded by cataclysmic events of cosmic proportions. (*See* Antichrist.)

PORNOGRAPHIC HELL. Sex sells today, and it did in the past. Everyone likes a vicarious thrill. It is no exaggeration to say that during the Middle Ages, apocalyptic tracts got out of hand; illustrated books about Hell and its sufferings grew positively pornographic.

Voyeuristic, sadistic illustrators, with a scatological bent, etched and charcoaled a Hell that would have been the envy of the Marquis de Sade. Nude men and women were tossed helter-skelter into heaps of humanity, male faces nestled in female crotches and bosoms, the juxtapositions being intentionally erotic. A horned Satan ravaged a buxom woman who was depicted in the throes of . . . was that agony or ecstasy? Only one of these illustrated tours of Hell, Dante's, is still a best-seller today.

DANTE'S *INFERNO*: 1310 TO 1314 ◆

The height of the artistry of Hell came with Dante Alighieri's *Inferno*, part one of his masterful *Divine Comedy*. Writing in the early fourteenth century, Dante lent Hell a complete landscape, replete with sights, sounds, smells, and sighs.

This narrative poem of Hell, written from about 1310 to 1314, is one of the world's great works of damnation literature. The *Divine Comedy* itself is divided into three sections—*Inferno*, *Purgatorio*, and *Paradiso*—the Christian Hell, Purgatory, and Heaven.

The narrative traces the journey of Dante, escorted by Virgil, who represents the epitome of human knowledge, through a deep, dark wood downward into the descending circles of Hades, Lucifer's lair. Narrowly, they pass the Devil to emerge on the beach of the island mountain of Purgatory, to witness repentant sinners being torturously purged of their pasts. At the gates of Paradise, Virgil departs: Human Knowledge, Do Not Enter. In Heaven, Dante meets up with Beatrice, the beauty who symbolizes divine mysteries. At the climax, Dante's allowed a glimpse, for an eye-blink, of the glory that is God.

So profound was Dante's work, eerily illustrated centuries later by Gustave Doré, that Hell during the Renaissance and the Enlightenment was synonymous with the *Inferno*. Our word "inferno" is from the Latin for "hell," *inferiorum*, literally, "the lower world."

We'll return to Dante's masterpiece in considering the origin of Purgatory.

REFORMED HELL: SIXTEENTH CENTURY C.E. ◆

With the dawning of the Reformation, the Christian faithful splintered, some believers in Christ becoming Lutherans, others Calvinists.

In Europe, Lutheranism would become the state religion of Norway, Sweden, Finland, and Denmark, and between the years 1520 and 1570, two-thirds of the people living in what is today Germany proudly proclaimed themselves Lutherans. Calvinism would for a time become the dominant theology in the Anglican Church.

Hell itself went in separate directions. Martin Luther's Hell was watched over by a God man could fear but not love carefree and wholeheartedly. John Calvin's Hell was created by a God who had already made up his mind about some people's sad fate. In Rome, an incensed pope painted the horrors of Hell a hotter hue of red to stem the exodus of apostates to the new branches of Christianity.

• *Lutheranism* is rooted in the doctrine of *sola fide*, man's salvation through "faith alone." A young Martin Luther received the epiphany that would power the Protestant Revolt; he wrote: "*The just man shall live by faith.* At this I felt myself to have been born again, and to have entered through open gates into paradise itself."

• *Calvinism* is built on the doctrine of *sola Scriptura*, salvation through "Scripture alone." Divine revelation is the entirety of religion. The Gospels are of paramount importance.

This is something of a simplification, since there is overlap between the two beliefs, but it sums up the Reformation's emphasis on faith and the Gospels as superior to artifacts and theological arguments posited by a Church hierarchy of priests and a pope in Rome.

*The Temptation of
Saint Anthony.*

HOW LUTHERANS AVOID HELL: POST-SIXTEENTH CENTURY ◆

Martin Luther, in his seminary days, had studied Saint Augustine. He believed the saint to say that only God could save humans from damnation. Salvation was something essentially private between the individual and his Creator. The Church in Rome, said Luther, with its emphasis on intercession through saints, the Virgin Mary, even pious priests, had wrongly interposed herself between the individual and his Creator.

Luther came to regard the Church establishment as false, and the pope "as possessed by Satan," and the papal chair as the "throne of Antichrist." He concluded that only three sacraments had biblical origins and thus were valid: baptism, penance, and the Eucharist. (*See* Sacraments.)

Worse, charged Luther, Rome had deliberately manipulated the concept of Hell, spinning off a kinder, gentler place called Purgatory, a tepid, temporary Hell for lukewarm sinners that had no clear biblical basis. Luther argued that Hell was dire and eternal, and that Purgatory probably did not exist but was a counterfeit artifact of Rome, a fanciful superstition from which the Church reaped a handsome profit by selling indulgences that lessened one's time in Purgatory.

Indeed, it seemed to the general public at the time that Rome would allow a vile, wealthy sinner to buy his way out of Hell and back into God's good graces. A dying noblemen, scared down to his feverish trembling feet, would gladly bequeath his estate to Holy Mother Church in return for a guarantee of salvation. (*See* Indulgences; Purgatory.) For Luther, only God could intercede and save a person's soul.

For Luther, man and woman, as children of a sinful Adam, are under the power of Satan. "Our free will has no power whatsoever in virtue of which man can prepare himself for justice or even seek it out," said Luther. How then can a Lutheran possibly avoid eternal fire? "Fallen man," explained Luther, "does not cease to be a rational creature . . . able somewhat to discern the good from the bad and even freely to do some things and desist from others." God appreciates a human's struggle, and a man or woman of faith, working hard to be good, can be saved by God's mercy alone.

CALVIN'S HELL AND THE PILGRIMS' REGRESS: POST-SIXTEENTH CENTURY ◆

John Calvin, in embracing the notion of strict predestination, went much further than Martin Luther in leaving the decision as to who went to Hell in God's hands.

"Some men are predestined unto everlasting life," went the Calvinist doctrine, "and others are foreordained to everlasting death." Thus, Jesus Christ did not die on the cross for all men, but for a select few; for the elect. Forget salvation through prayer, indulgences, deathbed repentance; if you are marked for Hell in the Lord's master plan, nothing but a midnight reprieve from God himself can save you.

Calvin preached that the nature of fallen man is "utterly devoid of goodness" and is "odious and abominable to God." Human will is not free, but God's grace is irresistible and men and women must seek it through prayer. The sacraments are channels of grace, but only for the elect. The hierarchical priesthood Calvin rejected outright.

The Calvinist Puritans, in the journals and autobiographies they left behind, show that they were obsessed with a terror that they would not be saved. Frequently, they subjected themselves to severe humiliation to get into God's good grace, and the emotional mood swing took them from extreme desolation to feverish elation. The Puritans' heavy emphasis on Hell and damnation drove many of them to profound depression; suicide, from all accounts, seems to have been prevalent. Puritans attributed this to Satan, who seemed as powerful a presence in their lives as God.

Hell under Calvin filled up fast. Today, Calvinistic sects have greatly modified the doctrine of "absolute predestinarianism."

JESUIT HELL: 1540 TO 1850 C.E. ◆

Jesuit missionary priests from the Society of Jesus, founded in 1540 by Saint Ignatius Loyola, carried their own visions of Hell to converts in Asia, the Indies, and the Americas. Educated in theology and science, spiritually devout and intellectually shrewd, Jesuits viewed their mission chiefly as a way to win

converts to a Church whose faithful had been siphoned off by the Reformation and Protestantism.

Hell, in Jesuit hands, became a nightmare of urban squalor. From Alice
Turner's *The History of Hell*:

> *The Jesuit Hell was unbearably, suffocatingly, repulsively crowded. In a dank,
> claustrophobic amalgam of dungeon and cesspool, dainty aristocrats and prosper-
> ous merchants jostled, cheek to jowl, buttock to belly, mouth to mouth, with
> coarse, foul-smelling, verminous peasants, lepers, and slum-dwellers. Just as the
> bodies of the saved were to be glorified at the Resurrection, those of the damned
> would be deformed, bloated, flabby, diseased, repugnant, "pressed together like
> grapes in a wine-press." There were no latrines. The infernal stench was human
> stench, and it was disgusting and everlasting and composed of filth and feces and
> pestilence and running sores and bad breath and everything else creative Jesuits
> came up with.*

The Jesuits borrowed imagery from the real-life urban squalor spawned in
big cities by the Industrial Revolution, where the poor were relegated to un-
sanitary slums and subsisted in overcrowded, ramshackle huts. The horrors of
real life were used to drive desperate folk to Christ and sanitary Christian
salvation. Hell couldn't get much worse. In general, Hell is and always has
been what people fear most in life. The imagery of Heaven, on the other
hand, always has been life idealized.

Has this been true in Eastern cultures as well?

HINDU HELL—ONE STOP ON A LONG JOURNEY: INDIA, 1500 B.C.E. ◆

Whereas Western religions, especially Christianity, are obsessed with Hell,
Eastern religions are not overly concerned with the concept of eternity.
Their belief in *reincarnation* denies the concept of One Life, One Afterlife.

In Hinduism, Hell is just one road stop in the soul's long journey to spiritual perfection. In fact, there are more than twenty Hells in the Hindu
netherworld. Since a Hindu is continually reincarnated, the time spent in
any one Hell is not of great significance. Eventually, the soul will return to
the world and enter a new physical life, even though many earth lifetimes
might elapse before this rebirth occurs.

Hindu Hell is not unlike that kind of remedial Christian Hell promoted
by Clement of Alexandria, which never caught on with Christian theologians.

*Hindu gods and the cycle
of reincarnation.*

ORIGIN OF HINDUISM. Hinduism, perhaps more than any other faith, is a collection of spiritual beliefs, dating from about the second millennium B.C.E. The spiritual ideals of nomadic Aryan tribes who invaded the Indian subcontinent blended with tenets prevalent in the Indus Valley and forged a religion unique in that, unlike others, it has no individual founder, but is based on a loose confederation of personal and local deities.

The religion is administered by the Brahman caste, consisting of priests. In Hinduism, caste is an innate attribute of humankind, determining one's station in life, one's ability to marry, and one's status in the afterlife. The family you are born into is of supreme importance.

Contained in the sacred texts of the Vedas (c. 1400 B.C.E.; assembled at the time Moses was writing the Hebrew Book of Genesis) and the Upanishads (c. 900 B.C.E.; dating from the Hebrew Books of Samuel) are all the instructions on how a Hindu must live.

A Hindu's ultimate destiny is determined by all of his actions, and even their unpredictable consequences, during the successive phases of his life. The sum total is his karma. A good life in the present will bring him the reward of a higher life later. A debauched life might result in his being reincarnated into a more difficult life, or even as a lowly animal next time. The process of continual birth and death comes to an end only when the soul reaches a state of perfection.

CHINESE HELL: SECOND CENTURY C.E. ◆

Chinese Hell, tempered by reincarnation, is based on Buddhist concepts and modified by Taoist philosophy.

At the moment of death, a person is escorted by spirit messengers to the "god of walls and moats," named Ch'eng Huang. The god grants the deceased a preliminary hearing on his good and bad deeds. The supremely virtuous may pass straight to one of the many Buddhist Paradises, such as K'un-lun Mountain, the dwelling place of the Taoist immortals; those slightly less virtuous go to the Court of Hell for immediate rebirth into the physical world, in order to perfect the soul.

The lowly sinner goes a different route. After forty-nine days in the grave, he descends to the realm of Hell Below that is located at the base of Mount Meru. Here the sinner endures a fixed period of remedial punishment, in preparation for his rebirth into the physical world. Eventually, he drinks the "broth of oblivion," forgets his past, then climbs on to the wheel of transmigration that spins him to the next stage of physical existence. Everyone gets a second chance. Or third. Or fourth.

ORIGIN OF TAOISM. This Chinese religion originated in the sixth century B.C.E. with the philosopher Lao-tzu (604–531 B.C.E.). His ideology was based on a belief that *Tao*—"The Way" to the Ultimate and Unconditioned Being—was correct conduct and the virtuous practice of thrift, humility, and compassion. In Taoism, ceremonial pomp, pageantry, and elaborate vestments are irrelevant. Among its principles are simplicity, patience, contentment, and harmony. In today's stress-filled world, Taoism has gained popularity in the West precisely for the appeal of these principles.

JAPANESE HELL: SIXTH CENTURY C.E. ◆

The Japanese Buddhist-inspired Hell is composed of eight hot and eight cold levels, located far beneath the earth. It is ruled over by Emma-o, the male Lord of Death, who judges the deeds of the dead with the help of a counting register that tallies sins. Emma-o is assisted by two disembodied heads, one male, one female, perched on pillars on either side of him. The female head, symbolic of intuition, is called Miru-me, and she has the power of perceiving the sinner's most secret private faults merely by eyeing him. The male head, called Kagu-hana, has the power to ferret out any actual misdeeds the person performed in life.

Damnation is not eternal. The wicked are sentenced to a fixed period of remedial punishment, which can be shortened or commuted through the prayers of the living. In this sense of intervention, the Japanese Hell is very much like the Roman Catholic Purgatory, in which the living, through prayer, can shorten the suffering of dead relatives and friends, hastening their entrance into Heaven.

ORIGIN OF BUDDHISM. Buddhism began with an Indian prince, Siddhartha (563–483 B.C.E.), a member of the Sakya clan, who wandered for six years formulating his spiritual beliefs; then he meditated forty-nine days until he achieved enlightenment or *Nirvana*. Henceforth, Siddhartha was known as the Enlightened One, or Gautama Buddha, or simply Gautama.

Linguistically, as Jesus is The Christ (*christos*, Greek for "anointed one"), Gautama is The Buddha (Sanskrit for the "enlightened one"). A Christian says Jesus Christ, a Buddhist says Gautama Buddha.

The Buddha taught salvation in Bihar, west of Bengal, until he died at the age of eighty. Buddhism embodies four Noble Truths:

1. A person suffers from one life to the next incarnation.
2. The origin of human suffering is craving either pleasure, possessions, or cessation of pain.
3. Craving is cured by detaching oneself from all things, including the self.
4. Detachment is achieved through the Eightfold Path: Right Conduct, Right Effort, Right Intentions, Right Livelihood, Right Meditation, Right Mindfulness, Right Speech, and Right Viewpoint.

Buddhist monks are celibate and adhere to vows of nonviolence, poverty, and vegetarianism.

END NOTE ◆

In this chapter on Hell, one point most sharply distinguishes Western from Eastern beliefs. In the West, Hell is eternal damnation from which there is no redemption. In the East, Hell is remedial punishment before rebirth and a second chance to get it right. The Western view is dualistic and close-looped. The Eastern view open-ended and cyclical. One is left to wonder what the ultimate Creator of humankind really intends for his creations. Does the soul live on through many lifetimes, as half the world's religions believe? Or, as the other half maintains, is one lifetime all we get to prove our mettle?

CHAPTER
━━━━━
3 1

𝔓urgatory

Divine Comedy *to Sale of Indulgences*

THE ROMAN CATHOLIC DEFINITION ◆

Purgatory, in Roman Catholic doctrine, is the third otherworldly place, situated nearer to Heaven than to Hell.

Purgatory is a temporary resting place for the souls of those who die in the state of grace, but who are not yet free from all imperfections. In Purgatory, they undergo remedial punishment, which may be swift or protracted, slight or searingly severe. In Purgatory, the soul makes expiation for venial sins unforgiven at the time of death, and for the temporal punishment due to venial and mortal sins confessed and forgiven on earth but which have left residual stains on the soul.

Only a totally purified soul, purged of unconfessed trivial sin and the stain from all confessed sin, is allowed entry into Heaven.

OUR APPROACH ◆

The theology of Purgatory is tricky; poorly understood even by most parish priests. For instance: Is there *real fire*? Do souls suffer pain? (Indeed, can a disembodied spirit feel pain?) How long does the remedial torture last? Once purified, does a soul depart Purgatory immediately for Heaven? We'll address these issues in this chapter.

The origin of Purgatory, we'll see, is murky to say the least; it seems to be a blend of biblical interpretation, tradition, and wishful thinking.

The noun "purgatory" is relatively new; it did not come into existence until late in the twelfth century, just in time to be included in Dante's *Divine Comedy*. The origin of the word, we'll discover, is a story only recently uncovered.

The Roman Catholic doctrine of Purgatory did not become official Church teaching until the mid-1200s. Later, the Council of Trent (1545–63) emphatically declared: "The Catholic Church . . . [teaches] that there is a purgatory, and that the souls detained in it are helped by the prayers of the faithful."

A century earlier, the Council of Florence had said that souls in Purgatory "are benefited by the suffrages [prayers of intercession] of the living faithful, namely the Sacrifice of the Mass, prayers, alms, and other works of piety."

These two statements, one dogma, one doctrine, occurred during a time of great ferment in the Church, when numerous heresies circulated Europe and the Protestant Revolt threatened. As we'll see, the Church in Rome, to solidify its power, elevated Purgatory to an article of faith in reaction to the adversity it perceived all around it. What Luther denies, the pope dignifies.

Let's begin, as we have in previous chapters, with what the Jews and their Scripture say about the concept.

JEWISH PURGATORY—A SHORT STAY IN HELL: SECOND CENTURY B.C.E. ◆

Although the doctrine of Purgatory is not explicitly stated in the Bible, the belief stems from the Jews' trust in God's fairness and justice.

Jews in the century before the birth of Jesus Christ believed that a person after death is judged according to his or her lifetime of deeds, and that friends and family could pray—and should pray—that God would shower mercy on the soul of the deceased.

The only Old Testament passage that can be cited in support of the doctrine of Purgatory is 2 Maccabees 12:39–46, written mid–second century B.C.E. and part of a book that is noncanonical to Jews and Protestants but canonical to Roman Catholics:

> It is therefore a holy and wholesome thought to pray for the dead that they may be loosed from sins. (2 Macc. 12:46)

In other words, prayer and offerings for the dead can redeem their souls from . . . from where? The Jews weren't sure where souls went to be purified. Maybe Hell? This vagueness didn't concern them, though. The Jews never developed an elaborate map and theology of Purgatory the way Christians would.

In rabbinical literature of the first century C.E., Gehenna or Hell is where souls of the deceased stop off to be scoured pure before continuing on to

Heaven. Some rabbis derived this interpretation from the words of Zechariah:

> *And I will bring the third part through the fire and will refine them as silver is refined; and I will try them as gold is tried. (Zech. 13:9)*

The school of Jewish theology lead by the rabbi Shammai explicitly taught that expiation of sin from a soul is accomplished in the blast furnace of Hell.

The Christian Gospel writers, surprisingly, do not pick up on this Jewish theme. At least not directly.

CHRISTIAN PURGATORY: NEW TESTAMENT EVIDENCE ◆

It is standard Roman Catholic teaching today to point to certain passages of the New Testament that support the doctrine of Purgatory, but the evidence for such support is not clear-cut. Martin Luther was troubled by the Gospel writers' muteness on a subject of such importance.

Traditionally, four passages are cited, none of which is straightforward in suggesting there exists a "third place" for expiation of sin:

• "Whoever speaks against the Holy Spirit, it will not be forgiven him, either in this world or in the world to come" (Matt. 12:32). And: "You shall not come out from *it* until you have paid the last penny" (Matt. 5:26). This is the strongest evidence; *it* is taken to be an indefinite pronoun for Purgatory.

• "May the Lord grant him to find mercy from the Lord on that day" (2 Tim. 1:18). This is Paul's prayer for Onesiphorus, and it seems to hint at a "third place," where the soul, after escape from the body, can find mercy. The reasoning goes: The soul is not yet in Heaven, but still has a chance of getting there.

• The final, and most subtle, citation is in Paul's parable in 1 Corinthians 3:10–15. Indeed, it is so subtle that no single line can be quoted. The parable concerns various Christian preachers working to spread the kingdom of God, and one needs considerable imagination to spot the evidence of Purgatory.

In truth, the Catholic doctrine of Purgatory is based on tradition, not on Sacred Scriptures, which is precisely why Martin Luther and John Calvin denounced it. Luther hedged a bit, granting that *if* Purgatory did indeed exist, and is bright with flames, souls there "sin without intermission so long as they crave for rest or shrink from pain."

CATHOLIC DOCTRINE: FIRST COUNCIL OF LYONS, 1245 C.E. ◆

Christians were rightly troubled by the severity and permanency of Hell. Hell was forever. The furnace was always on "high." There had to be some gentler way to work off the wages of sin before gaining entrance into Heaven.

Church fathers Ambrose, Jerome, and Origen all speculated that there existed a "third place" where a soul dwells between death and the Last Judgment, suffering and meriting grace.

Two theologians, Clement of Alexandria and Origen, were convinced of the existence of such a place because they believed there were two kinds of sinner: the incorrigible one who's hopeless, despicable, and not worth saving; and the occasional offender, racked with guilt, who should be saved. Here we see an emerging distinction between dastardly *mortal sin*, which if unconfessed damns a soul to Hell, and trifling *venial sin*, which if unconfessed at least can be seared off in the "third place."

The problem for Church fathers was where to locate this realm spatially. Some argued that Purgatory—as yet unnamed—was a large antechamber to Heaven, an overheated foyer with no windows, the very place where holy Jews like Abraham had gone before Jesus Christ had opened the gates of Heaven to deceased mortals.

Others wondered if Purgatory might not be located in Upper Gehenna, Upper Hell—a top tier that was bearably hot, tolerably torturous. The very intermediacy of Purgatory's function confounded its spatial indeterminacy.

The First and Second Councils of Lyons (1245 and 1274, respectively) authoritatively established the existence of Purgatory. The Council of Florence in the mid-1400s backed the belief. But it was the Council of Trent in the next century that really put Purgatory on the Christian map. Acting specifically in reaction against Protestant Reformers who denied Purgatory had any Scriptural basis, the council defined Purgatory's location and function, the temperature of the fire, the duration of one's stay, the conditions for leaving, and other theological fine points.

The best way to approach this complex theology is in a question-and-answer format:

IS THERE REAL FIRE IN PURGATORY? Yes, there is. The etymology of the word "purgatory"—purge, Latin *purgare*, "to cleanse"—suggests as much. The official teaching is that the purifying agent is flame. Intense heat is needed to burn off the stain of sin, and punish the sinner. However, a

Roman Catholic is not bound to believe in fire—though Purgatory is dogma, its fire is only preferred teaching.

HOW INTENSE ARE THE FLAMES? This question is discussed less today than in medieval times, when it was the subject of scholarly dissertations. The current belief is that suffering is proportional to the stain of sin on one's soul. The more sin, the more fire needed to cleanse the soul.

For Saint Bonaventure, the delay in seeing God face-to-face in Heaven—the Beatific Vision—was itself more painful than Purgatory's licking flames. Saint Catherine of Genoa claimed that the desire of the soul for God was "an ardent fire" more consuming than any earthly flame.

The Council of Trent suggested, wisely, that priests dignify the profound mystery of Purgatory by excluding from their sermons any fantastic imagery of its fires; that imagery should be saved for Hell. Priests were told that providing details of Purgatory does not edify the faithful, but just confuses them. It "savors of idle curiosity and superstition," as one source put it.

HOW CAN AN IMMATERIAL SOUL SUFFER PAIN? This question was a stumper. Theologians really had to put their heads together to come up with an answer. The soul in Purgatory, though separated from the body, retains in some mysterious way aspects of the material world that render it susceptible to real pain. The soul becomes truly liberated from the material world only after the Final Judgment and bodily resurrection in the Kingdom of God.

This relationship of the soul to matter, even after death, provides a metaphysical basis for fire as the purifying agent.

IF I'M IN PURGATORY, AM I GUARANTEED EVENTUAL SALVATION? You have already achieved salvation, despite the flames. Appearances are deceiving. As a definitive Catholic sourcebook states: "Whether the fact of their salvation becomes known to the departed souls, it is plain that this awareness is one of the greatest joys of Purgatory, preventing it from being merely a place of torture and suffering."

The Beatific Vision will be delayed while fire removes "the last dross and imperfection" from your soul, but now nothing can imperil your salvation and final happiness.

CAN PRAYERS FROM LIVING FAMILY MEMBERS SHORTEN MY STAY IN PURGATORY? The answer is yes, and that's based on the doctrine of the "communion of saints," the commonly bound community of saints in Heaven, souls in Purgatory, and the pious on earth. This implies that the good actions of any one member of the community spiritually benefit all the others, though how this happens, and to what degree each person benefits, remain a formidable mystery. Souls in Purgatory can be assisted by people on earth through prayer, almsgiving, fasting, Mass, various personal sacrifices—and through indulgences.

It was abuse of this last category—a theologically challenging one—that caused the most significant upheaval in the history of Christianity: the Reformation.

WHAT IS AN INDULGENCE? Here, from the *Catholic Encyclopedia*, is an official definition, in legalese, based on the Code of Canon Law. Indulgences are:

> *Authoritative grants from the Church's treasure of Grace for the remission or payment in whole (plenary indulgences) or in part (partial indulgences), valid before God, of the debt of temporal punishment after the guilt of sin has been forgiven.*

PURCHASED INDULGENCES: EARLY ELEVENTH CENTURY C.E. ◆

Grace for cash. Cattle and jewelry to buy off sin. By the sixteenth century, the sale of indulgences had become big business.

There were even accredited brokerage agents of the Church who bartered deals. The financial house of Fugger of Augsburg was a major player in the indulgence market. People were willing participants, believing they'd go straight to Heaven when they died if they just contributed enough money while they were alive. The elderly surrendered their life savings. And no dead person ever came back from the grave to report whether or not the cash-for-grace scheme worked.

The money was supposed to go for the rebuilding of Saint Peter's Basilica in Rome, but some of it was siphoned off by agents, and much of it went into bishops' pockets and the pope's own coffers. The bureaucracy at Rome was costly to maintain. This was a sad era of Church history.

On October 31, 1517, the very day Martin Luther nailed his famous ninety-five grievances on the door of the castle church in Wittenberg, he wrote this harsh critique:

> *Papal indulgences for the building of St. Peter's are hawked about under your illustrious sanction. I regret that the faithful have conceived some erroneous notions about them. These unhappy souls believe that if they buy a letter of pardon they are sure of their salvation; also that souls fly out of purgatory as soon as money is cast into the chest; that the grace conferred is so great that there is no*

Papist indulgence peddlers in the jaws of Hell. From a satiric sixteenth-century Reformation engraving.

sin whatever which cannot be absolved thereby, even if, as they say, taking an impossible example, a man should violate the mother of God.

Had the Church not so egregiously abused indulgences, as we'll see, it is quite likely that Martin Luther's grievances with Rome would have been quietly ironed out, that the Church would have reformed itself, and that Protestantism never would have come into existence. Christianity might have remained *catholic*—from the Latin *catholicus*, meaning "universal," and from the Greek *katholikos*, meaning "completely whole."

The kind of indulgence Luther railed against—the payment of money in lieu of penance—did not exist in Christianity until early in the eleventh century, when it became standard practice to absolve the penitent *before* the fulfillment of his or her penance. Previously, a sinner had been absolved *after* the performance of the penance.

Under the New Deal, a penitent could offer cash to his confessor right in the confessional, or promise livestock or land, and thus avoid having to do penance at all. His contribution "to the building of cathedrals," he was assured, was sacrifice enough to expiate his sins. The system was clearly ripe for abuse.

COMMUNION OF SAINTS: SAINT PAUL, FIRST CENTURY C.E. ◆

Paul had preached in the mid–first century C.E. that membership in the new Church was simultaneously enrollment in the Body of Christ. This collectivism became known as the communion of saints.

This "communion" refers to ongoing communications among three interrelated groups:

- The Blessed already in Heaven, called the *Church Triumphant*;
- The souls being purified in Purgatory, called the *Church Suffering*;
- The faithful on earth, struggling for salvation for themselves and conversion of others, called the *Church Militant*.

The Church father Tertullian expressed the threefold corporate nature of the Church or Body of Christ: "The body cannot rejoice over the misery of one of its members; rather the whole body must suffer and work together for a cure." Thus, from early on, special efficacy was attached to the intercession achieved for all Christians by the suffering of each individual martyr for the faith.

In fact, it was called the *Martyr's Privilege*. A martyr's pain could somehow be credited through confession to minimize the penance required of a sinner. At least in these days money didn't change hands. Just grace. Which, though never cheap, was abundant.

By the ninth century, popes and individual bishops were freely dipping into the Church's treasure of grace to grant certain of the faithful absolution from sin on special holy days. The cleric would announce an "absolution grant" in a parish letter that opened with the phrase "I absolve," and contained a solemn prayer all penitents had to recite to receive the blessing.

PARTIAL INDULGENCE:
FRANCE, EARLY ELEVENTH CENTURY C.E. ◆

The first true indulgences—that is, the remission of temporal punishment for sin that has already been forgiven, thus lessening one's time in Purgatory—were issued by bishops in the south of France early in the eleventh century. Certain short prayers, repeated a prescribed number of times, reduced the number of days, months, or even years one would otherwise have to burn in Purgatory.

These were called *partial* indulgences because they did not purify the soul totally; the soul would still be required to spend some remedial time in Purgatory before passing on to Heaven.

The Church was entering into a period of cathedral-building and construction money was needed. Thus the idea arose that a person who confessed his sins and received, say, a penance of three days of fasting, could, by contributing to the regional building coffer, have his fasting reduced to two days. For a larger contribution, reduced to one day. Money had begun to change hands, and thus arose the potential for abuse.

PLENARY OR CRUSADE INDULGENCES:
POPE URBAN II, 1095 C.E. ◆

The Crusades were a series of military expeditions organized by the Church against the Muslims who, by the end of the eleventh century, had captured the traditional Holy Lands of Christianity. The pope wanted "the infidels" routed out.

The First Crusade, called the "People's Crusade," was launched by Pope Urban II late in the year 1095. Sturdy Christian warriors were needed in large numbers, and the pope offered a deal, saying essentially this: Anyone who joins the Crusade to win back the Holy Land, and dies in battle, will go straight to Heaven; all remedial time that would have been spent in Purgatory is wiped out. This was the first plenary, or full, indulgence.

The 1095 Council of Clermont, under the auspices of Urban II, stated it this way:

> *Whoever from devotion alone, and not for the purposes of gaining honors and wealth, shall set out for the liberation of the Church of God at Jerusalem, that journey will be reckoned in the place of all penance.*

Urban II, in a sermon, made one thing absolutely clear: the plenary indulgence was granted only to those people who had *already confessed their sins*. That was the requirement for skipping Purgatory and going straight to Heaven. Pious men by the thousands enrolled in the First Crusade. Death on the battlefield meant direct ascent to God's abode.

Crusades would continue against the Moors, the Albigenses, and the Turks. For a period of about a hundred years, popes were parsimonious in passing out plenary indulgences. However, by the end of the twelfth century,

Pope Urban II (1088–99) offered full indulgences for any Christian killed in the First Crusade.

Pope Innocent III was handing out full-credit indulgences for anyone who even *assisted* in the Crusade effort—making clothes, signing up recruits—*whether or not he or she went to battle*. This kind of laxity quickly escalated into full-scale abuse of indulgences.

JUBILEE INDULGENCES: POPE BONIFACE VIII, 1300 ◆

Pope Boniface VIII needed money for the papal treasury. On Christmas Day in 1300, he announced the jubilee indulgence: Anyone who made a pilgrimage to Rome, and a monetary contribution to the papacy, received full exemption from Purgatory for sins already confessed. Boniface proclaimed there would be such a jubilee indulgence offered only once every hundred years.

Pope Paul II revised the jubilee grant in the mid-1400s—it would now occur once every twenty-five years. The bureaucracy at Rome had expanded and was costly to support. More money was needed. Now, theoretically, every quarter-century any Catholic could have all residual punishment for sins confessed wiped clear from his or her immortal soul. And now the physical pilgrimage to Rome was no longer mandatory—your contribution could be deposited with the local bishop.

WILD ABUSES ◆

In short, it came to the point where even priests were selling grace. In truth, many cardinals were living like kings, with their own country houses, staffs, chefs, and personal boys' choirs. The selling of indulgences became a quick way to raise cash and sustain a lifestyle.

When clerics hired lay agents, working on commission, to hawk indulgences, the situation spiraled out of control. The agents were called *quaestores*, "promoters."

Pope Sixtus IV (1471–84) extended indulgences to include souls in Purgatory.

In 1476, Pope Sixtus IV extended indulgences to souls already in Purgatory. These were called *indulgences for the dead*. Thus, a loving son could spring his mother's soul from the fires of Purgatory with the appropriate deposit of prayer—and often cash. The sick on their deathbeds made pleas that living relatives purchase postmortem indulgences on their behalf.

It is not an exaggeration to say that now much of an ordinary Catholic's devotional life centered around the greedy acquisition of indulgences, partial and plenary. Indeed, the *Raccolta* was a popular book listing prayers that merited indulgences of specific duration, giving the formulas for winning days, months, and years from burning in Purgatory. Agents for the Church bartered indulgences for livestock and produce from peasants. Many agents were hoaxers, who didn't even represent the Church.

LUTHER'S LAST STAND ◆

Abuse mounted. By the early 1600s, cathedrals and even universities were built with monies acquired through the sale of indulgences. In Germany, theologian and biblical translator Martin Luther decried the abuses and eventually split with Rome, changing the course of the history of religion.

On June 15, 1520, the pope issued the bull *Exsurge Domine*, "Lord, cast out," condemning forty-one of Luther's teachings, and in Rome, Luther's writings were burned.

In a counter-tantrum, Luther and his students staged a bonfire in Wittenberg, burning the papal bull, with Luther proclaiming before the flames: "Because you have corrupted God's truth, may God destroy you in this fire."

In January of the next year, the pope issued the bull of formal excommunication, *Decet Romanum pontificem*. On April 17, Luther, now an official heretic, faced notables of the Church at the Diet of Worms and uttered his final defiance: "Here I stand. I can do no other."

REFORM ◆

Less than twenty years after Luther's death in 1546, the Council of Trent finally ended the abusive practices; shortly thereafter, Pope Pius V (1566–72) revoked all indulgences for which money changed hands: "every indulgence . . . for which a helping hand must be offered, and which contains in any way whatsoever permission to make collections." Thus the Church lost considerable revenue. But gained in integrity.

In 1967, Pope Paul VI, in his Apostolic Constitution *Indulgentiarum Doc-*

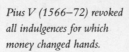

*Pius V (1566–72) revoked
all indulgences for which
money changed hands.*

trina, severely restricted the easy granting of plenary indulgence. Today, the Code of Canon Law limits the power to grant indulgences to the pope, and people he delegates.

DANTE'S *PURGATORIO*: 1319 ◆

The abuse of indulgences helped popularize Purgatory in the popular imagination, and the publication of Dante's *Divine Comedy* was Purgatory's poetic triumph. For literate Christians, Dante showed in graphic detail the tortures that awaited them. No other single work so strongly shaped the images of Purgatory.

The first two books of the trilogy, the *Inferno* (Hell) and the *Purgatorio* (Purgatory)—the third covers Paradise or Heaven—were completed in 1319. They assembled fragmentary themes of Christian damnation into a symphony of indelible sights and sounds. Dante, in a very real sense, *created* the Purgatory that earlier saints and theologians had been struggling to piece together.

Purgatory is divided into seven circles, their circumferences diminishing as a soul moves closer to the summit and escapes into Heaven. Each circle is related to one of the seven deadly sins, which, beginning with the outer circle, are: *pride, envy, wrath, sloth, avarice, gluttony,* and *lust.* (*See* Seven Deadly Sins.) In layering Purgatory, Dante gave to the "third place" the spatial representation and spiritual logic that had eluded Augustine, Clement, and others. It took a poet to bridge the gap between theology and cosmography. For countless Christians, Purgatory became the "Second Kingdom," situated cozily beneath Heaven, and comfortably above Hell.

And, too, it was Dante's genius to structure Purgatory as a climbable mountain, with a harrowingly steep slope, beckoning one on to the glorious summit and a glimpse of God. In the poem, Virgil, the tour guide, literally

RELIGIOUS REALMS

pulls an exhausted Dante along, both men ascending on all fours. The mountain metaphor was the perfect symbol for the soul's purification progress in Purgatory; with each incremental ascent, the soul gets whiter and whiter. When, in the mid-1500s, Church members met at Trent in northern Italy to nail down the doctrine of Purgatory, Dante's masterpiece already had had major influence.

**DEFINING CATHOLICISM:
COUNCIL OF TRENT, 1545 TO 1563 ◆**

Martin Luther had been excommunicated. The German Reformation was underway. Roman Catholicism was under attack. The supremacy of the papacy was being challenged throughout Germany.

Thus, the Council of Trent, the nineteenth such ecumenical council of the Roman Catholic Church, convened by Pope Paul III (1534–49) in an emergency session on December 13, 1545, initiated both sweeping decrees of self-reform and dogmatic definitions that clarified virtually every doctrine contested by Luther and the Protestants.

In addition to making belief in Purgatory dogma, the council, operating between the years 1545 and 1563, made these historic decisions:

• The canon of Old and New Testament books was fixed as the Roman Rite Bible.

• Tradition was accepted as a valid source of faith, and as adequate basis for issuing papal decrees.

• The Latin Vulgate Bible was declared the basis for doctrinal proofs.

• The number of sacred sacraments was fixed at seven: baptism, confirmation, penance, Holy Eucharist, holy orders, matrimony, and extreme unction. (*See* Sacraments.)

• The nature and consequence of original sin were defined. (*See* Original Sin.)

Pope Paul III (1534–49) convened the Council of Trent, which defined "Catholicism."

• The Nicene Creed was accepted as the basis of the Catholic faith. (*See* Creeds.)

• The Transubstantiation or Presence of Christ's body and blood was defined in terms of the Eucharist.

• The Mass was delineated, and defined as a true sacrifice.

• The veneration of saints and relics was officially approved.

Rome was responding to the Reformation by clearly defining, sometimes redefining, what it meant to be a Catholic.

By the end of the sixteenth century, many of the abuses that had motivated the Reformation had disappeared, and the Roman Catholic Church, through strenuous housecleaning, had reclaimed many of its followers throughout Europe.

THE WORD "PURGATORY" IS BORN: 1170 TO 1180 ◆

A remarkable job of linguistic sleuthing is presented by French historian and medievalist Jacques LeGoff in his 1981 book *The Birth of Purgatory*. "The crucial moment came in the second half of the twelfth century when the noun *purgatorium* was added to the vocabulary," writes LeGoff. "Curiously enough, this linguistic event, which in my view is the sign of an important evolution in beliefs about the other world, has until now escaped notice by historians of Purgatory."

LeGoff claims that the noun very probably made its first appearance between the years 1170 and 1180. And he proves that several earlier appearances of the word were, in fact, nothing more than the result of later translations that substituted "purgatory" for vague terms like the "third place."

LeGoff's detective work is masterful. For instance, in an eleventh-century sermon of priest Peter Damian, we find the domain for temporary punishment called *loca purgatoria*—which seems quite explicit. But, in fact, the sermon turns out to be not the work of Peter Damian but of a later notorious forger, Nicholas of Clairvaux, secretary to Saint Bernard. LeGoff disproves many such early appearances of the noun "purgatory" as either deliberate forgeries or retranslations of texts in which the word was added.

LeGoff concludes that the noun *purgatorium* is first found in a letter sent in 1176 by the English Benedictine monk Nicholas of Saint Albans—to the Cistercian monk Peter of Celle. The Latin sentence containing the new word is: "*Porro facto levi per purgatorium transitu intravit in gaudium Domini sui"*—"In turn, having been released from purgatory, he proceeded into the joy of his Lord."

Furthermore, the two corresponding monks, in addition to one Peter Comestor, a secular master in the school of Notre Dame in Paris, had for a few years been bandying the word about.

LeGoff discovered that for vernacular languages, the earliest mention of Purgatory in French occurs in the form *espurgatorie* around 1190, in a text by Marie de France, *Espurgatorie Saint Patriz.*

Finally, dictionaries and glossaries of medieval Latin do not record the noun *purgatorium* until the year 1254. The "third place" got a proper name. Of course, the noun did not materialize suddenly out of linguistic thin air. The medieval monks had shaped the proper noun from the old Latin verb for "cleansing," *purgare.*

What's the present state of belief on Purgatory?

Roman Catholics must believe in the doctrine; and the Blessed Virgin Mary holds the title Queen of Purgatory, that is, Mary is the major intermediary between God and the prayers of the living on behalf of souls suffering in Purgatory.

Most members of Protestant and Eastern Orthodox Churches still challenge the concept of Purgatory as unbiblical. Some theologians of Eastern Christianity, though not all, concede the existence of a "third place" between Heaven and Hell, but regard it as more of a place for meditation and spiritual growth than for expiatory suffering through flames.

Limbo

Original Sin to the Harrowing

To BE "in limbo" is popular jargon for being trapped in an indeterminate state midway between more solid locations. The word is from the Latin *limbus*, meaning "edge" or "borderland."

In Christian theology, Limbo is the name of a celestial locale. The concept arose early in Church history in response to two thorny dilemmas:

DILEMMA NUMBER ONE: Where does the soul of an innocent infant go if the baby dies before being baptized? To consign the child to Hell seemed harsh. However, to allow the child's soul, soiled by Adam's sin, access to Heaven contradicts the basic Christian concept of salvation through a water rebirth.

SOLUTION: The Church created a new celestial realm called *limbus infantum*, Children's Limbo, cosmographically bordering Heaven just to the "south"; *below*, that is. All unbaptized infants and dead fetuses, throughout all time, are still in Limbo awaiting the Last Judgment, when they'll be resurrected in body, cleansed of original sin, and ushered into Heaven. At which time, *limbus infantum* will become a ghost town.

DILEMMA NUMBER TWO: Abraham and the Old Testament patriarchs were holy men, disadvantaged (in Christians' eyes) by having died before Jesus Christ redeemed humankind and opened the gates of Heaven to the souls of mortals. So, too, were honorable pagans like Aristotle and Plato. Where, in the intervening centuries, had virtuous souls languished?

SOLUTION: The Church created a nexus Limbo, *limbus patrum*, the Fathers' Limbo, specifically for Old Testament saints and good-hearted pagans. *Limbus patrum* has already been emptied out due to Christ's opening of Heaven to the souls of mortals. Abraham, Plato, and the others have spiritually ascended, breaking through the glass ceiling into Heaven.

> **THE FATE OF GOOD JEWS** ◆ *It should be pointed out that today some Catholic theologians refuse to dismantle Fathers' Limbo. Instead, they reserve it for the souls of good modern Jews, benevolent Buddhists, holy Hindus, moral Muslims—all decent but disadvantaged non-Christians who don't qualify for Christian Heaven. Only after the Last Judgment will Heaven swing open its pearly gates to righteous peoples of all faiths.*

EARLY BAPTISM ◆

Limbo has always been a murky, makeshift construct, and it's given theologians nothing but difficulty for centuries. No pope has dared make Limbo dogma, and to this day, Limbo remains one of the few unsettled fine points of theology. Limbo is in limbo.

To avoid sending innocent newborns who die to Limbo, the Holy Office of the Pope, as recently as 1958, advised parents and parish priests:

> *The practice has arisen in some places of delaying the conferring of Baptism for so-called reasons of convenience. . . . The Holy Father warns the faithful that infants are to be baptized as soon as possible.*

Who dreamed up the mythic realms of Children's Limbo and Fathers' Limbo?

First, we must examine the origin of the doctrine of original sin, which is, after all, the hereditary taint of guilt that makes the concept of Limbo necessary.

ORIGINAL SIN: SAINT PAUL, MID–FIRST CENTURY c.e. ◆

Wit and atheist Oscar Wilde is alleged to have quipped: "No sin is worth committing unless it's original."

In Christian theology, original sin is the hereditary smudge on the soul of every mortal (except the Blessed Virgin Mary) due to the disobedience of the first man, Adam.

OLD TESTAMENT EVIDENCE. Hebrew Scriptures make no explicit reference to the transmission of hereditary guilt to the entire human race. However, the roots of the concept are clearly present. The fall of man, as recounted in chapter three of Genesis, results in the sorriest aspects of the human condition: pain, suffering, death, injustice, and an inclination to wickedness.

In the Gospels, too, we find no explicit definition of hereditary sin, only allusions that link Adam's lawbreaking and universal dishonor.

The concept of original sin, as formally defined by the Council of Trent in the sixteenth century, comes first from the writing of Saint Paul, and is elaborated upon some three hundred years later by Saint Augustine. Paul can be vague on the matter; Augustine, on the other hand, is strident, unbending, and unequivocal.

PAUL'S TEXT. The primary scriptural affirmation of original sin is found in Paul's Letter to the Romans, written about 57 C.E. The lines are contained in a difficult passage (5:12–19) in which Paul establishes a parallel between Adam and Christ, stating that whereas *sin and death* entered the world through Adam's fall—"death reigned from Adam to Moses, even over those who had not sinned"—*grace and eternal life* have come through Christ's Redemption.

Paul, an inveterate traveler, was probably in Corinth at the time, writing to Rome, capital of an empire that stretched from Britain to Arabia, wealthy, cosmopolitan, with all the accompanying temptations. Paul's most often quoted line to back universal sin is: "By one man's disobedience many were made sinners."

Centuries before, in the same spirit, an Old Testament psalmist wrote (51:5): "I was brought forth in iniquity, and in sin did my mother conceive me."

AUGUSTINE'S CONDEMNATION OF THE UNBAPTIZED: FOURTH CENTURY C.E. ◆

Augustine pushed the concept of original sin to perplexing depths. The Church still frets over and regrets the great saint's venomous attack on innocent infants:

> *Those unfortunate children who die without baptism must face the judgment of God. They are vessels of contumely, vessels of wrath, and the wrath of God is upon them.*

In public debates, Augustine often worked himself into a righteous rage on the matter:

Baptism is the only thing that can deliver these unfortunate infants from the kingdom of death and the power of the devil. If no one frees them from the grasp of the devil, what wonder is it that they must suffer in flames with him?

He answers rhetorically: "There can be no doubt about the matter: they will go into eternal fire with the devil."

Later theologians argued that Augustine didn't really mean what he so vehemently shouted. The saint, said apologists, was only lashing out at a group of heretics known as the Pelagians, who denied original sin; Augustine had to be harsh in defense of the doctrine. If privately Augustine had compassion for the souls of innocents, he never committed those gentle views to paper.

Unfortunately, the Church, often with a hard swallow, agreed with Augustine for the next five centuries. No one can estimate the number of unbaptized babies that "went to Hell" due to errant theology.

As we're about to see, a somewhat softer stand, and one supported by Thomas Aquinas, claimed that unbaptized infants, who do not possess the intellect to sin on their own, suffer the "pain of loss" of God but not the "pain of sense" of fire. In direct contradiction to Augustine's fiery view.

CHILDREN'S LIMBO:
PETER ABELARD, ELEVENTH CENTURY c.e. ◆

The man who finally broke with Augustine's stern view was Peter Abelard (1079–1144), a brilliant scholar, logician, moral philosopher, unwilling eunuch at an early age, and all-around maverick of the Middle Ages.

In *Sic et Non*—"Yes and No"—the controversial young teacher collected religious and biblical quotations that pricked the inconsistencies in Church doctrine. In Paris, where he taught at the university, Abelard fathered a child by his beautiful private pupil Heloise, whom he then secretly married. The young woman's wealthy and enraged uncle had Abelard arrested, bound, and brutally castrated. Hot-blooded Heloise was dispatched to a nunnery, a common fate for passionate women at the time. The emasculated Abelard entered the abbey of Saint-Denis, unrepentant, and penned a testy autobiography of his turbulent life, *Historia calamitatum*, "History of My Troubles."

His clever idea was simple enough: Yes, unbaptized children are tainted with Adam's sin, but upon death, they are not condemned to Hell. Nor are they allowed in Heaven proper, where souls rejoice in the presence of the Creator. Rather, the children go to a suburb of Heaven, not yet named Limbo, from which they cannot catch a glimpse of God. Thus, the punishment for uncleansed souls is to suffer the grief of separation from the Lord. "Darkness," as Abelard portrayed the bittersweet state.

"Punishment," said Abelard, "consists of this alone: that they are in darkness, that they are deprived of the vision of the divine majesty without any hope of attaining it." His views were concisely summed up at the time by the archbishop of Paris, Peter Lombard, in his theological tract *Sentences*, on which Thomas Aquinas cut his doctrinal teeth. Subsequent saints and scholars—especially Aquinas and Bonaventure—embraced Abelard's humane idea wholeheartedly. Limbo for children was so much more charitable a fate than Hell.

Albert the Great is believed to have coined the name "Limbo"—though in Albert's day, Limbo was thought to border Hell, not Heaven.

As to Peter Abelard's fate: after he was condemned for challenging the concept of the Trinity, he became an abbott, joined forces with his beloved Sister Heloise, and the abbott and the nun founded a new religious order of nuns. In death, the lovers were buried side by side.

MODERN LIMBO: POPE PIUS XII, 1939–58 ◆

Over the next three centuries, Abelard's view of a benign "darkness" for the unbaptized was kept alive through a popular catechism of the period: the *Elucidarium* of theologian Honorius of Autun. Written in Latin and translated into German and French (more than sixty French copies survive), Honorius's "Elucidation" accomplished exactly what its title promised: it spelled out church teachings in straightforward language for priests and their flocks.

The Church allowed theologians to debate the validity of the doctrine of Children's Limbo. Several Church councils—especially the sixteenth-century Council of Trent—wrestled with prickly fine points of Limbo and original sin. For instance, do all human beings—Chinese, Africans, Eskimos—descend from Adam and Eve? If Eskimos are unaware of their biblical ties to Adam and his sin, is it fair to stigmatize them with hereditary guilt from ancestors they don't even know they have?

Truly, can any newborn child be held responsible for a four-thousand-year-old crime of its ancient forebear?

Ironically, just when popular piety among ordinary folk was beginning to question the existence of Limbo, a pope spoke out strongly in its favor.

TEST TUBE EMBRYOS. Pope Pius XII (1939–58) addressed a convention of Italian midwives on the necessity of baptism, when he seemed, in the opinion of many theologians, to go too far: "In an adult, an act of love may suffice to obtain him sanctifying grace and so supply for the lack of baptism. To the child still unborn, or newly born, this way is not open."

Nor is any other way, the pontiff told the attentive audience. The midwives, he advised, have a duty to quickly summon a priest to baptize each newborn or else that infant will . . .

Well, the pope didn't explicitly say. But he seemed to imply that an unbaptized infant is condemned to Peter Abelard's "darkness." To *limbo infantum*. No previous pope had ever come so close to nailing down Limbo as doctrine. Although the pontiff had not been speaking infallibly, many conservative theologians immediately claimed that Pius XII had officially embraced the concept of Limbo.

Today, more than ever, due to modern conception technology, Limbo is a theologically relevant concept. Infants with souls are conceived in test tubes; other embryos with souls are frozen and perhaps later destroyed. What is the fate of these unbaptized souls?

MODERN VIEWS. Many Christians—particularly those of the Anglican, Roman Catholic, Lutheran, Eastern Orthodox, Methodist, and Presbyterian Churches—believe that Adam's sin stains the soul of each newborn. Yet, when pressed on the issue, most Christians refuse to believe that an innocent newborn who dies without baptism would be deprived of the glory of Heaven.

On the other hand, the doctrine of original sin itself is denied by most members of the Baptist, Assemblies of God, and Pentecostal Churches. They cannot conceive of a merciful God tainting the soul of any newborn. Simply put: Sin cannot be inherited. Not even Adam's.

Was any human ever born free of original sin?

Only the Virgin Mary, Mother of God; according to Saint Augustine: "[All are born sinners] except the Holy Virgin Mary, whom I desire, for the sake of the honor of the Lord, to leave entirely out of the question when the talk is of sin."

Fourteen centuries later, on December 8, 1854, Pope Pius IX made Saint Augustine's wish Church law. In his papal decree *Ineffabilis Deus*, he authenticated the doctrine of the Immaculate Conception of Mary: the Mother of God was not only born free of original sin, but born "without concupiscence," without the weakness to sin in any human way. (*See* Immaculate Conception.)

HARROWING OF HELL: MATTHEW AND LUKE, C. 65–75 C.E. ◆

The idea that Jesus Christ died and was entombed on a Friday and was resurrected on Sunday morning raises the question: How did Jesus spend the three-day interim, known theologically as the *triduum*?

He was not idle. In fact, the question has had two answers.

DESCENT INTO HELL. The first answer has Jesus descending into Hell to rout the forces of Satan, and conquer the powers of death and evil. This mission goes by the chilling name of the Harrowing. It is a central part of the major Christian creed, the Apostles' Creed: "[Christ] suffered under Pontius Pilate, was crucified, died, and buried; he descended into hell. The third day he rose again from the dead."

One origin traditionally given in support of this concept is Matthew 12:40: "For even as Jonas was in the belly of the fish three days and three nights, so will the Son of Man be three days and three nights in the heart of the earth."

An even less explicit statement is found in Luke's Acts of the Apostles 2:24: "God has raised him up, having loosed the sorrows of hell, because it was not possible that he should be held fast by it."

In truth, the concept of the Harrowing grew in popular legend during the second and third centuries. It had ample precedent in mythology. Descent into the underworld was a journey undertaken by numerous Greek and Roman gods and heroes, including Odysseus, Hercules, Persephone, and Aeneas. In fact, a god's mettle was measured by his face-to-face confrontation with demons in their own domain. If he emerged unscathed, he was a greater god.

A VISIT TO FATHERS' LIMBO. The second and later answer as to how Jesus Christ spent the *triduum* has the Savior dropping in on Adam, Eve, Old Testament patriarchs, and virtuous Greeks like Plato and Socrates.

In support of this view, which had gained popularity by the fourth century, Church fathers pointed to Peter's First Epistle (3:18–19), written about 64 C.E.: "Put to death in the flesh, he was brought to life in the spirit, and he went and preached to the spirits in prison." In the prison of Fathers' Limbo.

Still another text has Jesus enter Fathers' Limbo to preach the Christian Gospel of salvation to old-time Jews and Greeks, then ushering the new converts into Heaven. Here the *triduum* is presented as an evangelical mission to save the souls of those who had died before the Christian faith existed.

The word "harrowing" supports this second view: "harrow" is from the Old Norse *harfn*, meaning "to harvest." The risen Jesus harvested the souls from Fathers' Limbo.

"TESTAMENT OF THE TWELVE PATRIARCHS": FIRST CENTURY B.C.E. ◆

It is possible that the true origin of the Harrowing of Hell is a popular Jewish tale, "Testament of the Twelve Patriarchs," which dates from a century before Christ's birth. In this story, the Messiah-to-come visits the nether kingdom of Baal, the ruler of Hell, in order to rescue righteous men and women whom the Devil has unjustly imprisoned there.

Early Christian writers might well have borrowed from the story, and at least by the third century, the Gospel of Bartholomew clearly has substituted Jesus Christ as liberator of the patriarchs.

The most complete and influential account of Christ's descent into Hell/Limbo is found in the fifth-century Gospel of Nicodemus, a bizarre rewrite of text from the canonical Gospels. Nicodemus elaborates on Christ's trial and Crucifixion, supposedly using as his source word-of-mouth tradition. In a section titled the "Harrowing of Hell," he has two sons of the high priest Simeon, who have risen from the grave themselves to bear witness to Christ's Resurrection, continue the story. It seems that Christ's Crucifixion was arranged by Satan, but the event backfired when the dead Christ descended into Hell to give Satan a tongue-lashing and liberate souls unjustly imprisoned there.

Surprisingly, few Christian theologians questioned Nicodemus's account. Probably because it filled two crucial functions. First, it liberated from Hell Old Testament saints like Abraham, plus Adam and Eve, plus good pagans like Plato. Indeed, Jesus comes off as the Great Liberator. Second, the story paints Jesus as a warrior-prince, waging vigorous battles with the Devil and his demons. Jesus triumphs; Satan is shamed. The story was too good to pick apart.

Consequently, subsequent popes and saints accepted as fact that Christ, between midday Good Friday and early Easter Sunday morning, routed the Devil and his denizens. By entering the Apostles' Creed, the Harrowing became an integral part of Christ's Passion.

Only centuries later, when the concept of the Fathers' Limbo gained favor, did theologians claim that Christ had descended not into Hell but visited *limbus patrum*.

DANTE ON LIMBO ◆

In his *Divine Comedy*, Dante struggles with the confusing existence of two parallel Limbos, one for sages of the ancient world, one for unbaptized babies of the Christian world. Rather than clarifying things, his great masterwork actually makes the matter of Limbo more of a muddle. The denizens of these two realms obsess Dante throughout his long pilgrimage in the netherworld. In *Il Purgatorio*, he specifically mentions Aristotle and Plato as being liberated by Christ's Harrowing. But liberated sages, as well as the freed souls of unchristened children, do not go to Heaven, but to the cooler, uppermost reaches of Hell, its so-called First Circle, which boasts a *nobile castello* (noble castle), surrounded by "a green meadow" that blooms year-round.

No pope, theologian, or saint has ever been really comfortable with the makeshift construct called Limbo. Limbo remains to this day a foggy shade of theological gray. It seems to exist only to solve the two dilemmas presented at the opening of this chapter.

PART

XII

N. S. DE MISERICORDIA, CON SUS TRES MARTI.
VENERADOS EN SU ERMITA DE LA VILLA DE REUS.

Acts
of Faith

iracles

Raising the Dead to Stigmata

WHAT A MIRACLE IS ◆

"The dearest child of faith" is Goethe's description of a wondrous deed attributed to divine power.

"Miracles are propitious accidents, the natural causes of which are too complicated to be clearly understood" is Santayana's critical view.

"A miracle does not happen in contradiction to nature," espoused Saint Augustine, *"but in contradiction to that which is known to us of nature."*

"Believe the works," advised Jesus of his own wonderworks, *"that you may know and understand that the Father is in me"* (John 10:38). To that, Saint Thomas Aquinas said: "Christ was either a liar, lunatic, or Lord."

Poet Walt Whitman effused: *"To me every hour of the light and dark is a miracle, Every cubic inch of space a miracle."*

About eighteen hundred years ago, a number of Talmudic scholars held a view of miracles somewhat similar to that of Santayana's. Their concern was over the Bible's many "mighty works"—Moses' parting of the Red Sea, the mysterious manna from Heaven, Elijah's fireball from the sky—and how to harmonize such sudden supernatural ruptures with nature's otherwise seamless order. After all, seas don't normally split open and conveniently shut.

The rabbis concluded, cleverly, that the biblical happenings called miracles were actually preordained events, which at the time of Creation God programmed into nature as part of natural order. "God made an agreement with the sea" at the time of Creation, explained one rabbi, "that it would split in half when it would be approached by the Israelites" epochs later. Hence, a miracle is not a break with natural order, but fulfillment of the master plan. Maybe this is what Saint Augustine had in mind, too.

Many devoutly religious people have been deeply troubled by miraculous

*Jesus cures a man
blind from birth*

happenings. Even Jesus, who performed some forty spectacular feats, repeat-edly cautioned witnesses to "tell no one what you saw" (Luke 8:56). Jesus feared that some folk would jump to conclusions and confuse a miracle with magic; faith with trickery; a prophet with a sorcerer.

No wonder, given the marvels Christ produced. On at least eight occa-sions, he pulled heavenly rank on the forces of nature: Jesus *calmed a storm* (Matt. 8:23–27), *walked on water* (14:25), *withered a fig tree* (21:18–22), *multi-plied five barley loaves and two fishes* to feed thousands (14:15–21), and *turned water into wine* at his mother's behest (John 2:1–11).

And, overriding the forces of life and death, Jesus brought back from the grave *Lazarus* (John 11:1–44), the *widow's son at Nain* (Luke 7:11–15), and *Jairus's daughter* (8:41–42). Most numerous of all, though, where Christ's heal-ing miracles—more on this later.

WORD ORIGIN. In ancient times, people did not suspect that there ex-isted impersonal "laws of nature." Rather, they believed that gods and god-desses governed everything that happened in the world. The miracles recounted in the Hebrew Scripture were not considered violations of natural laws but rather signs that revealed God's ever-present sovereignty.

Today, we use the word "miracle"—from the Latin *miraculum*, meaning "a strange thing"—to describe an occurrence that contradicts scientific laws. But in the primitive past, a miracle was not unlike a scientific explanation.

That a miracle is something wonderful is inherent in the derivation of the Latin *miraculum*, which is preceded by the Indo-European root *mei*, meaning "to be surprised," and the Sanskrit *mayati*, meaning "he smiles." Implying: Something strange happens and one smiles.

Today, too, we in the West tend to overlook the fact that other cultures hold starkly different views of miraculous happenings. In fact, as we'll see, even within modern America, Jews, Protestants, charismatics, and Roman Catholics regard miracles in different ways.

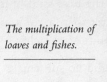

The multiplication of loaves and fishes.

Before examining miracles in the Judeo-Christian tradition, there is wisdom to be gleaned from how the world's other religions regard miraculous events.

HINDUISM—"MAGIC" EVERYONE CAN PERFORM: 1500 B.C.E. ◆

In India's major religion, the view on miracles is remarkably democratic. Miracles spring quite naturally from the performance of ascetic rituals and the chanting of mantras. Thus, any man or woman who follows the path of Yoga—the Hindu philosophy that teaches how to rise above mind and body toward enlightenment—can possess miraculous powers.

Miracles are innumerable, and go unchallenged, in the Hindu world. This is why India was long known as the "land of wonders." Anything could happen. To anyone. At any time. For most ordinary folk, this still holds true.

Holy texts like the Upanishads and the Brahmanas consider a person's supreme aim not the performance of miracles, though, but the individual attainment of insight and mystical enlightenment. Yet, neither text belittles miracles, nor questions their reality, nor the holiness of people who perform them. Miraculous wonders are, in short, side effects of individual spirituality.

BUDDHISM—THREE KINDS OF WONDERS: SIXTH CENTURY B.C.E. ◆

The Buddha refused to spread his teachings merely by impressing his audience with the dazzle of miracles—and yet miraculous happenings trailed in his wake. Like Jesus "The Christ" ("anointed one"), Gautama "The Buddha" ("enlightened one") walked from village to village and miracles happened all around him. He deprecated the powers he possessed as devoid of spiritual significance. (Nonetheless, his relics or mortal remains—several teeth and two collarbones now in various shrines—are still believed to be working wonders today. *See* Relics.)

Rather, Gautama Buddha viewed the best kind of miracle as one that *instructs*; all others were not much better than a conjuror's tricks. In fact, the Buddha taught that there are three kinds of miracles:

• The miracle of *magic*—all show and no substance;

• The miracle of *thought reading* or telepathy, worthwhile at times to read into a person's heart but intrusive and not to be encouraged; and

• The miracle of *instruction*—the only miracle worthy of awe and reverence.

The appropriate counterpart in Christianity to a "miracle of magic" is the dramatic physical upheavals that accompany Christ's three-hour Agony on the cross: flashy, ominous ruptures in natural law. For instance: at noon, "there was darkness over the whole land" (Mark 15:33), "the curtain of the temple was torn in two, from top to bottom" (Matt. 27:51), an earthquake struck at the moment of Jesus' death, and "the tombs also were opened, and many bodies of the saints who had fallen asleep were raised" (Matt. 27:52). This is the miracle as "special effects"—it doesn't so much teach as terrify.

Like the Buddha, scholars from all faiths have argued over the centuries that perhaps miracles are best understood as allegorical and poetic expressions of God's greatness; the miracle as parable—meant only to teach a lesson.

ISLAMIC MIRACLES—ALLAH'S CONTINUAL RE-CREATION OF NATURE: SEVENTH CENTURY C.E. ◆

The Prophet Muhammad, according to the Koran, explicitly rejected the idea of proving his vocation by performing miracles, though later narratives of his life embellished it with numerous miraculous moments. Muhammad claimed that the Koran itself was the greatest miracle of miracles, and that he was no wonder-worker but merely a human messenger preaching repentance.

Today, the Islamic faith holds that Allah works miracles and has done so in the past through such prophets as Moses, Solomon, and Jesus, but, significantly, not through the Islamic Prophet Muhammad himself. The Koran, the "miracle of miracles," is viewed as God's final revelation to humankind, superseding both the Old and New Testaments, and since there will be no more Sacred Scriptures ever, there is no longer a need for miracles that im-press, inspire, and strike awe and fear in the human heart. The Last Great Miracle was the Koran.

Nonetheless, everyday people like an occasional miracle. Indeed, people of all faiths seem to *need* miracles. Thus, popular Islam, particularly Sufi mysticism, abounds in miraculous cures, as well as pilgrimages to the tombs of wonder-working saints, sites equivalent in the Christian world to Lourdes and Fátima.

A peculiar feature of Islamic theology is that, unlike Christian and Jewish theologies, it did not adopt the idea of nature operating in accordance to fixed laws ordained by the Creator at the beginning of time. Rather, the universe is continually being re-created by Allah, altered and reshaped as time passes. Thus, technically, what a Muslim sees as a "miracle" is in truth merely Allah departing from his regular habits to do a bit of re-creating.

Muslim dogmatics distinguish between two kinds of wonders:

• *Marvels* or *karamat* that Allah allows his saints to perform as evidence of his approval of them, and of people's petitions made through the saints; and

• *Signs* or *ayat*—also *mu'jizat*; literally, "acts of an overwhelming nature." These wonderworks are wrought by Allah to prove the genuineness of his holy men and to overwhelm and reduce to silence their opponents. The Jewish prophets of the Old Testament often worked these "political" miracles to intimidate their oppressors; as did Christ's disciples. This is the miracle as put-down—God saying: "I'll show you whose side I'm on."

Not all Muslims believe in miracles. Orthodox zealots, such as the Wahhabis, have on numerous occasions destroyed the tombs and shrines of saints because they consider the cult of veneration—and the magic of "bogus" miracles—incompatible with true Islam.

Next we look at the "mighty works" in Judaism, then in Christianity—for the two faiths hold drastically different views on miracles.

HEBREW MIRACLE WORKERS—A METHOD TO THEIR MADNESS: OLD TESTAMENT TIMES ◆

In Judaism, miracles are taken for granted throughout the Old Testament. Indeed, miraculous events provide the entire framework for biblical history, from the opening line of Genesis: "In the beginning God created the heavens and the earth." Thus the tone for the text that follows is mightily struck. Miracles are to be everywhere in the Old Testament.

At least two *animals talk*: the serpent in the Garden of Eden, and the ass belonging to the Mesopotamian seer named Balaam. In Numbers 22:28, God "opened the mouth of the ass" and the poor donkey complained about its abusive treatment.

Heavenly fire is one of the most frequent miracles, and symbols of God's power. "The Lord your God is a devouring fire" (Deut. 4:24), so Moses warned the Israelites. When God first appears to Moses, it is "in a flame of fire out of the midst of a bush" (Exod. 3:2). God guides his people during their Exodus in a "pillar of fire" by night (Exod. 13:21), and he descends on Mount Sinai "in fire" (19:18). And at least four times the Bible describes "divine fire" that consumes a sacrifice, thereby demonstrating God's approval of the offering.

A PATTERN. In the Old Testament, miracles reveal an interesting pattern: *extraordinary events occur most often in times of profound crisis or bewildering transition.* Something "extraordinary" happens in times when the "ordinary" will not do. Often the prophets are mad and make miracles happen.

At the time of the Israelites' daring flight from Egypt, God gave them their first superior miracle worker, eighty-year-old Moses—who'd been absent from both his own people and the court of Egypt for forty years. Moses needed to work flashy, flamboyant miracles to convince the Israelites he was their liberator. In order to carry out God's various plans, Moses' *staff changes into a snake, he calls down ten plagues on Egypt, parts the Red Sea,* and *coaxes water to flow from rock.*

At another time of peril, a whole series of miracles marks Joshua's conquest of Canaan—from the *parting of the Jordan River,* to the *fall of the walls of Jericho,* to the *sun standing still at Gibeon* as a sign God took Joshua's side in the battle against the five Amorite kings.

Two of the greatest Hebrew miracle workers were Elijah and Elisha, born after the tumultuous division of Israel into northern and southern kingdoms. More trouble; more miracles. The Books of Kings show how the supernatural works of Elijah and Elisha—*parting the Jordan, purifying water, separating poison from stew*—helped the Israelites keep their faith alive when it was threatened by the worship of the pagan god Baal.

In fact, Elijah punishes Israel's King Ahab for worshiping the rain and storm god Baal by miraculously invoking a drought on the region. Before he prays for the drought's end, he challenges Ahab's 450 pagan prophets to a miracle contest on Mount Carmel. Elijah watches the pagan magicians hour after hour implore Baal to send down his fire to burn their offering. When they are exhausted, Elijah prays to his God and immediately fire descends, devouring his offering and the altar on which it lay. Then he promptly, and miraculously, slays all 450 of Baal's prophets. This last, in Buddhism, is the kind of miracle that teaches a lesson; in Islam, it is the kind of "political" miracle that intimidates the opposition.

"JESUS DID NOT PERFORM MIRACLES"—THE JEWISH VIEW: TALMUDIC TIMES ◆

The Jews, who through the Old Testament gave the world some of its greatest miracles, soon backed off from their belief in miraculous happenings. In fact, they did an about-face. Many Talmudic and post-Talmudic scholars held the opinion that miracles were to be taken as allegorical expressions of God's greatness. The miracle as metaphor.

For instance: Exodus, in relating Israel's battle with its archenemy, the Amalekites, says (17:11): "And it came to pass, when Moses held up his hand, Israel prevailed; and when he put down his hand, Amalek prevailed." The rabbis of the Talmud insisted that the event was not to be taken literally—indeed, miracles are not literal happenings—but as merely a message, by way of allegory, that as long as the Children of Israel "look up" (Moses' raised hand) to their Father in Heaven, they will prevail; if they "look down" (Moses' dropped hand) they will be defeated.

By parallel argument, consider Jesus' walking on water:

Fierce winds batter the boat carrying Christ's disciples across the stormy Sea of Galilee. It's past 3 A.M., they've been rowing since nightfall and are exhausted and frightened, when from out of the dim gray moonlight materializes a fluttering figure in white. "It's a ghost!" the disciples cry. As they stare, paralyzed with terror, a voice speaks to them: "Take heart, it is I; have noth-

Jesus walking on the water.

ing to fear." Peter challenges Christ. "Lord, if it is you, bid me come to you on the water." Jesus beckons: "Come" (Matt. 14:27–29). With his eyes raised and fixed on Jesus, Peter steps on the raging waves. But the instant he glances away from Jesus—down at the dark depths—he's gripped with fear and sinks.

The moral: Throughout life, a Christian must keep his or her eyes focused on Jesus, for only Christ can save. Glance away and you're lost.

This figurative manner of interpreting the Bible's great wonderworks was given wide acceptance by the greatest Jewish scholars, men like Saadya Gaon, and the philosopher, jurist, and physician Moses Maimonides. Maimonides, in fact, the foremost intellectual figure of medieval Judaism, stated flatly in his masterwork, *Guide for the Perplexed*—a book that influenced Jewish and non-Jewish scholars alike—that all miracles described in the Bible in connection with the careers of the prophets must be understood only as prophetic visions, never as literal happenings.

Since Talmudic scholars reject the idea that the laws of nature can be contravened, it's not surprising that Jews refuse to accept Jesus as a miracle worker. Jesus was a prophet; Jesus was a holy man; but Jesus could not bend and twist the laws of nature. Mainstream Judaism teaches that God himself would never pull rank on the natural laws he so lovingly put in motion at the beginning of time.

Even those Jews who today might believe in miracles do not do so with the aggressiveness that Christians do. For many Jews, miracles might have happened in their past but don't today.

For Christians, however, miracles are happening every day. This should not be surprising, since the greatest number of miracles in the Bible, Old and New Testaments combined, occur bunched into the brief ministry of Jesus Christ.

NEW TESTAMENT—CHRIST, THE BIBLE'S CHIEF WONDER-WORKER: EARLY CHRISTIANITY ◆

Jesus Christ himself had an ambiguous attitude toward miracles—though he performed at least forty, according to the New Testament.

On the one hand, Christ performed miracles as a sign of his mission and the impending coming of the Kingdom of God. "Believe the works that you may know and understand that the Father is in me and I am in the Father" (John 10:38). As proof, he fed five thousand men, women, and children with only five barley loaves and two fishes. Interestingly, this is the only miracle of Christ's ministry that appears in all Four Gospels. (His postmortem miracle, when he appears to his disciples following his Resurrection, doesn't count, since by then, he's indisputably God.) The miracle of the loaves and fishes recalls the time the Old Testament prophet Elisha fed a hundred people with twenty small barley loaves, and had leftovers to spare.

On the other hand, Jesus disapproved of people's desire for "mighty wonders." "Why does this generation ask for a sign?" an angry Jesus demanded. That is why he refused the Devil's dare to jump from the highest point of the Temple to reveal the manner of man he was. He repeatedly forbade his disciples to publicize his miracles—"Tell no one what you saw"—insisting that it was faith alone that worked miracles. If a person has faith, Christ said, then the miraculous can happen.

This is very much in tune with the modern-day perspective on, say, miraculous healings from incurable diseases. Many a modern Christian would say: Belief that a cure from cancer is possible can actually bolster that person's immune system, which in turn brings about the cure. We say "Christ healed a leper" (Matt. 8:2–3), but Christ said that the diseased man's belief in the Son of God caused his body to rally and conquer his leprosy. Faith heals; though human nature likes to personify a miracle by attributing it to a prophet.

The same could be said for all the lame who walked in Christ's presence, all the mute who spoke, the blind who saw—even the dead who woke; they might have been in comas. At least this is how many Christians today justify miraculous healings to themselves.

In fact, many prominent Christian scholars argue that the miracles of the New Testament are meant as metaphor and allegory—literary attempts by the writers of the Four Gospels to paint a persuasive and an indelible picture of Jesus Christ.

RAISING LAZARUS FROM THE DEAD:
GOSPEL OF JOHN, 11:1–44 ◆

This famous event is not mentioned anywhere in the three synoptic Gospels of Mark, Matthew, and Luke. Which is odd, for the miracle of raising Lazarus from the dead, so vividly pictured by John, is the very climax of Jesus' wonderworks on earth.

Indeed, the episode is described as taking place in public, witnessed by many who are dumbstruck, and it achieves such instant fame as to be the final straw that drives the Pharisees to have Jesus convicted and executed. How could Mark, Matthew, and Luke have overlooked such a seminal happening?

*The raising of
Lazarus from the
dead, at Bethany.*

As John tells his story:

Jesus is teaching east of the Jordan when he receives word that his close
friend Lazarus, who lives with his two sisters, Mary and Martha, in the town
of Bethany, Jerusalem, is gravely ill. But Jesus doesn't hurry back. Calmly, he
completes two more days of teaching in the region, then sets off for Bethany.

He arrives to find Lazarus dead, and already entombed for four days.
Martha, acquainted with Jesus' healing powers, laments: "Lord, if you had
been here, my brother would not have died." Lazarus's friends surround Jesus.
Why did he take so long to get there? Everyone weeps. Including Jesus.

Then, unexpectedly, Jesus orders: "Take away the stone."

Martha speaks for everyone when she says: "Lord, by this time there will
be an odor, for he has been dead four days."

Jesus reproaches her. "Did I not tell you that if you would believe you
would see the glory of God?" Then Jesus' voice, echoing through the gaping
tunnel of the burial cave, thunders: "Lazarus, come out."

Lazarus, still bound by his burial shroud, struggles his way out into the
sunlight. All are awestruck.

"I am the resurrection and the life," Jesus says, driving home the point of
the story. "Whoever lives and believes in me shall never die."

The tale reads as unambiguous allegory. Indeed, Jesus' verbal summation
seems to pointedly underscore the metaphor: "Whoever lives and believes in
me shall never die." The Kingdom of Heaven awaits all believers.

WATER TO WINE: GOSPEL OF JOHN, 2:1–11 ◆

The apostle John uses two miracles as bookends to Christ's ministry. Raising
Lazarus from the dead caps Christ's career as his final public wonderwork;
and John is also the only Gospel writer who relates Jesus' first miracle—so
different from his many others.

Again, John tells a detailed narrative:

Water to wine, at the wedding at Cana.

On returning from the Jordan River and an encounter with John the Baptist, Jesus finds himself at a wedding celebration. The host is mortified, since the wine has run out and guests might go home. Mary begs her son to intercede and he snaps, sharply and cryptically, "O woman, what have you to do with me? My hour has not yet come" (2:4).

Mary, the strong-willed mother, shrugs off her son's rebuff and orders the host: "Do whatever he tells you" (2:5). Jesus, ever the obedient son, requests that six stone jars be filled with water—something over 120 gallons—and before the "steward of the feast" can taste the water, it has transformed into wine. And a fine wine, too.

Intriguingly, this first miracle of Jesus'—something that should draw wide attention—goes virtually unheeded by guests at the wedding. Equally troubling, the miracle, Christ's first, goes unreported by Mark, Matthew, and Luke. Only Jesus' disciples who are present at the feast gasp in awe. Jesus has, John drives home his story's point, "manifested his glory, and his disciples believed in him" (2:11). That is, the disciples believed wholeheartedly that Jesus Christ had to be the Messiah. Has John once again used a miracle as metaphor?

WHAT IS ONE TO BELIEVE? ◆

In Roman Catholicism, a strong stand on miracles was taken by the First Vatican Council in 1870: "If anyone should say that no miracles can be performed . . . let him be anathema"—anathema being a solemn ban or curse pronounced by ecclesiastical authority. Thus, belief in miracles is obligatory for Roman Catholics—though belief in any specific miracle is not so unambiguously binding. Orthodox Christians equally condemn anyone who claims Christ's miracles were literary devices contributed after his death.

In the final analysis, the miracles of God the Father, of Jesus Christ, of Allah, of the Buddha, of all ancient Oriental and Occidental deities, were never meant to create a faith; they were meant, instead, to strengthen an already existing faith. As a Roman Catholic philosopher explained: "Miracles are miraculous only to those who are already prepared to recognize the operation of God in the commonest events and actions."

Jesus Christ gave his disciples the power to do miracles—"gifts of the Holy Spirit," as Saint Paul put it—and thus handed down a tradition that thrives to this day. At Lourdes. At Fátima. (*See* Lourdes; Fatima.)

STIGMATA—THE MIRACULOUS APPEARANCE OF CHRIST'S FIVE WOUNDS: SAINT FRANCIS OF ASSISI, 1224 ◆

To Christianity belongs one of the oldest and most perplexing of ongoing miracles: stigmata.

The origin of stigmata is perfectly clear. On September 14, 1224, two years before his death, Saint Francis of Assisi, then a forty-two-year-old monk, was undergoing yet another of his protracted, self-imposed fasts. His fasts were of incredible severity. One Lent, for instance, isolating himself on a small island, the hermit ate only half a loaf of bread during the entire forty days.

On this September day in 1224, the mystic was in a thatched hut in the woods on Monte La Verna, and into his fourth week of fasting and praying; he'd begun on August 15, the Feast of the Assumption of the Blessed Virgin Mary into Heaven. This day, the fourteenth, was Holy Cross Day, a time for contemplation on Christ's Crucifixion.

This time, Francis was refusing to eat in honor of the angels in Heaven, to whom he had a great devotion. As dawn broke, he emerged from his spartan hut and knelt in sunlight, praying while he contemplated Christ's five wounds. Suddenly, blood began to ooze from his hands, feet, and side, as if he'd been crucified.

As the so-called *Fioretti* or "Little Flowers" biography of his life relates the episode:

> *While he was thus inflamed by this contemplation [of Christ], he saw a seraph with six shining, fiery wings descend from heaven. This seraph drew near to Saint Francis in swift flight, so that he could see him clearly and recognize that he had the form of a man crucified. . . .*
>
> *As Saint Francis gazed on him he was filled with great fear, and at the same time with great joy. . . . After a period of secret converse this marvelous vision faded, of Christ.*

Francis was embarrassed by the bleeding and said nothing to the companions who were on retreat with him in the woods. But:

They nevertheless noticed that he did not uncover his hands or feet, and that he could not set his feet to the ground. And finding that his habit and undergarment were stained with blood when they washed them, they knew for certain that he bore the image and likeness of Christ crucified imprinted on his hands and feet, as well as in his side.

This is the first recorded case of the miracle of stigmata. The word itself is from the Greek, meaning "a prick with a pointed instrument"—indeed, the kind of chicanery that many later mystics would be accused of self-inflicting.

WHO ARE STIGMATICS? ◆

Since Francis's experience, the Catholic Church has confirmed over three hundred occurrences of stigmata around the world, including the much-publicized case of Padre Pio in Italy.

PADRE PIO (d. 1968). Pio was in the middle of a prayer when suddenly he screamed and fell unconscious. Blood poured from what appeared to be nail holes in his hands and feet. His wounds never healed. They never became infected. And they continued to trickle blood for the next fifty years of his life. Occasionally, they'd scab, but the scabs quickly fell off.

Some not-insignificant specifics:

Pio, born in 1887 to devoutly Catholic parents, was christened Francesco, or Francis; his patron saint was Francis of Assisi. When he chose a religious vocation, it was the Franciscan order; thereafter, he took the name "Pio," "pious." Not long after his ordination, in September 1915—the week of the anniversary of Saint Francis's stigmatization—Pio was home visiting his parents, praying in their garden in a small hut he'd built in imitation of Francis's, when he ran out waving his hands in the air as if they'd been strung by bees. The palms were bloody.

Most significant of all:

Pio's first bout of stigmata cleared up. However, three years later, after he'd become a Capuchin friar, the most austere branch of the Franciscan order, the bleeding suddenly returned. Kneeling in prayer, Pio was, significantly, deep in contemplation of a particularly gory statuette of the Crucifixion—Christ's hands and feet were liberally smeared with red paint, the nails were formidable black spikes, Christ's chest was peppered black with scourge marks, and his gnarled knees bloody and broken from repeated falls while carrying the cross.

Might Padre Pio have been a highly suggestible person?

Remarkably, in virtually all of the more than three hundred confirmed cases of stigmata since Saint Francis's time—280 female stigmatics; 41 males; a curious seven-to-one ratio—each woman or man was at the time of onset of bleeding (or near to it) contemplating a crucified Christ. In picture or statuette, these images were often quite graphic in their gore.

As pointed out in an earlier chapter, the historical origin of the phenomenon of stigmata is curiously coincidental with the manufacturing of crosses bearing lifelike statues of Jesus Christ in his suffering; previously, crosses had been bare. (*See* Latin Cross.)

Furthermore, in each case, the sufferer had been in a state of severe physical or mental duress prior to the onset of symptoms, often through self-imposed fasting.

Of the more than three hundred cases of bleeding wounds, the Catholic Church has been conservative in its approach to the phenomenon. Only sixty-two sufferers from the list have been beatified or canonized, and invariably they've won their status for saintly qualities other than enigmatic bleeding.

BY NATIONALITY. Interestingly, one study has shown that a third of all stigmatics were Italians—as was Saint Francis; seventy were French, forty-seven Spanish, thirty-three German, fifteen Belgian, thirteen Portuguese, five Swiss, five Dutch, three Hungarian, one Peruvian.

A high proportion of these people were cloistered priests or nuns who belonged to a major religious order, in particular, the Franciscans; as well as the Cistercians, and the Dominicans.

Troublingly, Jesus Christ was not crucified through his palms; the bones of the hands are too thin to support the weight of the body. All crucifixions in Roman times were done with nails driven between the large bones of the wrists. Nonetheless, full stigmatics bleed from the palms—in accordance with paintings and statuary that portray, incorrectly, Christ's wounds.

Curiously, before Saint Francis's stigmatization of the 1220s, there were no stigmatics in Christian history. After his much-publicized bout of bleeding, cases began to appear almost overnight:

DODO OF HASCHA (d. 1231). This holy monk's dead body developed open wounds in the hands, feet, and side. The first case of postmortem stigmata.

SAINT LUTGARDE OF TONGRES (d. 1246). She suffered the so-called "bloody sweat of Gethsemane" when in states of extreme ecstasy. The blood was so copious that it bathed her body and soaked her robes.

BLESSED HELEN OF VESZPRIM (d. 1249). This nun of a cloistered Dominican convent in Hungary first was stigmatized in only her right hand—and on the feast day, October 4, of Saint Francis. Thereafter, she miraculously bled from her side.

SAINT CHRISTINA OF STOMMELN (d. 1312). At age twenty-six, she received stigmata in her hands, feet, side, and holes in her forehead, as if from a crown of thorns. Subsequently, she bled every Easter Sunday, the day of Christ's glorious Resurrection—not on Good Friday, the day Christ received his mortal wounds. Most stigmatics bled on Good Friday. Or on Fridays in general. Her skull, preserved at a shrine in France, is said to bear a curious circlet of indentations, as if made by a crown of thorns.

ELIZABETH OF HERKENRODE (d. 1275). This Cistercian nun from a town near Liège relived Christ's bloody Passion every twenty-four hours, a draining experience. She did not live long.

The above are only a few cases from Saint Francis's own century. The next century celebrated two major stigmatics:

SAINT CATHERINE OF SIENA (d. 1380). She first suffered the "pain of the Passion" in 1373, at age twenty-six, with the sensation of Christ's crown of thorns pressed into her head. In the spring of 1375, she was fully stigmatized with the five wounds. She prayed they'd disappear and they did, leaving her, she claimed, with severe pain all her short life. She virtually refused to eat from age twenty onward—and vomited when food was forced upon her; anorexic and bulimic. She withered away at age thirty-three.

SAINT RITA OF CASCIA (d. 1457). Her forehead wound, as if from a crown of thorns, turned uncharacteristically septic; then, when the putrid hole threatened to prevent her from attending a papal jubilee in Rome, it miraculously healed.

One of the earliest male stigmatics after Saint Francis was:

JOHANN JETZER (d. 1515). His case is strange. Son of poor Swiss Catholic farmers, Johann joined the Dominican friary of Berne at age twenty-three. Immediately, the place's quietude was shattered by mysterious bangs, knocks, and rowdy poltergeist tantrums. A former prior, deceased, appeared to Johann and demanded mortifications—which the young man promptly self-inflicted.

At that point in history, the Church was deep into debate over the Virgin Mary's possible Immaculate Conception—her birth without original sin on her soul. The Dominicans opposed the doctrine. Mary appeared to Johann in an apparition and stigmatized his hands, and warned—or promised, Johann wasn't sure—she'd inflict other wounds. They duly manifested, as did body flailing and cataleptic seizures.

When a statue in the friary of Mary wept, Johann was called before a court convened by the chief Benedictine bishop at Lausanne. He was caught in many lies; four of his companion priests were tortured until they owned up to staging pranks in the friary, then they were burned at the stake. Johann, awaiting his own judgment, was smuggled female clothes by his mother and escaped jail in drag. He subsequently married and took up the tailoring trade.

The phenomenon of stigmata continued down through the centuries. Up to our time.

THERESE NEUMANN, KONNERSREUTH, BAVARIA (b. 1898). Born on Good Friday, she fought off two rapes as a teenager and received stigmata in her late twenties: the five standard wounds—hands, feet, and side—plus a bleeding shoulder (Christ hauled the cross on his shoulder), and bloody knees (Christ fell three times to his knees). She bled only on Fridays, and mainly during Lent. Jesus spoke to her in Aramaic, his native tongue; she translated, though she'd never studied languages.

She went blind for a time, then her sight was restored on the day Saint Teresa of Lisieux was beatified, April 29, 1923. She was paralyzed for a time, but mobility returned on the day Saint Teresa was canonized, May 17, 1925. Though she spelled her Christian name "Therese," her patron was Saint Teresa.

From Christmas of 1926 until her death during the Kennedy presidency, she is said to have eaten not a morsel, drunk not a drop. Her only sustenance was one daily Communion wafer. She was watched by two nuns for two weeks, then her father, who some allege smuggled her food, called off the scrutiny.

She suffered a paralyzing stroke in 1940, but Mary appeared and cured her fully. For her suffering in the name of Saint Francis's stigmata, she was received into the Third Order of Saint Francis in 1946. She died in 1962.

TERESA MUSCO, ITALIAN SEAMSTRESS (b. 1943). She received stigmata during a vision in 1969. Though illiterate, in trance she'd speak in Aramaic—it sounded like Aramaic to listeners—and write out whole passages from the Bible. She predicted she'd die from her "pain of the Passion" at age thirty-three; Christ's age at his death. And she did.

JANE HUNT, DERBYSHIRE, ENGLAND (b. 1957). Deaf until the age of six, with limited schooling—and after suffering three miscarriages—she received well-documented stigmata to her hands on July 25, 1985. In fact, that morning, she'd awakened with itching and burning in her palms. At 10:00 A.M., leaving her house to go shopping, she experienced needlelike pangs in her palms and dropped the grocery bag she was carrying. Rushing back inside, she showed her bleeding hands to her husband and daughter. Blood seeped through unbroken skin and trickled down her fingers.

Jane, the semiliterate daughter of a coal miner, claimed not to know what stigmata were. Her pastor at the local Anglican church first recognized the "signs of Saint Francis." Embarrassed, Jane took to wearing gloves, and when the gloves got bloody, she'd pull down her sleeves—or sit on her hands.

The bleeding continued for two years. Sometimes, her feet bled; the intensity varied from day to day. The local pastor, Rev. Norman Hill, held Jane's hands up to a window and could see light shine translucently through the wounds that went front to back. The holes were particularly transparent on Sundays, especially Easter. At those times, Jane would drip a pint of blood a day. During quiescent phases, the wounds were a purplish black, with deep indentations.

Jane Hunt's stigmata was the first case recorded on film, in close-up, for a half-hour British television documentary, "Just Jane" (droll British understatement), as part of a 1980s series, *The Human Factor*, which aired in 1986.

Then, mysteriously, and quite suddenly, the condition disappeared entirely after Jane underwent a full hysterectomy in 1987.

The word "hyster + ectomy" is Greek for "removal of the womb"—*hystera*, "uterus"—and it's related to our word "hysteria," from the old notion that women were hysterical far more often than men. One might be inclined to say that Jane Hunt had her "hysteria" removed.

CLORETTA ROBINSON, WEST OAKLAND, CALIFORNIA (b. 1962)
This young Baptist girl—presumably, the first African-American stigmatic—began to bleed from the left palm, in class, during school one day in March 1972; she'd just recently read a religious book detailing Christ's bloody Crucifixion. For the next nineteen days, up until Good Friday, she exhibited stigmatized hands, feet, and forehead. Then the condition cleared up.

It should be pointed out that many of the cases the Church has looked into have turned out to be fraudulent, the result of self-inflicted wounds. Some would say that all such cases, from Saint Francis's time onward, can be accounted for by overpious, well-intentioned fraud. Others might point to the complex, yet not completely understood, connection between the mind and the body.

STIGMATA REPLICATED THROUGH HYPNOSIS:
TWENTIETH CENTURY ◆

The power of suggestion is potent. Especially under hypnosis. For instance, a hypnotized subject can be made insensitive to pinpricks.

On the other hand, a good hypnotic subject—one who is highly suggestible—can have his palm touched by a pencil eraser but told it's actually a lighted cigarette. Most likely, he'll yank his hand immediately away. But a few excellent hypnotic subjects will develop a redness in the very spot touched by the cool eraser. And, from among these, a few extraordinary subjects will develop an actual blistering of the skin, an accumulation of water beneath the surface that is characteristic of a burn reaction.

But it's possible to go further in replicating stigmata. The palm of a rare supersuggestible subject when touched with a cool pencil eraser will not only blister, but the skin will open and bleed—a severe third-degree burn produced by the power of suggestion. Such an experiment was conducted by a German psychiatrist and hypnotherapist in the late 1920s, Dr. Alfred Lechler.

Not only are such people—rare as they are—extraordinarily suggestible, but many of them appear to suffer from what is called *dermagraphia*: skin so sheer and sensitive that a pattern traced with a blunt instrument will leave a visible trace for quite some time; often the trace will be elevated in bas-relief.

A medical encyclopedia defines the type of people likely to exhibit dermagraphia as "hysterical women" (that sexist association again), "multiple personalities," "some epileptics," and "victims of disorders of the nervous system." Indeed, Dr. Lechler's star subject, identified in the medical literature only as "Elizabeth K.," suffered from multiple personalities. Her case is special.

ELIZABETH K.—THE MOST STUDIED STIGMATIC. Born in southern Germany in 1902, Elizabeth was a terribly troubled child.

For starters, she suffered from countless neuroses, and she was a true somnambulist—she could sleepwalk with uncanny accuracy and no awareness or recall. At six, her mother died. A bright student, she soon began to suffer from shaking limbs, severe headaches, and numbness and body paralysis on the right side. Often, she couldn't swallow food or speak. Her bladder and bowels regularly dysfunctioned. She subsisted on virtually no food, and slept only two to three hours each night. Yet she seemed to have limitless, manic energy.

She came under the care of Dr. Lechler in 1929. In fact, she moved in with the doctor, so he could observe her round-the-clock. Immediately, the psychiatrist noticed that Elizabeth took on the pains and ailments of people around her. She actually suffered from the illnesses—experiencing aches, pains, chills, fever—that those around her experienced. That meant, to Lechler, that Elizabeth was highly suggestible.

On Easter Sunday of 1932, Lechler showed Elizabeth a series of religious slides, including vivid, quite gory scenes of Christ's Crucifixion and death. That night, the young woman complained of severe piercing pains in her hands and feet. Later, hypnotizing her, Lechler instructed Elizabeth to concentrate on the hand and foot pains; to imagine actual wounds.

She began to bleed through porous openings in the flesh, and when ordered to cry, she did, and her tears were filled with copious amounts of blood. When she was asked to imagine a crown of thorns on her head, she bled from the forehead. While it is known that subjects in a trance have a deep tendency to do as told, Elizabeth was clearly more obliging than most. She was exceptional.

Lechler's experiments with Elizabeth K. leave many questions unanswered; and his causal methodology is not beyond attack. Suffice it to say here, Lechler concluded that stigmata can be replicated in certain highly gifted—or severely disturbed—individuals.

Might many of the mystic stigmatics have been highly suggestible like Elizabeth K.? Might some of them have had thin, sensitive skin that displayed dermagraphia?

It is interesting to note that the historical facts we have about Saint

Catherine of Siena's stigmata include the observation made shortly after her death that she had extraordinarily thin and translucent skin. Almost transparent, it was said at the time.

Of course, looking at the phenomenon of stigmata from the opposite direction, it is quite common in the East for meditating mystics to *prevent* the flow of blood from a wound as they pierce their tongues, cheeks, and flesh with long needles. If the human mind can stop the flow of blood, might it allow diluted blood to seep through thin, porous skin? Is the phenomenon of stigmata unwittingly self-induced in certain pious persons transfixed on a crucifix and the wounds of Christ?

If Christ himself produced this miracle, it seems likely that he would have the holy victim bleed from the wrists, as he did, and not from the palms—which supports the idea that stigmata somehow come from within the individual.

CHAPTER

---

3 4

𝕺irginity
of the 𝕺irgin

Immaculate Conception to Virgin Birth

"ALL GENERATIONS WILL CALL ME BLESSED."
LUKE 1:48

MIRIAM OF NAZARETH: BORN C. 20 B.C.E., JERUSALEM ◆

How did a simple, perhaps unschooled, teenage Jewish virgin named Miriam—of whom nothing is known prior to her unexpected teenage pregnancy at age fourteen—become the single most famous and influential woman in Western history? The icon to lord over all other icons? The subject of more etchings, oils, pastels, lithographs, drawings, statuary, medallions, and amulets than any other human being living or dead?

It wasn't easy. It didn't happen overnight. It didn't happen without heated infighting within the Church.

And it didn't happen without vicious attacks from outside the Church: charges that Catholicism worshiped the Hebrew maiden from the tiny town of Nazareth as a member of the Godhead, held her in higher esteem than the Holy Spirit; charges that Rome had gone Mariocentric.

Historically, little is known of Mary; really nothing outside the New Testament. And within the New Testament, it's the Gospel of Luke, relating the narratives of Jesus' infancy and childhood, that is the principal source of information about Christ's mother.

Mary enters the Bible in the story of the Annunciation, when the angel Gabriel shocks her with news that she's pregnant; or about to be—the angel's wording is ambiguous, as we'll see.

Mary exists in the Bible in Acts, when she is seen in the company of those who are praying after Jesus' Ascension into Heaven.

Born in Jerusalem, or Sepphoris in Galilee, about 18 or 20 B.C.E. (even this is derived from counting backward from Christ's birth c. 6 to 3 B.C.E.), Mary is the child of Jewish parents, Joachim and Anne, of whom even less is known. From relative obscurity, however, she rises to stellar prominence, and is gifted with some of the most spectacular, stupendous miracles ever recorded:

THE IMMACULATE CONCEPTION. The belief that Mary was conceived in her mother's womb without original sin on her soul. For this to have happened, some scholars have argued that Mary's mother, Anne, had to conceive her daughter without experiencing any sexual pleasure.

THE VIRGIN BIRTH. The belief that Mary conceived Jesus Christ, yet retained her virginity; and that she physically gave birth to the infant without labor pains or vaginal exit; "as a beam of light passes unobtrusively through a windowpane" goes one apt analogy.

THE ASSUMPTION. The belief that Mary was spared standard human death and decay, and was "assumed" incorrupt, body and soul, into Heaven at the behest of her son Jesus Christ.

APPARITIONS OF MARY. Scores of claims over the centuries that the Jewish Blessed Virgin, usually appearing young, Anglo-Saxon, and robed in blue and white (colors of later iconography), reappears regularly, invariably to illiterate, childlike peasants in Third World countries, with messages from her son.

Before examining the origins of these wondrous happenings, let's take a close look at Mariology, for within the Roman Catholic Church, the study of Mary has evolved into a rigorous theological discipline.

MARY'S THREE STAGES OF VIRGINITY: FIRST TO FOURTH CENTURIES ◆

"Ever-Virgin," or *Sempre Virgo*, is the theological phrase, popular from the fourteenth century onward, which sums up the threefold mystery of Mary's virginity, a central pillar of the Catholic faith. Mary's three stages of virginity are conceptually challenging, and at least one is unfamiliar to most Catholics, and probably to all Protestants.

Three stages to the virgin birth: conception, parturition, and postpartum.

1. "VIRGIN BEFORE BRINGING FORTH." Mary's virginal conception of Christ, or *virginitas ante partum*. This became accepted Church teaching by the end of the first century C.E. It is the most familiar stage of Mary's virginity, and the one accepted by all branches of Christianity, commonly called the "virgin birth." It is the Roman Catholic dogma that Jesus Christ was "fathered" not by Joseph but by the Holy Spirit.

2. "VIRGIN DURING BRINGING FORTH." Mary's virginity in parturition, or while giving birth to Christ: *virginitas durante partu*. That is to say, Mary's hymen never ruptured because the infant Jesus exited from her womb but not down a dilated birth canal. How? Truly, only God knows. Even Mary, claims Church theology, was not privy to this birthing miracle.

In addition, there was no "breaking of water" from the amniotic sac, and no placental afterbirth. And, too, no pains of labor. Theologically, Mary, Ever-Virgin, cannot have experienced any vaginal sensations that might be construed as pain or pleasure.

This phase of the Blessed Virgin's virginity—called "the preservation of the bodily integrity of Mary" in the field of Mariology—did not become accepted Church teaching until the year 390 C.E. At that time, the doctrine was spelled out in a letter from Saint Ambrose and the synod of bishops in Milan to Pope Siricius (384–99). In fact, the pope, two years later, excommunicated the monk Jovinian because he insisted that Mary had lost her hymen in bearing the Savior. Most Roman Catholics are unaware of this technical aspect of Mary's virginity.

3. "VIRGIN AFTER BRINGING FORTH." Mary's remaining a virgin after the birth of Jesus for the rest of her life upon earth, or *virginitas post partum*. This, despite strong scriptural evidence that Jesus had many siblings, named brothers, and unnamed sisters.

Mary's lifelong virginity was a popular Church doctrine in the second century, and achieved dogmatic status at the Council of Chalcedon in 451 C.E.—and is therefore a binding belief for Eastern Orthodox and Roman Catholics. In addition, it's maintained by many Anglican, some Lutheran, and a few other Protestant groups. Many Protestants believe that after Christ's virgin conception, Mary had several natural children.

Of the above three conditions on virginity, Catholics must believe 1 and 3; they are Church dogma. Number 2, today, is not regarded as dogma but is revered as long-standing patristic tradition. It might be added that no woman theologian, of course, had a hand in creating any of the above Church teachings on female virginity and birthing.

Had there been virgin births before Mary's time? If so, were Christians familiar with these miraculous events?

VIRGIN BIRTHS—COMMON IN THE CLASSICAL WORLD: PRE-CHRISTIANITY ◆

Birds do it, bees do it, and even certain kinds of fleas do it—parthenogenesis, that is, the female production of offspring without sperm from a male. Even turkeys are known on occasion to do it. And frogs.

The word "parthenogenesis" is from the Greek *parthenos*, "virgin," and *genesis*, "birth." We'll shortly return to this tantalizing word and provocative concept.

Early Christians were not ignorant of the mythology of their time, and tales of virgin births were not at all uncommon.

In many ancient cultures, we find a male deity who impregnates a mortal female to sire a hybrid human-divine offspring. It's standard mythologic sex in both the East and the West. Typically, the mixed duo beget a demigod or distinguished mortal.

The Greek god Zeus, for instance, impregnates the mortal virgin Danae, who gives birth to Perseus. Similarly, the god Apollo begets Asclepius; the god Mars begets Romulus; Zeus also fathers Hercules.

In historical times, such legends flourished around famous men. Alexander the Great was "conceived" by the god Zeus in the form of a snake intertwining the groin of the lovely mortal Olympias. The Greek mathematician Pythagoras and the Greek philosopher Plato were assumed to be sons of the god Apollo. Greatness in a mortal man was often accounted for by the assumption that he had a celestial father.

India, too, is rich with such hybrid human-divine sex.

However, in all of these pagan examples, the coupling of a god and a mortal is *sexual*—and often highly charged. Amorous and promiscuous Zeus, for instance, impregnates a mortal woman over three long, sultry nights. Clearly, these pagan tales are not concerned with the preservation of the mortal woman's virginity, which is the entire point of the Christian version. An angel of the Lord visits Mary; no serpent seduces the fourteen-year-old Jewish maiden.

Jesus' virgin birth is definitely unique; and it is more than just a prudish Christian twist to the older cross-cultural tales.

CHRIST IS "BREATHED" INTO MARY'S WOMB ✦

Technically, Mary's is not a tale of impregnation at all, but of asexual conception by divine fiat, by direct decree of God.

The divine power of the Holy Spirit overshadows Mary to induce "pneumatological" conception—from the Greek *pneuma*, "breath" or "to breathe." The seed of Christ was breathed into Mary's womb. And the seed was not semen, as in all the preternatural pagan myths of conception. The seed, it is argued, was grace.

Luke, who best tells the biblical narrative, makes only the slightest concession to sexual imagery—perhaps unintentional at that—when the angel Gabriel informs Mary that "the Holy Spirit shall come upon thee" (1:35). The agent being a "spirit" of course precludes any idea of physical intercourse.

Before going further, it should be said that today not all Christians, and fewer religious scholars than in the past, believe in Mary's perpetual virginity. Modern scholars are immensely troubled, for instance, by the fact that among the four Gospel writers, Mark and John essentially ignore Christ's virginal conception, a seminal article of the faith—though silence can never prove anything definitively; it's at best suggestive.

Ultimately, of course, the issue of Jesus' virgin birth is decided by a person's faith and interpretation of Scripture.

That said, let's pursue the origin of this unique biblical mystery.

JESUS' VIRGINAL CONCEPTION:
GOSPELS OF MATTHEW AND LUKE, C. 65 TO 75 C.E. ✦

We have only two historical sources to turn to, Matthew and Luke, since Gospel writers Mark (6:3) and John (1:13–14; 6:42) make at best only vague allusions to the miracle. Furthermore, the evangelist Paul, who wrote so voluminously about Christianity, nowhere mentions the Christ's virgin birth.

Even Matthew, who presents the miracle with astonishing understatement, attaches no deep theological significance to it. He seems more interested in having Christ's birth fulfill ancient Hebrew prophesy.

However, in postbiblical literature—from about the year 100 C.E. up until our own time—the most voluminous discussions of Mary have centered on her virginity and Christ's virginal conception.

Mary is first mentioned in Luke's story of the Annunciation, chapter 1; the first time we meet Mary she is a virgin, and perhaps carrying a child in her womb. She's certainly caught by surprise (Luke 1:26–34):

> The angel Gabriel was sent from God unto a city of Galilee, named Nazareth, to a virgin espoused to a man whose name was Joseph, of the house of David, and the virgin's name was Mary.
>
> And the angel came to her and said, "Hail, O favored one, the Lord is with you!"
>
> But she was greatly troubled at the saying, and considered in her mind what sort of greeting this might be.
>
> And the angel said to her, "Do not be afraid, Mary, for you have found favor with God. And behold, you will conceive in your womb and bear a son, and you shall call his name Jesus . . ."
>
> And Mary said to the angel, "How shall this be?"

Mary's first recorded state of mind is bewilderment, and her first recorded speech is a nature question: "How shall this be?"

(Luke emphasizes that Mary is a virgin, but he does not imply—at least not yet, and never explicitly—that she'll conceive in a virginal manner. It's Matthew who more clearly states the virginal conception of Jesus.)

Mary, at the time of this Annunciation, was a young teenager betrothed to Joseph, presumably an older man, a customary pairing at that time. Startled, Mary asks: "How shall this be, seeing I know not a man?"

It is an odd question since she's about to become Joseph's wife. Actually, in the Hebrew world, betrothal was tantamount to marriage. Some scholars suggest that by her remark perhaps Mary means that she intends to remain forever a virgin.

Has Mary already conceived Christ? Perhaps not, for Gabriel answers Mary's question in the future tense: "The Holy Spirit shall come upon thee."

Despite such vagueness, Luke's intent is clear: a woman who has never had sexual relations has been, or will be, miraculously impregnated.

Furthermore, the detailed nature of the dialogue between Mary and Gabriel—the question-and-answer format—suggests that Luke, writing his account about 65 C.E., was responding to specific questions asked of him, or questions under general discussion, concerning the virgin birth of Christ. Luke tells the story in a way that seems intended to clear up doubts about a virginal conception.

In addition, Luke later (3:23) returns to the virgin birth theme in his genealogy of Jesus, when he says that Jesus was "the son (as was supposed) of Joseph."

We need to turn to Matthew in order to dig deeper into this profound mystery.

VIRGIN CONCEPTION AS PROPHESY FULFILLED: MATTHEW 1:18–25 ◆

Matthew wrote his Gospel perhaps a decade after Luke's. And he takes a very different approach to the virginal conception of Jesus. He tells Joseph's side of the story.

An unnamed angel appears to Joseph, who has discovered, much to his horror, that his wife-to-be is pregnant. Joseph is ready to break off the engagement, but the angel commands him to see the marriage through, since the child in Mary's womb was fathered by the Holy Spirit.

As in Luke, Matthew makes it clear that Mary and Joseph have not had sexual relations prior to this moment. (Though textual variations of Matthew use the seemingly contradictory phrase "Joseph begat Jesus.") Matthew states that Joseph "did not know her until she had borne a son." That might mean the two had never met face-to-face; or that after Jesus' miraculous birth, Joseph got to "know" Mary sexually, and had children with her.

But Matthew's agenda is broader than Luke's.

Matthew is bent on proving that Jesus is the Messiah by showing how his life fulfills Hebrew Scriptures. He presents an Old Testament passage, from Isaiah 7, about the future of Judah and threats from its enemies.

In brief, the prophet Isaiah claims that God will send a sign: A "young woman"—*alma* in Hebrew—who is pregnant will bear a son, and before the child is old enough to tell good from evil, the enemies that threaten Judah will be defeated:

> *Behold, a young woman shall bear a son and shall call his name Immanuel.*
> *(Isa. 7:14)*

WORD ORIGINS. Immanuel means "God [is] with us"—implying "God is on our side"—in Hebrew.

The point of this Old Testament story has nothing to do with virginity; its intention is to set a timetable for the approaching threat to Israel: from the child's birth until the age he can distinguish good from evil. There is nothing miraculous about the young woman, *alma*; nothing divine about her conception.

Matthew, we know, used a Greek translation of the Hebrew Old Testament. As mentioned, the Hebrew word *alma* means simply "young woman," without any implication of virginity. The standard Greek word used to translate *alma* is *parthenos*, which actually has the broader double meaning of either "young woman" or "virgin." Hence, our English word "parthenogenesis," "virgin birth."

Thus, Matthew, writing some thirty to forty years after Christ's death, and wishing to cast Christ as the fulfillment of Hebrew prophesy, reinterprets Isaiah (7:14): Christ becomes the foretold Immanuel, and the male name meaning "God with us" takes on a literal meaning that equates Christ to God; and Christ is now born to a *parthenos*, a virgin.

Isaiah's original meaning is superseded by the identification of Jesus as Immanuel (in Greek, *Emmanouel*), "God [is] with us." Compare three texts from three different times and in two different languages:

ISAIAH 7:14. From the Hebrew; written about the eighth century B.C.E.: "*Behold, a young woman shall bear a son and shall call his name Immanuel.*"

MATTHEW 1:23. From the Greek; written about 75 C.E.: "*Behold, a virgin shall bring forth a son and they shall call him Emmanuel, which being interpreted is, God with us.*"

LUKE 1:31. From the Greek; written about 65 C.E.: "*Behold, thou shall conceive in thy womb, and bring forth a son, and shall call him Jesus.*"

Those who doubt the virgin birth argue that Matthew and Luke twisted Isaiah to create their own tapestry, weaving an image of Jesus as the Messiah. Furthermore, they claim that the story was strongly supported by the early Church as a way of honoring the coming of Jesus as the Son of God; and, too, of explaining the idea of how God incarnated in the flesh on earth.

The critics are right on one point:

The virgin birth was embraced early by the Apostolic Father Saint Ignatius of Antioch, who was martyred in 110 C.E. by being thrown to the lions in the Colosseum.

Ignatius, the first person to write about Mary after the Gospel authors, was the third bishop of the ancient church where Saint Peter established his chair before going to Rome, and Peter's second successor—called an "Apostolic Father" because his witness is during the lifetime of some of the apostles. He battled a group of heretics known as the Judaizers, who did not accept the New Testament—including the virgin birth story—and clung to such Jewish practices as observance of the Sabbath.

To quiet critics, Ignatius knew something had to be done about Christ's several brothers and sisters.

CHRIST'S SIBLINGS:
GOSPELS OF MATTHEW AND MARK, C. 60 TO 75 c.e. ◆

As Christian doctrine of the virgin birth developed, it became a preeminent statement of faith, as well as the ultimate test of belief in biblical inerrancy. The New Testament did not lie. Its words were divinely inspired.

However, siblings of Jesus are referred to collectively twice in the Gospels (plus in the Acts of the Apostles and in 1 Corinthians 9:5, and Galatians 1:19). In Matthew (12:46–50), Jesus' mother and brothers come to speak to him while he is teaching. He refuses to see them, however, saying that his true sister, brother, and mother are those who do the will of God.

When Jesus teaches at the synagogue in his hometown of Nazareth, his wisdom and mighty works antagonize the crowd of listeners (Matt. 13:53–58; Mark 6:1–6). Simply put, the locals doubt that a hometown boy, one of their own, whom they watched grow up, could suddenly be endowed with miraculous powers. The crowd emphasizes that, after all, "We know your mother, father, brothers and sisters."

The brothers are listed by name: James, Joseph ("Joses" in Mark's Gospel), Simon, and Judas.

The sisters are listed only as a group.

Mark, who does not recount the virgin birth in his Gospel, wouldn't, of course, be bothered by Christ's siblings.

However, Matthew, who does recount the virgin birth story, should be highly troubled by Christ having brothers and sisters. Unless, of course, *after* Christ's birth, Mary and Joseph had children in the normal, sexual way. Did Mary eventually forfeit her virginity?

COUSINS? STEPCHILDREN? Saint Jerome, late in the fourth century, argued that the "brothers of the Lord" were really his cousins. However, there existed a simple Greek word for "cousins"—why hadn't the Bible interpreters used it?

The issue bothered the early Church, and it continues to split Roman Catholics from many other Christian denominations. Catholicism teaches that Mary was a virgin before, during, and after Christ's birth—called, as we've seen, *ante partum*, *durante partu*, and *post partum*; Mary is *Sempre Virgo*, "Ever-Virgin." This led the Church to identify Christ's siblings as his cousins, or as stepbrothers and stepsisters from some previous marriage of Joseph's, though no evidence for such a marriage exists.

Many theologians are repulsed by the idea that Joseph, the male role model for Jesus, *ever* had sex. With any woman. And for that matter that the Blessed Virgin Mary ever experienced sexual stimulation.

Saint Augustine initially accounted for Christ's siblings as Joseph's children from a previous marriage, then denounced his own view, turned off by the imagery of Joseph ever having copulated with any woman. The spouse of the Virgin Mary and the foster father of Jesus Christ should be a lifelong virgin himself.

Today, this ticklish topic is best handled—if it comes up at all—by saying that the kin mentioned in the New Testament were "cousins from Joseph's side of the family," children of Joseph's brothers and sisters who, for reasons unclear, came to live with Joseph, Mary, and Jesus.

MARY—THE "NEW EVE": SECOND CENTURY C.E. ◆

With the virgin birth as part of Church doctrine, second-century Church father Saint Irenaeus was free to cast Mary as a Second Eve, or, more accurately, as the New and Improved Eve. Eve, the first woman, was a virgin who disobeyed God; Mary was a virgin always obedient to the Lord.

This analogy suited the new Church because it neatly paralleled a picture of Christ in the New Testament as the New Adam: "As in Adam all die, so also in Christ shall all be made alive" (1 Cor. 15:22). Adam disobeyed God and unleashed sin on the world; Christ, the New Adam, obeyed God and won redemption for all from sin.

Christianity is founded on the New Testament, the New Adam, and the New Eve.

In essence, the New Adam (Christ) and the New Eve (Mary) start God's creation cycle all over again, this time on a superior footing. Saint Irenaeus pursued this analogy: "For Adam had necessarily to be restored in Christ, that mortality be absorbed in immortality," he wrote. Aristotle warns against pushing any analogy too far; the leading head circles back and bites the premise.

COREDEMPTRIX. What the above parallel does is ascribe to Mary an active role in the redemption of the human race—something that would enrage many later theologians who thought the Church was trying to deify Mary, shape her into a fourth Godhead.

The logic goes like this: All men died in Adam. Eve was part of the sin that brought this on. All men are saved in Christ. Mary brought forth the life that made this redemption possible. Ergo, Mary made the redemption possible.

The Second Vatican Council (1962–65), in its Dogmatic Constitution, *Lumen Gentium*, gave Mary an approving nod: "Rightly, therefore, the Fathers [of the Church] see Mary not merely as passively engaged by God, but as freely cooperating in the work of man's salvation through faith and obedience."

Many non–Roman Catholic Christians think this is extending Mary's role too far. Mary gave birth to Christ, Mary was a holy woman, Mary lived an exemplary life, but Christ was the sole redeemer of humankind. This is the Protestant view.

The original source of Mary's title as Coredemptrix is from Luke (1:38), when Mary accepts her commission and guarantees the Incarnation of Christ: "Let it be to me according to your word." In a sense, by fully pledging herself to God's plan for the redemption of humankind, Mary automatically becomes an active part of that plan. How active, though? Two thousand years after Luke wrote those words, Christian theologians are still arguing about the day-to-day job of a Coredemptrix.

"MOTHER OF GOD" VS. "MOTHER OF CHRIST"— THEOTOKOS VS. CHRISTOTOKOS: THIRD CENTURY C.E. ◆

The first widespread controversy over Mary involved the wisdom—or lack thereof—of honoring her with the supreme title Theotokos, "God-bearer," or "Mother of God." It is certainly the highest rank any woman can achieve in Christendom. And, it should be added, it is not a title that pleases Jews or Muslims, who worship the same God as Christians.

The title arose in the third century, probably in Alexandria, Egypt, and grew out of public devotion. It seemed to many a logical deduction from the doctrine of Christ being divine. But to many others at the time it seemed to ignore Christ's human side. After all, he was human *and* divine.

Thus argued the patriarch of Constantinople, Nestorius: Let us honor Mary with the title Christotokos, "Christ-bearer," or "Mother of Christ." Isn't that more to the point? said the patriarch.

Well, Nestorius's objections were bluntly condemned at the Council of Ephesus in 431 C.E., and Theotokos was unconditionally approved.

Greek (top) and
Roman monograms
for "Mother of God"—
Theotokos.

It is clear that at this point the Church was already constructing a fortress theology surrounding Mary. A cult of the Virgin. Not much had been revealed about Mary in Scripture, but Church fathers, through their own writings, deliberations, and decrees, were fleshing out a full-scale biography of the Blessed Virgin Mary, or BVM, a respectful and acceptable acronym in Catholicism.

The cult would flower fullest in the Roman Catholic, Anglo-Catholic, and Orthodox churches. In time, the litany for Mary would become more extensive than that for her son Jesus Christ. And she'd enjoy at least sixteen liturgical celebrations in the Roman Rite—four called solemn (S), three feasts (F), five memorials (M), four optional memorials (OM):

Immaculate Conception, December 8, S
Our Lady of Guadalupe, December 12, M
Mary, Mother of God (Theotokos), January 1, S
Presentation of the Lord, February 2, F
Our Lady of Lourdes, February 11, OM
The Annunciation of the Lord, March 25, S
The Visitation, May 31, F
Immaculate Heart of Mary, Saturday following second Sunday after
    Pentecost, OM
Our Lady of Mount Carmel, July 16, OM
Dedication of Saint Mary Major, August 5, OM
The Assumption, August 15, S
Queenship of Mary, August 22, M
Birth of Mary, September 8, F

Our Lady of Sorrows, September 15, M
Our Lady of the Rosary, October 7, M
Presentation of Mary, November 21, M

IMMACULATE CONCEPTION DOGMA: DECEMBER 8, 1854 ◆

The origin of this mystery—that Mary was conceived in her mother Anne's womb without original sin on her soul—is discussed in part elsewhere in this book. (*See* Feast of the Immaculate Conception.)

Here we'll take a different approach, employing Scripture and tradition.

First: There is no explicit biblical revelation of the dogma that came to be called the Immaculate Conception of Mary. In fact, it did not become dogma—a truth or "article of faith" Roman Catholics must believe—until December 8, 1854, when Pope Pius IX, speaking "infallibly," declared it such in his papal bull *Ineffabilis Deus*.

It had already enjoyed a long tradition in the Church.

Even some maverick theologians in the fourth and fifth centuries, who argued that Mary may have committed "actual sins" in her lifetime (never a universal view), conceded that she was not born with original sin on her soul.

But how was Mary, the only human to enjoy this honor, spared the stain of original sin?

Thomas Aquinas, the most important medieval theologian in the West, taught that Mary's conception was "tarnished," as was that of all humans—springing as conception does from a sexual act—but that God extinguished the ember of original sin in Mary at some (unspecified) moment before her birth.

This position sounded good for a time. But it was opposed by the doctrine of the Immaculate Conception espoused in the thirteenth century by British Scholastic theologian John Duns Scotus—and defined as Roman Catholic dogma by Pope Pius IX in 1854. Accordingly, Mary was not only pure throughout her lifetime and at the moment of her birth into the world, but (as the pontiff declared).

> at the first instant of her conception was preserved immaculate from all stain of original sin, by the singular grace and privilege granted her by Almighty God, through the merits of Christ Jesus, Savior of mankind.

How did Pius IX arrive at this certainty?

Three biblical references are called upon to support the weighty dogma of the Immaculate Conception; they vary greatly in their cogency:

LUKE 1:28. "And he [Gabriel] came to her and said, 'Hail, full of grace, the Lord is with you.' "

LUKE 1:42. ". . . and she [Elizabeth] exclaimed with a loud cry, 'Blessed are you among women, and blessed is the fruit of your womb!' "

These two were used by Pius IX in his 1854 bull *Ineffabilis Deus*. Vatican II, also referring to the angel Gabriel's salutation at the Annunciation, argued that Mary was "enriched from the first instant of her conception with the splendor of an entirely unique holiness."

The third biblical passage is:

GENESIS 3:15. "I will put enmity between you and the woman, and between your seed and her seed; he shall bruise your head, and you shall bruise his heel."

Does this ancient Eden text about the crushing of the serpent's head have anything to do with the later-day Immaculate Conception? Is this "woman" in Genesis Mary?

Here is what Vatican II, in its Constitution *Lumen Gentium*, has to say on the matter:

The earliest documents, as they are read in the Church and are understood in the light of a further and full revelation, bring the figure of the woman, Mother of the Redeemer, into a gradually clearer light.

Considered in this light, she is already prophetically foreshadowed in the promise of victory over the serpent which was given to our first parents after their fall into sin.

SEX AND ORIGINAL SIN ◆ *Christians have always tended to connect original sin with sex, and assume that an infant's soul receives its taint from the sexual coupling of its parents. Specifically, from the lust and pleasure the parents experience from their first moment of arousal through climax.*

This prudish notion springs quite naturally from the Genesis tale of Adam and Eve, the serpent, and the tree of forbidden knowledge. No mere fruit tree, surely. More likely, the knowledge forbidden to the pure unclothed Adam and Eve was S-E-X. As metaphor, the seductive, winsome serpent couldn't be a better phallic substitute. In an act of disobedience, Adam and Eve "bit into each other," and the knowledge they acquired was that they "knew" each other in the so-called "biblical sense." Thus, inherited original sin is a sex stain. Wiped away by baptism.

Thus, claims the Church, the Immaculate Conception is *implied* by Mary's absolute opposition to evil as witnessed by the crushing of the serpent head's in Genesis.

Without tracing the reasoning in detail, suffice it to say that the Church concluded that the "woman" in Genesis is the foreshadowment of the Mary in Luke's Gospel, in Acts, and in John's Gospel, and of the "woman" who bears "Marian symbolism" in Revelation (12:1) as "the woman clothed with sun."

DID ANNE AND JOACHIM CONCEIVE MARY WITHOUT LUST? ◆

If so, Mary presumably would be born without original sin on her soul.

While neither dogma nor doctrine, passionless procreation at once had been entertained as a basis for the Immaculate Conception. Saint Augustine, the fourth-century bishop of Hippo, lays the framework for sex without lust, or ejaculation without orgasm, in his masterwork, *De Civitate Dei*, "The City of God." He does so in the chapter intriguingly titled: "Were Adam and Eve Troubled by Passion Before They Ate of the Tree of Knowledge?"

Says Augustine, if the pure First Parents had not sinned and been evicted East of Eden, they'd have been able to produce Cain and Abel in Paradise through "innocent conception." As the Church father speculates: "In Paradise, then, generative seed would have been sown by the husband, and the wife would have conceived . . . by deliberate and not by uncontrollable lust." Sex without arousal.

Augustine gets quite explicit on how sensationless sex works:

> At a time when there was no unruly lust to excite the organs of generation . . . the seminal flow [of Adam] could have reached the womb [of Eve] with as little rupture of the hymen and by the same vaginal ducts as is at present the case, in reverse, with the menstrual flux.

As we've seen earlier, one condition of the Blessed Virgin's virginity is that her hymen was not broken in giving birth: *virginitas durante partu*. Mary's bodily integrity was kept intact.

Catholics do not have to believe that Anne and Joachim begot Mary through the kind of passionless procreation that Adam and Eve might have ended up engaging in—had they not become sexual creatures through an act of disobedience. Pius IX did not employ the concept in promulgating the dogma of the Immaculate Conception. Indeed, it's no longer discussed.

Today, most religious texts tersely state that Mary was conceived in an "ordinary manner" and say no more.

DOGMA OF MARY'S ASSUMPTION, BODY AND SOUL: NOVEMBER 1, 1950 ◆

The Assumption into Heaven of Mary's incorrupt body and spotless soul was made Church dogma by Pope Pius XII on November 1, 1950, in the papal bull *Munificentissimus Deus*.

In an earlier chapter, we examined the "Feast of the Assumption." Here we search for the miracle's biblical origins—a search that the pontiff himself had difficulty with.

To backtrack a bit:

Once the Immaculate Conception of Mary was made dogma in 1854, the Vatican began to receive petitions that the pope next define as dogma the Assumption of Mary—since this was already a popular belief and long celebrated in the Feast of the Assumption. During the century that followed, from 1854 to 1950, the Vatican was deluged with more than eight million petitions, from Catholics around the world.

Yet Rome hesitated. Deliberately dragged its feet.

Little wonder. The problems were major.

The date and circumstances surrounding Mary's "death" were unknown. It was not even certain where she'd lived out the remainder of her life after Christ's Crucifixion. Rumor was that she lived with John, the son of Zebedee, in Jerusalem and died there.

No tomb has ever been found—although there is a grave in Jerusalem that some claimed had once contained Mary's body.

No account existed of witnesses to Mary's bodily assumption off the face of the earth. At best, there was a tradition of oil paintings that depicted her "dormition," or gentle "falling asleep" as she passed from this life. (Latin *dormire*, "to lie dormant or sleep.") Some argued that this actually occurred in the ancient Ionian city of Ephesus.

No reference—or inference—exists in the New Testament to a glorious assumption of Christ's mother.

With no evidence whatsoever, how could an infallible dogma be promulgated by a sitting pontiff without making him look at least a little ridiculous?

Yet, on November 1, 1950, in *Munificentissimus Deus*, Pius XII, speaking infallibly, said:

We pronounce, declare, and define it to be a divinely revealed dogma: that the Immaculate Mother of God, the ever Virgin Mary, having completed the course of her earthly life, was assumed body and soul into heavenly glory.

Of course, the key phrase here is "divinely revealed." Revelation cannot be challenged. Revelation *is* the basis of all religions; without divine revelation, there is no Judaism, no Islam, no Christianity. No faith.

Had the pope pulled rank?

INSINUATIONS OF AN ASSUMPTION. "There is no explicit reference to her glorious Assumption in the Bible," writes a leading Dominican Mariologist, Father Frederick Jelly. "But that does not mean that there is no biblical basis for it."

What is that basis?

As Father Jelly points out: "Insinuations in biblical revelation become explicit under the guidance of the [Holy] Spirit in the Church, who inspired them originally." In other words, the Holy Spirit both reveals and insinuates, is explicit and works through innuendo.

Suffice it to say, Pius XII, in promulgating the dogma of the Virgin's Assumption, draws heavily on tradition:

• The fact that Christians for centuries were celebrating Mary's Assumption.

• That during the sixth-century reign of Emperor Mauricius Flavius, the liturgical feast of "Mary's Dormition" or "falling asleep" was already observed on August 15.

• That under the eighth-century pope Saint Adrian I, the word "Dormition" or "falling asleep" became "Assumption" or "rising up."

In addition, the pope argued that Mary's rising up to Heaven—like smoke—was hinted at in the Bible:

• In the Song of Songs 3:6—"Who is that coming up from the wilderness like a column of smoke?"

• In Psalms 45:10–16—which describes a king receiving a princess into his palace: "Her clothing is of wrought gold. She shall be brought unto the king in raiment of needlework; the virgins her companions that follow her."

• In Psalms 132:8—"Arise, O Lord, and go to thy resting place, thou and the ark of thy might"—the argument being that the ark symbolizes the Virgin.

• The image of Mary as the "New Eve," and as the "woman" of Genesis 3:15, and as the "woman clothed with the sun" in Revelation.

• And from teachings of Saint Paul, specifically: "When the perishable puts on the imperishable, and the mortal puts on immortality, then shall come to pass the saying that is written: 'Death is swallowed up in victory' " (1 Cor. 15:54).

This reference from Paul is of particular importance since it calls on Mary as the New Eve. In a nutshell, it says:

Since the glorious Resurrection of Christ (the New Adam) was a victory over sin and death, so, too, Mary, as the New Eve, shares in the victory over sin and death. Her victory over *sin* is summed up in the miracle of the Immaculate Conception, whereas her victory over *death* is expressed in the dogma of her Assumption body and soul into Heaven.

It should be understood that the Church never seriously intended such biblical texts to matter. The appeal is to tradition.

MARY'S "DEATH," DATE AND PLACE UNKNOWN ◆

Did Mary actually die before she was assumed into Heaven? That is, did she pass out of consciousness, out of touch with this world?

After all, the Jewish patriarchs Enoch (Gen. 5:24) and Elijah (2 Kings 2:11) were spared physical death. Was Mary, as Christ's mother, similarly spared?

Two thousand years after the fact, the issue remains unresolved. Tradition favors death. The major fathers of the Church believed Mary died. The great Scholastic theologians thought so. Theoteknos, the fifth-century bishop of Livias, argued that it was fitting for the human body of Mary to be "entrusted to the earth for a little while"—a very little while, not long enough for decomposition to begin—then raised up in glory.

All agree that Mary's body never decayed in any way. This, based on the argument that Christ took his own flesh from Mary, and his body never decayed; thus, he'd never allow hers to suffer corruption.

As a Church homily goes: "It was fitting that she, who in childbirth kept her virginity undamaged, should also after death keep her body free from all corruption."

WITNESSES TO MARY'S "DEATH"? Late in the fifth century, a fascinating Greek narrative surfaced, falsely attributed to John. So compelling was the tale that versions soon circulated in Latin, Syriac, Arabic, Coptic, and Ethiopic. Here is that story of Mary's death:

Mary, assumed into Heaven, and present at the Last Judgment; German woodcut, 1493.

Mary spent her last days in Jerusalem. She often prayed at her son's tomb, requesting she be reunited with him. One day, an angel appeared to her at the tomb and announced that her wish was to be granted.

Mary begged to be allowed to see her son's apostles one last time before her death. They were scattered around the world—John in Ephesus, Peter in Rome, Thomas in India. Nonetheless, the Holy Spirit buoyed them up on clouds and brought them over many miles to Jerusalem. Paul was among them.

Mary, now weak and on her deathbed, roused herself and conversed with the guests. Angels appeared around the house. Sick people in the town miraculously recovered.

Presently Christ himself came to summon his mother. As he stood by the bed, her soul passed visibly into his hands. Her body went limp.

The apostles carried Mary's lifeless body from the house for burial. Jews menaced the funeral procession. They spit out slurs, but the stones they hurled at the mourners were miraculously repelled. Seeing this, many Jews converted.

Mary's body was laid in the tomb, the vault sealed. Soon thereafter, the apostles went to check on the Virgin's grave and discovered the door open and Christ standing inside the sepulcher. He was reinfusing Mary's soul into her body. The two of them—Christ and his Mother—then ascended into Heaven.

As said earlier, no account of Mary's death has the weight of authentic tradition behind it. Mary is unequivocally the most significant woman in Western history, and yet nothing is known with certainty about her final days and death.

Might we one day know? Perhaps—through archaeological discoveries of authentic texts or of a tomb.

That is why Vatican II, in supporting the doctrine of Mary's Assumption, has left open for further theological inquiry and discussion such questions as the circumstances surrounding her death, the site of her burial, and even the possibility that her body did undergo some degree of corruption, which was miraculously reversed before her Assumption.

Today, the Roman Catholic Church stresses that all doctrines pertaining to Mary must be viewed in the context of two other doctrines: that of Christ, and of his Church. That is, Christians know and honor Mary through Christ and his Church. This emphasis is deliberate: it's intended first to stem any extravagances of a Marian cult, and second to squelch criticism that the discipline of Mariology has exceeded the bounds of biblical scholarship and ecclesiastical wisdom. The Islamic Koran honors Mary, and all Christian Churches venerate her, but Protestants reject the Marianist doctrines in any form. Some feel that with the Immaculate Conception and Assumption, Mariology became Mariolatry.

MARIAN RELICS ◆

SHROUD OF THE VIRGIN. What is assumed to be the wrap of cloth that served briefly to cover Mary's dead or sleeping body is venerated in Aachen, Germany, at the cathedral built by the emperor Charlemagne, which also possesses the Infant Jesus' swaddling cloth. Encased in a golden shrine, the "Shroud of Our Lady" is displayed to the public once every seven years and is the cause of large pilgrimages to Aachen.

MARY'S VEIL. Pieces of a cloth veil that allegedly belonged to the Virgin Mary exist in several churches throughout Europe. No attempt has ever been made to assemble the fragments to see if they're of the same material; the largest swath, of silk, is in France at the Cathedral of Chartres, and it first surfaced in the tenth century. Encased in a golden reliquary, the cloth is the focal point of a large annual procession through the streets of Chartres commemorating Mary's Feast of the Assumption.

BELT OF THE BLESSED MOTHER. Encased in a gold reliquary with a crystal window at the Cathedral of Prato, Italy, is a green ribbon, woven from goat's hair and fine golden threads; it measures about four feet in length and is studded along one side with small olive-shaped buttons for fastening. This cincture, allegedly worn by the Virgin, first surfaced in the twelfth century (its earlier history is obscure), and later the Medici family of

*Pope Clement V (1305–14; left)
recognized Mary's house worthy
of veneration.
Pope Benedict XIII (1724–30)
ordered a basilica built over
the house.*

Florence had a reliquary especially constructed to house it. For several centuries, priests were only allowed to touch the ribbon if they wore silk gloves.

Aside from the above Marian relics, others are of even more dubious origins:

In the tenth century, several parts of tunics alleged to be Mary's were venerated in churches at Munchmunster, Regensburg, and Trier; the bishop of Verdun claimed to have an entire tunic intact. In the twelfth century, the bishop of Coutances in France claimed he possessed strands of Mary's hair; additional strands soon were being venerated in Spain and at Santa Maria Maggiore in Rome. From the eleventh century onward, vials, supposedly containing the Virgin's breast milk not consumed by the Baby Jesus, became astonishingly numerous.

MARY'S HOUSE FROM NAZARETH. According to tradition, the small house in which Mary was immaculately born, grew up, and where she virginally conceived Jesus was miraculously transported from Nazareth to Loreto, Italy, in the 1290s, carried aloft by a group of angels. The angels made two temporary stops en route, first setting the house down at Tersato, where it remained for three years, then stopping again at Recanati. Both sites are now shrines themselves. Eventually, the house ended up in Loreto.

A less popular legend has the stone house being dismantled rock by rock during the period of the Crusades, and transported by knights fearful that the house would be desecrated by the Infidels occupying the Holy Land. The first papal recognition of the house as a relic worthy of veneration was set forth in a bull by Pope Clement V in 1310.

Today, the small stone house is enclosed within a magnificent basilica, built in 1728 by order of Pope Benedict XIII, and is the focus of pilgrimages from around the world. Several modern pontiffs have visited the site, including Pope John XXIII on October 4, 1962, and Pope John Paul II on September 8, 1979.

Uisions
of the Uirgin

Guadalupe to Medjugorje

FIVE APPARITIONS FROM AROUND THE WORLD: FIFTEENTH TO TWENTIETH CENTURIES ◆

In pursuing the origins of the many apparitions of the Blessed Virgin Mary, let's begin with a brief overview of five notable cases, seeking out similarities.

DECEMBER 9, 1531, GUADALUPE, MEXICO. A woman in white appears at the town of Tepeyac to a local Indian recently baptized Juan Diego. Her instruction: Build a church in my honor on this site. Roses fall from Diego's mantle, on which a painting of the apparition materializes.

UPDATES:
1533. A small church is built as requested; expanded three years later due to the size of the crowds; dedicated in 1709.
1945. Pope Pius XII names Our Lady of Guadalupe patroness of the Americas, assigns her feast day as December 12, and issues the prayer to be said at the basilica on the site: "God of power and mercy, you blessed the Americas at Tepeyac with the presence of the Virgin Mary of Guadalupe. May her prayers help all men and women to accept each other as brothers and sisters. Through your justice present in our hearts, may your peace reign in the world."

NOVEMBER 27, 1830, PARIS, FRANCE. A woman in white, standing atop a half-globe, with rays of light emanating from her fingers, appears to nun Catherine Laboure in the chapel on rue du Bac. A message materializes in air: "Mary conceived free from sin, pray for us who have re-course to thee." A crucifix materializes. Then the letter *M*. Then a heart gar-landed with thorns. Another heart pierced by a sword, haloed in twelve stars. "Strike a medal of this vision," whispers the apparition, "all who wear it will receive great grace."

UPDATES:

1831. Visions continue through September of this year.

1832. The archbishop of Paris has the medal struck and fifteen hundred are issued in June; miracles associated with the medal begin. A book on the apparition enjoys huge sales, and is translated into many languages, including Chinese.

1838. A confraternity is founded with the "Miraculous Medal" as its shield of arms.

1854. The Vatican promulgates the dogma of the Virgin's Immaculate Conception, inspired in part by this apparition.

1947. Catherine Laboure is canonized a saint.

SEPTEMBER 19, 1846, LA SALETTE-FALLAVAUX, FRANCE. A woman in white appears to two children tending cattle high on a moun-tainside. She's crying because, she whispers, of all the irreligious people in the world, of those who do servile work on the Lord's Day and use abusive language. "Tell everyone I was here," she instructs as she vanishes.

UPDATE: A shrine is built on site; a new society of priests organize, call-ing themselves Missionaries of La Salette, and they arrive in the United States in 1892. In France, thousands stop servile work on Sundays.

FEBRUARY 11, 1858, LOURDES, FRANCE. A woman in white, rosary draped over her arm, appears at the mouth of a shallow grotto on a

Visions of the Virgin have always drawn crowds of believers—and skeptics.

rocky cliff to a fourteen-year-old peasant girl named Bernadette Soubirous, who is out gathering firewood. The vision says nothing. The mysterious woman appears to be no taller than, or older than, the peasant girl herself.

The woman reappears on March 25 and announces: "I am the Immaculate Conception"—a pointed reference to the dogma proclaimed just four years earlier.

UPDATES:

1862. The sitting pope declares the visions to be authentic and he authorizes a cult of Our Lady of Lourdes. An underground spring in the grotto, revealed to the teenager, is determined to have miraculous curative qualities.

1889. A basilica is built on site; soon it proves too small for crowds.

1933. The Vatican canonizes Bernadette Soubirous as a saint; feast of Our Lady of Lourdes, February 11.

1958. The inauguration of an immense prestressed concrete underground church on the site, seating twenty thousand.

1983. August 15, Pope John Paul II visits the shrine; first pontiff to do so.

1994. Some three million pilgrims now visit annually, among whom fifty thousand are sick or disabled.

MAY 13, 1917, FÁTIMA, PORTUGAL. A woman in white, announcing she comes from Heaven, appears to three children in the mountainous countryside. She tells them to accept suffering for the sake of sinners, orders them to pray for world peace, instructs them to return to the same site monthly, on the same day, at the same hour, for six months.

She reappears on June 13 and repeats the instructions.

On October 13, the sun "dances in the sky," light and heat intensify, a crowd of seventy thousand witness "miraculous solar phenomenon": the sun plummets toward earth, and people panic, believing the world's about to end. The woman in white appears, and requests a chapel be built on site in honor of the "Lady of the Rosary." She foretells the end of World War I, and asks for prayers for the conversion of Russia.

UPDATES:

1918. World War I ends.

Within three years of the apparitions, two of the original children, Francisco and Jacinta Marto, have died. The third child, Lucia dos Santos, enters a cloistered convent.

1930. The Church authenticates the apparitions and authorizes a cult of Our Lady of Fátima. Papal indulgences are granted to pilgrims.

1958. A basilica on the site is dedicated. It has a 213-foot tower surmounted by a large bronze crown and a crystal cross; it is flanked by hospitals and retreat houses; numerous healing cures by now have been reported.

1967. May 13, fiftieth anniversary of first vision; an estimated one million pilgrims gather to hear Pope Paul IV celebrate Mass and pray for peace.

CURRENT STATUS: The shrine's popularity remains strong. The secret message given by the Virgin to Lucia, suspected of forecasting worldwide disaster, and long concealed by the Vatican, remains a secret still.

Mary is alleged to have appeared countless times since her death in the first century C.E.; mostly to poor, uneducated, pious, adolescent girls. But only a handful of visions, the above five included, have been studied and authenticated by the Roman Catholic Church and approved worthy of devotion. A miracle is a wonder, a ray of supernatural light piercing the swathe of human history. For an instant, the Up There comes Down Here. Faith supersedes reason.

In the past, visions of the Virgin were easier to accept than they are in today's technological world when a transplanted heart is no longer a miracle. In addition, today the Virgin's simple, solitary appearances, to simple, solitary folk, must compete with the extravagant theatrics and spectacles of the secular wonders of our age.

The Catholic Church is extremely cautious when it comes to visions of the Blessed Mother. As a document prepared by America's bishops states:

> *Even when a "private revelation" has spread to the entire world, as in the case of Our Lady of Lourdes, and has been recognized in the liturgical calendar, the Church does not make mandatory the acceptance either of the original story or of particular forms of piety springing from it. . . . We remind true lovers of Our Lady of the danger of superficial sentiment and vain credulity.*

ORIGIN OF MARY'S APPARITIONS: ELEVENTH CENTURY ◆

As when analyzing UFO sightings, one attempts to isolate similarities from among Mary's many visions. What did Mary look like? Who reported seeing her?

One also attempts to pin down the very first time the extraordinary event occurred, with the hope that it correlates to some significant human historical happening. A devastating earthquake, say, a deluge, or a decimating plague.

It's sensible to assume that the apparitions of the Virgin did not begin until after her death. The date of her death is unknown, but we do know that Mary was a girl of fourteen or fifteen when she bore Jesus Christ. At the time of his Crucifixion some thirty-three years later, she'd have been around forty-eight. So even if she lived a long human life, she'd most likely have died by the end of the first century C.E.

Did she start appearing as an apparition right away?

Did she look Semitic then, as opposed to the distinctly fair, Anglo-Saxon visage she later adopted—or was perceived as having by her European sighters?

Were her clothes from the start always a long white gown, white head cape, and pale blue accessories?

Was her message always a request for a shrine on the site and prayers for peace?

Let's start with the first apparition.

LITTLE WALSINGHAM, HAMLET IN NORFOLK, ENGLAND: 1061 C.E. ◆

From the best sources, it seems that Mary did not start appearing in a simple fashion to ordinary folk—as opposed to appearing to martyrs and mystics in the throes of agony and ecstasy—until a little more than a thousand years after her death.

Why? Only God knows. Certainly it was not because the Dark Ages were without travail and people not in need of spiritual uplift.

One of the earliest Virgin sightings, with the site still an important center of pilgrimage, occurred in the year 1061 at Little Walsingham, in Norfolk, England. As the legend goes (it was not written down for another three hundred years):

The Virgin appeared on three different occasions to one Mrs. Richeldis, the lady of the manor. Descriptions of the Virgin have not survived, nor has most of the exchange between Mary and Mrs. Richeldis. In each vision, Mary appeared as a housewife inside her own humble home at Nazareth, where Jesus had grown up.

Mrs. Richeldis was instructed to replicate the Middle Eastern stone house on her own estate at Walsingham. Mary, in fact, gave specific dimensions, then parted, saying: "This little house at Walsingham shall be held in remembrance of the great joy of my salutation when Gabriel told me I should through humility be the mother of God's son."

Mrs. Richeldis instructed her craftsmen to build the Nazareth home. One night, the building, then under construction, changed location on its own, moving seventy yards. When completed, Christ's cottage was in unmistakable eleventh-century Norfolk style, without a single identifiable Palestinian element. It looked exactly like all of the simple homes in Little Walsingham. Nonetheless, this English-style house became the first Marian shrine in Europe.

This first recorded case of the sighting of the Virgin does not inspire confidence—though it has inspired a wealth of healing cures and conversions. The shrine, still popular, has never been officially recognized by the Church.

Europe is the center for the largest number of early apparitions. Many were collected in a book, *Miracles of the Blessed Virgin Mary*, written around 1435 by one Johannes Herolt. The contents, in brief: Mary always takes a close interest in local Church matters, family affairs, education, and politics. She always promises miracles in return for devotion, she requests prayers for peace, and she suggests that character is built by sacrifice and self-denial.

In truth, not a single apparition before the one in Guadalupe, Mexico, in 1531 is believed by the Church to be authentic.

OUR LADY OF GUADALUPE—MARY ARRIVES
IN THE AMERICAS: DECEMBER 9, 1531 ✦

This case marks the first Church-certified instance of a Marian apparition.

Yet even this much-touted incident was not written down until 1560, twenty-nine years after the fifty-seven-year-old Aztec Indian who'd recently been christened Juan Diego spotted the Virgin. Till then, the case had survived—and was embellished and romanticized—by word of mouth. Here are the bare bones of the story:

Sunrise on the morning of December 9. Juan Diego, of Aztec Indian heritage—his Nahuatl name is "Singing Eagle"—is racing to attend Mass at the

Our Lady of Guadalupe—Mary's first appearance in the Americas.

church closest to his small Mexican village. As he reaches the base of a 130-foot-high hill known as Tepeyac, site of a past temple to the Aztec Mother Goddess, an eerie silence and stillness fill the air. Juan pauses, glances around. Day has barely broken, yet Juan is bathed in glowing sunlight.

The strange quiet is finally broken by a frail, youthful, female voice calling his name. Climbing up the hill from where the sound emanated, Juan reaches the arid top and spots a floating apparition: a beautiful young Mexican girl, about fourteen years old, with long dark hair, who Juan immediately assumes is Christ's mother, the Virgin Mary.

Issues of ethnicity did not concern him. And why should they, since Mary speaks in Nahuatl: "*Nopiltzin, campa tiauh?*" ["Where are you going?"]

Mary requests a chapel, a *teocali* or "temple," be built on the site. She instructs Juan to relay her request to Bishop Zumarraga, five miles away, in Mexico City (Tenochtitlán), at its original island location. He rushes off on foot.

The bishop is suspicious, but says he'll think it over.

Juan, on the way home, again encounters the Virgin Mary. She tells him to try the bishop again on Sunday. He'll be more receptive then.

After Sunday Mass in the town of Tlaltelolco, Juan confronts Zumarraga once again with the Virgin's simple request. A small chapel, that's all, not a cathedral. More tolerant this time, Zumarraga suggests that Juan coax the young teenage apparition to prove her identity by way of miracles. Juan does; and his uncle who's seriously ill instantly recovers. Following the Virgin's newest instructions, Juan picks fresh roses from a barren bush, and carries the miraculous blooms to the bishop concealed in his long ratty outer cape, a *tilma*.

In front of the bishop and his entire household—who'd all detected a powerful scent of roses coming from inside Juan's coarse-woven cape—the peasant Juan rips open the *tilma* and releases a shower of unseasonal flowers. And painted on the cape's inside is a magnificent full-color image of the Virgin, which everyone scrambles to see. House servants snatch up roses as relics. Juan himself is speechless. Convinced he's witnessed a miracle, the bishop falls to his knees and begs that he may have the dirty, threadbare cape—which he hangs on the wall of his private chapel.

The Virgin whispers to Juan: "Call me and my image Santa Maria de Guadalupe."

EFFECT LEGITIMIZES CAUSE. Within seven years of the Guadalupe apparitions, eight million Latin American pagans were baptized. On one day alone, one thousand natives were married through the Christian sacrament of matrimony. On Easter Sunday, 1540, twelve warring tribes assembled peacefully for services at a Catholic church. As is often the case with miracles, beneficial effects legitimize paranormal causes.

In whatever manner the curious image may have originated on Juan Diego's cape, the garment is still on display in Mexico—the Marian equivalent of Christ's shroud at Turin, Italy.

AZTEC TRANSLATION FACTOR? There is one strange twist to this tale, which might explain the remarkable conversion power of the Virgin over the native population.

Mary had asked, in Juan's native Nahuatl, to be called Santa Maria de Guadalupe. The Aztec alphabet has no letter for *G* or *D*—or for *R*; Maria is pronounced "Malia." One linguist has suggested that to Aztec ears, "de Guadalupe," spoken by Spaniards, easily could have sounded like "de Guatlashupe," close to their *tetlcoatlaxopeuh*, a pagan epithet that means "Stone Serpent Trodden Upon"—a reference to the Aztec's bloodthirsty god Quetzalcoatl, once idolized as a feathered serpent to whom countless men, women, and children were excruciatingly sacrificed.

This opens the possibility that the Virgin's requested title "Santa Maria de Guadalupe" was interpreted by locals to mean that the Mother of God had come to crush the head of their horrible serpent. "Stone Serpent Trodden Upon." Christ's Mother, the Coredemptrix, as local savior. In other words, the apparitions announced that Mary would suppress and supplant the ferocious feathered beast.

In vanquishing the savage god Quetzalcoatl, had Christ's mother fulfilled an ancient Aztec prophesy?

Or was Genesis 3:15, which relates the crushing of the serpent's head— and which later would be invoked by Rome to establish the dogma of Mary's Immaculate Conception—unwittingly being played out in Latin America through a language error?

Or, then again, was this the far-reaching hand of God himself, benevolently stroking a continent of heathens, showing them the way?

In any case, the fact is that Christianity swept rapidly through the region. Native Indians embraced the symbols of the new faith—rays of light, stars, crucifixes, images of a beautiful Mexican Virgin in white. Jesus Christ had died on the cross for them, too, and now he'd sent his mother to them directly, and speaking their native Nahuatl tongue, she had announced that she'd trodden on the serpent's head.

Today, descendants of the Aztecs praise God's Mother, "Teotl Inantzin," and honor her by her title "Coatlalupej," and sing of how "She freed us from great evil, She crushed the serpent!"

A SAD NOTE. The Spaniards brought with them to the New World not just Christianity, but guns and smallpox. Later, mumps and measles. The Aztecs had no immunity. No guns, either, a distinct disadvantage once the Spaniards decided to claim the land for themselves.

By 1595, the Aztec death toll from arms and disease was 18.5 million; eighty years earlier, the natives had numbered 25 million. Mary, who'd crushed their mythical serpent, couldn't save them from the real threats of the Spaniards's guns and microorganisms. For the Aztecs, Christianity nearly was genocide.

MODERN VISIONS OF MARY: TWENTIETH CENTURY ◆

From the number of claimants, the Blessed Virgin has been busy in our own century. Indeed, she's never been more frequently sighted than in the last 150 years. This period is called "The Marian Age."

The much-publicized apparitions at Fátima, Portugal, in 1917 seem to have triggered a sensitivity in simple children to spot the Virgin—or, as critics charge, children have found a way to get attention, to add a little luster and commotion to their otherwise ordinary lives.

After Portugal, Mary is spotted more than forty times in two Belgian towns:

BEAURAING IN 1932; BANNEUX IN 1933 ◆

Beauraing is a village of about two thousand people, sixty miles southeast of Brussels, a few miles from the French border. The story:

Mary appears to five children in a small grotto near a convent; the nuns had constructed the shrine as a replica of that at Lourdes. Mary is seen as a bright light, which one child initially thinks is a car headlight. The nuns, when called outside, see nothing.

In subsequent visions, Mary has a halo of golden rays crowning her head. She wears a white dress with blue sash, her face is so radiant one child exclaims: "It looked like she had an electric bulb inside." Mary speaks in French, and her message to the children is sensible: Be good, obey your parents.

One day, one child asks: "Must we build a chapel for you here?" (One wonders if the child had been reading of past apparitional requests.)

Mary nods, Yes.

Transcripts later reveal that the child consistently asked leading questions, which the Virgin had merely to affirm or deny.

One night, a child in town is miraculously cured of suppurating leg sores. Throngs of people flock to the grotto and pray.

In all, the children count thirty-three separate visions of the Virgin.

The final vision is a sad one indeed. Startled by a photographer's flash, a spectator in the crowd shouts, enthusiastically: "A ball of fire!"

"Yes! Yes! The Virgin!" screams one of the children, dropping to her knees, prostrating herself on the ground, overcome by fits of ecstasy at the arrival of the fireball. The child's writhing goes on for several minutes. The crowd, who had seen the flash come from the camera, quietly disperses. The other children assist the hysterical one to her feet. They explain about the flash.

On their way home, all five children are crying; one says to a witness: "The lovely days are over."

Twelve days after the last apparition at Beauraing, Mary is spotted at Banneux, by a young girl, Marietta Beco: "Mamma, there's a woman in the garden."

"I am the Virgin of the Poor," says the figure. She requests—what else?—"a little chapel." On the site.

Subsequent visions are unspectacular, even banal, and can be downright sad: one day, the Virgin abandons Marietta in a freezing downpour, refusing to appear. Distraught in front of witnesses, the child lay huddled on the wet ground, hiccuping, sobbing convulsively, gulping out Hail Marys, which fall on deaf ears.

Most apparitions are believed by locals and by the town priest or regional bishops. Despite the banality of the visions at Banneux, it is now the site of a magnificent shrine, a grotto and a gathering of buildings that match in splendor any other center of pilgrimage and miraculous healing.

The same is true of Beauraing. Said the bishop who headed an investigation into the thirty-three visions and many "authentic" miracles: "We are able in all serenity and prudence to affirm that the Queen of Heaven appeared to the children of Beauraing during the winter of 1932–33 . . . for the conversion of sinners."

OUR LADY OF MOUNT CARMEL:
GARABANDAL, SPAIN, 1961–65 ◆

The extraordinary worldwide devotion to Mary as Our Lady of Mount Carmel—shrines, films, feasts—is disproportionate to the quality of the more than two thousand visions in Garabandal, Spain; it's more in line with the quantity of those apparitions.

Never has the Virgin made more trips to a site, been first heralded by an angel, later accompanied by two archangels, or departed with so tantalizing a message: a promise, we'll see, that continues to bring the devout to the Spanish shrine in droves.

It must be stated that the Feast of Our Lady of Mount Carmel, celebrated on July 16, originated with the Carmelite nuns about the year 1380, soon after the order was approved. Pope Sixtus V, in 1587, officially sanctioned the feast, and it proved to be a particularly popular devotion to the Spanish.

The Garabandal story:

Again, children are involved. Four this time. All from peasant families. Conchita, Loli, and Jancita, age twelve; Mari, age eleven. Over four years, they will see Mary some two thousand times, often more than once a day.

Sunday, June 18, 1961. The children are playing marbles with stones when Conchita spots an angel. From her diary, written a year later:

He was wearing a long seamless blue robe. He had fairly big pink wings. His face was small. . . . His eyes were black. He had fine hands and short fingernails. He looked about nine years old. But, although he was a child to look at, he gave the impression of being very strong.

July 1. After several brief appearances, the angel speaks for the first time, announcing that the Virgin Mary will appear the next day as Our Lady of Mount Carmel. Two diary entries:

At each side of Her there stood an angel. One was St. Michael; we did not know the other . . . one would have said that they were twins . . . on a level with Our Lady, we saw a very large eye, which seemed to us to be the eye of God.

Our Lady comes wearing a white robe and blue cloak. She has a crown of golden stars: her feet are not visible. Her hands are slender with a scapular on her right wrist. The scapular is reddish. Her hair is long, wavy, and dark brown, parted in the middle. Her face is long, her nose is long and slender and her

mouth is dainty and very lovely; her lips are just a little bit thick. Her complex-
ion is quite dark but lighter than the angel's and she has a very beautiful voice,
very unusual. . . . Our Lady seems to be about eighteen years old.

Eucharistic Hosts miraculously appear on Conchita's tongue; or at least
they're present when she sticks out her tongue. Mary imparts dire warnings
of impending disaster:

Many cardinals, many bishops, and many priests are on the road to perdition,
and are taking many souls with them. Less and less importance is being given to
the Eucharist. You should turn the wrath of God away from yourselves by your
efforts. If you ask His forgiveness with sincere hearts, He will pardon you. I,
your Mother, through the intercession of St. Michael the Archangel, ask you to
amend your lives. You are now receiving the last warnings. I love you very much
and do not want your condemnation.

No wonder the Vatican was skeptical about Garabandal. The "road to
perdition" seems to be a reproach for modernization within the Church.
Conchita, the ringleader of the group, was a clever little girl. The unusual
twist to the Garabandal message is this: The end of the world as we know it
will be forecast, in detail, at the site at eight-thirty in the evening on a Thursday. Which Thursday, only Conchita knows. Every Thursday is a popular
night at the shrine. On the final Thursday, whenever that turns out to be, the
Virgin will perform a colossal miracle that will permanently alter the site in
some stupendous way, and a visible warning of impending destruction will
echo round the world. It is this expectancy of Apocalypse that continues to
draw believers to Garabandal, Spain. Any Thursday might be *the* Thursday.
As our twentieth century draws toward a close and claims of Armageddon
mount—as happens with the end of a millennium—the site at Spain could
become standing room only.

MEDJUGORJE, BOSNIA-HERCEGOVINA, JUNE 24, 1981 ◆

Mary could not forestall a bloody civil war on the borders of Croatia, site of
the now-famous on-again/off-again apparitions at Medjugorje—the town's
name means "between the hills."
Again, adolescents are involved. Two: fifteen-year-old Ivanka, and sixteen-
year-old Mirjana. Eventually, many children will claim to see the Virgin—as
will the Franciscan parish priest, Father Jozo Zovko. The events:

June 24, 1981. The visions begin with Mary revealing herself as the "Queen of Peace."

Communist authorities forbid crowds of believers from gathering at the hillside site; Mary moves to a village church.

A local bishop forbids use of the church; Mary moves to the parish house.

Church officials feud among themselves. The Franciscan priests who minister to Saint James Parish, which serves the village, are true believers. However, Bishop Pavao Zanic, of the Diocese of Mostar, in which the apparitions take place, publicly doubts their authenticity, and bluntly calls them "collective hallucinations."

July 27. Mary announces: "Men must be reconciled with God and with one another. For this to happen, it is necessary to believe, to pray, to fast, to go to confession."

June 28. Fifteen thousand people arrive to view the encounter with the Virgin. Local police grill the adolescents but come up with no medical rationale to commit them to a psychiatric hospital.

July 13. Communist authorities block roads to the site, for the crowds hopeful of miracles are now out of hand.

August 6. A word appears written in the sky: *Mir*, meaning "peace." Thousands claim to see it; the Virgin's message, they say, isn't to be stopped by a roadblock.

August 15, feast of Mary's Assumption into Heaven. Thousands flock to the site; the frustrated police arrest Pastor Zovko, charge him with "subversion." The priest sees the Virgin, too. The Communists are paranoid that the visions are a papal plot to draw worldwide attention to the repressive government regime. "I am the Queen of Peace," stresses Mary that day.

October. Mary predicts and chastises: "Russia is the people in which God will be most glorified. The West has advanced civilization, but without God, as though it were its own creator."

In 1991, the bishops of then Yugoslavia, in a vote of 19 to 1, declared: "On the basis of research conducted so far, one cannot affirm that supernatural apparitions are involved."

About the same time, the influential Jesuit priest Father Giandomenico Mucci stated: "All the messages I've seen from Medjugorje can be reduced to one word, conversion. One does not understand why Mary must repeat herself like that. Nor can one understand the banality of the language."

WHY MARY APPEARS TO CHILDREN ◆

Or to childlike adults. Fifty-five-year-old Juan Diego of Guadalupe, for instance, was a naïve, poorly schooled, credulous soul.

Critics point to children's fertile imaginations and need for attention from adults. Believers underscore a child's purity and innocence.

In his survey of Marian apparitions, *A Woman Clothed with the Sun*, John Delaney, a believer, lays out the Church's point of view. Why does Mary not "appear to learned scholars, people in important positions, or the great of the world?" he asks. Aren't these people better suited to spread her message and finance new shrines?

Mary, he acknowledges, has repeatedly appeared "to the poorest, humblest, most unlearned and illiterate of her children." Because:

> *These were people whose minds were uncluttered with the pretentious philosophies and skepticisms of the day or whose outlook on life was not befuddled by the complexities of the great savants' knowledge and teaching.*
>
> *These were the little children who would acknowledge . . . that the Mother of God had appeared to them, unhesitatingly and unquestioningly. Directly and unequivocally, they would deliver the message she had given them exactly as she had given it to them, and no amount of questioning and bullying would change their stories.*

When one believes in miracles, where does one draw the line? When does a miraculous happening become incredible? Or any more incredible than it was initially?

Consider an adolescent involved in one of the most famous Marian apparitions ever:

MARIE BERNARDE ("BERNADETTE") SOUBIROUS: LOURDES, FEBRUARY 11, 1858 ◆

Born at Lourdes, France, in 1844, first child of a poverty-stricken miller named François and his young wife, Louise, Marie was so diminutive, frail, and sickly that her parents called her Bernadette. Undersized, shy, emotionally sensitive, she suffered asthma and was handicapped by a lack of schooling.

Her health was not helped by a bout of cholera, contracted during the epidemic of 1854, when she was ten. Nor were her asthma and allergies (as we'd call the symptoms today) helped by her living in a dank, dark, moldy basement with an earthen floor, with no sanitary provisions.

A few years before her early death in 1879, at age thirty-five, and after she'd been admitted to the convent of the Sisters of Charity at Nevers, she'd answer inquiries about her work by saying: "I am getting on with my life's work. Being ill."

It was to this frail, sickly, unschooled girl out in the countryside that the Virgin chose to show herself on February 11, 1858. Bernadette was fourteen. Mary—appearing to be about sixteen years old herself—would continue to materialize another seventeen times in a shallow cave on the bank of the river Gave, departing on July 18 of that year. Others often were present, but only Bernadette saw the teenage Virgin.

Mary, identifying herself as the "Immaculate Conception"—not insignificantly the title that was made dogma in 1854, year of the cholera epidemic—asked that a chapel be constructed on the site.

One day, the Virgin instructed Bernadette to drink from a nearby spring—an existing but forgotten spring? Or one miraculously created? Legend has it that the ground was dry and that frail Bernadette dug and dug until water bubbled up, filling a stream—which to this day produces a prodigious twenty-seven thousand gallons of curative healing water per week— the renowned waters of Lourdes.

Bernadette appears not to have been an hysterical girl given to pious flailing in fits of ecstasy, like so many visionaries. Indeed, she seems to have been a stable individual, cursed with poor health—which only deteriorated under the incessant attention and scrutiny that is part and parcel of witnessing apparitions. Despite grueling cross-examination about Mary's visits, young Bernadette never wavered in her story.

Nor did Bernadette play any part in elevating the site of the shallow cave and copious stream to the status of a sacred shrine. Quite the contrary. Wishing to escape the unwanted publicity, which was equal measures of awe and skepticism, she entered a convent. She did not even attend the 1876 consecration of the basilica on the site, the chapel the Virgin had requested.

Bernadette Soubirous lived out her sickly, self-effacing life as a nun, dying at age thirty-five. Lourdes became one of the greatest pilgrim shrines in the history of Christendom.

She was beatified in 1925, and when she was finally canonized by Pope Pius XI in 1933, it was not so much for her eighteen visions of the Virgin, but for the integrity, humility, and holiness of her life. Saint Bernadette's feast day is April 16.

U.S.A. ◆

In America, in this century alone, there have been more than two hundred reported cases of apparitions. What are we to make of them?

"They are evidence of a great spiritual hunger among the people," says the Reverend Thomas Thompson, director of the Catholic Church's Marian Library at the University of Dayton, Ohio, which holds the world's largest collection of materials on the Virgin Mary. "A hunger that grows when times become difficult."

According to Thompson, the Church has approved only fourteen apparitions over the last 160 years. And, as we've seen, approval does not mean that Catholics are encouraged to believe the events, merely that they are not forbidden to do so.

The Vatican is loath to debunk a vision of Mary for fear of treading upon the faith of thousands. Yet Rome wants to keep miracles separate from magic and fraud. Though the Vatican has banned Church-sponsored pilgrimages to Medjugorje—suggesting that the apparitions were the hoax of local priests—the site remains immensely popular and has a large following in America.

When the current pope was asked if *he* believed in the Virgin's appearances at Medjugorje, he answered more like a politician than a pontiff: Just because there is a natural explanation for an event, said the pontiff, does not mean that it can't be an occasion for spiritual renewal.

Papal Infallibility

Tradition to Dogma

PAPAL INFALLIBILITY: THE HISTORY ◆

Emperors, kings, and czars have reigned absolutely. So, too, have dictators, duces, and führers.

But the lofty decrees of such secular autocrats were never binding on their successors. A new emperor could negate, cancel, contradict, deny, revoke, or denounce the judgment by a predecessor.

However, no Roman Catholic pope can ever refute, impugn, rebut, debate, or contradict the infallible findings of any previous pontiffs. That can make life hard for the sitting bishop of Rome.

Times change. Society and the world changes. Moral codes change. But past infallible decisions cannot be changed. For this reason, one bishop cursed the doctrine of papal infallibility as "the work of the Devil."

The extraordinary saga, little known, of how one supreme pontiff in the summer of 1870 "decreed" himself and all his successors forever infallible on matters of faith and morals is the subject of this chapter. It is a tale that probably the most devout Roman Catholics have never heard told before—an escapade of infighting, power plays, political intrigue, and papal arm-twisting that is not taught in Catholic schools.

A few clarifying facts first:

EXACTLY WHAT IS PAPAL INFALLIBILITY? It is the doctrine in Roman Catholic theology which asserts that the pope, acting as the religion's supreme teacher, cannot err when he teaches on matters of faith and morals: when he teaches *ex cathedra* or "from the chair" of Saint Peter (from the Latin *cathedra*, "chair").

The doctrine is based on the belief that the Church has been divinely entrusted with the teaching mission of Jesus Christ; therefore, God himself, in the voice of the Holy Spirit, in essence speaks *through* the pope on certain matters of faith and morals. This is why an infallible decision cannot be in error, and cannot be reversed. Simply put, God does not make mistakes; therefore, God need never change his mind.

Popular in the United States in the early 1860s was a Roman Catholic catechism bearing the official imprimatur (Latin *imprimere*, "imprint") of the archbishop of New York. There any Catholic could read:

QUESTION: Must not Catholics believe the pope himself to be infallible?

ANSWER: This is a Protestant invention, it is no article of the Catholic faith; no decision of his can bind on pain of heresy, unless it be received and enforced by the teaching body, that is, the bishops of the Church.

A few years later, the doctrine of infallibility was made binding dogma and all the catechisms had to be destroyed.

WASN'T THE POPE, AS SAINT PETER'S SUCCESSOR, ALWAYS INFALLIBLE? No. That may come as a surprise to many Catholics. But the truth is, the term "infallibility" was rarely mentioned in the early and medieval Church. Granted, early Church fathers and later theologians felt confident in the fidelity of papal teachings, but no supreme pontiff up until the summer of 1870 was ever officially infallible.

The first infallible pope was Pius IX, the 253rd successor of Saint Peter, who reigned from 1846 to 1878.

Pius IX "decreed" his own inerrancy on matters of faith and morals on July 18, 1870—against fierce opposition from numerous bishops. Many bishops, then in Rome for the First Vatican Council, walked out of the assembly rather than concede to Pius's insistence that he and all his successors, for all time, be made infallible. Rather than cast a vote against their conscience, they packed their bags and departed from the Vatican, fearful that the new dogma would ultimately destroy the Catholic Church.

"All power tends to corrupt; absolute power corrupts absolutely," wrote British historian and philosopher Lord Acton to Bishop Mandell Creighton in 1887.

Since the doctrine of infallibility has been, from the day it was promulgated, the source of heated debate within and outside the Church, it's fitting to present the Vatican's own definition of the dogma—which by the final vote of bishops at Vatican Council was greatly watered down from the harsher wording Pius IX had originally demanded:

> *The Roman Pontiff, when he speaks* ex cathedra, *that is, when in the exercise of his office as the pastor and teacher of all Christians, he defines by virtue of his supreme apostolic authority the doctrine concerning faith and morals to be held by the universal Church, is, by the divine assistance promised to him in the person of St. Peter, possessed of that infallibility wherewith the divine Redeemer wished His Church should be endowed in defining doctrine concerning faith and morals; and that for this cause such definitions of the Roman Pontiff are irreformable of themselves and not because of the consent of the church.*

That last phrase—"and not because of the consent of the church"—is an eye-opener. It means, simply, that the pope need not consult, or collect a consensus opinion from, bishops, archbishops, or cardinals. No matter how strong their opposition to an issue, how large their majority, how cogent their arguments, they cannot overrule the pope. Technically, on matters of faith and morals, the pontiff is truly supreme.

In practice, a pope does, of course, consult with his bishops. But he is not bound by their counsel.

WORD ORIGIN: A "CURIA" OF MEN. In the day-to-day exercise of his jurisdiction, the pope relies on the assistance of the Roman Curia, a name first used for the body of papal helpers in the eleventh century. "Curia" is Latin for "assembly of men"—and derives delightfully from *co viria*, "together virile."

The Curia, by the way, had its origin in the local body of presbyters (priests), deacons (lower than priests), and notaries (secretaries) who assisted the early bishops of Rome.

From within the Roman Curia emerged, in 1179, the Sacred College of Cardinals, the corporate body with the exclusive right to elect a pope. Upon the death of a pope, the College of Cardinals automatically steps to the helm of Holy Mother Church—the way the U.S. vice-president takes over upon the death of a president.

**NEW TESTAMENT EVIDENCE:
GOSPELS OF LUKE AND MATTHEW** ◆

In arriving at the vote for papal infallibility in 1870, the Vatican Council cited two major biblical references to support the dogma. First, Christ's promise to the apostle Peter at the Last Supper:

> *But I have prayed for you that your faith may not fail; and when you have turned again [converted], strengthen [confirm] your brethren. (Luke 22:32)*

And Christ's words to Peter that established the so-called Petrine primacy— that is, the claim of all bishops of Rome for their position as head of the Christian faith worldwide:

> *And I tell you, you are Peter, and on this rock I will build my church, and the powers of death [the gates of hell] shall not prevail against it. I will give you the keys of the kingdom of heaven, and whatever you bind on earth shall be bound in heaven, and whatever you loose on earth shall be loosed in heaven. (Matt: 16:18–19)*

Vatican I, in defining the pope as the direct successor of Saint Peter, employed, in addition to the reference from Matthew, two quotations from John:

> *Feed my lambs. . . . Tend my sheep. (21:15–6)*

> *Jesus beheld him [Simon Peter] and said, "Thou art Simon . . . thou shall be called 'Cephas,' which by interpretation is stone." (1:42)*

This last seems to identify Peter as the "rock" in "on this rock I will build my church." At least this is the Roman Catholic interpretation. (More on this to follow.)

Indeed, when the pope celebrates Mass—standing over Peter's "mortal remains"—two hundred feet above his head, in letters five feet high, is: *Tu es Petrus, et super hanc petram aedificabo ecclesiam meam, et portae inferni non praevalebunt adversus eam*—"You are Peter, and on this rock I will build my church, and the gates of hell shall not prevail against it."

Before getting into the real origins of papal infallibility, it is necessary to address the origin of the papacy itself.

PETER, FIRST BISHOP OF ROME: TO 65 c.e. ◆

First there was the title *bishop of Rome*. It is a clear reference to the traditional belief that the apostle Peter preached at Rome, established a congregation there, was its "overseer," and was martyred there, perhaps in 65 C.E.

The word "bishop" is from the Greek *episkopos*, meaning "overseer."

Evidence in the New Testament (Acts 20:17–28) suggests that originally the terms "bishop" and "presbyter" (Greek *presbyteros*, "elder"; from which

Peter, first bishop of Rome
(c. 33–c. 65).

we derive the word "priest") were interchangeable. A bishop/presbyter made sacrifices and performed other sacred rites.

The earliest Christian communities most likely were governed by colleges of elders, as were Jewish synagogues. In the course of time, the need developed to have a single liturgical president, and by late in the first century C.E. that authority had centered in one leader called a bishop or "overseer."

Furthermore, the chief overseer at Rome soon was honored by the additional title of "pope," from the Greek *papas*, "father." Origin of our endearment "papa." Thus the head bishop at Rome was "father" of all the faithful, "papa" of all congregations of Christians everywhere.

This came as quite a shock to congregations outside Rome that also laid claim to apostolic foundations. Not all Christians lived in Rome, under the bishop of Rome.

In truth, the bishop of Rome became increasingly important after the imperial Roman government was transferred to Constantinople in the fourth century. This left an enormous political, administrative, and emotional gap to fill, and the bishops of Rome gladly stepped in. They started to elevate the apostle Peter over the evangelist Paul, claiming, in fact, that Paul had labored under Peter's jurisdiction. Whereas the New Testament clearly speaks of Peter as the apostle to the Jews and Paul as the apostle to the Gentiles, the bishops of Rome now cast Peter as Paul's superior. Thus the groundwork was laid for the bishops of Rome to claim for themselves direct papal lineage back to Peter and the biblical quotation: "You are Peter, and on this rock I will build my church."

It is little known, but not until the fourth century did the Church at Rome insist, emphatically, that it was the *Apostolic See*—the word "see" from the Latin *sedes*, meaning "seat" or "center of authority."

In fact, before that time, early Church fathers had argued that Christ's word "rock"—"on this rock I will build my church"—made reference not to Peter and his church at Rome, but to Christ himself and his faithful followers wherever they resided under their own bishops.

TEXTUAL EVIDENCE. Peter, originally called Simon, a native of Bethsaida, a village on the Sea of Galilee, and a fisherman by trade, clearly was Christ's chief apostle. On this all four Gospels agree. Peter is mentioned with conspicuous frequency, his name appears first in all lists of the twelve, and he belongs to the inner group present at significant events:

- Raising Jairus's daughter from death (Matt. 9:18–26)
- The Transfiguration (Matt. 17:1–8)
- Christ's Agony in the Garden (Matt. 26:37)
- First disciple to enter Christ's tomb (Luke 24:12)
- First to whom the risen Christ showed himself (Luke 24:34)
- The disciple who explained the meaning of Pentecost (Acts 2:14–40)
- Opened the Church to Gentiles by having Cornelius baptized without undergoing circumcision (Acts 10:9–48)

According to tradition, because Peter readily recognized Christ as the Messiah, Jesus bestowed on him the Aramaic name Cephas, meaning "stone" or "rock," and rendered "Peter" in Greek. Roman Catholics believe Peter is the "rock" on which Christ founded his Church. Other Christians believe Christ meant that Peter was a "rock of faith." Stone-solid in his belief.

TOMB OF SAINT PETER. Few archaeologists endorse the Church claim that excavations in the 1940s, 1950s, and 1960s under Saint Peter's Basilica unearthed Peter's tomb, containing his mortal remains. Most agree that the excavations reveal that a Christian congregation at Rome, in the early third century, believed that Peter's grave was on the site and revered the area. As we saw earlier, the skeleton in the crypt is that of a man five feet four inches tall; tradition has Peter being a very large man.

It is because the bishop of Rome claims to be the successor to Saint Peter, prince of the apostles, that he holds the "Petrine chair" and thus wields supreme legislative, executive, and judicial powers—an old-fashioned absolute monarchy.

By the fifth century, the bishop of Rome had laid claim to the additional title *supreme pontiff*, or *Summus Pontifex* (literally, "Highest Bridge Builder"), which had previously been held by pagan Roman emperors who headed the college of presbyters or priests.

Jesus washing Peter's feet, as "servant of the servants of God."

In the early Middle Ages, he picked up the title *Vicar of Christ*—"vicar" from the Latin *vicarius*, meaning "vicarious." Thus, the pope is the "deputy" or "representative" of Christ on earth.

Today, the official Vatican directory, the *Annuario Pontificio*, lists the pope's full set of titles as:

> *Bishop of Rome. Vicar of Christ. Successor of the Prince of the Apostles. Supreme Pontiff of the Universal Church. Patriarch of the West. Primate of Italy. Archbishop and Metropolitan of the Roman Province. Sovereign of the State of Vatican City (created in 1929). Servant of the Servants of God.*

That last humble title, Christian to its core, seems incongruously meek in the shadow of its royal antecedents. Yet, when a pope issues a solemn pronouncement of great importance to the whole Church, he signs off not with one of his autocratic titles, but with this subservient pastoral designation, "servant of the servants of God."

As the great fourteenth-century writer Petrarch observed while on a visit to Rome in which he glimpsed papal finery: "I am astounded to see these men loaded with gold and clad in purple. We seem to be among the kings of the Persians, before whom we must fall down and worship. O apostles and early popes, is it for this ye labored?"

In reference to the Vatican's thousands of rooms, countless treasures of art, summer palace Castel Gandolfo (slightly larger than the Vatican) on Alban Lake with its sumptuous swimming pool (which Pope John Paul built for himself), Peter De Rosa, dean of theology at Corpus Christi College, London, asked: "If Peter were to arise from his tomb under the dome and be told that all this was erected in his honor, how would he react?"

Jesus renounced possessions. He repeatedly taught: "Go, sell all you have and give to the poor, then come and follow me."

PROTESTANT REVOLT AND GREEK SCHISM ◆

At the Reformation, the title of "bishop" was retained by Anglicans and some Lutherans, but "pope" was rejected—both the title and the man.

Martin Luther argued that the New Testament did not create a single Apostolic See at Rome; rather, it was the bishops of Rome, from about the fourth century onward, who created the papacy centered at Rome by insisting that Peter's inheritance was *theirs* and no one else's. The Gospels did not create the papacy; the papacy, once set up in Rome, turned to the Gospels to support its uniqueness.

However, even the Protestant Reformers retained the notion that the Church itself (conceived as the community of the faithful) cannot err totally, that is, cannot drift too far from Christ's intentions—this by virtue of Christ's own promise that his Church is indestructible and infallible:

Matthew 16:18—". . . on this rock I will build my church, and the powers of death shall not prevail against it."

John 21:15—"Feed my lambs. . . . Tend my sheep."

Luke 22:32—"But I have prayed for you that your faith may not fail; and when you have turned again, strengthen your brethren."

Furthermore, the Protestant Reformer would not tolerate the notion that the human bishop of Rome was himself infallible—something that was not yet dogma but was insinuating itself into doctrines. In fact, these two separate ideas—the inerrancy of Christ's Church, and the inerrancy of all of Saint Peter's successors—were only combined in the seventeenth century by the so-called Ultramontane (pro-papal) School of Theologians, under Cardinal Robert Bellarmine (d. 1621).

Today, most Christian faiths have bishops; only Roman Catholicism has a pope. These other denominations recognize a bishop's traditional laying on of hands as necessary for ordination to the priesthood, and retain the office for reasons of historical succession.

The pope's power is total. The 1917 Code of Canon Law states: "There cannot be an ecumenical council which is not convoked by the Roman Pontiff" and "the First See is under the judgment of nobody." That means, simply, there is no higher authority in the Church, not even an ecumenical council, to which an appeal can be made from a papal judgment.

In this century, the Eastern Orthodox Churches have been unanimously adamant in their rejection of the papal claims to primacy (that only bishops of Rome are direct successors of Saint Peter) and infallibility.

The schism between the Latin and Greek Churches occurred in 1054, when papal leadership *in* the Church was replaced by papal monarchy *over* the Church, when Rome began to exercise the muscle of *plentitudo potestatis*, "full authority." The split was deepened when the bishop of Rome began to sell indulgences and benefices (Church offices and titles for a fee) in order to support the burgeoning army of bureaucrats at Rome. And promulgation of the dogma of papal infallibility in July of 1870 only rubbed salt in long-festering wounds.

Most Christian denominations argue that by the word "rock" Christ meant himself; upon himself he founded his Church—not upon Saint Peter and all his successors who happened to reside in Rome.

This idea might be shocking—or blatant sacrilege—to most Roman Catholics. But the truth is, the great fathers of the Church—Cyprian, Origen, Cyril, Hilary, Jerome, Ambrose, Augustine—all viewed Christ as the Rock on which the Church rests. It is Peter's *faith* that Christ elsewhere refers to as "stone" or "rock."

Furthermore, all the councils of the Church—Ecumenical Councils (those summoned by civil power; language, Greek) and General Councils (summoned by popes; language, Latin) from Nicaea in the fourth century to Constance in the fifteenth century: Nicaea I (325 C.E.) and II (787); Constantinople I (381), II (553), III (680), and IV (869); Ephesus (431); Chalcedon (451); Lateran I (1123), II (1139), III (1179), and IV (1215); Lyons I (1245) and II (1274); Vienne (1311); Constance (1414–18)—agreed that Christ himself is the only foundation of the Church, not any human mortal.

As mentioned earlier, the modern-day attitudes of papal primacy and infallibility gradually took hold in the sixteenth and seventeenth centuries—paving the way for the nineteenth-century dogma of inerrancy when a pope speaks "from the chair of Peter," *ex cathedra*.

DOGMA OF PAPAL INFALLIBILITY: JULY 1870 ◆

Papal infallibility was officially granted to Pius IX and his successors in July of 1870, but the seeds were sown sixteen years earlier: on December 8, 1854. That's when Pius IX, exerting extraordinary authority, defined as dogma Mary's Immaculate Conception in his bull *Ineffabilis Deus*.

As the pope's private secretary, Monsignor Talbot, confided to a friend: "The most important thing is not the new dogma, but the way it is proclaimed." Essentially, through papal infallibility. For while the doctrine of the Immaculate Conception had received enthusiastic support from bishops of Italy, Spain, and Portugal, bishops from other countries did not embrace it.

They preferred to allow Catholics to believe whatever they wished about Mary's conception with or without original sin.

As we saw earlier, until the twelfth century, Christians took for granted that Mary was conceived in original sin. Pope Gregory the Great, Peter's sixty-third successor, in the late sixth century stated emphatically: "Christ alone was conceived without sin." He, and other popes, believed that the sex act always involved sin. Mary was conceived through sex, and therefore in sin. The Greek and Russian Orthodox Churches never altered in this belief.

With the Immaculate Conception as dogma, no Catholic's soul could be saved without embracing the concept 100 percent. This is what had many bishops uncomfortable.

Pius IX was a very political man. He'd floated the dogma of the Immaculate Conception in 1854 as a pilot balloon for the upcoming definition of papal infallibility.

Why, after all these centuries, was it suddenly necessary to dogmatize so controversial an idea as infallibility?

BISHOPS SUMMONED TO ROME. Pius IX knew when he took office in the late 1840s that the days of the Papal States were numbered. In fact, no sooner did he become pope than a temporary republic was set up in Rome. Italy was coalescing into a country. Papal States would soon be forcibly annexed to burgeon the boarders of the new Kingdom of Italy.

Feeling himself stripped of temporal power, Pius IX moved to exploit his spiritual authority. The government could take away his jurisdiction over lands, but not over souls. He'd already tested the waters. Sixteen years earlier, he'd passed as dogma an idea that did not have the full support of the world's bishops. And they'd done nothing to stop him.

Thus, when the bishops were summoned to Rome in 1869 for the First Vatican Council, many were wary.

Most ominously, the date the pope chose to open the First Vatican Council was December 8, the anniversary of his papal definition of the Immaculate Conception. The bishops knew what they were going to be asked to vote on this time. Papal infallibility. They feared a schism in the Roman Catholic Church.

There might be scriptural evidence to support the infallibility of Christ's Church, as most Christians believed, but not to support the infallibility of its human head. As Cardinal Manning of Westminster moaned: "Oh, the dogma must overcome history."

And that popular catechism in the United States—the one that blamed "Protestant invention" for the widespread Catholic assumption that popes were infallible—would have to be burned. To its question "Must not Catholics believe the pope himself to be infallible?" the new answer was going to be: "Now they must. By Catholic invention."

BISHOPS ASKED TO VOTE. As the day of the vote on infallibility approached, many bishops became conveniently sick and left Rome. On the actual day of the session, many more bishops dodged the assembly and left the Vatican rather than vote against their conscience. The doctrine was too hot to make dogma.

On the "first ballot," only 451 bishops voted yes, fewer than half of the 1,084 members entitled to take part in the council—and less than two-thirds of the seven hundred bishops who'd arrived at Rome for the opening session.

Any vote was meaningless, however. Pius IX had already let it be known that the papacy was going to be infallible "without the consent of the Church." He'd scribbled in his own hand a message to be passed around: "Don't waste your words where there is no one to heed them." Opponents were soon in the minority.

No source tells the story better than *How the Pope Became Infallible*, by August Bernard Hasler, Vatican Secretariat for Christian Unity:

"Just before the solemn vote on July 18, 1870," writes Hasler, "the minority made a desperate attempt to change the pope's mind. But all their efforts, including the visit by a delegation of six archbishops and bishops, got nowhere. On the contrary, their request . . . antagonized the pope." Now these bishops left Rome in protest.

Believe it or not, the pope threatened suspension or excommunication for bishops who opposed him. As Bishop Joseph Hefele of Rottenburg later wrote: "The position of a suspended and excommunicated bishop strikes me as something terrible. I could hardly bear it."

At the last meeting of the council on July 18, the number of yes votes rose to 535. Only two bishops voted no—Bishop Luigi Riccio of Cajazzo and American bishop Edward Fitzgerald of Little Rock, Arkansas. Immediately after passage of the doctrine, both men submitted to papal might and right.

"As the dogma was being proclaimed," writes Hasler, "a violent electrical storm burst over St. Peter's. The thunder rolled and growled, the lightning flashes threw a ghostly light into the darkness which had filled the cathedral—for some a sign of God's approval, for others of his wrath."

UPDATES:
• *July 22, 1870.* "Almost all the bishops of Austria-Hungary now returned from Rome are *furious* over the definition of infallibility," wrote the

nuncio in Vienna, Mariano Falcinelli. "The few who have visited me did not dare to talk about the Council."

• A theology professor denounced Pius IX as a "heretic and devastator of the Church."

• *August 7, 1870.* Bishop Philipp Krementz laments in a letter to a friend: "It is hard for me to reconcile what has been decided in Rome with my old theology and the facts of history."

• In France, six recalcitrant bishops who refused to accept the dogma were either forced to resign or strongly urged to do so—the circumstances surrounding their removal remain unclear.

• In the United States, Archbishop Peter Richard Kenrick of St. Louis, a vocal opponent of infallibility, finally succumbed to pressure from other American bishops. In Rome, the authorities of the Roman Inquisition, as the body is named, accepted his declaration of submission.

In a short time, all bishops would succumb to Pius's wishes for the sake of Church unity. After all, he was now officially infallible.

Exactly how bishops gave in is best expressed in Bishop Philipp Krementz's about-face. Three months after he'd written the above lament, he wrote to a friend on November 8, 1870:

> *Since the Church has reached this solemn decision, it is therefore certain and self-evident that her resolution is grounded in Holy Scripture and tradition, the two sources of Christ's teaching, which she interprets unerringly.*

SEALED FOLIOS AND VANISHING FILES. The official Historian for Vatican I was Archbishop Vincenzo Tizzani—one of the few men in the Curia ("together virile") strongly opposed to the doctrine of infallibility. He'd taken extensive notes, but published nothing. When he died in 1892, the Vatican bought all of his manuscripts from his niece, the Countess Lucrezia Gazzoli (and paid only a fifth of the agreed-upon price, which led to litigation). To this day, Tizzani's papers are under lock and key in the Vatican secret archives.

The notes of a second bishop who had planned to publish the opposition's view of the council have vanished entirely.

In December of 1966, the Vatican secret archives opened up to researchers "all materials" touching on the pontificate of Pius IX—but boxes already had been "tidied up."

"To this day," wrote Hasler in 1979, "no one has published a history of the First Vatican Council based upon [primary] sources."

After its passage in 1870, the dogma of papal infallibility was not invoked again until 1950, when in the bull *Munificentissimus Deus*, Pius XII declared as dogma Mary's Assumption, body and soul, into Heaven.

The Second Vatican Council (1962–65) confirmed the dogma of papal infallibility—how could it denounce it?—but did not discuss the touchy topic. In fact, no one likes to discuss it anymore. It's become an embarrassment.

Swiss theologian Hans Küng challenged the basis of papal infallibility—from both the Bible and tradition—in the 1960s with his book *Infallible? An Inquiry*. In December of 1979, Küng, probably the world's best-known theologian, was stripped of his right to teach the Catholic faith, and thus lost his post at the University of Tübingen.

To this day, the dogma of papal infallibility, and its intrinsic corollary of the primacy of the bishops of Rome, is the single greatest obstacle to unity among the world's Christians.

DOCTRINE OF "CREEPING INFALLIBILITY" ◆

Peter De Rosa, in *Vicars of Christ*, neatly sums up the evidence against papal infallibility.

1. Saint Peter himself was fallible, having blundered many times before and after Christ's Crucifixion.

2. There is no proof in the New Testament that Peter alone possessed some divine power that all his successors would inherit.

3. According to early Church fathers, Peter had no single successor. They viewed all bishops as succeeding to the apostles—not an individual bishop at Rome (a pope) succeeding to an individual apostle (Peter).

4. All the great doctrinal statements of the Church, especially the creeds, came not from individual bishops of Rome but from councils of bishops. It never occurred to the early bishops of Rome that they could define doctrine for the whole Church.

5. The First Vatican Council really needed to explain why, if papal infallibility is crucial to the Church, there is no mention of it in the creeds and councils, and why it was not imposed until 1870. Before then, belief in papal infallibility was in no way demanded of Catholics. They could deny it—and whole countries did—without any suggestion that they were bad Catholics.

"Papal infallibility does nothing to enlighten the church," argues De Rosa. "It seems to have less to do with truth than with control."

De Rosa makes the potent point that the pope's prestige and power rest not on the dogma of infallibility—which is infrequently invoked—"but on what has been called 'creeping infallibility.' " That is, the doctrine of infallibility is so intimidating and formidable that the very idea imbues the pope with an aura of total inerrancy such that *all* his words appear to Catholics as being infallible—all the many words he does not speak *ex cathedra*. "Creeping infallibility" makes even a modern pope's statements on world politics and matters not of faith and morals appear to carry a divine imprimatur of inerrancy.

References
and Reading

Is THERE A SUBJECT that's been more voluminously covered than religion? I know of none. In order to maximize accuracy and minimize dispute, I've leaned heavily on standard religious encyclopedias and dictionaries. These works cover a wide spectrum of sacred origins. At other times, I've had to seek the origins of a particular devotion, amulet, or sacramental in a more obscure source. The essential bibliography includes:

Asimov's Guide to the Bible. Vols. 1, 2. Isaac Asimov. Avenel Books, 1981.

The Catholic Encyclopedia. Robert C. Broderick, ed. Thomas Nelson Publications.

Catholicism. Vols. 1, 2. Richard P. McBrien. Minneapolis, Minn.: Winston Press.

Dictionary of Catholic Devotions. Michael Walsh. Harper San Francisco, 1993.

Eerdmans Handbook of the Bible. David Alexander and Pat Alexander, eds. Grand Rapids, Mich: Eerdmans Publishing Co., 1994.

Encyclopedia of Catholic History. Matthew Bunson. Huntington, Ind.: Our Sunday Visitor Publishing, 1995.

Encyclopedia Judaica. Vols. 1–16. Cecil Roth, ed.-in-chief. Jerusalem: Keter Publishing House.

The Encyclopedia of Judaism. Geoffrey Wigoder, ed.-in-chief. Macmillan Publishing Co.

The Encyclopedia of Religion. Vols. 1–15. Mircea Eliade, ed.-in-chief. Macmillan Publishing Co.

Expression of Catholic Faith. Kevin Orlin Johnson. Ballantine, 1994.

The Interpreter's Bible. Vols. 1–12. George Arthur Buttrick, ed. New York: Abingdon Press.

The Lion Encyclopedia of the Bible. Pat Alexander, ed. London: Bloomsbury.

New Catholic Encyclopedia. Vols. 1–17. William J. McDonald, ed.-in-chief. Catholic University of America Press.

The New Schaff-Herzog Encyclopedia of Religious Knowledge. Vols. 1–15. Samuel Macauley Jackson, ed.-in-chief. Grand Rapids, Mich.: Baker Book House.

The Oxford Companion to the Bible. Bruce Metzger and Michael Coogan, eds. Oxford University Press, 1993.

Reader's Digest:ABC's of the Bible. Pleasantville, N.Y.: The Reader's Digest Association, 1991.

I ALSO FOUND handy several religious almanacs, atlases, and catechisms. These books, while seldom delving into historical origins, present concise factual knowledge and statistics, which I've used to flesh out my text:

American Jewish Yearbook 1994. David Singer, ed. Scranton, Pa.: Haddon Craftsmen.

Catechism of the Catholic Church. Doubleday, 1995.

Essential Truths of the Christian Faith. R. C. Sproal. Illinois: Tyndale Publishers, 1992.

A Guide to Jewish Religious Practices. Isaac Klein. The Jewish Theological Seminary of America; KTAV Publishing House, USA.

The Jewish Almanac. Richard Siegel and Carol Rheins, eds. New York: Bantam.

1995 Catholic Almanac. Felician A. Foy, ed. Huntington, Ind.: Our Sunday Visitor Publishing.

The State of Religion Atlas. Joanne O'Brien and Martin Palmer. Simon and Schuster, 1993.

IN ATTEMPTING TO present a cross-cultural picture of religious customs and practices, I've relied on several standard and popular works:

A Handbook of Living Religions. John Hinnells, ed. Penguin, 1991.

Our Religions. Arvid Sharma, ed. Harper San Francisco, 1993.

Sacred Writings, Jaroslav Pelikan, ed., Quality Paperback Book Club, 1992; six volumes—which present, authoritatively, the world's major religious texts:
    Vol. 1, Judaism: *The Tanakh*
    Vol. 2, Christianity: *The Apocrypha and New Testament*
    Vol. 3, Islam: *The Koran*
    Vol. 4, Confucianism: *The Analects of Confucius*
    Vol. 5, Hinduism: *The Rig Veda*
    Vol. 6, Buddhism: *The Dhammapada*

World Religions. Charles R. Monroe: Amherst, N.Y.: Prometheus Books, 1995.

World Religions: From Ancient History to the Present. Geoffrey Parrinder, ed. New York: Facts on File, 1983.

FOR THE CHAPTERS on the origins of religious symbols, the following texts were used to varying degrees. All are highly recommended to any reader wishing to delve further into this subject:

Catholic Sacramentals. Ann Ball. Huntington, Ind.: Our Sunday Visitor Publishing, 1991.

A Dictionary of Symbols. J. E. Cirlot. New York: Philosophical Library, 1971.

Our Christian Symbols. Friedrich Rest. Cleveland, Ohio: The Pilgrim Press, 1982.

Outward Signs: The Language of Christian Symbolism. Edward West. New York: Waller & Co., 1991.

The Secret Language of Symbols. David Fontana. San Francisco: Chronicle Books, 1993.

ANY READER WISHING to further explore the fascinating histories of such places as Heaven, Hell, Purgatory, and Limbo would not be disappointed with these detailed, often cross-cultural, works (which I refer to, and comment upon, throughout my text):

The Birth of Purgatory. Jacques Le Goff. Chicago: University of Chicago Press, 1981.

Heaven: A History. Colleen McDonnell and Bernhard Lang. New Haven: Yale University Press, 1988.

A History of Hell. Alice K. Turner. Harcourt Brace, 1993.

Limbo: The Unsettled Question. George J. Dyer. New York: Sheed and Ward, 1964.

WHEN IT COMES to evil, I've used, and highly recommend:

Antichrist: Two Thousand Years of the Human Fascination with Evil. Bernard McGinn. HarperCollins, 1994.

Naming the Antichrist: The History of An American Obsession. Robert Fuller. Oxford University Press, 1995.

The Origin of Satan. Elaine Pagels. New York: Random House, 1995.

Who Killed Jesus? Exposing the Roots of Anti-Semitism in the Gospel Story of the Death of Jesus. John Dominic Crossan. Harper San Francisco, 1992.

IN REGARD TO my chapters on saints and their mortal remains, I highly recommend:

American Martyrs, From 1542 to the Present. Albert J. Nevins. Huntington, Ind: Our Sunday Visitor Publishing, 1987.

Angelic Doctor: The Life and World of St. Thomas Aquinas. Matthew Bunson. Huntington, Ind.: Our Sunday Visitor Publishing, 1994.

The Avenel Dictionary of Saints. Donald Attwater. Avenel Books, 1979.

Butler's Lives of Patron Saints. Michael Walsh, ed. Harper and Row, 1987.

Butler's Lives of the Saints. Complete ed., 4 vols. Herbert Thurston and Donald Attwater. Westminster, Md.: Christian Classics.

A Guide to the Saints. Kristin White. New York: Ivy Books, 1991.

Lives of the Saints, with Excerpts from their Writings. Joseph Vann, ed. Crawley Publishers, 1954.

Making Saints. Kenneth Woodward. Simon and Schuster, 1990. The best single volume on the process of how a holy human being is transformed into a postmortem icon.

Patron Saints. Michael Freze. Huntington, Ind.: Our Sunday Visitor Publishing, 1992.

Relics. Joan Carroll Cruz. Huntington, Ind.: Our Sunday Visitor Publishing, 1995. A comprehensive book on Christian relics.

St. Peter: A Biography. Michael Grant. Scribners, 1995.

Saints. Alison Jones. New York: Chambers Encyclopedia Guides, 1992.

Saints Preserve Us: Everything You Need to Know About Every Saint You'll Ever Need. Sean Kelly and Rosemary Rogers. Random House, 1993.

Stigmata. Ian Wilson. Harper and Row, 1989. A comprehensive work on this fascinating phenomenon.

The Twelve: The Lives of the Apostles After Calvary. C. Bernard Ruffin. Huntington, Ind.: Our Sunday Visitor Publishing, 1984.

FOR FASCINATING READING on God—the concept, the man, the woman:

Eunuchs for the Kingdom of Heaven: Women, Sexuality and the Catholic Church. Uta Ranke-Heinemann. Penguin, 1990.

A History of God. Karen Armstrong. Knopf, 1993.

The Myth of the Goddess. Anne Baring and Jules Cashford. Penguin/Arkana, 1993.

When God Was a Woman. Merlin Stone. Dorset Press, 1976.

FOR BIOGRAPHIES and facts on popes:

The Oxford Dictionary of Popes. J. N. D. Kelly. Oxford University Press, 1986.

Pontiffs: Popes Who Shaped History. John Jay Hughes. Huntington, Ind.: Our Sunday Visitor Publishing, 1994.

The Shepherd and the Rock: Origins, Development and Mission of the Papacy. J. Michael Miller. Huntington, Ind.: Our Sunday Visitor Publishing, 1994.

MUCH HAS been written about angels recently. Of particular interest, I found:

A Handbook of Angels. H. C. Moolenburgh. C. W. Daniel Ltd., 1992.
Your Guardian Angels. Linda Georgian. Simon and Schuster, 1994.

TWO FASCINATING BOOKS on Christianity and homosexuality:

Christianity, Social Tolerance and Homosexuality. John Boswell. Chicago: University of
    Chicago Press, 1980.
Same-Sex Unions. John Boswell. Villard Books, 1994.

A MOST UNUSUAL book on the Bible, written by a lawyer, and fascinating from
cover to cover:

A New Look at Biblical Crime. Ralph W. Scott. New York: Dorset Press, 1979. How
    would the Bible's greatest crimes play out in today's courts? Who would get the
    electric chair? Who would go free?

YOU MIGHT ALSO look into:

The Bible as History. Werner Keller. Morrow, 1981.
The Book of J. David Rosenberg and Harold Bloom. Grove Weidenfeld, 1990. Were
    the early books of the Old Testament penned by a woman?
Brush Up on Your Bible! Michael Macrone. HarperCollins, 1993. Fun to browse for
    biblical quotations and clichés that have crept into our common speech.
What the Bible Really Says. Morton Smith and R. Joseph Hoffmann, eds. Harper
    San Francisco, 1993.
Who Wrote the Bible? Richard Elliott Friedman. Summit Books, 1987.

THREE ENTERTAINING VOLUMES that answer hundreds of religious questions, often
about the origins of customs and holidays:

The Christian Book of Why. John C. McCollisters. Middle Village, N.Y.: Jonathan
    David Publishers, 1983.
The Jewish Book of Why. Vols. 1, 2. Alfred J. Kolatch. Middle Village, N.Y.: Jonathan
    David Publishers, 1981.

Index